HANDBOOK OF RESEARCH INTERNATIONAL HUMAN RESOURCE MANAGEMENT

Handbook of Research in International Human Resource Management

Edited by

Günter K. Stahl

Associate Professor of Organizational Behaviour, INSEAD, France and Singapore

Ingmar Björkman

Swedish School of Economics, Finland and Adjunct Professor of Asian Business, INSEAD, France and Singapore

Edward Elgar
Cheltenham, UK • Northampton, MA, USA

Published by
Edward Elgar Publishing Limited
Glensanda House
Montpellier Parade
Cheltenham
Glos GL50 1UA
UK

Edward Elgar Publishing, Inc.
136 West Street
Suite 202
Northampton
Massachusetts 01060
USA

A catalogue record for this book
is available from the British Library

Library of Congress Cataloguing in Publication Data
Handbook of research in international human resource management / [editors],
    Günter K. Stahl, Ingmar Björkman.
        p. cm. — (Elgar original reference)
    Includes bibliographical references.
        1. International business enterprises—Personnel management. I. Stahl,
    Günter K., 1966– II. Björkman, Ingmar. III. Series.

    HF5549.5.E45H36 2006
    658.3—dc22   2005051829

ISBN 978 1 84542 128 1 (cased)
ISBN 978 1 84720 258 1 (paperback)

Printed and bound in Great Britain by MPG Books Group

Contents

Contributors   viii

1 International human resource management research:
   an introduction to the field   1
   Ingmar Björkman and Günter K. Stahl

PART I   THE ROLE OF INTERNATIONAL HUMAN
RESOURCE MANAGEMENT

2 Strategic international human resource management in
   multinational enterprises: developments and directions   15
   Helen De Cieri and Peter J. Dowling
3 The dual logics behind international human resource
   management: pressures for global integration and local
   responsiveness   36
   Philip M. Rosenzweig
4 The human resource department: roles, coordination and
   influence   49
   Philip Stiles and Jonathan Trevor
5 Comparing HRM policies and practices across geographical
   borders   68
   Chris Brewster
6 International human resource management and firm
   performance   91
   Jaap Paauwe and Elaine Farndale
7 Global knowledge management and HRM   113
   Paul Sparrow

PART II   RESEARCH ON GLOBAL STAFFING,
PERFORMANCE MANAGEMENT AND
LEADERSHIP DEVELOPMENT

8 Global staffing   141
   David Collings and Hugh Scullion
9 The compensation of expatriates: a review and a future
   research agenda   158
   Jaime Bonache

10 Global performance management systems   176
    Wayne F. Cascio
11 Developing global leadership capabilities and global mindset:
    a review   197
    *Joyce S. Osland, Allan Bird, Mark Mendenhall and Asbjorn
    Osland*
12 Diversity management   223
    Joerg Dietz and Lars-Eric Petersen

PART III RESEARCH ON INTERNATIONAL ASSIGNMENTS

13 Expatriate adjustment and performance: a critical review 247
    David C. Thomas and Mila B. Lazarova
14 Issues facing women on international assignments: a review of
    the research   265
    Hilary Harris
15 International business travellers: a challenge for IHRM   283
    Denice E. Welch and Verner Worm
16 International assignee selection and cross-cultural training
    and development   302
    Paula Caligiuri and Ibraiz Tarique
17 The evolution from repatriation of managers in MNEs to
    'patriation' in global organizations   323
    Michael Harvey and Milorad M. Novicevic

PART IV RESEARCH ON INTERNATIONAL TEAMS,
         ALLIANCES, MERGERS AND ACQUISITIONS

18 Decoupling and coupling in global teams: implications for
    human resource management   347
    Jennifer L. Gibbs
19 Global virtual team dynamics and effectiveness   364
    Martha Maznevski, Sue Canney Davison and Karsten Jonsen
20 International joint venture system complexity and human
    resource management   385
    Randall Schuler and Ibraiz Tarique
21 Managing culture and human resources in mergers and
    acquisitions   405
    Philip K. Goulet and David M. Schweiger

PART V   THEORETICAL PERSPECTIVES ON
INTERNATIONAL HUMAN RESOURCE
MANAGEMENT

22 A resource-based view of international human resources:
toward a framework of integrative and creative capabilities   433
Shad S. Morris, Scott A. Snell and Patrick M. Wright
23 International human resource management and economic
theories of the firm   449
Marion Festing
24 International human resource management research and
institutional theory   463
Ingmar Björkman
25 International human resource management and social
network/social capital theory   475
Mark L. Lengnick-Hall and Cynthia A. Lengnick-Hall
26 International human resource management, fairness and
trust: an organizational support theory framework   488
Ellen Whitener
27 Gender and international human resource management   502
Jeff Hearn, Beverly D. Metcalfe and Rebecca Piekkari
28 Critical theoretical perspectives on international human
resource management   523
Tuomo Peltonen
29 Language effects in multinational corporations: a review from
an international human resource management perspective   536
Rebecca Piekkari

Index   551

Contributors

Allan Bird, University of Missouri, USA

Ingmar Björkman, Swedish School of Economics, Finland

Jaime Bonache, Universidad Carlos III, Spain

Chris Brewster, Henley Management College, UK

Paula Caligiuri, Rutgers University, USA and Bocconi University, Italy

Sue Canney Davison, Pipal International Consultants Nairobi, Kenya

Wayne F. Cascio, University of Colorado, USA

David Collings, University of Limerick, Ireland

Helen De Cieri, Monash University, Australia

Joerg Dietz, Richard Ivey School of Business, The University of Western Ontario, Canada

Peter J. Dowling, University of Canberra, Australia

Elaine Farndale, Erasmus University, Netherlands

Marion Festing, ESCP-EAP, France

Jennifer L. Gibbs, Rutgers University, USA

Philip K. Goulet, University of South Carolina, USA

Hilary Harris, HH Associates and Cranfield University, UK

Michael Harvey, University of Mississippi, USA

Jeff Hearn, Swedish School of Economics, Finland

Karsten Jonsen, IMD, Switzerland

Mila B. Lazarova, Simon Fraser University, Canada

Cynthia A. Lengnick-Hall, University of Texas at San Antonio, USA

Mark L. Lengnick-Hall, University of Texas at San Antonio, USA

Martha Maznevski, IMD, Switzerland

Mark Mendenhall, University of Tennessee, USA

Beverly D. Metcalfe, University of Manchester, UK

Shad S. Morris, Cornell University, USA

Milorad M. Novicevic, University of Wisconsin-La Crosse, USA

Asbjorn Osland, San Jose State University, USA

Joyce S. Osland, San Jose State University, USA

Jaap Paauwe, Erasmus University, Netherlands

Tuomo Peltonen, University of Oulu, Finland

Lars-Eric Petersen, University of Halle-Wittenberg, Germany

Rebecca Piekkari, Helsinki School of Economics, Finland

Philip M. Rosenzweig, IMD, Switzerland

Randall Schuler, Rutgers University, USA

David M. Schweiger, University of South Carolina, USA

Hugh Scullion, University of Strathclyde, UK

Scott A. Snell, Cornell University, USA

Paul Sparrow, Manchester Business School, UK

Günter K. Stahl, INSEAD, France and Singapore

Philip Stiles, Cambridge University, UK

Ibraiz Tarique, Pace University, USA

David C. Thomas, Simon Fraser University, Canada

Jonathan Trevor, Cambridge University, UK

Denice E. Welch, Mt Eliza Business School, Australia

The late **Ellen Whitener**, University of Virginia, USA

Verner Worm, Copenhagen Business School, Denmark

Patrick M. Wright, Cornell University, USA

1 International human resource management research: an introduction to the field

Ingmar Björkman and Günter K. Stahl

The field of 'international human resource management' (IHRM) research has grown extensively over the last few decades. Since André Laurent in 1986 described the field as being in the infancy stage of development (Laurent, 1986), we have witnessed a rapid transformation of the field of IHRM research. The establishment in 1991 of the *International Journal of Human Resource Management*, that mostly publishes articles within IHRM, was an important milestone. For the first time there was a 'home journal' for scholars pursuing IHRM research. At the same time, a significant number of IHRM articles were published in prestigious management journals like *Academy of Management Journal, Administrative Science Quarterly* and *Organization Science*. The number of conferences and workshops dedicated to IHRM research has also increased. By the time this book is in print, the Eighth Conference on International Human Resource Management will have been held.

While growing in size, the field has also expanded in scope. It has shifted from an early focus on the topic areas of top management attitudes and staffing decisions in multinational corporations (MNCs) (Edström & Galbraith, 1977; Perlmutter, 1969) and expatriate adjustment and performance (Torbiörn, 1982; Tung, 1981) to a field characterized by a high degree of diversity, cross-fertilization of ideas from different disciplines, and ambiguous delineations of what is included in the field and what is not. In this *Handbook* we define the field of IHRM broadly to cover all issues related to the management of people in an international context. Hence our definition of IHRM covers a wide range of human resource issues facing MNCs in different parts of their organizations. Additionally we include comparative analyses of HRM in different countries.

Development of the field of IHRM research

Although the coining and spreading of the term 'international human resource management' took place only in the late 1980s and early 1990s, the history of what we view as IHRM research arguably covers a time span of some 30 years. Much of the early work focused on staffing decisions in

1

MNCs and how to manage expatriate managers from the corporation's home country. Perlmutter's seminal article 'The tortuous evolution of the multinational corporation' (1965 [in French]/1969) is arguably the first influential article published within IHRM. In this article the author distinguishes among three different attitudes of MNC headquarters executives: ethnocentric (home country-oriented), polycentric (host country-oriented) and geocentric (world-oriented). In MNCs where headquarters has an ethnocentric attitude, managers from the home country are seen as superior to those of the other countries in which the MNC has operations. In the IHRM literature, Perlmutter's headquarters orientations became the standard way to classify international HRM strategies, in particular staffing policies and practices, and the terms 'ethnocentric', 'polycentric' and 'geocentric' are today widely used (Collings & Scullion, this volume; Harzing, 2004a). Heenan and Perlmutter (1979) later added a fourth category: 'regiocentric'.

Subsequent to Perlmutter's important contribution, two streams of work soon began to emerge: one focusing on the management of expatriates, where much of the emphasis was on the expatriate job choice process and factors that contributed to the adjustment and performance of the expatriate (for example, Ivancevich, 1969; Miller, 1973; Miller & Cheng, 1978); the second focusing on the roles that the transfer of people across units played in the management of the MNC (for example, Franko, 1973; Heenan, 1970), with some authors trying to integrate the two research streams (for example, Robock & Simmonds, 1973; Zeira, Harari & Nundi, 1975). Empirical studies focused almost exclusively on US MNCs and expatriates. Tung (1981, 1982), in her work on international staffing, was one of the first to examine how MNCs from different regions (USA, Europe and Japan) selected and trained managers for overseas assignments.

Throughout the 1980s and in the early 1990s much was written about the management of expatriates (for example, Black, 1988; Black, Mendenhall & Oddou, 1991; Harvey, 1998; Mendenhall & Oddou, 1985), reflecting the heavy emphasis on expatriate management issues among the HR staff responsible for IHRM in the MNC headquarters organization (see also Thomas and Lazarova, this volume, for a critical review of research on expatriate adjustment and performance, and Caligiuri and Tarique's chapter on expatriate selection, training and development). For instance, Reynolds (1997) reports that IHRM staff in US MNCs in the 1970s devoted almost all their time to managing expatriate assignments.

Edström and Galbraith's (1977) research on the motives for transferring managers across units became highly influential among IHRM researchers. They describe three motives for international assignments: to fill positions when qualified local nationals are not available; as management development (that is, to develop the expatriates through the experiences they gain during their international assignments); and as organization development (through socialization of expatriates, as well as through the development of interpersonal linkages across MNC units). Studies published in German by, among others, Pausenberger and Noelle (1977) and Welge (1980) (cf. Harzing, 2004b) presented similar if not identical classifications of motives for the deployment of expatriate managers. This line of research later became integrated with a growing literature on international business strategy and the management/organization of MNCs (Bartlett & Ghoshal, 1989; Hedlund, 1986; Prahalad & Doz, 1987). Researchers who at the turn of the century began studying interpersonal and inter-unit relationships within MNCs from social network or social capital perspectives (for example, Tsai & Ghoshal, 1998) are at least indirectly building on the classic piece by Edström and Galbraith (1977).

One of the many management issues facing MNCs is the extent to which to transfer management practices across borders. Some of the early work on this issue developed from Hofstede's (1980, 1991) research on cultural differences among the countries in which the IBM corporation operated. Other scholars, such as Laurent (1986), strongly argued that national cultural differences have a significant impact on HRM practices and that MNCs need to pay attention to cultural factors when deciding upon HRM policies in their foreign operations. It was also proposed that cultural features of the home country of the MNC had an impact on the kind of HR policies and practices used by the MNC. However, in the 1990s, some of the emphasis among IHRM scholars shifted from a cross-cultural perspective on HRM to studying MNC practices in overseas affiliates within institutional theory (for example, Rosenzweig & Nohria, 1994) and national business system (for example, Ferner & Quantanilla, 1998) perspectives. The potentially positive aspects of transferring HRM found to be efficient elsewhere to other parts of the MNC have also received attention in the literature (for example, Evans, Pucik & Barsoux, 2002).

Another trend that emerged was an increased emphasis on the strategic role of HRM. The early to mid-1980s saw the emergence of the term 'human resource management' (HRM) and hence HRM as a recognized field of study. Most observers trace the birth of the field to the foundational conceptual models of the 'Harvard' (Beer *et al.*, 1984) and 'Michigan' (Fombrun, Tichy & Devanna, 1984) schools. A central aspect of HRM that clearly distinguishes it from the previously dominating 'personnel management' is the link between HRM and strategy. HRM scholars such as Guest (1987) argued that HRM is long-term, proactive and strategic, and that it constitutes an integrated approach to the management of people. The new HRM discourse originated in the USA and was focused on the domestic operations of US corporations, but it did not take long for scholars based outside North America as well as researchers doing work on HRM within MNCs to become influenced by the new HRM concept. This led, not only to a surge in studies aiming at examining how HRM was related to organizational performance (for example, Arthur, 1994; Huselid, 1995; Macduffie, 1995), but also to critical reactions towards the alleged and/or proposed trends towards HRM (for example, Storey, 1995; see also Peltonen, this volume) and critique of the notion that there might be a universal model of HRM regardless of the national context within which the corporation operates (for example, Brewster, 1995; Brewster, this volume).

In this way, the new HRM discourse contributed to reinvigorate the comparative studies of industrial relations and personnel practices in different countries that had already been carried out for some time. The interest in comparative research had to no little degree been a result of the rise of large Japanese corporations in the 1970s and 1980s, and the rich literature on the people management practices found in these corporations (for example, Boxall, 1995; Pucik, 1984). More recently, research on HRM practices found in foreign affiliates, the increasing reliance on alliances and joint ventures, and a surge in mergers and acquisitions of firms from different countries have contributed to an increased cross-fertilization of insights from comparative studies of HRM in different countries with research focusing on the operations of MNCs (Budhwar & Sparrow, 2002). For many years already, there has been a large group of IHRM scholars carrying out comparative research on HRM across countries not only with an interest in understanding the effect of cultural and institutional factors on HRM but also with an agenda to shed light on cross-national processes of convergence and divergence of HRM (Brewster, Mayrhofer & Morley, 2000, 2004; Brewster, this volume).

However the biggest impact of the HRM concept on IHRM research was probably in terms of its influence on efforts to link HRM policies and practices to the organizational strategy of MNCs. Within this body of literature – sometimes called Strategic International HRM, and building increasingly on recent developments in strategy and organizational research such as the resource-based view of the firm (Barney, 1991) – scholars, among others, have developed comprehensive models of the causal factors influencing HRM policies and practices in MNCs (Schuler, Dowling & De Cieri, 1993; Taylor, Beechler & Napier, 1996). But researchers have also come to believe that there are strong opposing forces facing MNCs, dualities that firms need to understand as they develop HRM policies and practices in a world where successful operations require multidimensional organizational capabilities (Evans & Doz, 1989; Evans et al., 2002). One particularly important duality that global organizations must manage and that has major implications for IHRM policies and practices is that of centralization (or global integration) versus decentralization (or local responsiveness) (see Prahalad & Doz, 1987; Rosenzweig, this volume).

In addition to the streams of research outlined above, IHRM researchers have expanded their work into a wide range of other topic areas. For instance, extensive work has been conducted on the management of people in alliances, mergers and acquisitions (Stahl & Mendenhall, 2005) Scholars have also devoted much attention to studying multinational (and often virtual) teams, global leadership development and career issues, performance management, cross-border transfer of knowledge and organizational learning, global outsourcing and organizational culture development – all from an IHRM perspective. And the HR function itself and the roles it plays in the functioning of the MNC have also received increased attention. Finally IHRM scholars have increasingly framed their research in terms of organization theories (cf. Wright & McMahan, 1992). In short, the field of IHRM research has developed into a large, complex and constantly developing field of study.

Objectives and scope of this handbook

The work with this *Handbook of Research in International Human Resource Management* was triggered by what we saw as a gap in the IHRM literature. Although several excellent books have been written on IHRM (recent book publications include Briscoe & Schuler, 2004; Dowling & Welch, 2004; Evans, Pucik & Barsoux, 2002; Harzing & Van Ruysseveldt, 2004; Scullion & Linehan, 2005; Sparrow, Brewster & Harris, 2004), their foci and objectives are somewhat different from ours. The present volume is directed to the scholarly community: our intention was to put together a book on IHRM studies that would serve as a guide to existing and future IHRM researchers from all parts of the world. Hence our main target audience is our own colleagues, doctoral students and others interested in IHRM research.

Our goal with this book has been to bring together leading IHRM scholars to provide a comprehensive overview of the field, including emerging topic areas and exciting new research findings that may shape the field of IHRM research in the years to come. The 48 authors of the 29 chapters that form this *Handbook* were encouraged not only to review critically previous research within the scope of their chapters, but also to provide a foundation for and concrete suggestions regarding how, through forthcoming research, we are to further develop our knowledge of important issues in the area of IHRM. The authors are affiliated with academic institutions located in Europe, North America, Africa, Asia and Australia, lending the

Handbook a truly global flavour. While the authors differ widely in their academic backgrounds, paradigmatic orientations and theoretical and methodological approaches to IHRM, they all share an active interest in augmenting our understanding of people management issues in the global arena.

Before presenting an outline of this book a word of caution about its limitations seems warranted. The study of IHRM is a relatively new area of research, as described earlier in this chapter; it is also a highly dynamic and constantly evolving field, with new themes emerging that transcend traditional approaches. The chapters in this volume provide insights into the latest theoretical thinking and cutting-edge research on IHRM. However, in spite of the many important contributions that have been made, it would be unwise to state that the research efforts described are much more than a first step towards a thorough understanding of the phenomena under investigation. There is a rich research agenda here, and the chapters in this book open up a number of questions and avenues for future studies. However definite answers to the questions raised are unlikely to be found any time soon, because the underlying phenomena are, by their very nature, highly dynamic and complex. Chris Brewster (in this volume) captured some of this complexity when he summarized the convergence–divergence debate and concluded:

> The situation is, inevitably, complex. And the evidence can be selected to suit almost any position. . . . [S]ome aspects of industrial societies tend to converge, whilst others diverge, depending upon time and circumstances. . . . An alternative approach would be to consider whether some parts of the overall HR system might be converging, in some regions or geographies, whilst other parts might be diverging. Moreover, since HR operates at multiple levels including philosophy, policy, programme, practice and process . . . there might be convergence at one level but divergence at another, even within one firm, never mind between nations.

IHRM scholars face similar complexities in most other areas of inquiry within this field.

Content and outline of this handbook

IHRM scholars (for example, Dowling & Welch, 2004; Sparrow *et al.*, 2004) have argued that IHRM involves the same activities and dimensions as domestic HRM but operates on a much larger scale, with more complex strategic considerations, more complex coordination and control demands and some additional HR functions. Additional HR functions are considered necessary to accommodate the need for greater operating unit diversity, more external stakeholder influence, higher levels of risk exposure and more personal insight into employees' lives and family situation.

However others (Bird & Osland, 2004; Lane, Maznevski & Mendenhall, 2004; Prahalad, 1990) have argued that global management – including people management – differs from management in a domestic context not only in *degree* (broader scope, more complex coordination demands and so on) but also in *kind*, because the challenges faced by individuals and the organization are qualitatively different from those faced in a domestic context. These demands include increased ambiguity surrounding decisions and related outcomes; wider and more frequent 'boundary spanning'; a more challenging and expanded list of competing tensions that need to be balanced; a heightened need for cultural understanding; and more challenging ethical dilemmas relating to globalization. As Bird and Osland (2004) put it, 'the transition from purely domestic to global is a quantum leap' (p.61). This is particularly true for HRM, and throughout this book we are reminded of the significantly greater challenges faced by global HR functions, compared to the role of HRM in a domestic context.

This *Handbook of Research in International Human Resource Management* is divided into five parts:

I   The Role of International Human Resource Management
II   Research on Global Staffing, Performance Management and Leadership Development
III Research on International Assignments
IV   Research on International Teams, Alliances, Mergers and Acquisitions
V   Theoretical Perspectives on International Human Resource Management

The chapters comprising Part I provide the overall context for the rest of the book. The theoretical approaches and empirical studies presented in these chapters explore the role of IHRM from a variety of perspectives. The authors look at the nature of HRM from a comparative perspective and consider the dual logics behind IHRM, namely pressures for global integration and local responsiveness; they explore how IHRM is associated with global knowledge management and organizational learning; and they consider the role of the HR function in global corporations and the link between IHRM and organizational performance. Throughout this part of the book, the authors emphasize the importance of linking IHRM policies and activities to organizational strategy.

The chapters in Part II review research on a variety of global HRM issues related to staffing, performance management, leadership development and diversity management. The emphasis here is on broader HR issues than expatriate management, reflecting how the field of IHRM has evolved from its early focus on the selection and training of expatriate managers to encompass a much broader spectrum of topics and issues. However international assignment issues still figure prominently in this book, owing to their importance in the global coordination and integration of resources and operations (Evans *et al.*, 2002) and the continuing stream of research on expatriation (Dowling & Welch, 2004; Harzing & Van Ruysseveldt, 2004).

Consequently Part III of the book deals with a variety of international assignment issues, from the perspective of both the individual and the organization. Its five chapters cover activities relating to expatriate management, such as career-pathing, selection, training, support and repatriation of expatriates, as well as other issues deemed critical in managing international assignments. These issues include the antecedents of expatriate adjustment and performance, the challenges confronting women while on international assignments, and dual career issues. The contributors also show why it is important that organizations take a wider view of mobility, including short-term assignments and frequent flying, and examine how the international HR function can manage both the organizational and the personal implications of mobility.

In Part IV of the book, the contributors consider the role that IHRM can play in the management of global teams – be they colocated or virtual – as well as the management of cross-border alliances, mergers and acquisitions: topic areas that have recently received increased research attention thanks to their special relevance to global organizations.

The *Handbook* concludes with a synopsis of the rich theoretical foundations of and influences on the field of IHRM research. The theoretical perspectives discussed in Part V include the resource-based view of the firm, institutional theory, social network and social capital theory, and economic theories of the firm. In addition, contributors explore IHRM processes and issues from a variety of perspectives, such as fairness and trust, linguistic, gender and feminist perspectives, and apply critical theory to the study of IHRM. These chapters illustrate that IHRM research is theoretically eclectic, drawing upon a range of paradigms and perspectives; and, second, that the field has overcome the theory deficit that was characteristic of the early days of IHRM research.

The chapters in this book address a range of critical issues involved in the management of people in a global context from rich, novel perspectives. Thus this book attempts to act as a catalyst for scholars who work in the field of IHRM by providing them with a wider scope of theoretical understanding regarding the complexity of variables and processes that affect the effectiveness of IHRM policies and practices. It is our hope that this book will spur innovation in both theory and practice in IHRM.

Acknowledgment

The authors are grateful to Paul Evans for his helpful comments on the chapter.

References

Arthur, J. 1994. Effects of human resource systems on manufacturing performance and turnover. *Academy of Management Journal*, **37**: 670–87.

Barney, J.B. 1991. Firm resources and sustained competitive advantage. *Journal of Management*, **17**: 99–120.

Bartlett, C.A. & S. Ghoshal. 1989. *Managing across borders: The transnational solution.* Boston, MA: Harvard Business School Press.

Beer, M., B. Spector, P.R. Lawrence, D. Quinn Mills & R.E. Walton. 1984. *Managing human assets.* New York: Free Press.

Bird, A. & J. Osland. 2004. Global competencies: an introduction. In H. Lane, M. Maznevski, M. Mendenhall & J. Mcnett (eds), *The handbook of global management*: 57–80. Oxford: Blackwell.

Black, J.S. 1988. Work role transitions: a study of American expatriate managers in Japan. *Journal of International Business Studies*, **19**: 277–94.

Black, J.S., M.E. Mendenhall & G.R. Oddou. 1991. Toward a comprehensive model of international adjustment: an integration of multiple theoretical perspectives. *Academy of Management Review*, **16**: 291–317.

Boxall, P. 1995. Building the theory of comparative HRM. *Human Resource Management Journal*, **5**(5): 5–17.

Brewster, C. 1995. Towards a 'European' model of human resource management. *Journal of International Business Studies*, **26**: 1–21.

Brewster, C., W. Mayrhofer & M. Morley. (eds) 2000. *New challenges in European human resource management.* London: Macmillan.

Brewster, C., W. Mayrhofer & M. Morley. (eds) 2004. *Human resource management in Europe. Evidence of convergence?* Oxford: Butterworth-Heinemann.

Briscoe, D.R. & R.S. Schuler. 2004. *International human resource management.* Second edition. London: Routledge.

Budhwar, P.S. & P.R. Sparrow. 2002. An integrative framework for understanding cross-national human resource management practices. *Human Resource Management Review*, **12**: 377–403.

Dowling, P.E. & D.E. Welch. 2004. *International human resource management.* Fourth edition. London: Thomson Learning.

Edström, A. & J.R. Galbraith. 1977. Transfer of managers as a co-ordination and control strategy in multinational organizations. *Administrative Science Quarterly*, **22**: 248–63.

Evans, P. & Y. Doz. 1989. The dualistic organization. In P. Evans, Y. Doz & A. Laurent (eds), *Human resource management in international firms: change, globalization, innovation.* Oxford: Blackwell.

Evans, P., V. Pucik & J.-L. Barsoux. 2002. *The global challenge: frameworks for international human resource management.* New York: McGraw-Hill/Irwin.

Ferner, A. & J. Quantanilla. 1998. Multinationals, national business systems and HRM: the enduring influence of national identity or a process of 'Anglo-Saxonization'. *International Journal of Human Resource Management*, **9**: 710–31.

Fombrun, C.J., N.M. Tichy & M.A. Devanna. 1984. *Strategic human resource management.* New York: John Wiley.

Franko, L.G. 1973. Who manages multinational enterprises? *Columbia Journal of World Business*, **8**: 30–42.

Guest, D. 1987. Human resource management and industrial relations. *Journal of Management Studies*, **24**: 503–21.

Harvey, M. 1998. The expatriate family: an overlooked variable in international assignments. *Columbia Journal of World Business*, **20**(1): 84–92.

Harzing, A.W. 2004a. Strategy and structure of multinational companies. In A.W. Harzing & J. Van Ruysseveldt (eds), *International human resource management*: 33–64. London: Sage.

Harzing, A.W. 2004b. Composing an international staff. In A.W. Harzing & J. Van Ruysseveldt (eds), *International human resource management*: 251–82. London: Sage.

Harzing, A.W. & J. van Ruysseveldt. (eds) 2004. *International human resource management: An integrated approach*. Second edition. London: Sage

Hedlund, G. 1986. The hypermodern MNC: A heterarchy? *Human Resource Management*, **25**: 9–35.

Heenan, D.A. 1970. The corporate expatriate: assignment to ambiguity. *Columbia Journal of World Business*, **5**(3): 49–54.

Heenan, D.A. & H.V. Perlmutter. 1979. *Multinational organization development*. Reading, MA: Addison-Wesley.

Hofstede, G. 1980. *Culture's consequences: International differences in work-related values*. Beverly Hills: Sage.

Hofstede, G. 1991. *Cultures and organizations: Software of the mind*. London: McGraw-Hill.

Huselid, M.A. 1995. The impact of human resource management practices on turnover, productivity and corporate financial performance. *Academy of Management Journal*, **38**: 635–72.

Ivancevich, J.M. 1969. Perceived need satisfaction of domestic versus overseas managers. *Journal of Applied Psychology*, **53**: 274–8.

Lane, H., M. Maznevski & M. Mendenhall. 2004. Globalization: Hercules meets Buddha. In H. Lane, M. Maznevski, M. Mendenhall & J. Mcnett (eds), *The handbook of global management*: 3–25. Oxford: Blackwell.

Laurent, A. 1986. The cross-cultural puzzle of international human resource management. *Human Resource Management*, **25**(1): 91–103.

Macduffie, J.P. 1995. Human resource bundles and manufacturing performance: organizational logic and flexible production systems in the world auto industry. *Industrial and Labor Relations Review*, **48**: 197–221.

Mendenhall, M. & G. Oddou. 1985. The dimensions of expatriate acculturation. *Academy of Management Review*, **10**: 39–47.

Miller, E.L. 1973. The international selection decision: a study of some dimensions of managerial behavior in the selection decision process. *Academy of Management Journal*, **16**: 239–52.

Miller, E.L. & J.L. Cheng. 1978. A closer look at the decision to accept an overseas position. *Management International Review*, **3**: 25–33.

Pausenberger, E. & G.F. Noelle. 1977. Entsendung von Fuhrungskraften in Auslandische Niderlassungen. *Zeitschrift für Betriebswirtshaftliche Forschung*, **29**: 346–66.

Perlmutter, H. 1969. The tortuous evolution of the multinational company. *Columbia Journal of World Business*, **4**(1): 9–18.

Prahalad, C.K. 1990. Globalization: The intellectual and managerial challenges. *Human Resource Management*, **29**(1): 27–37.

Prahalad, C.K. & Y. Doz. 1987. *The multinational mission: balancing local demands and global vision*. New York: The Free Press.

Pucik, V. 1984. White collar human resource management in large Japanese manufacturing firms. *Human Resource Management*, **23**: 257–76.

Reynolds, C. 1997. Expatriate compensation in historical perspective. *Journal of World Business*, **32**(2): 118–32.

Robock, S.H. & K. Simmonds. 1973. *International business and multinational enterprises*. Homewood: Irwin.

Rosenzweig, P.M. & N. Nohria. 1994. Influences on human resource management practices in multinational corporations. *Journal of International Business Studies*, **25**: 229–51.

Schuler, R.S., P.J. Dowling & H. De Cieri. 1993. An integrative framework of strategic international human resource management. *Journal of Management*, **19**: 419–59.

Scullion, H. & M. Linehan. 2005. *International human resource management*. London et al.: Palgrave.

Sparrow, P., C. Brewster & H. Harris. 2004. *Globalizing human resource management*. London: Routledge.

Stahl, G.K. & M.E. Mendenhall. (eds) 2005. *Mergers and acquisitions: Managing culture and human resources*. Stanford: Stanford University Press.

Storey, J. (ed.) 1995. *Human resource management: A critical text*. London: Routledge.

Taylor, S., S. Beechler & N. Napier. 1996. Toward an integrative model of strategic international human resource management. *Academy of Management Review*, **21**: 959–85.

Torbiörn, I. 1982. *Living abroad: Personal adjustment and personnel policy in the overseas setting*. New York: Wiley.

Tsai, W. & S. Ghoshal. 1998. Social capital and value creation: the role of intrafirm networks. *Academy of Management Journal*, **41**: 464–76.

Tung, R.L. 1981. Selecting and training of personnel for overseas assignments. *Columbia Journal of World Business*, **16**(2): 67–78.

Tung. R.L. 1982. Selection and training procedures of US, European and Japanese multinationals. *California Management Review*, **25**(1): 57–71.

Welge, M. 1980. *Management in Deutschen multinationalen unternehmen*. Stuttgart: Poeschel.

Wright, P.M. & G.C. McMahan. 1992. Theoretical perspectives for strategic human resource management. *Journal of Management*, **18**: 295–320.

Zeira, Y., E. Harari & D.I. Nundi. 1975. Some structural and cultural factors in ethnocentric multinational corporations and employee morale. *Journal of Management Studies*, **12**: 66–82.

PART I

THE ROLE OF INTERNATIONAL HUMAN RESOURCE MANAGEMENT

2 Strategic international human resource management in multinational enterprises: developments and directions

Helen De Cieri and Peter J. Dowling

Globalization has brought remarkable developments in the diversity and complexity of international business and multinational enterprises (MNEs).[1] Concomitant with these developments has been increasing awareness that the management of a global workforce is a critical dimension of international business. A major aspect of MNE management relates to the area of 'strategic international human resource management' (SIHRM) (Milliman, Von Glinow & Nathan, 1991; Schuler, Dowling & De Cieri, 1993), which we relabel as 'strategic human resource management in MNEs' (De Cieri & Dowling, 1999). This field of research and practice draws upon HRM as a disciplinary base, and is embedded in the context of international business.

The first aim of this chapter is to explain the development of the field of SHRM in MNEs and to review the theoretical perspectives that inform research in this field. Second, we present a revised framework of SHRM for MNEs, based on recent developments and emerging directions in research and practice. Our third aim is to discuss the implications of this framework, to provide some guidance for future research in this field.

Strategic human resource management in multinational enterprises

The field of international human resource management has been characterized by three broad approaches (Dowling, 1999). Early work in this field (for example, Laurent, 1986) emphasized cross-cultural management issues. A second area of research has been developed in comparative HRM research (for example, Brewster, 1998; Hendry, 2003; Rowley, Benson & Warner, 2004). Third, much of the research in international HRM has focused on aspects of HRM in MNEs. This latter area is most widely recognized as international HRM, involving the same elements as HRM within a single country, yet with added complexity due to diversity of national contexts and inclusion of different national categories of workers (Dowling & Welch, 2004). A major aspect of international HRM research has developed

15

understanding of micro-level variables related to the cross-national transfer of employees and management practices (for example, Caligiuri, 2000; Engle, Mendenhall, Powers & Stedham, 2001; Zhang, 2003).

Parallel to the development of research on strategic HRM issues, international HRM researchers and practitioners have paid increasing attention to more macro-level issues, such as the strategic nature of international HRM and implications for organizational performance (McWilliams, Van Fleet & Wright, 2001). This work raised awareness of the emergence of SIHRM, which has been defined as:

> human resource management issues, functions, and policies and practices that result from the strategic activities of multinational enterprises and that impact the international concerns and goals of those enterprises. (Schuler *et al.*, 1993: 422.)

This definition is consistent with, yet expands upon, the definition of strategic HRM offered by Wright and McMahan (1992). Schuler *et al.* (1993) sought to build upon the work of Wright and McMahan (1992) and to build connection, rather than separation, between *strategic* and *international* HRM. This definition has been adopted by other writers in the field (for example, Taylor, Beechler & Napier, 1996).

The identification of SIHRM as a distinct area of research has been a useful step in differentiating the emergent 'strategic' and 'international' issues, but we argue that this has been an interim step which may be of greater benefit if we balance our search for distinctiveness from 'domestic' HRM with recognition of the similarities. We suggest that it is more appropriate to speak of 'strategic HRM in MNEs' when describing this area.

Schuler *et al.* (1993) presented an integrative framework of SIHRM, in which they concluded that a fundamental issue is the tension between the needs for global coordination (integration) and local responsiveness (differentiation) (Doz & Prahalad, 1991; Quintanilla & Ferner, 2003; Rosenzweig & Nohria, 1994). The framework showed factors exogenous and endogenous to an MNE that influence SIHRM issues, functions, policies and practices, thereby influencing the realization of MNE concerns and goals. Schuler *et al.* (1993) presented their framework as a conceptual model for exploratory analysis, and the framework has been noted as a useful tool that brings together the strategic and international dimensions of HRM (Kamoche, 1996; Taylor *et al.*, 1996).

In an important development in this field, Taylor *et al.* (1996) developed a theoretical model of the determinants of SIHRM systems in MNEs. These authors acknowledged the importance of the endogenous factors identified by Schuler *et al.* (1993), namely strategy, international experience of the firm, organizational structure and headquarters' international orientation, and suggested the importance of additional endogenous factors, such as organizational life cycle. Taylor *et al.* (1996) also recognized the influence of external factors on an MNE, and particularly on SHRM. They identified reciprocal influences between organizational factors, such as MNE strategy or life cycle stage, and SIHRM. Further they present a simplified version of SIHRM constituents, reducing Schuler *et al.*'s (1993) 'SIHRM issues, functions, policies and practices' to 'SIHRM orientation' (analogous to HR function strategy) and 'SIHRM functional focus' (comprising all HR practices). Similarly, De Cieri and Dowling (1999) presented a revised framework, highlighting the theoretical bases informing the framework and reviewing empirical research that reflected the substantive developments in this field throughout the 1990s.

While previous frameworks have provided useful and informative steps in the development of SHRM in MNEs, recent global events, represented by tumultuous events such as corporate scandals, terrorism and the 2004 tsunami disaster in Asia, suggest the need for a paradigmatic shift in our research approaches and practical applications, in order to build a contemporary vision of SHRM in MNEs. For example, Czinkota, Knight & Liesch (2004) make the point that the impact of terrorism is geopolitical and pervasive and has influenced risk management in MNEs in a fundamental way. In this context, it is pertinent to note that risk management has received scant attention in the extant literature related to SHRM in MNEs. Czinkota *et al.* (2004) discuss the increase in the level of *uncertainty* in the following areas:

1.   consumer demand for the firm's goods and services;
2.   supply of needed inputs, resources and services;
3.   government policies and laws enacted to deal with terrorism, thereby altering the business environment and the ease with which business is conducted;
4.   macroeconomic phenomena; and
5.   the nature of relations among countries.

SHRM in MNEs is involved closely with the first three of these five areas. The HR function in MNEs has been particularly affected by changes in the economic, geopolitical, social and biospheric environment. A comprehensive understanding of SHRM in MNEs in the new global context requires much more than a traditional focus on micro-level IHRM issues. Macro-level factors, particularly those external to the MNE, demand attention and investigation to reveal their implications for SHRM policies and practices in MNEs, and inevitably for MNE concerns and goals. We suggest that developments in these areas bring the need for a revised framework for

SHRM in MNEs. The complexity of globalization and global events invites multitheoretical, multi-level analysis. Following Guillén's (2001: 255) sociological analysis of the debate surrounding globalization, we suggest that we need a framework to encourage the integration of theoretical perspectives and research methodologies that bridge the micro–macro gap, 'i.e., that move across levels of analysis from the world-system to the nation-state, the industry, sector, community, organization, and group'. Before presenting our framework, in the following sections we acknowledge the theoretical and empirical bases for this framework.

Theoretical perspectives of SHRM in MNEs
Several theoretical perspectives have been applied to SHRM in MNEs, including institutional, economic and behavioural theories (see subsequent chapters of this book for detailed discussions). The theoretical perspectives vary in their philosophical assumptions and their foci: from exogenous (market-based) to endogenous (intraorganizational); from macro-level to micro-level; from strategic to non-strategic (De Cieri & Dowling, 1999). Although few of the theories were developed with human resources in mind, their application to SHRM in MNEs is worthwhile. Our framework, and those upon which it is built, draws from various theoretical perspectives, including institutional theory (Meyer & Rowan, 1977), resource dependence theory (Pfeffer & Cohen, 1984), transaction cost theory (Williamson, 1981), strategic choice theory (Child, 1972) and resource-based theory (Penrose, 1959).

In the following section we briefly review those perspectives which have received most research attention, which represent a broad spectrum of views and which appear most promising for explication of SHRM in MNEs.

The institutionalism perspective
The institutionalism perspective (DiMaggio & Powell, 1983; Scott, 1987) encompasses a broad range of perspectives. A common assumption is that 'the structural forms (as well as the identities and values sustaining these) of relevant external institutions map themselves on to organizations which depend on them for legitimacy, resourcing or staffing' (Child, 1997: 45). Institutional analysis focuses on the manner in which societal bodies accord social legitimacy to organizations and thereby contributes to achievement of organizational success and survival (Meyer & Rowan, 1977; Powell & DiMaggio, 1991).

When applied to HRM, an institutional perspective may help to explain the institutional pressures that may be powerful influences on HR strategy, programmes and practices. For example, it has been suggested that 'larger organizations should adopt more sophisticated and socially responsive HRM activities because these more visible organizations are under more pressure to gain legitimacy' (Jackson & Schuler, 1995: 245–6). An institutional (or neoinstitutional) perspective highlights the importance of external stakeholders such as regulatory bodies or communities of practice (Tregaskis, 2003). Overall a wide range of external factors, across the contexts of industry, nation and region, may influence organizational factors, SHRM in MNEs and the achievement of MNE concerns and goals.

The resource dependence perspective

In common with institutional theory, resource dependence theory (Pfeffer & Cohen, 1984; Pfeffer & Salancik, 1978) is focused upon relationships between an organization and its constituencies. A resource dependence perspective, however, considers that central to these relationships are exchanges of resources, in contrast to institutional theory's emphasis on concerns about social acceptability and legitimacy (Pfeffer & Cohen, 1984). A resource dependence perspective views the environment as the source of scarce and valued resources, which are essential for organizational survival. This perspective is focused on power relationships, identifying the ability of external parties to have command of resources that are vital for the operations of an organization as the basis for power over that organization (Child, 1997). An organization will be vulnerable if external parties control vital resources, such as knowledge, and the organization will strive to acquire control over those resources that minimize their dependence. Tregaskis (2003: 432–3) suggests that combining ideas from neoinstitutional and resource dependency theory is 'particularly powerful given the conflict between the need both for conformity (in response to isomorphic pressures) and for differentiation (in terms of having critical and valued resources), and given the diversity of institutional contexts influencing multinationals' operations'. As one example of application in research, these theories could help to explain the acquisition and transfer of knowledge through interorganizational and intraorganizational networks.

Taylor *et al.* (1996: 960) also viewed the resource dependence perspective as useful in the identification of 'situations in which MNCs will exercise control over the SIHRM system of their affiliates'. These authors combined resource dependence with a resource-based perspective and applied these to develop their theoretical model of the determinants of SIHRM systems in MNEs. Therefore we suggest that a resource dependence perspective supplements our knowledge of the influence of both external and organizational factors and their reciprocal relationships with SHRM policies and practices in MNEs.

The transaction cost perspective

This perspective, which informs much of international business theory (Buckley, 1996), has been noted as a potentially useful perspective for strategic HRM (Wright & McMahan, 1992). Transaction cost economics focus on the 'adaptative adjustments which organizations need to make in the face of pressures for maximizing efficiency in their internal and external transactions' (Reed, 1996: 39). From the transaction cost perspective, it is assumed that firms choose governance structures which economize transaction costs associated with establishing, monitoring, evaluating and enforcing agreed upon exchanges (Williamson, 1975, 1981). Several environmental factors and human factors will influence organizational efforts to minimize the costs associated with these exchanges. This perspective has direct implications for SHRM in MNEs, and the manner in which SHRM practices may be utilized to achieve a governance structure which enables the management of multiple implicit and explicit contracts between employers and employees (Wright & McMahan, 1992). Transaction cost economics may have particular applicability in the case of multinational joint ventures or strategic alliances. For example, Kabst (2004) has used this perspective to argue that selective control via functional gatekeepers, such as expatriate managers assigned to key joint venture positions, will provide an efficient mechanism to reduce opportunistic behaviour in joint venture relationships.

The transaction cost perspective has not received a great deal of attention in the SHRM literature, with some notable exceptions (cf. Festing, 1997; Kabst, 2004). While recognizing that transaction cost economics provides additional support for the idea that there are reciprocal relationships between endogenous factors, SHRM and MNE concerns or goals, we note that a criticism of this perspective is that it fails to provide 'any sustained interest or concern with social power and human agency' (Reed, 1996: 39).

The strategic choice perspective

A strategic choice perspective focuses on the interaction of people and environment (Child, 1972, 1997). For example, organizational members belong to external bodies, and can influence them, through actions such as lobbying, or through social networks. Strategic choice is defined as 'the process whereby power-holders within organizations decide upon courses of strategic action . . . Strategic choices are seen to be made through initiatives within the network of internal and external organizational relationships – through *pro-action* as well as *re-action*' (Child, 1997: 45–6). Strategic choice is essentially a political phenomenon, and the term 'strategic' is used to identify matters of importance to the organization as a whole, particularly issues with impact on performance.

From a strategic choice perspective, it is argued that managers create and select environments by choice of domain, representing a view of managers as more proactive than the contingency view. Child (1997) recognizes constraints on managers, but argues that they still have significant latitude for decision making. The influence of environmental factors is recognized, but is viewed as mediated by managerial choice. The process of strategic choice may be viewed as a dynamic social process. Actors, both individuals and firms, are capable of learning, and organizational structures and routines are both affected and modified by the learning process (Child, 1997). HR managers' values influence strategies and practices, and determine decisions made across a range of areas. Hence the HR manager in an MNE has the opportunity to play a strategic role in the adoption of strategies that deal with a variety of demands and have potential for significant positive outcomes for the organization.

We suggest that a strategic choice perspective contributes to our understanding of SHRM in MNEs by emphasizing the influence of organizational factors, such as managers' international orientation and experience, on SHRM and MNE concerns and goals. The work by Brewster, Tregaskis, Hegewisch and Mayne (1996) highlights the reciprocity between HR function strategy and the organizational factors of corporate-level and business-level strategy.

Resource-based perspective

The resource-based view of the firm has been applied in research related to SHRM in MNEs; for example, relationships between strategic issues and SHRM in MNEs have been highlighted by research applying a resource-based perspective (Kamoche, 1997; Li, 2003; Park, Mitsuhashi, Fey & Björkman, 2003). However several scholars have identified challenges or limitations encountered by resource-based approaches to HRM (for example, Coff, 1997; Lei, Hitt & Bettis, 1996). As Delery (1998: 290) has noted, 'while the resource-based view provides a nice backdrop, explaining the importance of human resources to firm competitiveness, it does not deal with how an organization can develop and support the human resources it needs for competitive advantage'. Recognizing such limitations, several researchers have advocated an integrative approach, recognizing the explanatory power of other theoretical perspectives, which complement or build upon the resource-based view (for example, Colbert, 2004).

In addition to the theoretical perspectives discussed above, we note the emergent application of other perspectives. For example, political influence theory (Judge & Ferris, 1991, cited in Novicevic & Harvey, 2001) has been applied to explicate the increasing influence of the corporate HR function in MNEs. This perspective appears to have potential to provide useful new insights, and to raise new areas for research in SHRM in MNEs, to complement the understanding gained via strategic and rational perspectives. Furthermore we note some emerging interest in critical and post-modern perspectives of international management (Welge & Holtbrügge, 1999) and SHRM in MNEs (De Cieri, Wolfram Cox & Fenwick, 2001).

Each of the perspectives discussed above, and others, holds potential for useful contributions to understanding of SHRM in MNEs. However we acknowledge that, overwhelmingly, the SHRM field has been influenced in the past decade or so by the resource-based view of the firm (Penrose, 1959; Boxall & Purcell, 2003; Wright, Dunford & Snell, 2001). Overall SHRM in MNEs may be best understood via integration of multiple disciplinary bases and theoretical perspectives, to explain the complex phenomena under investigation. Indeed there are 'signs that a more integrated, eclectic approach is emerging . . . as researchers strive to weave together elements taken from a variety of theoretical perspectives' (Quintanilla & Ferner, 2003: 364).

Development of research on SHRM in MNEs

While early work in the international management field was criticized for being atheoretical or monotheoretical, the past decade has shown substantial progress in theory development and empirical research design applied to SHRM in MNEs. Despite progress, some problems are enduring. Many studies of SHRM in MNEs suffer from small sample size and low response rates. Much of the research has been restricted to quantitative analysis, often using proxy measures, although there is increasing use of qualitative methodologies and multi-method approaches. A large proportion of research on SHRM in MNEs uses HR managers as the sole respondent for each MNE represented in their sample. Use of reports directly from managers and employees (parent, host and third country nationals) would serve to validate the reports of HR managers, particularly with respect to the perceived effectiveness of SHRM strategy and practices.

Overall early research related to SHRM in MNEs has been atheoretical or monotheoretical. While this has been an important research phase, it was necessary to move on to the next iteration, by implementing theory-based, hypothetico-deductive research designs. More recent research is theory-driven, with integrative, multitheoretical approaches and more rigorous research designs. To assist in the development of this research, we propose a conceptual framework to build upon extant literature and to provide some guidance for future research seeking to examine relationships between the factors relevant to SHRM in MNEs.

Development of a framework of SHRM in MNEs

As mentioned earlier in this chapter, Schuler *et al.* (1993) presented an integrative framework of SIHRM. In our view, developments in research and practice relevant to SHRM in MNEs have brought the need for continuing revision of the framework (De Cieri & Dowling, 1999). A revised framework of SHRM in MNEs is shown in Figure 2.1 and discussed in the following sections, including examples of recent developments relevant to each section of the framework. It is important to acknowledge that our framework provides a somewhat simplified representation of the dynamic interrelationships between the elements shown in the various boxes. It should also be noted that, while Schuler *et al.* (1993) presented the integration–differentiation balance as the management of strategic MNE components, an issue separated from other elements of SIHRM, research by Kamoche (1996) has suggested that this balance is perhaps more accurately represented as integral to the concerns and goals of MNEs; we represent this balance in our revised framework in this way.

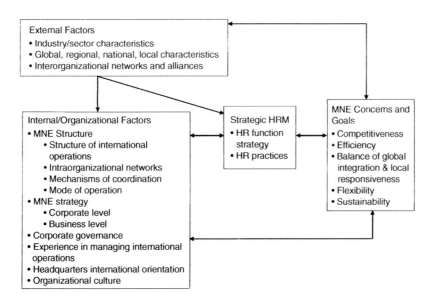

Source: Adapted from H. De Cieri & P.J. Dowling. 1999. Strategic human resource management in multinational enterprises: theoretical and empirical developments. In P.M. Wright, L.D. Dyer, J.W. Boudreau & G.T. Milkovich (eds), *Research in personnel and human resources management: strategic human resources management in the twenty-first century*: 318. Supplement 4, Stamford, CT: JAI Press.

Figure 2.1   A framework of strategic HRM in multinational enterprises

External factors
MNEs operate in the context of worldwide conditions, including the influences of industry or sector, and global, regional, national and local markets, which include geopolitical, legal, cultural and economic characteristics (Cheng & Hitt, 2004; Hitt, Keats & DeMarie, 1998; Katz & Darbishire, 2000). Recent research suggests that external factors exert direct influence in a number of ways. We suggest that external factors have direct influence on both internal/organization factors and SHRM strategy and practices. Furthermore we suggest that external factors have a direct influence on MNE concerns and goals. For example, research in countries undergoing significant economic transformation, such as Poland or China, indicates that the human resource function has been substantially influenced by the changing external environment (Weinstein & Obloj, 2002; Zhu, Cooper, De Cieri & Dowling, 2005). Furthermore concerns about security and global risks (Suder, 2004) have led many MNEs to rethink their approaches to SHRM strategies and practices, such as those related to global mobility of employees (Cendant Mobility, 2002; GMAC Global Relocation Services, National Foreign Trade Council & SHRM Global Forum, 2003). In this context, SHRM in MNEs might include, for example, reducing the use of expatriates; altering the nature of international assignments, relying more on virtual assignments (Harris & Brewster, 2003; Welch & Fenwick, 2003) and/or ceasing operations in a location that has become too difficult. These options involve important decisions with implications for management of employees, management of risk (financial and personal) and the strategic management of the MNE.

Another feature of the external environment is the emergence of the global knowledge economy as a challenging competitive environment for business and management (Doz, Santos & Williamson, 2001). In order to compete effectively in global markets, managers need to move away from competition and imitation as the basis for relationships with other organizations and focus on adding value and innovation through cooperation (Kim & Mauborgne, 1999). Studies show that interorganizational networks and alliances have increased and are a crucial aspect of globalization (Pettigrew *et al.*, 2003). Interorganizational networks and alliances may be complex relationship webs based upon personal relationships and trust; non-binding social contracts that may be, nevertheless, long-term, pervasive and strong in nature (Gulati & Gargiulo, 1999). Networks may include parent country managers and employees, host country managers and employees, host country governments, and investors. Central to network management is an emphasis on human resources that recognizes that knowledge, power and perceived trustworthiness are often person-specific rather than organization-specific. One implication for SHRM in MNEs is that interorganizational networks need to attract, motivate and retain people who have strong personal networks and who excel in collaborative work (Tung, 2002).

Internal/organizational factors

Internal/organizational factors have been a major focus of international business and SHRM research throughout recent decades. These factors are suggested to hold implications not only for areas such as SHRM, but also for overall organizational MNE performance. Following developments in the literature (for example, Taylor *et al.*, 1996), we suggest that there are reciprocal relationships between internal factors, SHRM and MNE concerns and goals.

Referring to Figure 2.1, internal factors are shown in order of most 'tangible' to most 'intangible'. First, the *organizational structure* literature has shown the importance, not only of the structure of MNEs (Kidger, 2002), but also of intraorganizational networks (Wolf, 1997), mechanisms of coordination (Harvey & Novicevic, 2002; Hedlund, 1994) and mode of operation, for SHRM in MNEs (Barkema, Bell & Pennings, 1996). Second, we note that developments in the *organizational strategy* literature have substantial implications for SHRM (McWilliams *et al.*, 2001; Wright *et al.*, 2001). Of particular relevance here, the relationship and possibility for reciprocity between organizational strategy and human resource management, and their relationship with firm performance, have received much attention over the past two decades (for example, Björkman & Xiucheng, 2002; Li, 2003). Third, issues related to *corporate governance* and incorporating ethical principles and values into international business practice have become increasingly important for MNE managers, particularly in light of cases of corporate wrongdoing, yet this is fraught with challenges for SHRM in MNEs (Dowling & Welch, 2004). For example, HR managers may be required to play important roles in corporate governance, such as the design, implementation and maintenance of corporate codes of conduct (Beatty, Ewing & Tharp, 2003), but training in and enforcement of codes of conduct are difficult across the complex context of an MNE (Dowling & Welch, 2004). Fourth and fifth, we note that *experience in international business* and *headquarters' international orientation* (Caligiuri & Stroh, 1995; Kidger, 2002) are well established as important factors for SHRM in MNEs. Finally we include *organizational culture*, the 'sense of common identity and purpose across the whole organisation' (Kidger, 2002: 81), in our framework. Researchers have recently investigated the relationship between organizational culture and SHRM in MNEs. For MNEs, particularly those seeking a high level of global integration, organizational culture, sustaining a shared global mindset, may provide a valuable resource to support HR practices and enhance firm performance (Chan, Shaffer & Snape, 2004; Engle *et al.*, 2001).

SHRM: HR function strategy and practices
Referring again to Figure 2.1, we now focus on the elements of SHRM: HR function strategy and HR practices. As with other functional areas of management, such as information technology and marketing, it is necessary to identify the relevant HR function strategy at the relevant level of the MNE (corporate- or business-level). Dyer (1985) suggested that the HR function should be integrated into processes of strategy formulation and strategy implementation. Dyer (1984) differentiated the content and process of strategy making in HRM, and emphasized the fluid, dynamic nature of emergent strategy. He emphasized the importance of the presence of an HR director at board level, proactivity in the HR function and coherence between HR strategy and practices. More recently globalization of business has increased the pressure for the HR function in MNEs to perform at a strategic level, influencing and enabling systems for global leadership development, managing diversity and global mobility management (Dowling & Welch, 2004; Novicevic & Harvey, 2001; Scullion & Starkey, 2000). For example, the HR function can play valuable strategic roles when it broadens its function to that of change agent developing global mindsets in a boundaryless world (Sanchez, Spector & Cooper, 2000).

HR practices involve attracting, motivating and retaining staff to support business goals and objectives (Dowling & Welch, 2004; Hiltrop, 2002). These practices typically include all HR programmes conducted in MNEs across national borders (see later chapters in this book for detailed discussions of HR practices). These may include global shared services, worldwide training programmes, expatriation management, and so on. Their role in enhancing less formal aspects of organization, such as relationship building and network development has recently been noted (Novicevic & Harvey, 2001). Several studies have shown that HR practices such as expatriate management are influenced by both external and internal/organizational factors, and have positive implications for organizational outcomes. One example of the strategic value of human resources and organizational learning is evident in the knowledge acquired by expatriates on assignment and transferred across the organization (Hocking, Brown & Harzing, 2004).

Effective SHRM is expected to improve MNE competitiveness overall. This view is influenced by the emerging body of SHRM literature that examines the relationships between internal/organizational factors, HR strategy and practices, and MNE performance. A recent trend in research on SHRM in MNEs has been to examine the overall system of HR practices, rather than individual HR practices. Empirical findings overall have provided some support for the hypothesis that a 'high performance' HR system will contribute to organizational performance, including firm financial outcomes (for example, Björkman & Xiucheng, 2002), although the relationship between HRM and organizational performance has been hotly debated in the HRM literature (see, for example, Paauwe, 2004; Wright, Gardner & Moynihan, 2003). While a focus on large MNEs has dominated this research field, it is recognized that small and internationalizing firms also face significant issues with regard to their human resources (De Cieri & Dowling, 1999; Dowling & Welch, 2004).

MNE concerns and goals
Consistent with Schuler *et al.* (1993), we suggest that MNEs have numerous strategic concerns and goals, which may include *competitiveness, efficiency, balance of global integration* and *local responsiveness, flexibility* and *sustainability*. These concerns and goals relate to outcomes towards which each MNE is striving; the importance and relevance of each outcome will vary across organizations; organizational outcomes are related to and result, at least in part, from each of the preceding elements in our framework.

The first four of these outcomes have been discussed in previous research (see, for example, De Cieri & Dowling, 1999). In revising the framework, we have added corporate *sustainability* as a desired MNE outcome. As noted earlier with regard to organizational factors, HR managers in MNEs are under increasing pressure to establish and maintain high standards of corporate governance, in order to achieve the goal of corporate sustainability. The traditional focus of corporate governance with regard to MNE concerns and goals is on financial performance, reporting to shareholders and protecting shareholders' interests. However society in general, and employees and customers in particular, expect executives and managers to demonstrate the highest standards of ethics, transparency and responsiveness. Hence there is increasing pressure for the focus of corporate governance to broaden, to address the concerns of all stakeholders (Daily, Dalton & Cannella, 2003) and to aim for corporate sustainability, which refers to the continuing, voluntary commitment by companies to establish and maintain a systematic approach to the management of environmental, social, economic and governance issues. This requires companies and managers to behave in ethical ways and to contribute to economic development while improving quality of life for employees, their families, the local community and society in general (Global Reporting Initiative, 2002; Hemingway & Maclagan, 2004).

In endeavouring to achieve desired outcomes, such as sustainability, organizations increasingly derive value from human resources; this strategic importance of the global workforce makes decisions about SHRM in

MNEs critical to organizational success. Therefore we suggest that HR metrics that show a connection between HR and key organizational outcomes are essential (De Cieri & Boudreau, 2003).

Often links between the HR function in an MNE and organizational success are not easy to demonstrate as the assessment of HR performance and its relationship with organizational performance is a complex and often difficult task. A simple indicator may not adequately measure performance, as organizations have different goals relating to effectiveness and efficiency. A recent survey of 249 executives worldwide conducted on behalf of Deloitte Touche Tohmatsu by the Economist Intelligence Unit found that the majority of board directors and senior executives considered specific factors such as customer satisfaction, innovation, supplier relations and employee commitment as critical to corporate success, although they recognized that these factors are difficult to measure. When they were asked why board members and senior managers lacked information on intangible assets, such as the contribution of HR, respondents identified two main barriers: the absence of developed tools for analysing non-financial measures and scepticism that such measures would directly affect the bottom line (*Human Resources*, 2004). A well-thought-out measurement system needs to act as a guide for evaluating HR's contribution to strategy implementation and provide a valid and systematic justification for resource allocation decisions (Becker, Huselid & Ulrich, 2001). A measurement system should provide the HR function with the opportunity to demonstrate its contribution to organizational success.

Overall SHRM in MNEs requires a comprehensive and flexible framework to fit a great variety of situations because managing across national boundaries requires attention to and measurement of external factors, internal/organizational factors, HR strategy and practices and MNE concerns and goals.

Future directions for SHRM in MNEs
In the following sections we consider the potential directions for SHRM in MNEs, with respect to theory, research, teaching and practice in this field.

Implications for theory development
The various theoretical perspectives discussed in this chapter and in subsequent chapters of this book are all valuable but unlikely to be sufficient for an explanation of SHRM in MNEs. Thus we argue that future research will be most likely to benefit from multiple theoretical perspectives. It is recognized that progress will be iterative and protracted, but, as Jackson and Schuler (1995: 256) have suggested, 'research driven by incomplete theories is more likely to accumulate to form a meaningful body of knowledge,

compared to research driven by no theory at all'. Cross-fertilization of ideas and issues seems a productive approach to take to the development of theory and empirical research for SHRM in MNEs.

Implications for research

Although research on SHRM in MNEs has made several important steps forward, inadequacies remain. The frameworks that have been developed, including our own, tend to be broad and somewhat unspecified. While intended to provide a comprehensive and useful overview of issues/factors to consider when examining SHRM issues in MNEs, the frameworks contain few specified relationships between the different boxes and between items within each of the boxes. We suggest that there are a number of areas that require attention in future research. Researchers may seek to develop understanding of the implications of various theoretical perspectives for SHRM in MNEs. We present our framework as an exploratory model of SHRM in MNEs. We encourage researchers to adapt and revise the framework further as understanding of the field develops. For example, much of the research in this field has focused on large, stand-alone, profit-based MNEs. To retain broad applicability in the 21st century, testing of the framework in application to diverse organizational forms is recommended. While this is intended to be a general and comprehensive framework, it may need adaptation to be applicable to international non-government organizations (INGOs) (Ramia, 2003; Teegan, Doh & Vachani, 2004). There is widespread recognition of the emerging importance of INGOs, which are in part different because they are *value-driven* (the INGO response to the tsunami disaster in Asia is an excellent example). SHRM in INGOs may have much in common with SHRM in MNEs but additional factors, such as the voluntary workforce and value-driven nature of INGOs, would need to be considered as organizational factors (Fenwick, in press). Terrorism is also value-driven and this is the hallmark of the change to risk management for MNEs dealing with the problem (Czinkota *et al.*, 2004). Future research is needed to explicate the role of SHRM in MNEs in developing effective risk management in the 21st century.

It may be worthwhile to re-examine the factors we have identified and to further explore the relationships within and between the elements in our framework of SHRM in MNEs. In order to do so, researchers may choose to develop specific research propositions or hypotheses that operationalize their particular research focus.

Further work is needed to overcome methodological problems and develop an integrative and multidisciplinary understanding of the field with theoretical rigour and concrete operationalization of terms (Schuler & Florkowski, 1996). Sundaram and Black (1992) have suggested that the multidisciplinary nature of MNEs has implications for the manner in which scholars are trained, as it may be necessary to train scholars who are willing and able to assimilate views outside a particular discipline. An alternative approach would be to build research teams incorporating various specializations, to overcome the limitations of any individual's area of knowledge or expertise. Research on SHRM in MNEs may require multidisciplinary and multicultural collaborations in order to understand and explore complex phenomena, although there are inherent challenges to the conduct of such research (cf. Brewster *et al.*, 1996; Teagarden *et al.*, 1995).

Implications for practice
On some issues related to SHRM in MNEs, it is evident that a research–practice gap exists, with research lagging behind the current needs of HR practitioners and managers in MNEs. The gap may not be easy to fill, as there are complex issues to define, measure and address. The complexities of international research remain daunting. There is also a practice–research gap, with SHRM practice in MNEs in some aspects lagging behind research. In many organizations it could be said that the state of practice lags far behind the state of knowledge (De Cieri, Fenwick & Hutchings, 2005; Wasti & Robert, 2004). We encourage knowledge sharing between academics and practitioners, to bridge these identified gaps and develop the field.

Conclusion
As global integration builds up and more businesses expand their operations across national borders, issues around SHRM in MNEs have become critical to organizational sustainability and success. As this occurs, the importance of SHRM in MNEs as a field of academic endeavour is becoming more pronounced. While there are many complexities and challenges for the development of SHRM in MNEs, the opportunities for progressing this field are substantial.

Note
1.   Throughout this chapter, the term 'multinational enterprise (MNE)' is used as a generic title for organizations identifiable by the various criteria offered by Sundaram and Black (1992), and Bartlett and Ghoshal (1992).

References
Barkema, H.G., J.H.J. Bell & J.M. Pennings. 1996. Foreign entry, cultural barriers and learning. *Strategic Management Journal*, **17**: 151–66.
Bartlett, C. & S. Ghoshal. 1992. *Transnational management: Text, cases, and readings in cross border management*. Boston, MA: Irwin.
Beatty, R.W., J.R. Ewing & C.G. Tharp. 2003. HR's role in corporate governance: present and prospective. *Human Resource Management*, **42**: 257–69.

Becker, B.E., M.A. Huselid & D. Ulrich. 2001. *The HR scorecard: Linking people, strategy and performance*. Boston, MA: Harvard Business School Press.

Björkman, I. & F. Xiucheng. 2002. Human resource management and the performance of Western firms in China. *International Journal of Human Resource Management*, **13**: 853–64.

Boxall, P.F. & J. Purcell. 2003. *Strategy and human resource management*. Basingstoke, UK: Palgrave Macmillan.

Brewster, C. 1998. Strategic HRM: questions raised by international and comparative data. In P.M. Wright, L.D. Dyer, J.W. Boudreau & G.T. Milkovich (eds), *Research in personnel and human resources management: strategic human resources management in the twenty-first century*, Supplement 4, Greenwich, CT: JAI Press.

Brewster, C., O. Tregaskis, A. Hegewisch & L. Mayne. 1996. Comparative survey research in human resource management: a review and an example. *International Journal of Human Resource Management*, **7**: 585–604.

Buckley, P.J. 1996. The role of management in international business theory: a meta-analysis and integration of the literature on international business and international management. *Management International Review*, **36**(1): 7–54.

Caligiuri, P. 2000. Selecting expatriates for personality characteristics: a moderating effect of personality on the relationship between host national contact and cross-cultural adjustment. *Management International Review*, **40**(1): 61–80.

Caligiuri, P.M. & L.K. Stroh. 1995. Multinational corporate management strategies and international human resource practices: bringing IHRM to the bottom line. *International Journal of Human Resource Management*, **6**: 494–507.

Cendant Mobility, 2002. *2002 worldwide benchmark study: new approaches to global mobility.* Bethesda, MD: Cendant Mobility Services Corporation.

Chan, L.L.M., M.A. Shaffer & E. Snape. 2004. In search of sustained competitive advantage: the impact of organizational culture, competitive strategy and human resource management practices on firm performance. *International Journal of Human Resource Management*, **15**(1): 17–35.

Cheng, J.L.C. & M. Hitt. (eds) 2004. *Managing multinationals in a knowledge economy: economics, culture and human resources*. London: JAI Press.

Child, J. 1972. Organizational structure, environment and performance: the role of strategic choice. *Sociology*, **6**: 1–22.

Child, J. 1997. Strategic choice in the analysis of action, structure, organizations and environment: retrospect and prospect. *Organization Studies*, **18**(1): 43–76.

Coff, R.W. 1997. Human assets and management dilemmas: coping with hazards on the road to resource-based theory. *Academy of Management Review*, **22**: 374–402.

Colbert, B. 2004. The complex resource-based view: implications for theory and practice in human resource management. *Academy of Management Review*, **29**: 341–58.

Czinkota, M.R., G.A. Knight & P.W. Liesch. 2004. Terrorism and international business: conceptual foundations. In G.G.S. Suder (ed.), *Terrorism and the international business environment. The security–business nexus:* 43–57. Cheltenham, UK and Northampton, MA, USA: Edward Elgar.

Daily, C.M., D.R. Dalton & A.A. Cannella Jr. 2003. Corporate governance: decades of dialogue and data. *Academy of Management Review*, **28**(3): 371–82.

De Cieri, H. & J.W. Boudreau. 2003. Global human resource metrics. In J. Scott, J. Edwards & N. Raju (eds), *The human resources program evaluation handbook*: 493–513. Thousand Oaks, CA: Sage.

De Cieri, H. & P.J. Dowling. 1999. Strategic human resource management in multinational enterprises: theoretical and empirical developments. In P.M. Wright, L.D. Dyer, J.W. Boudreau & G.T. Milkovich (eds), *Research in personnel and human resources management: strategic human resources management in the twenty-first century*: 305–27. Supplement 4, Stamford, CT: JAI Press.

De Cieri, H., M. Fenwick & K. Hutchings. 2005. The challenge of international human resource management: balancing the duality of strategy and practice. *International Journal of Human Resource Management*, **16**: 588–602.

De Cieri, H., J. Wolfram Cox & M. Fenwick. 2001. Think global, act local: from naïve comparison to critical participation in the teaching of strategic international human resource management. *Tamara. Journal of Critical Postmodern Organization Science*, **1**(1): 68–78.

Delery, J. 1998. Issues of fit in strategic human resource management: implications for research. *Human Resource Management Review*, **8**: 289–309.

DiMaggio, P.J. & W.W. Powell. 1983. The iron cage revisited: institutional isomorphism and collective rationality in organizational fields. *American Sociological Review*, **23**: 111–36.

Dowling, P.J. 1999. Completing the puzzle: issues in the development of the field of international human resource management. *Management International Review*, **39**(Special issue 3): 27–43.

Dowling, P.J. & D.E. Welch. 2004. *International human resource management. Managing people in a multinational context*. Fourth edition. London: Thomson.

Doz, Y. & K. Prahalad. 1991. Managing DMNCs: a search for a new paradigm. *Strategic Management Journal*, **12**: 145–64.

Doz, Y., J. Santos & P. Williamson. 2001. *From global to metanational: how companies win in the knowledge economy*, Boston, MA: Harvard Business School Press.

Dyer, L. 1984. Studying human resource strategy: an approach and an agenda. *Industrial Relations*, **23**(2): 156–69.

Dyer, L. 1985. Strategic human resources management and planning. In K.M. Rowland & G.R. Ferris (eds), *Research in personnel and human resources management*: 1–30. Greenwich, CT: JAI Press.

Engle, A.D., M.E. Mendenhall, R.L. Powers & Y. Stedham. 2001. Conceptualizing the global competency cube: a transitional model of human resources. *Journal of European Industrial Training*, **25**: 346–53.

Fenwick, M.S. In press. Extending strategic international human resource management research and pedagogy to the non-profit multinational. *International Journal of Human Resource Management*.

Festing, M. 1997. International human resource management strategies in multinational corporations: theoretical assumptions and empirical evidence from German firms. *Management International Review*, **37**(Special issue 1): 43–63.

Global Reporting Initiative. 2002. *Sustainability reporting guidelines*, Global Reporting Initiative: Boston MA, http://www.globalreporting.org/guidelines/, accessed 10 October, 2004.

GMAC Global Relocation Services, National Foreign Trade Council & SHRM Global Forum 2003. *Global relocation trends 2002 survey report*. New Jersey: GMAC Global Relocation Services.

Guillén, M. 2001. Is globalization civilizing, destructive or feeble? A critique of five key debates in the social science literature. *Annual Review of Sociology*, **27**: 235–60.

Gulati, R. & M. Gargiulo. 1999. Where do interorganizational networks come from? *American Journal of Sociology*, **104**: 1439–93.

Harris, H. & C. Brewster. 2003. Alternatives to traditional international assignments. In W. Mayrhofer, G. Stahl & T. Kuhlmann (eds), *Innovative anstatze im internationalen personalmanagement (Innovating HRM)*, Munich/Mering: Hampp Verlag.

Harvey, M. & M.M. Novicevic. 2002. The co-ordination of strategic initiatives within global organizations: the role of global teams. *International Journal of Human Resource Management*, **13**: 660–76.

Hedlund, G. 1994. A model of knowledge management and the N-form corporation. *Strategic Management Journal*, **15**: 73–90.

Hemingway, C.A. & P.W. Maclagan. 2004. Managers' personal values as drivers of corporate social responsibility. *Journal of Business Ethics*, **50**: 33–44.

Hendry, C. 2003. Applying employment systems theory to the analysis of national models of HRM. *International Journal of Human Resource Management*, **14**: 1430–37.

Hiltrop, J.M. 2002. Mapping the HRM practices of international organizations. *Strategic Change*, **11**: 329–38.

Hitt, M., B. Keats & S. DeMarie. 1998. Navigating in the new competitive landscape: building strategic flexibility and competitive advantage in the 21st century. *Academy of Management Executive*, **12**(4): 22–42.

Hocking, B.J., M. Brown & A.-W. Harzing. 2004. A knowledge transfer perspective of strategic assignment purposes and their path-dependent outcomes. *International Journal of Human Resource Management*, **15**: 565–86.

Human Resources. 2004. Boards struggle with non-financials, 17 November.

Jackson, S.E. & R.S. Schuler. 1995. Understanding human resource management in the context of organizations and their environments. *Annual Review of Psychology*, **46**: 237–64.

Kabst, R. 2004. Human resource management for international joint ventures: expatriation and selective control. *International Journal of Human Resource Management*, **15**: 1–16.

Kamoche, K. 1996. The integration–differentiation puzzle: a resource capability perspective in international human resource management. *International Journal of Human Resource Management*, **7**: 230–44.

Kamoche, K. 1997. Knowledge creation and learning in international HRM. *International Journal of Human Resource Management*, **8**: 213–25.

Katz, H. & O. Darbishire. 2000. *Converging divergences: worldwide changes in employment systems*. Ithaca, NY: Cornell University Press.

Kidger, P.J. 2002. Management structure in multinational enterprises. *Employee Relations*, **24**(1/2): 69–85.

Kim, W.C. & R. Mauborgne. 1999. Strategy, value innovation, and the knowledge economy. *Sloan Management Review*, **40**(3): 41–54.

Laurent, A. 1986. The cross-cultural puzzle of international human resource management. *Human Resource Management*, **5**: 581–608.

Lei, D., M.A. Hitt & R. Bettis. 1996. Dynamic core competences through meta-learning and strategic context. *Journal of Management*, **22**: 549–69.

Li, J. 2003. Strategic human resource management and MNEs' performance in China. *International Journal of Human Resource Management*, **14**: 157–73.

McWilliams, A., D.D. Van Fleet & P.M. Wright. 2001. Strategic management of human resources for global competitive advantage. *Journal of Business Strategies*, **18**: 1–24.

Meyer, J.W. & R. Rowan. 1977. Institutional organizations: formal structure as myth and ceremony. *American Journal of Sociology*, **83**: 340–63.

Milliman, J., M.A. Von Glinow & M. Nathan. 1991. Organizational life cycles and strategic international human resource management in multinational companies: implications for congruence theory. *Academy of Management Review*, **16**: 318–39.

Novicevic, M. & M. Harvey. 2001. The changing role of the corporate HR function in global organizations of the twenty-first century. *International Journal of Human Resource Management*, **12**: 1251–68.

Paauwe, J. 2004. *HRM and performance – achieving long term viability*. Oxford: Oxford University Press.

Park, H.J., H. Mitsuhashi, C.F. Fey & I. Björkman. 2003. The effect of human resource management practices on Japanese MNC subsidiary performance: a partial mediating model. *International Journal of Human Resource Management*, **14**: 1391–1406.

Penrose, E.T. 1959. *The theory of the growth of the firm*. Oxford: Blackwell.

Pettigrew, A.M., R. Whittington, L. Melin, C. Sanchez-Runde, F.A.J. Van Den Bosch, W. Ruigrok & T. Numagami. 2003. *Innovative forms of organizing*. London: Sage.

Pfeffer, J. & Y. Cohen. 1984. Determinants of internal labor markets in organizations. *Administrative Science Quarterly*, **33**: 588–606.

Pfeffer, J. & G. Salancik. 1978. *The external control of organizations: a resource dependence perspective*. New York: Harper & Row.

Powell, W.W. & P.J. DiMaggio. 1991. *The new institutionalism in organizational analysis*. Chicago, IL: University of Chicago Press.

Quintanilla, J. & A. Ferner. 2003. Multinationals and human resource management: between global convergence and national identity. *International Journal of Human Resource Management*, **14**: 363–8.

Ramia, G. 2003. Global social policy, INGOs and strategic management. *Global Social Policy*, **3**(1): 79–101.

Reed, M. 1996. Organizational theorizing: a historically contested terrain. In S.R. Clegg, C. Hardy & W.R. Nord (eds), *Handbook of organization studies*: 31–56. London: Sage.

Rosenzweig, P.M. & N. Nohria. 1994. Influences on human resource management practices in multinational corporations. *Journal of International Business Studies*, **25**: 229–51.

Rowley, C., J. Benson & M. Warner. 2004. Towards an Asian model of human resource management? A comparative analysis of China, Japan and South Korea. *International Journal of Human Resource Management*, **15**: 917–33.

Sanchez, J.I., P.E. Spector & C.L. Cooper. 2000. Adapting to a boundaryless world: a developmental expatriate model. *Academy of Management Executive*, **14**(2): 96–106.

Schuler, R.S. & G.W. Florkowski. 1996. International human resources management. In B.J. Punnett & O. Shenkar (eds), *Handbook of international management research*: 351–401. Cambridge, MA: Blackwell.

Schuler, R.S., P.J. Dowling & H. De Cieri. 1993. An integrative framework of strategic international human resource management. *Journal of Management*, **19**: 419–59.

Scott, W.R. 1987. The adolescence of institutional theory. *Administrative Science Quarterly*, **32**: 493–511.

Scullion, H. & K. Starkey. 2000. In search of the changing role of the corporate human resource function in the international firm. *International Journal of Human Resource Management*, **11**: 1061–81.

Suder, G.G.S. (ed.) 2004. *Terrorism and the international business environment. The security–business nexus*, Cheltenham, UK and Northampton, MA, USA: Edward Elgar.

Sundaram, A.K. & J.S. Black. 1992. The environment and internal organization of multinational enterprises. *Academy of Management Review*, **17**: 729–57.

Taylor, S., S. Beechler & N. Napier. 1996. Towards an integrative model of strategic international human resource management. *Academy of Management Review*, **21**: 959–85.

Teagarden, M.B, M.A. Von Glinow, D.E. Bowen, C.A. Frayne, S. Nason, Y.P. Huo, J. Milliman, M.A. Arias, M.C. Butler, J.M. Geringer, N.K. Kim, H. Scullion, K.B. Lowe & E.A. Drost. 1995. Towards building a theory of comparative management research methodology: an idiographic case study of the Best International Human Resources Management Project. *Academy of Management Journal*, **38**: 1261–87.

Teegan, H., J.P. Doh & S. Vachani. 2004. The importance of nongovernmental organizations (NGOs) in global governance and value creation: an international business research agenda. *Journal of International Business Studies*, **35**: 463–83.

Tregaskis, O. 2003. Learning networks, power and legitimacy in multinational subsidiaries. *International Journal of Human Resource Management*, **14**: 431–47.

Tung, R.L. 2002. Building effective networks. *Journal of Management Inquiry*, **11**(2): 94–101.

Wasti, S.A. & C. Robert. 2004. Out of touch? An evaluation of the correspondence between academic and practitioner concerns in IHRM. In J.L.C. Cheng & M.Hitt (eds), *Managing multinationals in a knowledge economy: Economics, culture and human resources:* 207–39. London: JAI Press.

Weinstein, M. & K. Obloj. 2002. Strategic and environmental determinants of HRM innovations in post-socialist Poland. *International Journal of Human Resource Management*, **13**: 642–59.

Welch, D.E. & M. Fenwick. 2003. Virtual assignments: a new possibility for IHRM? In R. Wiesner & B. Millett (eds), *Human resource management: challenges and future directions*. Brisbane, Australia: Wiley.

Welge, M.K. & D. Holtbrügge. 1999. International management under post-modern conditions. *Management International Review*, **39**: 305–22.

Williamson, O.E. 1975. *Markets and hierarchies: analysis and antitrust implications*. New York: Free Press.

Williamson, O.E. 1981. The modern corporation: origins, evolution, attributes. *Journal of Economic Literature*, **19**: 1537–68.

Wolf, J. 1997. From 'starworks' to networks and heterarchies? *Management International Review*, **37**(Special issue 1): 145–69.

Wright, P.M. & G.C. McMahan. 1992. Theoretical perspectives for strategic human resource management. *Journal of Management,* **18**: 295–320.

Wright, P.M., B.B. Dunford & S.A. Snell. 2001. Human resources and the resource based view of the firm. *Journal of Management,* **27**: 701–21.

Wright, P.M., T.M. Gardner & L.M. Moynihan. 2003. The impact of HR practices on the performance of business units. *Human Resource Management Journal,* **13**(3): 21–36.

Zhang, M. 2003. Transferring human resource management across national boundaries. *Employee Relations,* **25**: 613–26.

Zhu, C.J., B. Cooper, H. De Cieri & P.J. Dowling. 2005. The problematic role of a strategic approach to human resource management in industrial enterprises in China. *International Journal of Human Resource Management,* **16**: 517–35.

3 The dual logics behind international human resource management: pressures for global integration and local responsiveness
Philip M. Rosenzweig

The many chapters of this handbook address a full range of dimensions of international human resource management, from HRM practices and tasks, to the distinctive contributions of headquarters to the responsibilities of local HR management, to the difficult challenges of successful execution. This chapter examines IHRM through the lens of what has been an important and useful organizing principle, that of global integration and local responsiveness. This framework has helped bring an incisive and valuable perspective to the field of international business in general, and is highly useful for understanding the topic of interest: human resource management in multinational organizations. The chapter proceeds in three parts. First, we trace the origins of the framework, from its general application to organizations, to its more recent use in MNCs, and finally to the HRM function. Second, we review some of the research that has been conducted about HRM, noting the ways the framework has illuminated finer distinctions and tradeoffs. Third, we offer an evaluation of where this line of research stands and suggest how it might be advanced.

The integration–responsiveness framework: an overview
The roots of the integration–responsiveness framework can be traced back at least as far as the work of Paul Lawrence and Jay Lorsch (1969), who defined a central management problem as that of achieving requisite internal differentiation, usually in response to environmental complexity and turbulence, while also developing sufficient integrating mechanisms to coordinate the organization's activities. Their treatment was about organizations in general, with only slight mention of organizations that span national lines. Soon, however, the basic framework was explicitly applied to multinational corporations by Doz, Bartlett and Prahalad (1981) in an article whose title laid out the central argument: 'Global competitive pressures versus host country demands: managing tensions in multinational corporations'. An MNC is, after all, composed of a set of organizations

which operate in their respective local environments and must be sufficiently differentiated to respond to the demands of these locales, which may be regions, or countries, or even smaller areas within countries. If a company fails to respond to local differences, perhaps in a misguided belief that being 'global' means doing the same things everywhere, it may fail to compete successfully against more nimble and sensitive rivals, able to fine-tune their offerings for local customers and to compete effectively against national rivals. On the other hand, an MNC is a single organization that needs to coordinate its far-flung operations to capture fully the benefits of scale and scope. If an MNC does not realize these benefits, it remains a collection of independent local entities – and forfeits many of its potential advantages (Hout, Porter & Rudden, 1985).

Over the years, the basic tradeoff was explored more deeply. Prahalad and Doz (1987) explicitly presented the challenge facing multinational firms in terms of a need to pursue a global vision while meeting local needs. This balance was, they said, the distinctive mission of the multinational firm. Bartlett and Ghoshal (1989) extended the tradition by describing the challenge facing multinationals as that of simultaneously achieving global integration and local responsiveness while also facilitating worldwide learning – not merely balancing opposing pressures. Achieving the best of both called for a new generation of organizational capabilities, the so-called 'transnational solution', which replaced a hub-and-spoke model of the MNC with a network model, emphasizing the many dense connections among nodes around the world.

Bartlett and Ghoshal extended the integration–responsiveness framework in several directions. First, they showed that the forces for global integration and local responsiveness exerted different pressures by *industry*: consumer electronics, for example, offered high benefits for integration, owing to scale economies in manufacture and research, but did not require extensive local responsiveness; whereas consumer packaged goods demanded very high attention to local needs, owing to differences in taste and preference, but did not offer high benefits for integration, owing to the relative lack of scale economies in manufacture. They also showed how the framework could help elucidate pressures at play on finer levels *within* the corporation, namely business divisions, functions and tasks. A diversified corporation might have many business divisions, each of which would be somewhat differently shaped by pressures of integration and responsiveness for its particular industry. As an example, Unilever's chemical, detergent and packaged good businesses would need to be managed differently given the different forces impinging on each for integration and responsiveness.

Next, within a given business there might be a full range of functions and these, too, could usefully be understood as shaped by pressures for global integration and local responsiveness. As a rule, upstream functions show a greater need for global integration, and downstream functions tend to demand local responsiveness. Thus a company may have one or just a few centres of basic research, since this activity has very high scale economies but little need for adaptation to local markets; it may have practised manufacturing in a handful of sites, perhaps one in each major region, based on the tradeoff between economies of scale and transportation costs; and procurement, as well, may benefit from global coordination for at least a handful of items that are expensive and bought in high volumes. Of course this is a stylized general model; there are wide differences by industry, where, for instance, manufacturing in consumer electronics may lend itself to very high benefits of integration thanks to high economies of scale in production and low transportation costs in distribution, whereas building materials may require local manufacturing because of a relatively high transportation to value ratio. Similarly, as we move downstream, functions may require greater tailoring to local tastes, demands for functionality, levels of disposable income, climate, regulations, and more. In general, marketing, sales and customer support tend towards local responsiveness.

The usefulness of the integration–responsiveness framework does not end there. Within a given function, certain tasks may also tend more to integration and others toward local responsiveness. As an example, Bartlett and Ghoshal depicted the marketing function as involving tasks ranging from product policy to advertising, to pricing, to distribution, to promotion, again demanding either greater attention to global integration, as in consistency for product standards or a single message in advertising, or greater local responsiveness, as in point of sale promotion or customer support.

Over the years, the basic integration–responsiveness framework became rather well entrenched in the international business field. The dual pressures on MNCs were also described in organization-theoretic terms, thinking in terms of pressure for internal consistency on one hand and pressure for isomorphism with the local environment on the other (Rosenzweig & Singh, 1991). Drawing on institutional theory, they identified three motivations for local isomorphism: mimetic, coercive and normative isomorphism (DiMaggio & Powell, 1983).

HRM and the integration–responsiveness framework

In recent years, considerable research has been directed towards the human dimension of international management. This emphasis is well placed, for no matter how sound the strategy of a multinational corporation (MNC), or how carefully designed its structure, success or failure is likely to depend upon the MNC's ability to attract, develop and deploy talented employees in a multinational setting, and to get them to work together effectively despite differences in culture, language and location (O'Hara-Devereaux & Johansen, 1994).

As noted above, Bartlett and Ghoshal used the integration–responsiveness framework to illustrate the pressures on particular functions, showing how upstream functions tended more to offer benefits from global integration while functions closer to the customer demanded greater local responsiveness. They did not, however, explicitly address activities such as finance, legal or regulatory affairs, health and safety, and our present concern, human resource management. These support functions are pervasive, not limited to upstream or downstream, and therefore do not fit neatly into the basic diagram.

Yet the integration–responsiveness framework can be useful for understanding these activities, as well. For support functions, no less than in those that move materials from procurement to final customer use, there are pressures on one hand to operate as a single integrated entity as well as to respond to the local environment. Indeed the relevance of the framework was evident in the same year that Bartlett and Ghoshal wrote their seminal work, while Evans, Doz and Laurent (1989) noted that HRM practices, too, are shaped by the dual pressures for internal consistency and local adaptation.

HRM compared to other functions

Some early empirical research suggested that, of all the functions, human resource management tends to be the one which most closely adheres to local practices (see, for example, Kobayashi, 1982). In a study of the management practices of 249 US affiliates of foreign-owned firms, the author found that, of four functions studies (marketing, manufacturing, finance and human resource management), only the finance function tended to resemble more closely practices in the parent country than those of the local market (Rosenzweig, 1994). Furthermore, of the three functions that tended more closely to resemble local firms, the resemblance was significant but moderate for manufacturing, stronger for marketing, and by far the strongest for HRM. This overall tendency of HRM within MNC affiliates to resemble practices of the local environment was not surprising, as HRM practices are often mandated by local regulation or shaped by strong local conventions. Moreover since an MNC affiliate, in most instances, has little choice but to hire its employees from competitive local labour markets, it is hard to diverge too far from local norms. Thus, using the vocabulary of institutional theory, HRM faces coercive isomorphism when it comes to following laws and regulations and mimetic isomorphism when it comes to wanting to look like local companies, overcoming a liability of foreignness, as well as normative isomorphism, meaning adoption of policies and practices that are more effective for reasons quite apart from regulatory demands or a desire to appear local.

The general tendency for HRM to be closely linked to the local environment was also evident when it came to the nationality of key executives. The same study asked about the nationality of three key executives, the top officer, the head of finance and the head of human resources, asking whether he or she was a host country national, a parent country national or a third country national. The respondents reported that of their top officers, were 60 per cent American, 33 per cent parent country nationals and 8 per cent third country nationals. (When Japanese companies were removed, the numbers were 68 per cent, 22 per cent and 10 per cent, respectively.) Heads of finance were 73 per cent American, 24 per cent parent country nationals and 3 per cent third country. (When Japanese countries were removed, the numbers shifted to 84 per cent, 12 per cent and 4 per cent.) The heads of human resources, meanwhile, were overwhelmingly host country nationals: fully 94 per cent were American, with just 5 per cent parent country nationals and 1 per cent third country nationals. (Removing Japanese companies brought the numbers to 97 per cent, 2 per cent and 1 per cent.) Once again, we find evidence that HRM is the most local of functions: the one most closely shaped by local responsiveness, or isomorphism with the local environment.

Extending the integration–responsiveness framework

After these initial empirical studies, the integration–responsiveness framework was used to probe more deeply into several dimensions of human resource management in MNCs. The dimensions examined included HRM tasks, MNC home country, MNC host country, MNC strategy and level of employee. Some studies looked at just one of these dimensions, while others examined more than one.

Regarding tasks, HRM covers a broad range of elements, which, based on Huselid (1995) can be grouped into the following: (1) recruitment and selection; (2) education and training; (3) job design; (4) labour–management relations; (5) performance appraisal; (6) incentive compensation and benefits; (7) career progression planning. Another scheme organizes HRM into (1) staffing, including recruiting and job selection; (2) training, including technical training and management development; (3) performance evaluation systems, including developmental, results and behavioural measures; (4) compensation, including variable or performance- based plans (Youndt, Snell, Dean & Lepak, 1996). These various elements are analogous to the tasks which, as Bartlett and Ghoshal describe, may respond differently to pressures for global integration and local responsiveness.

In a study of US affiliates of foreign-based MNCs, conducted in 1991, Rosenzweig and Nohria (1994) tested whether HRM practices were closer in their resemblance either to local firms or to the parent firm in its home country. Six practices were identified to represent a range of HRM practices: extent of employee benefits, extent of annual paid time off, extent of variable compensation for managers, extent of participation in executive decision making, gender composition in management and extent of employee training. They found that four of these (paid time off, employee benefits, gender composition and training) were much closer to local practices than to parent country practices, with a statistical significance of $p < 0.0001$. The two remaining practices, variable compensation and participation in executive decision making, were very slightly closer to local practices but not at a statistically significant level.

The close similarity of four practices to local practice very likely reflects the presence of local labour laws, as in the case of paid time off and employee benefits, which may compel the adoption of specific practices (so-called 'coercive isomorphism'), as well as perhaps also very clear local practices – in the case of training and gender participation – which induce the local affiliate to want to adopt local practices (mimetic isomorphism). The remaining two practices pertain largely to executives rather than to the workforce in general, and in these instances any pressure for local isomorphism is offset by a need to achieve consistency within the MNC. In sum, the authors inferred that HRM practices for which there are well-defined local norms, and which affect the rank-and-file of the affiliate organization, were likely to conform most closely to the practices of local competitors, whereas practices for which there are diffuse or poorly defined local norms, or which are seen as being critical to maintaining internal consistency or arriving at critical decisions, were less likely to conform to local norms.

By extension, it is likely that, in a multinational corporation, the forces for integration and responsiveness do not affect all levels equally; and indeed, from a normative standpoint, forging policies that take into account organizational level may be wise. For employees at lower levels of the organization, where the great majority of employees are likely to be local nationals, hired from the local population, working locally, the forces for local responsiveness are likely to be strongest. Elements of HRM should be expected to conform more strongly to local practices for lower-level employees than they do for employees further up the hierarchy. As we move up the hierarchy the relative importance of integration and responsiveness is likely to shift, in part because of a lessening need for local responsiveness, but much more as a reflection of a growing need to manage the workforce as an integrated, coherent whole.

Here the reasons have to do with equity among managers in different countries, as well as the ability to optimize the workforce through career progression and international assignments. MNCs will want to bring about a consistency in outlook and purpose, as described by Bartlett and Ghoshal (1989) as the forging of a shared vision among managers and a common sense of purpose. Moreover MNCs often rely on a strong core of managers, often home-country expatriates, to manage far-flung subsidiaries. Examples include Philips' 'Dutch Mafia', Heineken's Dutch brew managers and cadres of Japanese executives who lead overseas affiliates. Edstrom and Galbraith (1977) note that the use of expatriates is a way to ensure coordination and control. MNCs therefore may feel pressure to bring about consistency in such things as performance appraisal and incentive compensation, as inequities among managers around the world may present obstacles to the smooth flow of managers, thus discouraging much-needed transfers for development and deployment. Deployment of executives, too, can be optimized when there are consistent policies relating to education and development, as well as career assignments. As an example, managers at Colgate-Palmolive were hired locally and spent the first years of their career locally; but if they progressed to a level where they would be sent for key jobs abroad, they shifted from a home-country HRM system and became global employees, with benefits and retirement pension planning that conformed to a worldwide policy. Only 100 or so managers worldwide were part of this programme, and they held the most important positions in key countries as well as the top positions in regional and corporate headquarters. Bringing about consistency in career evaluation, progression and compensation was critical for a smoothly functioning global managerial pool.

Research that was explicitly based in the integration–responsiveness framework, this time based on data from 100 subsidiaries of Japanese, US and European MNCs in Taiwan, was conducted by Hannon, Huang and Jaw (1995). They found that the nature of HR practices was largely shaped by the interaction of two forces: an environmental force including host country pressures, and internal forces that included firm strategy and the parent culture. On the topic of firm strategy, they found support for the typology set out by Jarillo and Martinez (1990) that classified subsidiaries as 'autonomous' (high responsiveness, low integration), 'receptive' (high integration, low responsiveness) or 'active' (high responsiveness and high integration), meaning some degree of autonomy in the host country, but closely coordinated with the rest of the organization. They concluded, 'When a subsidiary is highly dependent on the parent to provide crucial resources, it is common for the MNC to exert control through formal coordination mechanisms and through IHR strategies' (Hannon, Huang & Jaw, 1995: 548–9). The result was an effort to adopt HR strategies that could lessen the tensions of needing to balance global integration and local responsiveness.

Dowling (1999: 30) argued that 'complexities of operating in different countries and employing different national categories of workers is a key variable that differentiates domestic and international HRM, rather than any major differences between the HRM activities performed'. He suggested that the activities of the HRM function are moderated by five elements: cultural environment, industry, extent of reliance on home country or domestic market, attitudes of senior management, and complexity involved. Scullion and Starkey (2000) found support for this claim, noting that MNCs could usefully be typified in terms of their degree of global centralization or decentralization, and that, not surprisingly in centralized/global firms, the corporate HR function played a more active role, undertaking a greater degree of management development, succession and career planning, making key staffing decisions, including the deployment of expatriate managers, and also determining rewards for top managers. Given these differences, they found significant variation in the role played by the corporate HR function in different types of international firms.

The global integration–local responsiveness framework has also been used in the study of European MNCs. Particularly important has been an extensive database of HR practices gathered since the late 1980s by the Cranfield network on European human resource management (Cranet-E). Using this database, Tregaskis *et al.* (2001: 34) asked whether 'foreign subsidiaries act and behave as local firms, or adopt practices that resemble those of the parent'. Examining data on 600 organizations based in the UK and Ireland, they found that MNCs adapt their practices to accommodate local differences: 'Results support the hypotheses proposed, namely that MNCs operating in Ireland and the UK adapt their practices in light of country differences' (ibid.: 44). They also found significant differences among HR practices, noting that localization is stronger in 'career traditions' and 'labour market', but that MNCs maintain a more similar internal approach to 'training frameworks': need identification and delivery. Gunnigle *et al.* (2002) also used the Cranet-E database to examine firms in the UK, Ireland, Denmark, Germany and Sweden. They found that subsidiaries of US MNCs in Europe were less localized and used more standardized HRM policies than their European counterparts, suggesting the importance of home country preferences. They also found evidence, consistent with the predictions of institutional theory, that home country influence was reduced as host country regulation increased, forcing MNCs to adhere to local practices.

Finally, the global integration–local responsiveness framework has been used in examining the HR practices of Chinese enterprises (Zhu &

Dowling, 2002). During the Communist era, state-owned enterprises (SOEs) followed Maoist policies of full employment, centralized labour allocation and lifetime tenure. With enormous economic development, including both the stimulation of privately owned Chinese enterprises (POEs) and mushrooming foreign direct investment, leading to the establishment of a large number of Foreign Investment Enterprises (FIEs), a key question is whether HR practices are also experiencing transition. Zhu and Dowling asked whether convergence in staffing practices could be observed in China's industrial enterprises. In particular, they asked: 'To what extent have the staffing practices commonly used in the advanced Western market economy, such as job analysis and selection processes, been adopted by the Chinese industrial enterprises?' (ibid.: 570). Their study of 440 Chinese companies concluded that 'we are witnessing the emergence ·of a more complex, hybrid management model' (ibid.: 592) with a growing adoption of Western practices, especially within FIEs and POEs, yet with many distinctive features retained from the traditional Chinese model, especially in the SOEs. Once again, we find that thinking in terms of similarity to local practices or adoption of Western management models has been a useful organizing framework.

Assessing the global integration–local responsiveness framework
From the studies reviewed above, it is clear that the global integration–local responsiveness framework has been widely embraced and largely fruitful in the study of MNCs during the 1990s. The basic logic of integration and responsiveness remains widely used to this day, and for good reason, as it resonates with the challenges facing managers in MNCs. It can be used to suggest, among other things, the appropriate design for a complex organization. Galbraith (2000) identifies the so-called 'front–back' organization as one that groups upstream activities organized by business division, and downstream activities organized by geography, so as to take full advantage of the integration benefits upstream while also ensuring local responsiveness downstream. The framework also remains central in discussions of IHRM. Evans, Pucik and Barsoux (2002) explicitly draw on the integration–responsiveness framework to describe the forces that shape the HRM function. They write that achieving an alignment with corporate goals, bringing about a desired standardization of activities, and also achieving specialization of particular affiliates, are all furthered by effective HR policies. Furthermore a key element in achieving global integration is through the use of expatriates, which again relies on effective HR policies. At the same time, the authors note, MNCs must be locally responsive, which calls for the development of local staff through recruitment, training and development, and retention.

As a basic organizing principle, identifying some inherent tradeoffs, the framework has been and is likely to continue to be useful. We should, however, pause to evaluate the record of these empirical studies. In the main, a decade and a half of empirical studies have tended to show two things: first, that the framework is usefully applied at a relatively fine-grained level, isolating patterns that apply, not to the MNC as a whole, nor even to the HRM function, but for different HRM tasks, related to employees at different hierarchical levels, in companies of different strategies, and in host countries with different cultures and regulatory pressures; second, looking across the many studies mentioned above (which do not even constitute an exhaustive list) the general sense is that, while there are statistically significant patterns of difference, they tend mainly to confirm the hypotheses advanced. Put another way, a considerable amount of research has yielded relatively few surprises.

The question, then, is: *What next?* Is the global integration–local responsiveness framework still able to pose the most incisive questions for study, or should we be moving on increasingly to different frameworks? This is not a new question. Indeed, as early as in the mid-1990s, the framework was thought by some to be reaching a point of diminishing returns. (In 1994, I took part in a conference at the University of Michigan, organized by Tom Murtha and C.K. Prahalad, at which the late Gunnar Hedlund voiced some dismay at the ubiquity of the integration–responsiveness framework and asked whether we could not get beyond it. He was not criticizing it for any particular shortcoming, but merely wondering if a reliance on the framework was limiting our research and preventing us from posing new questions.) If it was already a bit stale in the 1990s, could it be that this framework, for all its inherent strengths, runs the risk of being a cliché today, an easy and natural way of conceiving of issues but one which may indeed distract attention from other, more promising, avenues of inquiry?

My sense is that, whereas the global integration–local responsiveness framework remains relevant, and has an intuitive appeal to practitioners and theorists alike, there are diminishing returns to continuing to go over the basic areas of empirical work. Instead, I would hope that fresh thinking might be pursued along a few dimensions, as indicated below.

The link to performance

Almost all studies have been purely descriptive, observing patterns of similarity and difference, whether by nationality or host country environment or by HRM task. Researchers have revealed statistically significant findings based on their testing of hypotheses about these differences. Rarely addressed are underlying performance issues. Do MNCs that allow internal differentiation achieve higher performance? Does erring too far on the side of integration stifle local initiative or lead to subsidiaries being unable to attract and retain key employees? Does erring too far on the side of local responsiveness lead to fragmentation and chaos? Surely there are some anecdotes to support these claims, but can we show some systematic relationship to performance? There are, naturally, many methodological challenges to studying firm performance, especially at the subsidiary level, and these must not be minimized. Yet if a link to performance can be established, the value of the global integration–local responsiveness framework would get a new breath of life.

Convergence among local environments
We live in an age where host country environments show signs of converging, both because of commercial and cultural interchange, and because of the influence of regional institutions such as the European Union and NAFTA. In the vocabulary of institutional theory, changes in the environments themselves may take place for both mimetic and coercive reasons. Thus the nature of local responsiveness is itself undergoing change, and is surely a topic worthy of study. So far, most empirical treatments have taken local environments as fixed, but to capture their evolution, too, may be a valuable area of inquiry.

Change in ownership patterns
The advent of large scale outsourcing, most recently regarding high-technology jobs to India, as well as contract manufacturing with companies like Flextronics, has opened up an important area of study that fits uneasily in the integration–responsiveness framework. Simply put, the basic variable of interest – the foreign subsidiary or affiliate, with some ownership interest, leading to classification as foreign direct investment – is no longer the inevitable or even most interesting form of organization for global enterprise. While joint ventures have been a major area of study for 20 years, they still constitute FDI. The advent of a myriad of supplier and outsourcing relations raises a further set of questions.

Special attention to China and India
Linked to the preceding point is the enormous influence, growing in the present and of monumental importance in the future, of China and India. China is already one of the great recipients of FDI, which few if any MNCs are prepared to ignore. Yet its scale and industrial policy have already shown it is able to rewrite rules by which companies manage their global activities. It is a good sign that numerous scholars have already focused on China (see, for example, Zhu & Dowling, 2002, mentioned above) and it is to be wished that such efforts continue.

As an enduring and useful way to think about managing MNCs (in all functions, but certainly in the case of IHRM) the global integration–local responsiveness framework is not likely to become obsolete any time soon. It is likely to remain an important organizing principle, valuable both to academics and to practitioners. For it to remain at the forefront of research, however, it would be most useful to see new areas of study along the above four dimensions, and perhaps others. It is to be hoped that researchers will not simply continue to refine an existing framework, but to push it into new areas, and thereby invigorate what has been a valuable means to understand international business.

References

Bartlett, C.A. & S. Ghoshal. 1989. *Managing across borders: The transnational solution.* Boston, MA: Harvard Business School Press.

DiMaggio, P. & W.W. Powell. 1983. The iron cage revisited: institutional isomorphism and collective rationality in organizational fields. *American Sociological Review,* **48**: 147–60.

Dowling, P.J. 1999. Completing the puzzle: issues in the development of the field of international human resource management. *Management International Review,* **39**(Special Issue 3): 27–43.

Doz, Y., C.A. Bartlett & C.K. Prahalad. 1981. Global competitive pressures versus host country demands: managing tensions in multinational corporations. *California Management Review,* **23**(3): 63–74.

Edstrom, A. & J. Galbraith. 1977. Transfer of managers as a coordination and control strategy in multinational corporations. *Administrative Science Quarterly,* **22**(June): 248–63.

Evans, P., Y. Doz & A. Laurent. 1989. *Human resource management in international firms: change, globalization and innovation.* London: Macmillan.

Evans, P., V. Pucik & J.-L. Barsoux. 2002. *The global challenge: frameworks for international human resource management.* New York: McGraw Hill-Irwin.

Galbraith, J.R. 2000. *Designing global organizations.* San Francisco, CA: Jossey-Bass.

Gunnigle, P., K. Murphy, J.N. Cleveland, N. Heraty & M. Morley. 2002. Localization in human resource management: comparing American and European multinational corporations. *Advances in International Management,* **14**: 259–84.

Gupta, A.K. & V. Govindarajan. 1991. Knowledge flows and the structure of control within multinational corporations. *Academy of Management Review,* **16**(4): 768–92.

Hannon, J.M., I.-C. Huang & B.-S. Jaw. 1995. International human resources strategy and its determinants: the case of subsidiaries in Taiwan. *Journal of International Business Studies,* **26**(3): 531–54.

Hout, T., M. Porter & E. Rudden. 1985. How global companies win out. *Harvard Business Review,* September–October: 98–108.

Huselid, M. 1995. The impact of human resource management practices on turnover, productivity, and corporate financial performance. *Academy of Management Journal,* **38**: 635–72.

Jarillo, J.C. & J.I. Martinez. 1990. Different roles for subsidiaries: the case of multinational corporations in Spain. *Strategic Management Journal,* **11**: 501–12.

Kobayashi, N. 1982. The present and future of Japanese multinational enterprise. *International Studies of Man and Organization,* **12**(1): 38–58.

Lawrence, P.R. & J. Lorsch. 1969. *Organization and environment: managing differentiation and integration.* Homewood, IL: Irwin.

O'Hara-Devereaux, M. & R. Johansen. 1994. *Global work: Bridging distance, culture, and time.* San Francisco, CA: Jossey-Bass Publishers.

Prahalad, C.K. & Y. Doz. 1987. *The multinational mission: balancing local demands and global vision.* New York: The Free Press.

Rosenzweig, P.M. 1994. Are 'they' just like 'us'? Management practices in U.S. affiliates of foreign-owned firms. *The International Executive*, July–August.

Rosenzweig, P.M. & N. Nohria. 1994. Influences on human resource management in multinational firms. *Journal of International Business Studies*, 25(2): 229–51.

Rosenzweig, P.M. & J. Singh. 1991. Organizational environments and the multinational enterprise. *Academy of Management Review*, 16(2): 340–61.

Scullion, H. & K. Starkey. 2000. In search of the changing role of the corporate human resource function in the international firm. *International Journal of Human Resource Management*, 11(6): 1061–81.

Tregaskis, O., N. Heraty & M. Morley. 2001. HRD in multinationals: the global/local mix. *Human Resource Management Journal*, 11(2): 34–56.

Youndt, M.A., S.A. Snell, J.W. Dean Jr & D.P. Lepak. 1996. Human resource management, manufacturing strategy, and firm performance. *Academy of Management Journal*, 39: 836–66.

Zhu, C.J. & P.J. Dowling. 2002. Staffing practices in transition: some empirical evidence from China. *International Journal of Human Resource Management*, 13(4): 569–97.

4 The human resource department: roles, coordination and influence

Philip Stiles and Jonathan Trevor

There have been many predictions for the future role of the HR department, its role, function and size. The predominant tenor of such calls has been for the HR function to be more strategic and to create value within organizations (Beatty & Schneider, 1997; Beer, 1997; Bennett *et al.*, 1998; Pfeffer, 1994; Ulrich, 1997). HR functions have traditionally come under fire because of their perceived unresponsiveness, their administrative rather than strategic focus and their perceived nature as cost centres rather than wealth creation centres (Truss *et al.*, 2002). In the face of growing internationalization of organizations, the HR function is seen to be a key subunit in the development of capability and the coordination of practice (Ferner, 1997). But, as Pucik (1997: 321) argues, 'paradoxically, in spite of the value adding opportunities for HR contribution to competitive advantage driven by the demands of business globalizations, in many companies today the HR function is still perceived not as a full partner in the globalization process'.

The rise of the resource-based view of the firm and the development of human capital management have given cause for optimism about the future role of HR (Barney, 1991; Ulrich, 1997, 1998; Wright & McMahan, 1992) but, as Hunt and Boxall (1998: 770) argue, 'the dominant view in the international literature is that HR specialists, senior or otherwise, are not typically key players in the development of corporate strategy'. A good deal of research has shown HRM's importance to business performance (Becker *et al.*, 1997; Becker & Huselid, 1998; Huselid, 1995; Schuler, 1990; Ulrich, 1997) but the influence of the HR department within the organization has been less evident. Though Sisson (2001) finds evidence in the Workplace Employee Relations survey (WERS98) to show that HR departments are becoming more strategic than once thought, the weight of evidence suggests that most HR departments play a tactical role, with little consistency in HR interventions (Ulrich, 1998; Purcell & Ahlstrand, 1994; Kochan & Dyer, 1995; Torrington, 1998). This may be because the HR function is subject to a number of ambiguities in its role (Legge, 1978; Purcell & Ahlstrand, 1994). These include a clear distinction between the HR and line; doubts over the professional expertise of HR staff being encroached upon by line and top management; a lack of clarity over roles and responsibilities; marginality in management decision-making processes, especially at a strategic level; lack of clarity or account-ability in specifying the goals, business outcomes or the contribution of the HR function; and tensions in sustaining an ethos of mutuality in the face of the opposing interests between management and employees (Legge, 1978; Storey, 1992; Tyson & Fell, 1986; Watson, 1977).

An additional tension for international HR departments is the require-ment to balance the demands for central integration with the need to retain and develop local responsiveness. For HR to work effectively there must be consistency and fairness of practice and delivery, but cultural difference and local market conditions, and legislation, require variation and differentiation (Caliguiri & Stroh, 1994; Martin & Beaumont, 2001; Scullion & Starkey, 2000). Little is known about the way international HR departments organize and structure themselves to meet such challenges. The aim of this chapter is to assess how the HR function operates in multi-national companies. Our aim is to examine three major aspects of the inter-national HR function. The first is to explore the roles the HR function is supposed to carry out. Though there are calls for a greater strategic role, we shall argue that such calls should be viewed against a backdrop of ambi-guity and tension with other roles the HR department is given. Second, we shall explore the balance between centralization and decentralization. This is held to be the definitive tension within the management of the HR department. Third, we shall examine issues of power within the HR depart-ment and how the HR department in international firms attempts to move beyond stereotypes of low departmental power to make claims for greater added value within organizations.

This chapter uses data from two multinational companies to illustrate issues that emerge from the preceding review. In the first case, a Japanese multinational, we draw on extensive empirical work in Japan and China to understand the context of the company, its current state in terms of human resource practices and the structure and capabilities of its human resource department. In all, 40 interviews were conducted at both head office and plant level, with HR corporate managers, HR line managers and line man-agers included in the sample. The second case is intended by way of com-parison, and draws heavily on secondary data to develop a picture of a European multinational's approach to structuring and managing the HR department and its operations in China.

Multinational firms and the HR function
Roles
Reviews of HR department development stress the function's traditional 'personnel' past, where the focus was on administration and industrial/

employee relations issues. The term 'personnel' department seems to date from around 1909 and grew strongly in 1920s, following the industrial welfare movement and the growth of recruitment and selection tests and motivational instruments developed in World War I, as well as the growth of trade unions. The human relations movement provided the rationale for improving workers' conditions and jobs and social environment. The development of system theory encouraged the view that strategy and the management of people could be interlinked and so HR could have wide consequences for the prosperity of the firm. Though this growth in understanding the human resource of organizations has been considerable, the HR department has remained locked into operational and transactional issues until recently (Schuler, 1990; Ulrich, 1997, 1998). A number of scholars have argued that a shift towards greater strategic presence has emerged, however, with an emphasis away from traditional auditing and back-office record keeping, to embrace work on the management teams of businesses, involvement in change and organizational design (Ulrich, 1997; Mohrman, Lawler & McMahan, 1995). However, as Ulrich himself states: 'most assessments of HR roles are wanna be statements made by HR people who "wanna-be" involved, respected and admired by their client' (Connor & Ulrich, 2000).

As with HR functions in traditional organizations, the emphasis in the literature on the MNC HR department is to call for greater attention to the strategic element of the function. Pucik (1997) has argued that increasing internationalization of organizations will lead to a more strategic role for HRM. The enabling of strategy through facilitating change and building capabilities are claimed to be of central importance (Evans *et al.*, 2002), an argument reinforced by the resource-based view of the firm (Barney, 1991). The role of the international corporate HR function in supporting globalizing strategies of MNCs was recognized by Ghoshal and Bartlett (1990), who argued that the recruitment, training and management development of managers was crucial to MNC success. Brewster *et al.* (2002) identified four major roles: talent management, management through global networks, development of intellectual integration through the management of knowledge, and the global e-enablement of HR processes. Scullion's work on international management cadres (1995) also places the development of senior management teams with international experience as a prime responsibility of the corporate HR department. The ability to capture and promote diversity and to have a clear understanding of cultural issues have been seen as key HR disciplines (Pelled, Eisenhardt & Xin, 1999). However there is recognition that such high-profile activities must not be done at the expense of traditional administrative roles and the fostering of traditional technical HR expertise. The e-enablement of HR has been viewed as an important mechanism to ensure that key administrative tasks and services can be standardized and made available across the businesses, departments and functions of the organization (DeFidelto & Slater, 2001) with some commentators claiming that such enablement can be used at a transformational level as well as at a transactional level (Harris *et al.*, 2002), with the implication that the HR function becomes gatekeeper of what is centralized, what is decentralized and how information and knowledge are transferred from one location to another (Brewster *et al.*, 2002).

Though evidence has been collected to show that HR departments are becoming more strategic around the world (Bowen *et al.*, 2002; Harris *et al.*, 2002), research remains patchy. Bowen *et al.* (2002) provide evidence to show that there is cross-country variation in the status of HR departments across the world, according to national cultural and strategic posture dimensions. Harris *et al.* drawing on CRANET data, state that 'in around half of the organizations in the UK, the personnel manager is a member of the top management team. In Sweden, on the other hand, and even more so in France and Spain, at least three quarters of their organizations have an HR representation on the board. Some countries, such as Germany or those in Central and Eastern Germany, have much lower levels' (2002: 71). It is debatable whether board representation is an accurate proxy for the HR department's strategic influence, nevertheless these data are revealing. However it may be with this aspect of the HR department's role, a number of commentators have urged that the emphasis on the strategic role should not detract from the other putative roles the HR department should play.

The work of Ulrich has been prominently trying to understand the roles of the HR function. He defines four main roles for the HR professional along two axes: strategy versus operations and process (HR tools and systems) versus people. The four roles are (1) strategic partner, (2) administrative expert, (3) employee champion, and (4) change agent (Ulrich, 1997). He argues that human resources are the 'dominant lever for creating value' and that managers, employees, consultants and HR professionals will all work together to achieve this overarching goal (ibid.: 42). Ulrich argues that each of the four roles is important and the typology should not be viewed as hierarchical, but though this model has become pervasive, it is heavily prescriptive and seems to gloss over the possibility of conflict between these roles (Caldwell, 2003).

In the literature of international HR departments, Ulrich (1997) has devised a model of HR activities based on degrees on integration and differentiation. On this account, for some HR activities, high integration and high differentiation interventions such as leadership development, would be in the domain of a corporate HR department, whereas low integration and low differentiation interventions, such as payroll or blue-collar recruitment, would be candidates for outsourcing. In the conceptual middle (moderate integration and differentiation) service centres or centres of excellence could be located, where expertise is brought together in one space to service regions or global operations, often encompassing compensation and benefits, performance management, pensions and benefits (Evans *et al.*, 2002; Ulrich, 1997).

However, typologies such as these suffer from their static nature and 'a reduction of the complexities of organizational behaviour to one or two dimensions' (Edwards *et al.*, 1996: 24), as well as emphasizing a structural determinism. The issue of possible conflict between roles is also pertinent here. Certainly there can be conflict between these roles; for example, moves to become a strategic partner can increase the sense of the HR function as a consultancy role, thus losing much of its traditional power base and influence as an employee champion and administrator. Also the HR department, unlike many organizational subunits, has to contend with multiple objectives and multiple constituencies. As Tsui (2000) argues, the HR department has to serve simultaneously the institutional (advising executives and ensuring compliance with employment law), the instrumental (providing a capable and motivated workforce) and the individual (providing training and development and coaching that enhances individual talent and opportunities). Such multiple objectives and constituencies also make measuring the performance of HR problematic, 'not because of the lack of goals, but because of the presence of multiple objectives that are often divergent and potentially inconsistent' (ibid.).

Devolution and coordination
A number of statements of multinational HR operations have stressed the issue of synergy, with vertical and horizontal integration between operating units, or financial control, with the management of business units made on the lines of financial rewards or sanctions (Marginson *et al.*, 1995; Edwards *et al.*, 1996). This reflects work in the strategy field on the issue of parenting styles within multinational organizations (Goold & Campbell, 1987). In this literature, a range of practice between HQ and subsidiary operations is identified, and a threefold classification proposed, reflecting whether the HQ acts as strategic control, strategic planning and financial control, where explicit financial targets and returns are monitored and used as a discipline to ensure subsidiary performance. For the central HR department, adopting an appropriate 'parenting' style with the diverse local HR units is an important consideration. The role of the centre is generally considered to have four elements (Goold & Campbell, 1987): standalone influence, linkage influence, influence through central functions and services, and corporate development activities. Stand-alone influence refers

to the involvement the centre has with each individual division, the extent to which it is engaged with agreeing and monitoring performance and budgetary targets and approving major capital expenditures and selecting heads of the division. Linkage influence refers to the centre's creation of value by developing cooperation and synergy between the divisions. The provision of central functions and services is intended to support business effectiveness and bring certain economies of scale. Corporate development activities would include acquisitions, divestments, alliances and new ventures. There are potential downsides to the centre's involvement in these activities and, if practised inappropriately, they can destroy value, for example, in the stand-alone influence role, setting inappropriate targets, misallocating resources; and selecting the wrong partners to head the divisions can be highly counterproductive.

Scullion and Starkey argue that 'corporate HR has a key role to play in the international firm and that this needs to be understood in terms of the dilemmas surrounding the tension between integration/differentiation and . . . learning' (2000: 1063). Within multinational firms, techniques of formalization and centralization are used to provide consistency of practice and to reduce uncertainty and to underpin the legitimacy of the corporate decision making process (Ghoshal & Bartlett, 1990).

A number of HR mechanisms have been suggested as likely to improve control and coordination, in particular strategic global staffing, global task forces and global leadership programmes (Taylor & Beechler, 1993). These integrating mechanisms are intended to develop into the 'soft' structures within global organizations, which function both as informal control monitoring devices and as cocoordinating 'inducers' of subsidiary collaboration and competition for strategic projects (Birkinshaw & Hood, 1999).

Recent work by Sparrow and colleagues (2002) has highlighted three major roles for HR, transactional work, capability development and business development, supported by key delivery mechanisms for HRM such as e-enabling HRM: using new information and communications technology, knowledge management and cost-reduction strategies, and creating centres of excellence to avoid replication and duplication of effort. But these authors and others admit that variation among multinational firms in terms of their HR practice and HR function operation remains, in terms of industry, employee and life cycle effects, but also in terms of the effects of nationality (Bowen *et al.*, 2002; Ferner & Quintanilla, 1998). This later issue, 'the extent to which MNCs take elements of their national "baggage" with them when they operate abroad' (Ferner & Quintanilla, 1998: 710) has been shown to have a clear impact on organizational approaches to managing (Rosenzweig & Nohria, 1994). Japanese firms, for example, 'have been portrayed as global firms that limit the roles of overseas subsidiaries to the assembly and sale of standardized products designed and developed in Japan' (Whitley *et al.*, 2003: 644). This does not necessarily imply that formal systems and standard policies are apparent and there has been a strong reliance on expatriate managers to ensure tight control with Japanese ways of working (Debroux, 2003; Ferner & Quintantilla, 1998; Whitley *et al.*, 2003).

Power and influence

But though the HR department may want to become more strategic, much depends on issues of power, influence and status to enable this to happen. This theme, however, has received scant attention in the literature. Subunit power has focused on departments other than the HR department. One exception is the study by Galang and Ferris (1997), which examined 242 organizations and concluded that symbolic actions such as espousing values and norms similar to those of senior management and being the embodiment of social values within the firm predicted greater HR departmental power and greater access to organizational resources. 'Hence, merely being present in an organization is not enough; taking an active role may differentiate the more influential HR departments from those who enjoy less power' (ibid.: 1418).

Tsui (2000) examined the effectiveness assessments of different constituencies for the influence of HR departments. She found that HR departments used one of two strategies: cooptation was linked to the satisfaction of managers with the performance of the HR unit, and responsiveness was linked to employee satisfactions, both confirming resource dependence theory.

Legge (1978) identified two strategies used by HR departments to increase power and influence: conformist innovation and deviant innovation. In an economic environment characterized by difficult conditions, the conformist innovation strategy is deemed more appropriate, chiefly owing to the absence of slack resources within the organization. Here the personnel specialist 'defines his professionalism in terms of acquiring expertise that will enable him to demonstrate a closer relationship between his activities (means) and organizational success criteria (ends)' (ibid.: 79). A deviant innovation strategy is considered more effective in more benign economic circumstances, and represents an opportunity for the personnel manager to extend his or her influence on the organization by influencing organizational strategies and building a different set of criteria for the effectiveness of the organization (Townley, 2004). Conformist HR strategies may focus on HR accounting techniques and manpower planning, whereas a deviant HR strategy may be informed by organizational development programmes and corporate social responsibility considerations (ibid.).

In terms of the international HR department, Novicevic and Harvey (2001) argue that explicit norms of control within the businesses of the MNC must be supplemented by informal personnel control: 'To be an effective and relevant actor in a leadership-driven globally diversified organization, the corporate HR has to redefine its traditional role of the bureaucratic administrator or the quasi-strategic partner [of the top management team] and become an effective political "influencer".' The means of influence are cited as global staffing, the development of worldwide competencies and labour bargaining. This prescriptive argument is supported by work by Ferner (2000) who also advocates a political approach to the running of bureaucratic control systems such as HR within MNCs; 'the existence of formal systems does not mean they will be implemented in practice. Systems may operate ineffectually or have fallen into disuse. The exercise of central "will" in the form of the deployment of power resources is required to activate formal systems' (Ferner, 1997: 537).

But as Novicevic and Harvey (2001) argue, such mechanisms are 'not sufficient because, in addition to the explicit internal/external sources of uncertainty in a global organization, there are many latent sources of uncertainty in the decision-making environment' (ibid.: 1255). This political approach stresses the need to show the interlinkage between formal bureaucratic control systems and the informal control dependent on the deployment of power resources. Much depends, Ferner claims, on the 'power of the centre to make things happen [which] has to confront the power of local units to resist or subvert the operations of formal systems' (Ferner, 2000: 537).

This work provides insights into the issues of power and influence, and there seems to be a consensus that the HR department should take on a more active strategic role but is hampered by a number of considerations: 'becoming a strategic partner remains an elusive goal for many HR professionals' (Connor & Ulrich, 2000: 46). Measurement has been cited as one issue (Connor & Ulrich, 2000), involving a lack of clear metrics to show the impact of HR and the HR department. Despite the prevalence of human capital measures and benchmarking techniques, plus the installation of HR scorecards, this remains largely true.

Two case illustrations
In this section we examine evidence from two MNCs, J-Electric and Philips, and consider their HR structure, roles and the management of devolution and coordination.

J-Electric
J-Electric, founded in 1950, has a capitalization of 150.0 billion yen, with net sales in 2002 of 1780.0 billion yen. The company operates in the

electronics and engineering sectors, with chief product categories: electronic devices, industrial and commercial equipment, home appliances and audio-visual equipment. Headquartered in Tokyo, Japan, J-Electric has over a 100 business bases worldwide and employs 65000 people.

Four SBU groups drive the organization: consumer, commercial, component and services. These business units are supported by a headquarters that provides platform services in finance, research and development, market development and human resources.

The strategy of the firm is to move towards a business model which stresses innovation and 'ideas generation' and away from a standard manufacturing model of incremental product improvement, embracing a much more market and customer-driven approach. The company has ambitious financial growth targets, and is seeking capitalization of regional and global emerging markets, such as digital products and Asia Pacific consumer markets. In difficult conditions, J-Electric is attempting to consolidate its brand and market position in established 'white' goods markets.

J-Electric's presence in China is extensive, with 50 subsidiary and affiliate companies, and all major divisions represented in the country. It is headquartered in Beijing, and employs more than 20000 people in China. Sales in China in 2004 were worth US$2000 million. The company entered China in 1986 when China was changing to a market economy. Each division has its own HR department, with a small HR team at each of the factory/manufacturing sites. Budgetary control for HR remains in Japan but otherwise there is almost total discretion for HR practice within each division. However, this discretion is more apparent than real, since the divisions in Japan are run almost exclusively by Japanese expatriates who instil a 'Japanese mindset' including HR processes and practices from Japan.

Philips

Royal Philips Electronics of the Netherlands is Europe's largest electronics company, with sales of EUR 32.3 billion in 2001. Its 184000 employees in more than 60 countries are active in the areas of lighting, consumer electronics, domestic appliances, components, semiconductors and medical systems (Ghemawat & Nueno, 2003).

Philips is organized into the following divisions: Components, Consumer Electronics, Domestic Appliances, Personal Care (DAP) and Lighting, and five regions, Western Europe, North America, Latin America, Asia Pacific and Eastern Europe. Philips has operations in 60 countries and has service companies in 150 countries (Ghemawat & Nueno, 2003).

Philips' trading record with China stretches back to the 1920s and its investment in 2002 was more than US$2.5 billion, with sales revenue of

US$6.7 billion. The company has over 20 manufacturing plants in China and has total employee numbers there of 20 244. Since the expansion of Philips into China, the organization grew to have 22 HR departments in different units and 171 HR staff. The Towards One Philips programme, introduced in late 2001, aimed to reduce this proliferation, and the first step was to set up shared service centres – Philips People Services' (PPS) – to serve all the Philips companies, plants and units in China (Mobley & Fernandez, 2004).

The two cases reveal some differences and also strong similarities between the European and Japanese MNCs in the way the HR function is managed and used to control and coordinate HR practice and knowledge. First, in terms of similarity, in both companies there is a tripartite approach to managing the HR function; corporate HR, line HR and an internal consultancy function, intended to give coverage of both strategic and operational HR to all stakeholders within the organization. These stakeholders are predominantly located in product divisions, to which a large degree of autonomy has been ceded by corporate HQ. But though this structural similarity exists, it masks differences in terms of the relationships between the various parties, and the level of embeddedness within the organization they have achieved.

Within J-Electric, the three-part HR function comprises corporate HR, line HR and a consultancy business, J-Electric HR consulting. The human resources strategy has placed strong emphasis on globalizing J-Electric. As a result of the divisionalization of J-Electric into four product groups, with each division having its own distinctive context and business demands and environmental pressures, responsibility for HR matters is devolved to the divisions, except for a number of core activities, including global staffing, specifying headcount targets, and certain performance management frameworks, in particular the common appraisal scheme. However this has worked only for the Japanese operations of the product divisions. For the country operations, HR has no formal link to Japan at all, save for budget and headcount reporting.

At Philips, the three HR roles are administrative, business and functional. Administrative HR focuses on non-business specific HR processes. The role is performed by shared service centres. The objective is to provide shared services to all the Philips companies, plants and units, centralizing the resources in one place. By centralizing administrative HR services, the shared service centres could lower HR operational costs and improve efficiency. These shared service centres were in recruitment, HR administration, HRIS (HR Information Systems) administration, payroll and benefits administration, relocation, rewards management and people development (Mobley & Fernandez, 2004; Ghemawat & Nueno, 2003).

The business HR role is to concentrate on strategic HR at the division level to align people and businesses. In performing this role, HR will act as a consultant and a business partner to the division management team and help translate business needs into HR solutions. Also business HR supports the execution of business-specific HR policies and programmes, such as performance management, talent management and management development. The business HR personnel are within the product divisions, because all product divisions had different strategies and different positions in the market (Mobley & Fernandez, 2004).

The role of Functional HR is to ensure HR programme excellence and also to ensure that the link between shared services and business HR is effective. This is present at global, regional and country levels: 'The functional HR is to ensure consistency and coherence among global, regional and country HR processes; rewards management, industrial relations, recruitment/employment branding, people development' (company documentation, 2003).

In the case firms, there were different operating assumptions in terms of devolution and coordination. In J-Electric, traditionally, the corporate HR function designed and developed HR practices and systems and it was the responsibility of the groups to implement these as far as possible. But the changes to corporate structure have brought an increasingly more fragmented HR approach, with each division developing its own practices to suit its particular conditions. At Philips, the building block of the One Philips vision is the consistent sharing and streamlining of support functions in IT, finance, purchasing and HR and, wherever possible, sharing internal resources.

At J-Electric the parenting role of HR is minimal. In China, there is a highly fragmented regional structure, with no horizontal integration of practice across the group of Chinese businesses, and vertical integration extends between the individual China-based operation and the Japanese business unit headquarters. There is little or no consistency of practice, with no transfer of knowledge and best practice, and strong duplication of work. For example, there is no common recruitment policy or provider, even for different operations employing the same staff in the same localized labour market. There is also a good deal of inconsistency in practices, such as a high dispersion of pay and working conditions for employees doing work of equal value.

The HR department fulfils the role of personnel administrator rather than strategic partner in China. Employees are considered 'an element of the production process' and there is a highly transactional employment relationship. This is to be expected, given that the business model is low-cost manufacturing and that the basic practices are staffing, grievance, discipline and dispute resolution, payroll and welfare. The regional centre is on hand to provide HR support and guidance, but, in reality, their services are not called upon. Nor is Japanese corporate HR consulted. In each of the divisions, there is total local management discretion about staffing, contingent on production levels, a highly informal system of appraisal based on supervisor discretion, rewards based on fixed local market rates, and no performance link to pay. Training and development are likewise informally and sporadically run.

At Philips, the world-class HR campaign that led to three distinct roles for HR was rolled out to China. Three shared service centres, one for commercial and two for the industrial group, were set up, and run on a contract basis to the businesses. The business HR groups were located in the product divisions and were responsible for aligning HR with the distinctive context of the particular product division's strategy. The functional HR aim was to standardize processes across regions and countries. The application of intranets allowed greater speed and ease of use with this. Philips created a career centre, e-learning systems, people performance management and a salary automated system, all of which were e-enabled. Continuity and consistency among practices and processes within Philips was therefore a major aim, with coordination tightly managed (Mobley & Fernandez, 2004).

Both companies stressed the need for corporate HR to have strong parenting roles in certain key aspects, primarily through the use of global staffing and global leadership programmes. These linking mechanisms are at different stages of maturity, with J-Electric just initiating, while Philips has had such approaches in place for a number of years. In this scenario, the corporate or global headquarters houses the leadership development effort and local, regional and/or business HR units should cooperate with corporate HR in their efforts to coordinate management development (MD) programmes and to glue the units together.

At J-Electric an internship programme involves the director of J-Electric Human Consulting and colleagues forming networks with major business schools worldwide and selecting strong international potential candidates for the organization. This is the ground work to make J-Electric into 'a truly global' company. Each year 40 interns are selected and brought to Japan to work in various divisions and from these a number are selected and offered job contracts.

The high potential scheme, just launched, identifies the global 1000 high potentials and has a dedicated team which has developed a competency framework and series of assessments to determine high potential within J-Electric.

At Philips, the foundation of the management development process is the Philips Leadership Competencies, a set of common personal characteristics to be found in leaders, which are needed for outstanding performance. The six competencies define the behaviour that is required to achieve business success. It is implicit that the criteria for management development effectiveness are generally applicable across product divisions (PDs) and countries and are measurable and observable. Management at every level is accountable for recognizing and developing the skills and talents of its employees, the importance of early identification, the structural approach to individual career development and succession planning.

Succession planning takes place across the company, with a strong awareness that managers needed international skills if their career was to progress within the company. In J-Electric, however, the HR department lacks such formal coordination and a clear link to strategy and corporate competitiveness. It also lacks any kind of database or coordinating mechanism to track managerial and leadership talent across the J-Electric group.

In terms of common practices across countries, there is wide variation. At J-Electric, the corporate HR function generates a suite of global practices, called 'global standards', for use in business units, including the performance management system and the pay system, but though the term 'global' is used, in reality these practices do not extend beyond Japan and the corporate HR is given the informal title 'domestic corporate HR'. The corporate HR also seems to lack a coordination process with HR in line, except for twice-yearly meetings, and there seems to be little by way of monitoring whether the businesses are actually implementing these practices/standards correctly. There seem to be few mechanisms for transferring best practice across HR activity, and indeed seemingly little desire on the part of line HR to seek this out. HR in the strategic business units is engaged in support to the line, but, according to the line managers, has variable value. Line HR members are seen to have reasonable expertise and knowledge of the business, but the lack of formal reporting relationships to corporate HR is a key issue in terms of effectiveness.

At Philips, the major programme, One Philips, was intended to transform Philips from a conglomerate into a more homogeneous company. The 'One Philips' idea summarizes what working together as one company entails: leveraging the potential in the enterprise by working together as one global team, sharing knowledge, technology, processes, customers, talent and one brand (Ghemawat & Nueno, 2003).

Discussion and conclusions
The international HR department has much in common with other staff functional units: it aspires to a more strategic role, it has strong claims for its central contribution to organizational success, and it has problems in

terms of power and influence that have seen its de facto role as primarily tactical and often marginalized. We have examined the existing literature on the HR department from three perspectives: its roles, the nature of devolution and coordination that exists within the HR department and its units, and its power and influence.

With respect to the first issue, the strategic role is a complex problem. Despite the welter of prescriptions there is only patchy evidence to suggest that the HR department in international firms is really playing this role. The HR department is a multi-role unit, answering to multiple constituencies (Caldwell, 2003; Tsui, 2000) and so focusing on the strategic role alone cannot reflect the reality of the department's endeavour. Prescriptive notions that suggest that the multiple HR department roles (strategic partner, change agent, administrator, employee champion – Ulrich, 1997; Storey, 1992) are reconcilable and consistent seem wide of the mark; in truth a theoretical position that embraces the notion of tensions or paradoxes or dilemmas seems to be the most accurate reflection of the lived experience of HR professionals (Evans *et al.*, 2002).

The second issue we examined concerned devolution and coordination. The literature here supports a contingency model of HR department approaches to 'fit', depending primarily on strategic posture and national cultural issues. The requirements of integration and differentiation (Ulrich, 1997) have different implications for the international HR department depending upon issues of strategy and synergy and internationalization approach. Even within the same industry and with the same expansion plans, we saw with the two case illustrations that the variation in HR department approaches could be very different indeed. The Japanese model highlights a traditional country-of-origin effect (Ferner & Quintanilla, 1998) with the MNC's pattern of managing its subsidiary one of 'application rather than learning from local institutions and practices' (Whitley *et al.*, 2003: 646). Expatriate managers dominated on the operational side, though in the HR department, this was less so. The autonomy given to local operations of product divisions was high but, in reality, the firm required chiefly low-skilled employees and given labour market conditions, and the need to build commitment amongst employees was low (Debroux, 2003). However, given the importance of China to J-Electric's growth ambitions and their stated aim of increasing the innovative potential of their employees, greater attention is being given to these issues. Within this organization there are signs of movement towards the European MNC in terms of approach and HR department structure and even in terms of coordination. However to understand whether any kind of convergence is taking place more generally would require a study that includes longitudinal dimensions and broader sample of cases.

The third issue, the power and influence of the HR department, has long been a subject of attention, with barely concealed bafflement that, given the recognized importance of human resources for the success of the business, the role of the HR department seems mired in perceptions of ineffectiveness and moribundity. Like most subunits, the HR department suffers through a perceived lack of accountability and problems of measurement or outcomes and, perhaps because of this, a lack of visibility to the organization as a whole, except for delivering routine processes such as payroll and recruitment, or, in the worst case, enforcing redundancy programmes. The importance of the HR department influencing mechanism and how it seeks to build a power base has rarely been examined. Our view is that, for the international HR department, given the issues of coordination and control and the need to build a case for corporate HR that exhibits added value, notions of power and influence are central to understanding the nature of international HR departments (Novicevic & Harvey, 2001; Ferner, 1997, 2000; Galang & Ferris, 1997). A common assertion on the part of organizations is that, for the HR department to get a seat at the strategic table, it must first perform the basic HR practices efficiently and effectively (Gratton *et al.*, 1999). This thought suggests that the way to build power and influence is to secure credibility for delivering HR in a professional manner and to secure understanding of the HR requirements of the organization and its context. The wealth of studies highlighting a gap between the rhetoric and reality of human resource management within organizations indicates that such delivery is problematic in many cases (Watson, 1977, 1986; Guest & King, 2004).

Future research
A simple recommendation would be to call for more research into the HR department period. There is much received wisdom and many myths that surround what the international HR department does (or should do). While much of the HRM literature has focused on the link between HR practices and organizational effectiveness, little attention has been given to the delivery of many HR practices and the designer of HR systems, the HR department. Perhaps this research neglect is a reflection of the traditional low status of the HR department, in which case this is a particularly vicious cycle of neglect.

A related further issue for research is the extent to which isomorphic pressures are driving changes in HR departments in international countries and the need to examine where these influences are experienced and how organizations respond to them. Though a number of articles (for example, Sparrow, Schuler & Jackson, 1994; Von Glinow *et al.*, 2002) have sought to examine whether there is a convergence worldwide around certain HR practices, the degree to which HR departments are being structured and assigned roles in light of responses to normative or coercive forces remains unknown. Institutional theory has focused on practice adoption, but little on departmental structure convergence, and this may add a fruitful line of inquiry for both theoretical disciplines.

We would support calls to study the power relations within and around HR departments and to examine the enablers and constraints to their influence (Galang & Ferris, 1997). Other support functions, such as IT and finance and marketing, have been subjected to detailed investigation, while HR has remained unattended. For the international HR function to increase its influence, detailed case studies of HR departments, preferably conducted over time, showing the processes of interaction between behavioural dynamics within and around the HR department and the prevailing structural conditions, would be valuable.

Last we would urge the examination of the HR department at multiple levels of analysis. If the HR department serves the organization, group and individual levels (Tsui, 2000), then the interconnections and interactions between these levels should be explored and greater insights found into the roles and effectiveness of the HR department, beyond traditional and rather narrow concerns over strategic contribution (Ostroff & Bowen, 2000).

References

Barney, J. 1991. Firm resources and sustained competitive advantage. *Journal of Management*, **17**: 99–120.
Beatty, R. & C. Schneider. 1997. New HR roles to impact organizational performance: from partners to players. *Human Resource Management*, **36**: 29–37.
Becker, B. & M. Huselid. 1998. High performance work systems: a synthesis of research and managerial implications. *Research in Personnel and Human Resource Management*, **16**: 53–101.
Becker, B., M. Huselid, P. Pickus & M.F. Spratt. 1997. Human resources as a source of shareholder value: research and recommendations. In D. Ulrich, M. Losey & G. Lake (eds), *Tomorrow's HR management*: 227–40. New York: Wiley.
Beer, M. 1997. The transformation of the human resource function; resolving the tension between a traditional administrative and a new strategic role. *Human Resource Management*, **36**: 49–56.
Bennett, N., D. Ketchen & E. Schultz. 1998. An examination of factors associated with the integration of human resource management and strategic decision-making. *Human Resource Management*, **37**: 3–16.
Birkinshaw, J. & N. Hood. 1999. An empirical study of the development process in foreign-owned subsidiaries in Canada and Scotland. *Management International Review*, **4**: 339–64.
Bowen, D.E., C. Galang & R. Pillai. 2002. The role of human resource management: an exploratory study of cross country variance. *Human Resource Management*, **41**(1): 103–22.
Brewster, C., H. Harris & P. Sparrow. 2002. *Globalising HR*. Executive brief. London: CIPD.
Caldwell, R. 2003. The changing roles of personnel managers: old ambiguities, new uncertainties. *Journal of Management Studies*, **40**: 983–1004.
Caligiuri, P. & L. Stroh. 1994. Multinational corporation management strategies and international human resource practices: bringing IHRM to the bottom line. *International Journal of Human Resource Management*, **6**: 494–507.

Connor, J. & D. Ulrich. 2000. The changing role of the HR department. *Human Resource Planning*, **41**: 42–53.

Debroux, P. 2003. *Human resource management in Japan: Changes and uncertainties*. London: Ashgate.

DeFidelto, C. & I. Slater. 2001. Web-based HR in an international setting. In A.J. Walker (ed.), *Web-based human resources: The technologies that are transforming HR*. London: McGraw-Hill.

Edwards, P., A. Ferner & K. Sisson. 1996. The conditions for international human resource management: two case studies. *International Journal of Human Resource Management*, **7**: 20–40.

Evans, P.A., V. Pucik & J.L. Barsoux. 2002. *The Global Challenge: Frameworks for international resource management*. New York: McGraw-Hill.

Ferner, A. 1997. Country of origin effects and HRM in multinational companies. *Human Resource Management Journal*, **7**(1): 19–37.

Ferner, A. 2000. The underpinnings of 'bureaucratic' control systems: HRM in European multinationals. *Journal of Management Studies*, **37**: 521–42.

Ferner, A. & J. Quintanilla. 1998. Multinationals, national business systems and human resource management: the enduring influence of national identity or a process of 'Anglo-Saxonization?' *International Journal of Human Resource Management*, **9**(4): 710–31.

Galang, M.C. & G.R. Ferris. 1997. Human resource department power and influence through symbolic action. *Human Relations*, **50**(11): 1403–26.

Ghemawat, P. & P. Nueno. 2003. *Revitalizing Philips*. Harvard Business School, Case 9-703-501.

Ghoshal, S. & C. Bartlett. 1990. The multinational corporation as an interorganizational network. *Academy of Management Review*, **15**: 603–25.

Goold, M. & A. Campbell. 1987. *Strategies and styles*. London: Macmillan.

Gratton, L., V. Hope-Hailey, P. Stiles & K. Truss. 1999. *Strategic human resource management*. Oxford: Oxford University Press.

Guest, D. & Z. King. 2004. Power, innovation and problem-solving: the personnel managers' three steps to heaven? *Journal of Management Studies*, **41**: 401–24.

Harris, H., C. Brewster & P. Sparrow. 2002. *International human resource management*. London: CIPD.

Hunt, J. & P. Boxall. 1998. Are top human resource specialists strategic partners? Self-perceptions of a corporate elite. *International Journal of Human Resource Management*, **9**(5): 767–81.

Huselid, M. 1995. The impact of human resource management practices on turnover, productivity and corporate financial performance. *Academy of Management Journal*, **40**(1): 171–88.

Kochan, T. & L. Dyer. 1995. Human resource management: an American view. In J. Storey (ed.), *Human resource management: A critical text*. London: Thompson Learning.

Legge, K. 1978. *Power, innovation and problem solving in personnel management*. London: McGraw-Hill.

Marginson, P., P. Armstrong, P.K. Edwards & J. Purcell. 1995. Extending beyond borders: multinational companies and the international management of labour. *International Journal of Human Resource Management*, **6**: 702–19.

Martin, G. & P. Beaumont. 2001. Transforming multinational enterprises: towards a process model of strategic human resource management change. *International Journal of Human Resource Management*, **12**: 1234–48.

Mobley, W. & J. Fernandez. 2004. *Philips China: Towards one Philips program*. Shanghai: CEIBS.

Mohrman, S.A., E.E. Lawler & G. McMahan. 1995. *New directions for the human resource organisation*. Los Angeles, CA: Centre for Effective Organisations.

Novicevic, M.M. & M. Harvey. 2001. The changing role of the corporate HR function in global organizations of the twenty-first century. *International Journal of Human Resource Management*, **12**: 1251–68.

Ostroff, C. & D.E. Bowen. 2000. Moving human resources to a higher level: human resource practices and organizational effectiveness. In K. Klein & S.W. Kozlowski (eds), *Multilevel theory, research and methods in organizations*. San Franscisco, CA: Jossey Bass.

Pelled, L.M., K.M. Eisenhardt & K.R. Xin. 1999. Exploring the black box: an analysis of work diversity, conflict and performance. *Administrative Science Quarterly*, 44(1): 1–28.

Pfeffer, J. 1994. *Competitive advantage through people*. Boston, MA: Harvard University Press.

Pucik, V. 1997. Human resources in the future: an obstacle or a champion of globalization? In D. Ulrich, M. Losey & G. Lake (eds), *Tomorrow's HR management*: 320–27. New York: Wiley.

Purcell, J. & B. Ahlstrand. 1994. *Human resource management in the multi-divisional company*. Oxford: Oxford University Press.

Rosenzweig, P.M. & N. Nohria. 1994. Influences on human resources management practice in multinational companies. *Journal of International Business Studies*, 25(2): 229–51.

Schuler, R. 1990. Repositioning the human resource function: transformation or demise? *Academy of Management Executive*, 4: 49–60.

Scullion, H. 1995. International human resource management. In J. Storey (ed.), *Human resource management: A critical text*. London: Routledge.

Scullion, H. & K. Starkey. 2000. In search of the changing role of the corporate human resource function in the international firm. *International Journal of Human Resource Management*, 11(6): 1061–81.

Sisson, K. 2001. Human resource management and the personnel function: a case of partial impact? In J. Storey (ed.), *Human resource management: A critical text*. Second edition, London: Thompson Learning.

Sparrow, P., C. Brewster & H. Harris. 2002. *Globalization of human resources: tracking the business role of international HR specialists*. London: Heinemann.

Sparrow, P., R. Schuler & S. Jackson. 1994. Convergence or divergence: human resource practices and policies for competitive advantage worldwide. *International Journal of Human Resource Management*, 5(2): 267–99.

Storey, J. 1992. *Developments in the management of human resource management*. Oxford: Blackwell.

Storey, J. (ed.) 2001. *Human resource management: A critical text*. Second edition, London: Thompson Learning.

Taylor, S. & S. Beechler. 1993. Human resource management system integration and adaptation in multinational firms. *Advances in International Comparative Management*, 8: 115–74.

Torrington, D. 1998. Crisis and opportunity in human resource management: the challenge for the personnel department. In P. Sparrow & M. Marchington (eds), *Human resource management: The new agenda*. London: Pitman.

Townley, B. 2004. Managerial technologies, ethics and managing. *Journal of Management Studies*, 41: 425–46.

Truss, C., L. Gratton, V. Hope-Hailey, P. Stiles & J. Zaleska. 2002. Paying the piper: choice and constraints in changing HR functional roles. *Human Resource Management Journal*, 12(2): 39–63.

Tsui, A. 2000. A multiple constituency approach to human resource effectiveness. *Academy of Management Journal*, 35: 458–83.

Tyson, S. & R. Fell. 1986. *Evaluating the personnel function*. Cheltenham: Nelson Thornes.

Ulrich, D. 1997. *Human resource champions*. Boston, MA: Harvard University Press.

Ulrich, D. 1998. A new mandate for human resources. *Harvard Business Review*, 76(1): 124–34.

Von Glinow, M.A., E.A. Drost & M.B. Teagarden. 2002. Converging on IHRM best practices: lessons learned from a globally distributed consortium on theory and practice. *Human Resource Management*, 41: 123–40.

Watson, T. 1977. *The personnel managers: a study in the sociology of work and employment*. London: Routledge.

Watson, T. 1986. *Management, organization and employment strategy*. London: Routledge & Kegan Paul.

Watson, T. 2004. HRM and critical social science. *Journal of Management Studies*, **41**: 447–68.
Whitley, R., G. Morgan, W. Kelly & D. Sharpe. 2003. The changing Japanese multinational: adaptation and learning in car manufacturing and financial services. *Journal of Management Studies*, **40**: 643–72.
Wright, P.M. & G. McMahan. 1992. Theoretical perspectives for strategic human resource management. *Journal of Management*, **18**: 295–320.

5 Comparing HRM policies and practices across geographical borders
Chris Brewster

Comparative Human Resource Management can be distinguished from international human resource management (Boxall, 1995; Harris, Brewster & Sparrow, 2003). International human resource management (IHRM) is concerned with the way that organizations that operate across national borders manage their employees, and increasingly the term is applied to all their employees and not just those who are working internationally (Sparrow, Brewster & Harris, 2004). This is a significantly more complex task than managing human resources in one country (Dowling, 1988), given the dual requirements of systematizing their management processes (global integration) and remaining aware of the differences between countries (local responsiveness), which mean that it is not possible, or rational, to manage people in exactly the same way in different circumstances (Ashkenas et al., 1995; Hamal & Prahalad, 1985; Yip, 1995). Comparative human resource management is about understanding and explaining what differences exist between countries in the way that human resources are managed. Whereas most of the rest of this book is concerned with IHRM, this chapter focuses on comparative human resource management.

Comparison is the method used in social sciences to replace the experiment in the natural sciences. Most studies of HRM take place within one country and their findings relate to that country even if they are often assumed to be universally applicable. International comparisons are not only a good way of checking our assumptions about the systems and practices that operate in HRM, they are also a valuable way of checking our basic assumptions about the meaning and understanding of HRM.

HRM research has been focused on North America and Europe, although many writers have accommodated the Japanese system, and more recently the other 'East Asian Tigers'. Few include the full range even of European systems; other Arab, Asian, South American and African countries have only more recently begun to feature in the literature.[1]

It is not possible, even in summary, to avoid 'the danger of lapsing into either vacuous description or superficial comparison' (Shalev, 1980: 40) with any attempt to cover all differences between nation states in their management of human resources; nor is it possible to cover all the elements of

HRM or all the theoretical or practical issues that arise in international comparisons of HRM. This chapter, therefore, has just three aims: to explore some of the assumptions of the universalist approach to HRM; to compare that with the national differences argument (and to examine some of the reasons advanced for there being these national differences); and then to consider whether these differences are diminishing (the convergence thesis) as globalization becomes more widespread.

The universalist model

It has been argued, amongst the 'classic' management theorists, that efficiency imperatives create pressure to identify and adopt a 'one best way' in management, irrespective of cultural or national context (Smith & Meiskins, 1995). Thus Taylor, Barnard, Mayo, Mouton and Blake, among others, were seeking to identify management principles which can be universally employed as 'best practices'. One consequence of the increasing pressures of competition and globalization is a growing need to learn systematically from management practices regarded as the most successful (see, for example, Levitt, 1983; Mueller, 1994) and, given the economic power of the USA, that has tended to be seen as a recipe for following the US models of management. Very similar arguments can be applied to the human resource aspect of management.

And at one level, of course, human resource management (HRM) clearly is universal. Every organization has to utilize and, hence, in some way, to manage, human resources. However HRM practices vary across the world. There are significant differences in the way human resource management is conceptualized, the research traditions through which it is explored and the way HRM is conducted. In conceptual and research terms two different (ideal type) paradigms might be classified as the *universalist* and the *contextual* (Brewster, 1999a, 1999b).[2] The notion of paradigm is used here in Kuhn's (1970) sense as an accepted model or theory. The corollary is that different researchers may be using competing models or theories.

The *universalist paradigm*, which is dominant in the USA, and is widely used elsewhere, is essentially a nomothetic social science approach. Generalizations of an abstract and lawlike character are created and tested empirically against a 'yes/no' criterion in a way that can lead on to prediction. As in other related areas of the social sciences, the universalist paradigm tends to seek general laws. This paradigm assumes that the purpose of the study of our area of the social sciences, HRM, and in particular strategic human resource management (SHRM); (see, for example, Fombrun, Tichy & Devanna, 1984; Ulrich, 1987; Wright & McMahan, 1992; Wright & Snell, 1991), is to improve the way that human resources are managed strategically within organizations. The ultimate aim of this work is to improve organizational performance, as judged by its impact on the organization's declared corporate strategy (Tichy, Fombrun & Devanna, 1982; Huselid, 1995), the customer (Ulrich, 1989) or share-holders (Huselid, 1995; Becker & Gerhart, 1996; Becker et al., 1997). It is implicit that this objective will apply in all cases. Thus the widely cited def-inition by Wright and McMahan states that SHRM is 'the pattern of planned human resource deployments and activities intended to enable a firm to achieve its goals' (1992: 298). Boxall and Purcell (2003) focus on the close link between HRM and business strategies in HRM and even deal with social legitimacy as primarily a firm-level issue. Much of the research base in this paradigm is centred on a small number of private sector 'leading edge' exemplars of 'good practice', often large multinationals, gen-erally from the manufacturing or even specifically the high tech sector.

The value of this paradigm lies in the simplicity of focus and the coales-cing of research around this shared objective. It also has a clear relation-ship with the demands of industry, which often funds such research either directly or indirectly. The disadvantages lie in the ignoring of other potential focuses, the resultant narrowness of the research objectives and the ignoring of other levels and other stakeholders in the outcomes of SHRM (Guest, 1990; Poole, 1990; Pieper, 1990; Legge, 1995; Kochan, 1999).

There is no agreed list of what constitutes 'good' HRM policies and prac-tices. However, in general, there is a coalescing of views around the concept of 'high performance work systems'. These have been characterized by the US Department of Labor (1993) as having certain clear characteristics:

- careful and extensive systems for recruitment, selection and training,
- formal systems for sharing information with the individuals who work in the organization,
- clear job design,
- local-level participation procedures,
- monitoring of attitudes,
- performance appraisals,
- properly functioning grievance procedures, and
- promotion and compensation schemes that provide for the recogni-tion and financial rewarding of high performing members of the workforce.

Whilst there are many other attempts to develop such lists, and they all differ to some degree, the Department of Labor list can be taken as an exemplar of the universalist paradigm: few US researchers in HRM would find very much to argue with in this list, particularly if they are likely to label their studies as SHRM. However, in other countries, researchers and practitioners might find such a list contrary to experience and even to what they would conceive of as good practice. Thus they might argue for sharing information with representative bodies such as trade unions or works councils, for flexible work boundaries, for group reward systems. They might argue that the 'low trust' inherent in attitude monitoring, appraisal systems and so on are culturally inappropriate. And they might identify quite different meanings in the term 'careful' recruitment, and others.

Differences in national contexts

This section of the chapter addresses our second issue: the argument for the importance of focusing on national differences in our attempts to understand HRM. This section explores an alternative paradigm for understanding and researching HRM and uses that to critique the relevance of the universalist model outside the USA; examines the problems of researching comparative HRM; identifies some of reasons that have been advanced for those differences; and attempts to draw some messages about understanding these static distinctions before briefly considering time and change as a lead-in to the final section on the concept of convergence.

The contextual paradigm (Brewster, 1999a, 1999b) is idiographic, searching for an overall understanding of what is contextually unique and why. It is focused on understanding what is different between and within management in various contexts and what the antecedents of those differences are. Hence the research mechanisms used are inductive. Here theory is drawn from an accumulation of data collected or gathered in a less directed (or constrained) manner than would be the case under the universalist paradigm. Research traditions are focused less upon testing and prediction and more upon the collection of evidence. There is an assumption that, if things are important, they should be studied, even if testable prediction is not possible or the resultant data are complex and unclear. The policies and practices of the 'leading edge' companies (something of a value-laden term in itself) are of less interest to contextualists than identifying the way markets and organizations work and what the more typical organizations are doing. This affects, not just the contingencies within which the firm operates, but also our notions of the management process. Clark and Mueller (1996: 126), for example, argue that 'firms are so embedded, constrained and encultured by their national homes that the room for corporate agency and its zones of manoeuvre could be, and perhaps is, rather small'.

Currently a powerful strand in this line of argument is Business Systems Theory, summarized by Whitley (1999) as arguing that specific nations are locked on a particular developmental trajectory reflecting differences in both institutional configuration and corresponding social agency; these variations are reflected in the role and structuring of firms. Thus, amongst the classical studies of management, Bendix (1956) argues that managerial authority is contingent on the use of ideology; this inevitably varies from context to context and is moulded by the relative extent of government controls and patterns of political decision making. The outcomes reflect predominant cultural dynamics and the specific nature of national class formation. For Whitley (1999) business systems constitute mechanisms and structures for regulating market relations. Whilst, at least partially, they may be backed up by coercive power, they are most visible in shaping, moulding and making possible everyday exchange relationships through imitation and network ties.

Most, perhaps, of the exponents of such theories have tended to work with rather simplistic binary models. Thus Dore (2000) argues that important differences persist between the shareholder-driven Anglo-Saxon model and varieties of capitalism where the rights of owners are circumscribed by the rights of other stakeholders, including employees, customers, suppliers and community. Applebaum *et al.* (2001) argue that the development and persistence of 'high performance work systems' are closely bound up with the regulatory environment. Hall and Soskice (2000) draw a sharp distinction between 'co-ordinated market economies' and 'liberal market' (Anglo-American) ones; the former are reconstituted through systemic checks and balances (see also Lincoln & Kalleberg, 1990; Gooderham *et al.*, 1999).

Whitley's *Business Systems Theory* (1999) is rather more ambitious in seeking to identify a greater number of systemic archetypes, characterized by a wider range of defining features. The book is not coherent or consistent in its analysis, but does go a long way towards reflecting the messy reality of comparative research: the world is not coherent or consistent. Whitley emphasizes the fact that institutional effects comprise both formal regulatory and associated administrative structures (including the state, education and financial systems) and personal ties, attitudes, norms and values. Thus human resource management is explicitly accorded a distinctive role in defining the difference between these systems.

HRM is the aspect of management most subject to local influences (Hendry, 1991; Müller, 1999; Rosenzweig & Nohria, 1994) and the aspect, therefore, where the contextual paradigm is most relevant. What matters to HRM specialists working in this paradigm are explanations – any link to firm performance is secondary. It is assumed that HRM can apply to societies, governments, regions and firms. The focus is more likely to include public sector organizations. There is no necessary assumption that an organization's objectives and strategy will be 'good' either for the organization or for society: indeed there are plenty of examples where this is clearly not the case. Nor, in this paradigm, is there any assumption that the interests of everyone in the organization will be the same, or any expectation that an organization will have a strategy that people within the organization will 'buy into'. The assumption is that not only will the employees and the unions have a different perspective from the management team (Keenoy, 1990; Storey, 1992; Purcell & Ahlstrand, 1994), but that even within the management team there may be different interests and views (Hyman, 1987; Kochan *et al.*, 1986; Koch & McGrath, 1996). These, and the resultant impact on HRM, are issues for empirical study. This paradigm emphasizes external factors as well as the actions of the management within an organization. Thus it explores the importance of such factors as culture, ownership structures, labour markets, the role of the state and trade union organization as aspects of the subject rather than external influences upon it. The scope of HRM goes beyond the organization to reflect the reality of the role of many HR departments, particularly in Europe: for example, in lobbying about and adjusting to government actions, in dealing with legislation or in working with trade unions and tripartite institutions.

It has been argued that the USA is an inappropriate model for Europe (see Brewster, 1993, 1995b; Cox & Cooper, 1985; Pieper, 1990; Thurley & Wirdenius, 1991), for Japan (Dore, 2000; Okazaki-Ward, 1993; Sano, Morishima & Seike, 1997) and for many other countries (see, for example, Kamoche *et al.*, 2004; Budhwar, 2004). The vision of the US models of HRM is culture-bound; in particular a view of HRM as based on the largely unconstrained exercise of managerial autonomy has been attacked as being peculiarly American (Guest, 1990; Brewster, 1995b). In most other places in the world, organizations are not so autonomous. They exist within a system which constrains (or supports) them, at the national level, by culture and by extensive legal and institutional limitations on the nature of the contract of employment and, second, at the organizational level, by patterns of ownership (by the state, by the banking and finance system and by families) which are distinct from those in the USA. The very subject matter of HRM in the contextual paradigm is wider. The firm is less often the focus since more coordinated market systems such as Germany and Japan involve a close linkage between the firm, the educational system, sector-level arrangements for industrial training and public policy. Outside the USA, much research into HRM is located in the contextual paradigm, concerned to develop a critique of the relationship between owners and/or managers and the employees and the society in which the organizations operate. It is worth noting here that there are powerful calls from North Americans for a contextual paradigm to be used in the USA too (see, for example, Schuler & Jackson, 1987; Dyer & Kochan, 1995; Kochan, 1999).

Researching comparative HRM

Comparative research in HRM has been rare (comparative research in the fields of industrial and employment relations, rooted in institutional explanations, has been more common). The main reason for this is that it is difficult. There are, as one recent article (Mayrhofer & Brewster, 2005) put it, 'noble and not so noble' problems: those of conceptualization and the practical difficulties.

Different scientific traditions in methodological and epistemological terms exist across countries. In the Latin countries of continental Europe, for example, there is a long tradition of interpretative research. Struggling with the issue of 'likeness' and equivalence is one of the big topics in international comparative research (Cavusgil & Das, 1997). The same empirical phenomena can be labelled differently in different countries and, vice versa, different things can carry the same labels. Likewise the same data-gathering procedures can yield quite different results. Therefore comparative research 'is concerned with attempting to compare like with like. In international settings this is not an easy task' (Tregaskis *et al.*, 2004: 440). Practically, given the complexity of people from one culture trying to understand differences in other countries, effective comparative research requires the creation and maintenance of international teams of researchers. There are also complex problems of identifying comparable research issues, databases, methodologies and analytical methods (Cavusgil & Das, 1997; Elder, 1976; England & Harpaz, 1983; Mayrhofer, 1998; Sanders, 1994; Sekaran, 1983; Tregaskis *et al.*, 2004). Keeping research teams together over a long time period is particularly difficult, which partly explains why we have such limited data on the crucial issue of convergence.

Nonetheless comparative HRM has experienced a steady growth in research efforts and publications, especially in the last few years. European researchers in particular have made a number of significant contributions to theoretical, empirical and methodological advances in the field of comparative HRM (for example, Brunstein, 1995; Pieper, 1990; Poole, 1990; Gooderham *et al.*, 1999; Brewster, Mayrhofer & Morley, 2004). There have also been important contributions from other parts of the world: in Asia (see, for example, Budhwar, 2004; Zanko, 2002; Zanko & Ngui, 2003), in Africa (Kamoche *et al.*, 2004) and in the developing countries (Budhwar & Debrah, 2001a, 2001b).

Explaining national differences

Inevitably, trying to explain the differences found by this research is complex and difficult. Broadly, two types of explanatory factors have been identified: the cultural and the institutional (Sorge, 2004). The cultural explanatory factors argue that national values are deeply embedded in a society and, though often invisible to the actors involved, structure the way that 'big questions' (good or bad, decent or indecent, fair or unfair, and so on) are answered. The management of people is an obvious area where these cultural differences come to the fore. The institutional explanator has two strands: one arguing that, as institutions respond to the same features across the world, they will create convergence (the role of MNCs is seen as crucial here); the other arguing that, since most countries have unique institutions, these will create and sustain national differences.

Culturally a distinction has been made between emic and etic approaches (see, for example, Ronen, 1986; Thomas, 1993; Holzmüller, 1995). 'Whereas emics apply in only a particular culture, etics represent universality – they apply to all cultures in the world' (Ronen, 1986: 47). At the most general level, while the empirical data on national cultural differences are limited (see, for example, Hofstede, 1980, 1991, 2001; House *et al.*, 2004; Schwartz, 1992, 1994), they do demonstrate considerable diversity. Cultural differences have a direct impact on HRM. It does not require much experience of international travel and particularly international work to understand that the way people respond to authority, the way they relate to their peers, the impact of gender and the importance of face-to-face contact, to mention just a few items, vary considerably from country to country.

Critiques of this literature would point to the limited databases used, the static nature of the evidence and in particular to the (con)fusion of culture and country. There are countries in the Arab world, and in Africa, for example, where the boundaries have been drawn only recently and cut across traditional boundaries. There are countries as different as Switzerland and India, which include several different linguistic, religious and national groupings. A fascinating recent study of the bicultural state of Belgium (Buyens *et al.*, 2004) concluded that, in some of the HR practices, the two communities (French Catholics and Flemish-speaking Protestants) are very close together, whilst in others the French-speaking region is closer to France and the Flemish-speaking region to the Netherlands.

At the institutional level, a wide range of institutions affects HRM. Institutions represent 'a system of patterned expectations defining the proper behaviour of persons playing particular roles' (Parsons, 1951). Business systems theory takes as fundamental the view that it is nationally based institutions that make the difference. Institutions such as the educational system, the labour market, macroeconomic policy making by government, employment legislation and trade unions are nearly always national (with a few exceptions amongst, for example, employment legislation in the European Union and US/Canadian and UK/Irish unions). In most countries, mechanisms for determining basic pay and conditions of employment continue to operate primarily at the national level. Two significant

institutional variations between countries lie, first, in the persistent centrality of state power (cf. Burnell, 2003: 247; Traxler, Blaschke & Kittel, 2001),
with its associated formal regulatory structures and, second, in patterns of
ownership (Brewster, 1993). Public ownership, which links the two, has
decreased to some extent in many European countries in recent years; but
here as around the world it is still far more widespread than in the USA.

These two explanators are not necessarily mutually exclusive. Organizations are not completely (or even in some cases, very) rational. Issues of
history and personality play a great part. Of course, just as individual
behaviour and social structure are reciprocally constituted (Giddens, 1986),
so are cultures and institutions. Thus the culturalists point out that institutions within a state will reflect the culture of that territory; and institutionalists tend to include national culture as an institution. The conclusion
must be that 'both institutional and cultural dimensions . . . have an important impact on HRM practices in different countries' (Romani, 2004: 163).
Institutional configurations are, anyway, nested at a range of levels from
subregional to transnational (cf. Hollingsworth & Boyer, 1997b) so that it
is unsurprising that elements of HRM operate at each level.

A major critique of both the cultural and institutional literature (though
particularly the cultural texts) is that, generally, it takes no account of
change over time. Indeed, as indicated in the section above on research
difficulties, many articles either supporting or, particularly, opposing convergence take their evidence from one time point, which, simply logically,
cannot provide any data on the presence or absence of convergence.
Equally much of the discussion on convergence is theoretical and prescriptive and lacks time series evidence.

But situations do change over time: and sometimes at a quite fundamental level. For example, a recent study of managers in Hong Kong found
that, not only did their work values differ from those of other territories,
but these values changed over time according to economic and political circumstances. On a wider and more general scale, the contribution of HRM
practices to the success of the Japanese economy during the 1970s and
1980s (Inohara, 1990), which was presented as an inspirational role-model
(Ouchi, 1981; Peters & Waterman, 1982), is now less often perceived as
being worth learning from (Smith, 1997; Yoshimura & Anderson, 1997).

This raises the questions of time and change. An overemphasis on comparative national differences is in danger of becoming a purely static analysis, unable to cope with change over time. In particular it raises the question
of convergence (and, by implication, divergence and stasis). If the Japanese
model has fallen out of favour, are we moving towards the US models, or
towards some other alternatives, or is each country continuing to go its own
way?

Evidence of convergence?
This third section of the chapter explores (necessarily briefly) the concept of convergence in HRM policies and practices around the world. Convergence is the process of structures, practices and values in different countries, in this case, becoming more similar. The concept accepts the fact that policies and practices are different, but argues that these differences are being, or will be, decreased. Are the differences between countries being reduced as the pressures to conform become stronger; and, if so, what are they converging towards?

Convergence and non-convergence in the management literature
Many of the seminal management and, specifically, HRM texts are written as if the analysis applies at all levels: what Rose (1991) has called 'false universalism'. The early management theorists were generally clear that practice in all countries would converge towards the most efficient model. Powerful market forces ensure that more productive firms with lower costs will be successful and in a process of organizational evolution others will be driven to copy them to survive. Given the power of the US economy, this 'was, after all, premised on the rest of the world copying the US' (Smith & Meiskins, 1995: 244). Authors who focus on the importance of learning from best practice in order to increase national competitiveness are more positive about cross-national convergence (see, for example, Child & Kieser, 1979; Hannerz, 1996; Tomlinson, 1999; Toynbee, 2001). An institutional version of this theory (sometimes termed the 'North-American phenomenological neo-institutionalism' – Djelic & Bensedrine, 2001) argues that institutions reflect power relationships and so there will be coercive pressure to ensure that similar structures and practices are adopted throughout the world (such as the deregulation 'strings' typically tied to IMF loans to underdeveloped countries). It has been argued that one effect of this global institutional isomorphism is that the role of nation states becomes less significant (Meyer, 2000). Normative pressures (from professional bodies, international associations and the growing internationalization of executive education) and cognitive isomorphism (as international organizations attempt to spread their policies and cultures around the world) are reinforcing this trend (DiMaggio & Powell, 1983). More recently, 'transaction cost theorists argue that there is one best organizational form for firms that have similar or identical transaction costs' (Hollingsworth & Boyer, 1997b:34; see also Scott, 1995).

An alternative version of the institutional analysis sees room for regional convergence. For example, there are developments at the level of the European Union which have an impact upon all organizations in Europe. In a historically unique experiment, European Union countries have agreed to subordinate national legislative decision making to European-level legislation. These developments have indirect effects upon business and management through their effects on the market and economy of the region and direct effects through the EU's adoption of legislation supporting and constraining businesses. Thus this strand of the debate would see convergence, not on a worldwide basis, but rather towards different regional groupings based on the developing regional institutions.[3] The European Union, where these institutions are far stronger than they are in any other regional bloc, is a test case and may create a convergence towards a distinctly European practice – different from the market convergence model.

A different view is, of course, taken by those authors who stress the embeddedness of management in its national cultural and institutional context. They see little room for convergence. This view may be based upon an institutionalist perspective, in which organizational choice is limited by institutional pressures, including the state, regulatory structures, interest groups, public opinion and norms (DiMaggio & Powell, 1983; Meyer & Rowan, 1983; Oliver, 1991; Hollingsworth & Boyer, 1997a). Or it may be based on the notion that cultural differences mean that the management of organizations (and particularly of people) is, and will remain, fundamentally different from country to country. National differences in ownership, structures, educational systems and laws all have a significant effect on the architecture and the practices of employing organizations.

These are non-convergence rather than divergence theorists. They argue, not that countries are getting further apart in their management policies and practices, but that, since national, and in some cases regional, cultures and institutional contexts are slow to change, they are unlikely to move together either. They argue that change is path-dependent. In other words, even when change does occur this can only be understood in relation to the specific social context in which it occurs (Maurice *et al.*, 1986; Poole, 1986). The goals of business leaders in different countries might be quite distinct (Hofstede *et al.*, 2002) so there seems little reason to expect that their behaviours would be becoming increasingly alike. Performance criteria or goals are, at any point in time, socially rather than economically or technologically selected, so that they reflect primarily the national culture and the idiosyncratic principles of local rationality.

Convergence and non-convergence in the HR literature
Similar arguments have been applied to HRM. The univeralists tend to be also convergers and often assume that the convergence will be towards the US pattern. Müller (1999: 126) argues that the American concept of HRM 'has emerged as one of the most important prescriptions for

a world-wide convergence of managerial practices'. There are signs of policies of deregulation and decontrol of labour markets, for example, spreading from the USA to Europe (Locke *et al.*, 1995) and signs too that this is spreading to other countries. The world financial institutions often make deregulation of the labour market, for example, a condition of their loans (Stiglitz, 2002). The ILO has sought to spread collective bargaining systems throughout the former socialist Central and Eastern Europe states (Martin & Bamber, 2004). In the business world, MNCs attempt to create global human resource strategies, with sophisticated policies and practices rolled out internationally, policed by a central human resource function (Brewster, Sparrow & Harris, 2005; Dowling, Welch & Schuler, 1999; Ferner & Quintanilla, 1998; Sparrow, Harris & Brewster, 2004). It is argued that human resource management is a dependent variable that evolves in response to technological and economic change, rather than with reference to the sociopolitical context, so that 'much of what happens to management and labor is the same regardless of auspices' (Kerr, 1983).

In HRM too there is a regional version of convergence, perhaps, at least in the European case, more persuasive than in the general management context, given the attention that the European Union pays to social issues. Thus some researchers see the current economic and political integration of European Union countries reflected in a convergence towards a distinctly European practice (Due, Madsen & Jensen, 1991). This concept would see regional convergence, but not global convergence, potentially generating a 'European' model of HRM (Brewster, 1995b).

As with the more general management literature, there is a stream of writers on HRM who emphasize national differences. Indeed it seems that human resource management is increasingly acknowledged to be one of the areas where organizations are most likely to maintain a 'national flavour' and is the point at which business and national cultures have the sharpest interface. A number of studies show the differences between various aspects of HRM in European countries (for example, Pieper, 1990; Vickerstaff, 1992; Brunstein, 1995; Brewster, Mayrhofer & Morley, 2004). A large survey of HR directors of the biggest firms in Germany, the USA and Japan (Pudelko, 2000) found that 'statistically significant differences between the three countries can be reported in 57 out of 80' HR issues. There is recent evidence that, even in the most centralized MNCs, forms of control (Harzing & Sorge, 2003), work systems (Geppart, Williams & Matten, 2003) and teamwork (Woywode, 2002) vary by country and that, in practice, the form of implementation of 'worldwide' policies is negotiated or varied at national level (Ferner, 1997; Wächter *et al.*, 2003). Industrial relations theory, in particular (as Martin & Bamber, 2004, point out) has maintained a national focus, with limited comparative work (though see, for example, Bamber & Lansbury, 1998; Katz & Darbishire, 2000; Traxler, Blaschke & Kittel, 2001) and almost no international versions. However some authors here have found evidence, not just that these countries are different, but that they stay different over time: non-convergence. Traxler and colleagues, for example, note that, between 1980 and 1996, the coverage of collective bargaining increased in five countries (Finland, France, the Netherlands, Portugal and Spain), declined in five (Australia, Britain, Germany, Japan and the USA), stayed the same in two (Belgium and Sweden), with incomplete data for three (Austria, Canada and Denmark) (Traxler, Blaschke & Kittel, 2001: 197).

Another look at the convergence debate in HRM
The situation is, inevitably, complex. And the evidence can be selected to suit almost any position. As Piore and Sabel (1984) observed, some aspects of industrial societies tend to converge, whilst others diverge, depending upon time and circumstances. Objective and transnational institutions and associated cultural forces do not have simple homogenizing effects; they are reshaped, resisted and redeployed by the socially embedded processes of the host locale (Comaroff & Comaroff, 2001: 14). Global market forces are moulded and ameliorated by the strengths and homogeneity of institutional configurations (D'Aunno et al., 2000: 680). Equally, national business systems are subject to the pressures of isomorphism. It is no surprise that elements of both convergence and divergence can be seen in most areas of management. In HRM, the convergence–divergence debate tends to assume that the HRM system as a whole has to converge or remain divergent. An alternative approach would be to consider whether some parts of the overall HR system might be converging, in some regions or geographies, whilst other parts might be diverging. Moreover, since HR operates at multiple levels including philosophy, policy, programme, practice and process (Schuler, 1992) there might be convergence at one level but divergence at another, even within one firm, never mind between nations.

We might also examine the notion of convergence itself. The meaning most commonly assumed in the literature (even if rarely stated explicitly) is of movement leading to greater similarity. At the comparative national level of HRM this would mean countries becoming more like each other in the way that they manage their human resources. Much of the evidence that is adduced for this, however (found in the literature cited above), comes either from a single point in time, or from the identification of similar trends across countries. Logically these cannot prove movement towards greater similarity. An attempt has been made, therefore, to disaggregate the notion of convergence in comparative HRM so that we can consider three forms of convergence (Mayrhofer *et al.*, 2002). These forms are 'directional convergence' in which the trends tend in the same direction (but different starting points may mean that countries remain parallel, staying in the same relationship to each other, or even diverging somewhat); final convergence, where the practice of HRM in these countries becomes more similar (even though that might, on occasion, mean that different countries are heading in different directions); and 'majority convergence' where organizations within one country become more alike (again, perhaps by some heading in opposite directions to others).

The best evidence that we have on convergence comes from the European part of the repeating Cranet studies (see Brewster, Mayrhofer & Morley, 2004). Indeed there are significant differences between the countries in all major functional areas of HRM. There is little room here to go into detail, or to explore the many caveats that are necessary, but Table 5.1 indicates the range of practice in Europe for a few chosen HR domains. The table illustrates a remarkable degree of difference: what is widespread or standard practice in one country plays much less of a role in others.

Table 5.1   *Range of selected HRM practices in Europe (percentage of organizations, 1999/2000)*

	EU average	Highest	Lowest
Formal representation of HR function at the highest board	54.5	88.2 (F)	29.9 (P)
Involved in development of corporate strategy from the outset	58.1	72.0	43.5
Internal recruitment of senior management	52.0	65.9 (GR)	7.0 (DK)
>10% of workforce on part-time contracts	24.9	63.3 (NL)	2.3 (P)
No part-timers employed	7.4	68.7 (P)	0 (NL)
Proportion of annual salaries bill spent on training & development			
<1%	12.9	26.3 (I)	0.3 (F)
1–1.9%	27.3	42.0 (E)	7.8 (F)
2–2.9%	20.1	31.2 (DK)	12.1 (P)
3–4.9 %	19.4	37.5 (F)	9.6 (E)
5–9.9%	15.6	31.1 (F)	1.8 (I)
>10%	4.9	9.3 (P)	1.5 (FIN)

Note: F = France; P = Portugal; GR = Greece; DK = Denmark; NL = Netherlands; I = Italy; E = Spain; FIN = Finland.

Source: Mayrhofer and Brewster (2005).

*Table 5.2   Change in selected HRM practices in Europe
(percentage of organizations, 1999/2000)*

Formal representation of HR on board	1991	1995	1999/2000
Spain	86	75	75
France	86	82	87
Germany	30*	42	46
Sweden	89	80	79
UK	50	52	47

>10% workforce on part-time contracts	1991	1995	1999/2000
Spain	5	5	11
France	13	26	17
Germany	22*	31	21
Sweden	43	43	38
UK	25	22	31

Note: * West Germany only.

Over time the pattern is that HRM in these countries tends not to change very much and that countries tend to hold their position in relation to each other. Table 5.2 gives two examples. The role of HRM at board (or equivalent) level changes very little and the countries retain their positions, with the single exception of a clear trend in Germany towards more organizations having an HR director on the board. A completely different example, the number of companies with more than 10 per cent of their workforce on part-time contracts, shows more fluctuation, but less sign of any obvious pattern or trend.

These examples could be multiplied, but overall there are consistent developments towards *directional* convergence in Europe to be found in four areas: decreases in the size of the HR department relative to the overall workforce, small rises in the percentage of the annual salaries bill spent on training (which, of course, may reflect a growing disparity between wage growth and the growing costs of training rather than a 'real' growth in the amount of training), increases in the amount of information being given to employees about company strategy and financial performance, and a more frequent use of contingent compensation systems. This was termed strong evidence of directional convergence. (In other areas of HRM, such as the use of flexible work arrangements, the level at which the HR policy is determined and the responsibility shift from HR departments to line managers, the evidence is mixed or rather weak.) It would seem that, where economic necessities, institutional requirements and/or management folklore point in the same direction, a more or less consistent trend could be seen. Good examples of this may be the reduction in the comparative size of the HR department or the increasing amount of money spent on training and development.

In terms of *final* convergence, however, the overall evidence, for all the HR practices analysed, is unequivocal: there is no trend towards final convergence. Moreover the data show a relatively constant picture throughout the 1990s. This should be an antidote to the 'change frenzy' that has infiltrated much of scientific and practitioner-oriented writing about HRM. The combination of the heterogeneity of national differences and this stability adds a further weapon to the critique of 'ultimate solutions' and 'best practices' that are supposed to lead inevitably to organizational success and related models (Marchington & Grugulis, 2000).

In general, it seems clear that we need a more nuanced view of convergence in HRM policies and practices than has been apparent hitherto. Manifestly there are differences between countries and, while things appear to change slowly in HRM, there seems to be at least some clear indication of directional convergence in some areas. However, looking at final convergence, it is obvious that the country recipe remains very powerful. HRM varies by country, sector and size of organization, by subjects within the generic topic of HRM, and by the nature of the organization (life-stage, governance, market and so on). And we need to separate the policy intentions of those at the top of organizations from practice on the ground. Overall, however, the internationally comparative dimension of HRM is one that is demanding ever more attention from practitioners as they strive to cope with globalization: researchers are increasingly paying comparative HRM the same attention.

Conclusions

Adding a comparative dimension to HRM adds a further level of complexity. Simplistic notions of similarity or difference, of cultural or institutional explanations for the differences, of convergence or non-convergence, are simply inadequate. Simplifying complexity so that we can see some of the patterns in social activity is an important tool for the social sciences but we also have to remember the complexity and factor it back in when we try to understand the significance of what actors are doing. In HRM in particular, because our subject concerns the social actors, there is a continual tension between the isomorphic pressures for similarity and the local resistance to such pressures: in both cases, perhaps, mostly invisible to those involved. Through deliberate delay or obfuscation, through genuine misunderstanding or through well-intentioned actions that, in a different context, have different consequences, what is proposed from the centre of an organization rarely looks the same at the local level. When getting to the local level involves crossing national boundaries, the problem for the centre is exacerbated.

In each of these dichotomies, there is sufficient evidence for the committed to come down firmly on one side or the other, but the impartial observer will note that, whilst strictures and structures may tend towards commonality, values and practices probably remain fundamentally local.

There is a rich research agenda here. In many areas of comparative HRM we lack adequate theory to explain the complexity of the differences between the meaning, policies and practices of HRM in different countries. There are many countries in the world about which we still have little information; and in many cases the information we have is stereotyped, inadequate or non-comparable. At this point in our knowledge we still need the deep, but narrow, understanding of meaning and process that can be provided by detailed comparative case studies; the wide, but shallow, evidential base that large-scale surveys can bring; and the further exploration of the secondary data provided by governments and international organizations. And if our evidence about and understanding of national differences remains a research gap, there is a research chasm in developments over time that can only be filled by longitudinal research.

Although comparative and international HRM are distinct fields of study, the increasing reliance on strategic partnerships and joint ventures, coupled with a trend towards localization, has made the need to understand how HRM is delivered in different country contexts more important. Consequently there has been a degree of convergence in thinking between the comparative and international HRM fields (Budhwar & Sparrow, 2002). The future task will be, perhaps, to define an integrated theory covering both fields.

Notes

1. For good introductions to these less studied areas, see the stream of books in the Routledge Global Human Resource Management series. Other useful texts are, on Asia, Zanko (2002) and Zanko and Ngui (2003) and, on Africa, Debrah (2002) and Jackson (2002).
2. This notion of paradigms has been applied to HRM elsewhere (Wright & McMahan, 1992) and given similar but slightly different terminology and meaning, e.g., 'universalism/contingency' (Delery & Doty, 1996); 'culture-free/culture-bound' (Lammers & Hickson, 1979) and 'universalism/institutionalism' (Smith & Meiskins, 1995).
3. For attempts to summarize the differences between the North American and European models, see Brewster, 1995a, 1995b; Pudelko, 2000. In general, such comparisons are blighted by a lack of comparable evidence. For an attempt to summarize the regional blocs within Europe, see Brewster, 2005; Mayrhofer & Brewster, 2005; Ignjatovic & Sveltic, 2003.

References

Applebaum, E., T. Bailey, P. Berg & A. Kalleberg. 2001. *Manufacturing advantage: why high performance work systems pay off*. Ithaca, NY: Cornell University Press.

Ashkenas, R., D. Ulrich, T. Jick & S. Kerr. 1995. *The boundaryless organization*. San Francisco, CA: Jossey-Bass.

Bamber, G.J. & R.D. Lansbury. (eds) 1998. *International and comparative employee relations*. London: Sage

Becker, B. & B. Gerhart. 1996. The impact of human resource practices on organisational performance: progress and prospects. *Academy of Management Journal*, **39**: 779–801.

Becker, B., M. Huselid, P. Pickus & M. Spratt. 1997. HR as a source of shareholder value: research and recommendations. *Human Resource Management*, **36**(1): 39–47.

Bendix, R. 1956. *Work and authority in industry*. New York: John Wiley.

Boxall, P. 1995. Building the theory of comparative HRM. *Human Resource Management Journal*, **55**: 5–17.

Boxall, P. & J. Purcell. 2003. *Strategy and human resource management*. Basingstoke: Palgrave Macmillan.

Brewster, C. 1993. Developing a 'European' model of human resource management. *International Journal of Human Resource Management*, **44**: 765–84.

Brewster, C. 1995a. IR and HRM: a subversive European model. *Industrielle Beziehungen*, **24**: 395–413.

Brewster, C. 1995b. Towards a 'European' model of human resource management. *Journal of International Business Studies*, **261**: 1–21.

Brewster, C. 1999a. Different paradigms in strategic HRM: questions raised by comparative research. In P. Wright, L. Dyer, J. Boudreau & G. Milkovich (eds), *Research in personnel and HRM*: 213–38. Greenwich, CT: JAI Press.

Brewster, C. 1999b. Strategic human resource management: the value of different paradigms. *Management International Review*, **39**(Special issue): 45–64.

Brewster, C. 2005. European perspectives on human resource management. *Human Resource Management Review*, **14**(4): 365–82.

Brewster, C., W. Mayrhofer & M. Morley. (eds) 2004. *Human resource management in Europe. Evidence of convergence?* London: Butterworth Heinemann.

Brewster, C., P. Sparrow & H. Harris. (2005). Towards a new model of globalizing HRM. *International Journal of Human Resource Management*, **16**(6): 949–70.

Brunstein, I. (ed.) 1995. *Human resource management in Western Europe*. Berlin: Walter de Gruyter.

Budhwar, P. 2004. *Managing human resources in Asia-Pacific*. London: Routledge.

Budhwar, P.S. & Y.A. Debrah. 2001a. *Human resource management in developing countries*. London: Routledge.

Budhwar, P.S. & Y.A. Debrah. 2001b. Rethinking comparative and cross national human resource management research. *International Journal of Human Resource Management*, **12**(3): 497–515.

Budhwar, P.S. & P. Sparrow. 2002. Strategic HRM through the cultural looking glass: mapping the cognition of British and Indian managers. *Organization Studies*, **234**: 599–638.

Burnell, P. 2003. Conclusion. In P. Burnell (ed.), *Democratization through the looking glass*. Manchester: Manchester University Press.

Buyens, D., F. Dany, K. Dewettninck & B. Quninodon. 2004. France and Belgium: language, culture and differences in human resource management. In C. Brewster, W. Mayrhofer & M. Morley (eds), *Human resource management in Europe. Evidence of convergence?* London: Butterworth Heinemann.

Cavusgil, S.T. & A. Das. 1997. Methodological issues in empirical cross-cultural research: a survey of the management literature and a framework. *Management International Review*, **371**: 71–96.

Child, J.D. & A. Kieser. 1979. Organization and managerial roles in British and West German companies. An examination of the culture-free thesis. In C.J. Lammers & D.J. Hickson (eds), *Organizations alike and unlike. International and interinstitutional studies in the sociology of organizations*: 251–71. London: Routledge.

Clark, P. & F. Mueller. 1996. Organizations and nations: from universalism to institutionalism? *British Journal of Management*, **7**: 125–39.

Comaroff, J. & J. Comaroff. 2001. Millenial capitalism: first thoughts on a second coming. In J. Comaroff & J. Comaroff (eds), *Millenial capitalism and the culture of neoliberalism*. Durham, NC: Duke University Press.

Cox, C. & G. Cooper. 1985. The irrelevance of American organizational sciences to the UK and Europe. *Journal of General Management*, **112**: 27–34.

D'Aunno, T., M. Succi & J. Alexander. 2000. The role of institutional and market forces in divergent organizational change. *Administrative Science Quarterly*, **45**: 679–703.

Debrah, Y.A. 2002. Doing business in Ghana. *Thunderbird International Management Review*, **44**(4): 495–513.

DiMaggio, P.J. & W.W. Powell. 1983. The iron cage revisited: institutional isomorphism and collective rationality in organizational fields. *American Sociological Review*, **48**: 147–60.

Djelic, M-L. & J. Bensedrine. 2001. Globalisation and its limits: the making of international regulation. In G. Morgan, P.H. Kristensen & R. Whitley (eds), *The multinational firm*: 258–80. Oxford: Oxford University Press.

Dore, R. 2000. *Stock market capitalism: welfare capitalism. Japan and Germany versus the Anglo-Saxons*. Oxford: Oxford University Press.

Dowling, P.J. 1988. International and domestic personnel/human resource management: similarities and differences. In R.S. Schuler, S.A. Youngblood & V.L. Huber (eds), *Readings in personnel and human resource management*, Third edition. St. Paul, MN: West Publishing Co.

Dowling, P.J., D.E. Welch & R.S. Schuler. 1999. *International human resource management: managing people in a multinational context*. Cincinnati, OH: South-Western College Publishing.

Due, J., J.S. Madsen & C.S. Jensen. 1991. The social dimension: convergence or diversification of IR in the single European market? *Industrial Relations Journal*, **222**: 85–102.

Dyer, L. & T. Kochan. 1995. Is there a new HRM? Contemporary evidence and future directions. In B. Downie, P. Kumar & M.L. Coates (eds), *Managing human resources in the 1990s and beyond: is the workplace being transformed?* Queen's University, Kingston, Ontario: Industrial Relations Centre Press.

Elder, J. 1976. Comparative cross-national methodology. *Annual Review of Sociology*, **2**: 529–30.

England, G.W. & I. Harpaz. 1983. Some methodological and analytic considerations in cross-national research. *Journal of International Business Studies*, **fall**: 49–59.

Ferner, A. & J. Quintanilla. 1998. Multinationals, national business systems and HRM: The enduring influence of national identity or a process of 'Anglo-Saxonization'. *International Journal of Human Resource Management*, **9**(4): 710–31.

Fombrun, C.J., N. Tichy & M.A. Devanna. 1984. *Strategic human resource management*. New York: John Wiley.

Geppart, M., K. Williams & D. Matten. 2003. The social construct of contextual rationalities in MNCs and Anglo-German comparison of subsidiary choice. *Journal of Management Studies*, **40**(3): 617–41.

Giddens, A. 1986. *The constitution of society*. Berkeley and Los Angeles: University of California Press.

Gooderham, P.N., O. Nordhaug & K. Ringdal. 1999. Institutional and rational determinants of organizational practices: human resource management in European firms. *Administrative Science Quarterly*, **44**: 507–31.

Guest, D.E. 1990. Human resource management and the American dream. *Journal of Management Studies*, **274**: 377–397.

Hall, P.A. & D. Soskice. 2000. *Varieties of capitalism: The institutional basis of competitive advantage*. Oxford: Oxford University Press.

Hamal, G. & C.K. Prahalad. 1985. Do you really have a global strategy? *Harvard Business Review*. July/August: 139–48.

Hannerz, U. 1996. *Transnational connections*. London: Routledge.

Harris, H., C. Brewster & P. Sparrow. 2003. *International human resource management*. Wimbledon: CIPD Publishing.

Harzing, A-W. & A. Sorge. 2003. The relative impact of country of origin and universal contingencies on internationalization strategies and corporate control in multinational enterprises: worldwide and European perspectives. *Organization Studies*, **24**(2): 187–214.

Hendry, C. 1991. International comparisons of human resource management. Putting the firm in the frame. *International Journal of Human Resource Management*, **2**(3): 415–40.

Hofstede, G. 1980. *Culture's consequences: international differences in work-related values*. Beverly Hills, CA: Sage.

Hofstede, G. 1991. *Cultures and organizations: Software of the mind*. London: McGraw-Hill.

Hofstede, G. 2001. *Culture's consequences: comparing values, behaviors, institutions and organizations across nations*. Thousand Oaks, CA: Sage.

Hofstede, G., C.A. van Deusen, C.B. Mueller & T.A. Charles. 2002. What goals do business leaders pursue? A study in fifteen countries. *Journal of International Business Studies*, **33**(4): 785–803.

Hollingsworth, J.R. & R. Boyer. (eds). 1997a. *Contemporary capitalism*. Cambridge: Cambridge University Press.

Hollingsworth, J.R. & R. Boyer. 1997b. Coordination of economic actors and social systems of production. In J.R. Hollingsworth & R. Boyer (eds), *Contemporary capitalism*. Cambridge: Cambridge University Press.

Holzmüller, H.H. 1995. *Konzeptionelle und methodische Probleme in der interkulturellen Management- und Marketingforschung*. Stuttgart: Schäffer-Poeschel Verlag.

House, R.J., P.J. Hanges, M. Javidan, P.W. Dorfman & V. Gupta. 2004. *Culture, leadership and organizations: the GLOBE study of 62 societies*. New York: Sage.

Huselid, M. 1995. The impact of human resource management practices on turnover, productivity and corporate financial performance. *Academy of Management Journal*, **38**: 635–72.

Hyman, R. 1987. Strategy or structure? Capital, labour and control. *Work, Employment and Society*, **1**(1): 25–55.

Ignjatovic, M. & I. Sveltic 2003. European HRM clusters. *Estonian Business Review*, **17**(Fall): 25–39.

Inohara, H. 1990. *Human resource development in Japanese companies*. Tokyo: Asian Productivity Organization.

Jackson, T. 2002. Reframing human resource management in Africa: a cross-cultural perspective. *International Journal of Human Resource Management*, **13**(7): 998–1018.

Kamoche, K.N., Y.A. Debrah, F. Horwitz & G. Nkombo. 2004. *Managing human resources in Africa*. London: Routledge.

Katz, H.C. & O. Darbishire. 2000. *Converging divergences: Worldwide changes in employment systems*. Ithaca, NY: Cornell University Press.

Keenoy, T. 1990. HRM: a case of the wolf in sheep's clothing. *Personnel Review*, **19**(2): 3–9.

Kerr, C. 1983. *The future of industrial societies*. Cambridge, MA: Harvard University Press.

Koch, M.J. & R.G. McGrath. 1996. Improving labor productivity: human resource management policies do matter. *Strategic Management Journal*, **17**: 335–54.

Kochan, T. 1999. Beyond myopia: human resources and the changing social contract. In P.M. Wright, L.D. Dyer, J.W. Boudrea & G.T. Milkovich (eds), *Research in personnel and human resources management, Supplement 4*. Stamford, CT: JAI Press.

Kochan, T.A., H.C. Katz & R.B. McKersie. 1986. *The transformation of American industrial relations*. New York: Basic Books.

Kuhn, T. 1970. *The Structure of Scientific Revolutions*. Chicago: University of Chicago Press.

Lammers, C.J. & D.J. Hickson. 1979. Are organizations culture-bound? In C.J. Lammers & D.J. Hickson (eds), *Organizations alike and unlike. International and interinstitutional studies in the sociology of organizations*: 402–19. London: Routledge.

Legge, K. 1995. *Human resource management: rhetorics and realities*. Basingstoke: Macmillan.

Levitt, T. 1983. The globalization of the markets. *Harvard Business Review*, **3**: 92–102.

Lincoln, J. & A. Kalleberg. 1990. *Culture, control and commitment: a study of work organization in the United States and Japan*. Cambridge: Cambridge University Press.

Locke, R., M. Piore & T. Kochan. 1995. Introduction. In R. Locke, T. Kochan & M. Piore (eds), *Employment relations in a changing world economy:* i–xviii. Cambridge, MA: MIT Press.

Marchington, M. & I. Grugulis. 2000. 'Best practice' human resource management: perfect opportunity or dangerous illusion? *International Journal of Human Resource Management*, **11**(6): 1104–24.

Martin, R. & G. Bamber. 2004. International comparative employment relations: developing the political economy perspective. In B.E. Kaufman (ed.), *IIRA annual research volume: theoretical perspectives on work and the employment relationship*. Champaign, IL: IIRA.

Maurice, M., F. Sellier & J. Silvestre. 1986. *The social foundations of industrial power*. Cambridge, MA: MIT Press.

Mayrhofer, W. 1998. Between market, bureaucracy, and clan – coordination and control mechanisms in the Cranfield network on European human resource management, Cranet-E. *Journal of Managerial Psychology*, **133**(4): 241–58.

Mayrhofer, W. & C. Brewster. 2005. European human resource management: researching developments over time. *Management Review*.

Mayrhofer, W., M. Müller-Camen, J. Ledolter, G. Strunk & C. Erten. 2002. The diffusion of management concepts in Europe – conceptual considerations and longitudinal analysis. *Journal of Cross-Cultural Competence & Management*, **3**: 315–49.

Meyer, J.W. 2000. Globalization – sources and effects on national states and societies. *International Sociology*, **15**: 233–48.

Meyer, J.W. & B. Rowan. 1983. The structure of educational organizations. In J.W. Meyer & W.R. Scott (eds), *Organizational environments: ritual and rationality*: 179–97. Beverly Hills, CA: Sage.

Mueller, F. 1994. Societal effect, organizational effect and globalization. *Organizational Studies*, **15**: 407–28.

Müller, M. 1999. Unitarism, pluralism, and human resource management in Germany, *Management International Review*, **39**(3): 125–44.

Okazaki-Ward, L. 1993. *Management education and training in Japan*. London: Graham and Trotman.

Oliver, C. 1991. Strategic responses to institutional processes. *Academy of Management Review*, **16**(1): 145–79.

Ouchi, W.G. 1981. *Theory Z. How American business can meet the Japanese challenge*. New York: Avon Books.

Parsons, T. 1951. *The social system*. Glencoe: Free Press.

Pedersen, T. & S. Thomsen. 1999. Business systems and corporate governance. *International Studies of Management & Organization*, **29**(2): 42–59.

Peters, T.J. & R.H. Waterman. 1982. *In search of excellence. Lessons from America's best run companies*. New York: Warner Books.

Pieper, R. (ed.) 1990. *Human resource management: an international comparison*. Berlin: Walter de Gruyter.

Piore, M. & C. Sabel. 1984. *The second industrial divide*. New York: Basic Books.

Poole, M. 1986. *Industrial relations – origins and patterns of national diversity*. London: RKP.

Poole, M. 1990. Human resource management in an international perspective. *International Journal of Human Resource Management*, **11**: 1–15.

Pudelko, M. 2000. *Das personalmanagement in Deutschland, den USA und Japan. a) vol. 1: Die gesamtgesellschaftlichen rahmenbedingungen im wettbewerb der systeme. b) vol. 2: Eine systematische und vergleichende Bestandsaufnahme. c) vol. 3: Wie wir voneinander lernen können*. Cologne: Saborowski.

Purcell, J. & B. Ahlstrand. 1994. *Human resource management in the multi-divisional firm*. Oxford: OUP.

Romani, L. 2004. Culture in management: the measurement of differences. In A-W. Harzing & J. van Ruysseveldt (eds), *International human resource management*. London: Sage.

Ronen, S. 1986. *Comparative and multinational management*. New York: Wiley.

Rose, M.J. 1991. Comparing forms of comparative analysis. *Political Studies*, **39**: 446–62.

Rosenzweig, P.M. & N. Nohria. 1994. Influences on human resource development. Practices in multinational corporations. *Journal of International Business Studies*, **251**: 229–51.

Sanders, D. 1994. *Methodological considerations in comparative cross-national research*: 513–21. ISS, 42, UNESCO.

Sano, Y., M. Morishima & A. Seike. (eds) 1997. *Frontiers of Japanese human resource practices*. Tokyo: The Japan Institute of Labour.

Schuler, R.S. 1992. Strategic human resource management: linking the people with the strategic needs of the business. *Organizational Dynamics*, **21**(1): 18–32.

Schuler, R.S. & S.E. Jackson. 1987. Linking competitive strategies with human resource management practices. *Academy of Management Executive*, **13**: 207–19.

Schwartz, S.H. 1992. Universals in the content and structure of values: theoretical advances and empirical tests in 20 countries. In M.P. Zanna (ed.), *Advances in experimental social psychology*, vol. 25. New York: Academic Press.

Schwartz, S.H. 1994. Beyond individualism/collectivism: new cultural dimensions of values. In U. Kim, H.C. Triandis, C. Kagitcibasi, S.C. Choi & G. Yoon (eds), *Individualism and collectivism*. London: Sage.

Scott, W.R. 1995. Institutions and organizations. Thousand Oaks, CA: Sage.

Sekaran, U. 1983. Methodological and theoretical issues and advancements in cross-cultural research. *Journal of International Business Studies*, **14**(2): 61–73.

Shalev, M. 1980. Industrial relations theory and the comparative study of industrial relations and industrial conflict. *British Journal of Industrial Relations*, **18**(1): 26–43.

Smith, C. & P. Meiskins. 1995. System, society and dominance effects in cross national organizational analysis. *Work, Employment and Society*, **9**(2): 241–67.

Smith, P. 1997. *Japan. A reinterpretation*. New York: Pantheon.

Sorge, A. 2004. Cross-national differences in human resources and organization. In A-W. Harzing & J. van Ruysseveldt (eds), *International human resource management*. London: Sage.

Sparrow, P., C. Brewster & H. Harris. 2004. *Globalising human resource management*. London: Routledge.

Stiglitz, J. 2002. *Globalization and its discontents*. London: Allen Lane.

Storey, J. 1992. *Developments in the management of human resources*. Oxford: Blackwells.

Thomas, A. 1993. *Kulturvergleichende Psychologie – eine Einführung*. Göttingen: Hogrefe.

Thurley, K. & H. Wirdenius. 1991. Will management become 'European'? Strategic choices for organizations. *European Management Journal*, **92**: 127–34.

Tichy, N., C.J. Fombrun & M.A. Devanna. 1982. Strategic human resource management. *Sloan Management Review*, **232**: 47–60.

Tomlinson, J. 1999. *Globalization and culture*. Chicago: University of Chicago Press.

Toynbee, P. 2001. Who's afraid of global culture? In W. Hutton & A. Giddens (eds), *On the edge: living with global capitalism*: 191–212. London: Jonathan Cape.

Traxler, F., S. Blaschke & B. Kittel. 2001. *National labour relations in internationalised markets. A comparative study of institutions, change and performance*. Oxford: Oxford University Press.

Tregaskis, O., C. Mahoney & S. Atterbury. 2004. International survey methodology: experiences from the Cranfield network. In C. Brewster, W. Mayrhofer & M. Morley (eds), *European human resource management – evidence of convergence*. London: Butterworth Heinemann.

Ulrich, D. 1987. Organizational capability as competitive advantage: human resource professionals as strategic partners. *Human Resource Planning*, **10**: 169–84.

Ulrich, D. 1989. Tie the corporate knot: gaining complete customer commitment. *Sloan Management Review*, **1989**(summer): 19–28.

US Department of Labor. 1993. *High performance work practices and firm performance*. Washington, DC: US Government Printing Office.

Vickerstaff, S. (ed.) 1992. *Human resource management in Europe*. London: Thomson Learning.

Wächter, H., R. Peters, A. Tempel & M. Müller-Camen. 2003. *The 'country-of-origin-effect' in cross-national management of human resources*. Munich and Mering: Rainer Hampp.

Whitley, R. 1999. *Divergent capitalisms. The social structuring and change of business systems*. Oxford: Oxford University Press.

Woywode, M. 2002. Global management concepts and local adaptations: working groups in the French and German manufacturing industry. *Organization Studies*, **23**(4): 497–524.

Wright, P.M. & G.C. McMahan. 1992. Theoretical perspectives for strategic human resource management. *Journal of Management*, **18**(2): 295–320.

Wright, P.M. & S.A. Snell. 1991. Toward an integrative view of strategic human resource management. *Human Resource Management Review*, **1**: 203–25.

Yip, G.S. 1995. *Total global strategy*. Englewood Cliffs, NJ: Prentice-Hall.

Yoshimura, N. & P. Anderson. 1997. *Inside the kaisha: demystifying Japanese business behavior*. Boston, MA: Harvard Business School Press.

Zanko, M. 2002. *Handbook of human resource management policies and practices in Asia-Pacific economies*, volume 1. Cheltenham: Edward Elgar.

Zanko, M. & M. Ngui. 2003. *Handbook of human resource management policies and practices in Asia-Pacific economies*, volume 2. Cheltenham, UK and Northampton, MA, USA: Edward Elgar.

6 International human resource management and firm performance
Jaap Paauwe and Elaine Farndale

As interest has grown in the strategic dimension of human resource management (HRM), there has been an increasing desire to relate aspects of people management with firm performance. Particularly over the last decade, many popular articles and books appeared on this topic, exploring how organizations can achieve competitive advantage through their people (for a full overview, see Paauwe, 2004). In this chapter we will focus both on the HRM and firm performance relationship in general and on the specifics of the relationship in the context of multinational corporations (MNCs). We broadly take an institutional theory perspective to address issues that arise owing to the diversity of contexts in which MNCs are operating, which include different meanings of the concept of firm performance, and potentially different outcomes of HRM policies and practices.

The starting point for much of the work in the area of HRM and firm performance was an article by Huselid (1995) which appeared in the highly acclaimed *Academy of Management Journal*, arguing that high performance work practices are linked with increased sales and market value per employee for the firm. Equally the work by Pfeffer (1994, 1998) was influential in identifying so-called 'best practices' in HRM argued to contribute towards achieving sustained competitive advantage. Empirical work in this area has continued on both sides of the Atlantic since (see, for example, Boselie, 2002; Fey & Björkman, 2001; Guest & Peccei, 1994; Laroche, 2001; Wright & Gardner, 2001).

As this body of literature has grown, increasing attention has been paid to producing measurable outcomes of HRM practices in terms of firm performance, particularly in the USA-based literature. The academic interest in the relationship between HRM and firm performance has been paralleled by a more practitioner and consultancy inspired approach towards the development of metrics in order to establish the added value of HRM interventions. We have thus witnessed in the last decade growing interest in balanced scorecard techniques applied to HRM (see, for example, Becker *et al.*, 2001; Paauwe, 2004, ch.9; for an overview of related techniques and approaches).

Many of the early studies in the field of HRM and performance were based on work carried out in the USA. Only gradually were studies also carried out, firstly, in the United Kingdom and, later, in other countries across mainland Europe. As this geographical spread occurred, questions were raised about the extent to which there are actually HRM 'best practices' which firms can adopt to improve firm performance. Commentators started to ask why all firms should not have these identical best practice systems in place, especially in different countries around the world. This also raises the issue of firms adopting particular HRM practices beyond considerations of anticipated financial performance outcomes. Hence discussions emerged developing a distinction between universalistic, contingency and configurational approaches to HRM (Delery & Doty, 1996), a significant development which we will discuss in detail in this chapter.

Alongside the generic discussions of relationships between HRM and firm performance and how to measure this linkage, there are also more specific discussions relevant to the international HRM context and particularly to HRM and MNC performance. Little empirical work has as yet been carried out in this field (Park *et al.*, 2003). In this chapter, we develop the argument for a contingency model to analyse the link between HRM and firm performance in MNCs. We raise questions regarding the extent to which MNCs can and do adopt HRM best practices, and the extent to which the practices they do adopt are constrained by corporate, national and local considerations.

In summary, the chapter starts with an overview of the extant literature on HRM and firm performance, looking at the different models or lenses we can use to explore this relationship. Here we cover in depth the debate between 'best practice' and 'best fit' models of HRM and firm performance. We then raise some of the methodological challenges still outstanding in the HRM and firm performance literature which affect our interpretation of the linkage. In the following section we introduce the Contextually Based Human Resource Theory. This theory builds on previous models and addresses the factors we need to consider when exploring the linkage between HRM and firm performance in an international context. The chapter concludes by dealing with the concepts of leeway and strategic choice in order to highlight the room for manoeuvre within international organizations for creating optimal links between HRM and firm performance.

Relating HRM to firm performance
High firm performance is reliant on achieving (sustainable) competitive advantage, which, according to Pfeffer (1995) comprises three elements: it distinguishes an organization from its competitors; it provides an organization with positive economic benefits; and it is something that is not readily duplicated by other organizations. This definition is built upon a

resource-based view (RBV) of the firm, as is Huselid's (1995) seminal work on HRM and firm performance. This resource-based view emphasizes the effective and efficient utilization of organizational resources to achieve sustainable competitive advantage (Barney, 1991). This can only be achieved when the resources available are valuable, rare, imperfectly imitable and imperfectly substitutable – such as an organization's human resources (Huselid, 1995; Paauwe, 1994; Wright *et al.*, 1994).

Despite the overall desired outcome of competitive advantage, there are multiple ways of exploring the relationship between HRM practices and firm performance. These depend on what factors are considered important in the relationship and the causal link then created between these factors. One framework provided by Delery and Doty (1996) is a useful starting point for this discussion, as they distinguish between three categories of extant models in this field: *universalistic, contingency* and *configurational* models.

Universalistic models relate to the concept of 'best practice': there is one best way of performing a certain process in order to achieve maximum economic gain for the organization. This approach makes three assumptions: a linear relationship between HRM practices and organizational performance; best practices being universally applicable and useful; and firm performance being best measured through financial performance, such as profit, market share and sales levels (Paauwe, 2004: 53). As we have seen, this model is usually grounded in the resource-based view of the firm. Osterman (1994), Pfeffer (1994) and Huselid (1995) are examples of commentators taking this perspective, arguing that their models will produce superior performance across all types of organization.

In contrast, the contingency model suggests that relationships between individual independent HRM practice variables and dependent firm performance variables will be modified by other variables, predominantly company strategy (Delery & Doty, 1996: 807). Delery and Doty cite Schuler and Jackson (1987) and Gómez-Meija and Balkin (1992) as examples of this stream. Boselie *et al.* (2005) review of the literature in this area highlighted other significant contingency factors as being industry and firm size. Other factors may also include firm age, degree of unionization, capital intensity, geographical location, local demographics and technology. Particularly on an international scale, the different business systems and cultures of different countries are said to have an impact on both the specific combination and outcomes of HRM practices (Whitley, 1992). This contingency approach aligns itself closely with neoinstitutional theory, as we shall discuss further below.

The configurational model focuses on the bundling together of HRM practices in order to maximize firm performance. Whereas the contingency model looks at the way individual independent variables are related to the firm performance dependent variable, the configurational model is concerned with how the pattern of multiple independent variables is related to the dependent variable. For example, Arthur's (1994) control and commitment HRM systems are based on the idea that the closer an organization's HR practices resemble the correct prototypical system (for its business strategy) the greater the performance gains. HRM practices are thus seen as affecting firm performance not individually, but as interrelated elements in an internally consistent bundle or system of HRM practices (MacDuffie, 1995). However there is no single best configuration of HRM practice bundles: multiple unique configurations are capable of maximizing firm performance (Delery & Doty, 1996). The configurations used in this kind of research are very often ideal types rather than empirically observable phenomena. Also, in addition to achieving the synergistic internal fit between HRM practices within an HRM system, the overall system must be congruent with other organizational systems such as management accounting systems as well as organizational culture (Paauwe, 2004: 54).

Most existing studies exploring the link between HRM practices and firm performance have been carried out in a domestic setting, predominantly in the USA. Many of the studies that do look beyond national boundaries from a US perspective have largely explored the extent to which HRM best practice is being adopted. MNCs are argued to attempt to apply the management practices they are most familiar with or which appear to promise high returns in performance, regardless of the location of their subsidiary (Gooderham & Nordhaug, 2003). Although this approach can address the issue of strategic fit within multinational organizations by aligning practices internally, this can raise problems for environmental fit owing to operating in multiple businesses in multiple countries.

The idea of universalistic best practice is often associated with high performance work systems (HPWS) and the Japanese management practices of the 1980s, which companies elsewhere were encouraged to adopt to create lean and agile manufacturing systems (McCurry & McIvor, 2002). The characteristics of these systems were linked with four core HRM practices: employee development; flexible job design in terms of employee participation and teamwork; incentive-based payment systems; and investment in recruitment and selection (Boxall & Purcell, 2003; Boselie *et al.*, 2005). These practices became accepted amongst manufacturing companies as appropriate practices to adopt in order to improve firm performance. Empirical studies explored the transfer of these employment practices and found that US manufacturers that adopted a full system of innovative Japanese HRM practices achieved higher levels of productivity and quality than those manufacturers who only adopted certain individual practices

(Ichniowski & Shaw, 1999; Park *et al.*, 2003). However the number of US manufacturers found to be adopting full systems of Japanese HRM best practice remained minimal; this would imply that there are factors other than pure anticipated performance outcomes affecting the choice of HRM practices.

In general, we have thus seen a predominance of universalistic models in domestic empirical studies, and a scarcity of studies considering the contingency or control variables relevant to the HRM and firm performance literature (Björkman & Xiucheng, 2002). Although such variables are sometimes included, their relevance is often played down. When considering the added complexity of the international context of multinational corporations, this highlights a shortfall in empirical studies to date.

There are, however, some examples of studies focusing on the contingency perspective. Fey and Björkman's (2001) study, looking at the link between HRM and firm performance in a US MNC with subsidiaries based in Russia, emphasizes differences in national culture between the two countries. These include the stronger hierarchy in Russia, less willingness to share information and higher levels of employee–management mistrust. Although some support was found for previous domestic-setting findings linking HRM practices to firm performance, they conclude that specific bundles of practices aimed at specific categories of staff in Russian subsidiaries show the strongest links with firm performance, rather than a universal application of HRM best practices across all staff in all subsidiaries regardless of country location.

Some studies have considered the exogenous factors influencing the adoption of HRM practices which are then argued to lead to a certain level of firm performance. For example, Ten Have (1993) emphasizes the prescriptive and prohibitive influences in an organization's environment (such as legislation and collective agreements) restricting management's choice in the adoption of HRM policies and practices. This has led to a lack of fit between HRM practice and overall corporate strategy; however this lack of fit was not found to have an effect on firm performance. Despite Huselid's (1995) arguments emphasizing the need for vertical fit between HRM and strategy, as yet there is thus no conclusive empirical proof of this necessity to maximize firm performance (Paauwe, 2004).

Paauwe (1998) also argues that contingency factors affect the range of choices of both management and the organization as a whole. For example, Paauwe found that the majority of the 16 best practices identified by Pfeffer (1994) had all been in place in almost every Dutch company since the 1970s. This would imply that the majority of Dutch firms long ago predicted best practice in HRM, adopted these practices and now all have high performance outcomes. However the discussion is not so straightforward.

The underlying point being made by Paauwe (1998) is that we must look to find a clearer understanding of the reasons why firms adopt particular HRM practices beyond considerations of anticipated financial performance outcomes. Neoinstitutional theory is a useful mechanism for exploring this further.

Neoinstitutional theory rejects the optimization assumptions of economic rationality with actors capable of enacting strategic choice as advocated in functionalist contingency theories, and argues instead that societal expectations are more influential in deciding organizational practice (Paauwe, 2004). Organizations conform to contextual expectations in order to gain legitimacy and increase their probability of survival (Greenwood & Hinings, 1996). In the process of conforming, organizations become more alike, hence the isomorphic characteristics of institutionalization. DiMaggio and Powell (1983) describe institutional isomorphism in terms of three mechanisms: coercive, normative and mimetic forces. There are therefore external forces limiting the choice options for organizations in selecting HRM policies and practices.

So far, our discussion has largely taken a critical approach to adopting a best practice approach; however to assume that contingency models help us explain the HRM and firm performance relationship is also flawed. Institutional theory argumentation has been criticized in that it does not address issues of organizational strategic choice. The role of organizational self-interest and active agency need to be considered when exploring how organizations respond to the institutional pressures they face. As organizations use different strategies to respond to institutional pressures, similar environmental conditions do not necessarily lead to similar outcomes. Oliver (1991) puts forward a framework for predicting the occurrence of alternative corporate strategies in dealing with isomorphic pressures, suggesting that strategic responses range from passive conformity to proactive manipulation through stages of compromise, avoidance and defiance.

Institutional and strategic choice factors thus influence the shaping of HRM policies and practices and therefore have an impact on the HRM and firm performance linkage (Paauwe & Boselie, 2003). The choice between HRM strategies occurs at an interactive level between the organization and its environment. We therefore argue that it is imperative, particularly when conducting international research, owing to the complex diversity of institutional contexts of different countries, to adopt a contingency-based approach to observing the relationship between HRM and firm performance, and at the same time not to ignore the implications of corporate strategic choice. A similar plea has also been made in the broader HRM field calling for further development of institutionalist theories (Legge, 2005: 41). We will return to this important point later in the chapter after further consideration of the challenges still facing researchers in the broader HRM and firm performance field.

Methodological challenges for future research

Despite considerable research exploring the linkage between HRM and firm performance, and the interesting results which have been achieved to date, there are still significant gaps in our understanding and some important challenges facing the field. Below we highlight a number of these issues. Further issues can also be identified in other studies (see, for example, Guest, 1997; Wood, 1999; Wright & Gardner, 2001; Gerhart, 2004; Paauwe & Boselie, 2005); however here we focus on those issues especially relevant from the perspective of conducting research in an international setting.

The linkage between HRM and firm performance: how many boxes?

All of the models and theories described so far do little to explore the causal relationship between HRM and firm performance; rather they make assumptions about the outcomes of certain individual (or clusters of) HRM practices. Some conceptual models have, however, been developed to test empirically the causal relationships. Although it is inappropriate to go into the detailed outcomes of each of these studies here, a useful summary of findings can be found in the framework developed by Paauwe and Richardson (1997), as shown in Figure 6.1. The framework is based on an overview of more than 30 articles that have studied empirically the relationship between HRM practices, HRM outcomes and the subsequent effect on firm performance.

The debate centres on how many boxes need to be incorporated in a model representing HRM impact on firm performance, and what variables each of these boxes should contain. The overview framework presented by Paauwe and Richardson (1997) resembles an *open systems* approach of HRM activities, HRM outcomes and firm performance, all affected by contingency variables. Although this provides a good overview of research findings in this area, psychologists are more in favour of specifying the desired HRM outcomes in terms of worker attitude and subsequent effects on worker behaviour. If HRM activities indeed have an impact on HRM outcomes and firm performance it will only occur provided worker attitude, and especially worker behaviour, is affected in a certain way. The concept of the effect of behavioural outcomes on firm performance is emphasized in the framework by Guest (1997), shown in Figure 6.2. This framework assumes that only when all three HRM outcomes are achieved (high commitment of the workforce, high quality of staff knowledge and skills, and high functional flexibility) will this lead to behaviour change and higher firm performance.

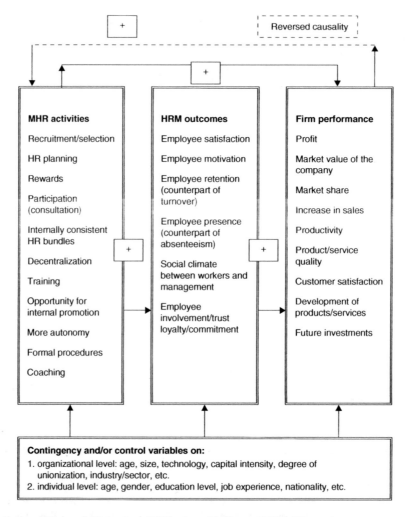

Source: Paauwe & Richardson (1997) adapted in Paauwe (2004: 60).

Figure 6.1 Linkage between HRM activities, outcomes and firm performance

There are also variations in opinions on what should appear in the 'firm performance' box. The majority of USA-based empirical research in the field adopts a shareholder perspective, focusing on productivity or financial performance indicators such as return on investment, assets or equity (see, for example, Arthur 1994; Huselid, 1995; Kalleberg & Moody, 1994; Koch & McGrath, 1996). These studies pay little attention to the impact of HRM

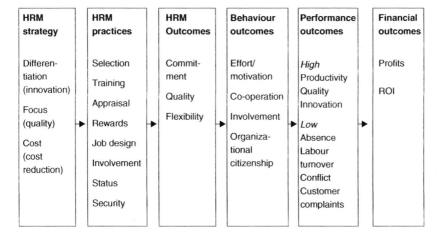

HRM strategy	HRM practices	HRM Outcomes	Behaviour outcomes	Performance outcomes	Financial outcomes
Differen-tiation (innovation) Focus (quality) Cost (cost reduction)	Selection Training Appraisal Rewards Job design Involvement Status Security	Commit-ment Quality Flexibility	Effort/ motivation Co-operation Involvement Organiza-tional citizenship	*High* Productivity Quality Innovation *Low* Absence Labour turnover Conflict Customer complaints	Profits ROI

Source: Guest (1997).

Figure 6.2 Linking HRM and performance

on other firm stakeholders such as employees, trade unions and society at large (Paauwe, 2004). In contrast, studies in the UK (Guest & Peccei, 1994; McNabb & Whitfield, 1997) and in the Netherlands (Boselie *et al.*, 2001) have tended to take more of a stakeholder approach, also adopting a contingency rather than universalistic approach to exploring HRM and performance relationships.

The meaning of HRM

There appears to be no consensus on what we mean by HRM. Is it the effectiveness of the HR department (Teo, 2002) at corporate and other levels? Is it the value of the human resources (employees) as human capital contributing to performance (Wright *et al.*, 1994)? Or is it the HRM practices themselves either separately (Batt, 2002) or aligned as systems (Cappelli & Neumark, 2001)? The majority of studies focus on the latter dimension: individual practices or systems (bundles) of practices and their link with firm performance. Analysing 21 academic papers, Boselie *et al.* (2005) conclude, however, that there is no consensus on which HRM practices to include. Nevertheless, they describe the most commonly used as being employee training, employee involvement in decision making, reward and compensation, and communication and information sharing. All of these practices appear to be relevant in both a domestic and an international firm setting.

Intended, implemented and perceived practices
The majority of prior research on HRM and firm performance is focused on intended HRM practices, designed at corporate level. For this reason Wright and Nishii (2004) make a plea for paying more attention to the difference between intended and actual HRM practices. This is especially important from the perspective of an internationally operating company. In MNCs, there is a large distance between corporate headquarter initiatives, which are transferred to regional and divisional levels, which are then passed on – very often in an adapted version – to operational level, where they finally take effect (or not). As a result the difference between intended and actual practice as perceived by the employees can be substantial.

It is also important to include the workers' perspective and their perception of HRM activities as an important link in the chain from HRM to firm performance (Bowen & Ostroff, 2004; Guest, 1999; Peccei, 2004; Wright & Nishii, 2004). Different employee groupings within the organization can have divergent views on the nature and intentions of HRM activities. There is also likely to be variation in the way in which practices are both accepted and implemented by line management and employees (Truss & Gratton, 2003). This is especially relevant for multinational corporations with an enormous variety of employee groupings, working in different countries, different cultures and different contexts.

Distance versus proximity
Related to the previous discussion, and also to that on the number of boxes there should be in an HRM and firm performance model, is the issue of relative distance. The distance between some of the firm performance indicators (such as profit and market value) and HR interventions is too large and potentially subject to other business interventions (for example, research and development activities and marketing strategies) (Guest, 1997; Kanfer, 1994). To study the effects of HR interventions, whether studying multiple individual HR practices or bundles of practices, it is preferable to use outcome variables that are presumably closely linked to these interventions, such as attitudinal outcomes (employee satisfaction, motivation, commitment, trust), behavioural outcomes (employee turnover, absence), productivity outcomes (output per unit effort) and quality outcomes in terms of services or products.

The notion and nature of strategy
The notion of strategic or vertical fit is one of the most prominent fits in HRM and firm performance research. The underlying idea is that matching the overall company strategy with the HR strategy will result in increased firm performance. Unfortunately there is no convincing empirical evidence

for this proposition (Purcell, 2004). Huselid (1995), for example, does not find any empirical evidence for increased performance when aligning the overall company strategy with the HR system of a specific organization.

As Paauwe and Boselie (2005) state, there are different plausible explanations for this lack of evidence. First, strategy is often defined in probably simplistic Porter-like definitions such as differentiation/innovation, focus/quality and cost reduction. The organizational reality is much more complex and not easy to capture in a simple dichotomy. The Porter-like definitions of the 1980s are rather static and do not take into account the possibility of hybrid strategies or combinations of strategies that companies might use, serving different markets at the same time. Second, both Gerhart (2004) and Purcell (2004) underline the complexity of management research in large companies, in particular multinational corporations. Often these large companies are conglomerates of strategic business units that all have their own markets, customers and products/services. Therefore Gerhart (2004) states that there are fewer reliability problems with plant-level analysis than in prior company-level analyses. In order to advance the field, we should therefore ensure in IHRM and firm performance research that we focus on the appropriate organizational level of analysis (preferably plant and/or subsidiary level) to be able to conclude something substantial about the relationship between strategy, HRM and firm performance.

Direction of causality
There is some discussion over the assumed linearity and direction of causality in the empirical models tested to date (Wright & Gardner, 2001). Most studies take a cross-sectional perspective from which causality is inferred, rather than adopting a longitudinal approach to test the causal link between HRM and firm performance over time. Paauwe and Richardson (1997) and Hiltrop (1999) explicitly raise the reverse causality argument by mentioning the effects of growth or decline of profit on the degree of investment in HRM policies and practices. This is confirmed in a study by Guest and colleagues (2003) based in the UK, which uses both cross-sectional and longitudinal (one year lag) data. The study applies subjective performance indicators of both productivity and financial performance. It supports a view that profitability creates scope for more HRM practices (reverse causality) rather than showing HRM practices to cause higher performance. Further empirical work is still required to explore this issue of causality in greater depth.

Time-lag issue
Finally there is no convincing theory or strong empirical evidence on the possible time-lag between an HR intervention and its effect on firm

performance. The few studies on HRM and firm performance that take a longitudinal perspective (d'Arcimoles, 1997; Guest *et al.*, 2003; Paauwe, 1989) suggest that the majority of HR interventions have a time-lagged effect on firm performance, sometimes even up to two or three years, before generating effects.

Some HRM practices (such as individual performance-related pay) might have a direct, short-term effect on firm performance (such as productivity), but the effect of most practices (such as training and development, participation, teamwork and decentralization) will probably take one, two or even three years to be seen; or potentially the effect is never directly observed. Initiatives from corporate headquarters in MNCs might fail to generate any real effect on firm performance in the short term, which may be being aggravated owing to the long distance (not only physically but also in terms of difference in mindset and culture) between corporate headquarters and local subsidiaries.

To summarize, if we measure a positive association between HRM activities and firm performance based on cross-sectional data, it might simply be a matter of reverse causality, a matter of coincidence, the accidental moderating effect of one or more unknown variables (for example, a sudden boost or collapse in the economy), or it might be the result of HRM practices implemented some two or three years earlier. These are some important issues which must be considered in the future development of the HRM and firm performance field.

A 'best fit' model of HRM and firm performance
In our exploration of existing models which claim to represent the relationship between HRM and firm performance, we have highlighted both positive and negative aspects of the universalistic and contingency/configurational models. On balance, there appears to be increasing evidence, particularly when looking at organizations on an international rather than domestic scale, that the principle of best practice is difficult to uphold. Contexts are so varied that it is difficult to see how multinational organizations are able to, and want to, implement exactly the same HRM processes in exactly the same way in all their subsidiaries around the world, hoping to generate the same kind of firm performance gains. Moreover there is a debate around the concept of firm performance and its meaning in different settings.

In this section, we therefore consider in greater detail the range of contextual factors affecting the linkage between HRM and firm performance in an international setting. We do so by making use of the Contextually Based Human Resource Theory, which can be used both from a comparative perspective (in terms of analysing different companies operating in different national contexts) and from the perspective of internationally operating companies. We will use this model in order to highlight the different contextual factors, but also the degree of leeway still available for making strategic choices; a topic which will be dealt with in more detail in the following section.

The Contextually Based HR Theory (CBHRT) developed by Paauwe (1994, 2004) is an example of a 'best fit' model incorporating contingency and configurational approaches to exploring the relationship between HRM practice and firm performance (see Figure 6.3). The underlying argument of the model is based on the resource-based view of the firm, which highlights that people fit the criteria of added value, rareness, inimitability and non-substitutability – all necessary conditions for organizational success, as we discussed earlier. At the same time, though, inspiration is also drawn from institutional and coevolution theory, emphasizing the importance of organizational context and managerial intentionality, as well as discussions surrounding strategic choice and power and politics within organizations.

The CBHRT model shows how two dimensions of the environment in particular (the product/market/technology competitive dimension and the social/cultural/legal institutional dimension) dominate the crafting of HRM. The P/M/T dimension is affected primarily by the choice of corporate or business strategy given changing developments in the product or service being delivered, the markets in which the company is operating and the technologies available to carry out corporate activities. The S/C/L dimension focuses on external factors such as local culture, national institutions and local legislation that have an impact on corporate activities. These S/C/L dimensions in the international HRM context are covered extensively in Brewster (this volume).

The third environmental dimension is the unique historical heritage and configuration of the organization which have a role to play in terms of organizational, administrative and cultural legacies. This organizational, administrative heritage is the outcome of past choices and constraints which the organization has endured, resulting in a unique pattern of relationships existing between HRM policies and practices and other organizational characteristics such as organizational culture and reputation (see, for example, Hartog & Verburg, 2004, on the effects of organizational culture, and Ferris *et al.*, 1998, on how reputation acts as an important moderator in the relationship between HRM systems and organizational effectiveness).

The CBHRT model incorporates four dimensions of fit (based on Wood, 1999):

- *strategic* fit: vertical fit between HRM practices and the competitive or corporate strategy of the organization (the P/M/T dimension);

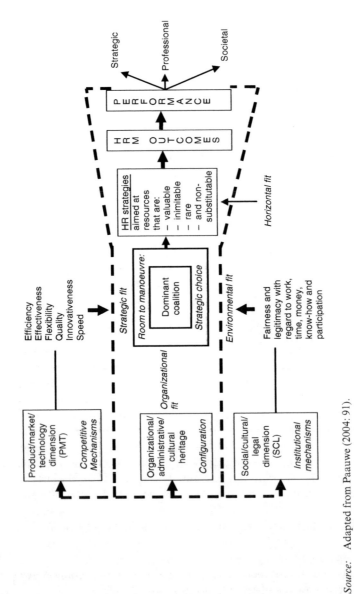

Source: Adapted from Paauwe (2004: 91).

Figure 6.3   A contextually based human resource theory

- *horizontal* fit: internal fit between HRM practices as coherent and consistent bundles (preferably shaped from a resource-based perspective in order to safeguard sustained competitive advantage);
- *organizational* fit: between HRM practices and other systems in the organization (the organizational and administrative heritage); and
- *environmental* fit: between HRM practices and the organization's social, cultural and legal environment (the S/C/L dimension).

The model also introduces the notion of leeway by adopting an actor's perspective (Lammers *et al.*, 2000), denoting the impact of the dominant coalition of the organization on the making of strategic choices. This element moderates the external and internal contingency factors noted so far, and gives an indication of the leeway available, the room for manoeuvre, for shaping HRM policies and practices within an organization. The dominant coalition may include top management, supervisory boards, works councils, shop stewards and the HR department, and its outcomes will depend on the (power) relationships between members and the way in which they differ or agree with respect to perceived constraints and opportunities.

HRM practices are therefore shown to be shaped by both external and internal contingency factors including strategic choice inputs. The resultant fits are thus designed to be organization-specific in order to deliver maximum HRM outcomes which in turn contribute to the performance of the firm.

Measuring performance
We raised earlier the question of how performance is actually measured and, particularly, how this might vary in an international setting. We have seen already how HRM practices themselves are affected by institutional factors in the organization's environment. Equally, different measures of performance become legitimized in different contexts based on institutionalization processes, as well as being a result of competing shareholder and stakeholder theories. The issue of ascertaining appropriate performance measures to judge the outcomes of HRM practices in different contexts is therefore discussed further here.

The most common approach to measuring the relationship between HRM and firm performance has been to adopt the open systems model which asserts that certain HRM activities lead to identifiable organizational and employee outcomes, which in turn lead to higher or lower levels of firm performance. However, as argued earlier, these three levels (inputs, outcomes and performance) are insufficient indicators alone, as they are all affected to a greater or lesser extent by contingency variables.

Equally there are multiple dimensions of performance which are not explored by many of the HRM and firm performance conceptual models. For example, as we have seen, the majority of performance metrics are related to financial indicators such as turnover and profit. However we are interested in the performance of the organization in meeting the needs of a broader range of stakeholders than shareholders alone: combining both economic and relational rationality. Paauwe (2004: 69–72), drawing largely on the work by Beer and colleagues (1984), has suggested a multidimensional model of HRM performance to address these issues, measuring a combination of *societal* and *professional* performance indicators in addition to *strategic* performance indicators which focus on the priorities of the board of directors, shareholders and financial institutions.

Societal performance considers aspects of company performance of relevance specifically to employees and their representatives, such as productivity, health and safety conditions, employment security, employee development, wages, employee satisfaction and work pressure. Governments are also keen to see organizations complying with both legislation and guidelines promoting particular employment practices to help boost the country's economy as a whole. Societal performance is thus largely a matter of meeting criteria for internal equity, fairness and legitimacy in the eyes of the major stakeholders, and hence achieving relational rationality.

Professional performance considers the particular activities of the HR department within the organization. Guest and Peccei (1994) have argued a link between the level of performance of the HR department and the overall effectiveness of HRM policies and practices. They argue in addition to the necessity of vertical and horizontal fit between HRM practices and corporate strategy as well as between individual HRM practices, that there also needs to be functional integration (appropriate staffing and location of the HR department to achieve organizational goals) and process integration emphasizing the efficiency and quality of HR processes and customer service.

In summary, the CBHRT model can be used in research to analyse the context of multinational corporations in terms of the different dimensions (the strategic P/M/T dimension, the socio-political S/C/L dimension, and the organizational, administrative heritage dimension) and how these forces influence the development of HR policies and their subsequent effects upon different dimensions of performance (strategic, societal, professional). It can be used at different levels of analysis: contrasting the subsidiaries of MNCs operating in different countries, or contrasting the corporate level of MNCs operating in the same sectors worldwide but which differ in country of origin (see, for example, Pot & Paauwe, 2004, who use the model to compare the shaping and performance effects of HRM policies for globally operating chemical companies, which differ in country of origin). In the following section, the centrally located dimension of the CBHRT model, room for manoeuvre and the role of the dominant coalition, are discussed in further detail.

Leeway and strategic choice

Based on an analysis of the various contextual factors, the dominant coalition has a certain degree of leeway, room for manoeuvre, for making strategic choices regarding the development and transfer of HRM practices across business unit boundaries and national borders, and for adapting them to meet local requirements. The underlying rationales for making these choices can be classified as follows (Edwards, 2004): *rational*, for reasons of efficiency and sharing best practice (economic rationality, competitive pressures); *culturalist*, meeting the need to adapt to local culture and institutions (relational rationality, institutional pressures); or *political*, enabling key agents to maintain or increase their power.

The previous sections here have explored the rational (best practice) and culturalist (best fit) reasoning for practice transfer and adaptation; however now we focus on the remaining reason, political elements of the organization environment, and particularly the role of strategic choice and the dominant coalition in a firm. The dominant coalition must balance competitive demands to gain competitive advantage against institutional demands to gain legitimacy. This balancing act is especially important for MNCs as they operate in a variety of countries and are normally highly visible because of their size of operation, reputation and brand.

Using a growing stream of research addressing the interaction between competitive and institutional forces (Baum & Oliver, 1991; Dacin, 1997; Oliver, 1997), Deephouse (1999) focuses our attention on the need for companies to be *different* in order to reduce competition and on the other hand to be *similar* in order to gain legitimacy. In this way, Deephouse develops an integrative theory of strategic balance, which claims that firms having intermediate levels of differentiation will benefit from reduced competition while maintaining legitimacy.

This theory can also be applied to the field of HRM and firm performance in an international setting, as MNCs face both competitive demands and institutional pressures in their diverse countries of operation. On the one hand, firms want to be unique in the marketplace by developing HRM policies and practices that will differentiate them from other firms and allow them to outperform others. On the other hand, institutional pressures (including state regulations, legislation, collective agreements and works councils) will lead to similar HRM policies and practices between organizations in a certain sector or country in order to avoid legitimacy challenges. There needs to be a tradeoff between competitive pressures (the P/M/T dimension of the CBHRT) and institutional pressures (the S/C/L dimension of the CBHRT) that pull the HRM system in two different directions.

This tradeoff has implications for the performance of the firm. When a company conforms to institutional pressures it is likely to perform well with respect to societal factors like internal equity, fairness and legitimacy, which enhance the company's reputation in society at large (societal performance). Yet at the same time the company risks lower financial performance because of this conformity and being less able to distinguish itself from its competitors. However, when the firm focuses on being different in order to escape competitive pressures, financial performance may improve, but at the same time the company faces the risk of losing legitimacy and damaging its reputation.

It therefore remains of interest to see how IHRM research in the future can explore how the dominant coalition (and who is part of it or not, and why) deals with this tradeoff between competitive pressures and institutional pressures in order to develop and shape HRM policies and practices, and the related firm performance outcomes. These outcomes will not limit themselves purely to financial firm performance indicators like growth, profitability or ROI, but will also focus on reputational and societal effects (based on organizational climate, culture or fairness). The latter will benefit the firm in terms of being better able to attract and develop the best possible human resources for operating in highly competitive international markets.

Conclusion/epilogue

In this chapter we have provided an overview of the extant knowledge regarding the linkage between HRM and firm performance. We have considered both a universalistic and a contingency/configurational framework to construct this linkage, and have argued that, within the context of multinational organizations, it is the contingency approach which appears most convincing.

Considering the HRM and firm performance link in the specific context of MNCs, we have discussed a range of challenges for future research in this area. Bearing in mind the importance of company context, we have presented the Contextually Based Human Resource Theory as a framework to enable researchers to understand and consider all the factors affecting the HRM and firm performance link. We have, however, also highlighted the point that, although contingency factors are important, they are not in themselves deterministic. Legislation in different countries may demand adaptation of corporate policy, but organizations still have an element of choice in how they deal with conflicting and competing demands: they must determine their own models of best fit for the organization in order to optimize the link between HRM and firm performance.

Although, as yet, there is only weak evidence of particular HRM best practices being guaranteed to deliver high firm performance, irrespective of the organization and its location, there are indications that some HRM practices more than others are capable of being implemented universally across organizations. In short, further research is still required in the HRM and firm performance field in general, and within the context of MNCs in particular, before we can be sure of the performance benefits of HRM practices and the right balance and tradeoff between adaptation and conformity on the one hand and differentiation and uniqueness on the other.

References

d'Arcimoles, C.H. 1997. Human resource policies and company performance: a quantitative approach using longitudinal data. *Organization Studies*, **18**(5): 857–74.

Arthur, J.B. 1994. Effects of human resource systems on manufacturing performance and turnover. *Academy of Management Journal*, **37**(3): 670–87.

Barney, J.B. 1991. Firm resources and sustainable competitive advantage. *Journal of management*, **17**(1): 99–120.

Batt, R. 2002. Managing customer services: human resource practices, quit rates and sales growth. *Academy of Management Journal*, **45**(3): 587–97.

Baum, J.A.C. & C. Oliver. 1991. Institutional linkages and organizational mortality. *Administrative Science Quarterly*, **36**(2): 187–218.

Becker, B.E., M.A. Huselid & D. Ulrich. 2001. *The HR scorecard: linking people, strategy and performance*. Boston, MA: Harvard Business School Press.

Beer, M., B. Spector, P.R. Lawrence, D.Q. Mills & R.E. Walton. 1984. *Managing human assets*. New York: Free Press.

Björkman, I. & F. Xiucheng. 2002. Human resource management and the performance of Western firms in China. *International Journal of Human Resource Management*, **13**(6): 853–64.

Boselie, P. 2002. *Human resource management, work systems and performance: a theoretical-empirical approach*. Tinbergen Institute Research Series, no.274. Thela Thesis, Netherlands.

Boselie, P., G. Dietz & C. Boon. 2005. Commonalities and contradictions in HRM and performance research. *Human Resource Management Journal*, **15**(3): 67–94.

Boselie, P., J. Paauwe & P.J. Jansen. 2001. Human resource management and performance: lessons from the Netherlands. *International Journal of Human Resource Management*, **12**(7): 1107–25.

Bowen, D.E. & C. Ostroff. 2004. Understanding HRM–firm performance linkages: the role of the 'strength' of the HRM system. *Academy of Management Review*, **29**(2): 203–21.

Boxall, P. & J. Purcell. 2003. *Strategy and human resource management*. Basingstoke: Palgrave Macmillan.

Cappelli, P. & D. Neumark. 2001. Do high-performance work practices improve establishment-level outcomes? *Industrial and Labor Relations Review*, **54**(4): 737–75.

Dacin, M.T. 1997. Isomorphism in context: the power and prescription of institutional norms. *Academy of Management Journal*, **40**(1): 46–81.

Deephouse, D.L. 1999. To be different, or to be the same? It's a question (and theory) of strategic balance. *Strategic Management Journal*, **20**(2): 147–66.

Delery, J.E. & D.H. Doty. 1996. Modes of theorizing in strategic human resource management: tests of universalistic, contingency, and configurational performance predictions. *Academy of Management Journal*, **39**(4): 802–35.

DiMaggio, P.J. & W.W. Powell. 1983. The iron cage revisited: institutional isomorphism and collective rationality in organizational fields. *American Sociological Review*, **48**(2): 147–60.

Edwards, T. 2004. The transfer of employment practices across borders in multinational companies. In A. Harzing & J. Van Ruysseveldt (eds), *International human resource management*: 389–410. Second edition. London: Sage.

Ferris, G.R., M.M. Arthur, H.M. Berkson, D.M. Kaplan, G. Harrel-Cook & D.D. Frink. 1998. Toward a social context theory of the human resource management–organization effectiveness relationship. *Human Resource Management Review*, **8**(3): 235–64.

Fey, C.F. & I. Björkman. 2001. The effect of human resource management practices on MNC subsidiary performance in Russia. *Journal of International Business Studies*, **32**(1): 59–75.

Gerhart, B. 2004. Research on human resources and effectiveness: selected methodological challenges. Working paper presented at the International seminar on HRM: What's Next? Organized by the Erasmus University Rotterdam, the Netherlands.

Gómez-Meija, L.R. & D.B. Balkin. 1992. *Compensation, organizational strategy and firm performance*. Cincinatti, OH: South-Western.

Gooderham, P.N. & O. Nordhaug. 2003. *International management: cross-boundary challenges*. Oxford: Blackwell Publishing.

Greenwood, R. & C.R. Hinings. 1996. Understanding radical organizational change: bringing together the old and the new institutionalism. *Academy of Management Review*, **21**(4): 1022–54.

Guest, D. 1997. Human resource management and performance: a review and research agenda. *International Journal of Human Resource Management*, **8**(3): 263–76.

Guest, D. 1999. Human resource management: the workers' verdict. *Human Resource Management Journal*, **9**(3): 5–25.

Guest, D. & R. Peccei. 1994. The nature and causes of effective human resource management. *British Journal of Industrial Relations*, **32**(2): 219–41.

Guest, D., J. Michie, N. Conway & M. Sheehan. 2003. Human resource management and corporate performance in the UK. *British Journal of Industrial Relations*, **41**(2): 291–314.

Hartog, D.N. den & R.M. Verburg. 2004. High performance work systems, organisational culture and firm effectiveness. *Human Resource Management Journal*, **14**(1): 55–78.

Hiltrop, J.M. 1999. The quest for the best: human resource practices to attract and retain talent. *European Management Journal*, **17**(4): 422–30.

Huselid, M.A. 1995. The impact of human resource management practices on turnover, productivity and corporate financial performance. *Academy of Management Journal*, **38**(3): 635–72.

Ichniowski, C. & K. Shaw. 1999. The effects of human resource management systems on economic performance: an international comparison of US and Japanese plants. *Management Science*, **45**(5): 704–21.

Kalleberg, A.L. & J.W. Moody. 1994. Human resource management and organizational performance. *American Behavioural Scientist*, **7**: 948–62.

Kanfer, R. 1994. Work motivation: new directions in theory and research. In C.L. Cooper & I.T. Robertson (eds), *Key reviews in managerial psychology*: 158–88. New York: Wiley.

Koch, M.J. & R.G. McGrath. 1996. Improving labor productivity: human resource policies do matter. *Strategic Management Journal*, **17**(5): 335–54.

Lammers, C.J., A.A. Mijs & W.J. van Noort. 2000. *Organisaties vergelijkende wijs: Ontwikkeling en relevantie van het sociologisch denken over organisaties*. Utrecht: Het Spectrum.

Laroche, P. 2001. The impact of human resource management practices and industrial relations on the firm performance: an empirical study in the French context. Paper presented at the Global HRM Conference, Barcelona, Spain.

Legge, K. 2005. *Human resource management: Rhetorics and realities.* Anniversary edition. Basingstoke: Palgrave Macmillan.

MacDuffie, J.P. 1995. Human resource bundles and manufacturing performance: Organizational logic and flexible production systems in the world auto industry. *Industrial and Labor Relations Review*, **48**(2): 197–221.

McCurry, L. & R. McIvor. 2002. Agile manufacturing: 21st century strategy for manufacturing on the periphery? *Irish Journal of Management*, **23**(2): 75–93.

McNabb, R. & K. Whitfield. 1997. Unions, flexibility, team working and financial performance. *Organization Studies*, **18**(5): 821–38.

Oliver, C. 1991. Strategic responses to institutional processes. *Academy of Management Review*, **16**(1): 145–79.

Oliver, C. 1997. Sustainable competitive advantage: combining institutional and resource-based views. *Strategic Management Journal*, **18**(9): 697–713.

Osterman, P. 1994. How common is workplace transformation and how can we explain who does it? *Industrial and Labor Relations Review*, **47**(2): 173–88.

Paauwe, J. 1989. *Sociaal ondernemingsbeleid: Tussen dwang en ambities.* Alphen aan den Rijn. Netherlands: Samson Bedrijfsinformatie.

Paauwe, J. 1994. *Organiseren: Een grensoverschrijdende passie.* Alphen aan den Rijn. Netherlands: Samson Bedrijfsinformatie.

Paauwe, J. 1998. HRM and performance: The linkage between resources and institutional context. RIBES Working Paper, Erasmus University Rotterdam, the Netherlands.

Paauwe, J. 2004. *HRM and performance: unique approaches for achieving long-term viability.* Oxford: Oxford University Press.

Paauwe, J. & P. Boselie. 2003. Challenging 'strategic HRM' and the relevance of institutional settings. *Human Resource Management Journal*, **13**(3): 56–70.

Paauwe, J. & P. Boselie. 2005. HRM and performance: what next? *Human Resource Management Journal*, **15**(4).

Paauwe, J. & R. Richardson. 1997. Introduction to special issue on HRM and performance. *International Journal of Human Resource Management*, **8**(3): 257–62.

Park, H.J., H. Mitsuhashi, C.F. Fey & I. Björkman. 2003. The effect of human resource management practices on Japanese subsidiary performance: a partial mediating model. *International Journal of Human Resource Management*, **14**(8): 1391–406.

Peccei, R. 2004. *Human resource management and the search for the happy work place.* Rotterdam: Erasmus Institute of Management (ERIM).

Pfeffer, J. 1994. *Competitive advantage through people.* Boston, MA: Harvard Business School Press.

Pfeffer, J. 1995. Producing sustainable competitive advantage through the effective management of people. *Academy of Management Executive*, **9**(1): 55–69.

Pfeffer, J. 1998. *The human equation: building profits by putting people first.* Boston, MA: Harvard Business School Press.

Pot, F. & J. Paauwe. 2004. Continuing divergence of HRM practices: US and European-based company-level HRM practices. In J. Paauwe (ed.), *HRM and performance: unique approaches for achieving long-term viability*: 155–78. Oxford: Oxford University Press.

Purcell, J. 2004. Business strategies and human resource management: uneasy bedfellows or strategic partners? Working paper presented at the International seminar on HRM: What's Next? Organized by the Erasmus University Rotterdam, the Netherlands.

Schuler, R.S. & S.E. Jackson. 1987. Linking competitive strategies with human resource management practices. *Academy of Management Executive*, **1**(3): 209–13.

Ten Have, K. 1993. *Markt, organisatie en personeel in de industrie: een empirisch onderzoek naar productieregimes als configuraties van arbeidsdeling en arbeidsrelaties.* Tilburg, Netherlands: Tilburg University Press.

Teo, S.T.T. 2002. Effectiveness of a corporate HR department in an Australian public sector entity during commercialization and corporatization. *International Journal of Human Resource Management*, **13**(1): 89–105.

Truss, K. & L. Gratton. 2003. The three-dimensional people strategy: putting human resources policies into action. *Academy of Management Executive*, **17**(3): 74–86.

Whitley, R. 1992. *European business systems. Firms and markets in their national contexts.* London: Sage Publications.
Wood, S. 1999. Human resource management and performance. *International Journal of Management Review,* **4**(1): 367–413.
Wright, P.M. & T.M. Gardner. 2001. Theoretical and empirical challenges in studying the HR practices: firm performance relationship. Paper presented at the ERIM Seminars, Erasmus University Rotterdam, Netherlands.
Wright, P.M. & L.H. Nishii. 2004. Strategic HRM and organizational behaviour: integrating multiple levels of analysis. Working paper presented at the International seminar on HRM: What's Next? Organized by the Erasmus University Rotterdam, Netherlands.
Wright, P., G.C. McMahan & A. McWilliams. 1994. Human resources and sustained competitive advantage: a resource-based perspective. *International Journal of Human Resource Management,* **5**(2): 301–26.

7 Global knowledge management and HRM

Paul Sparrow

Desouza and Evaristo (2003: 62) noted recently that 'the literature addressing management of knowledge in a global context is best described as sparse. To date there is yet to be a significant undertaking that looks at issues in managing knowledge across borders'. When analysing the capabilities that are deemed necessary to support a knowledge-based enterprise (Beckman, 1999; Grant & Baden-Fuller, 2004; Nevis, DiBella & Gould, 1997; Ruggles, 1998; Staples, Greenaway & McKeen, 2001) three clusters arise:

1. knowledge acquisition and creation: generation of new knowledge fundamental to the long-term viability of the enterprise;
2. knowledge capture and storage: creation of an inventory of knowledge so the organization knows what knowledge it possesses, and where it resides. The maintenance of current knowledge in usable form so that it remains valuable;
3. knowledge diffusion and transfer: subsequent mobilization and flow of knowledge within the organization that creates knowledge-based value.

There the consensus ends. If we ask *how* such capabilities may be put into action and what they actually look like there is much speculation. Theory often precedes any strong evidence base and there are still weaknesses in our knowledge about knowledge management. This chapter, it is hoped, contributes by highlighting a series of integration mechanisms that are necessary to assist in the acquisition, capture and diffusion of knowledge in international organizations. The chapter outlines five main forms of global knowledge management, or integration mechanisms: (a) organizational design and the specific issue of centres of excellence, (b) managing systems and technology-driven approaches to global knowledge management systems, (c) capitalizing on expatriate advice networks, (d) coordinating international management teams, and (e) developing communities of practice (COPs) or global expertise networks.

The successful development of each of these forms of global knowledge management in itself represents an important capability that has to be developed inside organizations. The theoretical bases that underlie analyses of these integration mechanisms include resource-based theory of the firm, institutional theory, social capital theory and concepts from within the field of organizational learning such as the development of absorptive capacity. Space does not allow for discussion of these theories (readers are directed to the appropriate chapters in this volume and to Sparrow and Braun, 2006) but the chapter does introduce a number of relevant concepts, theories and debates from strategy, international management, organization theory and organizational psychology fields. Throughout the chapter we will also discuss the roles that the HR function may play in these different 'forms' of knowledge management. The chapter concludes by examining the five forms of global knowledge management against the three knowledge management capabilities (knowledge generation, capture and storage, and diffusion and transfer).

The nature of knowledge management
Before examining each form of global knowledge management we must return briefly to the general topic. Two fields have been central to the operationalization of global knowledge management processes: information systems and human resource management (HRM). There has been little overlap of interest between these fields and indeed, even within the HRM field, there are very separate dialogues and academic discourses currently taking place. There is then little discussion between the psychology, economic and knowledge engineering research communities about the phenomenon of global knowledge management. The consequence? Our understanding of the field is fragmented, full of much prescription that does not work outside the narrow applications on which the prescription was based, and many analyses are distinctly subject-biased (a notable exception is the integration of strategic management and organization behaviour perspectives by Moingeon and Edmondson, 1996). Scarbrough (2005: 135) points out that 'the exploitation of knowledge as an organizational resource is . . . a complex endeavour which extends across technical, social and economic dimensions'. Economic perspectives view knowledge management as a response to the need to intensify the creation, exploitation and throughput of knowledge. Technical perspectives highlight the centralization of currently scattered knowledge and the codification of tacit knowledge. Social and political perspectives highlight the collectivization of very situational knowledge so that it no longer remains the exclusive property of individuals and groups.

What is meant by knowledge in the context of international management? Various taxonomies of knowledge exist (see, for example, Collins, 1993; Sackmann, 1991, 1992; Zack, 1999). They all show that knowledge is culturally dependent. Baba, Gluesing, Ratner and Wagner (2004: 549) observe that knowledge 'is both an integral component of cognition and one of its key products'. Knowledge represents aspects of cognition whose accuracy or correctness can be validated externally (Mohammed & Dumville, 2001) or it represents information that is validated through human action (Nonaka & Takeuchi, 1995). Beliefs arise when such knowledge is considered to be truthful, as evidenced through personal experiences and actions that demonstrate the veracity of the knowledge. Knowledge management therefore involves changes to cognitions and the way in which events or objects are described, and the content of the schemata of managers as a whole (changes in their descriptive theories of action, prescriptive theories of action, and/or their fundamental beliefs). It also requires changes in the way that knowledge is socially constructed, transfer through participation in social networks, and exploration and synthesis among different communities.

A review of the literature on organizational learning and knowledge structures (Hodgkinson & Sparrow, 2002) tells us that, whilst organizations do not think, there is knowledge that is socially recognized and codified and resides at the organizational level. Such knowledge is embedded in either organizational systems (such as rules, procedures for communication and strategies) or technical systems (hardware, software and technical operating procedures). It operates in much the same way that knowledge operates at the individual level (it serves as an interpretative scheme, the purpose of which is to inform managerial action) but it can only develop when organizations (or rather their members, via systems, structures and cultures as engineered through the actions of the managers) perceive, interpret, reconstruct and communicate new information.

The scale of the challenge of managing knowledge on a global scale is therefore obvious. Organizations are composed of many diverse, interdependent workgroups, such as new product development teams and manufacturing planning teams, all of which have unique decision domains and develop unique perspectives in response to differential tasks, goals and environments. Although managers can act autonomously within each of these decision domains, they are affected by each other's actions. Consequently mechanisms of integration (and the underlying capability to manage these integration mechanisms effectively) are needed above and beyond the simple summation of the different perspectives that exist within the organization (Scarbrough, Swan & Preston, 1999; Staples, Greenaway & McKeen, 2001).

Knowledge management by design: centres of excellence
The brokering of knowledge inside global organizations through formal structures is one such mechanism. Can organizations improve knowledge

management by design? The traditional and evolutionary progression of MNEs through international, multinational, global and transnational/ network/heterarchy is well understood and generally discussed in the context of the tradeoff between global integration and local responsiveness (see Rosenzweig, this volume). However, as MNEs change their organization design in response to the need to build more international capability, as part of their natural development they often establish dedicated organizational forms to facilitate this. One such form is the centre of excellence (Ohmae, 1990, 1996) and this is the first integration mechanism discussed in this chapter.

MNEs have relied on specialized and network-based structures to coordinate their activities for a while, but now have to coordinate increasingly dispersed activities. They have responded to this dispersion by adjusting their level of coordination and control to reflect the role of the subsidiary and the strategic importance of the mandate that it has (Bartlett & Ghoshal, 1989). A variety of missions can be assigned to subsidiaries, but one particular mission has recently gained prominence: that of the centre of excellence (COE) (Holm & Pedersen, 2000). A COE is an organizational unit that embodies a set of organizational capabilities. Frost, Birkinshaw and Prescott (2002) note that these capabilities must be explicitly recognized as an important source of value creation. There needs also to be a strategic remit, such as the intention to leverage or disseminate these capabilities to other parts of the firm. At the subsidiary level, COEs tend to be established as a consequence of a long and slow internationalization process within the organization, or as a deliberate part of organization design where HQ managers decide to grant autonomy to units that have also been given a specific strategic mandate. Increasingly small teams or units *within* either subsidiaries or central functions take a lead COE role in one area, with other units taking the lead in different areas of capability. While the leadership of a COE might be vested in a physical location, the centre itself may be virtual, spread across networks of teams in different geographies.

Various labels other than that of COE are now used to describe this process of progressive global knowledge transfer: centres of competence, centres of expertise or communities of practice. Common to all these forms is the fact that they take on a strategic role in the global organization that reaches beyond local undertakings, have to be tightly integrated with their surrounding technical or professional communities, and must have both high competence and high use of their competence throughout surrounding units if they are to survive (Sparrow, Brewster & Harris, 2004).

Helping the organization understand the role, design, competence and leadership needs of its own, COEs are a major challenge and opportunity for global HR functions as understanding of the managerial issues involved is rudimentary: '. . . a growing body of anecdotal evidence suggests that the COE phenomenon is increasing amongst the world's major MNEs, at the same time that this evidence also suggests that many firms are struggling with the managerial issues involved' (Frost, Birkinshaw & Prescott, 2002: 1016). Much of our knowledge is therefore normative. However, researchers should not decry this, or be tempted to overtheorize organization design decisions that are often not based on rational or logical criteria.

What is a more useful research enterprise is to understand what is necessary to build these more globally distributed centres of excellence into viable operations. The role of the global HR function initially has been reactive: coping with the need to relocate staff into new countries, considering the special terms and management conditions that should surround such units, and eventually applying the concept of COE to its own structures (Sparrow, Brewster & Harris, 2004). IHRM researchers should now consider more pertinent questions. What activities, processes and capabilities might constitute a COE and how should such units be mandated (that is, what has to happen in terms of capability building investments, decision-making autonomy, requisite levels of connectivity to other sources of competence inside the organization, leadership and processes of knowledge management)? What are the indicators of success under what contingencies? To what extent do institutional factors preclude or support long-term survival and contribution of COEs?

We know already that COEs are not just specialized in their own knowledge-base (Holm & Pedersen, 2000). In order to endure they must be able to maintain one or several critical fields of knowledge that have a long-term impact on the development of activity in the other subsidiaries and units of the MNE. COEs may be seen as high value subsidiaries that have a strategic role due to products, services or functions that cross geographic boundaries and markets (Moore & Birkinshaw, 1998). Examples include IBM's intelligent agent group, ITT's fluid technology group, Hewlett Packard's centre of manufacturing expertise in Singapore that handles the migration of low value activity to low cost activities. A COE might also only represent one part of the overall capability and mandate of a global unit, and therefore be considered instead as a source of best practice. In the latter context, the global HR function should help to devise roles and performance management systems that clarify the mandate and ensure that the design enables the unit and its key actors to act (a) as a focal point for knowledge development that serves people with related skills or disciplines, (b) as a conduit for the dissemination of knowledge within the firm, and (c) as a problem-solving unit that provides advice and fosters new competences within the firm.

Second, COEs must have the ability to manage dispersed capabilities and leverage pockets of expertise effectively as a source of competitive advantage. For a unit to be truly deemed a COE, it must have physical presence within a site or dispersed team; focus on a superior set of capabilities that create value including tangible resources (equipment, licences, patents) and intangible resources (knowledge, experience); have explicit recognition or declaration of its role; and have the intention of deriving value from the unit's capabilities for the broader organization (Frost, Birkinshaw & Prescott, 2002).

Third, the advice offered by the global HR function has to help the global firm manage the evolution and survival of COEs. Moore and Birkinshaw's (1998) work in service firms is helpful in this regard. They conducted 54 interviews in 18 global service firms in the consulting, financial service, engineering and transportation sectors (including Andersen Consulting, McKinsey, Ernst and Young, KPMG, IBM, Unisys, DHL, Royal Sun Alliance and Oxford University Press) and found that:

1. Competitive advantage was gained through their ability to transfer intangible assets such as the corporate name, image and reputation, proprietary services, operating procedures, and know-how about key customer bases.
2. New knowledge primarily came from interactions with clients and creative solutions developed within project teams.
3. The process of developing global COEs, even in MNEs, is often surprisingly individualized and small-scale. Three types of COEs could be placed in broad evolutionary sequence: charismatic (individual-based), focused (practice-based) and virtual (codification-based).

Some pragmatic observations should be made here. This researcher recently came across a decision on where to locate its European RHQ by a major consumer products multinational that was based on the CEO's connections with a well-known city orchestra rather than any business logic. Such idiosyncratic and theory-unpredictable decision making around the location of structural coordination mechanisms is not uncommon. In a strategic workshop with the senior IT management team of a European automobile firm it was evident that the development of centres of excellence was central to the global strategy and had already begun with the function, yet with such units already in existence there was no managerial consensus on their role, remit and success criteria and indeed limited understanding of how this structural solution would have to be enacted. Sadly action generally precedes comprehension even in the most apparently sophisticated organization. We should then beware decrying normative research and being tempted to overtheorize what is often an irrational and idiosyncratic design process. However we surely can test hypothesized links between assumed outcomes, the development of underlying knowledge management capabilities and the contribution of HR interventions (see the Conclusion and Table 7.1).

Global knowledge management systems

The second integration mechanism discussed is that of global knowledge management systems. The increased availability of computing and communication technologies has enabled more geographically dispersed transfer (or export) across this knowledge infrastructure and organizations have begun to seek better ways to invest, manage, and harvest their intellectual capital, responding broadly on two fronts:

1. E-commerce initiatives, to foster greater efficiency in their transaction processes. Attempts to better link the internal transactional systems and processes to the outside world, using different models (for example, business-to-business, and business-to-consumer) that link internal and external stakeholders of the organization.
2. Knowledge management initiatives, to leverage their intellectual capital by turning attention away from the pursuit of streamlined internal transactions and towards a focus on internal collaborative endeavours that facilitate the sharing of information and knowledge.

Kocharekar (2001) argues that two (currently unconnected) strategic drives inside global organizations towards transaction efficiency and intellectual capital effectiveness are converging through the use of global knowledge management systems. The resultant web of interactions has come to be known as the 'intraorganizational information market' (Hansen, 1999; Hansen & Haas, 2001; Hansen, Nohria & Tierney, 1999). Global managers act as information brokers, managing a web of natural 'interactions' that take place within the organization. Interactions and brokerage occurs in many forms. Global managers have to seek the right party with whom to exchange information, arrange the presentation of the information, manage its brokerage, integrate it with information from other databases and monitor the performance of the interaction. In these markets employees search internal databases and information media to help them complete their tasks. This information is associated with distinctive suppliers (individuals or subunits) such as practice groups and business functions that are responsible for gathering, selecting, editing, codifying and publishing codified knowledge.

A plethora of developments have taken place under the knowledge management umbrella that are highly reliant on information technology and the design of knowledge management systems (KMS) to handle and support tacit knowledge capture and transfer (Davenport & Prusak, 1998). Organization memory information systems, supported by distributed artificial intelligence programming techniques, are considered to contribute to knowledge-intensive and global work processes in a number of ways (see Decker & Maurer, 1999; Schwartz, 1999; Staples *et al.*, 2001).

Again most of the evidence is normative. Chiesa and Manzini (1996) looked at the transfer of knowledge within 12 MNEs and found that the main instruments and mechanisms for knowledge flows were electronic communication systems, forums, temporary assignments, international teams, internal markets, cross-border assignments, boundary spanning roles and personnel flows. Davenport *et al.*'s (1996) study of 31 knowledge management projects in 24 global companies showed that the success of the projects depended on the creation of an effective culture and process, common purpose, and creation of common language to help identify knowledge. Desouza and Evaristo (2003) interviewed 29 senior managers from 11 firms in the telecommunications, insurance, pharmaceutical, manufacturing, software and consulting sectors and considered how these organizations integrated disparate sources of knowledge across different geographical contexts and summarized the different competitive, IT system and knowledge management strategies that were found.

The knowledge management outcomes and associated HR roles are summarized in Table 7.1. From this table it is clear that, while these systems may be regarded as a prerequisite for knowledge management within global organizations and feature heavily in capture and storage, they are not sufficient in themselves. The table also shows that the main issues surrounding their effective operation are all HRM-related (see Barrett, Cappleman, Shoib & Walsham, 2004; Newell, Scarbrough & Swan, 2001; Shapiro, Furst, Spreitzer & von Glinow, 2002) and by inference solvable where an HR function is involved and given due influence in the design process. Knowledge management systems challenge the power and hegemony of global managers. It would be wrong, however, to conclude that technologically enabled systems are all bad. The informal networks that they can create, when suitably managed, can have great strategic importance (see, for example, the work of van der Merwe, Pitt & Berthon, 2004, on the creation of informal associations between individuals and organizations facilitated by Internet networks). What then needs to guide these informal associations and networks? Might some of the dysfunctions of a purely technological solution to global knowledge management be overcome? In the next sections we consider some of the more valuable ways in which networks contribute to global knowledge management.

Expatriates and their advice networks
The third integration mechanism discussed is expatriates and their advice networks. Expatriates are clearly an important vehicle more for knowledge capture and transfer than for knowledge generation (see Table 7.1). It is only relatively recently that there has been empirical study or detailed theorizing about this phenomenon (see Athanassiou & Nigh, 2000; Bonache & Brewster, 2001; Cerdin, 2003; Kostova & Roth, 2002; Makela, 2004; Smale & Riusala, 2004).

Attention focuses on the superior cognitive processes and social networks of expatriates. The earliest debates on international management strategy argued that strategic capability is ultimately dependent on the 'cognitive processes' of international managers and the ability of organizations to create a 'matrix in the minds of managers' or a transnational mentality (Bartlett & Ghoshal, 1989: 195). There are two aspects to this mentality: *attitudinal/values components* and *cognitive structures*. First, the 'attitudinal attribute' of an international orientation is assumed to correlate with both the extent and the quality of international experience (Kobrin, 1994). Researchers have developed measures that correspond to the core dimensions of managers' thinking about international strategy and organization and have shown how this mindset changes over time. For example, Murtha, Lenway and Bagozzi (1998) conducted a study of cognitive change towards a more global mindset in 410 managers over a three-year period within a single MNC. They identified a core value set or logic that was associated with global operations. Second, in relation to earlier comments about information markets, global managers need to have a 'good' mental model of how knowledge and information are shared across the people with whom they need to interact if they are to deliver an important global business process, product or service (Hodgkinson & Sparrow, 2002).

Social capital theory and social network theory are also crucial to our understanding of the management of global knowledge transfer (see Lengnick-Hall & Lengnick-Hall, this volume, for a full explanation of these perspectives) through expatriate networks (Wang & Kanungo, 2004). For an expatriate, the actors in the network can be individuals, such as peer expatriates, local working partners and local friends. These network ties serve as channels for social resources, such as informational, emotional, instrumental and appraisal support (Wang & Kanungo, 2004). Network size, network cultural diversity, network closeness and contact frequency have all been found to influence expatriate psychological well-being (Reagans & McEvily, 2003). For the global HR function, this suggests a change in emphasis away from traditional concerns with expatriate skill and international management competencies towards the need to assist expatriates in the development and quality of their social network.

While discussing issues of individual cognition and international mindset, it is important to note that a number of research streams show considerable stickiness when assessing the transfer of knowledge from one culture to another. It is unwise to assume that knowledge generation, capture and transfer are occurring in quite the depth that it might seem. Research at the individual level tends to demonstrate the deep persistence of nationality. If for example an international HR director gets HR managers from around the world together at a global forum and presents the HR strategy and constituent practices, even though country HR managers may nod at the mention of certain practices this means little in relation to the way in which they will (or will not) support the business logic behind the strategy, or the outcomes they intend to create by the pursuit of a particular practice. The first problem is that, even within an apparently like-minded cadre, team or network, there are often still different logic recipes involved. Sparrow and Budhwar (1997) showed that, when asked about the perceived relevance of specific HR practices to the competitive advantage of their organizations, there is a clear imprint of nationality. HR professionals packaged HR practices into a series of recipes concerning, for example, the range of practices that created a sense of empowerment through changes to organization structure, the range of practices that accelerated the pace at which human resources could be developed within the organization, the practices to develop an employee welfare, an efficiency orientation or a long-term perspective. Practitioners agree on the practices and the implicit logic represented by these underlying recipes, but they will rate their importance to the creation of competitive advantage in fundamentally different ways from one country to another. The second problem is that there may be different cognitive maps about the resultant cause and effect processes inherent in any intervention. Even when there is agreement around the assumed importance given to a best practice, there are marked differences in the perceptions: why such a practice might be important and the outcomes anticipated. Budhwar and Sparrow (2003) examined the logics of British and Indian HR professionals around the issues of integration of HR with the business strategy and devolvement of HR to line managers. Although in surveys both sets of professionals rated these policies as being extremely important, when cognitive mapping techniques were used to reveal why they were important and what the assumed cause and effect outcomes would be, the professionals were working to fundamentally different logics.

Researchers are therefore forced to consider whether *knowledge* and *belief* should be considered as separate or to be intertwined. Sadly there are still competing views on this question even amongst the cognitive scientists, let alone international management researchers. Some work on team cognition considers that knowledge and belief can be separated from each other, so that knowledge may be considered as objective and beliefs as more subjective. A more social-constructionist perspective considers that all forms of knowledge, whether declarative, procedural or evaluative, are built into cognitive structures, but there are complex networks of associations between cognitive schema that reflect actual experience and memory. These cognitive structures are then connected to beliefs that are validated by cultural experiences. This is not just some quaint academic debate and the answer needs resolving, for it has pragmatic implications for the sorts of tools, techniques, processes and mechanisms that global organizations must employ in order to get the knowledge generation, capture and transfer benefits suggested in Table 7.1.

Knowledge management within international and globally distributed teams
Much collaboration in international organizations takes place through virtual or globally distributed teams and they have long been a central topic within the field of IHRM (see, for example, Gibbs, this volume; Maznevski, Davison & Jonsen, this volume). This represents the fourth integration mechanism. In relation to global knowledge management, teams take on especial importance in two circumstances: when subsidiaries are considered to be rich in knowledge, or when it is appreciated that there are continuous changes in the state of knowledge within the organization (Ireland & Hitt, 1999).

They are considered to help renew organizations during times of heightened need for inter-unit learning, trust, commitment and coordination (Ghoshal & Bartlett, 1995; Mohrman, Cohen & Mohrman, 1995). Global teams therefore tend to facilitate global knowledge management in a number of ways (see Table 7.1). In order for the outcomes to be produced we need to better understand how knowledge must be managed in these teams. Work on shared cognition and team mental models (traditionally conducted by human factors experts and specialists in military training environments, for whom the study of team cognition was and is a necessity) is relevant in this regard (see, for example, Canon-Bowers *et al.*, 1993; Canon-Bowers & Salas, 2001; Klimoski & Mohammed, 1994). Hodgkinson and Sparrow (2002) reviewed the literature on team and collective cognition, team knowledge, team mental models, shared knowledge, transactive memory and shared mental models. No fewer than 20 labels have been used by work, social and cognitive psychologists, and experts in decision making and organizational behaviour to outline various concepts of shared cognition. However the methodologies used across these other fields to understand what is shared, what this sharing means, how such sharing might be measured and what outcomes result from effective sharing of cognition could well be applied to the study of international management teams.

Collective cognition is defined in terms of the group processes involved in the acquisition, storage, transmission, manipulation and use of information: 'collective cognition does not reside in the individuals taken separately, though each individual contributes to it. Nor does it reside outside them. It is present in the interrelations between the activities of group members' (Gibson, 2001: 123). It is an important indicator of a team's readiness or preparedness to take on a strategic task (Cooke *et al.*, 2000; Mohammed & Dumville, 2001). Hodgkinson and Sparrow (2002) developed three core competencies involved:

1. *Information sharing and sampling*: the process skills needed to overcome biased sampling and the introduction of favoured shared information
2. *Transactive memory*: complementary overlapping knowledge that reflects an understanding of the distribution of expertise within the wider team, the ability of team members to compensate for one another, predict each other's actions, provide information before being asked, and allocate resources according to member expertise.
3. *Cognitive consensus*: the integration of perceptions, judgments and opinions of group members to a greater degree through exchange of multiple views and the development of mutual perspective taking.

These competencies have their counterparts at the organizational level of analysis as well as within teams and individuals.

International HR functions need to take a more central role in fostering such shared cognitions. Currently they often (mistakenly) begin from a perceived need to elicit 'best practice'. Rather they need to instigate team processes that capture the underlying mindsets and belief structures that guide members of international teams and use these cognitions to 'educate' other team members (see Hodgkinson & Sparrow, 2002, for a discussion of various knowledge elicitation tools and techniques used in the study of top teams in this regard, such as policy capturing and causal mapping approaches).

Attention is also being given to globally distributed teams (as opposed to international management teams). This latter variant represents another specific challenge from a knowledge management perspective. They have been defined as interdependent workgroups comprising culturally diverse members based in two or more nations who share collective responsibilities for making or implementing decisions related to a firm's global strategy (Cohen & Mankin, 1999) or as semi-permanent groups assembled to facilitate cooperation and communications between headquarters and subsidiaries (Harvey & Novicevic, 2002). Team-based (that is, interdependent and with shared charters) structures, rather than looser workgroups, are increasingly used in order to facilitate both knowledge sharing and the creation of new knowledge (Mohrman, 1999). Effective communication in international teams seems particularly critical in this regard. Maznevski's (1994) review of research on diverse teams concluded that the common element in high performing groups with high member diversity was integration of that diversity. Diversity leads to a higher performance if members achieve mutual understanding, combine each other's ideas, and build on each other's ideas.

For such integration of diversity, communication is an absolute prerequisite and meaning has to be conveyed 'as it was intended' in order that global integration might take place. Maznevski (1994) argues that perspectives on reality within international teams are negotiated, as are the roles and norms for behaviour. This negotiation is particularly apparent in different cultures, as each culture adheres to different views of reality, which in turn leads to different interpretations of the same message. Maznevski and Peterson (1997) looked at integration in diverse teams depending on communication preconditions, and the role of sense-making approaches in explaining how members of international teams may differ in their event management, how this influences team interactions and how it can be managed. Although the international teams literature describes communication in ways in which cultures can differ with regard to communication styles, communication in international teams has generally not been studied in detail, especially in the context of new forms of work organization such as virtual teams.

However researchers (in particular anthropologists and psychologists) have begun to examine knowledge sharing and processes of mutual adjustment within international teams and are beginning to question the efficacy of globally distributed teams as a vehicle for knowledge sharing, and therefore challenge assumptions about performance gains which might arise from this coordinating mechanism. For example, Baba, Gluesing, Ratner and Wagner (2004) have examined the process through which the cognitive structures of globally distributed team (GDT) members become more similar to one another over time using longitudinal and ethnographic research methods. They studied six teams in a US manufacturing multinational from 1993 to 2001. The findings from a 14-month tracking of one of these teams (a 20-person team operating across one US and six European and Asian sites) support other studies in noting that shared cognition

across an international team in itself is not enough to account for performance gains in globally distributed teams. Because of a lack of four things
(observation of others at work, conversations that include joint problem
solving, testing of ideas and resolving discrepancies) cognitive differences
persisted. There were culturally-grounded beliefs about overall business
models that contradicted each other, which meant that team members
rejected certain aspects of knowledge held by the other (especially declarative and procedural types of knowledge).

Knowledge-sharing processes in themselves do not produce shared cognitions. Rather team members have to undergo separate but parallel learning experiences in a common context. Hidden knowledge in remote sites
has to be surfaced, often by third party mediators or knowledge brokers.
Issues of self-interest and power (historical, cultural and linguistic issues
can be exploited by team leaders to further their own agendas) have to be
shifted towards more collaborative and task-interdependence work
processes. In a cross-cultural context, sharing of knowledge has to include
the beliefs upon which evaluative knowledge is based. Using a biological
and genetic metaphor, Baba *et al.* (2004) argue that evaluative knowledge
acts as a control gene and regulates whether other forms of more structural
knowledge will be switched on (accepted and integrated into the team's cognitive structure) or switched off (rejected). It would be nice to see more
testing of such a proposition.

Maznevski and Athannasiou (2002) note that effective globalization
therefore requires recognizing and working with the complexity associated
with different cultures, institutions and economic and political systems.
To manage global business processes effectively organizations will have
to rethink many of their traditional management mechanisms (see
Maznevski, this volume). Global teams have created an explosion in the
quantity and complexity of interrelationships among the various national
systems that exist inside international organizations. As researchers, we
need richer and more complex tools to help them be effective and this
means conceptualizing, measuring and analysing the complexity of
interpersonal processes within MNEs by using new methodologies
(Athanassiou & Nigh, 1999, 2000, 2002). In their empirical study of 450
employees in 20 global account management teams in a large professional
services firm, Maznevski and Athanassiou (2002) looked at the teams
through the lens of social capital theory which they operationalized as the
assets contained in relationships among people, and the social networks, or
configurations of relationships, that hold and carry the social capital
(Borgatti, Candace & Everett, 1998; Lin, 2001) and argued that we must
build new models of decision-making processes to facilitate the various
modes for global expansion.

Transfer through communities of practice and global expertise networks

An important theme throughout this chapter is that, in order to integrate knowledge, organizations must be designed and administered in ways that first create, capture and protect valuable knowledge (Liebeskind, 1996), whilst the subsequent rapid transfer of knowledge across global units (whether business units or country operations) can only be achieved through the pursuit of broadened networks (see Lengnick-Hall & Lengnick-Hall, this volume). In discussing both the first integration mechanism of centres of excellence and the fourth mechanism of international management teams it was noted that global organizations can also comprise less formal networks of people who nonetheless are tasked with common strategic purpose. The fifth and final integration mechanism discussed is the transfer of knowledge through global expertise through a series of broadened networks. Networks are configurations of individuals that move in and out of some chartered purpose in a multidimensional and dynamic way. They represent much more loosely connected groups of people or units than might typically be found in globally distributed teams. They interact on a regular but more informal basis but are considered a powerful vehicle for organizational learning. In contrast, teams are more static and tend to be more formally constituted. Global expertise networks or communities of practice can produce the same generation, capture and transfer outcomes as those shown for international management teams in Table 7.1, but, depending on the nature of the network and its management, knowledge is considered to be capable of being generated, captured and transferred in a different manner. They can also serve a much stronger capability development role.

Knowledge management within broadened networks has been studied under the labels of 'communities of practice,' 'communities of interest' (Brown & Duguid, 1991; Orr, 1990), 'global expertise networks' or 'global leadership networks' (Sparrow, Brewster & Harris, 2004). The terms are sometimes used interchangeably. A community of practice (COP) is defined as 'a group of people who have common tasks, interact, and share knowledge with each other, either formally or informally' (Desouza, 2003: 29). The knowledge management literature tells us that, unlike more formally defined teams, these communities learn through the development of their own identities and skills. These identities and skills are generated because networks can operate in ways that allow them to create themselves and understand their own strategic trajectories. However, in order for communities to be effective, organizations have to have cultures, structures and systems that enable the acquisition of learning through such things as team processes of learning, reflection and appreciative enquiry, joint planning forums, long time-span projects, co-inquiry and discourses across

Table 7.1 The main forms of global knowledge management and theorized outcomes as integration mechanisms

Form of global knowledge transfer	Knowledge generation and creation	Knowledge capture and storage	Knowledge diffusion and transfer	Role of HR function
Centres of excellence and regional headquarters structures	• Focal point for knowledge development serving people with related skills or disciplines • New insights from client interactions and project teams • Identification of emerging practices • Concentration of resources around activities that generate mission-relevant knowledge • Role as a problem-solving unit fosters new competences as by-products of solutions	• Establish standardized processes for maintaining one or several critical fields of knowledge • Advice offered on problems captured and then internalized • Networks built up around charismatic individuals provide greater legitimacy to work, facilitating capture • Finance resources that can be dedicated to the upgrading of knowledge • Codification of knowledge when supported by databases and proprietary tools, systems and methods	• Remit to develop professional capability in others • Send signals about the fields of knowledge that create superior sets of capabilities • Add value to the organization by influencing resource allocation and workload systems • Progressively admit members into a 'guild' and provide a system by which key individuals keep in touch and share know-how • Develop activity in other subsidiaries/units • Bring expertise to related work, optimizing	• Audit the employment/location attractiveness • Relocate staff into new countries • Consider the special terms and management conditions that should surround such units to ensure knowledge generation, capture and transfer • Assess the quality of the strategy that surrounds such units and provide advice to ensure that conditions are in place to ensure units' survival and endurance • Communicate, recognize and declare specific roles needed,

Global knowledge management systems

- Record explicit or structured data against pre-developed database logics
- Create new knowledge demands as a result of linking internal transactional systems and processes to outside stakeholders, or integrating organizational processes across

- Established around internal collaborative endeavours that require sharing of information and knowledge
- Augment capability to identify, package, retrieve and update knowledge
- Association with a coordinating forum, systems or processes can be used to extract

- Knowledge from within silos made more freely available
- Social communities who participate in the knowledge expanded
- Knowledge maintenance roles delineate and clarify the distinctive suppliers of information (individuals or subunits)

- Routinization and institutionalization of knowledge into core skills in the organization, e.g. into training processes for others

- Transfer intangible assets (e.g. corporate image and reputation, proprietary services, operating procedures, organizational capability)

management practices

and articulate how they derive value for the broader organization

- Devise performance management systems that clarify the mandate and ensure that the design enables the unit and its key actors to act in line with the mandate
- Ensure that changes in business process/structure do not interfere with the skill intensity inside COEs

- Ensure that HRM processes allow for trust-based negotiations around the information
- Provide incentives to share knowledge and ensure staff receive rewards for their participation in the internal knowledge market through performance

Table 7.1 (continued)

Form of global knowledge transfer	Knowledge generation and creation	Knowledge capture and storage	Knowledge diffusion and transfer	Role of HR function
	interorganizational boundaries	and interpret culturally embedded knowledge • Act as organization memory information systems by introducing documents, models and 'war stories' and other artefacts into strategic exercises • (Potentially) capture and codify previously tacit knowledge (best practices, design rationales, process knowledge) into formal knowledge bases • Knowledge captured and brokered by market intermediaries, whose role is to add value to the communication		evaluations and social rewards such as status • Manage disruption of power structures and effort-withholding behaviours • Recognize dangers of homogenization and deskilling of different knowledge groups and subsequent reduction of diversity of knowledge inside the organization

Expatriate advice networks	• Boundary spanning roles enhance social capital and generate new knowledge through access to relevant sources of information/key actors • Technical expertise of expatriate renewed and deepened thanks to more focused, directed information search and task pursuits	or information flow by augmenting it • Superior cognitive attitudinal attributes (interpretative frame/international mindset of manager) allows access rather than denies entry to ideas • Richer cognitive maps about cause and effect relationships associated with global strategies lead to better capture	• Leverage expertise globally through high personal travel • Develop 'good' mental models of *how* knowledge and information are shared across the organization and the people with whom you must interact • Build high-quality networks that have strong business validity to support implementation • Diffuse knowledge into top teams through access to advice network and network ties (channels to informational resources)	• Develop better assessment methods of attitudinal and values facets of international mindset • Measure and consider social capital as part of expatriate selection, placement and performance evaluation processes • Mentor and assist expatriates in the development and quality of their social network • Monitor development of local successors and transfer of expatriate expertise (mental models) into units
International management teams	• Ideas exchange forum • Develop collective cognitions (team knowledge, team	• Direct knowledge capture to 'richer' local environments/ sources of learning	• Mediate headquarters– subsidiary conflicts leading to higher	• Shift selection and development systems to a focus on superior team competencies,

Table 7.1 (continued)

Form of global knowledge transfer	Knowledge generation and creation	Knowledge capture and storage	Knowledge diffusion and transfer	Role of HR function
	mental models) within important decision-making forums/strategic teams • Sharing of knowledge across team constituencies creates new insights into global connectivity of organization • Produce new complementary/over-lapping knowledge within team that reflects an understanding of the distribution of expertise within the wider team • Generation of new interpretations through observation of others at work,	• Greater sensitivity to and capture of changing knowledge levels in all local units • Surfacing of hidden knowledge in remote sites • Integrate perceptions, judgments and opinions of group members through exchange of multiple views and the development of mutual perspective taking • Capture of knowledge more efficient because the beliefs upon which evaluative knowledge is based are more transparent • Capture of separate but parallel learning	transfer of information • Build networks of expertise and transfer knowledge through involvement of access to decision implementers • Mobilize support for and then transfer knowledge through (subsequent) initiation of collaborative global projects • Facilitate inter-unit learning as members return insights into host unit • Facilitate development of global processes and protocols to coordinate teams which are then used	e.g. information-sharing and sampling behaviours, cross-cultural team skills • Instigate team processes that capture underlying mindsets and belief structures that guide members of international teams • Foster communication processes that allow for a negotiated reality between team members • Use captured cognitions to 'educate' other parts of the organization

Global expertise networks	conversations leading to joint problem solving, testing of ideas and resolution of discrepancies • Network formation/ecology reflects a bottom-up generation of new membership and expertise rather than a top-down logic about constituency relevance • Knowledge generated through the development of unique identities and skills as networks can choose and understand their own strategic trajectories • Reinforce a corporate culture that enables the acquisition of new learning	experiences in a common context • Progressive processes of knowing through joint planning forums, long timespan projects, coinquiry and discussions across communities	to work out development priorities, benchmarks for other activities • Learning from communities of practice acts as source of leadership for broader organization • Networks serve developmental role and build the level of capability within a wider geographical community	• Careful management of strategic charters of networks • Ensure there are strong team processes of learning, reflection and appreciative enquiry • Ensure linkage of networks through formal learning transfer processes such as corporate universities, learning directors and expertise transfer roles

Note: © Paul R. Sparrow, Manchester Business School.

communities (Elkjaer, 1999). The expert–student relationship created through headquarters control of country operations, or the presupposed constituency relevance of international teams, therefore rarely fosters effective knowledge management (Sparrow, Brewster & Harris, 2004).

A technological infrastructure to support the formation and initiation of COPs, while important, is not always necessary, and networks not strongly reliant on technical support can form an important part of strategic change processes (Sparrow, Brewster & Harris, 2004; Brewster, Sparrow & Harris, 2005). The findings of their research were as follows:

- Common global team processes (network management protocols) were established through which teams worked out their own development priorities, developed world-class and internal benchmarks against which the results of their initiatives would be compared, and formed their own networks of expertise and decision implementors.
- Once these networks were formed, and developed their own learning processes, this led to the development of protocols to 'manage' the network, driving subsequent consistency and communality into geographically dispersed operations through the use of a common process of 'finding out' what was happening, what could be learned to create a new global system, and what things going on in the business could be capitalized on.
- Global networks were used to develop organizational capability within wider geographical communities as global network leaders were tasked with getting country or local operations to a position where, if the network were no longer to provide the ideas exchange forum or service for them, the solution would still be implemented effectively.

Conclusion

Novicevic and Harvey (2001) note that the IHRM literature has generally not explained how the transition from the multidomestic MNC to a global integrated/coordinated networks changes the roles of the corporate HR function, but are clear that one of these new roles clearly has to be as managers of (or rather facilitators of) high-quality knowledge management. By way of conclusion, Table 7.1 takes each of the five forms of global knowledge management covered in this chapter and notes the role that they play in each of three knowledge management capabilities (generation, capture and transfer). The table lists a series of outcomes that (in theory) should result for each capability from each knowledge management form. In some cases the outcome may be positive or negative, depending on the actions of the organization. Table 7.1 then articulates the research agenda in the field, in that the creation of the outcomes represent propositions that need testing and validation.

Table 7.1 also highlights some specific implications for the HR function that result from the need to manage the three knowledge management capabilities. The HR function clearly has specific expertise in ensuring that this happens and so should put itself forward as a custodian of the activities and thought processes that result from these global forms of knowledge management. We also need to test whether the prescribed HRM roles in fact take place and, if so, whether they are associated with producing the outcomes. This raises an important point. It could be argued that other functions – indeed managers themselves – should or could take on many of these roles. To some extent this is true, but experience often shows that these knowledge management activities fall by the wayside. The HR function, in its role as business partner, is, it is hoped least likely to ignore these issues.

References

Athanassiou, N. & D. Nigh. 1999. The impact of company internationalization on top management team advice networks: a tacit knowledge perspective. *Strategic Management Journal*, **19**(1): 83–92.

Athanassiou, N. & D. Nigh. 2000. Internationalization, tacit knowledge and the top management team of MNCs. *Journal of International Business Studies*, **31**(3): 471–88.

Athanassiou, N. & D. Nigh. 2002. The impact of the top management team's international business experience on the firm's internationalization: social networks at work. *Management International Review*, **42**(2): 157–82.

Baba, M.L., J. Gluesing, H. Ratner & K.H. Wagner. 2004. The contexts of knowing: natural history of a globally distributed team. *Journal of Organizational Behaviour*, **25**(5): 547–87.

Barrett, M., S. Cappleman, G. Shoib & G. Walsham. 2004. Learning in knowledge communities: managing technology and context. *European Management Journal*, **22**(1): 1–11.

Bartlett, C.A. & S. Ghoshal. 1989. *Managing across borders: the transnational solution*. Boston, MA: Harvard Business School Press.

Beckman, T.J. 1999. The current state of knowledge management. In J. Leibowitz (ed.), *Knowledge management handbook*. Boca Raton: CRC Press.

Bonache, J. & C. Brewster. 2001. Knowledge transfer and the management of expatriation. *Thunderbird International Business Review*, **43**(1): 145–68.

Borgatti, S.P., J. Candace & M. Everett. 1998. Network measures of social capital. *Connections*, **21**(2): 27–36.

Brewster, C., P.R. Sparrow & H. Harris. 2005. Towards a new model of globalizing human resource management. *International Journal of Human Resource Management*, **16**(6): 953–74.

Brown, J.S. & P. Duguid. 1991. Organizational learning and communities-of-practice: towards a unified view of working, learning and innovating. *Organization Science*, **2**(1): 40–57.

Budhwar, P.S. & P.R. Sparrow. 2003. Strategic HRM through the cultural looking glass: mapping the cognition of British and Indian managers. *Organization Studies*, **23**(4): 599–638.

Canon-Bowers, J.A. & E. Salas. 2001. Reflections on shared cognition. *Journal of Organizational Behaviour*, **22**: 195–202.

Canon-Bowers, J.A., E. Salas & S. Converse. 1993. Shared mental models in expert team decision making. In N.J. Castellan (ed.), *Individual and group decision making*. Hillsdale, NJ: Lawrence Erlbaum Associates.

Cerdin, J.-L. 2003. International diffusion of HRM practices: the role of expatriates. *Beta: Scandinavian Journal of Business Research*, **17**(1): 48–58.

Chiesa, V. & R. Manzini. 1996. Managing knowledge transfer within multinational firms. *International Journal of Technology Management*, **12**(4): 462–76.

Cohen, S. & D. Mankin, 1999. Collaboration in the virtual organization. *Trends in Organizational Behaviour*, **6**: 105–20.

Collins, H. 1993. The structure of knowledge. *Social Research*, **60**: 95–116.

Cooke, N.J., E. Salas, J.A. Cannon-Bowers & R.J. Stout. 2000. Measuring team knowledge. *Human Factors*, **42**: 151–73.

Davenport, T.H. & L. Prusak. 1998. *Working knowledge: how organizations manage what they know*. Boston, MA: Harvard Business School Press.

Davenport, T.H., S.L. Jarvenpaa & M.C. Beers. 1996. Successful knowledge management projects. *Sloan Management Review*, **39**(2): 43–57.

Decker, S. & F. Maurer. 1999. Editorial: organisational memory and knowledge management. *International Journal of Human–Computer Studies*, **51**: 511–16.

Desouza, K.C. 2003. Knowledge management barriers: why the technology imperative seldom works. *Business Horizons*, January–February: 25–9.

Desouza, K.C. & R. Evaristo. 2003. Global knowledge management strategies. *European Management Journal*, **21**(1): 62–7.

Elkjaer, B. 1999. In search of a social learning theory. In M. Easterby-Smith, J. Burgoyne and L. Araujo (eds), *Organizational learning and the learning organization: developments in theory and practice*. London: Sage.

Frost, A., J.M. Birkinshaw & C.E. Prescott. 2002. Centers of excellence in multinational corporations. *Strategic Management Journal*, **23**(11), 997–1018.

Ghoshal, S. & C.A. Bartlett. 1995. Building the entrepreneurial organization: the new organizational processes, the new organizational tasks. *European Management Journal*, **13**(2): 139–55.

Gibson, C. B. 2001. From knowledge accumulation to accommodation: cycles of collective cognition in work groups. *Journal of Organizational Behaviour*, **22**: 121–34.

Grant, R.M. & C. Baden-Fuller. 2004. A knowledge accessing theory of strategic alliances. *Journal of Management Studies*, **41**(1): 61–84.

Hansen, M.T. 1999. The search–transfer problem: the role of weak ties in sharing knowledge across organization subunits. *Administrative Science Quarterly*, **44**: 82–111.

Hansen, M.T. & M.R. Haas. 2001. Competing for attention in knowledge markets: electronic document dissemination in a management consulting company. *Administrative Science Quarterly*, **46**(1): 1–28.

Hansen, M.T., N. Nohria & T. Tierney. 1999. What's your strategy for managing knowledge? *Harvard Business Review*, **77**(2): 106–16.

Harvey, M. & M.H. Novicevic. 2002. The co-ordination of strategic initiatives within global organizations: the role of global teams. *International Journal of Human Resource Management*, **13**(4): 660–76.

Hodgkinson, G. & P.R. Sparrow. 2002. *The competent organization: a psychological analysis of the strategic management process*. Buckingham: Open University Press.

Holm, U.I.F. & T. Pedersen. 2000. *The emergence and impact of MNC centres of excellence*. London: Macmillan Press.

Ireland, R. & M. Hitt. 1999. Achieving and maintaining strategic competitiveness in the 21st century: the role of strategic leadership. *Academy of Management Executive*, **13**(1): 43–57.

Klimoski, R. & S. Mohammed. 1994. Team mental model: construct or metaphor? *Journal of Management*, **20**: 403–37.

Kobrin, S.J. 1994. Is there a relationship between a geocentric mind-set and multinational strategy? *Journal of International Business Studies*, **25**(3): 493–51.

Kocharekar, R. 2001. K-commerce: knowledge-based commerce architecture with convergence of e-commerce and knowledge management. *Information Systems Management*, **18**(2): 30–35.

Kostova, T. & K. Roth. 2002. Adoption of an organizational practice by subsidiaries of multinational corporations: institutional and relational effects. *Academy of Management Journal*, **45**(1): 215–33.

Liebeskind, J.P. 1996. Knowledge strategy and the theory of the firm. *Strategic Management Journal*, **17**: 93–107.

Lin, N. 2001. Building a network theory of social capital. In N. Lin, K. Cook & R.S. Burt (eds), *Social capital: theory and research*: 3–29. New York: Aldine de Gruyter.

Makela, A.K. 2004. The social capital of expatriates and repatriates: knowledge sharing through interpersonal cross-border relationships. Paper presented at EIASM Workshop on Expatriation, Brussels, 18–19 October.

Maznevski, M. 1994. Understanding our differences: performance in decision-making groups with diverse members. *Human Relations*, **47**: 531–52.

Maznevski, M. & N. Athanassiou. 2002. Global teams as networks of social capital. Paper presented at US Academy of Management Conference, Denver, August.

Maznevski, M. & M.F. Peterson. 1997. Societal values, social interpretations and multinational teams. In C.S. Granrose & S. Oskamp (eds), *Cross-Cultural Work Groups*. London: Sage.

Mohammed, S. & B.C. Dumville. 2001. Team mental models in a team knowledge framework: expanding theory and measurement across disciplinary boundaries. *Journal of Organizational Behaviour*, **22**: 89–106.

Mohrman, S. 1999. The contexts for geographically dispersed teams and networks. *Trends in Organizational Behaviour*, **6**: 63–80.

Mohrman, S., S. Cohen & A. Mohrman. 1995. *Designing team-based organizations*. San Franscisco, CA: Jossey-Bass.

Moingeon, B. & A. Edmondson (eds). 1996. *Organizational learning and competitive advantage*. London: Sage.

Moore, K. & J.M. Birkinshaw. 1998. Managing knowledge in global service firms: centers of excellence. *Academy of Management Executive*, **12**(4), 81–92.

Murtha, T.P., S.A. Lenway & R.P. Bagozzi. 1998. Global mind-sets and cognitive shift in a complex multinational corporation. *Strategic Management Journal*, **19**: 97–114.

Nevis, E.C., A.J. DiBella & J.M. Gould. 1997. Understanding organizations as learning systems. *Sloan Management Review*, **36**(2): 73–85.

Newell, S., H. Scarbrough & J. Swan. 2001. From global knowledge management to internal electronic fences: contradictory outcomes of intranet development. *British Journal of Management*, **12**: 97–111.

Nonaka, I. & H. Takeuchi. 1995. *The knowledge creating company*. Oxford: Oxford University Press.

Novicevic, M.M. & M. Harvey. 2001. The changing role of the corporate HR function in global organizations of the twenty-first century. *International Journal of Human Resource Management*, **12**(8): 1251–68.

Ohmae, K. 1990. *The borderless world*. New York: Harper Collins.

Ohmae, K. 1996. *The end of the nation state*. Cambridge, MA: Free Press.

Orr, J.E. 1990. Sharing knowledge, celebrating identity: community memory in a service culture. In D. Middleton & D. Edwards (eds), *Collective Remembering*. London: Sage.

Reagans, R. & B.W. McEvily. 2003. Network structure and knowledge transfer: the effects of cohesion and range. *Administrative Science Quarterly*, **48**: 240–67.

Ruggles, R. 1998. The state of the notion: knowledge management in practice. *California Management Review*, **40**(3): 80–89.

Sackmann, S.A. 1991. *Cultural knowledge in organizations: exploring the collective mind*. Newbury Park, CA: Sage.

Sackmann, S.A. 1992. Culture and sub-cultures: an analysis of organizational knowledge. *Administrative Science Quarterly*, **37**: 140–61.

Scarbrough, H. 2005. Knowledge management. In D. Holman, T. Wall, C. Clegg, P. Sparrow & A. Howard (eds), *The essentials of the new workplace: a guide to the human impact of modern work practices*. Chichester: Wiley.

Scarbrough, H., J. Swan & J. Preston. 1999. *Knowledge management: a literature review*. London: Chartered Institute of Personnel and Development.

Schwartz, D.G. 1999. When e-mail meets organizational memories: addressing threats to communication in a learning organization. *International Journal of Human–Computer Studies*, **51**: 599–614.

Shapiro, D.L., S.A. Furst, G.M. Spreitzer & M.A. von Glinow. 2002. Transnational teams in the electronic age: are team identity and high performance at risk? *Journal of Organizational Behaviour*, **23**: 455–67.

Smale, A. & K. Riusala. 2004. Predicting stickiness factors in the international transfer of knowledge through expatriates. Paper presented at EIASM Workshop on Expatriation, Brussels, 18–19 October.

Sparrow, P.R. & W. Braun. 2006. HR strategy. Theory in international context. In M. Harris (ed.), *The handbook of research in international human resource management*. Mahwah, NJ: Lawrence Erlbaum.

Sparrow, P.R. & P. Budwhar. 1997. Competition and change in India: mapping transitions in HRM. *Journal of World Business*, **32**(3): 224–42.

Sparrow, P.R., C. Brewster & H. Harris. 2004. *Globalizing human resource management*. London: Routledge.

Staples, D.S., K. Greenaway & J.D. McKeen. 2001. Opportunities for research about managing the knowledge-based enterprise. *International Journal of Management Reviews*, **3**(1): 1–20.

van der Merwe, R., L. Pitt & P. Berthon. 2004. Elucidating elusive ensembles: the strategic value of informal internet networks. *European Management Journal*, **22**(1): 12–26.

Wang, X.Y. & R.N. Kanungo. 2004. Nationality, social network and psychological well-being: expatriates in China. *International Journal of Human Resource Management*, **15**(3): 775–93.

Zack, M. 1999. Managing codified knowledge. *Sloan Management Review*, Summer: 45–58.

PART II

RESEARCH ON GLOBAL STAFFING, PERFORMANCE MANAGEMENT AND LEADERSHIP DEVELOPMENT

8 Global staffing
David Collings and Hugh Scullion

Companies operating in the international business environment are faced with a great variety of cultural and institutional variations which make managing in a multinational context particularly complex (Doz & Prahalad, 1986). Managers of multinational corporations (MNCs) are increasingly realizing the importance of HR practices in ensuring the profitability and viability of their business operations, and global staffing is increasingly seen as a primary HR practice used by MNCs to control and coordinate their spatially dispersed global operations (Dowling & Welch, 2004). Indeed global staffing has emerged as a critical issue in international management for several reasons.

First, there is growing recognition that the success of global business depends most critically on recruiting the desired quality of senior management in the MNC (Schuler, 2000). Second, staffing issues are different and more complex in the international environment (Torbiorn, 1997). Third, the performance of expatriates continues to be problematic and the evidence suggests that the consequences of poor performance in international assignments are often costly in human and financial terms (Dowling & Welch, 2004). Fourth, shortages of international managers are a growing problem for international firms and frequently constrain the implementation of global strategies (Scullion, 1994). Fifth, global staffing issues are becoming increasingly important in a far wider range of organizations partly owing to the rapid growth of SME internationalization (Anderson & Boocock, 2002). Finally, recent research shows the growing importance of staffing strategies such as inpatriation which reflect the growing need for MNCs to develop a multicultural international workforce (Harvey et al., 1999b). The significance of staffing as a key HR concern in MNCs is not likely to diminish in the future owing to the rapid growth of emerging markets such as China and India (cf. UNCTAD, 2003, 2004) which is leading both to an increasing need for managers with the distinctive competences and the desire to manage in these culturally and economically distant countries and to a greater competition between MNCs for managers with the context-specific knowledge of how to do business successfully in these markets (Garten, 1997; Björkman & Xiucheng, 2002).

In evaluating the evolution of the literature on global staffing we can point to a number of key trends. Firstly, much of the early work on international staffing was drawn from research focused on North American MNCs and the main topic of attention was the explanation of expatriate failure, a concept which has recently received an amount of critical attention (Harzing, 1995). Much of this early work was largely descriptive, prescriptive and lacking in analytical rigour. A notable exception was the work of Tung (1981, 1982) which highlighted the fact that expatriate performance was a particular problem for US MNCs. The management of expatriates continued to be a key issue in international staffing and North American academics 'set the agenda' in this field through exercising a defining influence on research and theory in this field (Scullion & Brewster, 2001). However there was growing criticism that many American-based theories implicitly assumed universality despite a large body of empirical research substantiating the cultural diversity of values and the impact of such diversity on organizational behaviour (Hofstede, 2001).

A further critique suggested that staffing policies are often developed in isolation from other expatriation policies and companies often fail to connect expatriate selection to the company's international strategy (Brewster & Scullion, 1997). More recently, however, research has shifted towards considering staffing questions in a more strategic context. In an effort to consider the range of possible headquarters–subsidiary relationships, researchers are suggesting more 'variety' (Bonache & Fernandez, 1997) in approaches to staffing and other IHRM activities, and recent work has highlighted the advantages of mixed staffing approaches rather than adhering to a particular policy. Researchers are further drawing attention to the need to consider global strategy as well as local conditions in determining appropriate staffing approaches (Bonache & Cervino, 1997). Drawing on the theoretical notions of the resource-based view, recent research has attempted to explain the strategic dimensions of expatriate selection (Bonache & Fernandez, 1999). This reflects a new body of work which illuminates the linkage between expatriate assignments and competitive advantage by highlighting the importance of the transfer of tacit knowledge to new markets. It also highlighted the need to pay attention to the international transfer of teams and not just individual managers, which conflicts with the dominant trends in the literature.

During the last decade there has also been a rapid growth of research on international staffing outside North America, and particularly in Europe, which has added to our knowledge of expatriation by contributing to a deeper understanding of the importance of context in which international staffing takes place. This is an important development as studies suggest that there are major differences between US, Asian and European firms with regard to staffing practices (Ondrack, 1985; Kopp, 1994). This research also highlights the different staffing issues and challenges which firms face during the various stages of the internationalization process (Scullion & Brewster, 2001). Harzing's (1999) study highlights the importance of country-specific factors and reports large differences between European countries in international staffing practices. Also this study paid attention to the country of location of the subsidiary, the industry and the country of origin of headquarters as well as the characteristics of the subsidiary. While much of the research in this field is less descriptive and more analytical than earlier work, it still has an operational and practical orientation rather than a strategic orientation (Ferner, 1997).

In this chapter we will focus on some key themes and issues relating to international staffing. Following our introduction, the second section examines motives for using expatriates. The third section addresses the issues of staffing foreign subsidiaries. Inpatriation and top management staffing will be discussed in the fourth section. Finally, in the fifth section, we examine some recent developments in international staffing relating to new forms of international working as well as the strategic constraints which aspects of international staffing can have on the implementation of international strategies.

Motives for using expatriate employees

We begin our discussion by considering some of the reasons why MNCs use expatriate assignees to staff their foreign operations. This is significant as empirical research has shown that the reasons why expatriates are sent on assignment may have an impact on job performances, adjustment and roles performed (Shay & Baack, 2004) although it is important to note that many assignments generally have more than one rationale (Sparrow *et al.*, 2004) while there may be few 'pure' cases whereby assignments have a singular purpose. We first consider a seminal work in the field of international staffing, the Edström and Galbraith (1977) study.

Edström and Galbraith (1977) identified three key motives for utilizing international transfers. Firstly, when qualified local country nationals were not available, particularly in developing countries, expatriates were used to fill positions. Secondly, organizations use international assignments (IAs) as a means of developing individual employees. This type of assignment is aimed at developing the global competence of the individual manager and indeed organizations utilizing this type of assignee are likely to do so regardless of the competence of employees in the host environment. Finally, IAs could be utilized as a means of organizational development. In this instance IAs are used to transfer knowledge between subsidiaries and to modify and sustain organizational structure and decision process. The significance of Edström and Galbraith's study is reflected in the fact that, since its publication, it has formed the basis of almost all research on the functions of international assignments.

In theoretically developing Edström and Galbraith's typology, Pucik (1992) differentiates between demand-driven and learning-driven motives for expatriation. Assignments for the purposes of position filling or control are generally classified into the former category while assignments for the purposes of individual or organization development fit the latter. Drawing on Pucik's earlier work, and also taking into account the duration of international assignments, Evans *et al.* (2002) have, without empirical support, developed a framework for classifying the duration and purposes of international assignments; this is presented below (see Figure 8.1). This differentiation is important because, as Shay and Baack (2004: 218) postulate, on the basis of their empirical study: 'Managerial development reasons for the assignment will foster expatriate personal change and role innovation, whereas control reasons will focus attention on the expatriate making personal changes and on role innovation in the subsidiary.' Thus, in learning-driven assignments, the expatriate changes his/her frame of reference to adapt to the new environment and indeed adapts his/her behaviour to meet the requirements of the new environment. While in control-driven assignments, subordinates are expected to absorb the new demands of the expatriate manager and change their frames of reference, and further role requirements are adapted to meet the transferred manager's expectations (Shay & Baack, 2004).

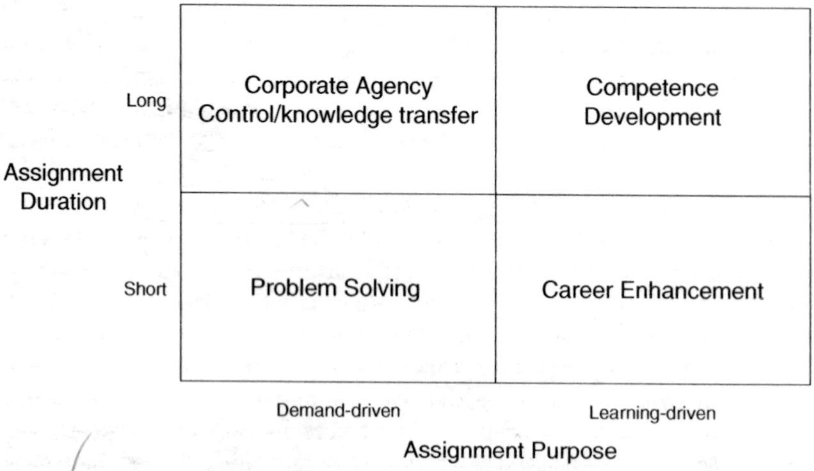

		Demand-driven	Learning-driven
Assignment Duration	Long	Corporate Agency Control/knowledge transfer	Competence Development
	Short	Problem Solving	Career Enhancement

Assignment Purpose

Source: Evans *et al.*, 2002: 119. Permission granted from McGraw-Hill.

Figure 8.1   The purpose of expatriation

Evans *et al.* (2002) posit that, traditionally, expatriate assignments were predominately demand-driven. Assignees of this type were considered either position fillers who acted as corporate agents by transferring knowledge or assisting in controlling newly established subsidiaries, or problem solvers. These assignments tend to be longer-term (that is, over three years' duration). Problem-solving expatriates perform similar roles but they are categorized as such by the singular purpose and duration of their assignment, which is determined by the length of time required to complete a specific task. These assignments are generally driven by short-term or start-up problems. Demand-driven assignments are usually utilized where there is a lack of suitably qualified host-country national's (HCNs) and are teaching-driven.

As the name would suggest, learning-driven assignments focus on learning rather than teaching. These assignments become more common as subsidiaries develop local managerial and technical capability, and the initial skills gap experienced by the firm reduces. Again learning-driven assignments can be categorized by duration and purpose. Assignments whose purpose is to increase cross-national, organizational coordination capabilities are generally longer-term assignments with the focus on developing a global mindset within the organization (see, for example, Osland *et al.* in this volume). Finally organizations are increasingly identifying high potential employees who, as part of fast track career programmes, are provided with the opportunity to gain international experience through short-term foreign assignments. These assignments are aimed at enhancing the careers of the employees concerned.

In examining the empirical evidence on the utilization of expatriates for demand-driven assignments we can point to a number of key trends. Firstly, Harzing (2001a) found a clear and consistent link between home and host countries and the purpose of expatriate assignment. Specifically she found that US and UK MNCs were most likely to utilise parent country nationals (PCNs) in position-filling roles, and thus IAs were demand-driven in these companies. The use of PCNs as position fillers was also more common in developing countries where local expertise was not available. Control and coordination-driven assignments emerged as the more significant in Japanese and German MNCs.

Looking next at learning-driven assignments, there is a growing emphasis on developing a global mindset in managers of MNCs in the IHRM literature. This global mindset is achieved primarily through learning-driven assignments. Thus these assignments are gaining increasing research attention in the literature. They were most common in German, Swiss and Dutch firms in Harzing's (2001b) study, where the emphasis was on individual management development. Learning-driven assignments have, however, recently received some critical attention in the literature. Indeed, on the basis of their empirical study, Shay and Baack (2004: 228–9) argue: 'It is not apparent that making an expatriate assignment for managerial development reasons results in any additional benefits than are already delivered by an assignment made for control reasons.' Thus they postulate that expatriate assignments should be made 'primarily, if not exclusively, for control reasons' (ibid.). They argue that linking expatriate assignments to control objectives helps to identify a link between the assignment and operational effectiveness of the firm and, thus, debates about the need and value of these assignments may be reduced or even eliminated.

Staffing foreign subsidiaries
Having examined the reasons why MNCs use expatriates in their foreign subsidiaries, we will now take a more strategic focus and look at the factors which influence the composition of senior staff in multinational subsidiaries. We take Perlmutter's (1969) seminal paper as our point of departure in this regard. Perlmutter introduced a classification of multinationals which differentiated between firms on the basis of their attitude toward the geographic sourcing of their management teams. Initially he identified three approaches to the staffing of MNCs: *ethnocentric*, where all key positions in subsidiary operations are filled by parent-country nationals (PCNs) or citizens of the country where the HQ is located; *polycentric*, where foreign subsidiaries are primarily staffed by host-country nationals (HCNs) or managers from the subsidiary location; and *geocentric*, which involves filling positions at both HQ and subsidiary level with the 'best person for the job' regardless of nationality; in later work he introduced a fourth approach, the *regiocentric* approach, where organizations are conceptualized on a regional basis and managers are generally selected on the basis of 'the best in the region' with international transfers generally being restricted to regions (Heenan & Perlmutter, 1979).

It is important to remember that this typology is primarily concerned with staffing policies for key positions within the MNC, and thus its focus is on top management team (TMT) positions at HQ and subsidiary locations (Torbiorn, 1985; Harzing, 2004). Furthermore the typology represents a number of ideal types of organization and it is unlikely that many MNCs will exactly fit any of the ideal types; indeed most organizations will display elements of more than one type (cf. Bonache & Fernandez, 1999). Nonetheless Perlmutter's work provides a useful starting point and indeed Schuler *et al.* (1993) posit that, by managing the mix of PCNs, HCNs and third-country nationals (TCNs) (nationals of one country, working in a second country and working for an MNC headquartered in a third country) (Gong, 2003b), an MNC may increase its ability to achieve learning, innovation and corporate integration. While a discussion of the advantages of filling key positions with these categories of managers is beyond the scope of this chapter owing to space restrictions (cf. Harzing, 2004: 253–6; Dowling & Welch, 2004: 63, for a discussion), we focus on the factors which influence the use of HCNs, PCNs and TCNs in filling key positions in MNCs.

In interpreting the findings of the studies referred to below it is important to be cognizant of a number of broadly consistent limitations of the literature on the broad area of international assignments. Firstly, many studies in the field fail to analyse the link between the expatriate policies pursued by the company and the international strategy of the company (Bonache *et al.*, 2001; Sparrow *et al.*, 2004), a consideration that we will return to below. Secondly, the literature has primordially focused on single aspects of the expatriate cycle and thus the literature is quite fragmented in parts. With a few notable exceptions (cf. Harzing, 2001b) the studies in this field are limited because of their small sample sizes. For example, Black's (1988) influential study was based on a sample of only 77 respondents. The data in these studies are also generally self-report data and thus there have been calls for more rigorous research designs to control better for cultural biases (Schuler *et al.*, 2002).

Although the evidence is not conclusive in a number of areas, a number of broadly consistent themes emerge in relation to staffing debates in MNCs (cf. Thomas, 1998, for a discussion of contradictions in the literature). We look first at the impact of an MNC's country of origin on the debate. At one extreme Japanese organizations are consistently identified as the most likely to utilize PCNs in key positions in subsidiary operations (Tung, 1982; Harzing, 1999). Perhaps surprisingly, given that it has been argued that ethnocentrism is inherent in US-based organizational theory and management education (Boyacigiller, 1990), US organizations represent the other extreme and they generally have lower levels of PCNs in subsidiaries than their Japanese and European counterparts (Harzing, 1999; Young *et al.*, 1985; Tung, 1982). It has been argued that the reduction of expatriates in US subsidiaries, which was largely in response to a posited high expatriate failure rate of US MNCs, had gone too far, resulting in problems of coordination and identity with corporate strategic objectives (Kobrin, 1994). While it has been argued that the majority of European firms rely heavily on PCN presence (Mayrhofer & Brewster, 1996; Scullion, 2001) it is important to note that the European case is one of heterogeneity, with empirical evidence suggesting that German firms are closer to the Japanese model while UK firms are more akin to their American counterparts (cf. Harzing, 1999). It has also been argued that pragmatic rather than strategic considerations influence staffing patterns in European MNCs (Torbiorn, 1994).

The host country also emerges as a significant moderating factor on the use of PCNs. In this regard, the extant research points to a lack of suitably qualified HCNs, particularly in developing countries (Harzing, 2001a; Boyacigiller, 1990) and also lower levels of educational attainment (Gong, 2003a; Harzing, 2004) as significant predictors of the presence of PCNs in key positions. If, however, the knowledge and skills required are generic, MNCs may train HCNs relatively easily and thus may not be required to utilize PCNs (Gong, 2003a), an option which may become more popular in the context of drives to reduce the cost of expatriate assignments (cf. Brewster & Scullion, 1997) and the fact that assignments in developing countries are increasingly being recognized as difficult assignments for expatriate managers in terms of quality of life and cultural adjustment (cf. Harvey *et al.*, 2001). Thus one needs to differentiate between generic, technical knowledge and corporate, context-specific resources such as corporate culture and managerial process. In the case of the latter the use of PCNs is called for because of their socialization into the company and also the potentially smaller shared knowledge base in developing countries (Gong, 2003a).

The cultural distance between the home and host country is also positively correlated to the use of PCNs in key positions in subsidiary operations (Gong, 2003a; Boyacigiller, 1990) although cultural distance raises a number of issues with regard to the willingness of PCNs to accept assignments. Harvey *et al.* (2001) argue that overseas work in developing countries may represent particularly challenging assignments for PCNs, particularly in terms of cultural adjustment. Thus they call on MNCs to focus on the possibility of hiring HCNs and TCNs and socializing them into the MNC through assignments in the HQ, a process they term 'inpatriation'. This, they argue, potentially increases subsidiary performance and minimizes the risk of costly expatriate failures. In considering the possible reasons why cultural distance may mediate the use of PCN employees, one can point to a number of plausible explanations. For example, the HQ may not trust employees in the host environment because of the dissimilarities in culture. This represents a promising area for future research and studies could focus on measures of trust or the proxy measure of confidence in subsidiary (HCN) managers while controlling for cultural distance.

On balance, the age of the subsidiary also appears to have an impact on the nationality of staff in key positions. While Boyacigiller (1990) found no relationship between the age of the subsidiary and the penetration of PCNs, a growing body of research points to an inverse relationship between the age of the subsidiary and the presence of PCNs in key subsidiary positions (Franko, 1973; Harzing, 2001a; Gong, 2003a). Thus the longer the subsidiary is in operation the lower the penetration of PCNs, although it is important to note the potential impact of other factors such as cultural distance on this finding. Closely related to age is the stage in the internationalization process through which the MNC is passing. Welch (1994) found that organizations' staffing requirements change to meet organizational needs as firms pass through different stages of the internationalization process (see also Adler & Ghadar, 1990; Milliman *et al.*, 1991). It is also apparent that the number of PCNs utilized by MNCs in the early stages of internationalization for control purposes is high; it then tends to grow for a short period and then levels off at a level necessary to ensure continuity in the international environment (Briscoe & Schuler, 2004).

A final area which requires consideration is the role of internationalization strategy on subsidiary staffing requirements. Studies in this area have generally failed to consider the impact of the internationalization of business on corporate HR roles. A notable exception was Scullion and Starkey's (2000) empirical study of 30 UK MNCs which examined the role of the corporate HR function specifically in the context of the international firm. They identified three distinctive groups of companies: centralized HR companies, decentralized HR companies and transition HR companies. The role of strategic staffing in each of these approaches will be discussed below.

The first group, the centralized HR companies, comprised ten companies with large corporate staffs operating in a large number of countries which were characterized by a high degree of coordination and integration of their foreign operations. These firms adopted a strategic approach to global staffing and centralized control was maintained over the careers and mobility of senior management positions worldwide, reflecting an increasingly strategic role for the corporate HR function. International assignments were increasingly linked to the career development process which became increasingly important for developing high-potential HCN and TCN managers (Evans & Lorange, 1989) (see the section on inpatriation below).

The second group, comprising 16 companies, operated with a decentralized approach which reflected the trend towards a reduction in the size of corporate offices in many UK organizations (Goold & Campbell, 1987; O'Donnell, 2000). These companies tended to have a small number of corporate HR managers who undertook a more limited range of activities than their counterparts in the first group. However a key finding of the research was that two-thirds of the decentralized companies reported an increased influence of corporate HR over global staffing, and in particular over the management of top management and senior expatriates in the previous five years, reflecting a shift away from the highly decentralized approach of the early 1990s (Storey *et al.*, 1997). In these firms the coordination of international transfers of managers was more problematic owing to greater tensions between short-term pressures and long-term strategic management needs. Empirical research highlighted a number of staffing strategies and methods which were used to address this problem, including job rotation, developing informal networks, forums to encourage cross-border transfer of knowledge and learning and, finally, encouraging other informal communication channels (Paauwe & Dewe, 1995).

The final group, the transition HR companies, comprised four highly internationalized companies who had grown mainly through acquisitions. They were transition HR companies in the sense that they were in the process of shifting away from the highly decentralized approach adopted in the first half of the 1990s. There was a greater degree of central control over global staffing, including the management of expatriates, than in the decentralized companies, and strategic staffing had emerged as an important issue thanks to the growing importance of international acquisitions. This supports recent findings which call into question the view that central control over staffing in the international firm has been abandoned (Arkin, 1999).

While this list is not exhaustive, and indeed it has been argued that we have 'a very incomplete picture of what might motivate firms to fill a position with an expatriate' (Thomas, 1998: 240), we point to a number of key variables which may affect the staffing of key positions in multinational subsidiaries. In developing research in this field we can point to a number of useful areas for future study. Firstly, research could focus on the impact of cultural and institutional distance on staffing decisions. Currently most of the literature in this regard is overly reliant on theorizing, without adequate empirical foundation. As noted above, research could also examine the link between corporate strategy and subsidiary staffing decisions. In particular these studies could focus on the strategic antecedents and outcomes of staffing decisions. Longitudinal studies of individual expatriate assignments through the entire expatriate cycle would be a useful addition to the literature. Qualitative studies could prove particularly useful, because most studies in this field to date have been mainly quantitatively based. While these studies are useful in providing a broad picture of the key patterns with regard to patterns and trends in expatriation, they are less useful in determining some of the underlying factors behind specific phenomena such as the adjustment/performance of expatriates. Well developed qualitative studies, which triangulate findings through cross-level interviewing could shed new light on these debates, and also help to reduce the criticism of self-report biases levelled at many quantitative studies. Finally research could focus on the link between foreign market entry strategy and staffing policy, an area which is likely to be of increasing importance given the increasing evidence of cross-border mergers and acquisition (cf. Schuler et al., 2004).

Top management staffing and inpatriation

In this section the role of inpatriation and strategic top management staffing will be discussed and linked to the previous discussion on the role of the corporate HR function in the international firm. The majority of the extant literature focuses on staffing multinational subsidiaries as opposed to headquarter operations. Indeed there is a paucity of research on the role of HCNs and TCNs in corporate top management teams (Evans *et al.*, 2002). Changes occurring within the globalization process have rendered traditional bureaucratic and unidirectional models of management staffing in MNCs less suitable for organizations operating in the global sphere (Harvey *et al.*, 2000) and this lack of global orientation also represents a constraint on the success of MNCs in the global business environment.

The practice of developing HCNs and TCNs through developmental transfers to corporate HQ, that is, inpatriation (Harvey *et al.*, 1999b), was becoming increasingly important in global firms referred to above. In these firms the growing importance of inpatriation as a strategy for developing the talent pipeline across global operations reflected an increasingly strategic role for management development. While inpatriation was also being used in the decentralized multinationals, this was often in the early stages of development, less systematic and more limited in scope compared to the global companies. In practice the implementation of inpatriation strategies in the decentralized businesses was more problematic because of the weaker corporate HR role in staffing and management development. Inpatriation was established as a more significant international staffing practice in the transition HR companies as their staffing strategy became more global, reflecting the more global orientation of their international strategy. The growing use of inpatriation strategies in such companies also reflected the shift away from decentralization with respect to strategic staffing and reflects the growing integration and coordination of foreign operations in globalizing companies (Scullion & Starkey, 2000).

There is a growing body of literature on inpatriation and it has been suggested that the impact of inpatriate managers may be more significant than the impact of the well-researched area of expatriate managers. This is because the majority of MNCs retain a large percentage of their personnel, production operation and research and develop capability in their home country (UNCTAD, 2003). The key drivers of the recruitment of inpatriate managers include (a) a desire to create a global core competency, a diversity of strategic perspective, or a multicultural frame of reference amongst the top management team (Harvey & Buckley, 1997; Harvey *et al.*, 1999b); (b) the emergence of developing markets, which, as noted above, are increasingly being recognized as difficult assignments for expatriate managers in terms of quality of life and cultural adjustment and thus less likely to be accepted by traditional expatriate pools (cf. Harvey *et al.*, 2001; Peterson, 2003); (c) a desire to increase the capability of organizations to 'think global and act local', which can be aided through including inpatriate managers in the decision-making process at HQ level (Harvey *et al.*, 1999b) and (d) the provision of career opportunities for high potential employees in host countries. The growing use of host and third country nationals was also increasingly linked to a more strategic approach to management development in the global environment (Harvey *et al.*, 1999b). Inpatriate managers not only provide a subsidiary perspective on decision making within the organization but also assist in a number of other strategic issues within the MNC (Reynolds, 1997).

Inpatriate assignments are not without their problems, however, and their successful integration into the HQ team presents a number of significant challenges for the MNC. Although it has been argued that the challenges associated with selecting and managing inpatriate managers are the same as those associated with expatriates, except in reverse (Briscoe & Schuler, 2004), a review of the literature would suggest that, while some of the issues are similar, the process is more complex. Specifically inpatriates not only have to adjust to a different external cultural environment, they may also be newcomers to the organization and thus may also have to adjust to the organizational culture (Harvey *et al.*, 1999a). Also, while PCNs assigned to subsidiaries also enhance their status as HQ employees in gaining acceptance in foreign operations, inpatriates may find they are not as well received in the HQ operation (ibid.). In addition, HQ employees may fear a loss of authority or power to successful inpatriates, which could lead to the former withdrawing cooperation and thereby limiting the effective integration of inpatriate employees (Harvey *et al.*, 1999b). In summary, while inpatriate assignments are not without significant challenges, there are a variety of reasons (discussed above) which suggest that they are likely to become a more common alternative for staffing in MNCs in the future. These issues will be increasingly important areas for future research in global staffing.

Discussion
This section will briefly discuss some of the major international staffing challenges and constraints faced by international firms who seek to develop a pool of global managers. It will highlight the strategic importance of these constraints in relation to the implementation of global strategies. These issues are becoming more significant as shortage of international management talent emerges as a critical strategic issue for many international firms and often constrains the implementation of global strategies (Evans *et al.*, 2002).

We begin by looking at constraints on the supply of international managers. First, we consider the position of women in international management. Despite the growing shortages of international management talent (Scullion, 2001), the evidence suggests that the participation of women in international management remains relatively low (Taylor *et al.*, 2002) and many women are denied opportunities to expand their career horizons through access to international careers (Adler, 2002). As global competition intensifies, competition for global leaders to manage overseas operations will steadily intensify and MNCs must develop new ways to identify, attract and retain new pools of international executive talent (Black *et al.*, 2000; Mayrhofer & Scullion, 2002), yet recent studies suggest that important formal and informal barriers remain to increasing women's participation in international management (Linehan, 2002).

The repatriation of managers has also been identified as a major strategic staffing problem for multinational companies in Europe and North America (Black *et al.*, 1999), and research shows that the failure by many companies to address this issue impacts adversely on the supply and staffing of international managers. There is growing awareness that potential expatriates will be more reluctant to accept the offer of international assignments in companies which fail to handle repatriation issues effectively (Scullion, 1994). Black *et al.* (1999) show that, while retention of expatriate managers was a growing problem for many US MNCs, in recent years the repatriation problem had also become more acute for European MNCs because internationalization had often taken place at the same time as downsizing of the domestic business, which reduced opportunities for expatriate managers on re-entry (Scullion, 1994). Studies confirm that many firms continue to adopt ad hoc approaches to repatriation and suggest the need for MNCs to develop a more strategic approach to repatriation and international career management (Lazarova & Caligiuri, 2001).

The growing barriers to international mobility are a further constraint on the ability of MNCs to implement their internationalization strategies. The demand for expatriates is increasing steadily, but the availability of people who are willing to accept global assignments is not increasing at the same rate (Adler, 2002). For many MNCs, finding the required numbers of people with the desired competencies for international assignments is a major strategic international HRM challenge (Gupta & Govindarajan, 2002). A recent review indicated that international mobility was becoming more of a problem in many firms due to several factors including uncertainties associated with re-entry, the growing unwillingness to disrupt the education of children, the growing importance of quality of life considerations and, finally, continued uncertainty regarding international terrorism and political unrest (Scullion & Linehan, 2004). There is some evidence to suggest that families are less willing to disrupt personal and social lives than was the case in the past (Forster, 2000). Dual career problems are also seen as major barriers to future international mobility in many different countries and pose considerable restrictions on the career development plans of multinationals (Harvey, 1998). The changing nature of the barriers to international mobility and their impact on international staffing is another promising area for future research.

Finally there is a need to comment briefly on the emergence of non-traditional forms of international assignment. There is a need to go beyond studying the traditional expatriate assignment in order also to examine the emergence of newer, shorter-term, international assignments. An excellent review of the different types of international assignment is provided in the chapter by Welch and Worm in the present volume. The two main reasons for the growth of non-standard forms of international assignment are the shortage of managers willing to accept long-term international positions (see above) and the high costs of expatriation (Dowling & Welch, 2004). The management of staffing issues in non-traditional and non-standard international assignments is a promising area for future research and the research questions around the psychological contract in these newer forms of international assignments are particularly challenging (Scullion & Pate, 2005). Recently there has been a rapid growth in virtual international teams, which are being utilized to help global firms to use the best talent wherever it is located (Welch & Welch, 1994). However, while there is a consensus that the capacity to develop and maintain trust-based relationships is critical to the performance of virtual organizations in the international context, role conflict, dual allegiance, identity issues and establishing trust have been identified as important areas for future research with respect to the management of virtual teams (Clases *et al.*, 2004).

Note

1.   In explaining the choices management make we assume a bounded rationality perspective (cf. Simon, 1957, 1982). Specifically, in making decisions regarding staffing subsidiaries, managers make rational decisions based on the information available. These decisions generally centre on maximizing the profitability of the subsidiary. The decisions are bounded as management may have imperfect information and limited mental schemas in making these decisions. An alternative perspective would be an institutional view where management make decisions based on seeking legitimacy from other external stakeholders which leads to mimetic effects.

References

Adler, N.J. 2002. Global managers: no longer men alone. *International Journal of Human Resource Management*, **13**: 743–60.

Adler, N.J. & F. Ghadar. 1990. Strategic human resource management: a global perspective. In R. Pieper (ed.), *Human resource management: an international comparison*: 235–60. Berlin: De Gruyter.

Anderson, V. & G. Boocock. 2002. Small firms and internationalisation: learning to manage and managing to learn. *Human Resource Management Journal*, **12**(3): 5–24.

Arkin, A. 1999. Return to centre. *People Management*, **6**(May): 34–41.

Björkman, I. & F. Xiucheng. 2002. Human resource management and the performance of western firms in China. *International Journal of Human Resource Management*, **13**: 853–64.

Black, J.S. 1988. Work role transitions: a study of American expatriate managers in Japan. *Journal of International Business Studies*, **19**: 277–95.

Black, J.S., A.J. Morrison & H.B. Gregerson. 2000. *Global explorers: the next generation of leaders*. New York: Routledge.

Black, J.S., H.B. Gregerson, M.E. Mendenhall & L.K. Stroh. 1999. *Globalizing people through international assignments*. Reading, MA: Addison-Wesley.

Bonache, J. & J. Cervino. (1997). Global integration without expatriates. *Human Resource Management Journal*, **7**(3): 89–100.

Bonache, J. & Z. Fernadez. 1997. Expatriate compensation and its link to the subsidiary strategic role: a theoretical analysis. *International Journal of Human Resource Management*, **8**: 457–75.

Bonache, J., V. Suutari & C. Brewster. 2001. Expatriation: a developing research agenda. *Thunderbird International Business Review*, **43**: 3–20.

Boyacigiller, N. 1990. The role of expatriates in the management of interdependence, complexity and risk in multinational corporations. *Journal of International Business Studies*, **21**: 265–73.

Brewster, C. & H. Scullion. 1997. A review and an agenda for expatriate HRM. *Human Resource Management Journal*, **7**(3): 32–41.

Briscoe, D.R. & R.S. Schuler. 2004. *International human resource management*. Second edition. London: Routledge.

Clases, C., R. Bachmann & T. Wehner. 2004. Studying trust in virtual organizations. *International Studies of Management and Organization*, **33**(3): 7–27.

Dowling, P. & D. Welch. 2004. *International human resource management: managing people in a global context*. Fourth edition. London: Thomson Learning.

Doz, Y. & C.K. Prahalad. 1986. Controlled variety: a challenge for human resource management in the MNC. *Human Resource Management*, **25**: 55–71.

Edström, A. & J.R. Galbraith. 1977. Transfer of managers as a coordination and control strategy in multinational organizations. *Administrative Science Quarterly*, **22**: 248–63.

Evans, P. & P. Lorange. 1989. The two logics behind human resource management. In P. Evans, Y. Doz & A. Laurent (eds), *Human resource management in international firms: change, globalization, innovation*. London: Macmillan.

Evans, P., P. Pucik & J.L. Barsoux. 2002. *The global challenge: frameworks for international human resource management*. New York: McGraw-Hill.

Ferner, A. 1997. Country of origin effects and HRM in multinational corporations. *Human Resource Management*, **7**: 19–37.

Forster, N. 2000. The myth of the 'international manager'. *International Journal of Human Resource Management*, **11**: 126–42.

Franko, L. 1973. Who manages multinational enterprises? *Columbia Journal of World Business*, **8**: 30–42.

Garten, J. 1997. *The big ten: the emerging markets and how they will change our lives*. New York: Basic Books.

Gong, Y. 2003a. Subsidiary staffing in multinational enterprises: agency, resources and performance. *Academy of Management Journal*, **46**: 728–39.

Gong, Y. 2003b. Toward a dynamic process model of staffing composition and subsidiary outcomes in multinational enterprises. *Journal of Management*, **29**: 259–80.

Goold, M.C. & A. Campbell. 1987. *Strategies and styles: the role of the centre in managing diversified corporations*. Oxford: Basil Blackwell.

Gupta, A.K. & V. Govindarajan. 2002. Cultivating a global mindset. *Academy of Management Executive*, **16**: 116–26.

Harvey, M. 1998. Dual-career couples during international relocation: the trailing spouse. *International Journal of Human Resource Management*, **9**: 309–31.

Harvey, M., M. Novicevic & C. Speier. 1999a. Inpatriate managers: how to increase the probability of success. *Human Resource Management Review*, **9**: 51–82.

Harvey, M., C. Speier & M.M. Novicevic. 1999b. The role of inpatriation in global staffing. *International Journal of Human Resource Management*, **10**: 459–76.

Harvey, M., C. Speier, & M.M. Novicevic. 2001. A theory-based framework for strategic global human resource staffing policies and practices. *International Journal of Human Resource Management*, **12**: 898–915.

Harvey, M.G. & M.R. Buckley. 1997. Managing inpatriates: building a global core competency. *Journal of World Business*, **32**: 35–52.

Harvey, M.G., M.M. Novicevic & C. Speier. 2000. Strategic global human resource management: The role of inpatriate managers. *Human Resource Management Review*, **10**: 153–75.

Harzing, A.W. 2001a. An analysis of the functions of international transfer of managers in MNCs. *Employee Relations*, **23**: 581–98.

Harzing, A.W. 2001b. Who's in charge? An empirical study of executive staffing practices in foreign multinationals. *Human Resource Management*, **40**: 139–58.

Harzing, A.W. 2004. Composing an international staff. In A.W. Harzing & J. van Ruysseveldt (eds), *International human resource management*. Second edition. London: Sage.

Harzing, A.W.K. 1995. The persistent myth of high expatriate failure rates. *International Journal of Human Resource Management*, **6**: 457–75.

Harzing, A.W.K. 1999. *Managing the multinationals: An international study of control mechanisms*. Cheltenham: Edward Elgar.

Heenan, D.A. & H.V. Perlmutter. 1979. *Multinational organizational development*. Reading, MA: Addison-Wesley.

Hofstede, G. 2001. *Culture's consequences*. Second edition. London, Sage.

Kobrin, S.J. 1994. Is there a relationship between a geocentric mindset and multinational strategy? *Journal of International Business Studies*, **25**: 493–511.

Kopp, R. 1994. International human resource policies and practices in Japanese, European and United States multinationals. *Human Resource Management*, **33**: 581–99.

Lazarova, M. & P. Caligiuri. 2001. Retaining repatriates: the role of organizational support practices. *Journal of World Business*, **36**: 389–401.

Linehan, M. 2002. Senior female international manager: empirical evidence from Western Europe. *International Journal of Human Resource Management*, **13**: 802–14.

Mayrhofer, W. & C. Brewster. 1996. In praise of ethnocentricity: expatriate policies in European MNCs. *International Executive*, **38**: 749–78.

Mayrhofer, W. & H. Scullion. 2002. Female expatriates in international business: empirical evidence from the German clothing industry. *International Journal of Human Resource Management*, **3**: 815–36.

Milliman, J., M.A. Von Glinow & M. Nathan. 1991. Organizational life cycles and strategic international human resource management in multinational companies: implications for congruence theory. *Academy of Management Review*, **16**: 318–29.

O'Donnell, S.W. 2000. Managing foreign subsidiaries: agents of headquarters or an independent network? *Strategic Management Journal*, **21**: 525–48.

Ondrack, D. 1985. International transfers of managers in North American and European multinationals. *Journal of International Business Studies*, **16**: 1–20.

Paauwe, J. & P. Dewe. 1995. Organizational structure of multinational corporations: theories and models. In A.W. Harzing & J. van Ruysseveldt (eds), *International human resource management*. Thousands Oaks, CA: Sage.

Perlmutter, H.V. 1969. The tortuous evolution of the multinational corporation. *Columbia Journal of World Business*, **4**: 9–18.

Peterson, R.B. 2003. The use of expatriates and inpatriates in Central and Eastern Europe since the Wall came down. *Journal of World Business*, **38**: 55–69.

Pucik, V. 1992. Globalization and human resource management. In V. Pucik, N.M. Tichy & C.K. Barnett, *Creating and Leading the Competitive Organization*. New York: Wiley.

Reynolds, C. 1997. Strategic employment of third country nationals: keys to sustaining the transformation of HR functions. *Human Resource Planning*, **20**(1): 33–40.

Schuler, R.S. 2000. The internationalization of human resource management. *Journal of International Management*, **6**: 239–60.

Schuler, R.S., P.S. Budhwar & G.W. Florkowski. 2002. International human resource management: review and critique. *International Journal of Management Reviews*, **4**: 41–70.

Schuler, R.S., P.J. Dowling & H. De Cieri. 1993. An integrative framework of strategic international human resource management. *Journal of Management*, **19**: 419–59.

Schuler, R.S., S.E. Jackson & Y. Luo. 2004. *Managing human resources in cross-border alliances*. London, Routledge.

Scullion, H. 1994. Staffing policies and strategic control in British multinationals. *International Studies of Management and Organization*, **4**(3): 18–35.

Scullion, H. 2001. International human resource management. In J. Storey (ed.), *Human resource management*. London: International Thompson.

Scullion, H. & C. Brewster. 2001. Managing expatriates: messages from Europe. *Journal of World Business*, **36**: 346–65.

Scullion, H. & M. Linehan 2004. *International human resource management: a critical text*. London: Palgrave Macmillan.

Scullion, H. & J. Pate. 2005. The changing nature of the psychological contract: traditional versus non standard international assignments. Unpublished working paper, Strathclyde International Business Unit, Glasgow.

Scullion, H. & K. Starkey. 2000. The changing role of the corporate human resource function in the international firm. *International Journal of Human Resource Management*, **11**: 1061–81.

Shay, J.P. & S.A. Baack. 2004. Expatriate assignment, adjustment and effectiveness: an empirical examination of the big picture. *Journal of International Business Studies*, **35**: 216–32.

Simon, H.A. 1957. *Models of man*. New York: Wiley.

Simon, H.A. 1982. *Models of bounded rationality*. Cambridge, MA: MIT Press.

Sparrow, P., C. Brewster & H. Harris. 2004. *Globalizing human resource management*. London: Routledge.

Storey, J., P. Edwards & K. Sisson. 1997. *Managers in the making: careers, development and control in corporate Britain and Japan*. London: Sage Publications.

Taylor, S., N.K. Napier & W. Mayrhofer. 2002. Women in global business: an introduction. *International Journal of Human Resource Management*, **13**: 739–42.

Thomas, D.C. 1998. The expatriate experience: a critical review and synthesis. *Advances in International and Comparative Management*, **12**: 237–73.

Torbiorn, I. 1985. The structure of managerial roles in cross-cultural settings. *International Studies of Management and Organization*, **15**(1): 52–74.

Torbiorn, I. 1994. Operative and strategic use of expatriates in new organizations and market structures. *International Studies of Management and Organization*, **24**(3): 5–17.

Torbiorn, I. 1997. Staffing for international operations. *Human Resource Management Journal*, **7**(3): 42–51.

Tung, R.L. 1981. Selection and training of personnel for overseas assignments. *Columbia Journal of World Business*, **23**: 129–43.

Tung, R.L. 1982. Selection and training procedures of US, European and Japanese multinationals. *California Management Review*, **25**(1): 57–71.

UNCTAD. 2003. *World investment report 2003: FDI policies for development: national and international perspectives*. Geneva: UNCTAD.

UNCTAD. 2004. *Prospects for FDI flows, transnational corporation strategies and promotion policies: 2004–2007*. GIPA Research note 1. Geneva: UNCTAD.

Welch, D. & L. Welch. 1994. Linking operation mode diversity and IHRM. *International Journal of Human Resource Management*, **5**: 911–26.

Welch, D.E. 1994. Determinants of international human resource management approaches and activities: a suggested framework. *Journal of Management Studies*, **31**: 139–64.

Young, S., N. Hood, N. Hamill and J. Hamill. 1985. *Decision making in foreign-owned multinational subsidiaries in the United Kingdom*. ILO Working Paper 35. Geneva.

9 The compensation of expatriates: a review and a future research agenda
Jaime Bonache

The academic research on the compensation of expatriates is an under-developed area. In a review of recent developments in international management in the 20 top management journals from 1996 to 2000, Werner (2002) has shown that the literature on expatriation has focused recently on a wide number of issues, including assignment acceptance (Aryee et al., 1996), concerns and expectations of dual career expatriates (Harvey, 1997), adjustment (Caligiuri et al., 1998; Shaffer et al., 1999), psychological withdrawal (Shaffer & Harrison, 1998), pre-departure thoughts (Garonzik et al., 2000), and commitment (Gregersen & Black, 1996). However no study focusing on expatriate compensation can be found in those journals in recent years. Going back further, we find this same lack of academic literature on this issue. For example, of 174 references selected in the early 1990s from *The International Journal of Human Resource Management* (May, 1994) on issues specially related to international HRM, only one of them (Reynolds, 1986) dealt with the compensation of expatriates in MNCs. This is in sharp contrast to the abundant references that exist from that same time on managerial compensation in the domestic human resources literature. In this field, according to a study by Gómez-Mejia (1994), more than 300 empirical studies on the determining factors of managers' compensation could be found.

To find analyses of this issue, it is necessary to refer to magazines and work more oriented towards practitioners (Becker, 1993; Bishko, 1990; Burns, 2003; Crandall & Phelps, 1991; Freeman & Kane, 1995; Hodgetts & Luthans, 1993; Hymer, 1993; O'Reilly, 1996; Reynolds, 1997, 2000; Senko, 1994; Wentland, 2003). This work reflects the concerns of professionals and there prevails a highly applied and descriptive orientation, focused on 'how' MNCs compensate their expatriates rather than on the causes and effects of their compensation strategies. Two issues dominate this highly descriptive literature: the difficulties that are encountered when designing an expatriates' pay system, and the approaches and elements usually included in an international compensation package. We will begin by reviewing these two issues and, after that, we will point out some areas that may guide further study.

Challenges and objectives

Designing a pay system is always a challenging process, but doing so in multinational corporations (MNCs) is particularly complex and difficult (Harvey, 1993a, 1993b; Suutari & Tornikoski, 2000, 2001). A set of situational factors not normally encountered in a strictly domestic situation must be taken into account when designing the compensation package of an expatriate. For example, the nationality of the individual, their family situation (number and ages of their children, work situation of the spouse), floating exchange rates, differences in living costs, taxes and inflation rates, the need to reconcile home and host-country laws and regulations for compensation and benefits, and the geographically imposed problems of communication and control are all of great importance. These issues increase the complexity of the situation, and the information needed as regards the individual and his/her destination (Suutari & Tornikoski, 2001).

In addition to these situational factors, there are a number of objectives that must be incorporated in the design of expatriates' pay packages. According to Freeman and Kane (1995) and Suutari and Tornikoski (2001), an ideal expatriate compensation system should include five main objectives: (1) to attract personnel in the areas where the multinational has its greatest needs and opportunities, (2) to facilitate the transfer of international employees in the most cost-effective manner, (3) to be consistent and fair in the treatment of all its employees, (4) to facilitate re-entry into the home country at the end of the foreign assignment, and (5) to contribute to organizational strategy (that is, to support organizational goals, foster corporate culture and help motivate employees to contribute their efforts to further organizational success). Taken individually, these objectives seem logical and achievable. However the implementation of one may well contradict another. As an example, let us consider the first objective in relation to the others.

Attracting personnel to international service by offering generous compensation packages is a widespread practice in many MNCs (Aryee *et al.*, 1996; Toh & Denisi, 2003; Bonache, 2005). This initiative is designed to break the frequent barriers to international mobility. In addition to family and personal issues (such as the growing unwillingness to disrupt the education of children and the growing importance of quality of life considerations; see Black *et al.*, 1992; Shaffer *et al.*, 1999), and the continued uncertainty regarding international terrorism and political and social unrest of certain destinations (Scullion, 1995), it is well documented that the career implications of international assignments are often frustrating. A lack of respect for acquired skills, loss of status and reverse culture shock upon return are recurring problems in many companies (Daily *et al.*, 2000;

Stahl, Miller & Tung, 2002). Because of these barriers, a logical way of encouraging individuals to accept a foreign assignment is to provide generous compensation packages for expatriates.

Yet this way of attracting individuals to the international service may conflict with other objectives of the system. Firstly, it leads to costly assignments. This, in turn, puts an economic strain on the company, and finally leads it to reduce the costs of assignments, in an attempt to save money. In doing so, the company might also reduce the pool of qualified candidates, thereby making the recruitment process all the more difficult (Hamil, 1989; Suutari & Tornikoski, 2001). Thus there is tension in the achievement of the first two objectives of the system. Second, it might also conflict with the repatriation objective. The incentives and allowances designed to encourage employees to take up a foreign assignment are not sustained when the expatriate return home, leading to a substantial loss of income. In fact, such a loss of income is cited as one of the main difficulties upon return (Harvey, 1989). In other words, a less attractive pay package facilitates re-entry but reduces the ability of the company to attract employees for the international service. Finally, the generous incentives designed to help attract overseas employment have the side-effect of creating large pay gaps between expatriates and local employees. The less fortunate position of the local employees relative to that of the expatriate may damage their perceptions of the company's procedural and distributive justice (Chen *et al.*, 2002; Toh & Denisi, 2003), thus failing to achieve the objective of fairness.

That some empirical studies have pointed out the relative dissatisfaction with the expatriate compensation system (Harvey, 1993b) is perhaps the logical consequence of the difficulty of satisfying objectives that may work in opposite directions. As in many other areas of human resources, the compensation policy for multinational expatriates is bound to confront various dilemmas and conflicts. For example, the company faces the potential conflict of maintaining some form of internal equity while providing sufficient incentive to attract and motivate oversees assignees (Torbiorn, 1982; Toh & Denisi, 2003). There is no magic formula that can solve these dilemmas, and so one should be wary of those who present this area of management as a science, with which one can limit oneself to applying technical solutions.

Approaches and components

Bearing in mind the situational factors and objectives outlined above, the MNCs have a number of ways to deal with the retribution of expatriates (Reynolds, 1986; Dowling & Schuler, 1990). Each way reflects the MNCs' priorities when paying expatriates. Three main approaches, each with its

Table 9.1 Retribution approaches and their impact on compensation objectives

Objectives of an international compensation system	Retribution approach		
	Host country	Home country	Global
1. To attract personnel for the inter national service	−	+	+
2. To be cost-effective	+	−	−
3. To be fair			
with respect to local employees,	+	−	−
with respect to other expatriates from a different nationality			
in the same location,	+	−	+
with respect to other expatriates			
in another location	−	+	+
4. To facilitate re-entry	−	+	−
5. To support the company's international strategy	0	0	0

Note: + = positive impact, − = negative impact, 0 = irrelevant.

strengths and weaknesses in achieving the five objectives (see Table 9.1), have been developed. The first is the *host-country approach*. The main intention of this approach is to fit the expatriate into the assignment location salary structure. This approach is satisfactory when a number of eligible candidates for the particular position have a personal interest in living abroad, and so a local salary does not seem unattractive. In addition to reducing costs, this approach helps to create a sense of equity between expatriates and local employees, since nobody feels underprivileged. However this method only has limited use in motivating international mobility, as worldwide variations and the consequent inconsistencies may inhibit the transfer of expatriates. This approach is usually adopted when the expatriate has become replaceable by a local hire but wants to remain abroad for personal reasons (O'Reilly, 1996).

The second is the *global approach*. The intention is to pay on an international scale, with allowances derived from that base. An international basket of goods would be used across all expatriates regardless of country of origin (Freeman & Kane, 1995). This approach is most relevant in the case of expatriates who are expected to move to more than one foreign country, thereby losing direct connection with either their home country or their host country grading and pay structure (O'Reilly, 1996). The high costs and difficulties of re-entry are often mentioned as the main shortfalls of this system (Dowling & Schuler, 1990).

The third is the *home-country approach*. The idea of this approach is to provide the expatriate with equivalent purchasing power abroad in order to maintain his/her standard of living in his/her home country. This is consistent with the so-called balance sheet approach (Senko, 1994). This system applies home country deductions and pays differential allowances (cost of living differential, housing allowance) to arrive at net disposable income which should maintain the expatriate's home country standard of living.

According to the 2002 Worldwide Survey of International Assignment Policies and Practices, conducted by the Organization Resources Counselors, Inc. (ORC), a New York-based consulting firm, most companies report that their intention is to provide expatriates with equivalent purchasing power abroad to help them maintain a home country lifestyle. This is the common practice among 70 per cent of European, 65 per cent of Asian, and 79 per cent of North American companies. The advantage of this approach is that, by keeping expatriates in line with conditions at home, they can readily fit back into their home country after their overseas posting. In addition, it enables a company to achieve worldwide consistency in its expatriate employment practices. However it is not without drawbacks, which arise when different nationalities work together in similar jobs. Yet there exist solutions to this problem too. For example, Endesa, a Spanish electrical company, gets around this problem by giving all peer group expatriates the same host country element, such as housing or goods and services allowance.

Moreover the home country approach is expensive, especially for some nationalities. For example, American expatriates are usually subject to higher income taxes abroad. The maximum marginal rate in the USA is 31 per cent, compared with 65 per cent in Japan, 53 per cent in Germany and 45 per cent in Spain (Mercer HR Consulting, 2003). Maintaining the same level of net salary entails receiving a higher level of gross salary. The employers will have to carry that cost as part of the assignment terms. One should consider the possibility that these higher costs of expatriates of some nationalities influence recruitment policies. For example, according to a survey by Kopp (1994), American MNCs are less inclined to use expatriates than their European and Asian counterparts. Although there are no figures to back up this supposition, it could be the case that the reason for the ethnocentricity of many North American companies is not only their general philosophy, but also economic factors.

Though we know the prevalence of the above three approaches in MNCs, we do not know the reasons or determinants that lead companies to adopt them. Nor do we know the connection they may have with the international strategy of the MNC. Despite the claim that expatriate pay should be consistent with the overall strategy of the MNC (Freeman & Kane, 1995; Reynolds, 1997), the truth is that no indication is provided as to how the design of expatriate compensation packages can help to implement the company's international strategy (Bonache & Fernández, 1997). This omission regarding the connection between compensation and strategy was noted from the beginning of the literature on expatriation. Thus Edstrom and Galbraith (1977: 253) justify the omission of the compensation system from the strategic dimensions involved in international transfers as follows: 'Compensation packages . . . do not differ with reasons for transfers; that is, all companies use compensation to maintain the expatriate's standard of living or slightly better it.' Subsequent empirical research has been developed along the same lines. For example, Welch (1994), in her analysis of four Australian multinational firms, showed that, in spite of their differences in strategy, all four adopted a standardized focus on expatriate compensation (the balance sheet). More recently another empirical study (O'Donnell, 1999) showed that few firms appear to be using compensation programmes as a tool for implementing subsidiary strategy. Many companies limit themselves to using only standard compensation policies.

These 'state of the art' compensation policies, mentioned by O'Donnell (1999), consist of including in the compensation package a series of key ingredients, such as cost of living and housing allowances, foreign service premiums (mobility premium, hardship pay), income tax reimbursements, assistance programmes (education, shipping and storage, travel and club membership) and performance incentives (for a detailed description of how these elements are typically built and combined in a compensation package, see Suutari & Tornikoski, 2000). The ORC 2002 survey (European edition) documents the prevalence of these different elements in an expatriate compensation package (see Table 9.2).

The sum of all these elements allows us to understand the high costs incurred by employing expatriates. The data are quite compelling. The average compensation package of expatriates, according to Reynolds (1997), is two to five times as much as that received by their counterparts at home, and a great deal more than that received by the local nationals in the developing countries. For instance, in China, it was estimated that expatriates earned between 20 and 50 times more than local employees (Chen *et al.*, 2002). Likewise, in a survey conducted in 1996 by the Conference Board, more than two-thirds of the 152 respondents reported that expatriates cost at least three times their salary.

Given such high costs, it is usual to debate the different ways or initiatives that companies can use to reduce the cost of expatriation, ways that

Table 9.2 Compensation components in European MNCs

Elements	European MNCs n = 187
Cost of living and housing allowances	
Cost of living allowance (COLA)	86%
Housing	
Free assignment housing	44%
Other (for example, housing differential)	48%
Foreign service premiums	
Mobility premium	
For moves within the same continent	56%
For moves from one continent to another	60%
Hardship pay	57%
Income tax reimbursements	
Tax policy	
Tax equalization	65%
Tax protection	8%
Tax free	4%
Other (for example, laissez-faire)	23%
Assistance programmes	
Education allowance	
Always	44%
If no suitable free education is available	47%
Shipping and storage cost	
Shipping costs	96%
Storage costs	75%
First or business class air travel	
For senior management	49%
Other expatriates	19%
Club membership	
For senior management	59%
Other expatriates	39%
Performance incentives	93%

Source: Based on *2002 Worldwide Survey of International Assignment Policies and Practices*, European edition, Organization Resources Counselors.

will help to minimize or eliminate some of the items in Table 9.2. Among these initiatives, one should mention the following:

- *Selection initiatives* To employ a greater number of local employees, expatriating only the most essential personnel (Dowling &

Schuler, 1990). Organizations should establish a selection process which ensures that only employees who are interested in expatriate assignments are assigned to overseas positions (Wentland, 2003). The consequence of this would be that foreign service premiums, hardship premiums and cost-of-living adjustments would be paid only to employees who accept assignments in undesirable or hazardous locations. Within Europe, where standards of living are converging, this initiative is relatively easy to implement, although there remain differences in tax systems, housing and education standards.

- *Career planning initiatives*   An alternative to selection initiatives is to require managers to have international experience as a criterion for promotion to higher-level positions (Bonache & Fernández, 1997; Yan *et al.*, 2002). This is fairly straightforward when dealing with a certain type of expatriate. Younger employees can be required to possess international experience if they want to move up the career ladder. They may then give up short-term earnings in exchange for long-term benefits. However this initiative is not viable when dealing with more mature employees.
- *Shorter assignments*   The figures show that short-term assignments are cheaper (Suutari & Tornikoski, 2001), as they do not include many of the items in Table 9.2. Perhaps because of this many MNCs have increased the use of short-term assignments (Bonache *et al.*, 2001).

Future research issues

The components included in Table 9.2, as well as the different alternatives that exist in each one of them, are the topics that attract the attention of professionals in this area. Often the focus is on the relative advantages of, for example, tax equalization (the employee pays no more or no less than he or she would have paid in the home country) over the tax protection policy (employee pays no more than he or she have paid in the home country, but may pay less in certain situations), or on the advantages of offering free housing over other alternative housing policies (for example, the company may pay a housing differential).

Though these issues will continue to attract the attention of practitioners, there are a number of topics which should also attract academics' interest and guide future research in this area. We will classify such topics around four main issues: satisfaction with expatriate packages, cost-efficiency, justice and strategy. The following is a brief analysis of these themes as well as the theories that can support their investigation.

Satisfaction with expatriate compensation packages
As has been mentioned before, MNCs often offer generous compensation policies to encourage international mobility. It would be reasonable to expect that this would lead to a high level of satisfaction among expatriates regarding their compensation. The evidence on this point is, however, contradictory. Suutari and Tornikoski (2001) studied the sources of salary satisfaction and dissatisfaction among Finnish expatriates and report a high degree of satisfaction among expatriates with the principles and levels of their compensation packages. Other studies on expatriates' attitudes, however, have uncovered low levels of salary satisfaction among these workers. For example, Black *et al.* (1992) assert that 77 per cent of expatriate employees are highly dissatisfied with their compensation systems. Similarly Hamil (1989) suggests that these low levels of salary satisfaction might explain the high rates of expatriate failure that have been widely documented by the international management literature. The issue of salary satisfaction among expatriates clearly deserves more attention.

Salary satisfaction can be explained in terms of the social comparison theory (Festinger, 1954; Adams, 1965). This theory asserts that satisfaction is a function of how 'fairly' an individual is treated at work. Satisfaction results from one's perception that work outcomes, relative to inputs, compare favourably to another's outcomes/inputs. Dissimilar ratios lead to perceptions of inequity. This proposition implies that the same organizational circumstance may be perceived as fair or unfair depending on which individual or group of individuals the worker chooses to compare himself to. Accordingly, a main concern when analysing people's satisfaction with their salary is identifying the referent used in the individual's comparisons (Chen *et al.*, 2002). The problem faced by expatriate workers is that there are multiple referents available to them when working abroad (Bonache *et al.*, 2001; Bonache, 2005). They can compare themselves not only to other expatriates within the same company and host country, but also to expatriates within the same company and other host countries, expatriates from other companies within their host country, local employees and so on. With all these referents, lack of equity with respect to other employees is a very likely possibility. From this point of view, the low levels of salary satisfaction among expatriates, reported by some studies, can easily be explained.

In any case, a low level of salary satisfaction is a very common problem among all types of employees (Gómez-Mejia *et al.*, 1995). This means that, even though expatriates might not feel satisfied with their pay, they might be relatively more satisfied than other groups of employees. However the evidence to hand does not lead to this conclusion. Thus in a recent study (Bonache, 2005) comparing job satisfaction among expatriates, repatriates and domestic employees with international experience, conducted on a large sample of employees from a Spanish multinational, some significant differences in the satisfaction ratings on job characteristics, career prospects and internal communication among these three groups of employees were found. The study, however, did not find differences in the average level of satisfaction regarding salary. More research is clearly required on this issue.

The influence of nationality in the expatriates' attitudes towards their salaries is another important topic to examine. Some studies analyse the cross-cultural and motivational utility of various compensation strategies on managers and the larger workforce (Gómez-Mejia & Welbourne, 1991; Lowe *et al.*, 2002; Townsend *et al.*, 1990). Their goal is to compare pay practices or preferences for pay practices across cultures. For example, when compared to individualist cultures, collectivist countries place more value on seniority. They see compensation according to needs as being fairer. Drawing on these studies, it would be illustrative to conduct in-depth academic cross-cultural research analysing the motivational utility of various compensation strategies on expatriates from different nationalities. Such research would aim at providing some clues for companies as to which expatriate compensation strategy is most likely to mesh with a particular culture's values.

The issue of costs
Until now, the high costs of employing expatriates has been stressed. It is therefore surprising that MNCs continue to show a strong preference for expatriates to fill certain managerial positions (Maryhofer & Brewster, 1996). In fact this is the case of Japanese companies, where 75 per cent of their subsidiaries' top managers are expatriates, according to a survey by Kopp (1994). European and American MNCs follow a very similar pattern, with 54 per cent and 51 per cent of their top managers being expatriates, respectively. Moreover, according to the ORC 2002 survey of international assignment policies and practices, only 23 per cent of companies from different countries declare a decreasing use of expatriates assigned in recent years. In other words, it is not clear why, in a business context under unremitting pressure to keep costs down, MNCs should continue to implement such a costly solution. To explain this apparent paradox would require more theoretical guidance than past work on expatriation has received.

On this point, the theory of transaction costs (Coase, 1937; Williamson, 1975, 1985, 1993) could be very useful, as it considers a set of costs which are ignored in traditional expatriate compensation literature, but which must be accounted for when an MNC is filling a management position in a subsidiary. Drawing on Jones and Wright's (1992) classification of transaction costs in the employment relation, there are four main types of transaction costs that can be incurred when filling a management position in an MNC: (1) selection and recruitment costs; these are the costs of gathering information about the candidate as well as the costs associated with negotiation and final drawing up of the contract with the appointed candidate; (2) training and socialization costs; these are costs associated with the development of the skills and firm-specific abilities of the managers in the subsidiary; (3) monitoring and evaluating a subsidiary's managers: the costs incurred in safeguarding the organization against moral hazard. These will include costs of managers from the HQs and managerial time spent on supervising the employees in the subsidiary, as well as costs associated with the implementation of appraisal and feedback systems; (4) enforcement: the organization will have to take action in the event of a breach of contract on the part of the subsidiary's manager. This will obviously produce new costs for the company.

The basic premise of transaction cost economics is that transactions will tend to take place in a form that minimizes the combined costs of the transaction. Accordingly, when deciding whether to recruit a local manager or an expatriate, relative salary levels are not the only economic items involved. Instead the organization will have to consider the total costs associated with each alternative and opt for the most efficient one; that is, the one that minimizes salary and transaction costs. Without a doubt, determining when the transaction costs of using expatriates are lower than those of using local managers is of interest.

The first step in this direction was made by Bonache and Pla (2005). Building on the existence of the above-mentioned transaction costs, we argue that, in companies with a lower level of international expansion, that are less technologically innovative, with a global strategy and with operations in very culturally distant environments, expatriates will have a lower level of associated transaction costs and, therefore, can be a cost-effective solution. We tested the viability of these arguments on a sample of 96 Spanish multinational companies. Our data did not support the hypothesis concerning the diminished use of expatriates when companies operate in increasingly culturally distant environments. However our empirical investigation supports our other three hypotheses, which illustrates the viability of this approach. Future research along these lines is clearly needed.

The issue of justice
In their review of HR literature, Ferris et al. (1999) insist upon the need to introduce the idea of justice into HR management. The topic of expatriate compensation provides an excellent opportunity to analyse the issue of justice. In fact it has been stated that a compensation programme should be fair in its treatment of all categories of employees (Milkovich & Newman, 1996). It is interesting to analyse this issue, not only from the point of view of the expatriates, but also from that of the local employees.

Equity theory is the point of reference from which to evaluate the extent to which employees judge the fairness of their compensation. According to this theory, employees compare what they give to what they receive. This is based on their own evaluation of their value, previous or later work, or what was promised to them. Such a comparison, as mentioned earlier, is made within a social setting, by taking other employees as referents for comparison. On occasion, the referents are employees that are considered to be 'similar', either in terms of age, seniority in the firm, or any other relevant variable. For example, the local employees may choose nationality as a variable and compare their level of compensation with that of other local employees, be it within the same MNC, other MNCs or in other local firms. Yet they also may choose 'different' people to whom they compare themselves, as would happen if local employees were to compare themselves to expatriates. As seen in Table 9.2, the different allowances, additions and deductions included in a typical expatriate package result in a pay package which is very different from that of other categories of employees (Guzzo *et al.*, 1993; Chen *et al.*, 2002). As compensation for their service abroad, it is logical that expatriates receive some of these elements (for example, overseas allowances, repatriation allowances), but other benefits (such as education allowances) are given to expatriates rather than to other groups (locals) with little justification.

Chen *et al.* (2002) analysed the reactions to such comparisons of Chinese employees working in MNCs. These workers were at a salary disadvantage compared to the expatriates, but at an advantage compared to other local employees. They found that local employees are more likely to feel a sense of injustice in compensation when comparing their salaries to expatriates' salaries rather than to locals'. This shows an egocentric bias: what they tend to see as fair is what benefits them the most.

The locals' perception of salary inequity when comparing themselves to expatriates is unfortunate because local nationals are valuable socializing agents, sources of social support, assistance and friendship to expatriates (Black *et al.*, 1992; Caligiuri & Cascio, 1998; Toh & Denesi, 2003). The disparity in pay may lead local nationals to become uncooperative or antagonistic, which may lower the effectiveness of the expatriate on the job (Crandall & Phelps, 1991; Wederspahn, 1992). Toh and Denisi (2003) have theoretically analysed factors that determine this perception of inequity. They state that this perception occurs when a local employee does not perceive a salary advantage over locals in other companies, when they do not see logical reasons for the high expatriate compensation and when expatriates do not have the appropriate interpersonal skills. Moreover Toh and Denisi assert that such perceptions are greatly influenced by the national culture of the local employee. For example, we can expect that differences in salaries will be better accepted in cultures characterized by high power distance than by those of low power distance. Empirical investigation regarding the determinants and effects of salary inequity among local employees and expatriates are clearly needed.

Finally, while equity theory is the traditional reference used to analyse organizational justice, other approaches regarding justice are also possible. One possible and complementary alternative is Rawls' theory of justice (see Bonache, 2004, for an analysis of this theory as applied to HRM). According to this theory, different work arrangements for expatriates and local employees will be fair in cases where (a) the groups have the same basic labour rights and opportunities, (b) greater rewards correspond to greater merits, and (c) the greater rewards of the expatriates group (the most favoured group) improve those of the less favoured local employees group. Theoretical and empirical research on the topic using this (or other) theoretical frameworks may be very instructive.

Link to the subsidiary strategic role

The fact that the majority of companies are simply using the 'state of the art' compensation policy highlights an important issue. It is widely recognized that expatriates may perform different strategic roles and use different behaviour in different subsidiaries (Edstrom & Galbraith, 1977; Boyacigiller, 1990; Brewster, 1991; Gupta & Govindarajan, 1991; Bonache & Fernandez, 1997). In some, for example, they are expected to transfer knowledge and procedures from the HQs while working independently with regard to other subsidiaries. Others, in contrast, are expected to develop their network of contacts with employees of other subsidiaries in order personally to import and export the knowledge within the integrated network of the multinational (see Gupta & Govindarajan, 1991). Given that managerial compensation is an important mechanism to elicit different managerial roles and behaviours (Finkelstein & Hambrick, 1989), how is it possible that multinationals limit themselves to the use of 'state of the art' compensation policies instead of adapting the expatriate compensation system to the different roles of expatriates?

Although the strategic use of expatriate compensation (that is, compensation used to foster those behaviours required for the strategy of the company) has not been practically analysed, we have some evidence that suggests its presence. For example, if we analyse the data in Table 9.2, we see that there are two types of incentives. One is classified under the category of premiums and allowances (that is, cost of living and housing allowances, foreign-service premiums, hardship allowances, danger money, mobility premiums and relocation allowances). These incentives are basically tools to encourage employees to take international assignments, and, as such, have had a prominent place in the traditional international compensation arena. We also see that performance incentives are used by around 93 per cent of European companies. These are expected to be a mechanism to elicit the managerial behaviours needed to implement the organization's strategy effectively. Little is known about these incentives, although they are the ones that hold a greater theoretic and strategic interest.

A useful perspective to analyse the strategic use of performance incentives is agency theory (Eisenhardt, 1989; Gómez-Mejia, 1994). This theory is relevant to situations that have a principal–agent structure. As Roth and O'Donnell (1996) have shown, the headquarters–foreign subsidiary responds to a principal–agent structure: HQ (the principal) delegates work and responsibilities to foreign subsidiaries (the agent). In this type of relationship, there is a risk that the 'agency problem' may arise. This refers to the possibility that agents will pursue their own interests, which may diverge from the interests of the principal (Eisenhardt, 1989). This is a real possibility in the multinational arena. For example, in a subsidiary located in a culturally different environment, it is possible for an expatriate to enjoy excellent work conditions while making very little effort. The resulting poor performance of the subsidiary can then be excused by attributing it to the lack of fit of the company's procedures to the local culture rather than to the expatriate's poor performance.

Incentive alignment is a traditional device used to address the agency problem. This is defined as the extent to which the reward structure is designed to induce managers to make decisions that are in the best interests of the principal (Gómez-Mejia, 1994). Properly designed, the reward structure promotes self-monitoring as it provides performance incentives that impel agents to minimize opportunism and promote their alignment with principal's interests. Through these performance incentives, expatriates, pursuing their own goals, will pursue the goal of the HQs.

From this theoretical perspective, one can analyse how different configurations of the incentives of the expatriates (that is, the proportion of bonuses and long-term incentives versus salary and benefits, the short and long time horizon of incentives, the quantitative and qualitative criteria used to trigger rewards) respond to the intentions of the multinational to solve the agency problem and procure an appropriate alignment of interests between the company and expatriates. Roth and O'Donnell (1996) carried out one such investigation in a sample of 100 foreign subsidiaries from five countries, yielding some relevant findings.[1] For example, they found that, when the senior manager of the foreign subsidiary has a lower level of parent commitment, the potential for opportunism increases and, as a result, (a) the percentage of senior management's incentive-based compensation increases, and (b) more weight is given to regional and corporate performance. Although more work is clearly needed, these findings provide some support for the agency theory insight according to which particular compensation components are designed to reduce the agency problem by inducing managers to make decisions that are in the best interests of the headquarters.

Not only is more research needed on the determinants of expatriate compensation systems but also more research is needed on the effects of these systems on firms' competitive advantages. In this regard, and contrary to the basic assumption underlying much of the research on traditional compensation literature, competitive advantage cannot be attained if companies simply implant a 'state of the art' compensation package. As is well explained by the resource-based view of the firm, a competitive advantage must come from a resource that is valuable, rare and difficult to imitate (Barney, 1991; Wright *et al.*, 1994). Accordingly, instead of focusing on standard compensation packages, competitive advantage will come from crafting compensation and reward systems to create employment relationships that extract the value of firm-specific resources (Milkovich & Bloom, 1998). We have no information about the way in which expatriate packages can be designed to create a shared mindset, extract tacit knowledge, encourage innovation, creativity and responsiveness, and stimulate the development of important relationships among people. Investigation along this line would undoubtedly be of great academic and professional interest.

Conclusion

Traditionally the literature on the compensation of expatriates has had a very descriptive and practitioner orientation. It basically describes the many difficulties encountered by MNCs in designing an 'attractive' and 'cost-efficient' compensation approach that enables them to standardize salary decisions and apply the approach uniformly throughout the multinational network. Such an approach, however, is not easy to develop. As noted, there are conflicting objectives to be achieved, forcing MNCs to face a dilemma of achieving one objective at the expense of giving up another.

The difficulty involved in finding a satisfactory compensation system may explain why expatriate compensation literature has been dominated by interests of practitioners and has been characterized by an operative focus. Although these practical issues will continue to attract the attention of both practitioners and academics, this chapter has tried to show that this topic also brings to light many more theoretical issues, such as justice, satisfaction, costs and strategy in expatriate compensation systems. The main challenge for academics is, from different theoretical perspectives, to shed light on these issues about which we still know very little.

Note

1. It is important to note that Roth and O'Donnell (1996) analyse subsidiary management compensation without controlling for the nationality of the managers.

References

Adams, J.S. 1965. Inequity in social exchange. In L. Berkowitz (ed.), *Advances in experimental social psychology*. New York: Academic Press.

Aryee, S., Y.W. Chay & J. Chew. 1996. An investigation of the willingness of managerial employees to accept an expatriate assignment. *Journal of Organizational Behaviour*, **17**: 267–83.

Barney, J. 1991. Firm resources and sustained competitive advantage. *Journal of Management*, **15**: 175–90.

Baron, J. & D. Kreps. 1999. *Strategic human resources: frameworks for general managers*. New York: John Wiley & Sons.

Becker, T.H. 1993. International executive compensation. In H.J. Bergadin & J.E.A. Russell (eds), *Human resource management: an experiential approach*. New York: McGraw-Hill.

Bishko, M.J. 1990. Compensating your overseas executives, part 1: strategies for the 1990s. *Compensation and Benefits Review*, **28**: 33–43.

Black, J.S., H.B. Gregersen & M.E. Mendenhall. 1992. *Global assignments*. San Francisco, CA: Jossey-Bass.

Bonache, J. 2004. Towards a re-examination of work arrangements: an analysis from Rawls' theory of justice. *Human Resource Management Review*, **14**(4).

Bonache, J. 2005. Job satisfaction among expatriates, repatriates and domestic employees. The perceived impact of international assignments on work-related variables. *Personnel Review*, **34**(1).

Bonache, J. & Z. Fernández. 1997. Expatriate compensation and its link to the subsidiary strategic role: a theoretical analysis. *The International Journal of HRM*, **8**: 457–75.

Bonache, J. & J. Pla. 2005. When are international managers a cost effective solution? The rationale of Transaction Cost Theory applied to staffing decisions in MNCs. *Journal of Business Research*.

Bonache, J., V. Suutari & C. Brewster. 2001. A review and agenda for expatriate HRM. *Thunderbird International Management Review*, **42**(1): 3–21.

Boyacigiller, N. 1990. The role of expatriates in the management of interdependence, complexity and risk in multinational corporations. *Journal of International Business Studies*, **21**(3): 357–81.

Brewster, C. 1991. *The management of expatriates*. London: Kogan Page.

Burns, S. 2003. Flexible international assignee compensation plans. *Compensation and Benefits Review*, **35**(3): 35–42.

Caligiuri, P.M. & W.F. Cascio. 1998. Can we send her there? Maximizing the success of western women on global assignments. *Journal of World Business*, **33**: 394–416.

Caligiuri, P.M., M.M. Hyland, A. Joshi & A.S. Bross. 1998. Testing a theoretical model for examining the relationship between family adjustment and expatriate's work adjustment. *Journal of Applied Psychology*, **83**: 598–614.

Chen, C.C., J. Choi & S.C. Chi. 2002. Making justice sense of local–expatriate compensation disparity: mitigation by local referents, ideological explanations, and interpersonal sensitivity in China–foreign joint ventures. *Academy of Management Journal*, **45**(4): 807–26.

Coase, R.H. 1937. The nature of the firm. *Economica*, **4** (New series): 386–405.

Crandall, L.P. & M.I. Phelps. 1991. Pay for a global workforce. *Personnel Journal*, **70**: 28–33.

Daily, C., C. Trevis & D. Dalton. 2000. International experience in the executive suite: The path to prosperity? *Strategic Management Journal*, **21**: 515–23.

Dowling, P. & R. Schuler. 1990. *International dimensions of human resource management*. Boston, MA: PWS-Kent publishing.

Edstrom, A. & J. Galbraith. 1977. Transfer of managers as a coordination and control strategy in multinational organizations. *Administrative Science Quarterly*, **22**: 248–63.

Eisenhardt., K. 1989. Agency theory: an assessment and review. *Strategic Management Journal*, **14**: 57–74.

Ferris, G., W. Hochwarter, M.R. Buckley, G. Harrell-Cook & D. Frink. 1999. Human resource management: some new directions. *Journal of Management*, **25**(3): 385–415.

Festinger, L. 1954. A theory of social comparison processes. *Human Relations*, **7**: 117–40.

Finkelstein. S. & D.C. Hambrick. 1989. Chief executive compensation: a study of the intersection of markets and political processes. *Strategic Management Journal*, **10**: 121–34.

Freeman, K. & J. Kane. 1995. An alternative approach to expatriate allowances: An international citizen. *The International Executive*, **37**(3): 245–59.

Garonzik, R., J. Brockner & P.A. Siegel. 2000. Identifying international assignees at risk for premature departure: the interactive effect of outcome favourability and procedural fairness. *Journal of Applied Psychology*, **85**: 13–20.

Gómez-Mejia, L.R. 1994. Executive compensation: a reassessment and a future research agenda. *Research in Personnel and HRM*, **12**: 161–222.

Gómez-Mejia, L.R. & T. Welbourne. 1991. Compensation strategies in a global context. *Human Resource Planning*, **14**: 29–41.

Gómez-Mejia, L.R., D.B. Balkin & R.L. Cardy. 1995. *Managing human resources*. Upper Saddle River, NJ: Prentice-Hall.

Gregersen, H.B. & J.S. Black. 1996. Multiple commitments upon repatriation: the Japanese experience. *Journal of Management*, **22**: 209–29.

Gupta, A.K. & V. Govindarajan. 1991. Knowledge flows and the structure of control within multinational corporations. *Academy of Management Review*, **16**: 768–92.

Guzzo, R.A., K.A. Noonan & E. Elron. 1993. Employer influence on the expatriate experience: limits and implications for retention in overseas assignments. *Research in Personnel and Human Resources Management*, **3**: 323–38.

Hamil, J. 1989. Expatriate policies in British multinational. *Journal of General Management*, **14**(4): 19–26.

Harvey, M.G. 1989. Repatriation of corporate executives: an empirical study. *Journal of International Business Studies*, Spring: 131–44.

Harvey, M.G. 1993a. Designing a global compensation system: the logic and a model. *Columbia Journal of World Business*, **28**: 56–72.

Harvey, M.G. 1993b. Empirical evidence of recurring international compensation problems. *Journal of International Business Studies*, **24**(4): 785–99.

Harvey, M.G. 1997. Dual-career expatriates: expectations, adjustment and satisfaction with international relocation. *Journal of International Business Studies*, **28**: 627–58.

Hodgetts, R. & F. Luthans. 1993. U.S. multinationals expatriate compensation strategies. *Compensation and Benefits Review*, **25**: 57–62.

Hymer, R.M. 1993. Executive compensation in the international arena. *Compensation and Benefits Review*, **25**: 49–54.

Jones, G. & P. Wright 1992. An economic approach to conceptualizing the utility of human resource management practices. *Research in Personnel and Human Resource Management*, **10**: 271–99.

Kopp, R. 1994. International human resource policies and practices in Japanese, European and United States multinationals. *Human Resource Management*, **33**(4): 581–99.

Lowe, K.B., J. Milliman, H. De Cieri & P. Dowling. 2002. International compensation practices: a ten-country comparative analysis. *Human Resource Management*, **41**(1): 45–66.

Mayrhofer, W. & C. Brewster. 1996. In praise of ethnocentricity: expatriate policies in European multinationals. *International Executive*, **38**(6): 749–78.

Mercer HR Consulting. 2003. *Estudio mundial sobre diferencias salariales*. Madrid: Mercer HR Consulting España.

Milkovich, G. & M. Bloom. 1998. Rethinking international compensation. *Compensation and Benefits Review*, **30**(1): 14–24.

Milkovich, G.T. & J.M. Newman. 1996. *Compensation*. Fifth edition. Homewood, IL: Irwin.

O'Donnell, S.1999. Compensation design as a tool for implementing foreign subsidiary strategy. *Management International Review*, **39**(2): 149–65.

O'Reilly, M. 1996. Expatriate pay: the state of the art. *Compensation and Benefits Review*, **12**(1): 54–60.

Organization Resources Counselors, Inc. 2002. *2002 Worldwide survey of international assignment policies and practices*. New York: Organization Resources Counselors, Inc.

Reynolds, C. 1986. Compensation of overseas personnel. In J.J. Famularo (ed.), *Handbook of human resources administration*. New York: McGraw-Hill.

Reynolds, C. 1997. Expatriate compensation in historical perspective. *Journal of World Business*, **32**(2): 118–32.

Reynolds, C. 2000. Global compensation and benefits in transition. *Compensation and Benefits Review*, **32**(1): 28–39.

Roth, K. & S. O'Donnell. 1996. Foreign subsidiary compensation strategy: an agency theory perspective. *Academy of Management Journal*, **39**: 678–703.

Scullion, H. 1995. International human resource management. In J. Storey (ed.), *Human resource management: a critical text*. London: Routledge.

Senko J. 1994. In defense of the balance sheet. *Benefits and Compensation International*, **23**(8): 15–22.

Shaffer, M.A. & D. Harrison. 1998. Expatriates' psychological withdrawal from international assignments: work, non-work and family influences. *Personnel Psychology*, **51**: 87–118.

Shaffer, M.A., D. Harrison & M. Gilley. 1999. Dimensions, determinants and differences in the expatriate adjustment process. *Journal of International Business Studies*, **30**(3): 557–81.

Stahl, G.K., E. Miller & R. Tung. 2002. Toward the bounderyless career: a closer look at the expatriate career concept and the perceived implications of an international assignment. *Journal of World Business*, **37**: 216–27.

Suutari, V. & C. Tornikoski. 2000. Determinants of expatriate compensation: findings among expatriate members of SEFE. *Finnish Journal of Business Economics*, **49**(4): 517–39.

Suutari, V. & C. Tornikoski. 2001. The challenge of expatriate compensation: the sources of satisfaction and dissatisfaction among expatriates. *International Journal of Human Resource Management*, **12**(3): 1–16.

Toh, S.M. & A. Denisi. 2003. Host country national reactions to expatriate pay policies: a model and implications. *Academy of Management Review*, **28**(4): 606–21.

Torbiorn, I. 1982. *Living abroad: personal adjustment and personnel policy in the overseas setting*. New York: Wiley.

Townsend, A.K, D. Scott & S. Markham. 1990. An examination of country and culture-based differences in compensation practices. *Journal of International Business Studies*, **21**: 667–78.

Wederspahn, G.M. 1992. Costing failures in expatriate human resources management. *Human Resource Planning*, **15**: 27–35.

Welch, D. 1994. Determinants of international human resource management approaches and activities: a suggested framework. *Journal of Management Studies*, **31**: 139–63.

Wentland, D. 2003. A new practical guide for determining expatriate compensation. *Compensation and Benefits Review*, **35**(3): 45–52.

Werner, S. 2002. Recent developments in international management research: a review of 20 top management journals. *Journal of Management*, **28**(3): 277–305.

Williamson, O. 1975. *Markets and hierarchies: analysis and antitrust implications*. New York: Free Press.

Williamson, O. 1985. *The economic institutions of capitalism: firms, markets, relational contracting*. New York: Free Press.

Williamson, O. 1993. Transaction cost economics and organization theory. *Industrial and Corporate Change*, **2**: 107–56.

Wright, P.M., G.C. McMahan & A. McWilliams. 1994. Human resources and sustained competitive advantage: a resource-based perspective. *The International Journal of Human Resource Manangement*, **5**(2): 301–26.

Yan, A., G. Zhu & D. Hall. 2002. International assignments for career building: a model of agency relationships and psychological contracts. *Academy of Management Review*, **27**(3): 373–91.

10 Global performance management systems
Wayne F. Cascio

Performance is what an organization hires one to do, and to do well (Campbell, Gasser & Oswald, 1996). Current theories of job performance suggest that the performance domain is multifaceted and it is likely to include dimensions that are not highly or even positively correlated with each other (Borman & Motowidlo, 1993; Campbell, McCloy, Oppler & Sager, 1993).

Borman & Motowidlo (1993) identified two broad categories of performance factors: *task* performance factors and *contextual* performance factors. Task performance factors represent the core technical activity of the organization (for example, software development, automobile manufacturing). Contextual performance factors represent the performance components that support the organizational, social and psychological environment in which the technical core must function. They include factors such as showing perseverance and conscientiousness, offering extra effort on the job, volunteering to carry out task activities that are not formally part of one's job, and helping and cooperating with others.

At its most basic level, performance management refers to the evaluation and continuous improvement of individual or team performance. It is every bit as important in the global context as it is in domestic operations. Indeed the special considerations associated with international assignments, and with managing host-country nationals, make global performance management particularly challenging, as we shall see. Managers who do it well address three important areas: they define performance, facilitate performance and encourage performance.

The purpose of this chapter is to review extant literature and findings with respect to international performance management, and to identify research needs in the years ahead. There is much to learn in this evolving area, and it promises to challenge researchers for years to come.

The chapter focuses particularly on performance management systems for two categories of employees: host-country nationals of multinational enterprises (MNEs), and expatriates, including both home and third-country nationals. An expatriate is anyone who works outside of his or her home country, with a planned return to that or a third country. A third-country national is an expatriate who has transferred to an additional country while working abroad (for example, a German working for a

US-based MNE in Spain). A key assumption throughout the chapter is that employees and their managers are colocated. Performance management strategies for global virtual teams are beyond the scope of the current chapter. For more on that subject see, for example, Cascio and Shurygailo (2003).

The chapter is structured as follows. We begin by considering the current status of global performance management systems, followed by a discussion of the purposes of such systems, that is, evaluation and development. We then consider the overall process of performance management in some detail, using the tripartite theoretical approach of define, facilitate and encourage performance. Since appropriate training in the use of global performance management systems is particularly important to their successful implementation, our next section focuses on one demonstrably effective approach, namely, frame-of-reference training. The next two sections of the chapter address cross-cultural dimensions that make the implementation of a uniform, global performance management approach difficult to do. To illustrate these differences we highlight alternative ways of communicating performance feedback in three different cultures. The final two sections of the chapter address what is known about performance management for host-country nationals and performance management for expatriates. Rather than identify emerging research needs in one section at the end of the chapter, these issues are interwoven throughout.

Current status of global performance management systems

A recent survey of performance management systems and practices in 278 organizations, two-thirds of which were multinational enterprises, from 15 different countries, reported the following key findings (Bernthal, Rogers & Smith, 2003):

- Fully 91 per cent use a company-sanctioned performance management system, and three-quarters of them use the same system for more than 70 per cent of their employees.
- While 58 per cent have a yearly review, 41 per cent have reviews more often than once a year.
- Only 20 per cent use online or software-based performance management systems, but another third plan to introduce them.
- Training for managers (55 per cent) and non-managers (28 per cent) has doubled in the past ten years, but fewer than 40 per cent of firms hold managers accountable for the effectiveness of the performance management system.
- Managers rely on a balance of subjective (66 per cent) and objective (71 per cent) data in performance reviews.

- Over the past five years forced rankings have become more common (34 per cent of organizations use them), but few managers find them to be effective.
- The most effective performance management systems are consistently used throughout the organization, integrated with other systems (for example, compensation, promotions, succession planning), involve senior managers and employees, and are linked to organizational strategy.
- Poor compliance or usage of the system (60 per cent of responding organizations selected this overall) is the greatest barrier to system effectiveness. This includes lack of monitoring to see if the system is working as designed, and lack of accountability for completing reviews.
- Organizations with strong performance management systems are 51 per cent more likely to outperform their competitors on financial measures, and 41 per cent more likely to outperform their competitors on non-financial measures (for example, customer satisfaction, employee retention, quality of products or services).

These findings are consistent with those of other recent research on performance management systems (Lawler, 2003), namely that they are important management tools that can have positive outcomes when done properly. Tying rewards to the results of such reviews makes them more effective for two reasons: (a) when rewards (pay, bonuses, stock options) are involved, all parties are likely to take the system seriously; (b) when significant financial rewards (and continued employment) are on the line, it is more likely that organizations will spend more time developing and training individuals to use their performance management systems properly.

Purposes of global performance management systems
On the surface, the purposes and goals of such systems are quite similar for domestic and international operations, but do not be fooled. As Briscoe and Schuler (2004) have noted, the major difference is that *implementation* is much more difficult in the international arena. To a large extent, the nature of the overseas job, the degree of support from and interaction with the parent company, the nature of the environment in which the performance occurs and the degree of expatriate and family adjustment all affect the ability of a global organization to achieve the goals of its performance management system. Broadly speaking, the goals comprise two domains: evaluation and development.

Evaluation goals for global performance management systems in the international environment include: (a) providing feedback to employees at all levels so they will know where they stand; (b) developing valid bases for employment decisions involving pay, promotions, job assignments, retention and termination decisions; and (c) providing a means to warn employees about unsatisfactory performance.

Development goals for global performance management systems in the international environment include: (a) helping employees at all levels to improve their performance and develop their professional skills; (b) diagnosing individual and organizational problems; (c) enhancing commitment to the organization through discussions of career opportunities, action plans and needs for training and development; and (d) using recognition to motivate continued or improved high performance.

The overall performance management process
Of necessity the process of performance management will be implemented somewhat differently in different situations, but it is important to highlight three features that appear to be common to the overall process. We might consider them to comprise a broad theory of the performance management process. While this approach tends to be normative or prescriptive in nature, many aspects of it have received strong research support. On the other hand, there is a pressing need to test its generalizability in non-Western cultures.

At a general level, therefore, performance management requires that managers responsible for implementation do three things well (Cascio, 1996, 2006): define performance, facilitate performance and encourage performance. The following sections explore each of these ideas briefly.

Define performance
A manager who defines performance ensures that individual employees or teams know what is expected of them, and that they stay focused on effective performance (Bernardin, Hagan, Kane & Villanova, 1998). How does the manager do this? By paying careful attention to three key elements: *goals, measures* and *assessment*.

Goal setting has a proven track record of success in improving performance in a variety of settings and cultures (Latham, 2004; Locke, 2004; Locke & Latham, 2002; Matsui, Kakuyama & Onglatco, 1987). How does it improve performance? Studies show that goals direct attention to the specific performance in question (for example, percentage of satisfied customers), they mobilize effort to accomplish higher levels of performance, and they foster persistence in achieving higher levels of performance (Latham, 2004; Tubbs, 1986). The practical implications of this work are clear: set specific, challenging goals, for this clarifies precisely what is expected and leads to high levels of performance (Knight, Durham &

Locke, 2001). Studies show that, on average, an individual can expect to improve his or her productivity by 10 per cent by using goal setting (Wood, Mento & Locke, 1987).

The mere presence of goals is not sufficient. Managers must also be able to measure the extent to which an employee has accomplished the goals that were set. Goals such as 'make the company successful' are too vague to be useful. Measures such as the number of defective parts produced per million or the average time to respond to a customer's inquiry are much more tangible. In the international context, goals might involve making customer contacts, establishing working relationships with union leaders and local government officials, community involvement, and improving the morale of the local workforce.

In defining performance, the third requirement is assessment. This is where performance appraisal and feedback come into play. Regular assessment of progress toward goals focuses the attention and efforts of an employee or a team. If a manager takes the time to identify measurable goals, but then fails to assess progress toward them, he or she is asking for trouble. As we saw in the survey of performance management practices cited earlier, more and more firms are assessing performance more than once a year. This is good practice, because it ensures that feedback will be provided in a timelier manner.

To define performance properly, therefore, it seems that those responsible for implementing performance management should do three things well: set goals, decide how to measure accomplishment, and provide regular assessments of progress (that is, evaluation and feedback). Doing so will leave no doubt in the minds of employees about what is expected of them, how it will be measured, and where they stand at any given point in time. There should be no surprises in the performance management process – and regular appraisals help ensure that there will not be.

Facilitate performance

Managers who are committed to managing for maximum performance recognize that one of their major responsibilities is to eliminate roadblocks to successful performance (Grensing-Pophal, 2001). Another is to provide adequate resources to get a job done right and on time, and a third is to pay careful attention to selecting employees.

Examples of obstacles that can inhibit maximum performance include lack of autonomy to accomplish important parts of one's job, outdated or poorly maintained equipment, delays in receiving supplies and ineffective work methods. In the international context, additional obstacles might include various types of government requirements (such as for permits, variances, inspections, reports), the need for representatives or intermediaries and, in dangerous or politically unstable areas, personal security. Employees are well aware of these obstacles; it is the manager's job to learn about them and to eliminate them.

The next step is to provide adequate resources: capital resources, material resources or human resources. After all, if employees lack the tools to meet the challenging goals they have set, they will become frustrated and disenchanted. Indeed one observer has gone so far as to say 'It's immoral not to give people tools to meet tough goals' (Sherman, 1995).

A final aspect of performance facilitation is the careful selection of employees. The costs of hiring people who are ill-suited to their jobs (for example, by temperament or training) are well known: overstaffing, excessive labour costs and reduced productivity. The topic of staffing for international assignments presents special challenges. We do not address them here because the whole of Part III of this Handbook addresses that issue.

At this point it is important to emphasize that, if organizations and individuals are truly committed to managing for maximum performance, they will address each factor that might affect performance and leave nothing to chance. That does not mean that managers are constantly monitoring the performance of their employees. On the contrary, it implies greater self-management, more autonomy, and opportunities to experiment, take risks and be entrepreneurial. In many domestic as well as international work environments, doing this is entirely appropriate.

Encourage performance
This is the last area of management responsibility in a coordinated approach to performance management. To encourage performance, especially repeated good performance, successful managers seem to do three more things well: (a) they provide sufficient rewards that employees value, (b) they do so in a timely fashion, and (c) they do so in a fair manner.

A simple approach is to ask people what is most important to them, for example pay, benefits, free time, merchandise or special privileges. Then a manager might consider tailoring a company-sanctioned awards programme so that employees or teams can choose from a menu of similarly valued options.

Next, the manager must provide rewards in a timely manner, soon after major accomplishments. For example, if an employee lands a major contract from a local government, or if another employee finds a way to complete an assigned project ahead of time and under budget, it is important to provide some type of recognition or reward reasonably soon after the accomplishment. If there is an excessive delay between effective performance and receipt of the reward, reinforcement theory tells us that the reward loses its potential to motivate subsequent high performance (Luthans, 2004).

Finally, rewards should be provided in a manner that employees consider fair. Fairness is a subjective concept, and it may be interpreted differently across cultures, but North American research suggests that fairness can be enhanced by adhering to four important practices (Gilliland & Langdon, 1998).

1. Voice – as long as it is appropriate in the culture in which one is operating, collect employee input through surveys or interviews.
2. Consistency – ensure that all employees are treated consistently when seeking input and communicating about the process for administering rewards.
3. Relevance – as noted earlier, include rewards that employees really care about.
4. Communication – explain clearly the rules and logic of the rewards process.

These practices might appear to be universally applicable, but we do not know that they are. There is a strong research need to identify their generalizability to countries and cultures outside of North America.

In summary, managing for maximum performance requires that managers do three things well: define performance, facilitate performance and encourage performance. Like a compass, the role of the manager is to provide orientation, direction and feedback.

Training for global performance management
In the survey cited earlier about the current status of global performance management systems, we noted that training for managers (55 per cent) and non-managers (28 per cent) has doubled in the past ten years, but that fewer than 40 per cent of firms hold managers accountable for the effectiveness of their organization's performance management system. Implementing a global performance management system without training all parties in the way to use it as designed is a waste of time and money. Training managers, but then not holding them accountable for implementing what they have been trained in, is just as bad. Almost no research has been carried out on training raters to use global performance management systems, or on the relative effectiveness of alternative approaches to such training. However there is much to learn from rater training in the domestic context.

Some key topics to address with respect to performance management training include the following (Pulakos, 2004):

● philosophy and uses of the system,
● description of the rating process,
● roles and responsibilities of employees and managers,

- how to define performance and to set expectations and goals,
- how to provide accurate assessments of performance, minimizing rating errors and rating inflation,
- the importance of continuing, constructive feedback in behavioural terms,
- how to give feedback in a manner that minimizes defensiveness and maintains the self-esteem of the receiver,
- how to react to and act on feedback in a constructive manner,
- how to seek feedback from others effectively,
- how to identify and address needs for training and development.

In terms of training raters to minimize rating errors (for example, central tendency, leniency, severity, halo) and to provide accurate ratings, a considerable amount of research has focused on helping raters to improve their observational skills by teaching them what to attend to, and how to develop common standards for evaluating behaviour.

Of the many types of rater training programmes available today, meta-analytic evidence has demonstrated reliably that frame of reference (FOR) training (Bernardin & Buckley, 1981) is most effective at improving the accuracy of performance appraisals (Woehr & Huffcut, 1994). Moreover the addition of other types of training in combination with FOR training does not seem to improve rating accuracy beyond the effects of FOR training alone (Noonan & Sulsky, 2001). Following procedures developed by Pulakos (1984, 1986), such FOR training proceeds as follows.

1. Participants are told that they will evaluate the performance of three ratees on three separate performance dimensions.
2. They are given rating scales and instructed to read them as the trainer reads the dimension definitions and scale anchors aloud.
3. The trainer then discusses ratee behaviours that illustrate different performance levels for each scale. The goal is to create a common performance theory (frame of reference) among raters such that they will agree on the appropriate performance dimension and effectiveness level for different behaviours.
4. Participants are shown a videotape of a practice vignette and are asked to evaluate the manager using the scales provided.
5. Ratings are then written on a blackboard and discussed by the group of participants. The trainer seeks to identify which behaviours participants used to decide on their assigned ratings, and to clarify any discrepancies among the ratings.
6. The trainer provides feedback to participants, explaining why the ratee should receive a certain rating (target score) on a given dimension.

FOR training provides trainees with a 'theory of performance' that allows them to understand the various performance dimensions, how to match these performance dimensions to rate behaviours, how to judge the effectiveness of various ratee behaviours, and how to integrate these judgments into an overall rating of performance (Sulsky & Day, 1992). In addition, the provision of rating standards and behavioural examples appears to be responsible for the improvements in rating accuracy. The use of target scores in performance examples and feedback on practice ratings allows raters to learn, through direct experience, how to use the different rating standards. In essence, the frame of reference training is a microcosm that includes an efficient model of the process by which standards for each performance dimension are acquired (Stamoulis & Hauenstein, 1993).

Nevertheless the approach described above assumes a single frame of reference for all raters. Research has shown that different sources of performance data (peers, supervisors, subordinates) demonstrate distinctly different frames of reference and that they disagree about the importance of incidents of poor performance (Hauenstein & Foti, 1989). These effects are likely to be magnified further in the international context, especially where diverse cultural backgrounds may lead to distinctly different frames of reference. Although this issue is extremely important, there is almost no research on it to date. Training should highlight these differences and focus both on the content of the raters' performance theories and on the process by which judgments are made (Schleicher & Day, 1998). Finally the training process should identify idiosyncratic raters so their performance in training can be monitored to assess improvement.

Rater training is clearly worth the effort, and the kind of approach advocated here is especially effective in improving the accuracy of ratings for individual ratees on separate performance dimensions (Day & Sulsky, 1995). In addition, trained managers are more effective in formulating development plans for their subordinates (Davis & Mount, 1984).

Once raters are trained, the next steps are to implement the performance management system and to provide feedback to ratees. This is a critically important process that must be managed well. It goes without saying that managers who are not held accountable for effective implementation of performance management (for example, by being rated themselves on the extent to which they effectively manage the performance of their subordinates) have no incentive to execute that part of their jobs well. Conversely we know that, when managers' own appraisals (and subsequent rewards) are on the line, they tend to take the process much more seriously (Lawler, 2003).

Cross-cultural differences and performance management systems
It is one thing to institute a performance management system with a home-country manager on an international assignment. It is quite another to do so with a local manager or local employees whose customs and culture differ from one's own. To put this issue into perspective, consider some brief comments about culture and its impact on people.

Triandis (1998) emphasizes that culture provides implicit theories of social behaviour that act like a 'computer program', controlling the actions of individuals. He notes that cultures include unstated assumptions, the way the world is. These assumptions influence thinking, emotions and actions without people noticing that they do. Members of cultures believe that their ways of thinking are obviously correct, and need not be discussed. Individuals and companies that seek to do business in countries outside their own ignore cross-cultural differences at their peril. To understand what cultural differences imply, consider one typology, the theory of vertical and horizontal individualism and collectivism.

Vertical and horizontal individualism and collectivism
Triandis (1998) notes that vertical cultures accept hierarchy as a given, whereas horizontal cultures accept equality as a given. Individualistic cultures emerge in societies that are complex (many subgroups with different attitudes and beliefs) and loose (relatively few rules and norms about what is correct behaviour in different types of situations). Collectivism emerges in societies that are simple (individuals agree on beliefs and attitudes) and tight (many rules and norms about what is correct behaviour in different types of situations).

Triandis argues that these syndromes (shared patterns of attitudes, beliefs and norms, and values organized around a theme) constitute the parameters of any general theory about the way culture influences people. Crossing the cultural syndromes of individualism and collectivism with the cultural syndromes of vertical and horizontal relationships yields a typology of four kinds of cultures. Additional culture-specific attributes define different kinds of individualism or collectivism. According to Triandis, the following four may be the universal dimensions of these constructs.

1. *Definition of the self* – autonomous and independent from groups (individualists), versus interdependent with others (collectivists).
2. *Structure of goals* – priority given to personal goals (individualists), versus priority given to in-group goals (collectivists).
3. *Emphasis on norms versus attitudes* – attitudes, personal needs, perceived rights and contracts determine social behaviour (individualists),

versus norms, duties and obligations as determinants of social behaviour (collectivists).

4. *Emphasis on relatedness versus rationality* – collectivists emphasize relatedness (giving priority to relationships and taking into account the needs of others), whereas individualists emphasize rationality (careful computation of the costs and benefits of relationships).

Culture determines the uniqueness of a human group in the same way that personality determines the uniqueness of an individual (Hofstede, 2001). There are many implications and patterns of variation of these important differences with respect to performance management. Two of them are goal setting and reward systems (individual versus team-wide or organization-wide) and communications (gestures, eye contact and body language in high-context cultures, versus precision with words in low-context cultures). These differences suggest propositions such as the following:

Hypothesis 1: Managers in individualistic and collectivist cultures will ascribe the causes of poor performance to different factors.

Hypothesis 2: Individual goals and individual rewards will be preferred in individualistic cultures. Team or organization-wide goals and rewards will be preferred in collectivist cultures.

With respect to performance feedback, characteristics of the culture, vertical/horizontal or individual/collectivist, interact with the objectives, style, frequency and inherent assumptions of the performance-feedback process. This suggests propositions such as the following:

Hypothesis 3: Participation in the performance management and feedback process is more common in horizontal/individualistic cultures than in vertical/collectivist cultures.

Hypothesis 4: There will be no differences in the frequency of performance feedback between individualistic and collectivist cultures, but substantial differences in the manner in which it is delivered.

We will have more to say about this issue in a later section, but the point is that, when providing feedback, it is critically important to respect local culture and customs. Failure to do so can lead to unintended consequences. With respect to assessment practices, different cultures prefer different approaches, and there is the possibility of variation in validity across cultures. This is an underresearched issue that could benefit handsomely from some systematic attention. As just one example, consider the following propositions about self-appraisals, keeping in mind that in some cultures (such as India) disagreeing with one's supervisor is viewed as disrespectful and inappropriate:

Hypothesis 5: Self-appraisals are used more frequently in Western than in Eastern cultures.

Hypothesis 6: The validity of self-appraisals is significantly lower in Eastern than in Western cultures.

Having discussed the broad process of performance management, and the need to tailor it to the customs and culture of the country or region in question, the next step is to identify relevant, important measures of performance. As we shall see, the 'criterion problem' is particularly thorny in the international environment.

Cross-cultural differences in performance feedback

A formal system for delivering performance feedback should be implemented because in the absence of such a system some employees are more likely to seek and benefit from feedback than are others. For example, consider the relationship between stereotype threat (that is, a fear of confirming a negative stereotype about one's group through one's one behaviour; see Farr, 2003) and the willingness to seek feedback.

A study that included 166 African American managers in utilities industries found that solo status in the workplace was related to stereotype threat and stereotype threat was negatively related to feedback seeking (Roberson, Deitch, Brief & Block, 2003). Thus, if no formal performance feedback system is in place, it is likely that employees who do not perceive a stereotype threat will be more likely to seek feedback from their supervisors and benefit from it. This, combined with the fact that people generally are apprehensive about both receiving and giving performance information, reinforces the notion that the implementation of formal performance feedback systems is necessary (London, 2003). On the other hand, it is important to respect the customs of the culture in question, particularly when providing performance feedback to host-country nationals.

Ideally a continuous feedback process should exist between superior and subordinate so that both may be guided. In individualistic cultures, such as the United States, Great Britain and Australia, a popular topic in first-level supervisory training programmes is how to conduct appraisal interviews. Indeed the ability to conduct performance appraisal interviews well and the ability to communicate 'bad news' are considered key skills for a successful manager in such cultures.

By contrast, in collectivist societies, such as Korea, Guatemala and Taiwan, discussing a person's performance openly with him or her is likely to clash head-on with the society's norm of harmony, and the subordinate may view it as an unacceptable loss of face. Such societies have more subtle, indirect ways of communicating feedback, as by withdrawing a normal favour or communicating concerns verbally via a mutually trusted inter-mediary (Hofstede, 2001).

The point is that it is crucial to be sensitive to local customs with respect to the process used to communicate feedback. Understanding those local customs, and mapping them across countries, is a continuing challenge for researchers interested in global performance management systems. As with domestic assignments, however, regular coaching and feedback are hall-marks of effective performance management systems, even though they may be expressed very differently in different parts of the world.

Table 10.1 illustrates some important differences in performance appraisal practices in three different cultures: Western culture (the United States), a Middle Eastern culture (Saudi Arabia) and a Far Eastern culture (Korea). Note the dramatic differences across these three cultures in every dimension listed in the left column of the table. Those responsible for implementing performance management systems ignore them at their peril.

Performance management for host-country nationals
Consider four broad constraints on the achievement of goals in the inter-national context (Dowling & Welch, 2005). First, differences in local accounting rules or labour laws, may make it difficult to compare the rela-tive performance of host-country managers of subsidiaries in different countries. Second, in turbulent international environments, long-term objectives need to be flexible. Third, separation by time and distance may make it difficult for performance management systems to take account of country-specific factors. Fourth, market development in foreign sub-sidiaries is generally slower and more difficult than at home. Hence host-country managers of MNEs need more time to achieve results.

Unfortunately, aside from anecdotal evidence, very little systematic research has been published on the performance effects of alternative approaches to performance management in different countries or on employee attitudes of host-country nationals toward these systems. In add-ition, psychological theories of motivation and performance (such as expectancy, equity and reinforcement theories) were developed in Western societies (principally North American) and much of the research that tests their theoretical propositions has been conducted in Western (that is, North American) settings. The fact is, we know very little about the extent to which the predictions of such theories will generalize to non-Western set-tings. Nor do we know very much about the relative effectiveness of glob-ally standardized performance management systems that some MNEs use.

We know that concepts such as individual rewards for individual perfor-mance, and making explicit distinctions in performance among employees are not universally accepted. Indeed, where the prevailing view is that it

Table 10.1 Some characteristics of performance appraisal systems in the USA, Saudi Arabia and Korea

Issue	United States	Saudi Arabia	Korea
Objective	Administrative decisions, employee development	Placement	Develop relationship between supervisor and employee
Done by?	Supervisor	Manager several layers up who knows employee well	Mentor and supervisor
Authority of appraiser?	Presumed in supervisor role	Reputation (prestige determined by nationality, age, sex, family, tribe, title, education)	Long tenure of supervisor with organization
Style	Supervisor takes the lead, with employee input	Authority of appraiser is important; never say 'I don't know'	Supervisor takes the lead, with informal employee input
Frequency	Usually yearly	Yearly	Developmental appraisal monthly for first year, annually thereafter
Assumptions	Objective: appraiser is fair	Subjective appraisal is more important than objective; connections are important	Subjective appraisal is more important than objective; no formal criteria
Feedback	Criticisms are direct; may be in writing	Criticisms more subtle; not likely to be in writing	Criticisms subtle and indirect; may be given verbally
Employee acknowledgement and possible rebuttal	Employee acknowledges receipt; may rebut in writing	Employee acknowledges receipt; may rebut verbally	Employee does not see or sign formal appraisal; would rarely rebut
How praised	Individually	Individually	Entire group
Motivators	Money, upward mobility, career development	Loyalty to supervisor	Money, promotion, loyalty to supervisor

Source: W. F. Cascio & E. Bailey. 1995. International HRM: the state of research and practice (p. 29). In O. Shenkar (ed.), *Global perspectives of human resource management*. Englewood Cliffs, NJ: Prentice-Hall.

takes contributions from everyone to achieve continuous improvement (that is, the concept of 'kaizen' in Japanese enterprises), the practice of singling out one employee's contribution may actually cause that employee to 'lose face' among his or her fellow workgroup members. In other cultures where nepotism is common and extended family members work together, the primary objective is to preserve working relationships. That objective may cause host-country managers to overlook results that more objective observers might judge to be inadequate. Situations like these should provide clues about relevant hypotheses that might shed light on the generalizability of widely accepted Western theories of motivation and performance. This leads to propositions such as the following.

Hypothesis 7: The fundamental objective of performance management, that is, improving performance versus preserving a relationship, differs in individualistic and collectivist cultures.

Hypothesis 8: Motivation to perform well is based on upward striving and monetary rewards in Western cultures, but on the desire to show loyalty and to improve the relationship with one's supervisor in Eastern cultures.

At a more basic level, we need both descriptive and inferential (theory-testing) studies about performance management practices in, for example, French enterprises, German enterprises, Russian enterprises, in Chinese, Vietnamese and Thai enterprises, and so forth. In fact there is almost no published empirical research on the relative effectiveness of alternative performance management practices for host-country nationals across subsidiaries in the many countries in which MNEs operate.

Throughout this chapter we have emphasized the impact of culture on performance management systems, yet this is but one possible approach to comparative studies of performance management systems across countries. Another useful theoretical framework is institutional theory, which has been applied to the study of human resource management practices in MNE subsidiaries (Björkman & Lu, 2001), but might also be used to provide a deeper understanding of country-specific performance management systems.

Performance management for expatriates
A number of factors affect the actual level of job performance of expatriate managers (Davis, 1998; Oddou & Mendenhall, 2000). These include technical knowledge (95 per cent of expatriates believe it to be crucial for job success), personal (and family) adjustment to the culture, and environmental factors (political and labour force stability, currency fluctuations and cultural distance from one's home culture). While technical knowledge is important, the expatriate who is an expert in his or her field, but who ignores cultural variables such as procedures and customs that are import-

ant to job performance, will likely be ineffective. This was the case with an expatriate of a construction firm who was sent to India. Unintentionally he ignored local work customs and became an object of hatred and distrust. The project was delayed by more than six months because of his behaviour (Oddou & Mendenhall, 2000).

The degree of support from headquarters (benefits and services, including job-search help for the spouse and financial support for his or her children's education) also affects an expatriate's job performance. Finally characteristics of the host-country environment have a powerful impact – its stage of economic development, its physical demands on the expatriate (heat, humidity, cold) and the type of business operation (for example, international joint venture versus wholly owned subsidiary).

Measures of performance (criteria) for expatriates
What indicators should organizations use to assess the performance of international assignees? Perhaps the biggest mistake is simply to use whatever makes sense in the domestic environment in all other countries in which a multinational enterprise (MNE) operates. As Briscoe and Schuler (2004) noted:

> MNEs cannot simply use standard appraisal criteria – developed in the domestic context – overseas and expect valid results. External factors usually influence the financial and operational results much more so in the overseas environment than they do domestically. Items like severe inflation, currency devaluations, local leave and holiday requirements, and thirteenth-month pay norms just are not issues in the domestic context for many MNEs. Thus MNEs need to construct criteria for evaluation according to each subsidiary's unique situation (Ibid.: 356).

A thorough review of research in this area led Sinangil and Ones (2001) to propose the following working model of the dimensions of expatriate job performance.

- Establishment and maintenance of business contacts – identification, development and use of such contacts to achieve goals.
- Technical performance, that is, task performance.
- Productivity: volume of work the expatriate produces.
- Ability to work with others: proficiency in working with and assisting others in the organization.
- Communication and persuasion – oral and written proficiency in gathering and transmitting information; persuading others.
- Effort and initiative: dedication to one's job, amount of effort expended in striving to do a good job.

- Personal discipline: avoidance of counterproductive behaviours at work.
- Interpersonal relations – the degree to which the expatriate facilitates team performance and supports others in the organization and unit.
- Management and supervision – proficiency in the coordination of different roles in the organization.
- Overall job performance: composite of all dimensions of expatriate job performance described above.

While this list is valuable, we know very little about the extent to which the various factors actually are measured when assessing expatriate job performance. To some extent, this may be a function of the stage of globalization of a given organization. Thus:

Hypothesis 9: Organizations with well-established international operations are more likely to assess factors in addition to technical proficiency and productivity indicators. Newly established international operations are more likely to focus exclusively on an expatriate's technical performance and productivity.

The list above reflects intangibles that are often difficult to measure (and usually are not measured) using typical performance appraisal methods. It also suggests that performance criteria for expatriates fall into three broad categories (Davis, 1998; Dowling & Welch, 2005): objective criteria, subjective criteria and contextual criteria.

Objective criteria include such measures as gross revenues, market share and return on investment. There are several potential problems with such measures. First, all financial figures are generally subject to the problem of currency conversion, and currency fluctuations may make accurate assessment of financial contribution difficult. Second, host governments may place restrictions on the repatriation of profits and also on currency conversion. Third, financial measures ignore the ways that results are obtained. That is, they ignore the behaviours used to generate the results. Especially when political or work environments are unstable (for example with frequent strikes), such behaviours are critical. These shortcomings suggest that additional criteria should be used to provide a deeper, fuller understanding of expatriate performance. Such criteria include subjective and contextual criteria. As we saw earlier in our examination of the current status of global performance management systems, most organizations use a combination of objective and subjective criteria.

Subjective criteria include judgments, usually by local executives, of factors such as the expatriate's leadership style and interpersonal skills. While local management tends to appraise the expatriate's performance from its own cultural frame of reference, such an evaluation is usually perceived as more accurate than that from the home office (Oddou & Mendenhall, 2000). Janssens (1994) suggests that performance appraisals of managers of subsidiaries using objective criteria are often supplemented by frequent visits by staff from headquarters and meetings with executives from the parent company. Subjective criteria can be used to complement objective criteria and take into account areas that are difficult to quantify, such as integrity, customer orientation and teamwork.

Contextual criteria take into consideration factors that result from the situation in which performance occurs. They include organizational citizenship behaviours (helping and cooperating with others, working with enthusiasm, volunteering for activities, being flexible and open to change) as well as indicators of cross-cultural skill development (for example, language, host culture, communication, networking) (Davis, 1998).

Who should do expatriate appraisals?
Earlier we noted that host-country managers can take contextual criteria into account in assessing an expatriate's job performance, but they may have culture-bound biases that prevent them from putting the expatriate's performance into a broader organizational context. The reverse is true of home-country managers. They may not be able to take contextual criteria into account, but they can put the expatriate's performance into a broader organizational context. What about the expatriate's self-evaluation? It is important to take his or her insights into account in order to provide a balanced perspective and to give him or her credit for relevant insights into the interdependencies among domestic and foreign operations. This suggests the following proposition:

Hypothesis 10: The greater the 'cultural distance' between home and host country, the more likely it is that multiple raters will be used to provide feedback about an expatriate's job performance.

Conclusions
The terrain of global performance management systems is largely uncharted. Research needs span every facet of the overall process. Specifically we need cross-cultural, comparative research on how managers define work and set expectations, how they facilitate performance (including identification of the barriers to effective performance that they encounter) and how content, frequency and administration rewards differ.

With respect to procedural fairness, although we know that it matters across cultures, we know little about the ways in which the constructs of employee voice, relevance, consistency and communication of perceptions of procedural fairness are expressed across cultures. Nor do we understand the relative contributions of these facets to perceptions of procedural fairness.

While there are anecdotal accounts of contextual variables that influence performance, it would be valuable to understand the determinants of expatriate and host-country national performance in terms of the relative contributions of objective, subjective and contextual criteria. Then we could begin to assign meaningful weights to the various components of performance in different contexts.

Finally, although commentators identify training in performance management as a sound practice, we know almost nothing about the behavioural outcomes or utility of such training. Likewise we know little about the relative payoff of culturally appropriate performance feedback. As should be obvious from this brief review of research needs, the overall domain of global performance management systems is rich with promise, along with the possibility of making meaningful contributions to the practice of international management.

References

Bernardin, H.J. & M.R. Buckley. 1981. A consideration of strategies in rater training. *Academy of Management Review*, **6**: 205–12.

Bernardin, H.J., C.M. Hagan, J.S. Kane & P. Villanova. 1998. Effective performance management. In J.W. Smither (ed.), *Performance appraisal: state of the art in practice*: 3–48. San Francisco, CA: Jossey-Bass.

Bernthal, P.R., R.W. Rogers & A.B. Smith. 2003. *Managing performance: building accountability for organizational success*. Pittsburgh, PA: Development Dimensions International, Inc.

Björkman, I. & Y. Lu. 2001. Institutionalization and bargaining power explanations of human resource management practices in international joint ventures – the case of Chinese–Western joint ventures. *Organization Studies*, **22**: 491–512.

Borman, W.C. & S.J. Motowidlo. 1993. Expanding the criterion domain to include elements of contextual performance. In N. Schmitt, W. Borman & Associates, *Personnel selection in organizations*: 71–98. San Francisco, CA: Jossey-Bass.

Briscoe, D.R. & R.S. Schuler. 2004. *International human resource management*. Second edition. London: Routledge.

Campbell, J.P., M.B. Gasser & F.L. Oswald. 1996. The substantive nature of job performance variability. In K.R. Murphy (ed.), *Individual differences and behavior in organizations*: 258–99. San Francisco, CA: Jossey-Bass.

Campbell, J.P., R.A. McCloy, S.H. Oppler & C.E. Sager. 1993. A theory of performance. In N. Schmitt, W. Borman & Associates, *Personnel selection in organizations*: 35–70. San Francisco, CA: Jossey-Bass.

Cascio, W.F. 1996. Managing for maximum performance. *HR Monthly* (Australia), September, 10–13.

Cascio, W.F. 2006. *Managing human resources: productivity, quality of work life, profits*. Seventh edition. Burr Ridge, IL: McGraw-Hill-Irwin.

Cascio, W.F. & S. Shurygailo. 2003. E-leadership in virtual teams. *Organizational dynamics*, **31**: 362–75.

Davis, B.L. & M.K. Mount. 1984. Effectiveness of performance appraisal training using computer-assisted instruction and behavior modeling. *Personnel Psychology*, **37**: 439–52.

Davis, D.D. 1998. International performance measurement and management. In J.W. Smither (ed.), *Performance appraisal: state of the art in practice*: 95–131. San Francisco, CA: Jossey-Bass.

Day, D.V. & L.M. Sulsky. 1995. Effects of frame-of-reference training and information con-figuration on memory organization and rating accuracy. *Journal of Applied Psychology*, **80**: 158–67.

Dowling, P.J. & D.E. Welch. 2005. *International human resource management: managing people in a multinational context*. Fourth edition. Cincinnati, OH: South-Western.

Farr, J.L. 2003. Introduction to the special issue: stereotype threat effects in employment set-tings. *Human Performance*, **16**: 179–80.

Gilliland, S.W. & J.C. Langdon. 1998. Creating performance management systems that promote perceptions of fairness. In J.W. Smither (ed.), *Performance appraisal: state of the art in practice*: 209–43. San Francisco, CA: Jossey-Bass.

Grensing-Pophal, L. 2001. Motivate managers to review performance. *HR Magazine*, March, 44–8.

Hauenstein, N.M. & R.J. Foti. 1989. From laboratory to practice: neglected issues in imple-menting frame-of-reference rater training. *Personnel Psychology*, **42**: 359–78.

Hofstede, G. 2001. *Culture's consequences: Comparing values, behaviors, institutions, and organizations across nations*. Second edition. Thousand Oaks, CA: Sage.

Janssens, M. 1994. Evaluating international managers' performance: parent country stan-dards as control mechanisms. *International Journal of Human Resource Management*, **5**: 853–73.

Knight, D., C.C. Durham & E.A. Locke. 2001. The relationship of team goals, incentives, and efficacy to strategic risk, tactical implementation, and performance. *Academy of Management Journal*, **44**: 326–38.

Latham, G.P. 2004. The motivational benefits of goal setting. *Academy of Management Executive*, **18**(4): 126–9.

Lawler, E.E. 2003. Reward practices and performance management system effectiveness. *Organizational Dynamics*, **32**(4): 396–404.

Locke, E.A. 2004. Linking goals to monetary incentives. *Academy of Management Executive*, **18**(4): 130–33.

Locke, E.A. & G.P. Latham. 2002. Building a practically useful theory of goal setting and task motivation. *American Psychologist*, **57**: 705–17.

London, M. 2003. *Job feedback: giving, seeking, and using feedback for performance improve-ment*. Second edition. Mahwah, NJ: Lawrence Erlbaum.

Luthans, F. 2004. *Organizational behavior*. Tenth edition. Burr Ridge, IL: McGraw-Hill-Irwin.

Matsui, T., T. Kakuyama & M.L.T. Onglatco. 1987. Effects of goals and feedback on perform-ance in groups. *Journal of Applied Psychology*, **72**: 407–15.

Noonan, L.E. & L.M. Sulsky. 2001. Impact of frame-of-reference and behavioral observation training on alternative training effectiveness criteria in a Canadian military sample. *Human Performance*, **14**: 3–26.

Oddou, G. & M.E. Mendenhall. 2000. Expatriate performance appraisal: problems and solu-tions. In M.E. Mendenhall & G. Oddou (eds), *Readings and cases in international human resource management*: 213–23. Third edition. Cincinnati, OH: South-Western.

Pulakos, E.D. 1984. A comparison of rater training programs: error training and accuracy training. *Journal of Applied Psychology*, **69**: 581–8.

Pulakos, E.D. 1986. The development of training programs to increase accuracy with different rating tasks. *Organizational Behavior and Human Decision Processes*, **38**: 76–91.

Pulakos, E.D. 2004. Research and practice-based guidelines for effective performance management. Alexandria, VA: Society for Human Resource Management Foundation.

Roberson, L., E.A. Deitch, A.P. Brief & C.J. Block. 2003. Stereotype threat and feedback seeking in the workplace. *Journal of Vocational Behavior*, **62**: 176–88.

Schleicher, D.J. & D.V. Day. 1998. A cognitive evaluation of frame-of-reference rater training: content and process issues. *Organizational Behavior and Human Decision Processes*, **73**: 76–101.

Sherman, S. 1995. Stretch goals: the dark side of asking for miracles. *Fortune*, 13 November, **132**(10): 231–2.

Stamoulis, D.T. & N.M. Hauenstein. 1993. Rater training and rating accuracy: training for dimensional accuracy versus training for ratee differentiation. *Journal of Applied Psychology*, **78**: 994–1003.

Sulsky, L.M. & D.V. Day. 1992. Frame-of-reference training and cognitive categorization: an empirical investigation of rater memory issues. *Journal of Applied Psychology*, **77**: 501–10.

Triandis, H.C. 1998. Vertical and horizontal individualism and collectivism: theory and research implications for international comparative management. In J.L. Cheng & R.B. Peterson (eds), *Advances in international and comparative management*: 7–35. Greenwich, CT: JAI Press.

Tubbs, M.E. 1986. Goal setting: a meta-analytic examination of the empirical evidence. *Journal of Applied Psychology*, **71**: 474–83.

Woehr, D.J. & A.I. Huffcut. 1994. Rater training for performance appraisal: a quantitative review. *Journal of Occupational and Organizational Psychology*, **67**: 189–205.

Wood, R.E., A.J. Mento & E.A. Locke. 1987. Task complexity as a moderator of goal effects: a meta-analysis. *Journal of Applied Psychology*, **72**: 416–25.

11 Developing global leadership capabilities and global mindset: a review

Joyce S. Osland, Allan Bird, Mark Mendenhall and Asbjorn Osland

What makes global leaders like Carlos Ghosn (President of Nissan Motors, Ltd and *Automotive News'* 2000 Industry Leader of the Year) tick? Born in Brazil and educated in France, Ghosn served seven years as head of Michelin in the United States and three years with Renault before becoming President and CEO of Nissan. He is responsible for Nissan's renowned turnaround effort and cross-border alliance with Renault.

Although cultural differences exacted a toll on other cross-border automotive alliances, such as Daimler-Chrysler, Ghosn sees them as opportunities. 'When you have taken the time to understand [that people don't think or act the same way] . . . and when you are really motivated and mobilized by a very strong objective, then the cultural differences can become seeds for innovation as opposed to seeds for dissention' (Emerson, 2001: 6). Ghosn contends that Europeans cannot call themselves 'international' after working in Italy, Germany or France: 'you have to go to countries that have a totally different way of thinking, a totally different way of organization, and a totally different way of life' (ibid.: 7).

With the rise of globalization, managers like Carlos Ghosn face complex challenges of leadership on a global scale. The nature of these challenges appears to be qualitatively different from those faced by international managers in the past. Consequently, there is a need to better understand what is required of these managers (Suutari, 2002) and to identify the mindset and personal qualities essential to effective global leadership.

The context of leading globally is complex and fraught with disorienting challenges. The term 'global' encompasses more than simple *geographic reach* in terms of business operations. It also includes the notion of *cultural reach* in terms of people and *intellectual reach* in the development of a global mindset. Lane and associates identify four aspects of the global context that combine to create significant challenges for global leaders (Lane, Maznevski, Mendenhall & McNett, 2004):

- *multiplicity* across a range of dimensions;
- *interdependence* among a host of stakeholders, sociocultural, political, economic and environmental systems;
- *ambiguity* in terms of understanding causal relationships, interpreting cues and signals, identifying appropriate actions and pursuing plausible goals;
- *flux* in terms of quickly transitioning systems, shifting values and emergent patterns of organizational structure and behaviour.

The authors maintain that the complexity of the global context can be addressed through attention to managing the following four processes (Lane *et al.*, 2004).

- *Collaborating*: working with others in relationships characterized by community, flexibility, respect, trust and mutual accountability.
- *Discovering*: transformational processes leading to new ways of seeing and acting which, in turn, lead to the creation of new knowledge, actions and things.
- *Architecting*: the mindful design of processes that align, balance and synchronize organizational behaviour.
- *Systems thinking*: seeing and/or discovering the interrelationship among components and levels in a complex system and anticipating consequences of changes in and to the system.

Rosen and associates (Rosen, Digh, Singer & Philips, 2000) took a different approach in delineating the context in which global leadership takes place. They sketched the specifics of globalization forces by identifying a host of worldwide trends that affect how multinational corporations operate and how global managers lead. On the economic front, they argued that international mega-mergers, the rise of regional economic powers, continued privatization of government-owned corporations, the expanding economic integration of Europe and China's growing economy and markets created new competitors and new consumers. On the social front, Rosen and associates pointed to increases in concern over the loss of national identities, increasing conflicts between the 'haves' and the 'have nots', ethnic strife, fundamentalist Islamic terrorists, a growing backlash against American influence and culture, significant demographic shifts due to rapidly aging populations in some countries, AIDS-devastated populations in some regions of the world, and escalating concerns about environmental degradation.

Within this context, corporate global leaders are often asked to accomplish near-Herculean tasks. To aid them, HR departments, consultants, coaches, researchers and universities are attempting to define the parameters of global leadership and global mindset and determine how they can be developed in both individuals and organizations. Suutari's (2002) literature review concludes that developing global competence in leaders is acknowledged as a need and a high priority for firms. For example, a US Fortune 500 survey found that 85 per cent of the firms did not have an adequate number of global leaders, and 67 per cent of existing leaders needed additional global skills and knowledge (Gregersen, Morrison & Black, 1998). Furthermore the adoption of a global mindset has been viewed as a prerequisite to effectively managing transnational corporations (Bartlett & Ghoshal, 1992; Ohmae, 1989; Doz & Prahalad, 1991).

In order to gain a better awareness of the contributions of academe to the understanding of these pressing issues, we next summarize and identify general problems in the literature, and raise questions and suggestions to guide future research. Subsequently we review literature on the development of global leadership and mindset and propose a non-linear framework to describe the process of global leadership development. The chapter ends with implications for future research on developmental activities for both individuals and firms.

Literature review of global mindset
How well individuals and firms observe and interpret the complex environment described in the introduction determines their success (Gupta & Govindarajan, 2002). Given Ashby's (1956) law of requisite variety, a complex global environment should be matched by internal complexity in the form of 'managerial mindset' (Boyacigiller, Beechler, Taylor & Levy, 2004). Bartlett and Ghoshal (1989) claimed that mindset was more important than sophisticated structures and procedures. In this vein, for instance, the mindset of the chief executive is perceived as critical to a company's strategy (Paul, 2000). Rhinesmith (1993: 24) defines mindset as

> a way of being rather than a set of skills. It is an orientation of the world that allows one to see certain things that others do not. A global mindset means the ability to scan the world from a broad perspective, always looking for unexpected trends and opportunities that may constitute a threat or an opportunity to achieve personal, professional or organizational objectives.

Maznevski and Lane (2004: 172) draw attention to the contextual application of Rhinesmith's 'orientation to the world' when they define global mindset as

> the ability to develop and interpret criteria for personal and business performance that are independent from the assumptions of a single country, culture, or

context; and to implement those criteria appropriately in different countries, cultures, and contexts.

The concept of global mindset first appeared in Perlmutter's (1969) taxonomy of ethnocentric (home country mindset), polycentric (host country mindset) and geocentric (world mindset) MNCs. Bartlett and Ghoshal (1989) expanded geocentrism, calling it the 'transnational' mindset. In the last decade, numerous articles have been published on global mindset (Begley & Boyd, 2003; Gupta & Govindarajan, 2002; Jeannet, 2000; Kedia & Mukherji, 1999; Kefalas, 1998; Maznevski & Lane, 2004; Paul, 2000; Rhinesmith, 1992, 1993; Srinivas, 1995) that are based either on consultants' experiences or on academics' conceptualizations. Global mindset is assumed to correlate with strategic success in MNCs (Bartlett & Ghoshal, 1992; Ohmae, 1989; Doz & Prahalad, 1991), but there are few empirical studies on the topic (see Table 11.1).

There is also little agreement on how to define, measure or develop global mindset (Bouquet, Morrison & Birkinshaw, 2003). As a result, scholars have operationalized global mindset in a variety of different ways. For example, cognitive complexity (Wills & Barham, 1994); cognitive maps of CEOs (Calori, Johnson & Sarnin, 1994), the international experience of top managers (Sambharya, 1996), judgments about international HR policies (Kobrin, 1994), cognitive orientation of top management teams (Levy, 2001), top management team (TMT) behaviour (Bouquet *et al.*, 2003), global orientation in managers (Nummela, Saarenketo & Puumalainen, 2004) and top management team global orientation (Beechler, Levy, Taylor & Boyacigiller, 2004).

The dependent variables in these studies are measures of global strategy or performance, such as internationalization or international sales. Several studies prove that global mindset correlates with greater international scope (Calof & Beamish, 1994; Kobrin, 1994; Sambharya, 1996; Nummela *et al.*, 2004), global strategic posture (Levy, 2001) and international financial performance (Nummela *et al.*, 2004). In contrast, one study discovered that too much top management team attention to global issues (the authors' operationalization of global mindset) was as harmful to performance as too little attention (Bouquet *et al.*, 2003). Global mindset also correlated with two internal measures: higher employee commitment and excitement about their job (Beechler *et al.*, 2004). Owing to the nature of their design, most of these studies cannot settle the question of causality. Murtha, Lenway and Bagozzi (1998) found that global mindset increased during the implementation of a new global strategy. Some findings suggest that global mindset may follow strategy rather than the general assumption that strategy follows mindset

Table 11.1   A chronological list of empirical research on global mindset

Authors	Operationalization of global mindset	Method	Findings
Wills & Barham (1994)	Cognitive complexity	Interviews with 60 successful international managers in global organizations	Successful international managers were characterized by cognitive complexity, emotional energy and psychological maturity, in addition to learned behaviours and skills
Calof & Beamish (1994)	Global mindset defined as geocentric	Surveys of 38 Canadian firms	Firms that characterized themselves as geocentric, rather than ethnocentric or polycentric, reported greater international sales and export intensity
Kobrin (1994)	International HR policies as indicators of geocentrism	Survey with geo-centrism index on international HR policies administered to 68 US manufacturing firms	Geocentric mindset is related to geographic scope of firm, but not to global strategy
Calori, Johnson & Sarnin (1994)	Cognitive complexity of CEOs defined as number of constructs and density of links between constructs	Sample of 26 French and British firms in four industries	CEOs of international firms have more complex maps of their industry than other CEOs. Cognitive complexity of the CEOs correlates with the geographic scope of the firm and interorganizational links, generally supporting 'requisite variety'
Sambharya (1996)	Cognitive state of the top management team as measured by their international work experience	Sample of 54 US manufacturing firms	International experience of top management team correlates with international diversification
Murtha, Lenway & Bagozzi (1998)	'Cognitive processes that balance competing country, business functional concerns' in managers	Longitudinal survey administered to 370 managers in 13 country and affiliates and US head office of an MNC	The change to a global strategy resulted in a cognitive shift toward increased global mindset across all managers

Table 11.1   (continued)

Authors	Operationalization of global mindset	Method	Findings
Levy (2001)	'Cosmopolitanism and cognitive diversity' in top management teams	Content analysis of letters to shareholders of 69 US-based tech firms	Global mindset in top management was linked to a global strategic posture
Bouquet, Morrison & Birkinshaw (2003)	Top management team behaviours: global scanning, CEO foreign travel, communication with overseas managers and discussions of globalization decisions	Questionnaires sent to 136 CEOs or presidents of MNCs	Global mindset is best explained by micro-level attention structures. Too little or too much attention to global issues decrease firm performance
Nummela, Saarenketo & Puumalainen (2004)	Global orientation attitude and international entrepreneurial behaviours	Web-based survey of 72 small Finnish information & communications technology companies	Managers' international work experience correlates with global mindset, as does the globalness of their market. Global mindset correlates with international financial performance
Beechler, Levy, Taylor & Boyacigiller (2004)	Global orientation of top management team	Surveys of 521 employees working in five countries for two Japanese MNCs	Employee perceptions of top management team's global orientation positively affected employee commitment and excitement about jobs

(Levy *et al.*, 1999). More research is needed to specify the contingencies that influence causality.

After reviewing how it has been used in the literature, Levy and her colleagues (1999) have attempted to define the global mindset construct. They reached the following conclusion: global mindset is a cognitive structure composed of two constructs, cosmopolitanism (an enthusiastic appreciation of other cultures) (Merton, 1957; Hannerz, 1996) and cognitive complexity (the ability to perceive situations as highly differentiated and to integrate these differentiated constructs) (Weick, 1979; Bartunek, Gordon & Weathersby, 1983). It remains to be seen whether or not this will be accepted as the standard definition of global mindset.

Problems with the global mindset research literature can be summarized in terms of three deficiencies. First, at present there is no generally accepted definition of the construct, and it has been operationalized in numerous ways. Second, some studies use international work experience as a surrogate measure, but not all international assignments have the same result, since some expatriates buffer themselves from the host culture and come home relatively unchanged without modifying their attitudes or world view. Third, the global mindset research has focused on various levels of analysis: individual managers and CEOs, top management teams, and firms as a whole. Is global mindset in individuals the same construct as it is for firms? Are there different types of global mindsets in firms with different strategies or in different industries depending on varying levels of required global/cultural knowledge and involvement?

Significant further effort is called for in addressing the following aspects of global mindset (GM) research.

- Further construct development or acceptance of the Levy *et al.* definition.
- Identification of different types of global mindset, perhaps at different levels of analysis.
- Creation and validation of a GM assessment instrument.
- Measurement of the impact of GM on performance outcomes.
- Identification of GM antecedents and clarification of causality.
- Determination of whether or to what extent GM can be developed in people.
- Identification of threshold personality characteristics, which can be used as selection criteria, that identify GM or facilitate its development.
- Identification of the cognitive processes related to GM.
- Identification of organizational and team contingencies related to GM.
- Exploration of different forms of GM and their relationship to global strategies or industries.
- Identification of GM capability in both teams and organizations.
- Development of GM process models that include interaction with the environment.
- Antecedents of GM effectiveness.
- Delineation of the relationship between GM capability and organizational culture.
- Determination of what constitutes an adequate level of GM capability for organizational effectiveness.
- Outcomes of GM development training methodologies.

Literature review of global leadership
Within the field of management science, the construct of global leadership was born out of the needs of corporations in the 1990s to adopt global strategies, expand internationally and compete in the global marketplace (Mendenhall & Osland, 2002; Von Glinow, 2001). Corporations realized that people with global capabilities were required to develop and implement their new strategic initiatives and, as a result, they created company-specific global leadership models to guide their management development efforts (Mendenhall & Osland, 2002). Because global leadership is a young field of study, many of these models and training programmes, including those offered by universities and consulting companies, are not based on an extensive body of empirical research that identifies effectiveness in global leadership or global leadership training.

In this chapter, global leadership is defined as a process of influencing the thinking, attitudes and behaviours of a global community to work together synergistically toward a common vision and common goals (Adler, 2001; Festing, 2001). To date, most scholars have approached the global leadership construct by asking two questions: 'What capabilities do global leaders need to acquire in order to be effective?' and 'How can managers most effectively develop these characteristics?' The earliest publications on global leaders were either extrapolations from the domestic leadership literature, interviews and focus groups or observations from the authors' consulting experiences (Kets de Vries & Mead, 1992; Tichy, Brimm, Charan & Takeuchi, 1992; Rhinesmith, 1993; Moran & Riesenberger, 1994; Brake, 1997). Two sources of current thinking, findings and implications for future research are the *Advances in Global Leadership* volumes (Mobley, Gessner & Arnold, 1999; Mobley & McCall, 2001; Mobley & Dorfman, 2003) and the edited volume by Mendenhall, Kühlmann and Stahl (2001). Additionally *Human Resource Management* (vol. 39, 2000), published a special issue on global leadership, and Mendenhall and Osland (2002), Hollenbeck (2001) and Suutari (2002) conducted reviews of the literature.

The extant empirical studies on global leadership are described in Table 11.2. Empirical studies of global managers (for example, Dalton, Ernst, Deal & Leslie, 2002; Leslie, Dalton, Ernst & Deal, 2002) and empirical work on comparative international leadership (for example, the GLOBE project) exist in the field as well. From the extensive study of the impact of culture on leadership in 62 nations, the GLOBE project identified 21 universally accepted leader attributes and the transformational leadership style as generally advisable (House, Hanges, Javidan, Dorfman & Gupta, 2004). Their subjects, however, were not global leaders, but middle managers and executives working in their own countries. These universal attributes may prove to be linked to effective global leadership; however

Table 11.2   A chronological list of empirical research on global leadership

Authors	Description	Method	Findings
Yeung & Ready (1995)	Identifies leadership capabilities in a cross-national study	Surveys of 1200 managers from ten major global corporations and eight countries	Capabilities: articulate vision, values, strategy; catalyst for strategic and cultural change; empower others; results and customer orientation
Adler (1997)	Describes women global leaders in politics and business	Archival data and interviews with women global leaders from 60 countries	Women global leaders are increasing. They come from diverse backgrounds; are *not* selected by women-friendly countries or companies; use broad-based power rather than hierarchical power; are lateral transfers; symbolize change and unity; and leverage their increased visibility
Black, Morrison & Gregersen (1999)	Identifies capabilities of effective global leaders and how to develop them	Interviews of 130 senior line and HR executives in 50 companies in Europe, North America and Asia, and nominated global leaders	Capabilities: inquisitive, character, duality, savvy. Development occurs via training, transfer, travel, teams
Kets de Vries & Florent-Treacy (1999)	Describes excellent global leadership	Case studies involving interviews with three global leaders	Identified best practices in leadership, structure, strategy, corporate culture
Ernst (2000)	Studies the impact of global leadership behavioural complexity on boss and subordinate perceptions of leadership effectiveness	Surveys of the bosses and subordinates of 174 upper-level managers from 39 countries working in four global organizations	Behavioural complexity variables were related to perceptions of leadership effectiveness. However the relationships were not stronger for leaders in global as opposed to local jobs

Table 11.2 (continued)

Authors	Description	Method	Findings
Rosen, Digh, Singer & Philips (2000)	Identifies leadership universals	Interviews with 75 CEOs from 28 countries; 1058 surveys with CEOs, presidents, managing directors or chairmen; studies of national culture	Leadership universals: personal, social, business and cultural literacies, many of which are paradoxical in nature
McCall & Hollenbeck (2002)	To identify how to select and develop global executives and understand how they derail	Interviews with 101 executives from 36 countries and 16 global firms nominated as successful global executives	Competencies: open-minded & flexible; culture interest & sensitivity; cognitively complex; resilient, resourceful, optimistic, energetic; honesty & integrity; stable personal life; value-added technical or business skills
Goldsmith, Greenberg, Robertson & Hu-Chan (2003)	To identify global leadership dimensions	Thought leader panels; focus and dialogue groups with 28 CEOs and an unspecified number of current and future global leaders from various firms; interviews with 202 high-potential next generation leaders; and 73 surveys from forum group members	Fourteen dimensions: integrity, constructive dialogue, shared vision, developing people, building partnerships, sharing leadership, empowerment, thinking globally, appreciating diversity, technologically savvy, customer satisfaction, maintaining competitive advantage, personal mastery, anticipating opportunities
Kets de Vries, Vrignaud & Florent-Treacy (2004)	Describes the development of 360-degree feedback instrument, GlobeInvent	Based on semi-structured interviews with a number of senior executives	Twelve dimensions/psychodynamic properties: envisioning, empowering, energizing, designing, rewarding, team building, outside orientation, global mind-set, tenacity, emotional intelligence, life balance, resilience to stress

further research that tests for the presence of these attributes among successful global leaders is needed. As Adler noted, 'A fundamental distinction is that global leadership is neither domestic nor multi-domestic; it focuses on cross-cultural interaction rather than on either single culture description or multi-country comparison' (2001: 77). In our review of the literature, we include only studies with a specified focus on *global* leadership.

As shown in Table 11.2, the methodology utilized to study global leadership has been limited to surveys and/or interviews, with the exception of Kets de Vries and Florent-Treacy's (1999) initial case studies. Ernst (2000) went beyond interview or self-reported data to include 360-degree feedback from bosses and subordinates on behaviours, but his findings did not distinguish between domestic and global leadership. Using semi-structured interviews, Kets de Vries and his colleagues (2004) developed an instrument to measure various psychodynamic properties associated with global leadership behaviour. Black *et al.* (1999) and Goldsmith *et al.* (2003) also developed instruments to measure global leadership. Perhaps because of their recent development, as yet none of these instruments has been validated using commonly accepted standards for development of psychological assessment and testing instruments (Anastasi & Urbina, 1997; Nunnally & Bernstein, 1994). Several studies employed exploratory designs, which is appropriate in a nascent field of study. No one, however, has replicated Mintzberg's (1971) landmark observation of managerial behaviour with global leaders or studied leader behaviour directly. Although cognitive complexity is frequently mentioned as a global leadership competency, no research has directly measured the cognitive processes of expert global leaders (Osland & Bird, forthcoming).

The majority of the research findings in Table 11.2 were published in books; only three studies were published in peer-reviewed research journals or well-respected practitioner journals (Yeung & Ready, 1995; Gregerson, Morrison & Black, 1998; and Kets de Vries *et al.*, 2004). Consequently it is more difficult to evaluate this research in terms of rigour.

While all of the global leader research in Table 11.2 makes a contribution to our understanding, and advances the field, the findings are not yet definitive. For example, the published research to date has not contributed much in the way of construct definition. No rigorous or collectively accepted definition of global leadership has emerged. In some studies the definition of the construct was left up to interviewees; in other cases the definition was merely assumed. As a result, there is conceptual confusion accompanied by enduring questions about whether there is a significant difference between global managers and global leaders, or between global and domestic leaders. In both sample selection and writing, the terms 'global leader' and 'global manager' are frequently used interchangeably, which is puzzling given the significant distinctions between managers and leaders in the leadership literature (Kotter, 1990).

Several studies asked global managers for their opinion about global leader capability without ensuring or clarifying whether they were in fact global leaders. Yeung and Ready (1995) used a global sample of 1200 managers who chose among survey items to elicit their description of global leaders. After identifying 43 political and 38 business women global leaders, Adler (2001) did content analysis using archival research and some interviews to describe their background, ascension and use of power. Black and his colleagues (1999) took a qualitative, exploratory approach. They asked 130 senior line and HR executives, as well as an unspecified number of nominated global leaders, for their opinion on global leadership capabilities and the methods of developing them. Rosen *et al*. (2000) interviewed 75 CEOs and surveyed 1058 CEOs, presidents, managing directors or chairmen about global leadership capabilities. Goldsmith and his colleagues (2003) took a three-pronged approach: (1) they asked the opinion of 18 well-known domestic leadership experts and futurists; (2) they held focus groups with 28 CEOs, an unspecified number of global managers and 2002 high potential leaders of the 'next' generation; and (3) they surveyed 75 forum members from various countries. McCall and Hollenbeck (2002) interviewed 101 executives from varied companies and countries who were nominated as successful global executives in high-level positions. They refer to their sample as global executives rather than leaders, although their sampling methods are similar to other global leader studies and they reviewed the global leadership literature prior to gathering data. Theirs is the only study to select all subjects solely on effectiveness, as perceived by others.

Black and his colleagues' subsample of nominated global leaders also took effectiveness into consideration. Kets de Vries and Florent-Treacy (1999) began their empirical work with case studies, utilizing a clinical orientation, of three global leaders who were acknowledged as highly successful global CEOs. As the basis of their subsequent research, an assessment instrument that measures global leader dimensions, they relied primarily on participants who attended INSEAD's senior executive seminar on Emotional Intelligence and Leadership and MBA programme. This convenience sample, drawn from a prestigious school, may well be composed of global leaders, but their selection criteria, as well as most of the research reviewed here, assume that global managers are indistinguishable from global leaders. In contrast, we contend that all CEOs and global managers are not, by definition, global leaders. Given the limited amount of research in this field, more could be learned from exploratory research on global leaders who are effective. Both of these contentions argue for more careful selection criteria in global leadership research.

Mendenhall and Osland's (2002) review of the empirical and non-empirical literature yielded 56 global leadership competencies, a list too large to be useful. Noting that there were numerous areas of overlap across the various lists, the authors concluded that global leadership is a multidimensional construct with at least six core dimensions of competencies: cross-cultural relationship skills, traits and values, cognitive orientation, global business expertise, global organizing expertise and visioning. This categorization seems applicable for the competencies identified in the empirical studies reviewed here, as shown in Figure 11.1.

One striking characteristic of the global leadership competency research is that it has, for the most part, taken a *content* approach. While such research is useful, it fails to explicate the process that global leaders utilize

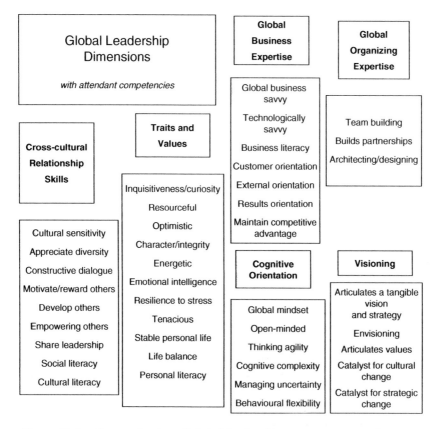

Figure 11.1   Categorization of global leadership competencies in the empirical research

or to identify the contingencies that influence their behaviour in specific contexts. Nor does it distinguish between essential and non-essential competencies. Are these competencies crucial at all times or important only in certain situations? Leadership requirements can vary by level, culture and situation, as well as by functions and operating units, so competency lists might not apply across the board (Conger & Ready, 2004: 45).

The competency approach also fails to answer the conundrum of exemplary global leaders who succeed despite glaring weaknesses. In reality, few leaders live up to the idealized view of leadership that competency lists portray (Conger & Ready, 2004). McCall and Hollenbeck (2002) note that complex, high-level executive jobs are accomplished in various ways by executives with multiple forms of talent. Therefore we would expect that global leaders can be effective without acquiring all competencies, but there is no research to prove or disprove this hypothesis.

Global leadership scholars may be distracted by the mythical lure of heroic leadership. The artist Andy Warhol stated, 'In the future, everyone will be world-famous for 15 minutes.' This may well describe some forms of global leadership. Leaders who accurately assess the shifting sands and rip tides of globalization may effectively harness the powers inherent in the situation and engage in '15 minutes' of global leadership. For that fleeting moment, their actions will be heroic. Do they then become heroes, destined like Spiderman to save us repeatedly from evil, and become true global leaders? Probably not; 15 minutes may be more than most could hope for, as evidenced in the rise and fall of certain well-known global business leaders and in cases of domestic leaders who surprisingly rise to the challenge of a one-time global leadership role. Hence another caveat is that scholars may well be reporting on episodic global leadership rather than finding subjects who act consistently as global leaders, modern examples of the archetypical heroic leader humankind so longs for. Our research needs to distinguish between global leaders and global leadership and between episodic and long-term global leadership behaviour.

In summary, global leadership is an emerging field, reminiscent of the first stage of domestic leadership research, which also began by examining traits and subsequently evolved more complex theories. Furthermore researchers have yet to focus on global leadership capability at the team or firm level, opting instead to study this topic only at the individual level of analysis. Future research is needed in the following global leadership (GL) topics.

- Construct definition for GL.
- Distinguishing between the roles and behaviours of global managers and global leaders.

- Definitively answering the question of whether and how global leaders differ from domestic leaders.
- Determination of competencies that are threshold characteristics that should be used as selection criteria in development programmes or promotion.
- Development and/or validation of GL assessment instruments.
- Identification of GL behaviours.
- Identification of GL thought processes and expert cognition.
- Identification of GL contingencies.
- Description of GL styles.
- Investigation of the relationship between global strategy and specific types of GL skills.
- Identification of GL capability in both teams and organizations.
- Development of GL process models that include interaction with the environment.
- Antecedents of GL effectiveness.
- Determination of how many global leaders firms need.
- Outcomes of GL development training methodologies.

The next literature review focuses on the development processes of global mindset and global leadership.

Developing global mindset and global leadership

One can develop attitudes, abilities and knowledge through international assignments and global projects, but personality characteristics such as openness, flexibility and reduction of ethnocentrism (which are closely related to cosmopolitanism and cognitive complexity) are, by definition, less amenable to change (Caligiuri & Di Santo, 2001). Therefore selecting and promoting those who already have the desired personality characteristics is a critical aspect in developing both global mindset and global leadership.

Global mindset development

There are no extant empirical studies on global mindset development. However, using research from cognitive psychology and knowledge development, Gupta and Govindarajan (2002: 120) assert that individual and organizational development of a global mindset are likely fostered by (a) curiosity about the world and a commitment to becoming better informed about how the world works, (b) an explicit and self-conscious articulation of current mindsets, (c) exposure to diversity and novelty, and (d) a disciplined attempt to develop an integrated perspective that weaves together diverse strands of knowledge about cultures and markets.

The authors hypothesized that global mindset can be developed by (a) hiring diverse employees and managers, (b) providing opportunities such as cross-border teams and projects, short immersion experiences, expatriate assignments, (c) holding meetings and business unit headquarters in foreign locations, (d) fostering social networks across cultures, and (e) taking formal education courses. It has also been hypothesized that global mindset can be developed with a focus on global issues with structural positions (global jobs, champions, teams), meeting topics and speakers, and incentives and accountability for global performance (Bouquet *et al.*, 2003).

Global leadership development
Few frameworks or models exist that describe the global leadership development process. (For a review of the literature on global leader development, see Suutari, 2002.) It is generally argued by scholars that the major challenges firms face in establishing global leadership development programmes are (a) establishing selection criteria, (b) agreeing on the competencies to develop and measure, (c) designing effective training programmes, and (d) retaining their highly sought-after 'graduates'.

Careful selection practices are essential. Certain personality characteristics that are desirable in global leaders (flexibility, ethnocentrism, openness) did not increase as a result of global assignments (Caliguiri & Di Santo, 2001). Caliguiri (2004) found that highly effective global leaders in one firm had significantly higher conscientiousness scores and significantly lower neuroticism than less effective ones. (They also had lived abroad with their families, had long-term international assignments, and were mentored by people from a different culture.) According to Kets de Vries and Florent-Treacy (2002), the basic foundation of global leadership development consists of: (1) family background that includes culturally diverse parents, early international experiences and bilingualism; (2) early education in international schools, summer camps and international travel; (3) later education involving exchange programmes, foreign language and international MBA programmes; and (4) spouses and children who are supportive, adventurous, adaptable and mobile. More research is needed to identify all traits and experiences that predict global leadership effectiveness. In general, selection practices must avoid ethnocentrism and be inclusive, since the traits, skills and management styles that result in a superior track record in the home country may be counterproductive abroad (Mendenhall, 2001; Ruben, 1989; Osland & Taylor, 2001).

International assignments have been viewed as the most powerful development tool in facilitating global leadership competencies (Gregersen *et al.*, 1998; Hall, Zhu & Yan, 2001; Mendenhall *et al.*, 2001), since they constitute a transformational experience that develops business savvy, continuous learning, cognitive complexity, behavioural flexibility, cross-cultural skills and the ability to manage uncertainty (Osland, 2001). However, a multi-method approach is recommended (Osland & Taylor, 2001) that utilizes international assignments, short-term developmental assignments, international teams, action learning groups/projects/task forces, international training and development programmes, international meetings and forums, international travel (Oddou, Mendenhall & Ritchie, 2000; Roberts, Kossek & Ozeki, 1998), 360-degree evaluations that include input from foreign organizational members, and assessment centres (Stahl, 2001). All methods have to be used mindfully by tying them to company strategy and ensuring that the necessary developmental learning occurs.

Fulkerson (2002) summarizes practical advice for developing global leadership based in part on his research with international executives. McCall & Hollenbeck's (2002) research makes a major contribution to clarifying the development process of global executives from both an individual and an organizational perspective. Their model consists of five components that lead to 'the right stuff' in global managers (what they need to implement business strategy): talent, mechanisms, experience in a global context and catalysts, the latter moderated by business strategy. They acknowledge several difficulties in assessing talent: identifying a common standard across cultures, country differences in assessing, promoting and developing managers, wide variability in global executive jobs, and the organization's openness to promoting executives from other nationalities (ibid.: 185–6). The mechanism variable in their model consists of selection, succession, development, discovery and recovery, which are elaborated below.

Selection and succession refer in part to the organization's need to identify people who are ready to assume global positions when unexpected staffing needs arise; in other words, replacement planning for critical jobs. Development occurs by placing people in jobs that will expand their cultural or business skills, which is often done with people from a culturally diverse background who have a clear interest in international work. Discovery mechanisms provide parochial employees with an opportunity early in their careers to ascertain whether they might have an interest in international work. Recovery pertains to the organization's efforts to integrate repatriates when they return home. Developmental catalysts, such as feedback, reward systems and so on, help executives learn. Finally, business strategy refers to a firm's specific development needs, which are based on their particular strategic intent and organizational design. Strategy and structure determine the number of international jobs, the types of global executives and their nationalities, and the skills they will need. Thus McCall and Hollenbeck (2002) view business strategy as a moderator in their global executive development framework. They confirm the findings of other scholars that global experience is crucial to global leadership development.

Global leadership development: a 'non-linear' perspective

The argument that global leadership is a process of personal transformation is an underlying theme in much of the literature. Assuming this thesis is cogent, it is likely that global leadership development is not a linear progression of adding competencies to an existing portfolio of leadership competencies, but rather a non-linear process whereby deep-seated change in competencies and world view takes places in the process of experiential overlays over time. This 'experiential crucible' includes experiences over which the company may have little or no control. Consequently traditional training cannot in and of itself be the primary tool through which global leadership competencies are inculcated within individuals. This process is akin to phenomena that are studied within the emerging field of non-linear dynamics.

Traditional social scientific philosophy, methodology and understanding are based on a core assumption: that relationships between variables in social phenomena are linear in nature (Capra, 1983, 1996). This cognitive and perceptual bedrock, which has been the centre of socialization for thousands of doctoral students since the 1920s in North American universities, has produced the development of social scientific theories that are reductionistic, deterministic and equilibrium-oriented in nature (Lichtenstein & Mendenhall, 2002). The superordinate goal of such social scientific theories is the prediction of human behaviour (Capra, 1983, 1996; Hayles, 1991; Dooley, 1997; Lichtenstein & Mendenhall, 2002). This unconscious, ubiquitous paradigm is a lens through which managers, as well as academics, perceive reality. Wheatley (1992: 6) summarized the subtle effects of our socialization when she observed:

> Each of us lives and works in organizations designed from Newtonian images of the universe. We manage by separating things into parts, we believe that influence occurs as a direct result of force exerted from one person to another, we engage in complex planning for a world that we keep expecting to be predictable, and we search continually for better methods of objectively perceiving the world. These assumptions . . . are the base from which we design and manage organizations, and from which we do research in all of the social sciences.

One reason for the sustained permanence of this core assumption is that linearity does exist in the world. Many systems and laws in the universe are inherently linear in nature. An understanding of linearity has allowed humankind to transport astronauts to the moon and, on a more mundane note, to know what time it is at any given moment of the day.

An overarching characteristic of linear, deterministic systems is their proportionality; that is, an input of *x* amount of force into a system results in a corresponding output which proportionately reflects the amount of force (*x*). Lichtenstein and Mendenhall (2002) note that the implicit belief that predictable, closed mechanical systems are the norm for natural and social science modelling (Harding, 1986; Turner, 1997) was the basis for virtually all models of biological and social process (Bateson, 1980; Berman, 1984).

Over the past two decades, however, discoveries of non-linearity in the natural sciences have led an increasing number of social scientists to explore the possibility that social phenomena have non-linear elements within them (Capra, 1996; Eylon & Giacalone, 2000). Some social scientists, such as George Herbert Mead, Joseph Schumpeter and Mary Parker Follett, saw and wrote about the relationship between non-linearity and social phenomena in the 1920s and 1930s, but their voices were drowned out by the tide of logical positivism that emerged at that time, and has continued to the present, to be the foundational philosophy of social science (Lichtenstein & Mendenhall, 2002).

The nature of non-linearity

Lichtenstein and Mendenhall (2002: 8) describe non-linearity as 'a common state of dynamic systems in which events and their outcomes are non-proportional. In the simplest sense, non-linear system inputs are not proportional to the system's outputs; for example 140° F is not twice as pleasant as 70° F, and eight aspirin are not eight times as effective as one.' Another description of non-linearity was provided by Meiss (1995: 1):

> Nonlinear is defined as the negation of linear. This means that the result may be out of proportion to the input. The result may be more than linear, as when a diode begins to pass current; or less than linear, as when finite resources limit Malthusian population growth. Thus the fundamental simplifying tools of linear analysis are no longer available.

Some scholars have begun to theorize that global leadership development has non-linear aspects and that firms need to understand this process better than they currently do in order to develop global leaders.[1] The multitudes of daily experiences that are encountered in a dynamic, intercultural milieu are not inherently linear. Certain intercultural experiences trigger either functional or dysfunctional global competency development out of proportion to their importance to all other factors in the situation, or to the business context itself. Seemingly innocent or minor intercultural interactions can career out of control, causing global managers to internalize false or skewed intercultural understanding of 'why' the event occurred and 'what' the event means. In responding to these events, global managers continually create a new reality. Mary Parker Follett (1924: 62–3) argued that such social interaction was a non-linear process:

> [an individual's] reaction is always reaction to a relating . . . I never react to you but to you-plus-me; or to be more accurate, it is I-plus-you reacting to you-plus-me . . . that is, in the very process of meeting, by the very process of meeting, we both become something different. It begins even before we meet, in the anticipation of meeting . . . It is I plus the-interweaving-between-you-and-me meeting you plus the-interweaving-between-you-and-me, etc., etc. If we were doing it mathematically we should work it out to the nth power.

Each intercultural situation that a global manager experiences – and there are myriad such experiences that occur daily – consists of 'non-linear relatings'. That is, the creation of global leadership competencies is like a continuing dance or tennis match with multiple partners. One is not independent of one's partners – the continual decisions and learning from decisions in response to continual behaviours enacted over time transform someone into either a competent or an incompetent global leader – and all points in between. Lichtenstein and Mendenhall (2002) contend that components and behaviours in non-linear dynamical systems cannot be separated, so independent forces do not bring about dependent outcomes. All elements in such systems are 'mutually constituting': they arise and evolve as an interconnected network (Capra, 1996). A cause does not have one and only one effect; therefore the customary linear connection among antecedents and outcomes does not hold true. Instead the 'mutual causality' that characterizes this interdependence among variables constitutes a core principle of the new sciences (Briggs & Peat, 1989).

On the assumption that global leadership development in an individual is a non-linear, mutually causal, emergent process moderated by a variety of key variables across time, we offer the following process model, depicted in Figure 11.2, as a first attempt to comprehend global leadership development through a non-linear, paradigmatic lens. The model is called, 'The Chattanooga model of global leadership development' as it was developed in a think-tank setting by global leadership scholars in Chattanooga, Tennessee in 2001, at the Frierson Leadership Institute.

At the left of the model, in the corner, an individual enters a global/cross-cultural context and is immersed in it (24-7) over a significant period of time. The person enters with basic, core immutable personality traits, which include fairly immutable competencies (ambition, desire to lead, sociability, openness, agreeableness, emotional stability and so on) and cognitive processes (attribution flexibility, category width, tolerance for ambiguity and so on). The individual also enters with existing levels of self-efficacy that are brought to bear on various aspects of living and working globally.

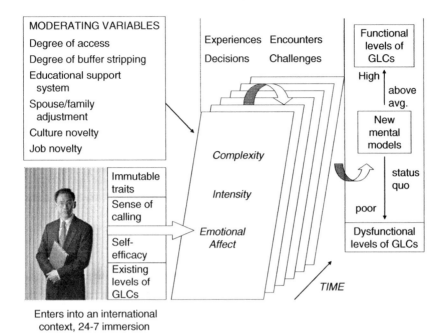

Enters into an international
context, 24-7 immersion

Figure 11.2   The Chattanooga model of global leadership development

The degree to which the individual perceives a 'call to do this', or, in other words, the degree to which people view themselves as global citizens and believe that this assignment fits 'who they really are' inside is an important factor in their motivation to lead in a global situation. Finally the person enters the global context with existing levels of global managerial/leadership competencies.

Each individual brings a unique configuration of these variables and brings this configuration to bear upon the multitude of daily experiences that are encountered in the new milieu. The 'folders' or 'pages' in Figure 11.2 represent experiences, interactions and challenges the individual passes through over time. Each of these experiences differs in the degree to which they confront the individual with complexity and the degree to which they are important to the individual, thus heightening the intensity of the experience for the individual. The combination of complexity and intensity contribute to the degree of emotional affect the individual experiences.

The recursive arrow in the model connotes the fact that a current experience can cause, through memory, an updating or reliving of past experiences. Thus the global leadership development process is not based on independent experiences; rather each experience is tied to past, multiple experiences and constitutes a sense-making process of learning and acquiring global leadership competencies. Bennis and Thomas (2002: 14) refer to the *gestalt* of these processes as constituting 'crucibles', situations 'characterized by the confluence of powerful intellectual, social, economic, or political forces' that severely test one's patience, and one's beliefs, and that produce a transformation in the individual, leaving him/her deeply different in terms of who they were before the crucible experience.

The nature of these various global/cross-cultural crucible experiences is critical to the formation of global leadership. The degree to which these experiences are buffered by organizational policies or the individuals themselves, or the degree to which access to these experiences is curtailed by companies (for example, expensive housing that separates the global manager from interaction with the host society) moderates whether or not these potentially transforming experiences instead become shallow and non-catalytic in terms of global leadership development. Additionally educational support systems, culture novelty, job novelty, and spouse/family adjustment can each enhance or detract from global leadership development.

Thus a key factor in individual global leadership development is 'access to high-level challenges'. Access to these challenges may produce, in some cases, solid global leadership competency development over time. However such access holds the potential to produce failure as well. Individuals may have the right kind of experiences, but be unable to handle them or learn from them because they are overwhelming. New mental leadership models are indeed created within the individual; however those models may be dysfunctional. It is important to note that, although these mental models become apparent at the end of the process depicted in Figure 11.2, in actuality they are being created over and over again in response to each experience the individual has. Consequently the developing framework is malleable, but it may harden into a dysfunctional systemic framework if experiences are not handled effectively over time.

In summary, the Chattanooga model depicts the global leadership development process as emergent in nature, and constantly dynamic. If a person's immutable personality traits, access to powerful challenges and so on are harmonious to working and learning in the global context, a functional global leadership process will ensue, and the individual will develop global leadership competencies. Similarly other levels of global leadership, ranging from 'status quo' to 'dysfunctional' may result as a consequence of an individual's unique processual experiences. At any point in time, one's trajectory can rise, fall or be moderated by the unique constellation of forces that impinge upon any given experience.

Much work remains to be done in the area of global mindset and leadership development. The Chattanooga model and others need to be tested, and the effectiveness and costs of different types of developmental methods need to be compared. The organizational aspect of development cannot be overlooked; the alignment of HRM and the organizational culture with the firm's efforts to develop global leadership and global mindset also require more investigation. What is required are systemic analyses of the factors that promote or impede global leadership and mindset. The caveat remains, however, that efforts to understand development will be hamstrung by the lack of consensus on the definition and parameters of global leadership and global mindset. Finally, to avoid a Western bias, future research on global mindset, leadership and their development should include globally diverse subjects and settings.

Note

1. A think-tank of global leadership scholars met at the Frierson Leadership Institute. Chattanooga, Tennessee to discuss the non-linear approach to global leadership development in 2001.

References

Adler, N. 2001. Global leadership: women leaders. In M. Mendenhall, T.M. Kuhlmann & G. Stahl (eds), *Developing global business leaders: policies, processes, and innovations*: 73–97. Westport, CN: Quorum; also in *Management International Review*, 1997, **37**(1): 171–96.

Anastasi, A. & S. Urbina. 1997. *Psychological testing*. Seventh edition. Upper Saddle River, NJ: Prentice-Hall.

Ashby, W.R. 1956. *An introduction to cybernetics*. New York: Wiley.

Bartlett, C.A. & S. Ghoshal. 1989. *Managing across borders: the transnational solution*. Boston, MA: Harvard Business School Press.

Bartlett, C.A. & S. Ghoshal. 1992. What is a global manager? *Harvard Business Review*, 124–31.

Bartunek, J.M., J.R. Gordon & R.P. Weathersby. 1983. Developing complicated understanding in administrators. *Academy of Management Review*, **8**(2): 273–84.

Bateson, G. 1980. *Mind and nature – a necessary unity*. New York: Bantam Books.

Beechler, S., O. Levy, S. Taylor & N. Boyacigiller. 2004. Does it really matter if Japanese MNCs think globally? The impact of employees' perceptions on their attitudes. In T. Roehl & A. Bird (eds), *Japanese Firms in Transition*, pp. 265–92. [Advances in International Management, 17]. Amsterdam and Oxford: Elsevier JAI.

Begley, T.M. & D.P. Boyd. 2003. The need for a corporate global mind-set. *Sloan Management Review*, **44**(2): 25–32.

Bennis, W.G. & R.J. Thomas. 2002. *Geeks and geezers: how era, values, and defining moments shape leaders*. Boston, MA: Harvard Business School Press.

Berman, M. 1984. *The Re-enchantment of the world*. New York: Bantam Books.

Black, J.S., A. Morrison & H. Gregersen. 1999. *Global explorers: the next generation of leaders*. New York: Routledge.

Bouquet, C., A. Morrison & J. Birkinshaw. 2003. Determinants and performance implications of global mindset: an attention-based perspective.

Boyacigiller, N., S. Beechler, S. Taylor & O. Levy. 2004. The crucial but illusive global mindset. In H. Lane, M. Maznevski, M. Mendenhall & J. McNett (eds), *Handbook of global management*: 81–93. Oxford: Blackwell.

Brake, T. 1997. *The global leader: critical factors for creating the world class organization*. Chicago, IL: Irwin Professional Publishing.

Briggs, J. & D. Peat. 1989. *Turbulent Mirror*. New York: Harper & Row.

Caliguiri, P. & V. Di Santo. 2001. Global competence: what is it and can it be developed through international assignment? *HR Resource Planning*, **24**(3): 27–36.
Caliguiri, P. 2004. Global leadership development through expatriate assignments and other international experiences. Paper presented at the Academy of Management, New Orleans, August.
Calof, J.L. & P.W. Beamish. 1994. The right attitude for international success. *Ivey Business Quarterly*, **59**(1):105–10.
Calori, R., G. Johnson & P. Sarnin. 1994. CEO's cognitive maps and the scope of the organization. *Strategic Management Journal*, **15**: 437–57.
Capra, F. 1983. *The turning point*. New York: Bantam Books.
Capra, F. 1996. *The web of life*. New York: Anchor Books.
Chattanooga think-tank on global leadership. 2001. Chattanooga, TN: Frierson Leadership Institute.
Conger, J. & D. Ready. 2004. Rethinking leadership competencies. *Leader to Leader*, **32**: 41–8.
Dalton, M., C. Ernst, J. Deal & J. Leslie. 2002. *Success for the new global manager: what you need to know to work across distances, countries and cultures*. San Francisco, CA: Jossey-Bass and the Center for Creative Leadership.
Dooley, K. 1997. A complex adaptive systems model of organization change. Nonlinear dynamics. *Psychology and the Life Sciences*, **3**: 230–49.
Doz, Y. & C. Prahalad. 1991. Managing DMNCs: a search for a new paradigm. *Strategic Management Journal*, **12**: 145–64.
Emerson, V. 2001. An interview with Carlos Ghosn, President of Nissan Motors, Ltd and Industry Leader of the Year (*Automotive News*, 2000). *Journal of World Business*, **36**: 3–10.
Ernst, C.T. 2000. The influence of behavioral complexity on global leadership effectiveness. Unpublished dissertation, North Carolina State University.
Eylon, D. & R. Giacalone. 2000. Introduction: the road to a new management paradigm. *American Behavioral Scientist*. **43**(Special issue): 1215–17.
Festing, M. 2001. The effects of international human resource management strategies on global leadership development. In M. Mendenhall, T.M. Kuhlmann & G. Stahl (eds), *Developing global business leaders: policies, processes, and innovations*: 37–56. Westport, CN: Quorum.
Follett, M.P. 1924. *Creative experience*. New York: Peter Smith.
Fulkerson, J. 2002. Growing global executives. In R. Silzer (ed.), *The 21st century: innovative practices for building leadership at the top*. San Francisco, CA: Jossey-Bass.
Goerner, S. 1994. *Chaos and the evolving ecological universe*. New York: Gordon & Breach.
Goldsmith, M., C. Greenberg, A. Robertson & M. Hu-Chan. 2003. *Global leadership: the next generation*. Upper Saddle River, NJ: Prentice-Hall.
Gregersen, H.B., A. Morrison & J.S. Black. 1998. Developing leaders for the global frontier. *Sloan Management Review*, **40**(1): 21–33.
Gupta, A.K. & V. Govindarajan. 2002. Cultivating a global mindset. *Academy of Management Executive*, **16**(1): 116–26.
Hall, D.T., G. Zhu & A. Yan. 2001. Developing global leaders: to hold on to them, let them go! In W. Mobley & M.W. McCall, Jr (eds), *Advances in Global Leadership*, vol. 2. Stamford, CT: JAI Press.
Hannerz, U. 1996. Cosmopolitans and locals in world culture. In U. Hannerz (ed.), *Transnational connections: culture, people, places*: 102–11. London: Routledge.
Harding, S. 1986. *The science question in feminism*. Ithaca, NY: Cornell University Press.
Hayles, N.K. 1991. Complex dynamics in science and literature. In N.K. Hayles (ed.), *Chaos and order: complex dynamics in literature and science*. Chicago, IL: University of Chicago Press.
Hollenbeck, G.P. 2001. A serendipitous sojourn through the global leadership literature. In W. Mobley & M.W. McCall, Jr (eds), *Advances in Global Leadership*, vol. 2. Stamford, CT: JAI Press.
House, R.J., P.W. Hanges, M. Javidan, P. Dorfman & V. Gupta. (eds). 2004. *Culture, leadership and organizations: the GLOBE study of 62 societies*. Beverly Hills: Sage.
Jeannet, J. 2000. *Managing with a global mindset*. London: Financial Times, Prentice-Hall.

Kedia, B. & A. Mukherji. 1999. Global managers: developing a mindset for global competitiveness. *Journal of World Business*, **34**(3): 230–50.

Kefalas, A.G. 1998. Think globally, act locally. *Thunderbird International Business Review*, **40**(6): 547–62.

Kets de Vries, M. & E. Florent-Treacy. 1999. *The new global leaders*. San Francisco, CA: Jossey-Bass.

Kets de Vries, M.F.R & E. Florent-Treacy. 2002. Global leadership from A to Z: creating high commitment organizations. *Organizational Dynamics*, **30**(4): 295–309.

Kets de Vries, M. & C. Mead. 1992. The development of the global leader within the multinational corporation. In V. Pucik, N.M. Tichy & C.K. Barnett (eds), *Globalizing management, creating and leading the competitive organization*. New York: John Wiley & Sons.

Kets de Vries, M., P. Vrignaud & E. Florent-Treacy. 2004. The global leadership life inventory: development and psychometric properties of a 360-degree feedback instrument. *International Journal of Human Resource Management*, **15**(3): 475–92.

Kobrin, S.J. 1994. Is there a relationship between a geocentric mind-set and multinational strategy? *Journal of international Business Studies*, **25**(3): 493–512.

Kotter, J. 1990. What leaders really do. *Harvard Business Review*, 103–11.

Lane, H.W., M.L. Maznevski, M.E. Mendenhall & J. McNett. (eds). 2004. *The Blackwell handbook of global management: a guide to managing complexity*. London: Blackwell.

Leslie, J.B., M. Dalton, C. Ernst & J. Deal. 2002. *Managerial effectiveness in a global context*. Greensboro, NC: Center for Creative Leadership Press.

Levy, O. 2001. The influence of top management team global mindset on global strategic posture of firms. Paper presented at the Annual Meeting of the Academy of Management, Washington, DC.

Levy, O., S. Beechler, S. Taylor & N.A. Boyacigiller. 1999. What we talk about when we talk about 'Global Mindset'. Paper Presented at the Academy of Management Annual Meeting, Chicago, August.

Lichtenstein, B. & M. Mendenhall. 2002. Non-linearity and response-ability: emergent order in 21st century careers. *Human Relations*, **55**(1): 5–32.

Maznevski, M. & H. Lane. 2004. Shaping the global mindset: designing educational experiences for effective global thinking and action. In N. Boyacigiller, R.M. Goodman & M. Phillips (eds), *Teaching and experiencing cross-cultural management: lessons from master teachers*. London and New York: Routledge.

McCall, M.W. Jr & G.P. Hollenbeck. 2002. *Developing global executives*. Harvard Business School Press.

Meiss, J.D. 1995. Frequently asked questions about nonlinear science (version 1.0.9). Newsgroup sci.nonlinear: Department of Applied Mathematics at University of Colorado at Boulder, 1–31.

Mendenhall, M. 2001. Introduction: new perspectives on expatriate adjustment and its relationship to global leadership development. In M. Mendenhall, T.M. Kuhlmann & G. Stahl (eds), *Developing global business leaders: policies, processes, and innovations*: 1–16. Westport, CN: Quorum.

Mendenhall, M. & J.S. Osland. 2002. An overview of the extant global leadership research. Symposium presentation, Academy of International Business, Puerto Rico, June.

Mendenhall, M., T.M. Kuhlmann & G. Stahl. (eds) 2001. *Developing global business leaders: policies, processes, and innovations*. Westport, CN: Quorum.

Merton, R. 1957. Patterns of influence: local and cosmopolitan influentials. In R.K. Merton (ed.), *Social theory and social structure*. Glencoe, IL: Free Press.

Mintzberg, H. 1971. *The nature of managerial work*. New York: Harper & Row.

Mobley, W. & P. Dorfman. (eds). 2003. *Advances in global leadership*, vol. 3. Stamford, CT: JAI Press.

Mobley, W. & M.W. McCall. Jr (eds). 2001. *Advances in global leadership*, vol. 2. Stamford, CT: JAI Press.

Mobley, W., M. Gessner & V. Arnold. (eds). 1999. *Advances in global leadership*, vol. 1. Stamford, CT: JAI Press.

Moran, R.T. & J.R. Riesenberger. 1994. *The global challenge: building the new worldwide enterprise*. London: McGraw-Hill.

Murtha, T.P., S.A. Lenway & R.P. Bagozzi. 1998. Global mind-sets and cognitive shift in a complex multinational corporation. *Strategic Management Journal*, 19(2): 97–114.

Nummela, N., S. Saarenketo & K. Puumalainen. 2004. A global mindset – a prerequisite for successful internationalization? *Canadian Journal of Administrative Sciences*, 21: 51–65.

Nunnaly, J.C. & I.H. Bernstein. 1994. *Psychometric theory*. Third edition. New York: McGraw-Hill.

Oddou, G., M. Mendenhall & J.B. Ritchie. 2000. Leveraging travel as a tool for global leadership development. *Human Resource Management*, 39(2, 3): 159–72.

Ohmae, K. 1989. Managing in a borderless world. *Harvard Business Review*, 67(3): 152–61.

Osland, J. 2001. The quest for transformation. In M. Mendenhall, T.M. Kuhlmann and G. Stahl (eds), *Developing global business leaders: policies, processes, and innovations*: 137–56. Westport, CN: Quorum.

Osland, J.S. & A. Bird. (Forthcoming). Global leaders as experts. In W. Mobley & E. Weldon (eds), *Advances in global leadership*, vol. 4. Stamford, CT: JAI Press.

Osland, J. & S. Taylor. 2001. Developing global leaders. *HR.Com*. February.

Paul, H. 2000. Creating a mindset. *Thunderbird International Business Review*, 42: 187–200.

Perlmutter, H.V. 1969. The tortuous evolution of the multinational corporation. *Columbia Journal of World Business*, 4(1): 9–18.

Rhinesmith, S.H. 1992. Global mindsets for global managers. *Training & Development*, 63–8.

Rhinesmith, S. 1993. *A manager's guide to globalization*. Alexandria, VA: Irwin.

Roberts, K., E.E. Kossek & C. Ozeki. 1998. Managing the global workforce: challenge and strategies. *Academy of Management Executive*, 12(4): 93–106.

Rosen, R., P. Digh, M. Singer & C. Philips. 2000. *Global literacies: lessons on business leadership and national cultures*. New York: Simon & Schuster.

Ruben, B.D. 1989. The study of cross-cultural competence: traditions and contemporary issues. *International Journal of intercultural relations*, 13: 229–39.

Sambharya, R. 1996. Foreign experience of top management teams and international diversification strategies of U.S. multinational corporations. *Strategic Management Journal*, 17(9): 739–46.

Srinivas, K.M. 1995. Globalization of business and the Third World: challenge of expanding the mindsets. *Journal of Management Development*, 14(3): 26–49.

Stahl, G. 2001. Using assessment centers as tools for global leadership development: an exploratory study. In M. Mendenhall, T.M. Kuhlmann and G. Stahl (eds), *Developing global business leaders: policies, processes, and innovations*: 197–210. Westport, CN: Quorum.

Suutari, V. 2002. Global leader development: an emerging research agenda. *Career Development International*, 7(4): 218–33.

Tichy, N., M. Brimm, R. Charan & H. Takeuchi. 1992. Leadership development as a lever for global transformation. In V. Pucik, N. Tichy & C.K. Barnett (eds), *Globalizing management, creating and leading the competitive organization*: 47–60. New York: John Wiley & Sons.

Turner, F. 1997. Chaos and social science. In R. Eve, S. Horsfall & M.E. Lee (eds), *Chaos, complexity, and sociology*. Thousand Oaks, CA: Sage Publications.

Von Glinow, M.A. 2001. Future issues in global leadership development. In M. Mendenhall, T.M. Kuhlmann & G. Stahl (eds), *Developing global business leaders: policies, processes and innovations*: 264–71. Westport, CT: Quorum.

Weick, K.E. 1979. Cognitive processes in organization. In B. Staw (ed.), *Research in Organizational Behavior*, vol. 1: 41–74. Greenwich, CT: JAI Press.

Wheatley, M. 1992. *Leadership and the new science*. San Francisco, CA: Barrett-Koehler.

Wills, S. & K. Barham. 1994. Being an international manager. *European Management Journal*, 12(1): 49–58.

Yeung, A. & D. Ready. 1995. Developing leadership capabilities of global corporations: a comparative study in eight nations. *Human Resource Management*, 34(4): 529–47.

12 Diversity management
Joerg Dietz and Lars-Eric Petersen

Many companies have an increasingly diverse labour force as a result of demographic trends in the population, new legal regulations, changing societal norms and the globalization of business (Bhawuk, Podsiadlowski, Graf & Triandis, 2002). In the USA, for example, the proportion of Latino and Asian employees has grown substantially, and in nearly all industrialized countries women are increasingly represented in the workplace. Diversity management helps to cope with the consequences of a diverse workforce (for instance, an increased risk of conflict). It has been defined as 'systematic and planned programs or procedures that are designed (a) to improve interaction among diverse people especially of different ethnicities, sexes or cultures and (b) to make this diversity a source of creativity, complementarity, and greater effectiveness' (Stockdale & Crosby, 2004: 12).

The importance of diversity management is related to the 'business case' for diversity. It links demographic diversity to bottom line results by drawing on three main arguments. First, there is an increasing shortage of qualified and talented staff in the knowledge economy; hence, organizations must exhaust all possible segments of the labour market, including minority employees, who traditionally have been underrepresented in most labour segments (with the exception of low-status work). Second, the demographic profile of customers is increasingly diverse (in particular with regard to ethnic diversity). The business principle of matching, which refers to the recruitment of applicants who fit the organization's and its clients' demographic profile, is seen as an important determinant of organizational success, although empirical evidence for this argument is sparse and inconsistent (Petersen & Dietz, 2005). Third, diverse teams produce better results because they bring more perspectives to the job than do homogeneous teams.

The problem with the business case for diversity is that the data largely do not support it. Williams and O'Reilly (1998: 120), upon reviewing the diversity literature, concluded that 'the preponderance of empirical evidence suggests that diversity is most likely to impede' how organizations function. In order to reap the benefits of workforce diversity, organizations must actively manage it. Today 'diversity management' has become one of the buzzwords in the human resource management community.

In this chapter we will discuss two approaches to diversity management. The macro or organizational-level approach speaks to organizational designs for diversity and suggests organizational change processes toward the multicultural organization. The micro approach draws on psychological models of discrimination and inter-group relations, thereby offering a platform for designing interventions that reduce conflict and maximize cooperation.

Macro models of diversity management
Over the years, scientists (for example, Cox, 1991, 2001; Cox & Blake, 1991; Golombiewski, 1995; R. Thomas, 1991, 1996) have proposed several macro or organizational-level models of diversity management. Here we first briefly review the model by Cox (1991, 2001) as a classic model of diversity management and that by D.A. Thomas and Ely (1996; Ely & D.A. Thomas, 2001) as a model that has been tested, at least partially, in the field. A discussion of empirical evidence follows, before we turn to suggestions for future research.

Cox's model
Cox (1991, 2001) developed his model on the basis of conceptual analyses and case examples. According to Cox (1991), up to the 1970s, *monolithic* organizations were dominant in the USA. These organizations essentially did not manage diversity, and the HR function was underutilized. Instead, through assimilation, minority members were expected to adjust to existing organizational norms, which had been shaped by the predominant demographic group (typically, white men). *Pluralistic* organizations, which first started to emerge in the late 1960s and represent the dominant organizational model today, engage in diversity management. They recruit and hire minority employees, monitor their compensation systems for fairness, and offer diversity training. Finally, the *multicultural* organization is the model for the future. In the multicultural organization, pluralism is the dominant value, and organizational members do not differ in their identification with the organization as a function of their demographics. Furthermore prejudice, discrimination and inter-group conflict are minimal. A key differentiator between the pluralistic and multicultural organization is that minority employees are not only valued as contributing to the organization, but also are formally and informally fully integrated (for example, across levels and tasks).

Cox and Blake (1991), in addition, specified the activities of diversity management. These include bias-free HR systems (such as training and development), policies that allow women to have the same career opportunities as men, education programmes, and the management of organizational cultures for diversity and inclusiveness. Cox (2001) revisited his earlier model, adding a cyclical five-step model toward becoming a multicultural organization. The five steps are leadership, research and measurement, education, alignment of management systems, and follow-up. Conceptually, this model can be viewed as an application of classic diagnostic models to diversity management (that is, leadership defines the diversity management issue, which is then systematically resolved and, in turn, leadership moves on to the next diversity issue).

Thomas and Ely's model
Thomas and Ely (1996) focused on processes by which diversity management affects the relationship between workforce diversity and organizational outcomes variables (for example, organizational effectiveness). Ely and Thomas (2001) argued that an organization's diversity perspective, which refers to organizational members' normative beliefs and expectations about cultural diversity and its role in their organizations, is a key moderator of the relationship between diversity and work outcomes. An organization's diversity perspective stands for the values that drive its diversity management practices. Ely and Thomas argued for three types of diversity perspectives: discrimination and fairness, access and legitimacy, and integration and learning. The authors tested and refined their arguments in a qualitative study of workgroups from three US firms. They observed that workforce diversity had the most positive effects on workgroup functioning when the workgroup stood for an integration-and-learning perspective. The effects of diversity perspective on group functioning were mediated by the quality of inter-group relations, feelings of being valued and respected, and the positivity of employees' racial identity at work.

On the basis of their theory-generating study, Ely and Thomas (2001) offered a refined description of the three diversity perspectives.

- The discrimination-and-fairness perspective focuses on ensuring equal and fair treatment and avoiding discriminatory practices. Diversity is not explicitly related to an organization's work, and the predominant diversity management strategy is colourblindness (demographics are ignored because they are assumed not to affect performance). Ironically the focus on fairness inevitably leads to concerns about unfairness, resulting in strained relationships among ethnic groups. These relationships are characterized by defensive claims of innocence. White employees become apprehensive about their racial identity, and employees of colour feel powerless. The discrimination-and-fairness perspective reduces the opportunities for learning from each other.
- The access-and-legitimacy perspective is characterized by using diversity as a means of gaining 'access to and legitimacy with a diverse

market' (Ely & Thomas, 2001: 265). The resulting staffing patterns (for example, more minority employees in inner-city markets versus more white employees in suburban areas) produce perceptions of differential status: the higher the percentage of white employees is in a business unit or function, the higher is its status. Minority employees question their value for the organization and feel uncertain about the value of their racial identity at work. The access-and-legitimacy perspective, like the discrimination-and-fairness perspective, prevents ethnically different employees learning from each other.

• The integration-and-learning perspective of diversity management assumes that 'the insights, skills, and experiences employees have developed as members of various cultural identity groups are potentially valuable resources' (2001: 240). These resources can influence organizational thinking on a variety of strategically important dimensions, such as market and product choices. Different cultural experiences are associated with different patterns of problem solution strategies and insights for optimizing organizational efficiency. Organizational members openly discuss the impact of their race-based experiences and value the input of ethnically different employees as an opportunity for learning.

Empirical research
Empirical research on diversity management at the macro or organizational level is sparse. Consistent with Ely and Thomas (2001), this research assumes that diversity management has a moderating effect on the relationship between diversity and organizational outcomes (in particular, organizational performance). The subsections below are organized by the assumptions about the linearity (ordinary linearity or curvilinearity) of the relationship between diversity and its outcomes.

The linear hypothesis   Figure 12.1 is a graphic representation of the role of diversity management for linear relationships between diversity and performance. A direct effect of diversity on organizational performance is not hypothesized, as the positive effects of diversity (variety of perspectives and problem-solving approaches; see, for example, McLeod, Lobel & Cox, 1996) are counterbalanced by its negative effects (dissimilarity-based conflicts, such as suggested by social identity theory, for example, Tajfel, 1978, and similarity attraction theory, Byrne, 1971; Berscheid & Walster, 1978). Diversity management is hypothesized to moderate the relationship between diversity and organizational performance so that this relationship is positive (or not negative) in the presence of diversity management, but negative in the absence of diversity management. The conceptual argument

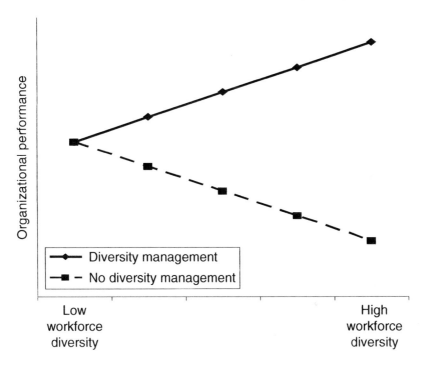

Figure 12.1   *The effect of diversity management on the linear relationship between workforce diversity and organizational performance*

is that, in order to take advantage of diverse perspectives and diverse access to networks, organizations need to manage carefully the potential conflicts and tensions resulting from diversity. When employees, through diversity management, become aware of the unique value that demographically different colleagues can offer, the likelihood of capturing the benefits of diverse perspectives are enhanced (cf. Ely & Thomas, 2001; Konrad & Linnehan, 1995).

Empirical tests of the linear hypothesis, as indicated above, are sparse. It is noteworthy that in several studies diversity was generally not related to organizational performance. Richard (2000) and Richard, McMillan, Chadwick and Dwyer (2003), in samples of US banks, did not find direct effects of racial diversity on bottom-line measures of organizational performance. Shrader, Blackburn and Iles (1997) reported, in a sample of 200 large US firms, that the percentage of women managers was related to financial profitability measures, such as return on assets, but Dwyer, Richard and Chadwick (2003) could not replicate this finding in a sample of 177 US banks.

In addition to Ely and Thomas's (2001) above-reviewed study, some evidence indicates a moderating effect of diversity management on the relationship between diversity and performance at the business unit of analysis. At the business unit and group levels of analysis, research in various organizations (Kochan *et al.*, 2003) has consistently shown that positive effects of racial diversity on business performance depended upon the extent to which organizations engaged in diversity interventions (for example, diversity training and emphasis on diversity as an organizational value). As the degree of diversity management increased, the effects of diversity on performance became more positive or at least less negative.

At the organizational level, we are not aware of research that indicates a moderating effect of diversity management on the relationship between diversity and organizational performance. A study by Wright, Ferris, Hiller and Knoll (1995), in a sample of 34 USA-based firms, indicated a direct effect. These researchers reported that the avoidance of diversity mismanagement (as indicated by awards for exemplary affirmative action programmes and avoidance of discrimination-related announcements) had a positive effect on stock price valuation. Bierman (2001), however, failed to replicate Wright *et al.*'s results in both the data of firms used by Wright *et al.* and a more extensive dataset. Bierman observed negative stock returns for the winners of exemplary affirmative action programmes.

The curvilinear hypothesis   Richard and his colleagues (Richard, Barnett, Dwyer & Chadwick, 2004; Richard & Murthi, 2004) recently argued for curvilinear relationships between organizational-level workforce diversity and organizational performance. These researchers suggested a U-shaped relationship on the basis of Blau's (1977) theory of heterogeneity. Richard *et al.* (2004), made this argument for the effects of diversity of management groups rather than entire workforces. According to Blau, homogeneous groups are characterized by positive social associations and interactions, which would contribute to effective organizational functioning. At increasing levels of diversity, communication would become more difficult as employees organized themselves in demographic subgroups, leading to between-group isolation and reduced effectiveness. At extremely high levels of diversity, however, demographic subgroups would be less likely to form because diversity would be more diffused and pressures to interact with demographically similar colleagues would be reduced. Instead pressures to interact with dissimilar colleagues would be increased, resulting in higher organizational performance.

Figure 12.2 is a graphical illustration of Richard and Murthi's (2004) arguments for the moderating effect of diversity management on the curvilinear relationship between diversity and organizational performance.

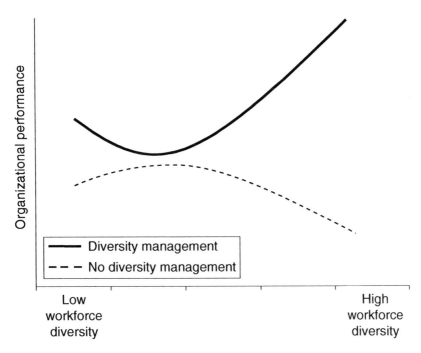

Figure 12.2   *The effect of diversity management on the curvilinear relationship between workforce diversity and organizational performance*

The authors suggested that, as the comprehensiveness of organizational diversity management systems increased, the U-shaped relationship between diversity and organizational performance would be stronger. For organizations with less comprehensive diversity management systems, however, the relationship between diversity and organizational performance would become increasingly negative.

As for the linear relationships between diversity and organizational performance, empirical evidence for the curvilinear relationship and the moderating role of diversity management is sparse. In a study of the 50 US organizations that were ranked as the most attractive employers for minorities by *Fortune* magazine, Richard and Murthi (2004) found a curvilinear U-shaped effect of racial diversity on productivity (operationalized as return on assets), such that productivity was highest when diversity was particularly low or particularly high. Richard *et al.* (2004), however, could not replicate this finding in a sample of 153 banks (neither for racial nor for gender diversity in the management groups of organizations).

Furthermore, Richard and Murthi (2004) observed that the U-shaped relationship between racial diversity and productivity was strongest in organizations with more comprehensive diversity management programmes. Their findings for highly diverse organizations were particularly remarkable. Whereas highly diverse organizations with high levels of diversity management reported the highest returns on assets across all organizations, those highly diverse organizations that engaged in less diversity management reported the lowest returns on assets across all organizations.

Future research
We noticed two key issues in reviewing macro-level research on diversity management. First, empirical research is rare. Second, and related to the first issue, the quality of the existing empirical research lags behind that of the theoretical work. The empirical research typically relies on rather crude assessments and categorizations of diversity management programmes. It is, however, obvious that testing full-fledged models of diversity management is an empirically arduous, if not impossible, task. The logical remedies are to scale down the conceptual models of diversity management, to test only the core assumptions or components of diversity management models (see, for example, Ely & Thomas, 2001, who focused on diversity perspectives) or to improve the empirical procedures. Regarding the latter point, researchers might choose multiple-study strategies, whereby each study assesses only a manageable number of diversity management elements.

The interpretability of the above-reviewed empirical research is hampered in several ways. First, some studies (for example, Richard, 2000; Richard *et al.*, 2003) relied on one informant per organization (typically an HR employee) (see Gerhart, Wright, McMahan & Snell, 2000, on the problems of single-informant designs and cross-sectional designs). An alternate methodology might include a representative sampling of employees within organizations in longitudinal designs. Second, theoretically critical variables have not been assessed. Examples include the distributions of diversity within organizations across locations, hierarchical levels and professions. Organizations might be diverse because of a range of social groups in their personnel, but the social groups might be clustered (Lefkowitz, 1994), resulting in a low potential for benefits and losses from diversity. Other variables that have not been assessed include the mediators of diversity effects on organizational performance, such as the interactions among organizational members (for an exception, see Ely & Thomas, 2001). Third, the vast majority of the research has been conducted in the USA on racial and gender diversity, and we sense a dire need for replications in other countries and for other forms of diversity.

Summary
At the macro level (business unit, organization) of analysis, diversity management is hypothesized to moderate the relationship between workforce diversity and performance, so that this relationship becomes more positive (or less negative) as the degree of diversity management increases. Empirical research to test this hypothesis is very sparse. It is noteworthy that very little research exists in the domain of international human resource management. For example, little is known about the effects of diversity management on the relationship between culturally diverse workforces (for example, the mix of home country nationals, host country nationals and third country nationals) and the performance of the subsidiaries of globally operating organizations.

Micro approaches to diversity management: stereotypes, prejudices and discrimination
Dietz and Petersen (2005) argued that a critical component of diversity management is understanding and managing stereotypes and prejudices. Figure 12.3 presents a model that may guide research on diversity management interventions on the basis of social psychological theories. Stereotypes and prejudices are seen as proximal or immediate antecedents of discrimination. The model acknowledges that other social psychological processes, such as the development of social identities (for example, Tajfel, 1978) and social categorizations (for example, Turner, 1985), the experience of realistic group conflict (Sherif, 1966; Sherif *et al.*, 1961; Campbell, 1965), contact with demographically different persons (Allport, 1954) and individual differences in social dominance orientation (Sidanius & Pratto, 1999; Sidanius, Pratto & Bobo, 1996) are critical for understanding discriminatory behaviour, but these social psychological processes are more distal antecedents of discrimination than are stereotypes and prejudices. Here, because of the immediate impact of stereotypes and prejudices on discrimination and because organizational researchers rarely attend to them, we focus on prejudices and stereotypes in the workplace and their implications for diversity management.

Stereotypes, prejudices and discrimination in the workplace
Stereotypes are descriptive 'pictures in our heads' (Lippman, 1922) about members of other social groups, such as people of a different ethnic or national origin or individuals with a different religious background. Prejudices are evaluative attitudes toward others based on their membership in a social group (for example, Brigham, 1971). For outgroups, both stereotypes and prejudices typically carry a negative connotation. Whereas stereotypes and prejudices are psychological constructs (that is, they are in

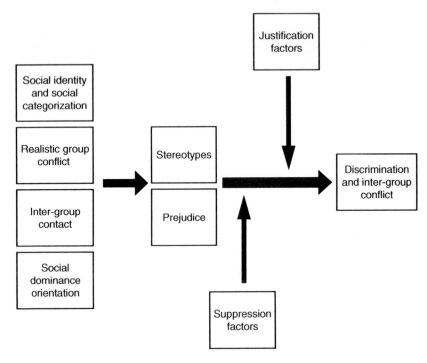

Figure 12.3   Prejudice, stereotypes and discrimination

the minds of people), discrimination refers to the behavioural treatment of the members of other social groups. Racial discrimination, for example, occurs when individuals are treated differently solely on the basis of their ethnicity. Figure 12.3 indicates that stereotypes and prejudices lead to discrimination, but this relationship is moderated by both suppression and justification factors, described below.

Suppression factors
In today's Western societies, the open expression of stereotypes and prejudices in the form of discriminatory behaviour is relatively rarely seen (compared to 30 to 50 years ago, when negative stereotypes and attitudes toward others as well as prejudicially motivated discrimination, such as serving only white or male customers, were widely tolerated) (for example, James, Brief, Dietz & Cohen, 2001; Petersen & Dietz, 2005). In the USA, for example, various polls taken since the passage of the Civil Rights Act of 1964 show that Whites' attitudes toward Blacks have become considerably more tolerant (for example, Schuman, Steeh, Bobo & Kryson, 1997). Only

a minority today endorses racial segregation. As Bobo (2001: 269) concluded: 'The single clearest trend in studies of racial attitudes has involved a steady and sweeping movement toward general endorsement of the principles of racial equality and integration.'

To explain this trend, the notion of suppression factors (cf. Crandall & Eshleman, 2003) is helpful. These factors stifle the expression of negative stereotypes and prejudices. Crandall and Eshleman viewed suppression factors as a set of psychological forces. For example, individuals might perceive that societal norms would not allow them to express their prejudice. They might also recognize that their endorsement of egalitarianism is not consistent with their negative stereotypes or prejudices. Or they simply might have behavioural standards of non-discrimination. Extending the notion of suppression factors, we consider them also at the organizational and societal levels. Some organizations have not only antidiscriminatory values and norms, but also formal rules against discrimination (for example, corporate codes, see Schwartz, 2001). These rules, if violated, lead to sanctions, such as poorer performance evaluations and lower bonuses or, in extreme cases, firings. At the societal level, laws and other legal regulations (such as Title VII in the USA) further suppress the expression of prejudice.

Research on so-called 'modern' or 'subtle' prejudice (see Dovidio & Gaertner, 1998, 2004; Pettigrew & Meertens, 1995, for reviews), which has emerged over the last 30 years, documents the suppression of prejudice at the individual level. Scientists in Europe and North America have studied the new prejudice using a variety of labels: modern prejudice (Pettigrew & Meertens, 1995), symbolic racism (Kinder & Sears, 1981), ambivalent racism (Katz & Hass, 1988) and sexism (Glick & Fiske, 1996), aversive racism (Dovidio & Gaertner, 1998, 2004) and modern racism and sexism (McConahay, 1983, 1986; Swim, Aikin, Hall & Hunter, 1995). One fundamental message of this research is that remnants of negative attitudes toward demographic others continue to exist, but they are often so latent, subtle and covert that those who harbour them are not aware of them. Pettigrew and Meertens (1995: 58) described the new subtle prejudice as 'cool, distant, and indirect', while the old blatant prejudice is 'hot, close, and direct'. Subtly prejudiced individuals do not openly endorse the differential treatment of minority members or negative stereotypes about them. They do, however, deny the existence of discrimination, and resist demands made by minorities and policies designed to support them. Typically subtly prejudiced individuals see themselves as non-prejudiced (Dovidio & Gaertner, 1998), arguing that they reject stereotypes about minority groups and that prejudice and discrimination are bad (McConahay, 1986).

Justification factors
A second fundamental message of subtle prejudice theories is that subtle prejudice only leads to discriminatory behaviours, when these behaviours can be justified in non-prejudicial ways (for example, Dovidio & Gaertner, 1998, 2004; McConahay, 1986). In other words, in order to act on their prejudice, subtly prejudiced individuals have to be able to justify, rationalize or explain away the prejudicial nature of their actions. These justifications can take many forms, in particular in organizations. Examples include: 'We only complied with orders from above'; 'No, we do not treat non-white customers poorly, but our white clientele because of its economic power deserves particularly good treatment'; 'Ethnically different employees would not fit well with the organization'; 'We should not hire women because they would not get along with our mostly male staff and/or clientele'; 'We did not hire this Indian applicant because she was Indian, but because her work experience and training were from India and she does not have Canadian work experience.' Although prejudice theories treat justification factors at the individual level, like suppression factors, they can be conceptualized at the individual, organizational and societal levels.

In summary, the model presented in Figure 12.3 shows that the path from stereotypes and prejudices to discrimination is not a simple one. Instead stereotypes and prejudices have gone underground and they only lead to discrimination when discrimination can be rationalized in non-prejudicial ways. Before speculating about interventions against discrimination, we present empirical evidence on the expression of prejudice in organizational settings.

Empirical research
Despite the importance of stereotypes and prejudice for diversity management, very few organizational scientists have studied and assessed them. Below, we review six laboratory studies and two field studies of prejudice in organizations.

Laboratory research   Studies by Brief, Dietz, Cohen, Pugh and Vaslow (2000) and Petersen and Dietz (2000, 2005) applied modern prejudice theory to hiring and selection decisions. Brief *et al.* reported two US studies of employment discrimination against African American applicants: white participants evaluated African Americans negatively or preferred not to invite them to interviews only when they were subtly prejudiced and had a 'business justification' to discriminate. As a justification, an organizational authority had expressed the belief that the demographic profile of new employees should match that of the existing personnel or clientele. In the absence of a business justification, modern prejudice did not predict discrimination. Petersen and Dietz (2000) observed similar effects of authoritarianism (for example, Altemeyer, 1988), which is related to prejudice, and a supervisor's demographic preference on employment discrimination in a German study. In a German follow-up study, Petersen and Dietz (2005) also demarcated the effects of modern prejudice from those of old-fashioned prejudice. These studies were the first to show that factors in the organizational context could provide prejudiced individuals with justifications behind which they hid their prejudicial attitudes.

In addition to research in the USA and Germany, a related stream of research by Dietz, Esses and their colleagues demonstrated similar effects in Canadian settings. In a study by Dietz, Esses, Bhardwaj and Joshi (2005) participants read one of four résumés of MBA graduates, who applied for a marketing job in a Canadian company. The MBA graduates were either Whites or African Americans, and they had received their degrees either in Canada or in South Africa. The results showed that participants evaluated negatively only the candidate who was African American and had an MBA degree from South Africa. If the candidate was African American and had a Canadian MBA degree, he was evaluated just as positively as the white candidate who received his MBA in Canada or South Africa. Importantly, if the South African MBA degree had been the 'true' or legitimate reason for a negative evaluation, the white applicant with a South African degree should also have been devalued. In a follow-up study, Esses, Dietz and Bhardwaj (forthcoming) found that prejudiced participants used a candidate's location of training (India versus England or Canada) as an excuse to discriminate against her, but only when the candidate also had Indian citizenship. When the candidate had Canadian citizenship, her Indian training was not used against her (not even by prejudiced participants). Participants would not just openly discriminate against an immigrant, but if that immigrant was also trained in a non-Western country, prejudiced participants had a seemingly non-prejudicial excuse (that is, a justification factor) to discriminate against immigrants.

Finally, to indicate further the importance of subtle prejudice theories for diversity management, consider the study reported by Dovidio, Gaertner, Kawakami and Hodson (2002). These researchers examined dyads of black and white students who worked on a problem-solving task. The white participants had been classified as non-prejudiced, subtly prejudiced and prejudiced. Following the completion of the problem-solving task, the Whites' and Blacks' impressions of the Whites' behaviours were assessed. As expected, non-prejudiced and subtly prejudiced Whites described their social interaction behaviours as friendlier than did prejudiced Whites. Blacks, however, perceived only non-prejudiced Whites to be friendlier than prejudiced Whites. Blacks also reported less trust in prejudiced Whites and, in particular, subtly prejudiced Whites. In addition to its effects on social relationships, Whites' level of prejudice also affected task performance. Dyads including a non-prejudiced White solved the task most quickly, followed by dyads with prejudiced Whites. The slowest dyads included subtly prejudiced Whites, leading Dovidio *et al.* to infer that the conflicting messages that subtly prejudiced individuals might send ('I am not prejudiced, but I do feel uncomfortable interacting with you, a Black person') likely hampered team efficiency.

Field studies   James, Brief, Dietz and Cohen (2001) examined how prejudicial attitudes can also result in negative work-related attitudes. These researchers argued that white employees' views of corporate affirmative action policies as benefiting African American employees were associated with negative job attitudes among white employees only when these white employees harboured prejudicial attitudes against Blacks. Their US study of 125 white employees in a highly diverse telecommunications organization was supportive of their arguments. Prejudice moderated the relationship between white employees' perceptions of affirmative action policies as benefiting African Americans and promotion satisfaction, such that only prejudiced employees reacted with reduced promotion satisfaction to perceptions of affirmative action policies as helping their African American colleagues.

Tsui, Egan and O'Reilly (1992) did not assess the prejudicial attitudes of white employees in their study, but they evoked prejudice to explain that Whites might react more negatively to increasing numbers of non-Whites in the workplace compared to non-Whites' reactions to increasing numbers of Whites. Their US study of 1705 employees from three organizations was consistent with these arguments: The organizational attachment of Whites decreased as the percentages of non-Whites in their workgroups increased, but the organizational attachment of non-Whites was not affected by the percentage of Whites in their workgroups.

Summary
Empirical research indicates that prejudice still affects the treatment of demographically different employees in organizations, albeit in more complex ways than 30 to 50 years ago. As the model depicted in Figure 12.3 indicates, justification factors have to be in place for subtle prejudice to lead to discriminatory behaviour and inter-group conflict. This research also indicates that, in organizational settings, such justification factors are often readily available. Diversity managers have to be aware of the complex joint effects of stereotypes, prejudices and the organizational context in order to design effective diversity management interventions.

Future research

The research reviewed above shows how stereotypes and prejudices can lead to discrimination in organizational settings, but it does not provide an evaluation of diversity management interventions against stereotypes and prejudices. The model depicted in Figure 12.3 provides a starting point for developing a programme of research on such interventions. They may aim at eliminating or reducing (a) negative stereotypes or prejudices, (b) justification factors, and (c) discrimination. Alternatively, interventions may lead to the enhancement of suppression factors. We discuss each of these points below. This discussion, in fact, complements the arguments raised in the previous section on organizational level models of diversity management by suggesting how organizational level interventions have to be designed to stamp out discrimination and inter-group conflict.

Eliminating negative stereotypes and prejudices   Diversity managers have to be aware that stereotypes and negative attitudes are generally difficult to change (cf. Dietz & Petersen, 2005), as they are ingrained in Western cultures. The model in Figure 12.3 indicates that interventions might include the redefinition of social identities and categorizations, the creation of settings that require inter-group cooperation (for example, shared goals) rather than conflict, the opportunity for contact among members of different social groups, and awareness of social dominance beliefs. Owing to space limitations, we cannot discuss these approaches in detail, but we will briefly elaborate on the contact hypothesis (see Dovidio and Gaertner, 2004, for a discussion of the implications of social identity and social categorization theories for reducing prejudice).

Brief and Barsky (2000) reached a rather pessimistic conclusion about the applicability of the contact hypothesis to organizational settings. These authors argued that, in organizational settings, the conditions for positive effects of inter-group contact, such as equal status, are typically not fulfilled. We concur with Brief and Barsky, but would like to add a slight twist on the basis of the 'extended contact hypothesis' by Wright, Aron, McLaughlin-Volpe and Ropp (1997), who hypothesized and found that, if an ingroup member had a close friendship with an outgroup member, more positive inter-group attitudes resulted. For example, if a white person's closest friend is of Asian Indian descent, this person can be expected to show more empathy in reaction to the news of natural catastrophes in India (even if her friend does not live in India and does not have relatives or friends there). To date, the viability of the extended group hypothesis has not been tested in organizations. A recent study by Bacharach, Bamberger and Vashdi (2005), however, indicates that organizations may be able to affect cross-racial friendships and peer relationships in the workplace.

In a study of 2342 employees from 60 work units in different organizations, these scientists found that cross-racial friendships and peer relationships were more prevalent in units characterized by a strong climate of peer support (these researchers, however, also found that the opportunity for contact alone was inversely related to the development of cross-racial relationships). These findings imply for the management of diversity that it is not sufficient to recruit a diverse workforce, but that, in addition, an organizational focus on peer support is critical for building positive inter-group relations. Future research will, it is hoped, replicate Wright *et al.*'s (1997) findings in organizations.

Finally, with regard to changing stereotypes and prejudices, diversity managers must understand that blatantly prejudiced, subtly prejudiced and non-prejudiced individuals would require different interventions (Brief & Barsky, 2000). It is particularly difficult to change the attitudes of subtly prejudiced individuals. They believe that they are not prejudiced and would readily agree that prejudice is bad and should be eliminated. In other words, changing the attitudes of subtly prejudiced individuals is like preaching to the choir (Dietz & Petersen, 2005; see, however, Dovidio & Gaertner, 2004, on techniques to address unconscious racial attitudes).

Eliminating discriminatory behaviours　If stereotypes and attitudes are difficult to change, then diversity managers may turn their attention to eliminating the discriminatory behaviours that result from them. In fact the enhancement of suppression factors and the elimination of justification factors, discussed below, speak to eliminating discriminatory behaviours. To begin with, however, diversity managers need to understand the degree of discrimination and inter-group conflict in their organizations. As theories of subtle prejudice suggest, they may not always do so. Because stereotypes and prejudices operate in subtle ways, the resulting discrimination often goes unnoticed as it is justified as non-prejudicially motivated (that is, as not being discrimination). Lefkowitz (1994) serendipitously found 'ethnic drift' in a job placement study in a US bank. In this bank, new employees tended to be assigned to supervisors of the same ethnic group, and this employee–supervisor congruence increased with reassignments. Bank managers, however, stated that they had not been aware of these homophyly effects. Hence effective diversity management starts with a diversity audit that allows an organization to see how it is doing on employment discrimination. A diversity audit is based on numbers, for example, comparisons among the demographic profiles of the labour pools, recruitment pools and the pool of new hires. These numbers tell top management whether their organization is 'walking the talk' of diversity management or not.

Enhancing suppression factors   Earlier we argued that suppression factors could be conceptualized at the individual, organizational and societal levels. At the organizational level, an organizational design approach suggests that an organization has to align its different components to build a climate for diversity (or a climate against prejudice and discrimination). For example, an organization's strategy may define learning from others as a key success factor (cf. Ely & Thomas, 2001). Furthermore, as the likelihood is low that changes in employees' stereotypes and prejudices will lead to behavioural changes, firm rules and norms against discrimination need to be in place. Such rules, as Brief and Barsky (2000) suggested, include enforceable consequences (that is, punishments, negative reinforcement) for violators and silent observers. Business unit leaders, for example, may be evaluated and rewarded on the diversity performance of their units (Coca-Cola, for example, has done so; see Bhawuk *et al.*, 2002). In addition to firm rules and norms against discrimination, positive rules and norms for diversity have to be established. Brief, Buttram, Reizenstein, Pugh, Callahan, McCline and Vaslow (1997) spoke of principled disobedience in response to instructions from organizational authorities that may lead to discrimination. Such principled disobedience entails the dispersion of authority, the redefinition of the role of the loyal subordinate, and the encouragement of peer discourse. Collectively the measures described above, in the long run, should contribute not only to a climate of diversity, but to a more stable and more deeply ingrained culture of diversity (Dietz & Petersen, 2005).

Eliminating justification factors   We assert that practitioners and students of diversity management often do not acknowledge justification factors that may trigger prejudicially based behaviours. Our earlier review of empirical research on stereotypes and prejudices in organizations revealed the disconcerting variety of these factors, such as person–organization fit, person–customer fit, foreign training and so on. Perhaps the most hypocritical justification factors for discrimination that have been observed in practice (see, for example, Gentile, Kaiser, Johnson, Harvey & Adler, 1991) are that minority employees (a) need to be protected from hostility in the workplace (for example, an African American employee should not be placed in a potentially racist environment) and (b) themselves are prejudiced (for example, Muslim employees may not tolerate women supervisors). The research by Brief *et al.* (2000), Petersen and Dietz (2000, 2005), and Dietz, Esses and their colleagues (2005) speaks to the importance of stating clear hiring and promotion criteria that are linked to job performance, as opposed to relying on ethnic group membership as a proxy for these criteria. In addition to the clarity of the criteria, the weights assigned to them must be clear and consistent across applicants from different ethnicities. A clear weighting, for example, might counteract the tendency to use foreign training as justification for not hiring immigrants, when the same foreign training is not held against local applicants.

Summary
To date, despite the importance of stereotypes and prejudices for diversity management, organizational research on them is sparse. Research on managing stereotypes and prejudices is even sparser. Nonetheless inferences about diversity management on the basis of prejudice theories provide scientists and practitioners with rationales for designing interventions to stamp out discrimination and inter-group conflict. These instructions may have to be harsh (behavioural change through punishments and negative reinforcement) rather than soft (attitude change).

Conclusion
When workforce diversity and diversity management became topics in organizations, many practitioners and researchers hoped that they could easily make the 'business case' for diversity, showing its positive consequences for employees, their employers and society at large. This chapter sends a different message. Demographic workforce diversity affects organizational outcomes in complex ways, including linear and curvilinear relationships that operate through mediators or are moderated by third variables. As a result, managing diversity is a very difficult task. So is studying diversity management. It is noteworthy that our discussion of macro and micro models of diversity management leads us to conclude that organizations are better off using colour-conscious rather than colourblind diversity management practices (cf. Konrad & Linnehan, 1995). If organizations rely on colourblind practices, the risk of latent prejudice breaking through unnoticed is high, and if organizations do not acknowledge the diversity of their workforce, they can hardly learn from it.

References
Allport, G.W. 1954. *The nature of prejudice*. Reading, MA: Addison-Wesley.
Altemeyer, B. 1988. *Enemies of freedom: understanding right-wing authoritarianism*. San Francisco, CA: Jossey-Bass.
Bacharach, S.P., P.A. Bamberger & D.F. Vashdi (2005). Diversity and homophily at work: supportive relations among white and African American peers. *Academy of Management Journal*, **48**(4).
Berscheid, E. & E.H. Walster. 1978. *Interpersonal attraction*. Second edition. Reading, MA: Addison-Wesley.
Bhawuk, D.P.S., A. Podsiadlowski, J. Graf & H.C. Triandis. 2002. Corporate strategies for managing diversity in the global workplace. In G.R. Ferris, M.R. Buckley & D.B. Fedor (eds), *Human resources management: perspectives, context, functions, and outcomes*: 122–64. Fourth edition. Upper Saddle River, NJ: Prentice-Hall.

Bierman, L. 2001. OFCCP affirmative action awards and stock market reaction. *Labour Law Journal*, **52**: 147–56.

Blau, P.M. 1977. *Inequality and heterogeneity*. New York: Free Press.

Bobo, L. 2001. Racial attitudes and relations at the close of the twentieth century. In N. Smelser, W.J. Wilson & F. Mitchell (eds), *America becoming: racial trends and their consequences*: 262–99. Washington, DC: National Academy Press.

Brief, A.P. & A. Barsky. 2000. Establishing a climate for diversity: the inhibition of prejudiced reactions in the workplace. In G.R. Ferris (ed.), *Research in personnel and human resources management*. Volume 19: 91–129. Amsterdam: JAI.

Brief, A.P., J. Dietz, R.R. Cohen, S.D. Pugh & J.B. Vaslow. 2000. Just doing business: modern racism and obedience to authority as explanations for employment discrimination. *Organizational Behavior and Human Decision Processes*, **81**: 72–97.

Brief, A.P., R.T. Buttram, R.M. Reizenstein, S.D. Pugh, J.D. Callahan, R.L. McCline & J.B. Vaslow. 1997. Beyond good intentions: The next steps toward racial equality in the American workplace. *The Academy of Management Executive*, **11**: 47–58.

Brigham, J.C. 1971. Ethnic stereotypes. *Psychological Bulletin*, **76**: 15–38.

Byrne, D. 1971. *The attraction paradigm*. New York: Academic Press.

Campbell, D.T. 1965. Ethnocentric and other altruistic motives. In D. Levine (ed.), *Nebraska symposium on motivation*. Volume 13: 283–311, Lincoln, NE: University of Nebraska Press.

Cox, T. 1991. The multicultural organization. *Academy of Management Executive*, **5**: 34–47.

Cox, T. 2001. *Creating the multicultural organization: a strategy for capturing the power of diversity*. Business school management series. Michigan: University of Michigan.

Cox, T. & S. Blake. 1991. Managing cultural diversity: implications for organizational competitiveness. *Academy of Management Executive*, **5**: 45–56.

Crandall, C.S. & A. Eshleman. 2003. A justification-suppression model of the expression and experience of prejudice. *Psychological Bulletin*, **129**: 414–46.

Dietz, J. & L.-E. Petersen. 2005. Diversity Management als Management von Stereotypen und Vorurteilen am Arbeitsplatz [Diversity management as management of stereotypes and prejudice at the workplace]. In G.K. Stahl, W. Mayrhofer & T.M. Kühlmann (eds), *Innovative Ansätze im Internationalen Personalmanagement* [Innovative approaches to international human resource management]. Mering: Rainer Hampp.

Dietz, J., V.M. Esses, A. Bhardwaj & C. Joshi. 2005. *Employment discrimination against ethnic immigrants: the role of foreign credentials*. Paper presented as part of a symposium at the 20th Annual Conference of the Society for Industrial and Organizational Psychology in Los Angeles.

Dovidio, J.F. & S.L. Gaertner. 1998. On the nature of contemporary prejudice: the causes, consequences, and challenges of aversive racism. In S.T. Fiske & J.L. Eberhardt (eds), *Confronting racism: the problem and the response*: 3–32. Thousand Oaks, CA: Sage Publications.

Dovidio, J.F. & S.L. Gaertner. 2004. Aversive racism. *Advances in Experimental Social Psychology*, **36**: 1–52.

Dovidio, J.F., S.L. Gaertner, K. Kawakami & G. Hodson. 2002. Why can't we just get along? Interpersonal biases and interracial distrust. *Cultural Diversity & Ethnic Minority Psychology*, **8**: 88–102.

Dwyer, S., O.C. Richard & K. Chadwick. 2003. Gender diversity in management and firm performance: the influence of growth orientation and organizational culture. *Journal of Business Research*, **56**: 1009–19.

Ely, R.J. & D. A.Thomas. 2001. Cultural diversity at work: the effects of diversity perspectives on work group processes and outcomes. *Administrative Science Quarterly*, **46**: 229–73.

Esses, V.M., J. Dietz & A. Bhardwaj. (forthcoming). The role of prejudice in the discounting of immigrant skills. In R. Mahalingam (ed.), *The cultural psychology of immigrants*. Mahwah, NJ: Erlbaum.

Gentile, M.C., J. Kaiser, J. Johnson, B. Harvey & N.J. Adler. 1991. The case of the unequal opportunity. *Harvard Business Review*, **69**: 14–25.

Gerhart, B., P.M. Wright, G.C. McMahan & S.A. Snell. 2000. Measurement error in research on human resources and firm performance: how much error is there and how does it influence effect size estimates? *Personnel Psychology*, **53**: 803–34.

Glick, P. & S.T. Fiske. 1996. The ambivalent sexism inventory: differentiating hostile and benevolent sexism. *Journal of Personality and Social Psychology*, **70**: 491–512.

Golombiewski, R. 1995. *Managing diversity in organizations*. Tuscaloosa, AL: University of Alabama Press.

James, E.H., A.P Brief, J. Dietz & R.R. Cohen. 2001. Prejudice matters: job attitudes as function of the perceived implementation of policies to advance disadvantaged groups. *Journal of Applied Psychology*, **86**: 1120–28.

Katz, I. & R.G. Hass. 1988. Racial ambivalence and American value conflict: correlational and priming studies of dual cognitive structures. *Journal of Personality and Social Psychology*, **55**: 893–905.

Kinder, D.R. & D.O. Sears. 1981. Prejudice and politics: symbolic racism versus racial threats to the good life. *Journal of Personality and Social Psychology*, **40**: 414–31.

Kochan, T., K. Bezrukova, R. Ely, S. Jackson, A. Joshi, K. Jehn, J. Leonard, D. Levine & D. Thomas. 2003. The effects of diversity on business performance: report of the Diversity Research Network. *Human Resource Management*, **42**: 3–21.

Konrad, A.M. & F. Linnehan. 1995. Formalized HRM structures: coordinating equal employment opportunity or concealing organizational practices? *Academy of Management Journal*, **38**: 787–820.

Lefkowitz, J. 1994. Race as a factor in job placement: serendipitous findings of ethnic drift. *Personnel Psychology*, **47**: 497–514.

Lippman, W. 1922. *Public opinion*. New York: Harcourt, Brace & Jovanovich.

McConahay, J.B. 1983. Modern racism and modern discrimination: the effects of race, racial attitudes, and context on simulated hiring decisions. *Personality and Social Psychology Bulletin*, **9**: 551–8.

McConahay, J.B. 1986. Modern racism, ambivalence, and the Modern Racism Scale. In S.L. Gaertner & J.F. Dovidio (eds), *Prejudice, discrimination, and racism*: 91–125. San Diego, CA: Academic Press.

McLeod, P.L., S.A. Lobel & T.H. Cox. 1996. Ethnic diversity and creativity in small groups. *Small Group Research*, **27**: 248–64.

Petersen, L.-E. & J. Dietz. 2000. Social discrimination in a personnel selection context: the effects of an authority's instruction to discriminate and followers' authoritarianism. *Journal of Applied Social Psychology*, **30**: 206–20.

Petersen, L.-E. & J. Dietz. 2005. Prejudice and enforcement of workforce homogeneity as explanations for employment discrimination. *Journal of Applied Social Psychology*, **35**: 144–59.

Pettigrew, T.F. & R.W. Meertens. 1995. Subtle and blatant prejudice in Western Europe. *European Journal of Social Psychology*, **25**: 57–75.

Richard, O.C. 2000. Racial diversity, business strategy, and firm performance: a resource-based view. *Academy of Management Journal*, **43**: 164–77.

Richard, O.C., T. Barnett, S. Dwyer & K. Chadwick. 2004. Cultural diversity in management, firm performance, and the moderating role of entrepreneurial orientation dimensions. *Academy of Management Journal*, **47**: 255–66.

Richard, O.C., A. McMillan, K. Chadwick & S. Dwyer. 2003. Employing an innovation strategy in a racially diverse workforce. *Group and Organization Management*, **28**: 107–26.

Richard, O.C. & B.P.S. Murthi. 2004. Does race matter within a multicultural context: alternate modes of theorizing and theory testing. Paper presented at the 2004 Academy of Management Conference in New Orleans.

Schuman, H., C. Steeh, L. Bobo & M. Kryson. 1997. *Racial attitudes in America*. Second edition. Cambridge, MA: Harvard University Press.

Schwartz, M. 2001. The nature of the relationship between corporate codes of ethics and behavior. *Journal of Business Ethics*, **32**: 247–62.

Sherif, M. 1966. *In common predicament: social psychology of intergroup conflict and cooperation*. Boston, MA: Houghton-Mifflin.

Sherif, M., O.J. Harvey, B.J. White, W.R. Hood & C.W. Sherif. 1961. *Inter-group cooperation and competition: the robbers cave experiment.* Norman, OK: University Book Exchange.

Shrader, C.B., V.B. Blackburn & P. Iles. 1997. Women in management and firm financial performance. *Journal of Managerial Issues,* **9**: 355–72.

Sidanius, J. & F. Pratto. 1999. *Social dominance: an intergroup theory of social hierarchy and oppression.* New York: Cambridge University Press.

Sidanius, J., F. Pratto & L. Bobo. 1996. Racism, conservatism, affirmative action and intellectual sophistication: a matter of principled conservatism or group dominance? *Journal of Personality and Social Psychology,* **70**: 476–90.

Stockdale, M.S. & F.J. Crosby. 2004. *The psychology and management of workplace diversity.* Malden, MA: Blackwell Publishers.

Swim, J.K., K.J. Aikin, W.S. Hall & B.A. Hunter. 1995. Sexism and racism: old-fashioned and modern prejudices. *Journal of Personality and Social Psychology,* **68**: 199–214.

Tajfel, H. (ed.) 1978. *Differentiation between social groups: studies in the social psychology of intergroup relations.* Oxford: Academic Press.

Thomas, D.A. & R. Ely. 1996. Making differences matter: a new paradigm for managing diversity. *Harvard Business Review,* **74**: 79–90.

Thomas, R.R. 1991. *Beyond race and gender: unleashing the power of your total workforce by managing diversity.* New York: Amacom.

Thomas, R.R. 1996. *Redefining diversity.* New York: American Management Association.

Tsui, A.S., T.D. Egan & C.A. O'Reilly. 1992. Being different: relational demography and organizational attachment. *Administrative Science Quarterly,* **37**: 549–79.

Turner, J.C. 1985. Social categorization and the self-concept: a social cognitive theory of group behavior. In E.J. Lawler (Ed.), *Advances in group processes: theory and research.* Volume 2: 77–122. Greenwich, CT: JAI Press.

Williams, K.Y. & C.A. O'Reilly. 1998. Demography and diversity in organizations. In B.M. Staw & R.I. Sutton (eds), *Research in organizational behavior.* Volume 20: 77–140. Stamford, CT: JAI Press.

Wright, S.C., A. Aron, T. McLaughlin-Volpe & S.A. Ropp. 1997. The extended contact effect: knowledge of cross-group friendships and prejudice. *Journal of Personality and Social Psychology,* **73**: 73–90.

Wright, P., S.P. Ferris, J.S. Hiller & M. Knoll. 1995. Competitiveness through management of diversity: effects on stock price valuation. *Academy of Management Journal,* **38**: 272–87.

PART III

RESEARCH ON INTERNATIONAL ASSIGNMENTS

13 Expatriate adjustment and performance: a critical review
David C. Thomas and Mila B. Lazarova

In this chapter we examine an assumption in the literature on international assignments, the belief in a direct positive relationship between the adjustment of expatriates and their performance. We first outline the historical basis for the overwhelming focus on adjustment. We then review the literature on the conceptualization and measurement of both adjustment and performance and on the adjustment–performance relationship. Finally, we reflect on the state of knowledge of this relationship and discuss implications for future research.

Historical basis for the study of adjustment
A vast amount of research on international assignments has as its focus the adjustment of expatriate managers and their families. While the move to a new environment may be the most novel aspect of international assignments, and a focus on adjustment might seem natural, this aspect of the international experience has dominated the expatriation literature, and has to a degree excluded the consideration of other outcomes. The focus on adjustment is so pervasive that in some empirical studies adjustment has been substituted for a wide range of outcome variables, effectively changing the nature of the phenomenon under investigation (Thomas, 1998). Moreover a strong positive relationship between adjustment and performance is often uncritically assumed, thus forming a lawlike generalization in the expatriate paradigm (for example, Andreason, 2003).

Perhaps the single most important event in generating the study of overseas adjustment was the advent of the Peace Corps in the United States in 1961 (see Lundstedt, 1963). The study of human behaviour in cross-cultural interactions had existed for some time, but this research was largely limited to the study of visiting students in the United States (for example, Smith, 1956), reduction of stress in military personnel (for example, Stouffer, 1949) or speculative theoretical expositions (for example, Schuetz, 1944). The Peace Corps was the first non-military endeavour engaged in the large-scale management of human resources in a variety of foreign locations, with 6554 people abroad in 1963 (Byrnes, 1966). Moreover the Peace Corps engaged social scientists, to help its members achieve cross-cultural effectiveness, who themselves drew on the existing sojourner literature (for example, Lysgaard, 1955; Oberg, 1960; Sewell & Davidsen, 1956), which focused on adjustment. For example, Smith's (1966) evaluation of the performance of Peace Corps teachers in Ghana and Mischel's (1965) study of Peace Corps volunteers in Nigeria both defined success in terms of adjustment. Thus this stream of research, which built on the sojourner adjustment literature (see Church, 1982, for a review), laid a strong foundation for adjustment as equalling success in overseas assignments.

Explicit in the research on expatriation during the 1970s and early 1980s (with some exceptions) was that adjustment was crucial to effectiveness on overseas assignments and that selection and training programmes should be designed to facilitate adjustment (for example, Hays, 1972, 1974; Howard, 1974; Miller & Cheng, 1978; Tung, 1981). The conventional wisdom derived from this literature was that, while firms tended to select expatriates on the basis of technical skills, their performance (or, more accurately, remaining on assignment the agreed upon period of time) depended on their ability to adjust. The tradition of focusing on adjustment as the key outcome of interest in the study of expatriates continued during the explosion of research on the topic that occurred from the late 1980s to the 1990s and to some extent continues today. The stated rationale for much of this research was the high cost of expatriate failure, with expatriate failure defined as premature return from assignment because of the failure of the expatriate (or spouse) to adjust.

A final factor that possibly influenced the dominance of adjustment as a central construct during this period was the interests of researchers. Social science research is inevitably influenced by the particular perspective of those conducting it (Mitroff, 1972) and a significant number of the most prolific researchers on this topic share the fact that as a part of their background they all engaged in an overseas missionary experience. These missionary postings are extraordinarily demanding, requiring significant pre-departure training, including fluency in the foreign language. And, like many expatriate assignments, the outcomes of missionary postings are long-term and difficult to measure accurately. Anyone who has spent a significant amount of time living and working overseas has felt the culture shock and experienced the difficulty adjusting to the foreign environment. Therefore, it is not surprising that researchers with this experience would consider adjustment as central to overseas effectiveness.

This discussion is not meant as a criticism of much excellent work, only as a partial explanation of the long-term and pervasive focus on adjustment as central to expatriate performance. That is, it is possible to discern an historical basis for the overwhelming focus on adjustment that is not necessarily warranted by the nature of the phenomenon itself. While adjustment is justifiably an important consideration in the expatriate experience, it may have enjoyed attention that is not consistent with its contribution to expatriate performance. A contributing factor is that the construct of adjustment itself has often been ill-defined. It is this issue to which we turn next.

Measurement of adjustment

Early definitions of adjustment conceptualized it in terms of overcoming culture shock (Oberg, 1960), the latter being defined as 'a normal process of adaptation to cultural stress involving such symptoms as anxiety, helplessness, irritability, and longing for more predictable and gratifying environment' (Church, 1982). This is the conceptualization implied in the work by Black and Gregersen (1991: 498) when they define adjustment as the 'degree of a person's psychological comfort with various aspects of a new setting'. Others have conceptualized adjustment as general satisfaction with one's life in the new environment (Hippler, 2000) or the 'degree of fit between the expatriate manager and the environment, both work and sociocultural' (Aycan, 1997a:433, 1997b), or as psychological well-being and sociocultural competence (Searle & Ward, 1990). Complicating matters, however, is the fact that it is not uncommon for researchers to use adjustment, adaptation and acculturation synonymously (Harrison, Shaffer & Bhaskar-Shrinivas, forthcoming) not to define adjustment explicitly, or to operationalize it through different constructs such as effective performance, satisfaction, degree of social interaction with host nationals, positive attitudes towards the host country, personal of professional growth, profile of mood states, mental health, absence of stress or premature return from assignment (see Church, 1982; and Thomas, 1998, for reviews). Thus, we are faced with the possibility of a conceptual overlap between adjustment and at least some aspects of performance. Finally some authors have distinguished between *anticipatory*, *in-country* and *repatriation* adjustment (for example, Black, Gregersen & Mendenhall, 1992). Our focus here is limited to the relationship between expatriate adjustment on assignment and performance.

Dimensionality and operationalization of adjustment

While some authors conceptualize adjustment as a single dimension, the vast majority of recent research adopts a multidimensional approach, with two multidimensional models of adjustment dominating the literature. By far the most popular conceptualization and measurement of adjustment among management researchers is the framework of Black and colleagues (Black, 1988; Black & Gregersen, 1991; Black *et al.*, 1991; Black & Stephens, 1989). In this model, adjustment is conceptualized as having three separate facets: *general*, *interaction* and *work* adjustment. Some early studies explicitly tested the dimensionality of this construct (for example, Parker & McEvoy, 1993) but more recent expatriate research simply accepts the model as axiomatic. The last two decades have accumulated sizeable (though sometimes contradictory) evidence for significant relationships between adjustment facets and specific antecedents and outcomes (Bhaskar-Shrinivas, Harrison, Shaffer & Luk, 2004; Thomas, 1998). Our review suggests some severe conceptual and measurement limitations of this construction.

First, a careful examination of the original work by Black and colleagues yields little in the way of theoretical clarity on construct definition and operationalization. In the seminal article, Black (1988) grounds his argument in the literature on work adjustment in domestic transfers when he points out that there exists '*some theoretical and empirical support* for the inclusion of adjustment to outside work factors as another facet of adjustment. Thus *it seems* that at a minimum there are *at least two facets* of adjustment: work adjustment and general adjustment' (Black, 1988: 279, emphases added), and goes on to say '*It seems*, expatriate managers adjust to 1) work roles; 2) interacting with host country nationals [. . .], and 3) the general culture and everyday life' (ibid.: 283, emphasis added).

Our review of the development of Black's (1988) 11-item scale suggested several other conceptual and measurement limitations, which we summarize in the following.

- The scale contains six items based on Torbiorn's (1982) work, which itself was not a comprehensive list of living conditions, but selected aspects based on general assumptions about people's needs (Hippler, 2000).
- Black's (1988) factor analysis was performed on an unacceptably small sample yielding inconclusive individual item loadings and factors with unsatisfactory reliability coefficients.
- The Black (1988) scale is a self-report instrument in the form of 'how adjusted are you to . . .' creating, as discussed below, additional measurement issues.
- Further development of the scale (Black & Stephens, 1989: 532), offered no theoretical argument as to the three specific dimensions, other than a passing reference to 'past theoretical and empirical work' (that is, Black's 1988 inconclusive article).
- Neither of Black's original publications contains confirmatory factor analysis, normally associated with construct development and validation.
- The theoretical article advancing a comprehensive model of international adjustment (Black *et al.*, 1991) is published *after* the

empirical work described above with reference only to 'research in the 80s' (namely, Black, 1988; and Black & Stephens, 1989). (To the credit of the authors, this article contains a fair warning: it points out that, even though a multifaceted conceptualization is proposed, 'the lack of systematic empirical evidence leaves the question open for future research': 305).

- Concurrently published work (Black & Gregersen, 1991) refers to the three facets as fully established by past research.

From this point forward, the conceptualization and related measurement become ubiquitous in further work on adjustment. Thus, a set of logical and intuitive, but ultimately data-driven, propositions that lack theoretical (and even empirical) substantiation established the standard for over a decade of subsequent research.

Recent years have provided statistical evidence for the operationalization of the dimensions of the construct and their structural equivalence across culturally dissimilar samples (Robie & Ryan, 1996; Shaffer, Harrison & Gilley, 1999). However this refers to the psychometric characteristics of the scales. It does not provide evidence that the domain of adjustment has been adequately represented. Recent research has pointed out that (a) the model may be inadequate to assess adjustment to a similar culture (Suutari & Brewster, 1998), (b) the categories overlap in some aspects yet do not identify other important elements of adjustment (Hippler, 2000), (c) there is significant redundancy in the interaction and the work adjustment items (Stahl & Caligiuri, 2005), and (d) items in the general adjustment scale are disproportionate to the work and the interaction scales (Harrison *et al.*, forthcoming).

Our discussion is not meant as a criticism of the research undertaken by Black and his colleagues. Their original publications clearly describe their propositions and provide sufficient technical details about their findings. Rather we find fault with the adoption of their conceptualization and scales without critical evaluation on behalf of subsequent research as well as with the resulting lack of interest in advancing our understanding of adjustment.

Another conceptualization of adjustment used extensively in cross-cultural adjustment research, but less popular among expatriate researchers, is presented by Searle and Ward (1990). They suggest the need to distinguish between two related but distinct facets of adjustment: *psychological* (referring to psychological and emotional well-being and satisfaction and reflecting the emotional/affective facet of adjustment) and *sociocultural* (referring to the ability to 'fit in', to acquire culturally appropriate skills and to negotiate interactive aspects of the host culture; and reflecting the behavioural facet of adjustment) (see Ward & Kennedy, 1992, 1999). Psychological adjustment can be best understood in terms of a stress and coping framework, and sociocultural adjustment – within a social skills and culture learning paradigm.

While Ward and associates provide a more solid theoretical basis of their conceptualization of adjustment than Black and his colleagues, they do not propose a comprehensive model of adjustment, and their early investigations of the antecedents of the two facets are, to some extent, piecemeal and empirically driven (for example, Ward & Kennedy, 1992). They measure psychological adjustment with an established depression inventory (Searle & Ward, 1990; Ward & Chang, 1997; Ward & Kennedy, 1992, 1994, 1999), which is not entirely consistent with other measures that have been used to capture psychological adjustment (Oguri & Gudykunst, 2002; Rogers & Ward, 1993; Ward & Kennedy, 1992).

Sociocultural adjustment was measured by items asking respondents to report the level of difficulty they experienced in various areas such as making friends, making themselves understood, or understanding local humour (Ward & Kennedy, 1999). Only minimal research reports the psychometric characteristics of the scale; there is insufficient clarity on exactly what the scale measures, other than generally defined sociocultural competence or social skills; and a recent review on the measure did not report validation and was inconclusive regarding scale dimensionality (Ward & Kennedy, 1999). Comparing results across the many studies using the scale is complicated because the scale is often modified according to the sample.

In summary, each of the conceptualizations of adjustment have specific strengths, both offer valuable insights into the experiences of adjusting to a new setting, but both need to be developed further to address important shortcomings.

Process of adjustment

An overwhelming majority of the work on cross-cultural adjustment in the last decade has been concerned with variables predicting the *degree* of adjustment. Because many of these variables can be traced back to the theoretical framework outlined by Black, Mendenhall and Oddou (1991) and related extensions (for example, Parker & McEvoy, 1993; Shaffer *et al.*, 1999) they have often been implicitly assumed also to predict performance, without regard for the process of this influence. Issues of mechanisms, strategies and time required to achieve adjustment remain underresearched. Several frameworks for exploring the *process* of adjustment, such as social learning principles and operant conditioning (Church, 1982), role transitions and socialization theory (Black & Gregersen, 1991), appraisal of acculturation experiences and coping (Aycan, 1997a) have been suggested. Unfortunately empirical research has largely ignored (for exceptions see Selmer, 1999; Shay & Baack, 2004; Stahl, 2000; Tung, 1998; Zimmermann, Holman & Sparrow, 2003) processes of adjustment, focusing on antecedents and outcomes, without specifying how people adjust (Zimmermann *et al.*, 2003). As discussed below, understanding the *how* of adjustment is one important avenue for understanding the adjustment–performance relationship.

Measurement of performance
In order to evaluate appropriately the relationship between adjustment overseas and performance on the expatriate assignment, it is important that we are also clear about what we mean by performance. Interestingly, the literature of expatriation has rarely focused on performance as an outcome variable, choosing instead to discuss overseas success. There is a pervasive assumption that success implies successful performance, but the evidence is far from established.

Success in an overseas posting has been defined in a variety of ways including, but not limited to, adjustment, intent to remain on assignment, satisfaction, commitment and task performance (Thomas, 1998). Early studies of sojourner effectiveness overseas (for example, Kealey & Ruben, 1983; Mischel, 1965; Smith, 1966) alluded to the multidimensional nature of overseas effectiveness, and Cushner and Brislin (1996) identified four criteria that summarized overseas success. Multidimensional measures of expatriate effectiveness have followed a similar pattern, with Caligiuri and Tung (1999) suggesting an interrelated measure consisting of adjustment, intention to return early and performance, and Shaffer *et al.* (2003) conceptualizing effectiveness as adjustment (Black's, 1988, three facets), task and contextual performance, and withdrawal cognitions. In the following section we briefly examine three of the most common performance-related constructs before turning our attention to direct measures of performance.

Intent to remain
By far the most pervasive outcome represented in the literature on expatriation is the intention to remain on assignment for the agreed-upon length of time, commonly operationalized as premature return home. A high rate of premature return coupled with the high cost of this phenomenon, has been the rationale for countless surveys of expatriates (see Harzing, 1995, for a discussion). In some cases premature return has been used as a proxy for failure to adjust (for example, Mendenhall & Oddou, 1985), an approach that is indicative of the circular logic and/or construct overlap prevalent in this literature.

Intent to remain is clearly an inadequate measure of successful expatriate performance. It is obvious that expatriates who stay on assignment but behave inappropriately or perform inadequately are conceivably more of a failure than those who return early. Conversely, staying on assignment the agreed-upon length of time is not a guarantee that tasks have been accomplished, relationships formed or personal development achieved. Finally, even though the term of the assignment has been met, the failure to reintegrate into the sponsoring organization (Black & Gregersen, 1991) or to capitalize on the skills gained overseas (Inkson, Pringle, Arthur & Barry, 1997) can also be regarded as a failure.

Job attitudes

Job attitudes (job satisfaction, commitment and so on) have also been assessed as an indicator of effective performance in overseas assignments. They have been treated as both a proxy for adjustment (for example, Newman, Bhatt & Gutteridge, 1978) and an outcome of adjustment (for example, Aryee & Stone, 1996; Takeuchi, Yun & Tesluk, 2002). However recent work suggests that job satisfaction and adjustment are unique outcomes (see Bhaskar-Shrinivas *et al.*, 2004). Clearly work-related attitudes are important in the evaluation of expatriates' overall relationship with their job and employer. However the tenuous relationship between attitudes and behaviour is well documented (Wicker, 1969). Therefore job-related attitudes are clearly inadequate as a measure of expatriate performance, but may play an important role as part of multidimensional effectiveness assessments or as mediating or moderating constructs.

Interaction with hosts

In addition to acting as a characteristic of adjustment (Black, 1988) the effective interactions with host nationals has a long-standing history as a measure of effective performance overseas. Both the sojourner (for example, Abe & Wiseman, 1983; Hammer, Gudykunst & Wiseman, 1978) and the expatriate (Tung, 1984, 1988) literatures have typically included this factor as a criterion of effectiveness, and also as a career development goal of overseas assignments (Feldman & Thomas, 1992). This ability is often cited as a key criterion of effective cross-cultural training (Cushner & Brislin, 1996).

Undoubtedly the ability to interact effectively with people who are culturally different is a critical element in performance on international assignments. Its importance is of such a magnitude that understanding individual differences in this ability has spawned a new area of research. The emerging study of this capability, which is being called *cultural intelligence* (Earley & Ang, 2003; Thomas & Inkson, 2004), shows promise for understanding individual differences in overseas performance. However this new literature does not entirely resolve the place of this construct within the adjustment–performance relationship.

Performance

An important consideration in the assessment of expatriate performance is the often conflicting performance expectations of host nationals and home office superiors (Mendenhall & Oddou, 1985; Suutari & Tahvanainen, 2002). This is a unique feature of the expatriate role which is difficult but necessary to balance. Not surprisingly, studies often find differences based on who (home or host country national) is evaluating performance (for example, Dalton & Wilson, 2000). Additionally the possibility of cultural differences in performance assessment exists (Abe & Wiseman, 1983).

Another consideration in the assessment of performance is, of course, the nature of the task to be performed. Early studies of sojourners and overseas managers were primarily concerned with such outcomes as teaching effectiveness (Smith, 1966) or technology transfer (Franko, 1973). Now performance typically means managerial performance (Thomas, 1998). Often this managerial performance has been assessed against expectations of the assessor on perceived overall effectiveness, achievement of expectations and/or achieving company goals (for example, Dalton & Wilson, 2000). Recent research identifies different dimensions of performance, with concomitant differences in the effect of antecedents (Caligiuri & Day, 2000). Obviously, any relationship between adjustment and performance depends in part on what aspect of performance is being assessed and who is conducting the assessment.

Where performance has been directly evaluated, it has often been regarded as a unitary construct (Caligiuri, 1997). If performance itself is multidimensional, what elements comprise an adequate measure of effective performance is somewhat circumspect (for examples, see Caligiuri & Day, 2000; Earley, 1987).

Two facets of performance have a long history of being distinguishable. These are task-based and relationship-based aspects of performance (Harrison *et al.*, forthcoming), which are also those elements that appear consistently in multidimensional definitions of expatriate performance (Caligiuri, 1997; Cushner & Brislin, 1996; Feldman & Thomas, 1992; Gregersen, Hite & Black, 1996). The first of these involves the accomplishment of goals, meeting objectives, which of course can be established from a variety of sources. The second involves establishing and maintaining relationships and effectively interacting with coworkers, supervisor and so on.

Adjustment–performance relationship

We now turn our attention to the somewhat limited body of literature that has directly examined the relationship between adjustment and performance. As we examine this literature it is important to keep in mind (a) that, to control for conceptual overlap, we limit our discussion to performance measures that exclude adjustment, job attitudes or intentions to remain as constituent elements, and (b) these data often involve self-reports of both constructs, a limitation to which we give attention ahead.

Some early studies of sojourners were not convinced of the direct positive relationship between adjustment and performance assumed in much of the subsequent expatriate literature. For example, Kealey (1989) and Ruben and Kealey (1979) suggested that the highest performing individuals, in terms of transferring skills and knowledge to host nationals, were also the most likely to experience severe culture shock. Earley's (1987) study of US managers sent to Korea for a short assignment found a composite measure of supervisor and self-reported performance to be negatively related ($r = -0.65$) to expatriates' perceived intensity of their adjustment (see Spradley & Phillips, 1972).

A number of studies have shown support for the influence of one dimension or another of adjustment (usually measured by Black's 1988 three-facet self-report scale) and some dimension of performance. For example, Nicholson and Imaizumi (1993), in a study of 91 expatriate managers, report that work adjustment, but not general or interaction adjustment, was positively related ($r = 0.49$) to self-reports of performance. Parker and McEvoy (1993) found that, while work adjustment was positively related ($r = 0.29$) to self-rated performance (Earley's 1987 scale), a significant negative relationship ($r = -0.18$) existed between general adjustment and performance, when work and interaction adjustment were controlled. Kraimer and associates (Kraimer, Wayne & Jaworski, 2001) found no significant relationship between general adjustment and either task or contextual performance (supervisor ratings); but work adjustment had a significant but small ($r = 0.17$) relationship with task performance, and interaction adjustment had a significant but also small ($r = 0.23$) relationship with contextual performance. Shaffer et al. (2003) found moderate relationships between self-reported adjustment (Black, 1988) and self-reported performance. Interaction adjustment was significantly related ($r = 0.35$) to contextual performance (three items from Caligiuri, 1997) and to overall task performance (fulfilling the requirements of the position; $r = 0.26$). Work adjustment was positively related to both contextual performance ($r = 0.30$) and overall task performance ($r = 0.40$).

In a departure from the three-facet self-report measure of adjustment, Shay and Baack (2004) failed to find a relationship between adjustment (measured by the extent to which the expatriates had made personal changes) and their self-rated performance, but reported a significant but small ($r = 0.19$) correlation between the extent to which expatriates had engaged in role innovation and self-rated performance. In another interesting departure from the dominant view, Clarke and Hammer (1995) found that performance and adjustment were predicted by different antecedents in a study of Japanese and American managers. That is, self-assertive skills predicted actual company performance appraisal scores ($r = 0.59$), while interpersonal skills predicted trainer-rated adjustment ($r = 0.44$).

A meta-analysis by Bhaskar-Shrinivas and colleagues (2004) claims, albeit with some disclaimers because of the small number of studies and other methods issues, to provide evidence of a reliable relationship between adjustment and expatriate performance. Specifically, however, cultural adjustment was found to be unrelated to self-reports of performance, but showed a significant if small ($p = 0.16$) relationship with multi-source measures of task performance. Cultural adjustment was positively related to both single and multiple source measures of 'relationship' performance ($p = 0.37$ and 0.17 respectively). Interaction and work adjustment (uncorrected for single source data) were found to be positively related to task performance ($p = 0.18$ and 0.33) and relationship performance ($p = 0.37$ and 0.29). The authors note, not surprisingly, that all relationships using same source data were stronger than those using multiple sources. In another recent meta analytic study (Hechanova, Beehr & Christiansen, 2003), evidence is presented that suggests both job satisfaction and organizational commitment as mediators of the adjustment performance relationship. And, consistent with Harrison *et al.* (forthcoming), the strongest relationship to adjustment was with job satisfaction (Hechanova *et al.*, 2003).

Our review indicated that the adjustment–performance relationship typically ranges from non-existent to what can only be considered as moderate. Additionally, the possibility that this relationship is mediated by other constructs has been suggested by a number of authors. Whether or not this evidence demonstrates the centrality of adjustment to expatriate performance may depend on the extent to which the conceptual or measurement limitations we discuss next have an impact on our thinking.

Reflections and observations

A number of conceptual and methodological issues contribute to our view that the adjustment–performance relationship is equivocal. Some of these issues are not unique to this particular relationship.

Cross-sectional studies

We are not the first to point out that expatriation is a longitudinal phenomenon that is not well suited to cross-sectional studies (see Harrison *et al.*, forthcoming; Hechanova *et al.*, 2003; Thomas, 1998). However this fact creates a specific additional issue in the study of the relationship between adjustment and performance. Because cross-sectional studies do not capture the processes involved, they implicitly assume similar rates and/or patterns of development in both adjustment and performance. That is, if we assume that adjustment follows the well-known U-shaped curve (Lysgaard, 1955), even though overwhelming evidence for this pattern is yet to be presented, then examining the relationship between adjustment and performance at various points in time along the adjustment curve assumes that performance follows a similar pattern. We simply do not know if performance and adjustment move in such a lock step fashion. For example, it seems entirely plausible to us that, as suggested in some of the early sojourner literature, expatriates who initially have difficulty adjusting will, through that experience, gain skills and abilities that make them higher performers in the longer term.

Self-report data
While supervisor ratings of performance (for example, Caligiuri, 2000; Caligiuri & Tung, 1999; Clarke & Hammer, 1995; Stoner, Aram & Rubin, 1972) and in rare cases subordinate ratings (Shay & Baack, 2004) have appeared in the literature, the vast majority of studies of expatriates have relied on self-reports of performance as well as adjustment. The tendency of individuals to be cognitively consistent in such studies trivializes these results to the extent that the magnitude of the relationships found could easily be accounted for by this common method problem. When studies have used a more objective measure of performance they typically continue to use self-reports of psychological adjustment. As Nisbett and Wilson (1977: 231) have cogently demonstrated, 'when people attempt to report on their cognitive processes . . . they do not do so with any true introspection. Instead their reports are based on a priori, implicit causal theories, or judgments about the extent to which a particular stimulus is a plausible cause of a given response'. In this case, it seems entirely probable that individuals who are performing well (even as rated by others) will believe that they have adjusted well. That is, 'I must be well adjusted because I'm performing well.' It is only through the use of more objective indicators of both adjustment and performance that we will solve this problem.

Adjustment as an antecedent
We believe that adjustment may have been miscast as a separable construct that is an antecedent to effective expatriate performance. Historically adjustment was either the label used for overseas effectiveness (for example, Cushner & Brislin, 1996) or was considered a facet of performance (Mischel, 1965; Smith, 1966). The myth of high failure rates (Harzing, 1995) and the centrality of adjustment as its alleged cause gave rise to a veritable industry to explain it. With the advent of the separable measure of adjustment (Black, 1988) a logical next question, based on the domestic

literature on adjustment to new roles (Nicholson, 1984), was the relationship to other outcomes, especially other aspects of the expatriate role that could be called 'performance'. However the position of adjustment in the causal chain from antecedents to performance is unclear. Adjustment, as conventionally measured, seems most highly related to job satisfaction, which in turn has a strong negative relationship to intent to leave the assignment (see Hechanova *et al.*, 2003). Thus adjustment may mediate the relationship to some outcomes, but its relationship to performance is potentially more distal. It is equally plausible that adjustment is an outcome of expatriation that parallels performance as conceptualized in a number of measures of expatriate effectiveness (for example, Caligiuri & Tung, 1999; Shaffer *et al.*, 2003).

Conceptualization of adjustment and performance
Previously we raised concerns about the conceptualization of the Black (1988) three-facet concept of adjustment. The most important of these concerns is, of course, the absence of any theoretical basis for the measure. It may be that adjustment as it is currently conceptualized in the expatriate literature is so ill-conceived and measured that it should be abandoned in favour of stress, strain, depression or other psychological indicators of failure to cope effectively with culture shock. If it is to be retained, a separable measure based on grounded theory and measured objectively needs to be adopted.

The measurement of performance is fraught with almost as many difficulties. While some studies (for example, Caligiuri & Tung, 1999; Clarke & Hammer, 1995; Shay & Baack, 2004) have measured performance with other than self-report ratings, the issue of the appropriate constituent elements remains. While measures tapping both goal accomplishment and relationship development may be defensible, they predominantly account for the firm's view on performance. From an employee perspective the development of a skill set that can transfer to other aspects of their career may be important (Feldman & Thomas, 1992) and the transference of knowledge and skills to the employer is a desirable outcome of expatriation (for example, Downes & Thomas, 2000).

Causal chain issues
The assumption of a positive relationship between adjustment and performance assumes a chain of causality that, for psychological adjustment, centres on absence of stress as a requisite for effective performance (see Beehr & Newman, 1978). However we find it equally plausible that, depending on the measure of performance (short term goal achievement, for example), individuals can perform exceptionally well at high levels of

stress (see Morris, Hancock & Shirkey, 2004). And, in some cases, the challenge of the international assignment may even facilitate superior performance (for example, Boswell, Olson-Buchanan & LePine, 2004).

The causal link between adjustment and performance is often confounded by the overlap that exists between sociocultural adjustment and relationship aspects of performance. Also examining this relationship in isolation denies the complexity of the phenomenon. If, for example, effective intercultural interactions are given a prominent role in the causal chain (for example Thomas, 2004), a host of individual moderators (for example hardiness, cultural intelligence) and situational moderators (for example job characteristics, time on assignment, cultural novelty) can be suggested.

In summary, the precise relationship between the adjustment and the performance of expatriates remains unresolved. Effectively evaluating this relationship awaits the development of a theoretically grounded measure of adjustment and also requires a clear specification of performance. Understanding the relationship would be facilitated by taking a process view of expatriation with the attendant implication for longitudinal studies. In that way, the causal linkages among constructs can be properly evaluated. Finally, given that we expect any relationship between adjustment and performance to be quite small, we should probably be more concerned with the process by which individuals deal with the inevitable culture shock of expatriate assignments and the characteristics of individuals and situations that allow them to perform well.

Acknowledgement

The authors are grateful to Laura Guerrero for research assistance in the preparation of this manuscript.

References

Abe, H. & R.L. Wiseman. 1983. A cross-cultural confirmation of the dimensions of intercultural effectiveness. *International Journal of Intercultural Relations*, **7**(1): 53–67.
Andreason, A.W. 2003. Expatriate adjustment to foreign assignments. *International Journal of Commerce & Management*, **13**(1): 42–60.
Aryee, S. & R.J. Stone. 1996. Work experiences, work adjustment and psychological well-being of expatriate employees in Hong Kong. *The International Journal of Human Resource Management*, **7**(1): 150–64.
Aycan, Z. 1997a. Acculturation of expatriate managers: a process model of adjustment and performance. *New Approaches to Employee Management*, **4**: 1–40.
Aycan, Z. 1997b. Expatriate adjustment as a multifaceted phenomenon: individual and organizational level predictors. *The International Journal of Human Resource Management*, **8**(4): 434–56.
Beehr, T.A. & J.E. Newman. 1978. Job stress, employee health and organizational effectiveness: a facet analysis, model and literature review. *Personnel Psychology*, **31**(4): 665–99.
Bhaskar-Shrinivas, P., D.A. Harrison, M.A. Shaffer & D.M. Luk. 2004. *What have we learned about expatriate adjustment? Answers accumulated from 23 years of research.* Paper

presented at the 2004 Annual Academy of Management Meeting, August, New Orleans, Louisiana.

Black, J.S. 1988. Work role transitions: a study of American expatriate managers in Japan. *Journal of International Business Studies*, **19**(2): 277–94.

Black, J.S. & H.B. Gregersen. 1991. Antecedents to cross-cultural adjustment for expatriates in Pacific Rim assignments. *Human Relations*, **44**(5): 497–515.

Black, J.S. & G.K. Stephens. 1989. The influence of the spouse on American expatriate adjustment and intent to stay in Pacific Rim overseas assignments. *Journal of Management*, **15**(4): 529–44.

Black, J.S., H.B. Gregersen & M.E. Mendenhall. 1992. Toward a theoretical framework of repatriation adjustment. *Journal of International Business Studies*, **23**(4): 737–60.

Black, J.S., M. Mendenhall & G. Oddou. 1991. Toward a comprehensive model of international adjustment: An integration of multiple theoretical perspectives. *Academy of Management Review*, **16**(2): 291–317.

Boswell, W.R., J.B. Olson-Buchanan & M.A. LePine. 2004. Relations between stress and work outcomes: the role of felt challenge, job control, and psychological strain. *Journal of Vocational Behavior*, **64**(1): 165–81.

Byrnes, F.C. 1966. Role shock: an occupational hazard of American technical assistants abroad. *The Annals of the American Academy of Political and Social Science*, **368**: 95–108.

Caligiuri, P. 1997. Assessing expatriate success: Beyond just 'being there'. *New Approaches to Employee Management*, **4**: 117–40.

Caligiuri, P.M. 2000. The big five personality characteristics as predictors of expatriates' desire to terminate the assignment and supervisor-rated performance. *Personnel Psychology*, **53**: 67–88.

Caligiuri, P.M. & D.V. Day. 2000. Effects of self-monitoring on technical, contextual, and assignment-specific performance: a study of cross-national work performance ratings. *Group & Organization Management*, **25**(2): 154–74.

Caligiuri, P.M. & R.L. Tung. 1999. Comparing the success of male and female expatriates from a US-based multinational company. *International Journal of Human Resource Management*, **10**(5): 763–82.

Church, A.T. 1982. Sojourner adjustment. *Psychological Bulletin*, **91**(3): 540–72.

Clarke, C. & M.R. Hammer. 1995. Predictors of Japanese and American managers' job success, personal adjustment, and intercultural interaction effectiveness. *Management International Review*, **35**(2): 153–70.

Cushner, K. & R.W. Brislin. 1996. *Intercultural interactions: a practical guide*. Second edition. Thousand Oaks, CA: Sage.

Dalton, M. & M. Wilson. 2000. The relationship of the five-factor model of personality to job performance for a group of Middle Eastern expatriate managers. *Journal of Cross-cultural Psychology*, **31**(2): 250–58.

Earley, P.C. 1987. Intercultural training for managers: a comparison of documentary and interpersonal methods. *Academy of Management Journal*, **30**(4): 239–52.

Earley, P.C. & S. Ang. 2003. *Cultural intelligence: individual interactions across cultures*. Stanford, CA: Stanford University Press.

Feldman, D.C. & D.C. Thomas. 1992. Career management issues facing expatriates. *Journal of International Business Studies*, **23**(2): 271–93.

Franko, L.C. 1973. Who manages multinational enterprises? *Columbia Journal of World Business*, **8**(2): 30–42.

Gregersen, H.B., J.M. Hite & J.S. Black. 1996. Expatriate performance appraisal in U.S. multinational firms. *Journal of International Business Studies*, **27**(4): 711–38.

Hammer, M.R., W.B. Gudykunst & R.L. Wiseman. 1978. Dimensions of intercultural effectiveness: an exploratory study. *International Journal of Intercultural Relations*, **2**: 382–92.

Harrison, D.A., M.A. Shaffer & P. Bhaskar-Shrinivas. (forthcoming). Going places: roads more and less traveled in research on expatriate experiences. In G. Ferris & J.J. Martocchio (eds), *Research in personnel and human resources management*, vol. 23.: Greenwich, CT: JAI Press.

Harzing, A-W.K. 1995. The persistent myth of high expatriate failure rates. *International Journal of Human Resource Management*, **6**(2): 457–75.

Hays, R.D. 1972. Ascribed behavioral determinants among US expatriate managers. *Journal of International Business Studies*, **2**: 40–46.

Hays, R.D. 1974. Expatriate selection: insuring success and avoiding failure. *Journal of International Business Studies*, **5**: 25–37.

Hechanova, R., T.A. Beehr & N.D. Christiansen. 2003. Antecedents and consequences of employees' adjustment to overseas assignment: a meta-analytic review. *Applied Psychology: An International Review*, **52**(2): 213–36.

Hippler, T. 2000. European assignments: international or quasi-domestic? *Journal of European Industrial Training*, **24**(9): 491–504.

Howard, C.G. 1974. Model for the design of a selection program for multinational executives. *Public Personnel Management*, Alexandria, VA: International Personnel Management Association.

Inkson, K., J. Pringle, M.B. Arthur & S. Barry. 1997. Expatriate assignment versus overseas experience: contrasting models of international human resource development. *Journal of World Business*, **32**(4): 351–68.

Kealey, D.J. 1989. A study of cross-cultural effectiveness: theoretical issues, practical applications. *International Journal of Intercultural Relations*, **13**(3): 387–428.

Kealey, D.J. & B.D. Ruben. 1983. Cross-cultural personnel selection criteria, issues and methods. In D. Landis & R.W. Brislin (eds), *Handbook of intercultural training. vol. 1: Issues in Training & Design*. New York: Pergamon.

Kraimer, M.L., S.J. Wayne & R.A. Jaworski. 2001. Sources of support and expatriate performance: the mediating role of expatriate adjustment. *Personnel Psychology*, **54**: 71–99.

Lundstedt, S. 1963. An introduction to some evolving problems in cross-cultural research. *Journal of Social Issues*, **19**(3): 1–9.

Lysgaard, S. 1955. Adjustment in a foreign society: Norwegian Fulbright grantees visiting the United States. *International Social Sciences Bulletin*, **7**: 45–51.

Mendenhall, M. & G. Oddou. 1985. The dimensions of expatriate acculturation: a review. *Academy of Management Review*, **10**(1): 39–47.

Miller, E.L. & J.L.C. Cheng. 1978. A closer look at the decision to accept an overseas position. *Management International Review*, **18**(3): 25–33.

Mischel, W. 1965. Predicting the success of Peace Corps volunteers in Nigeria. *Journal of Personality & Social Psychology*, **1**(5): 510–17.

Mitroff, I. 1972. The myth of objectivity or why science needs a new psychology of science. *Management Science*, **18**: 613–18.

Morris, C., P.A. Hancock & E.C. Shirkey. 2004. Motivational effects of adding context relevant stress in PC-based game training. *Military Psychology*, **16**(2): 135–47.

Newman, J., B. Bhatt & T. Gutteridge. 1978. Determinants of expatriate effectiveness: a theoretical and empirical vacuum. *Academy of Management Review*, **3**(3): 655–61.

Nicholson, N. 1984. A theory of work role transitions. *Administrative Science Quarterly*, **29**(2): 172–91.

Nicholson, N. & A. Imaizumi. 1993. The adjustment of Japanese expatriates to living and working in Britain. *British Journal of Management*, **4**(2): 119–34.

Nisbett, R.E. & T.D. Wilson. 1977. Telling more than we can know: verbal reports of mental processes. *Psychological Review*, **84**(3): 231–59.

Oberg, K. 1960. Cultural shock: adjustment to new cultural environments. *Practical Anthropology*, **7**: 177–82.

Oguri, M. & W.B. Gudykunst. 2002. The influence of self construals and communication styles on sojourners' psychological and sociocultural adjustment. *International Journal of Intercultural Relations*, **26**: 577–93.

Parker, B. & G.M. McEvoy. 1993. Initial examination of a model of intercultural adjustment. *International Journal of Intercultural Relations*, **17**(3): 355–79.

Robie, C. & A.M. Ryan. 1996. Structural equivalence of a measure of cross-cultural adjustment. *Educational and Psychological Measurement*, **56**(3): 514–21.

Rogers, J. & C. Ward. 1993. Expectation–experience discrepancies and psychological adjustment during cross-cultural reentry. *International Journal of Intercultural Relations*, **17**(2): 185–96.

Ruben, B.D. & D.J. Kealey. 1979. Behavioral assessment of communication competency and the prediction of cross-cultural adaptation. *International Journal of Intercultural Relations*, **3**(1): 15–47.

Schuetz, A. 1944. The stranger: an essay in social psychology. *American Journal of Sociology*, **49**: 499–507.

Searle, W. & C. Ward. 1990. The prediction of psychological and sociocultural adjustment during cross-cultural transitions. *International Journal of Intercultural Relations*, **14**(4): 449–64.

Selmer, J. 1999. Effects of coping strategies on sociocultural and psychological adjustment of Western expatriate managers in the PRC. *Journal of World Business*, **34**(1): 41–51.

Sewell, W.H. & O.M. Davidsen. 1956. The adjustment of Scandinavian students. *Journal of Social Issues*, **12**(1): 9–19.

Shaffer, M.A., D.A. Harrison & K.M. Gilley. 1999. Dimensions, determinants and differences in the expatriate adjustment process. *Journal of International Business Studies*, **30**(3): 557–81.

Shaffer, M.A., L.A. Ferzandi, D.A. Harrison, H. Gregersen & J.S. Black. 2003. You can take it with you: individual differences and expatriate effectiveness. BRC Papers on Cross-Cultural Management, Hong Kong Baptist University.

Shay, J.P. & S. Baack. 2004. Expatriate assignment, adjustment and effectiveness: an empirical examination of the big picture. *Journal of International Business Studies*, **35**: 216–32.

Smith, M.B. 1956. A perspective for further research on cross-cultural education. *Journal of Social Issues*, **12**(1): 56–68.

Smith, M.B. 1966. Explorations in competence: a study of peace corps teachers in Ghana. *American Psychologist*, **21**(6): 555–66.

Spradley, J. & M. Phillips. 1972. Culture and stress: a quantitative analysis. *American Anthropologist*, **74**: 518–29.

Stahl, G.K. 2000. Between ethnocentrism and assimilation: an exploratory study of the challenges and coping strategies of expatriate managers. Paper presented at Academy of Management.

Stahl, G.K. & P. Caligiuri. 2005. The effectiveness of expatriate coping strategies: the moderating role of cultural distance, position level, and time on the international assignment. *Journal of Applied Psychology*, **90**.

Stoner, J.A.F., J. D. Aram & I.M. Rubin. 1972. Factors associated with effective performance in overseas work assignments. *Personnel Psychology*, **25**: 303–18.

Stouffer, S.A. 1949. *The American soldier: combat and its aftermath*. Princeton, NJ: Princeton University Press.

Suutari, V. & C. Brewster. 1998. The adaptation of expatriates in Europe: evidence from Finnish companies. *Personnel Review*, **27**(2): 89–103.

Suutari, V. & M. Tahvanainen. 2002. The antecedents of performance management among Finnish expatriates. *International Journal of Human Resource Management*, **13**(1): 55–75.

Takeuchi, R., S. Yun & P.E. Tesluk. 2002. An examination of crossover and spillover effects of spousal and expatriate cross-cultural adjustment on expatriate outcomes. *Journal of Applied Psychology*, **87**(4): 655–66.

Thomas, D.C. 1998. The expatriate experience: a critical review and synthesis. *Advances in International Comparative Management*, **12**: 237–73.

Thomas, D.C. 2004. Cultural intelligence and the paradox of expatriate assignments. Paper presented to the annual meeting of The Academy of International Business, Stockholm.

Thomas, D.C. & K. Inkson. 2004. *Cultural intelligence: people skills for global business*. San Francisco, CA: Berrett-Koehler.

Torbiorn, I. 1982. *Living abroad*. New York: Wiley.

Tung, R.L. 1981. Selection and training of personnel for overseas assignments. *Columbia Journal of World Business*, **16**: 68–78.

Tung, R.L. 1984. Human resource planning in Japanese multinationals: a model for U.S. firms? *Journal of International Business Studies*, **15**: 139–49.

Tung, R.L. 1988. *The new expatriates: managing human resources abroad*. Cambridge, MA: Ballinger.

Tung, R.L. 1998. American expatriates abroad: from neophytes to cosmopolitans. *Journal of World Business*, **33**(2): 125–44.

Ward, C. & W.C. Chang. 1997. Cultural fit: a new perspective on personality and sojourner adjustment. *International Journal of Intercultural Relations*, **21**(4): 525–33.

Ward, C. & A. Kennedy. 1992. Locus of control, mood disturbance, and social difficulty during cross-cultural transitions. *International Journal of Intercultural Relations*, **16**(2): 175–94.

Ward, C. & A. Kennedy. 1994. Acculturation strategies, psychological adjustment, and socio-cultural competence during cross-cultural transitions. *International Journal of Intercultural Relations*, **18**(3): 329–43.

Ward, C. & A. Kennedy. 1999. The measurement of sociocultural adaptation. *International Journal of Intercultural Relations*, **23**(4): 659–77.

Wicker, A.W. 1969. Attitude versus action: the relationship of verbal and overt behavioral responses to attitude objects. *Journal of Social Issues*, **25** (Autumn): 41–78.

Zimmermann, A., D. Holman & P. Sparrow. 2003. Unraveling adjustment mechanisms: adjustment of German expatriates to intercultural interactions, work, and living conditions in the People's Republic of China. *International Journal of Cross Cultural Management*, **3**(1): 46–65.

14 Issues facing women on international assignments: a review of the research
Hilary Harris

Globalization of business has reinforced the importance of international assignments for career progression, both within an organization and across organizations. Under the 'boundaryless career' concept (Arthur & Rousseau, 1996; Parker & Inkson, 1999), managers increasingly view an international assignment as enhancing their internal rather than external careers (Tung, 1998). In a survey of US companies, while 65 per cent of HR executives thought an international assignment had a positive career impact, 77 per cent of expatriates felt it had a negative effect (Black *et al.*, 1999). Despite this, managers still continue to accept offers of international assignments as they see them enhancing their internal careers through skills acquisition, personal development and career development on the open market (Stahl *et al.*, 2002).

However the numbers of women international assignees remains stubbornly low. Most recent figures for international assignments show that women represent 18 per cent of the United States (US) international assignment sample (GMAC Global Relocation Services, 2003), 9 per cent of the European international assignment sample (Pricewaterhouse-Coopers, 2001) and 6 per cent of the Australian international assignment sample (Smith & Still, 1996). These figures stand in contrast with the numbers of women in middle management positions in the USA, Europe and Australia, where they represent between 30 and 45 per cent of the population on average.

Given the low numbers of women on international assignments, an obvious explanation is that women fail as assignees. Past research, however, does not support this contention. In contrast, it shows that women are successful in their global assignments. Adler (1987) reported a 97 per cent success rate for female expatriates working in Asian countries. These data were self-reported and might therefore reflect an inherent bias. However Adler reported that many women in her sample were promoted subsequently on the basis of their performance internationally.

Caligiuri and Tung (1999) compared male and female expatriates on three criteria of success: cross-cultural adjustment, supervisor-rated performance and desire to terminate the global assignment. Their results indicated that the percentage of men and women who wanted to terminate their global assignments did not differ. Men and women also did not differ on supervisor-related performance on the global assignment. The women, however, reported that they were less well adjusted cross-culturally than men in countries with low female workforce participation and low percentages of female managers.

It is only fair to say that the evidence is limited in terms of women's success while on international assignments. However, whilst there is no evidence of failure amongst female international assignees, there is substantial (if hotly debated) evidence of failure amongst male expatriates (Harzing, 1995). Reasons behind the paucity of women international managers need to be sought, therefore, in the reasons why so few women are selected. These are reviewed under four main categories: individual motivation, family characteristics, host nationals' attitudes towards women and organizational processes.

Individual motivation
A traditional answer given by organizational managers to the question 'Why are there so few women on international assignments?' is 'Well, they're not interested, they don't apply.' The reality of the situation is more complicated. Whilst motivation to take up international assignments may be similar in young male and female business students, perceptions of self-efficacy which are influenced by both family and socio-cultural factors may account for a lack of women applying for positions.

Motivation
The assumption that women did not want to go on international assignments was one of the first 'myths' investigated by Adler (1984b) in her research studies into women in international management in the early 1980s. Her survey of 1129 graduating MBA students in Canada, the United States and Europe showed that new women graduates expressed as much interest in international careers as their male colleagues. Later studies (Hill & Tillery, 1992; Lowe *et al.*, 1999) show similar results. Caution should be exercised when assessing the generalizability of these findings as these were business students and not international assignees. However these women were all very likely to enter organizations where a key facet of career advancement would be an international assignment, so their expressed desire to take up an assignment is likely to be based on a realistic assessment of career options. Linehan and Walsh's (1999) study of 50 senior female international managers confirmed this view, revealing that most of the women took up international assignments because they believed they constituted necessary experience for senior management positions.

A recent study by Van der Velde, Bossink and Jansen (forthcoming), conducted on 178 males and 122 female employees of a large Anglo-Dutch company found gender differences in willingness to participate in international assignments. In general, females' willingness depended on whether the position would be good in terms of personal growth, career advancement, good location, a satisfying life (both personal and family), positive cross-cultural experience and money. They would also have minimized uncertainty to do with security and political risk factors. In addition, the authors found that the salience of a woman's career affected motivation. The more important the career in terms of life goals, the more likely the participation in an international assignment.

Lowe *et al.* (1999) found that willingness to participate was affected by the level of development in specific countries. The study amongst graduate and undergraduate business students in the United States reported that gender was a significant predictor when specific referent countries were identified. Differences in cultural distance and human development explained substantial variance among males and females in their willingness to accept certain international assignments. In particular, Lowe *et al.* found that women did not want to participate in international assignments that were in countries such as Vietnam, Saudi Arabia and Indonesia. Political risk was not deemed to be a significant factor. These findings raise issues for organizations in terms of the amount of support needed to assist women to undertake assignments successfully in specific countries.

These studies show that young women are similar to young men in terms of desire to have international experience. However, even at business school stage, women are aware that they may face greater barriers than their male counterparts. They see this as mainly due to the impact of family roles and more traditional sociocultural norms in certain expatriate destinations, which in turn affects their perception of self-efficacy.

Family

The impact of family on women international assignees is usually viewed as a negative factor. Most research has focused on dual-career couples and highlights the tensions on women with male trailing partners. More recently researchers have placed a greater focus on the role of children. The reasons for family being seen as more of a problem for women than for men in general stems from continuing social norms of women's greater involvement with the family which suggest that women will experience greater conflict in trying to balance work and family responsibilities while on an international assignment. Perceptions of the difficulty of trying to combine home and work responsibilities in the context of an international assignment may even stop women from applying for assignments.

Work–family conflict
Work–family conflict is seen to be reciprocal in nature, that is, that work can interfere with family (WFC) and family can interfere with work (FWC), resulting in a wide variety of psychological and physical outcomes for individuals (Allen *et al.*, 2000; Adams *et al.*, 1996; Edwards & Rothbard, 2000; Kelloway *et al.*, 1999; Lieter & Durup, 1996). The nature of the reciprocal relationship suggests that, if work interferes with family, this may cause family issues as family obligations go unfulfilled and vice versa. An intervening variable is the extent of involvement of the individual within a domain (that is, high involvement with work) which is expected to have a direct and positive relationship with satisfaction in that domain (Adams *et al.*, 1996; Frone *et al.*, 1997).

An intervening factor in the potential for WFC or FWC is the role of social support, in terms of work or family social support (Burke, 1988; Carlson & Perrewe, 1999; Greenhaus *et al.*, 1987). Social support in the work domain may come from a variety of sources, including peers and supervisor support, as well as more formal social support mechanisms, such as organizational work–life balance programmes. Non-work social support, for example support from the family, has been found to play an important role in reducing work–non-work conflict (Caligiuri & Lazarova, 2002).

In domestic (one country) settings research findings on the influence of gender on the work–family interface are equivocal, with some reporting a link (Duxbury *et al.*, 1994; MacEwen & Barling, 1994) and others showing no evidence (Eagle *et al.*, 1997; Frone *et al.*, 1997). A possible reason for this was put forward by Gutek *et al.* (1991), who argued that most models of work–family conflict operate from a rational view, in which conflict is related linearly to the total amount of time spent in paid and family work. They posited that, according to the gender role perspective, gender role expectations mute the relationship between hours expended and perceived work–family conflict, and gender interacts with number of hours worked and work–family conflict. Their study findings provided partial support for this view, but also highlighted the complexity of the process, with changing expectations about appropriate roles from both men and women.

Work–family conflict in international assignments
In international working scenarios, which may involve the physical relocation of the entire family, however, both the impact of gender and work–family conflict itself are likely to increase. In such cases, the boundaries between work and home become blurred owing to the involvement of the whole family (Harvey, 1985). In dual-career couples, the partner's career may be disrupted and his or her sense of worth and identity may suffer (Harvey, 1997, 1998). For an international assignee with a male trailing

partner, acceptance by the overwhelmingly female expatriate spouse population may be an additional issue. The children's education may also be interrupted (Fukuda & Chu, 1994) and their social networks destroyed, which may affect their feelings of security and well-being (Harvey, 1985). In short, in international assignments, family life becomes more important because the whole family is uprooted.

Dual-career couples   From a gender role theory, sociocultural norms which see men as the primary breadwinners mean that males accompanying partners are more likely to be concerned with continuing their careers in the host country. In a survey asking men to rank activities which they felt organizations should undertake to assist accompanying partners (Punnett, 1997), four of the six top scoring activities dealt with issues concerning employment in the host country. However, many male partners are unable to obtain employment (Punnett, 1997; Windham International and National Foreign Trade Council, 1999). In these cases the male partner becomes dependent on the female expatriate and has to take on the non-traditional role of homemaker. These non-traditional roles of dependent and homemaker would be additional stressors for both the male and female partners (Caligiuri & Cascio, 1998; Harvey & Wiese, 1998; Punnett, 1997). Additional sociocultural barriers include the likelihood of the male spouse finding himself the lone man in a group of wives and the unavailability or inappropriateness of traditional volunteer activities which wives undertake in foreign locations, thus limiting the extent of productive activities for males (Punnett *et al.*, 1992). In these situations, the female partner may need to offer more support and empathy, thus increasing the demands placed on her from the family side.

The positive impact of a trailing male partner on the work performance of a female expatriate was, however, demonstrated by Linehan (2002) in her study of 50 senior female international managers. A majority of the married women in the study believed that progressing to the top of their managerial careers had been facilitated by the careers of their spouses being placed secondary to their own careers.

Family implications
The impact of an international relocation on the whole family has been examined by Caligiuri *et al.* (1998) using family systems theory (Minuchin, 1974) and family equilibrium. The authors argued that in the context of global assignments, pressures within the family, such as a child's maladjustment to his/her new school, or outside the family, such as unsatisfactory living conditions or difficulty in getting certain foods, can affect individual family members and thus the equilibrium of the family.

Under a family system approach, the *double ABCX model* (McCubbin & Patterson, 1982, 1983) examines family dynamics as they relate to family adaptation to stressors such as global relocation. The model suggests that three factors interact to produce a family's adaptation or adjustment: (a) the stressor (in this case, the international relocation), (b) the family's resources or characteristics to cope with the stressor, and (c) the family's perceptions of the stressor. The three family characteristics which most affect their ability to function are family support (or cohesion), family adaptability and family communication (Olson *et al.*, 1984). Family support refers to the cohesion or closeness that family members feel toward one another and the amount of emotional support that this engenders. Too little or too much emotional support can have negative consequences for family functioning. Family adaptability refers to the ability of the family to accommodate changes in its rules of functioning while maintaining family system continuity (Minuchin, 1974). The shift in roles for partners in the case of a female expatriate and trailing male partner will require a high degree of adaptability amongst all family members. Family communication refers to the ability to exchange opinions, respect differing opinions, establish decision-making rules, resolve conflicts, and so on. A healthy level of family communication will result in both effective support and adaptability.

The additional issues relating to family which face women in the decision process leading up to an international assignment and then once on assignment may well affect their sense of self-efficacy and indeed their overall motivation to take up such roles. The extent to which organizations offer appropriate support to women in this context is debatable. Linehan (2000) and Harris (1999) found that HR policies were geared more to the needs of the traditional male expatriate, with accompanying wife and children. They both argued that, unless these policies were re-examined and reassessed, women's participation in international assignments would remain low. Culpan and Wright (2002), however, found that international HR policies supported women in gaining their positions.

Host nationals' attitudes

One of the main reasons for the minimal participation of women in international assignments is the assumption that they will not be accepted in the host country. In her original research, Adler (1984a) found that one of the major reasons given by organizations for their reluctance to select female managers for foreign assignments was that foreigners are prejudiced against female managers.

Subsequent research by Adler (1987) amongst US women expatriates working in South-East Asian countries challenges the validity of this assumption by finding a very high rate of success amongst women international managers, largely due to the fact that women were seen as foreigners who happened to be women, not as women who happened to be foreigners – a subtle, but highly significant, distinction. Female expatriate managers were therefore not subject to the limitations imposed on local females.

More recent research by Napier and Taylor (2002) reiterates Adler's (1987) findings in looking at the experiences of women professionals working on assignments in China, Japan and Turkey. They all reported issues with gaining credibility in the initial stages of working abroad. In this respect, Japan was perceived as more difficult than China. However most of the women reported that they had found ways to overcome the resistance. In addition, they found that they were very 'visible' and had more responsibility than they would have had in an equivalent position in their home countries. The need to have and use interpersonal skills was another common feature of their experiences.

Interestingly the women reported most frustration with the non-work parts of their life. Being a woman in these countries, they felt that certain activities were 'restricted' or limited for women. They also felt that there was very little chance of developing a relationship with foreign men, or for that matter with local women as friends. Loneliness was therefore a factor. Many of the women joined associations or women's networks shortly after arriving in the host location as a way of alleviating this problem.

Several other studies have reiterated Adler's initial findings that managers in the home country organization believe that women will face prejudice from host country managers and employees in culturally different countries. Chusmir and Frontczak (1990) surveyed 222 women and men senior managers and found that the majority of them believed that attitudes towards women in foreign countries were slow to change. Smith and Still (1996) identified regions including the Middle East and parts of Asia (for example, Japan, India or Pakistan) which were seen to be inappropriate for female international assignees. In a somewhat unusual twist of events, Stone (1991) revealed that Asian and expatriate managers preferred males as international managers on the basis that female international assignees were discriminated against by (male) Western expatriates and their wives.

What is interesting when looking at the question of host-country cultural prejudices as a major barrier to women's chances of obtaining international assignments is that this issue appears to have been debated only from the point of view of women going to traditionally male-dominated cultures. Little research has been carried out into women's experiences when transferring to countries with similar or more relaxed cultural values, for instance, British women expatriates working in North America or Europe, or female expatriates from Pacific Rim countries working in Australia or North America, where the literature would argue there should be fewer problems of acceptance for female managers/professionals.

In fact, whilst there is no evidence that women fail once on assignment, there is a substantial body of research which shows that men experience difficulties adjusting (and hence performing) as a result of cross-cultural problems. There is increasing research into cross-cultural adaptation and its links to expatriate adjustment and performance. Hechanova *et al.* (2003), in their meta-review of employee's adjustment to overseas assignments, state that adjustment can refer to feelings of acceptance and satisfaction, acquisition of culturally acceptable skills and behaviours, lack of mental health problems such as stress or depression and the psychological comfort an individual feels in a new situation (Berry *et al.*, 1988; Brislin, 1981; Bochner *et al.*, 1977; Gregersen & Black, 1990). Why, then, do managers persist in using *assumptions* about possible prejudice as an excuse for not selecting women for international assignments?

Organizational processes
It is clear from the evidence above that, although women face complications in taking up international assignments, there are no blanket barriers to women being successful in such situations. Given that there is little evidence of women failing *once on* assignment, the low numbers of women international assignees may be explained by looking at organizational processes leading up to selection. It should be remembered that appointments to international positions are internal processes, closely linked to promotion and potential decisions. Two main pieces of research are reviewed here, both relating to international manager selection processes.

Supervisor–subordinate relationship
Varma and Stroh (2001) investigated reasons why women might not be made offers on international management assignments. They used the Leader–Member Exchange (LMX) model, which states that, because of time pressures, the leader can develop close relationships with only a few of his/her key subordinates (the 'in-group') while maintaining a formal relationship with the rest of his/her subordinates (the 'out-group'). Individual characteristics such as gender, race and educational background may be related to LMX and may determine the quality of the relationship between a supervisor and his/her subordinate. The authors argued that a poor quality relationship between female subordinates and primarily male superiors was the primary cause of the low number of female international assignees.

The results from the study were not conclusive, mainly owing to problems with the sample make-up (the survey targeted women who were on an international assignment, together with their current supervisors, and hence was unable to address the issues surrounding the LMX of potential women assignees and their supervisors). The focus on the informal inter-personal relationship between potential women assignees and their super-visors is, however, significant in the light of research into the role of the home country selection process as a key determinant of low female partic-ipation rates.

Line/senior managers' attitudes
In her original research into the myths surrounding women in international management, Adler (1984a) found only one to be 'true', this was that HR managers (and organizational managers) were reluctant to send women on international assignments. The attitude of managers in the home country organization is important as they are often responsible for the selection decision. A number of research studies have addressed the topic of man-agers' perceptions of women as suitable assignees. In general, these revealed a negative picture, with women being seen as unsuitable for a number of different reasons.

By far the most important reasons for negative attitudes on the part of managers towards women's participation in international assignments are family and marital status. Many managers believe that women would not be interested in international assignments because of family commitments (Adler, 1984c; Linehan, 2000, 2002; Smith & Still, 1996; Stroh *et al.*, 2000; Thal & Cateora, 1979). This includes women with accompanying spouses, where there is a general perception that problems with visas for the man will affect a woman's desire to take up an international assignment.

As stated in the previous section, many managers believed that prejudice on the part of host country nationals was a major deterrent to sending women on international assignments. A further set of perceptions shared by managers with regard to barriers to sending women on international assignments included worries about isolation and loneliness (Adler, 1984c), potential harassment (Izraeli *et al.*, 1980) and security risks (Thal & Cateora, 1979). Harris (1999), however, found that, with appropriate support and advice, women could work as effectively as men in hostile envi-ronments and also in countries with more traditional sociocultural norms.

Finally there is some limited evidence that managers perceive that women are not qualified or experienced enough to be sent on international assignments (Adler, 1984c; Harris, 1999).

Home country selection systems
The impact of managers' perceptions as to the suitability and acceptability of women as international managers is dependent on how international

assignees are selected. If the selection process allows managers to make selection decisions based on these perceptions, there is a greater likelihood that women will not be sent. The nature of the selection process is therefore a key determinant of the participation rate of women in international management. Harris (1999, 2002) examined the nature of selection systems for international managers in British-based multinationals. She discovered that they could be plotted on two axes, the first being 'open' and 'closed', the second being 'formal' and 'informal'.

In an 'open' selection system, all vacancies are advertised and all employees have equal access to applying. In a 'closed' system, on the other hand, positions are not advertised. Candidates are identified through nominations as a result of networking and reputation mainly. The components of a formal system include clearly defined selection criteria, clearly defined measures, training for selectors and panel discussions. In contrast, an 'informal' system have less defined criteria and measures, no training for selectors and no panel discussions.

The implications of the different typologies become apparent when looking at the extensive body of research in both North America and Europe highlighting the pervasive influence of discrimination in selection processes. This work addresses the issue of 'fit' from both a sociological and a social psychological perspective. From a sociological perspective, selection is seen as a *social* process, to be used by those in power within the organization as a means of determining the continuing form of the organization by recruiting and promoting only those individuals who most closely conform to organizational norms. Individuals would therefore be judged more on the basis of their *acceptability* than of their *suitability* (Jewson & Mason, 1986).

In the light of a continuing predominance of men in international management positions, the 'gender-blindness' of the majority of research into expatriate management is a problem. From a feminist perspective, the patriarchal nature of organizations, derived from the fact that organizational populations have traditionally been predominantly male, means that the holders of organizational power, in terms of shaping structures and beliefs, have been almost exclusively male. The need to acknowledge this perspective is seen to be critical as gender-role assumptions have been seen to be important components of decisions about 'fit' (Alimo-Metcalfe, 1993, 1995; Rubin, 1997; Webb, 1991).

The notion of 'fit' is taken further by sociopsychological studies into the use of schema and stereotyping in selection (for example, Futoran & Wyer, 1986; Heilman, 1983). Such studies suggest that individual selectors will develop schemata of ideal 'jobholders' and will use them as a yardstick against which all prospective candidates are measured during the process

Table 14.1 Typology of international manager selection systems

	Formal	Informal
Open	Clearly defined criteria Clearly defined measures Training for selectors Open advertising of vacancy (internal/external) Panel discussions	Less defined criteria Less defined measures Limited training for selectors No panel discussions Open advertising of vacancy Recommendations
Closed	Clearly defined criteria Clearly defined measures Training for selectors Panel discussions Nominations only (networking/reputation)	Selectors' individual preferences determine criteria and measures No panel discussions Nominations only (networking/reputation)

of selection. The less distinct the information concerning the vacancy and/
or the candidate, the more likely selectors are to use schemata and stereotypes. In occupations where there is a predominance of one gender over the
other there is a strong possibility that selectors may use gender-typed 'job-
holder' schema as part of the decision-making process (Perry *et al.*, 1994).

Harris (1999, 2002) theorized the outcome of the four different typologies as outlined in Table 14.1.

- *Open/formal* systems would be the most likely to produce equality of
  opportunity within international management selection thanks to
  the fact that employees have access to the selection process and that
  the necessity for selectors to assess candidates against formalized criteria and to determine the best 'fit' through continual comparison of
  their own assessments against other selectors' assessments would
  constrain the use of subjective judgments and generate a sharing of
  constructs. The objectivity of this type of system would be enhanced
  by the use of psychometric and other tests.
- *Closed/formal* systems imply that selectors are assessing candidates
  against formal criteria, but the lack of personal contact with the candidate, and hence the lack of any objective testing, may well lead to
  more subjective assessments. Equally the field of potential applicants
  is determined by the selector(s), with the attendant risk of omission
  of suitable candidates.
- *Open/informal* systems imply that, although employees have access to
  vacancies, decisions as to who should be selected are usually arranged

between relevant managers on the basis of personal recommendation and reputation and, although candidates may be put forward for interview, the selection decision is already made. In this scenario, the tendency for managers to select 'clones' of existing managers may well affect the possibility of women being considered for positions.
- *Closed/informal* systems are seen to be the worst situation for equality of opportunity in this area. Within this scenario, existing personal schematas of effective international managers, which may be more or less unclear, would be allowed to determine who is seen to be acceptable owing to the lack of influence of formal systems, the lack of open debate about criteria and the lack of accountability engendered by the fact that employees are unaware that the process is happening.

Investigating the typologies
In order to investigate the impact of the typology in practice, Harris (1999) chose three case study organizations. The first organization (Amstar) was in the oil industry and represented the *closed/informal* process. The second organization (Brymay) was in the airline industry and represented a more hybrid system. The selection process fell almost equally between the *open* and *closed* quadrant but was positioned more in the *informal* quadrant. The third organization (Cirus) was in the not-for-profit sector and represented the *open/formal* quadrant.

The degree to which differences in selection processes resulted in the posited outcomes with respect to the use of selectors' individual preferences in selection decision making was explored via Repertory Grid analyses (Kelly, 1955; Reger, 1990). A first set of analyses addressed the extent to which the type of selection process resulted in the posited outcomes with respect to clarity and consistency of thinking in relation to effective international managers and the degree to which the constructs derived from the Repertory Grid interviews with selectors matched formal company criteria. A further analysis addressed the potential for gender bias with respect to the way women international managers were viewed within the Repertory Grid responses and in respect of the degree to which the constructs used were masculine or feminine typed using the 92 item attribute inventory designed by Schein (1973, 1975). In the case where no match could be found, these were noted as neutral. The analysis of the constructs against the items from Schein's descriptive index (SDI) was carried out independently by Harris and a colleague and the results were then compared and a decision on best fit arrived at.

The results from the Repertory Grid interviews with selectors in each of the organizations supported the arguments posited for the outcomes of the various typologies. Under an *open/formal* system there was evidence of more consistency and clarity in thinking in relation to the characteristics of effective international managers. In addition, in Cirus, the selectors had clear views of the women international managers included on the grids and were therefore less likely to be picking clones of male managers when selecting. None of the grids showed any negative thinking about the managers being female. The position of the managers on the grid was determined exclusively by their indicators of performance. In addition, the SDI analysis of the constructs elicited through the Grid interviews showed a tendency towards a neutral/feminine gender typing, thus suggesting that equal opportunity considerations are used by selectors in the decision-making process.

In contrast, the *closed/informal* selection system in operation in Amstar did not force selectors to question their assumptions, resulting in a marked lack of consistency and clarity in thinking about criteria for effective international managers and little linkage with formal criteria. Also the majority of selectors were not clear in their thinking about the female managers included in the cognitive maps. Although the female managers were positioned on the cognitive maps in relation to their performance ratings, in general they were positioned closer to the centre of the maps, which indicates that they were seen to be less distinctive than the male managers. In addition the SDI analysis for the organization displayed a masculine-typed bias.

The picture at Brymay again provided tentative but limited support for the posited relationship between *closed/formal* and *open/informal* systems and the number of women entering international management positions. In terms of consistency and clarity of thinking in relation to characteristics of successful international managers and link with formal criteria, the organization was positioned between the two extremes of Amstar and Cirus. The number of women selected for inclusion on the grids and their general lack of distinctiveness for the selectors reflected the situation in Amstar, where thinking about women managers was generally less clear than in Cirus. It was argued that this situation would give rise to cloning of existing male international managers. The SDI results for Brymay, however, show a more equal split between masculine and neutral typed constructs, which might again reflect its positioning at the centre of the Typology of International Management Selection Systems.

The impact of the findings was reinforced by the actual numbers of women in international management positions within the three case study organizations (with Amstar having less than 5 per cent representation; Brymay having a representation of 25 per cent and Cirus having a representation of 45 per cent) despite all having fairly equal entry level ratios.

Harris's research focused attention on the pivotal, yet interlinked, role of home country organizational processes in determining the representation of women in international management. The study needs replication in different countries and with larger samples to create a more comprehensive picture of this key link in the chain. However the fact that relatively few women are sent on an international assignment suggests that both the perceptions of managers and the selection process are key determinants of participation.

Directions for further research
This review of research has highlighted several gaps in the literature and potential areas for further research. These are highlighted below.

- *Geographical scope*   Despite nearly 20 years of research interest in this area, the vast majority of studies still focus on women from the United States, the United Kingdom and Australia. Equally most of the expatriating organizations are based in these areas. Little is known of the situation for women in other countries. A multi-country qualitative study of the issues facing women and their organizations would provide a more comprehensive picture of the issues from a global perspective.
- *Assignment profile*   Again the majority of research carried out so far has focused on a traditional form of international working, the expatriate assignment. Alternatives to expatriation, including short-term assignments, commuting and self-initiated foreign assignments, are increasing and need to be examined in more depth in the women in international management literature.
- *Family considerations*   Issues relating to work–family constraints have taken a predominantly Western perspective. The impact of different sociocultural norms regarding family obligations and marital responsibilities on women from more traditional societies needs to be examined in relation to their ability to participate in international assignments. Anecdotal evidence suggests that work–family issues are less difficult for women from countries where it is accepted that the family has to separate to find work.
- *Methodology*: A majority of the studies in the women in management literature adopt a quantitative, survey methodology, with the notable exception of some qualitative studies such as Linehan's (2000, 2002). The rich and dynamic nature of the experience for both male and female international assignees calls for a more innovative and longitudinal approach to study methodology. Qualitative, longitudinal studies tracking the process of adjustment for male and female assignees from different countries would provide a wealth of insights which could be developed later into survey material, for example.

Conclusion

This chapter has reviewed the current research on women in international management. Our understanding of the factors influencing the numbers of women on international assignments encompasses the interlinkages between individual characteristics, family issues, host country barriers and organizational processes. The complexity of the issue is compounded by the need to adopt a more international approach in our research and to gain a fuller understanding of the nature of international assignments for women from every part of the globe. Our multinational organizations will only ever be able to claim true diversity if they count at the top of their management structures men *and* women from diverse nations. Critical, yet practical, research into the issues affecting participation in international assignments will, it is hoped, provide a sound framework from which both organizations and individuals can establish meaningful action plans.

References

Adams, G.A., L.A. King & D.W. King. 1996. Relationships of job and family involvement, family social support and work–family conflict with job and life satisfaction. *Journal of Applied Psychology*, **81**: 411–20.

Adler, N. 1984a. Women in international management: where are they? *California Management Review*, **26**(4): 78–89.

Adler, N. 1984b. Women do not want international careers, and other myths about international management. *Organizational Dynamics*, **13**(2): 66–79.

Adler, N.J. 1984c. Expecting international success: female managers overseas. *Columbia Journal of World Business*, **19**(3): 79–85.

Adler, N. 1987. Pacific basin managers: a Gaijin, not a woman. *Human Resource Management*, **26**(2): 169–92.

Alimo-Metcalfe, B. 1993. Women in management: organisational socialization and assessment practices that prevent career advancement. *International Journal of Selection and Assessment*, **1**(2): 68–83.

Alimo-Metcalfe, B. 1995. An investigation of female and male constructs of leadership and empowerment. *Women in Management Review*, **10**(2): 3–8.

Allen, T.D., D.E.L. Herst, C.S. Bruck & M. Sutton. 2000. Consequences associated with work-to-family conflict: a review and agenda for future research. *Journal of Occupational Health Psychology*, **5**(2): 278–308.

Arthur, M. & D. Rousseau. 1996. *The boundaryless career: a new employment principle for a new organizational era*. New York: Oxford University Press.

Berry, I., R. Kim & P. Boshi. 1988. Psychological acculturation of immigrants. In I.Kim & Y. Gudykust (eds), *Cross cultural adaptation: current approaches*. Beverley Hills, CA: Sage.

Black, J.S., H.B. Gregersen, M.E. Mendenhall & L.K. Stroh. 1999. *Globalizing people through international assignments*. New York: Addison-Wesley, Longman.

Bochner, S., B.M. McLeod & L. Anli. 1977. Friendship patterns of overseas students: a functional model. *International Journal of Psychology*, **12**(4): 277–95.

Brislin, R.W. 1981. *Cross-cultural encounters*. New York: Pergamon.

Burke, R.J. 1988. Some antecedents and consequences of work–family conflict. *Journal of Social Behavior and Personality*, **3**: 287–302.

Caligiuri, P. & W. Cascio. 1998. Can we send her there? Maximizing the success of Western women of global assignments. *Journal of World Business*, **33**: 394–416.

Caligiuri, P. & M. Lazarova. 2002. A model for the influence of social interaction and social support on female expatriates' cross-cultural adjustment. *International Journal of Human Resource Management*, **13**(5): 761–72.

Caligiuri, P.M. & R.L. Tung. 1998. Are masculine cultures female friendly? Male and female expatriates' success in countries differing in work value orientations. In G. Hofstede (chair), Masculinity/femininity as a cultural dimension. Paper presented at the International Congress of the International Association for Cross-Cultural Psychology: The Silver Jubilee Congress, Bellingham, WA.

Caligiuri, P.M. & R.L. Tung. 1999. Comparing the success of male and female expatriates from a US based multinational company. *The International Journal of Human Resource Management*, **10**(5): 763–82.

Carlson, D.S. & P.L. Perrewe. 1999. The role of social support in the stressor–strain relationship: an examination of work–family conflict. *Journal of Management*, **25**(4): 513–41.

Chusmir, L.H. & N.T. Frontczak. 1990. International management opportunities for women: women and men paint different pictures. *International Journal of Management*, **7**(3): 295–301.

Culpan, O. & G. Wright. 2002. Women abroad: getting the best results from women managers. *International Journal of Human Resource Management*, **13**(5): 784–801.

Duxbury, L., C. Higgins, & C. Lee. 1994. Work–family conflict: a comparison by gender, family type and perceived control. *Journal of Family Issues*, **15**(3): 449–66.

Eagle, B.W., E.W. Miles, & M.L. Icenogle. 1997. Interrole conflicts and the permeability of work and family domains: are there gender differences? *Journal of Vocational Behaviour*, **50**: 168–84.

Edwards, J.R. & N.P. Rothbard. 2000. Mechanism linking work and family: clarifying the relationship between work and family constructs. *Academy of Management Journal*, **25**: 178–99.

Frone, M.R., J.K. Yardley & K.S. Markel. 1997. Developing and testing an integrative model of the work–family interface. *Journal of Vocational Behavior*, **50**: 145–67.

Fukuda, K. & P. Chu. 1994. Wrestling with expatriate family problems: Japanese experiences in East Asia. *International Studies of Management and Organizations*, **24**: 36–47.

Futoran, G.C. & R.S. Wyer. 1986. The effects of traits and gender stereotypes on occupational suitability judgements and the recall of judgement-relevant information. *Journal of Experimental Social Psychology*, **22**: 475–503.

GMAC Global Relocation Services. 2003. *2002 global relocations trends survey.* Warren: GMAC Global Relocation Services.

Greenhaus, J.H., A.G. Bedeian, & K.W. Mossholder. 1987. Work experiences, job performance and feelings of personal and family well-being. *Journal of Vocational Behavior*, **31**: 200–215.

Gregersen, H.B. & J.S. Black. 1990. A multi-faceted approach to expatriate retention in international assignments. *Group and Organization Studies*, **15**(4): 461–85.

Gutek, B.A., S. Searle & L. Klepa. 1991. Rational versus gender role explanations for work–family conflict. *Journal of Applied Psychology*, **76**(4): 560–68.

Harris, H. 1999. Women in international management. In C. Brewster & H. Harris (eds), *International HRM: contemporary issues in Europe*. London: Routledge.

Harris, H. 2002. Think international manager, think male: why are women not selected for international management assignments? *Thunderbird International Review*, **44**(2): 175–203.

Harvey, M. 1985. The executive family: an overlooked variable in international assignments. *Columbia Journal of World Business*, **20**: 84–92.

Harvey, M. 1997. Dual-career expatriates: expectations, adjustment and satisfaction with international relocation. *Journal of International Business Studies*, **28**(3): 627–57.

Harvey, M. 1998. Dual career couples during international relocation: the trailing spouse. *International Journal of Human Resource Management*, **9**(2): 309–31.

Harvey, M. & D. Wiese. 1998. Global dual-career couple mentoring: a phase model approach. *Human Resource Planning*, **21**(2): 33–48.

Harzing, A.W.K. 1995. The persistent myth of high expatriate failure rate. *International Journal of Human Resource Management*, **6**(2): 457–75.

Hechanova, R., T.A. Beehr & N.D. Christiansen. 2003. Antecedents and consequences of employees' adjustment to overseas assignments: a meta-analytical review. *Applied Psychology: An International Review*, **52**(2): 213–36.

Heilman, M. 1983. Sex bias in work settings: the lack of fit model. *Research in Organisational Behaviour*, **5**: 269–98.

Hill, C.J. & K.R. Tillery. 1992. What do male/female perceptions of an international business career suggest about recruitment policies? *S.A.M. Advanced Management Journal*, **57**(4): 10–14.

Izraeli, D.N., M. Banai & Y. Zeira. 1980. Women executives in MNC subsidiaries. *California Management Review*, **23**(1): 53–63.

Jewson, N. & D. Mason. 1986. Modes of discrimination in the recruitment process: formalisation, fairness and efficiency. *Sociology*, **20**(1): 43–63.

Kelloway, E.K., B.H. Gottlieb & L. Barham. 1999. The source, nature and direction of work and family conflict: a longitudinal investigation. *Journal of Occupational Health Psychology*, **4**(4): 337–46.

Kelly, G.A. 1955. *The psychology of personal constructs*, Vols 1 and 2. New York: Norton.

Leiter, M.P. & M.J. Durup. 1996. Work, home and in between: a longitudinal study of spillover. *Journal of Applied Behavioral Science*, **32**: 29–47.

Linehan, M. 2000. *Senior female international managers: why so few?* Aldershot: Ashgate.

Linehan, M. 2002. Senior female international managers: empirical evidence from Western Europe. *International Journal of Human Resource Management*, **13**(5): 802–14.

Linehan, M. & J.S. Walsh. 1999. Senior female international managers: breaking the glass border. *Women in Management Review*, **14**(7): 264–72.

Lowe, K., M. Downes & K. Kroek. 1999. The impact of gender and location on the willingness to accept overseas assignments. *The International Journal of Human Resource Management*, **10**(2): 223–34.

McCubbin, H.L. & J.M. Patterson. 1982. Family adaptation to crises. In H.L. McCubbin, E. Cauble & J.M. Patterson (eds), *Family stress, coping and social support*: 26–47. Springfield, IL: Thomas.

McCubbin, H.L. & J.M. Patterson. 1983. The family stress process: the double ABCX model of adjustment and adaptation. In H.L. McCubbin, M.B. Sussman & J.M. Patterson (eds), *Advances and developments in family stress theory and research*: 7–37. New York: Haworth.

MacEwan, K.E. & J. Barling. 1994. Daily consequences of work interference with family and family interference with work. *Work and Stress*, **8**(3): 244–54.

Minuchin S. 1974. *Families and family therapy*. Cambridge, MA: Harvard University Press.

Napier, N.K. & S. Taylor. 2002. Experiences of women professionals abroad: comparisons across Japan, China and Turkey. *International Journal of Human Resource Management*, **13**(5): 837–51.

Olson, D.H., C.S. Russell & D.H. Sprenkle. 1984. Circumplex model of marital and family systems. In D.H. Olson & B.C. Miller (eds), *Family studies review yearbook*, vol. 2: 59–74. Beverly Hills, CA: Sage.

Parker, P. & K. Inkson. 1999. New forms of career: the challenge to human resource management. *Asia Pacific Journal of Human Resources*, **37**: 76–85.

Perry, E.L., A. Davis-Blake & C. Kulik. 1994. Explaining gender-based selection decisions: a synthesis of contextual and cognitive approaches. *Academy of Management Review*, **19**(4): 786–820.

PricewaterhouseCoopers. 2001. *International assignments: European policy and practice: key trends 1999/2000*. London: PricewaterhouseCoopers.

Punnett, B.J. 1997. Towards effective management of expatriate spouses. *Journal of World Business*, **32**(3): 243–57.

Punnett, B.J., O. Crocker & M.A. Stevens. 1992. The challenge for women expatriates and spouses: some empirical evidence. *The International Journal of Human Resource Management*, **3**(3): 585–92.

Reger, K.R. 1990. The repertory grid technique for eliciting the content and structure of cognitive constructive systems. In A.S. Huff (ed.), *Mapping strategic thought*. London: John Wiley & Sons.

Rubin, J. 1997. Gender, equality and the culture of organisational assessment. *Gender, Work and Organisation*, **4**(1): 24–34.

Schein, V.E. 1973. The relationship between sex role stereotypes and requisite management characteristics. *Journal of Applied Psychology*, **57**: 95–100.

Schein, V.E. 1975. Relationships between sex role stereotypes and requisite management characteristics among female managers. *Journal of Applied Psychology*, **60**(3): 340–44.

Smith, C.R. & L.V. Still. 1996. Breaking the glass border: barriers to global careers for women in Australia. *International Review of Women and Leadership*, **2**(2): 60–72.

Stahl, G.K., E. Miller & R. Tung. 2002. Toward the boundaryless career: a closer look at the expatriate career concept and the perceived implications of an international assignment. *Journal of World Business*, **37**: 216–27.

Stone, R.J. 1991. Expatriate selection and failure. *Human Resource Planning*, **14**(1): 9–18.

Stroh, L.K., H.B. Gregersen & S.J. Black. 2000. Triumphs and tragedies: expectations and commitments upon repatriation. *International Journal of Human Resource Management*, **11**(4): 681–97.

Thal, N.L. & P.R. Cateora. 1979. Opportunities for women in international business. *Business Horizons*, **22**(6): 21–7.

Tung, R.L. 1998. American expatriates abroad: from neophytes to cosmopolitans. *Journal of World Business*, **33**: 125–44.

Van der Velde, M.E.G., C.J.H. Bossink & P.G.W. Jansen. (forthcoming). Gender differences in the determinants of the willingness to accept an international assignment. *Journal of Vocational Behavior*.

Varma, A. & L.K. Stroh. 2001. Different perspectives on selection for international assignments: the impact of LMX and gender. *Cross Cultural Management*, **8**(3/4): 85–97.

Webb, J. 1991. The gender relations of assessment. In J. Firth-Cozens & M. West (eds), *Women at work: psychological and organizational perspectives*. Milton Keynes: Open University Press.

Windham International and the National Foreign Trade Council. 1999. *Global relocation trends 1999 survey report*. New York.

15 International business travellers: a challenge for IHRM
Denice E. Welch and Verner Worm

On average, I would go to Asia for two weeks and come back, go to the U.S. for two weeks and come back, go to Europe for two weeks and come back. And the next time I went to Asia [I would] probably go to a different part of it. I guess I was away – if you accumulated it – for 8 to 9 months of the year. (Senior Executive, Australian multinational)

The field of international human resource management (IHRM) has developed from its early status as an infant field of scientific inquiry, as the contents of this *Handbook* indicate. When it comes to the issue of international assignments, however, there remains a dominance of interest in, and research on, the management of traditional expatriates, primarily because they comprise the bulk of international assignees (Skovbro & Worm, 2002). Expatriates have tended to be the preferred choice when faced with strategic staffing decisions pertaining to subsidiary operations (see, for example, Dowling & Welch, 2004). However multinationals are finding that supporting a large contingent of traditional expatriates is becoming more difficult, even though the expatriate failure rate is not as high as is often reported (see, for example, Forster, 1997; Tung, 1998). It has long been recognized that expatriates are expensive. Also the rise of dual career couples has made international relocation more complicated. Therefore cost containment and staff immobility are two of the main driving forces for the observed increase in the use of what has been termed 'non-standard assignments' (PricewaterhouseCoopers, 1999, 2000). Non-standard assignments include commuting (special arrangements where the person concerned commutes from the home country on a weekly or bi-weekly basis to the place of work in another country); rotational (employees commute from the home country to a place of work in another country for a short, set period, followed by a break in the home country – used on oil rigs, for example); and contractual (used in situations where employees with specific skills vital to an international project are assigned for a limited duration of six to 12 months). Advances in telecommunications have enabled firms to experiment with a newer form, the virtual assignment, where the employee does not relocate to a host location but manages, from home-base, international responsibilities for a part of the organization in another country. With the rise in company use of these alternatives, research is beginning to examine the IHRM implications of these alternative forms of staffing international operations.

What has been relatively ignored in the IHRM literature (and indeed in the broader international business literature) has been the role of the international business traveller (IBT). This is somewhat curious, given that international travel remains the heart of international business. The international business traveller is one for whom business travel is an essential component of their work: for example, international sales staff whose jobs comprise a heavy component of international travel. Where this group is referred to, they are popularly termed 'road warriors', 'globetrotters' or 'frequent fliers'. These people are not relocated, so they do not come under the umbrella of 'international assignee' or 'expatriate'.

The aim of this chapter is to provide some redress by examining the nature of international business travel, in terms of its costs and benefits to the individual, and to the company. We then discuss the role of the corporate HR department in providing support for this category of employees: the IBTs or 'non-expatriates'. Suggestions for future research are then offered.

The nature of international business travel
As companies become more geographically dispersed, and foreign units more integrated into global activities, organizational pressures and requirements appear to increase the need for international movement. The volume of staff traffic appears to have remained largely unaffected by advances in electronic communications, such as e-mail and video conferencing. For example, a survey of 1400 business travellers across the world revealed that 91 per cent expected to maintain or increase their current business travel over the next year (American Express, 2002). This was despite the September 11 attack on the World Trade Center in New York the previous year, and the associated fear of further terrorist attacks in other locations and countries. The business reality is that, while certain transactions and information exchanges can be conducted electronically, others need to be handled personally. Face-to-face communication remains a primary, preferred medium.

Group and regional meetings, staff briefing sessions, joint training sessions, product development meetings and cross-border project work, opening or closing factories and solving technical problems are just some of the activities that involve travelling from one country location to another. Apart from these internal company activities, staff frequently travel to conduct business with external stakeholders in various international markets: negotiating deals and sales contracts, selling products and services, attending trade fairs and visiting host country government officials, alliance partners, subcontracting firms and foreign suppliers (Welch, Welch & Worm, 2003). The frequency and volume of host country visits vary according to circumstances and market dynamics. As multinationals exploit new opportunities in emerging and evolving markets, such as Russia, China and India, the number of staff making visits to support the new ventures tends to increase. In countries that are perhaps less volatile, and where operations are more mature with established standardized procedures and systems, visits by headquarters' staff may be less frequent.

IBTs are a diverse group of employees. Expatriates can also be international travellers, as their duties in a foreign country may involve regional responsibilities, or require frequent visits to headquarters, or other subsidiaries. As well, non-standard assignments, particularly the virtual assignment, will involve supporting visits. As HR activities and responsibilities are devolved to line managers, subsidiary managers and others, those responsible for managing IBTs would not necessarily share, or recognize the need to share, information regarding the nature of international travel and its demands on those who undertake it. Likewise, for HR staff, as the needs of this category of employee is not directly their responsibility, the needs of IBTs do not automatically come into their domain. Given the varied nature, roles and activities performed by international business travellers, it would be difficult for HR staff, particularly in the very large multinationals, to know just how many of their worldwide employees are travelling internationally at any given point in time.

To illustrate the various aspects involved, we draw on results of an exploratory study of five Australian and five Danish IBTs. Given the paucity of research on IBTs, a qualitative approach was considered appropriate, using the individual IBT as the informant, rather than the organization, as the focus was to explore issues pertaining to being an international business traveller. Each interviewee, therefore, was treated as a case. Semi-structured interviews were undertaken in 2003. Questions were asked regarding the perceived positives and negatives of constant international travel, the role of the home organization, the host location and the HR department. Interviewees were encouraged to relate critical incidents. Interviews were taped and transcribed by the authors. The five Australians were interviewed in English, and the five Danes in Danish. Two of the Danish interviewees were living abroad at the time of the study, so the questionnaire was posted to them and followed up with a telephone conversation of about half an hour's duration with each, in order to provide data clarification and extension where appropriate. Content analysis was conducted manually, with cross-case analysis within each country sample and between both country samples (Patton, 1990).

Interviewees were selected using purposeful intensity sampling that would provide information-rich cases. The six male and four female interviewees represented different IBT roles (for example, senior management, international sales and marketing, project management and troubleshooting). They were drawn from different-sized firms – large multinationals, subsidiary operations, small-to-medium enterprises and a family firm. Interviewees worked in various industries (including medical equipment, electrical appliances, resources, pharmaceuticals and consulting). The proportion of time spent on international activities per year ranged from 20 per cent to 100 per cent. The composite group's travel encompassed the globe.

Factors affecting international business travellers
The mention of international business travel conjures up images of comfortable airline seats, dedicated airport lounges, plush hotels and long lunches in exotic locations, all paid for by someone else. It is this common image of a glamorous life that perhaps has led to a perception that international business travellers do not require the same level of organizational support that traditional expatriates tend to receive. It is not uncommon for colleagues to envy the perceived lifestyle and discount any proffered examples of the negative aspects of international travel. As one interviewee described it: 'People always think travel is glamorous and there is a glamour component to it but in the end . . . it is a lot of hard work.' Our exploratory study confirms the limited research and anecdotal evidence that there is a range of physical, social and psychological demands associated with constant international travel that may counteract its positive side. These findings reflect the travel stressors identified in one of the few articles on IBTs. DeFrank, Konopaske and Ivancevich (2000) divide international travel into three stages and discuss the negative effects associated with each stage. The three stages are pre-trip, trip and post-trip. By separating international travel into distinct stages, the authors demonstrate how work arrangements, home and family issues, as well as the stresses encountered during the travel are compounded and may lead to poor performance and even illness.

What also emerged from our exploratory study was the importance of two other factors: the individual IBT's responses to the positive and negative factors encountered, and the level of support provided by the organization. These factors, along with the positive and negative factors, are depicted in Figure 15.1. It is recognized that the interaction between the different elements can be expected to vary, as individual interviewees gave different weighting to some of the positive and negative factors they identified. Furthermore, while the elements have been empirically derived, given the small sample of IBT cases involved, it is stressed that the figure is a conceptual model developed for analytical purposes. We use the various

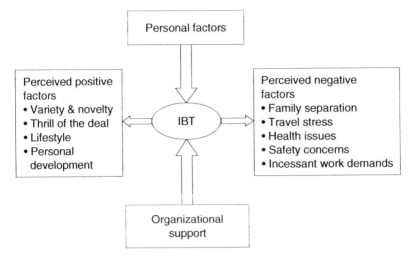

Figure 15.1   Aspects of international business travel

elements identified in Figure 15.1 to guide the discussion of the issues associated with each of the identified aspects.

Perceived negative factors
To a certain extent, some of the negative factors associated with international business travel (particularly family separation and incessant work demands) reflect arguments and issues raised in the broader community debate surrounding the quality of work life and the balance between work and private life (see, for example, Fagan, 2001; Hochschild, 1997). For example, increased connectedness through advances in telecommunications such as the Internet, e-mail and mobile telephone has sparked concerns about the intrusive nature of technology, and the growing expectation that a person is always available, including outside normal working hours. While an examination of the work–life balance debate is beyond the scope of this chapter, it can be argued that, because they operate in special situations, IBTs can be regarded as extreme case examples of the work demands confronting 21st-century employees, as the following discussion of the negative aspects of international travel illustrates.

Family Separation   The effect on family relationships of international travel emerged as a key factor. Interview data indicate how frequent absences put strain on home and family life. IBTs miss important anniversaries, children's birthdays, school events, family gatherings, and the like, as the following comments from two of the interviewees illustrate:

> The bigger impact [stress] is that you are away from your family for so long and you miss birthdays, you miss speech nights [school graduation ceremonies] and a lot of the responsibility that you otherwise share falls back on your wife.

> When the kids [children] were small it was hard. I sometimes felt like a visitor in my own house. Naturally they develop their own routines while you are out of the house. When you come back you are a guest and you actually disturb those routines. It is better for everyone to keep that in mind.

It is not surprising that the constant comings and goings can be disruptive to family relationships, and different expectations can cause tension, frustration and various coping mechanisms. As DeFrank *et al.* (2000) note, there are domestic chores waiting that may interfere with the IBT's wishes to spend 'quality time' with the children. The family, particularly children, may become so accustomed to the frequent absences that they cease to comment on the departure of the parent, which, in a perverse way, some interviewees found distressing. One interviewee reported that her decision to change to a home-based position within the Australian subsidiary was prompted by relationship concerns:

> As soon as I would go away, he would have his own life and then I would come back and we would have to adjust to each other again, and then I would have to go off again . . . it got to the point where we didn't actually bother trying to connect with each other . . . in the end, it was impacting on our relationship so I chose him over the travel.

Over time, trivial events can build into serious issues that have the potential to put strain on marital and familial relationships. For those without a permanent relationship, international travel can make it difficult to maintain friendships and keep social commitments, thus isolating the person. Mobile telephone technology facilitates the IBT's ability to maintain contact with spouse, partner and family members.

Frequency and length of trips have a bearing. Interview data suggest that many short trips that followed one upon the other created more family problems than more infrequent yet longer absences (that is, 30–60 days away) which allowed more continuity, as well as giving the family unit time to plan for the IBT's absence. Adjusting to sudden departures was found to be harder on the family. For example, a Danish interviewee involved in a virtual assignment arrangement recounted how he never knew what each workday would hold. It was not uncommon for work to entail an unexpected flight to a neighbouring country, without knowing how long the absence would be. He reported that international visits would often require social events that would prolong the visit:

Sometimes when I go to Stockholm I have to go out and have a beer with my people in Sweden and then go home next day . . . Life was easier when I was on [a] long-term assignment in Paris.

Respondents often expressed a feeling of being fully accepted neither in their work nor in their social/family life. A typical IBT comment goes like this: 'Sometimes I felt caught in the middle between responsibilities to my job and social responsibilities.'

Travel stress   Travelling itself can be stressful. DeFrank *et al.* (2000:59) define travel stress as 'the perpetual, emotional, behavioural, and physical responses made by an individual to the various problems faced during one or more of the phases of travel'. Jetlag is a physical consequence of crossing several time zones and may have performance implications as IBTs endeavour to cope with this phenomenon. Our interviewees had various coping mechanisms, and varied reactions to jetlag. For example:

I am a good sleeper so jetlag was not much of a problem.

You get into a pattern when you do a lot of it. It [jetlag] used to be the second night . . . so I tended to schedule a lighter day on the third day in a place where I was not making any critical decisions.

[Coping with jetlag] is hard during periods with excessive travelling. I sometimes use [a mild sleeping pill].

Tight airline connections, missed or delayed flights, coupled with long periods in flight are commonly cited as potential travel stressors. An Australian interviewee recounted a good example:

My flight to Singapore had not been reconfirmed [by her Australian secretary] so I could not get a seat out of the Philippines. It was Easter. My wallet was missing or stolen, my mobile phone was flat, the computer was down and I want an E-ticket so I can get out of the country. Then I am told that my connection in Singapore is cancelled.

Such hassles can be compounded by mix-ups with hotel accommodation, hectic meeting schedules and lack of sleep. The ability to sleep is important in order to cope with the various business challenges that IBTs confront (DeFrank *et al.*, 2000). Another feature was the expectation that the IBT would not need any time off work in order to recover from travel stress, nor experience jetlag, when back in the domestic situation. Interview data indicated an attitude that one was expected to report to work directly from the airport, even if the job entitlements specified a recovery period. One Australian interviewee explained:

> I have 17 days in lieu that I have owing for the travel that I did last year that I have never taken . . . It is just not done . . . It [the travel] is just part of the job that you sign on for . . . You are within your rights to take the leave . . . but it is not done, so I have not taken them.

In large multinationals, where people from the top management team are also travelling constantly, and they do not take time off to recover between these international trips, it is difficult for others to do so.

Age, coupled with the amount of time spent travelling, is also a consideration. It seems that, the older people get, the less they like to travel. Our study results suggest that older people find coping with the effects of jetlag more difficult.

Health issues   Outbreaks of infectious diseases affect international business, as evidenced by the recent Severe Acute Respiratory Syndrome (SARS) epidemic. Apart from the risk of contracting such diseases, it would appear that the constant travelling itself has negative consequences. These include poor diet, lack of physical exercise and weight gain, as the following interviewees explain:

> One gets some stress due to the heavy travelling in periods. [It is] nearly impossible to find time to relax . . . It becomes a very hectic lifestyle . . . You put on weight.

> I picked up colds easily, especially where my diet was concerned. I am a vegetarian so I had to relax that and start eating meat to stay healthy . . . I would get up early and go to the [hotel] gym. Exercise was one thing I did to keep healthy.

> Insomnia was incredible. Food became an issue . . . Weight gain or weight loss . . . You either had bad food or they [clients] feed you too much so you would gain weight.

One Danish IBT had collapsed with what seemed to be a minor heart attack. Other interviewees admitted that watching IBT colleagues collapse with health problems, such as a stroke, acted as a warning to focus on their own vulnerability. Corrective actions taken included exercise regimes, eating as healthily as possible, trying to get enough sleep and having regular medical check-ups. Most interviewees were accommodated in quality hotels with gymnasiums and swimming pools attached and, while it was possible to take advantage of these facilities, it often depended on time available. Business meetings could continue well into the evening and, in some cases, recommence early the following morning, or the IBT would be in flight to another destination, precluding time for exercise.

Safety concerns In the current global environment, physical safety has become a general travel concern for tourists and business people alike. Governments issue regular travel warnings regarding potential terrorist activity, and international operators take the risk of kidnapping seriously. For instance, one IBT was ordered out of a country when the political situation became too dangerous.

The female IBTs in our sample were also concerned about their physical safety when travelling unaccompanied in certain countries. Such concerns would limit their ability to explore their surroundings, and could result in their being isolated in a hotel room for several days. As one interviewee, whose sales responsibilities took her to countries such as Saudi Arabia, India, and the Philippines, described:

> They [her male counterparts] were able to go down to the hotel bar – that was acceptable . . . Once I realised that I had not spoken to another human being for four days . . . This happened often in India. Over the weekends, you would not speak to anyone . . . You would be thoroughly bored. There is only so much CNN you can watch.

Harassment was a concern. There was a feeling that white women in Asia were 'available', which led the female IBTs in our sample to take particular caution to dress appropriately and try to avoid placing themselves in situations where they might be open to harassment. They were careful only to use hotel-vetted taxicabs and cars.

Incessant work demands Modern technology (particularly e-mail and mobile phones) has proved to be both a benefit and an intrusion. The ability to utilize electronic media allows IBTs more easily to obtain information from headquarters or the home office that enables work in the foreign market to be more easily completed. Of course, the negative aspects of instant telecommunication means that home office business matters can intrude while one is away and may interfere with the international activity, or at least erode private time – usually sleeping hours.

Travellers are often confronted with a backlog of work when they return to home base, as one IBT explains:

> After being away for a couple of weeks there'd be a lot of paper work and other things to attend to – home office activities . . . And you would have to follow up issues that had arisen while away that needed review or authorisation.

This may encroach on the time available to spend with the family, thus compounding the unsatisfactory home situation. However, IBTs in our sample recounted how, while travelling internationally, they would try to use the time spent at airports or in flight to attend to work. E-mail access often permitted them to attend to pressing matters so that there was less work waiting when they came back, thus freeing time when they returned home to be with their families.

Perceived positive factors
Little has been written on the positive factors of international travel. For example, DeFrank *et al.* (2000) focus on the stresses and strains involved. While the IBTs in our sample mentioned the negative consequences of their travelling, they also raised positive aspects and most of them were willing to continue as an IBT. For some, the positive factors acted to moderate, if not negate, the negative aspects outlined in Figure 15.1 above. The positives listed by the IBTs were the variety and novelty of their jobs, the thrill of the deal undertaken in challenging environments, the lifestyle and the opportunities for personal development that international travel afforded them. Some IBTs considered that these factors made them somewhat addicted to the international travel, a side that those who were now domestically based missed.

Variety and novelty   A common positive was the variety of tasks, people and destinations involved, which meant that there was much that was new and novel, such as meeting people from different areas and countries. IBTs enjoyed the travel despite the negatives, particularly being away from home and family, as the following comments illustrate:

> I enjoyed the job because it had a lot of variety to it . . . It took me into areas and countries I had not been to before and therefore [was] exposed to more. There was something of a dichotomy. I enjoyed the travelling but did not enjoy being away from home.

> Being able to experience and work in countries that I would never go to as an individual . . . You take all the negatives and still do it! It was a buzz. There was adrenaline.

> It was the challenge of the job.

Thrill of the deal   Related to the variety and novelty that was seen to be inherent in international travel was what could best be described as the sense of accomplishment of performing well in difficult circumstances: what some IBTs referred to as 'the buzz'. For example, one IBT involved in selling medical equipment in Asia described it as follows:

> The romanticism and the exoticism of it [international travel] is one thing . . . but the other part – the buzz – is the deal, if the deal's come off. If you asked me to do the same deal domestically day after day there would be no buzz.

Lifestyle During interviews, IBTs concurred that there was an element of glamour attached to being a frequent traveller. They admitted that staying in top quality hotels, flying business class and shopping duty free were part of that. For some, international travel can become a lifestyle in itself that is almost addictive. One Danish interviewee, for example, recounted how taking early retirement from a working life of constant international travel was difficult. He had become accustomed to this way of life, and his wife was still working, so, to cope, he continued to travel, taking a charter tour a few times a year. He packed his suitcase with books and then went to Southern Europe for a week or so. He felt that it was like going on a business trip, and his wife seemed also to be satisfied, or at least not against his arrangements.

Personal development An important positive that was mentioned during the interviews was the developmental opportunities provided by the nature of the jobs involved. These included working with people from other cultures, coping with stressful situations and handling problems that would not be normally encountered. The jobs would be challenging, with more responsibilities, allowing self-development (such as 'broadening my horizons'). Danish interviewees regarded meeting people from different cultures as valuable to their personal development as well as professional development.

Personal factors
As indicated in Figure 15.1, and discussed in the above sections, individual responses to the stresses and strains of international travel may be moderated by personal factors, such as age, experience and family situation. While career objectives and aspirations were not directly addressed in interviews, several IBTs referred to expected career outcomes. For example, when discussing the positives of international travel, one interviewee mentioned how important it was to have international experience in order to advance within the company. The personal development aspect discussed above was indicative of the value placed on being able to function in a foreign context. In other words, taking on a role involving international travel delivered the same outcome in terms of international experience but without the disruption and adjustment that a full international posting would have imposed upon family members (the lesser of two evils). For others, the career path within the company had led to the international travel component or had been part of an international assignment.

In some cases, personal circumstances, particularly family relationships, did influence decisions to change jobs, or curtail the amount of international travel where possible. Job changes could be within the same company but at a different level or department. For others, it could mean changing companies. Those in our sample who deliberately switched to domestic-based jobs within the same company admitted that there was a lowering of job satisfaction as a result.

Thus how individuals cope with the demands of international travel has an important consequence in terms of job satisfaction and staff turnover. Voluntary separation from an organization has the potential for information and knowledge loss, given that individual IBTs are often the repositories of critical information about foreign operations and activities, and network connections with foreign government officials, key suppliers and clients, and the like (see, for example, Michailova & Worm, 2003; Lord & Ranft, 2000; Hedlund, 1994). IBTs who leave may take important information, knowledge and contacts to a competitor. A similar loss of knowledge and information can occur when IBTs move to a different section of the same company.

Organizational support

The level of support provided to the international business traveller is an influencing factor (positive or negative) and has an impact on the IBT's performance and job satisfaction. The degree to which organization support acted as a moderating factor in our exploratory study was dependent on the size of the organization, the level of position involved and the nature of the IBT's job in the foreign market. Those who worked for large, relatively mature multinationals had greater levels of assistance in the foreign market than did those from smaller firms. For instance, one interviewee was a senior manager in a large multinational. When he visited the company's subsidiaries, he received full support from regional and subsidiary staff, which ranged from assistance with mix-ups over hotel accommodation to provision of transport, the security of access to medical care if needed in a strange location, and local company contacts. Another interviewee who also worked for a large multinational held a more junior position and was expected to make her own travel and accommodation arrangements and to handle contacts at the various destinations. However this IBT had access to sophisticated telecommunications support while travelling, and was able to draw on the support of subsidiary staff, though the level of support and cooperation from local staff varied from country to country.

Conversely those from smaller companies had less support in the foreign market. One IBT travelled in China selecting and monitoring subcontracting firms for a small Australian whitegoods manufacturer. While in China, he relied on a local interpreter as a guide, but generally was expected to organize matters himself. He received very limited support from the Australian office. Another interviewee found the support from the home organization to be a negative as there were constant demands for weekly reports to be filed regardless of the travel demands and time zone differences, and requests for information and assistance were often ignored. This lack of support was attributed to a prevailing attitude of envy of those who travelled internationally that led to obstructive behaviour and direct comments about the glamorous life of the IBTs. One interviewee, from a small family-owned firm, relied heavily on the firm's foreign distributors and agents for support in meeting clients and potential customers, as well as accommodation and other travel advice.

Finally the nature of the work involved places demands on the individual's ability to operate in unfamiliar environments and handle cultural differences effectively. However the limited empirical evidence suggests that IBTs do not receive cross-cultural training, an area that is now recognized as important for those on expatriate assignments, as the relevant chapter in this *Handbook* identifies. Research on expatriate adjustment and retention has identified areas such as pre-departure training and on-assignment support as critical in terms of organizational commitment and expatriate turnover. Organizational commitment is considered as an influencer of the psychological contract – the relational element of the employment relationship. As with expatriates, IBTs may perceive lack of organizational support, or the non-delivery of promised support, to be a violation of the psychological contract – a breach of trust – and thus lessen their attachment (or affective commitment) to the organization (Welch, 2003). As mentioned above, IBTs can be regarded as knowledge transfer agents and, unless the organization has active mechanisms for the codification of their specific foreign market knowledge and information, critical tacit knowledge may be lost if these individuals leave the organization.

The role of the corporate HR function
The previous section has highlighted the potential for organizational support to act as a moderating variable. What is not clear is the extent to which the HR function is involved in providing such support. There is a paucity of research into the role of the corporate HR function in the burgeoning IHRM literature, apart from its identified responsibility for expatriate management and international relocation of personnel (Welch & Welch, 1997; Scullion & Starkey, 2000; Novicevic & Harvey, 2001). It would appear that HR departments have had limited involvement in the management of IBTs. In their UK-based study on the various forms of international assignments, Brewster, Harris and Petrovic (2001) report that 32 per cent of companies surveyed were not sure how many staff were 'frequent fliers', whereas all respondents had detailed figures for those on long-term assignments. This may be partly due to a perceived delineation

of roles and responsibilities, that HR directors regard IBTs as the responsibility of the function or line department concerned, whereas HR's role is confined to the management of staff transfers that involve relocation of the individual (and often the accompanying partner and family) into a foreign country for periods of over six months' duration.

In other words, IBTs are non-expatriates and therefore fall outside the domain of the HR function, a view that may be reinforced by line managers and the IBTs involved. For example, in a study of six Danish multinationals conducted by the second author in 2002, the HR directors interviewed considered non-expatriate staff as the responsibility of the line managers in the department concerned. From the perspective of the line managers interviewed, HR was a support department, which they contacted when they needed help, such as to 'calculate the compensation package', as one line manager explained. The line managers considered they could adequately handle the issues related to IBTs as there were no relocation aspects to address, thus reflecting a perception that HR's role was the management of expatriates. There was an attitude also that consulting the HR department would only create trouble. Such an attitude excludes the possibility of vital information, such as government travel warnings for certain countries, being passed from the HR department to the relevant departments and current or potential IBTs.

The HR managers in the Danish study were aware that to be effectively isolated from HR activities in other areas of the firms' activities was not satisfactory, given that HR staff had expertise that would be beneficial for both IBTs and their respective companies. As Brewster *et al.* (2001) found, it is difficult to formulate policies for IBTs, or monitor the costs (human and financial), without adequate information. Conversely vital knowledge about specific foreign operations that should be broadly available may remain contained within the department concerned as line managers would not necessarily see the need to share such knowledge. In what could be seen as an attempt to redress this attitude, an HR manager in a big American company was quoted as saying: 'We try to tell managers that when they have people travelling internationally – except for very short business trips – they need to contact HR' (Joinson, 2000: 96).

The separation between line management and the HR function is reinforced through the formal structure, as depicted in Figure 15.2. Here, the Sales/Marketing Department is very active in Country A. There is interaction between staff and the foreign intermediaries (export agents, distributors) and customers. There may be interaction with foreign suppliers, though often this is the responsibility of the Purchasing Department. Staff may also visit the firm's subsidiary in Country A. In other words, there is much staff traffic between the Sales/Marketing Department in the home

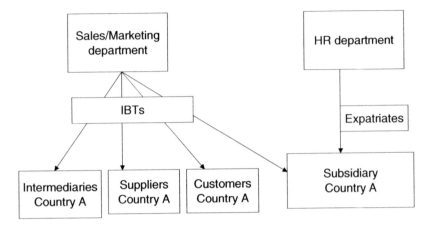

Figure 15.2   Compartmentalization

country and the firm's operations in Country A. However, as far as the Corporate HR Department is concerned, the only staff movement is that of the expatriates sent to Country A to formal positions within the subsidiary. In effect, the formal structure is supporting the development of silos in terms of IBTs.

Of course, Figure 15.2 assumes the existence of an HR department or function. In two of the companies involved in our exploratory study, there was no HR person or function owing, in one case, to the small number of employees (30) and, in the other, the company being a family-owned small firm with 22 employees where the four company directors shared employment responsibilities.

Subsidiary HR staff may be aware of visits by IBTs. There may be instances where the subsidiary HR staff are asked to host headquarters top managers making periodic, flag-waving visits to foreign operations, but these would be duties shared with other subsidiary managers. Expatriates assigned to subsidiary operations may travel within the region as part of their duties. Without a formal reporting requirement, information about IBTs, relating to issues such as health, safety and local travel that may reside at the subsidiary level, will not be shared with corporate HR staff.

If corporate HR management is kept at arm's length, then the flow of information and knowledge surrounding the management of IBTs may be negatively affected. For example, unilateral measures introduced in an attempt to contain the cost of utilizing international assignees, such as switching travel class entitlements from business to economy class, may not be appropriate for IBTs. A one-way trip to take up a traditional international assignment is different from making frequent trips to multiple destinations, often consecutively. Brewster *et al.* (2001) found little HR involvement in the control of costs of non-standard assignments or for IBTs. Rather responsibility to monitor such costs tended to be devolved to unit level line managers, and in some cases outsourced to travel agents. The HR function is therefore marginalized.

It is recognized that there are difficulties in generating consistent and equitable corporate policies for IBTs related to matters such as class of travel, level of accommodation and health aspects, given the variety and diversity of jobs they undertake. Equity of treatment is a contentious issue within the expatriate management literature and can become a performance issue. Development of corporate policies relating to compensation is seen as an essential step in removing disparities (Dowling & Welch, 2004). It is reasonable to assume that IBTs also compare their treatment with that of other IBTs. Communication between departments and the HR function would be an essential step in ensuring equity of treatment where international business travellers were concerned for issues such as taxation, class of travel and quality of accommodation.

A complicating factor may be the attitude towards international travel within multinational companies. Our interview data suggest that this attitude stems from senior management who travel extensively. If top management does not recognize jetlag and other travel-related stressors, it is difficult for these issues to be raised, either at the department level or through the HR function. For instance, an interviewee was one of five members of the international sales team, one of whom was also the managing director of the Australian subsidiary. While the managing director was appreciative of the physical and emotional strains involved, and tried to restrict the length of time per visit for each team member, his own schedule was as heavy and it was expected that others would follow his lead and place business performance before family commitments.

One interviewee who worked in the Australian subsidiary of a Canadian multinational offered her own view on the lack of HR involvement in the management of IBTs. She suggested that HR staff do not travel and therefore have little personal knowledge of stresses and strains of constant international travel, and that the 'corporate culture' is one epitomized as 'you were considered to be adults, therefore should be able to handle whatever the job entails'. The IHRM literature recognizes the importance of an international orientation within the HR function as important in terms of managing international assignments (see, for example, Dowling & Welch, 2004). HR staff who had experience as IBTs could be expected to appreciate the stresses and strains involved, and work to provide the required level of support to enhance work performance. As DeFrank *et al.* (2000)

concluded, there is a need for multinationals to take a more strategic approach that recognizes the importance of international travel to business success. This includes steps to monitor the health and well-being of IBTs.

IHRM research agenda

Given the seeming neglect of an important group of international operators, there is considerable scope for further scientific study of IBTs. Our data suggest interaction between the elements depicted in Figure 15.1: positive factors can affect negative factors; personal factors and organizational support may act as moderators, and this is an obvious starting point for further research. However broadening the sample is necessary to confirm, modify and extend the various elements that arose from our data analysis of ten IBT cases.

A more rigorous approach would be to interview all parties concerned – IBTs, family members and company personnel (line and HR managers) – to provide a more complete picture. More importantly this approach has methodological credibility, providing increased reliability and validity through data triangulation. Multiple methods, combining surveys with case studies for example, also yield the advantages of triangulation. The use of other methodological techniques such as critical textual analyses of the way international travelling is discussed in the media and by top managers of international companies may provide additional insights. It is important that scientific work is undertaken in this area that allows for theory development, given concerns that the field of IHRM has tended to be empirically driven.

The suggested connection between personal factors and staff turnover may provide a fruitful area of further research, not just in potentially confirming a suggested relationship, but in exposing other outcomes of international travel, such as the role of IBTs in knowledge transfer. Possible moderators may be career goals (linked to stage of life cycle), family commitments and quality of work life. A related area is the connection between organizational commitment, intactness of the psychological contract and organizational support. For example, cost containment actions by top management, such as reducing the class of travel, may be a moderating variable effecting a lessening of organizational commitment.

Job satisfaction emerged as a negative outcome for individual IBTs who resolved conflict between their job satisfaction and career objectives and family relationship concerns by accepting a more domestic position. This lessened their job satisfaction, at least in the short term. The relationship between aspects of international business travel, job satisfaction and performance is another line of scientific inquiry that has the potential to contribute to our understanding of the demands of working internationally.

The ability to transfer competencies around global operations is a strategic issue, and the role played by expatriates in such transfers has been acknowledged in the general international management and IHRM literature. IBTs can be expected to play similar roles (Welch, Welch & Worm, 2003). Further studies could examine how IBTs gather and disseminate foreign market information. How prepared are IBTs to share critical tacit knowledge in a work environment where loyalty to the organization and vice versa is considered an outmoded concept, accompanied by a growing expectation that a person should manage their own career? A related line of research is the role IBTs play in transferring competencies both internally (inter-unit transfer) and externally (such as in strategic alliances and international joint ventures).

As previously mentioned, researchers and practitioners have concentrated on expatriate management issues, and only recently has attention been given to non-standard assignments. The latter forms, particularly international commuting and virtual assignments, comprise international travel, so work on non-standard assignments could be expanded to include the international travel component. This line of inquiry would strengthen attention on the positive and negative aspects of international travel. It would also provide scope for comparative investigation; that is, the similarities and differences between IBTs and those on commuting and virtual assignments. Such data would have theoretical and practical outcomes: for example, given that companies continually search for alternatives to traditional expatriate assignments, it is important that the positive and negative consequences of alternative forms of staffing foreign operations, including the international travel component that some of these alternatives involve, be identified so that informed management of these alternatives is possible.

The role of corporate HR in providing support is a further line of inquiry. Further work in this area from the perspective of IBTs may make a valuable contribution to the general field of IHRM. The trend to devolve HR responsibilities to line management, and the rise of the field of strategic HRM, may in fact coalesce effectively to marginalize the HR function where international staffing issues are concerned. Decentralization may prove to be counterproductive in areas related to staff selection, training and development, and compensation. It is suggested that a degree of centralization is essential to provide an accessible repository of common information on managing internationally operating staff, to ensure equity of treatment among the various categories and to enhance the transfer of capabilities and competences. The compartmentalization between HR and functional areas identified in our exploratory study could be a starting point of research into this aspect of IHRM.

To conclude, as business activity continues to expand globally, international business travellers will continue to play an important strategic role in sustaining foreign operations. As one IBT interviewee stated: 'The job is the travel, and the travel is the job, and they are intertwined.' Research into this interrelationship is long overdue.

References

American Express. 2002. *International business travellers optimistic about travel for 2003*. New York, 9 October Press release. (Website accessed 19.5.03.)

Brewster, C., H. Harris & J. Petrovic. 2001. Globally mobile employees: managing the mix. *Journal of Professional Human Resource Management*, **25**: 11–15.

DeFrank, R.S., R. Konopaske & J.M. Ivancevich. 2000. Executive travel stress: perils of the road warrior. *Academy of Management Executive*, **14**(2): 58–71.

Dowling, P.J. & D.E. Welch. 2004. *International human resource management: managing people in a multinational context*. Fourth edition. London: Thomson Learning.

Fagan, C. 2001. Time, money and gender order: work orientations and working time preferences in Britain. *Gender, Work and Organization*, **8**: 239–66.

Forster, N. 1997. The persistent myth of high expatriate failure rates: a reappraisal. *International Journal of Human Resource Management*, **8**(4): 414–33.

Hedlund, G. 1994. A model of knowledge management and the N-form corporation. *Strategic Management Journal*, **15** (Special issue): 73–90.

Hochschild. A.R. 1997. *The time bind. When work becomes home and home becomes work*. New York: Metropolitan Books.

Joinson, C. 2000. Cutting down the days. *HR Magazine*, **45**(4): 92–7.

Lord, M.D. & A.L. Ranft. 2000. Organizational learning about new international markets: exploring the internal transfer of local market knowledge. *Journal of International Business Studies*, **31**(4): 573–89.

Michailova, S. & V. Worm. 2003. Personal networking in Russia and China: *Blat* and *Guanxi*. *European Management Journal*, **21**(4): 509–19.

Novicevic, M. & M. Harvey. 2001. The changing role of the corporate HR function in global organizations in the twenty-first century. *International Journal of Human Resource Management*, **12**(8): 1251–68.

Patton, M.Q. 1990. *Qualitative evaluation and research methods*. Second edition. California: Sage Publications.

PricewaterhouseCoopers, 1999. *International assignments. European policy and practices 1999/2000*. PricewaterhouseCoopers Europe.

PricewaterhouseCoopers, 2000. *Managing a virtual world: international non-standard assignments, policy and practices*. PricewaterhouseCoopers Europe.

Scullion, H. & K. Starkey. 2000. In search of the changing role of the corporate human resource function in the international firm. *International Journal of Human Resource Management*, **11**(6): 1061–81.

Skovbro, C. & V. Worm. 2002. Nailing the myths of international assignment. *European Business Forum*, **11**: 70–72.

Tung, R.L. 1998. American expatriates abroad: from neophytes to cosmopolitans. *Journal of World Business*, **33**(2): 125–44.

Welch, D.E. 2003. Globalization of staff movements: beyond cultural adjustment. *Management International Review*, **43**(2): 149–69.

Welch, D.E., & L.S. Welch. 1997. Pre-expatriation: the role of HR factors in the early stages of internationalisation. *International Journal of Human Resource Management*, **8**(4): 402–13.

Welch, D., L. Welch & V. Worm. 2003. *Just passing through: The international business traveller and knowledge transfer*. Paper presented at the European International Business Academy Meeting, Copenhagen, 11–13 December.

16 International assignee selection and cross-cultural training and development

Paula Caligiuri and Ibraiz Tarique

Multinational firms today compete on the effectiveness and competence of their core human talent around the world. Increasingly these core individuals are being required to operate effectively across a variety of national borders and in a greater number of cross-national job assignments. These international assignees, including all employees working outside of their own national borders (for example, parent country nationals, third country nationals, host country nationals), have collectively become vital for the success of multinational firms. These international assignees fill critical staffing needs in subsidiaries, manage key projects, transfer knowledge and corporate culture across geography, work on multinational teams and perform many other critical tasks for their firms.

International assignments can be very challenging personally. While immersed in new cultural environments, international assignees are out of their own comfort zones and are susceptible to a variety of challenges such as the inability to speak the host national language, the inability to cope with the stress of culture shock, the inability to interact effectively with host nationals, and the like. Past research suggests that individuals who are not predisposed or prepared to confront these challenges may perform poorly, be maladjusted and so on.

Given the criticality of their roles and the associated challenges of living and working in another country, maximizing the cross-national effectiveness of international assignees has become an increasingly important function for researchers and human resources (HR) practitioners alike. From a strategic perspective, optimizing the effectiveness of international assignees – core talent for most multinational firms – is a significant HR activity. Within an entire HR system, two specific functions which promote cross-cultural effectiveness among international assignees will be the focus of this chapter: first, selection and second, training and development. Other HR activities, such as compensation, performance management and repatriation, will not be discussed in this chapter yet should be integrated into a comprehensive HR programme for managing international assignees.

Within the selection and training functions, there are three major areas that have emerged in both the research and the practice of managing international assignees. The first includes the individual-level antecedents of international assignee success, such as personality characteristics, language skills and prior experience of living in a different country. The second includes the process issues for effectively selecting global assignees, such as realistic previews, self-selection and assessment. The third includes training and development issues for preparing international assignees to live and work in new cultural environments, such as designing effective cross-cultural training programmes. This chapter will cover these important areas and offer some suggestions for future research.

Individual-level antecedents of international assignee success

Personality characteristics

Researchers have found that successful and well-adjusted international assignees tend to share certain personality traits (for example, Black, 1990; Caligiuri, 2000a, 2000b; Church, 1982; Mendenhall & Oddou, 1985; Stening, 1979). Certain personality characteristics enable international assignees to be open and receptive to learning the norms of new cultures, to initiate contact with host nationals, to gather cultural information and to handle the higher amounts of stress associated with the ambiguity of their new environments (Black, 1990; Church, 1982; Mendenhall & Oddou, 1985) – all important for international assignee success. While many personality characteristics exist, research has found that five factors provide a useful typology or taxonomy for classifying them (Digman, 1990; Goldberg, 1992, 1993; McCrae & Costa, 1987, 1989; McCrae & John, 1992). These five factors have been found repeatedly through factor analyses and confirmatory factor analyses across time, contexts and cultures (Buss, 1991; Digman, 1990; Goldberg, 1992, 1993; McCrae & Costa, 1987; McCrae & John, 1992) and are labelled 'the Big Five'. The Big Five personality factors are extroversion, agreeableness, conscientiousness, emotional stability, and openness or intellect. Each of the Big Five personality characteristics has some relationship to international assignee success (Ones & Viswesvaran, 1997; Caligiuri, 2000a; Caligiuri, 2000b).

Some personality characteristics predispose international assignees to form stronger social bonds, which can encourage a higher level of cross-cultural adjustment (Caligiuri, 2000a). International assignees who are able to assert themselves enough to establish some interpersonal relationships with both host nationals and other international assignees tend to be more likely to learn effectively the social culture of the host country (Abe & Wiseman, 1983; Black, 1990; Caligiuri, 2000a, 2000b; Dinges, 1983; Mendenhall & Oddou, 1985, 1988; Searle & Ward, 1990); therefore *extroversion* which is important to help international assignees learn the work and non-work social culture in the host country relates to international assignee success. *Agreeableness* may also be important given that the ability to form reciprocal social alliances is achieved through this personality characteristic (Buss, 1991). Expatriates who are more agreeable (who deal with conflict collaboratively, strive for mutual understanding and are less competitive) report greater cross-cultural adjustment – and greater adjustment on the assignment (Caligiuri, 2000a, 2000b; Ones & Viswesvaran, 1997; Black, 1990; Tung, 1981).

Other personality characteristics may also predispose an international assignee for success. For example, trusted and *conscientious* employees are more likely to become leaders, gain status, get promoted, earn higher salaries and so on. In the domestic context, this has been supported through studies demonstrating a positive relationship between conscientiousness and work performance among professionals (for example, Barrick & Mount, 1991; Day & Silverman, 1989). This finding has been generalized to international assignee performance (Caligiuri, 2000a; Ones & Viswesvaran, 1997) and has been found to be a predictor of those who will be effective in international assignments.

In addition to the three personality characteristics described above, *emotional stability* may also be important for international assignee success. Emotional stability is the universal adaptive mechanism enabling humans to cope with stress in their environment (Buss, 1991). Given that stress is often associated with living and working in an ambiguous and unfamiliar environment (Richards, 1996), emotional stability is an important personality characteristic for international assignees' adjustment to the host country (Abe & Wiseman, 1983; Black, 1988; Gudykunst, 1988; Gudykunst & Hammer, 1984; Mendenhall & Oddou, 1985) and completion of an international assignee assignment (Ones & Viswesvaran, 1997).

Perhaps the most intuitively useful personality characteristic, as it relates to international assignee success, is the characteristic of *openness* or intellect. For an international assignee, the ability to assess correctly the social environment is more complicated given that the host country may provide ambiguous social cues (Caligiuri & Day, 2000). Successful international assignees will likely need to possess cognitive complexity, openness and intuitive perceptual acuity to perceive and interpret accurately the host culture (Caligiuri, Jacobs & Farr, 2000; Dinges, 1983; Finney & Von Glinow, 1988; Ones & Viswesvaran, 1997). Openness is related to international assignee success because individuals higher in this personality characteristic will have fewer rigid views of right and wrong, appropriate and inappropriate, and so on, and are more likely to be accepting of the new culture (for example, Abe & Wiseman, 1983; Black, 1990; Cui & Van den Berg, 1991; Hammer, Gudykunst & Wiseman, 1978).

Collectively these personality characteristics could be included in a valid selection system for prospective international assignees. It is important to note, however, that the absolute level of each personality characteristic would be contingent upon the type of international assignment under consideration. For example, the necessary level of openness and extroversion would be much higher for an executive in a networking role than it would be for a technician working predominantly with a system or machine. A better understanding of the level of necessary characteristics for given international contexts would be a useful focus for future research studies.

Language skills
There is a logical consensus with regard to the positive relationship between language skills and international assignee adjustment (for example, Abe & Wiseman, 1983; Church, 1982; Cui & Van den Berg, 1991). There is some disagreement, however, on the relative importance of language compared to other factors, such as personality characteristics (for example, Cui & Van den Berg, 1991; Dinges, 1983). The disagreement in the importance of language skills has its roots in whether interpersonal contact between people from different cultures leads to increased cultural understanding. Those who support contact theory believe that language skills, given that they are necessary for communication, are critical for cross-cultural adjustment. Others (for example, Cui & Van den Berg, 1991) suggest that merely interacting with host nationals is not enough to produce cross-cultural adjustment. They suggest that cross-cultural adjustment only occurs when international assignees have the cultural empathy to be open to different norms and fully accepting their host cultures (ibid.). In other words, one could both speak the host language fluently and know the 'correct' behaviours to display, and yet only be immersed superficially in the host culture (ibid.). Since it would be difficult for the opposite to be true (that is, that one could be immersed in a culture without language skills), basic language skills should, at the very least, be a minimum precondition for success as an international assignee. At a minimum, in most circumstances, an attempt should be made to find a qualified candidate with language skills, while for some positions the language skills may be more critical than with others.

Prior international experience
From a social learning perspective, the more contact international assignees have with host nationals and the host culture, the greater their

cross-cultural adjustment (Brein & David, 1971; Brislin, 1981; Guthrie, 1975). For example, past research has found that having friendships with host nationals greatly improves international assignees' ability to learn culturally appropriate social skills and behaviours (Searle & Ward, 1990). From this perspective, more prior experience with the host culture should produce greater cross-cultural adjustment. On the other hand, the social cognitive theorists contend that prior foreign experience with the host culture is positively related to adjustment *provided* that the experience does not serve to reinforce previously held stereotypical beliefs or foster negative, unrealistic expectations of the foreign culture. Social cognitive proponents agree that there is a direct relationship between foreign experience and cross-cultural adjustment when the experience provides an accurate and realistic representation of the host countries' norms, customs, values and so on, but the empirical evidence is inconclusive: the relationship between previous international experience and cross-cultural adjustment is more complex than is commonly believed. There is some evidence that previous experience abroad does not always facilitate adjustment to a new expatriate environment (for example, Black & Gregersen, 1991; Cui & Awa, 1992; Dunbar, 1992; Selmer, 2002). A recent study by Takeuchi, Tesluk, Yun and Lepak (2005), however, found support for unique moderating effects of past international experiences on the relationship between current assignment tenure and general and work adjustment.

Process issues for selecting international assignees

There are three key process issues in the research literature regarding international assignee selection. The first is the application of realistic previews to international assignments to help create realistic expectations during (or prior to) selection. The second is the concept of a formal self-selection process which enables international assignee candidates to determine whether the assignment is right for his or her personal situation, family situation, career stage and so on. The third is traditional candidate assessment that would include many of the dimensions identified in the previous section (such as personality, language skills and past experience) in a structured organizational selection programme. Each of these three international assignment process issues is discussed in greater detail below.

Realistic previews for international assignments

Preconceived and accurate expectations prior to an international assignment have been shown to influence the international assignment in many important ways (Caligiuri & Phillips, 2003; Searle & Ward, 1990;

Weissman & Furnham, 1987). Studies comparing international assignees' expectations prior to going abroad and their actual experience after relocation suggest that having moderately accurate expectations facilitates cross-cultural adjustment (Searle & Ward, 1990; Weissman & Furnham, 1987). Caligiuri and Phillips (2003) found that providing realistic previews prior to international assignments did not change candidates' interest in possible assignments, but did increase candidates' self-efficacy for an international assignment. This self-efficacy, in turn, could influence the outcome of the international assignment.

Both research and practice suggest that, in the selection phase (or prior to it), it is useful for firms to provide information, even informally, to assist candidates in making realistic decisions on whether an assignment is right for them and to help them form realistic expectations about a possible international assignment (Black, Gregersen & Mendenhall, 1992; Caligiuri & Phillips, 2003; Tung, 1988). Many firms have pre-selection programmes which pair repatriates with international assignee candidates to give international assignees the opportunity to form realistic expectations (Black, Gregersen & Mendenhall, 1992).

Self-Selection
Given that the demographic profiles and personal situations of the international assignee candidates will vary, self-assessment (or self-selection) has been found to be an effective method for encouraging realistic previews in a tailored and self-directed way (Caligiuri & Phillips, 2003). For example, an unmarried person who is a candidate for an international assignment might have a different set of concerns than a married candidate with a family (Caligiuri, Hyland, Joshi & Bross, 1998). Likewise, given the many personality characteristics related to cross-cultural adjustment, people who possess different personality characteristics may be differentially suited for certain types of international assignments (Caligiuri 2000a, 2000b; Dalton & Wilson, 2000; Ones & Viswesvaran, 1997, 1999).

Self-assessment provides a structured method for international assignment candidates to assess actively their fit with the personality and lifestyle requirements of the international assignment (Caligiuri & Phillips, 2003). Effective self-selection tools enable international assignee candidates to evaluate themselves critically on dimensions such as personality and individual characteristics, career issues and family issues (including issues of spouses and children). Self-selection instruments, used in a structured way, help employees make a thoroughly informed decision about whether to accept an international assignment (Caligiuri & Phillips, 2003).

Firms using self-assessment tools have found that this step fosters the creation of a candidate pool of potential international assignees.

This candidate pool can be organized to include information such as the availability of the employee (when and to what countries), languages the employee speaks, countries preferred, technical knowledge, skills and abilities and so on. The information retained, based on self-assessment, should be repeated and continually updated as much of the information (other than personality) can change over time. For example, language skills can diminish if not used, family situations change and so on.

Candidate assessment
Once the requirements of a given international assignment have been determined, many possibilities exist to assess the candidates on job-related dimensions. Given that international assignments are job contexts, rather than job descriptions, they require different levels of relevant attributes (for example, language fluency, openness and technical skills). For example, greater emphasis would be placed on personality characteristics (such as sociability and openness) when assessing a candidate for a developmental or strategic assignment, requiring much more host national contact, compared to a more technical international assignment (Caligiuri 2000a, 2000b, 2004). In a best case, a thorough assessment can be conducted through a variety of valid formal selection methods: paper and pencil tests, assessment centres, interviews, behavioural observations and the like.

While comprehensive, the reality of international assignment selection is not nearly as sophisticated. Most international assignee selection generally happens using the most informal methods: recommendations of peers or supervisors (Brewster & Harris, 1999) on basic dimensions such as work experience and willingness to relocate. That said, future research should attempt to close the gap between research and practice. For instance, two aspects of the international assignee selection process have shown promise for practical application but warrant further investigation. The first is to better understand ways to engage employees early, even before an international assignment is even available. The best candidates could build their efficacy for the assignment when their decision-making processes are engaged before a position becomes available (Caligiuri & Phillips, 2003). The second promising application for practice is to better understand ways to involve the family effectively as early as possible in the selection process. Research suggests that family members can greatly influence the assignment outcome (Caligiuri *et al.*, 1998) so their motivation and interest in the international assignment should not be disregarded in the assessment phase. It is generally accepted that the best selection decision will be mutual among the employees, their organizations and their families. While the best case for international assignee selection is understood, the dynamic interplay among employees, families and organizations – in terms of international assignment selection decisions – is not yet thoroughly understood and warrants further research.

Training and development for international assignees

In addition to comprehensive self-selection and selection programmes, success in international assignments may be facilitated through the training and development of cross-national competencies (for example, cross-cultural knowledge, skills and abilities). For example, providing an international assignee with knowledge of general dimensions on which most cultures differ and the impact of these differences may provide the individual with some awareness regarding expected norms and behaviours in the new culture (Black & Mendenhall, 1990). This awareness may lower anxiety, reduce culture shock and encourage appropriate behaviours when living and working in a host culture. For the organization, both international training activities and international development activities will help improve cross-national competencies among international assignees (Briscoe & Schuler, 2004; Dowling & Welch, 2004; Evans, Pucik and Barsoux, 2002; Gupta & Govindarajan, 2002).

International training and development activities

Organizations recognize the importance of international training and development activities and increasingly use them to prepare individuals for the challenges and opportunities associated with living and working in new cultural environments, with diverse teams, across national borders and so on (see Windham International & National Foreign Trade Council, 2003, 2002; Csoka & Hackett, 1998; Gregersen, Morrison & Black, 1998). The terms 'international training activities' (ITAs) and 'international development activities' (IDAs) tend to be combined to signify the set of activities used by firms to develop the competency base of their internationally oriented employees. The objective of both ITAs and IDAs is to foster learning among the organizational members and develop enriched and more capable workers who, in turn, can enhance organizational competitiveness and effectiveness internationally.

While similar in objective, the specific goals of ITAs and IDAs are, in fact, different. In general terms, ITAs focus on the competencies needed to perform more effectively in one's current job. In other words, ITAs tend to be oriented towards solving short-term performance concerns. In contrast, IDAs refer to the acquisition of competencies needed to perform in some future job. It is, however, important to note that certain activities such as cross-cultural training can be used for both training purposes (for example, Earley, 1987) and for developmental purposes (for example, Lievens,

Harris, Van Keer & Bisqueret, 2003). Some of the various international training and development activities are listed below.

- Cross-cultural training (specific and general): the most researched and most used in practice, when used as an ITA, the goal of cross-cultural training is to increase an international assignee's specific cross-cultural knowledge of a given country. When (albeit, less commonly) used as an IDA, cross-cultural training will be geared for individuals who must work across a variety of cultural contexts, without any one cultural context in mind.
- Pre-departure cross-cultural orientation: as an ITA, the immediate goal of cross-cultural orientation is to help an international assignee learn the basics (for example, currency, public transportation, working hours) to live and work comfortably in the host country.
- Diversity training: depending on the immediacy of the need, diversity training can be either an ITA or an IDA. The goal of diversity training is to increase one's ability to understand and appreciate multiple cultural perspectives.
- Language training: depending on the immediacy of the need for fluency in another language, language training can be either an ITA or an IDA, but in practice is most often offered when an international assignee will be moving to a country where different language skills are needed. Sometimes organizations offer language training in the corporate language for all who are interested. In this case, language training may be viewed more developmentally.
- Traditional education in international management: university or specific training programmes are often offered as a part of a larger developmental plan and therefore are more likely to be an ITA. The goal of the traditional programme is to increase international business acumen and knowledge.
- Cross-national coaching or mentoring: generally viewed as an IDA, cross-national coaches and mentors help international assignees build cultural awareness, work on cultural 'blind-spots' and help develop competencies for becoming effective in an international environment. Occasionally cross-national coaches are assigned for a specific task (for example, delivering an important speech in another country, negotiating an international joint venture) and, in those cases, will then be considered more of an ITA.
- Immersion cultural experiences: generally viewed as an IDA, the goal of immersion is to produce culture shock for the developmental purpose of increasing one's ability to recognize and appreciate multiple cultural perspectives.

- Cross-border global teams (with debriefing): both an ITA and an IDA; here individuals are debriefed after a multicultural team experience (such as a meeting) to receive feedback and, it is hoped, to improve their skills, on how to be a better leader, team member and so on in a multicultural context. The feedback is an ITA for the purpose of the immediate team and an IDA for long-term skill development.
- International assignments: international assignments can be the means by which people develop cross-cultural competence and the outcome that the more immediately focused ITAs hope to influence. In the developmental context, as an IDA, living and working in another country may have a long-term effect on an individual's cross-national competence. Believing in their developmental power, many firms view successful international assignments as the indicator of cross-national competence.

We encourage future research to investigate the various ITAs and IDAs with their specific goals in mind. Research, to date, has overgeneralized the short-term and long-term outcomes of these diverse training and development interventions. An investigation of the various interventions, relative to the short-term and long-term goals, would help organizations better understand the implications of the activities in which they engage. In some cases, long-term benefits may be present as a direct result of a short-term intervention (for example, a language course gives an individual some cultural exposure and appreciation). The concern, however, is that the opposite may also be the case – that a long-term intervention (such as an international rotational assignment) may have only a short-term gain. In the case of an international assignment, this concern suggests that an individual has learned to be competent within one particular culture, but has not developed any international competencies that could generalize to other cross-border contexts. This is an open, and very important, area for scholarly investigation.

Cross-cultural training

As the non-exhaustive list suggests, there are many types of ITAs and IDAs with different goals and objectives. From this list, the most frequently used and researched activity is cross-cultural training. Traditionally multinational firms have used cross-cultural training to increase the knowledge and skills of international assignees to help them operate effectively in the unfamiliar host culture (Mendenhall, Kuhlmann, Stahl & Osland, 2002; Morris & Robie, 2001; Kealey & Protheroe, 1996).

A well-designed cross-cultural training initiative may enhance the learning process of the international assignee and thus facilitate effective cross-cultural interactions and cross-cultural adjustment (Black & Gregersen, 1991; Caligiuri, Phillips, Lazarova, Tarique & Burgi, 2001). To understand the systematic approach to designing cross-cultural training initiatives, Tarique and Caligiuri (2003) propose a five-phase process as a general strategy to follow in designing effective cross-cultural training initiatives:

1. identify the type of global assignment for which cross-cultural training is needed;
2. determine the specific cross-cultural training needs (from the organization level, assignment level and individual level);
3. establish the goals and measures for determining cross-cultural training effectiveness;
4. develop and deliver the cross-cultural training programme;
5. evaluate whether the cross-cultural training programme was effective.

The first phase includes identifying the type of global assignment for which cross-cultural training is needed. Research has shown that there are different types of global assignments (for example, Caligiuri & Lazarova, 2001; Hays, 1974; Oddou, 1991) and cross-cultural training will differ according to the goals required for the successful completion of each assignment (Tarique & Caligiuri, 2002; Tarique 2002). The second phase determines the specific cross-cultural training needs. This involves conducting a cross-cultural training needs analysis across three levels: the organizational level, the individual (or international assignee) level and the assignment level. The organizational-level analysis determines the organizational context for cross-cultural training. This analysis considers how cross-cultural training can assist both headquarters and subsidiaries in supporting the firm's strategy. The individual (or international assignee) level analysis identifies any special needs that have to be addressed in cross-cultural training for the individuals who are on the receiving end of the cross-cultural training, the international assignees themselves. This analysis includes examining the international assignee's prior international experience, his or her existing levels of cross-cultural competencies, how he or she perceives the issues the cross-cultural training initiative is designed to address, and the needs of the international assignee's entire family. The assignment-level analysis determines the cross-cultural competencies required to complete the given assignment effectively. This includes identifying the important tasks required on the global assignment and the type of cross-cultural competencies needed to perform those tasks effectively.

Phase three involves establishing short-term goals and long-term goals for determining cross-cultural training effectiveness. Cross-cultural training goals should be stated in detailed and measurable terms (for example, Noe, 2004). Short-term cross-cultural training goals can bring about cognitive, affective and behavioural changes (Gudykunst, Guzley & Hammer, 1996). Cognitive goals focus on helping international assignees understand the role of cultural values in behaviour in the destination country, in both social and business contexts. Affective goals aim at helping international assignees effectively manage their attitude toward the new culture and successfully handle negative emotions. Behavioural goals help international assignees form adaptive behaviours by emphasizing the transnational skills international assignees require in order to interact successfully with individuals from other cultures. While the short-term goals of cross-cultural training will vary from assignment to assignment, the long-term goal of many cross-cultural training initiatives is to improve the rate of cross-cultural adjustment. Improving cross-cultural adjustment is important for all international assignees and should generalize across assignments.

The fourth phase develops and delivers the cross-cultural training initiative. This phase involves determining the specific instructional content needed in order to achieve the stated goal and the methods to deliver the instructional content, and the sequencing of the training sessions. Using the cross-cultural and intercultural communication research (for example, Brislin, Cushner, Cherrie & Yong, 1986; Copeland & Griggs, 1985; Harris & Moran, 1991), Harrison suggests that content structure should follow an integrated approach consisting of both general cultural orientation (to understand factors that may influence one's receptiveness to effective cross-cultural interactions and to understand how cultures differ and the impact of these differences on international assignees) and specific cultural orientation (to help international assignees understand more about the specific culture to which they are being assigned).

Gudykunst, Guzley and Hammer (1996) suggest that the methods to deliver the instructional content can be categorized into four categories: didactic culture general, didactic culture specific, experiential cultural general and experiential cultural specific. Didactic culture general methods provide cultural general information to international assignees and include lectures, seminars, reading material, discussions, videotapes and culture-general assimilators. Didactic culture-specific methods, in contrast, present information on a particular culture. Methods used in this category include area studies, videotapes, orientation briefings, case studies and the like. Experiential cultural methods help international assignees experience the impact of cultural differences on their behaviours. Methods in this category include immersion programmes or intensive workshops. Experiential culture-specific methods, in contrast, help international assignees experience and learn from interactions with individuals from the host culture. This approach generally includes methods like role-playing, look-and-see trips, in-country cultural coaching and language training (Gudykunst, Guzley & Hammer, 1996).

Lastly, phase five evaluates whether the cross-cultural training initiative was effective. Cross-cultural training evaluation refers to the systematic process of gathering information necessary to determine the effectiveness of cross-cultural training. Cross-cultural training effectiveness is generally defined in terms of the benefits the international assignees receive from cross-cultural training and is determined by the extent to which international assignees have changed as a result of participating in cross-cultural training. The evaluation process involves establishing measures of effectiveness and developing research designs to determine what changes (for example, cognitive, affective and behavioural) have occurred during the training. Results from the cross-cultural training evaluation should help the organization decide whether cross-cultural training should be continued in its current form or modified.

Future research on these proposed phases and the various categories of cross-cultural training content (proposed by Gudykunst *et al.*, 1996) is an important area for investigation. The optimal combination of delivery methods and content for producing the desired outcome has not yet been determined. For example, are some content areas better covered before (or while) an individual is experiencing a culture? Currently many cross-cultural training programmes are delivered prior to the international assignment, with questionable influence on adjustment (Mendenhall *et al.*, 2004). Also a better understanding of the limits and generalizability across organizational, cultural, national and individual contexts for cross-cultural training is an important area to explore in future research.

The intersection between selection and training: future research directions
As mentioned earlier, many international organizations provide ITAs and IDAs for their employees in order to improve their global work performance. However, despite the plethora of research advocating the use of ITAs and IDAs as mechanisms for improving global work performance, the current research has generally assumed that everyone benefits equally from ITAs and IDAs. Given the extraordinary high costs (financial and emotional) of developing global managers, it is important to understand who will benefit the most from ITAs and IDAs. Caligiuri (2000a), for example, notes that academics and practitioners alike should identify those individuals with the requisite individual characteristics (such as personality), and then offer cross-cultural training to those identified. Cross-cultural training may only be effective when trainees are predisposed to success in the

first place (Caligiuri, 2000a). Certain personality traits, in particular openness to experience, extroversion and agreeableness, and early international experiences may provide the conditions under which ITAs and IDAs will lead to greater learning of cross-national competencies.

Personality, training and development
There is some evidence in the domestic training and development literature that personality traits are related to learning outcomes (for example, Salas & Cannon-Bowers, 2001; Colquitt & Simmering, 1998; Barrick & Mount, 1991). Barrick and Mount's (1991) meta-analysis found that the personality traits of conscientiousness, extroversion and openness were related to training proficiency. In another example, Salgado's (1997) meta-analysis of 36 studies found that the personality traits of openness and agreeableness were valid predictors of training proficiency.

The contact hypothesis or association hypothesis (Allport, 1954; Amir, 1969; Zajonc, 1968) can provide theoretical justification for personality traits as predictors of learning through a training or development intervention. The contact hypothesis or association hypothesis was originally developed to examine the race relations in the United States in the 1950s and 1960s, and suggests, in brief, that the more interaction (that is, contact) a person has with people from a given cultural group, the more positive his or her attitudes will be toward the people from that cultural group (Allport, 1954; Amir, 1969; Zajonc, 1968). Church (1982) suggested that the principles of the contact hypothesis could be applied to the interpersonal interactions between international assignees and host nationals. More recently, Caligiuri (2000a) used the contact hypothesis to suggest that international assignees often learn appropriate cultural norms and behaviours through cross-cultural interactions and that international assignees vary on the personality traits necessary for relating to others.

The predisposition to cross-cultural interactions can facilitate the learning of cross-national competencies during international training and development. This is based on the assertion that interaction with people from different cultures will affect the extent to which an individual is able to use the learned skills and behaviours. The more an individual interacts with people from different cultures, the more likely he or she will be to use and apply the learned skills and behaviours. In addition extensive interpersonal interactions will help individuals to experience the consequences of using behaviour or skills and to observe others, and seeing the consequences of their behaviours. Such consequences would help them to determine which behaviours result in positive outcomes and to prevent the development of unwanted or inappropriate behaviours. The dynamic interplay between individual differences and international training and development activities for improving cross-national competence is an area which warrants additional scholarly research.

Early international experience, training and development
One type of experience that has not been given much attention by researchers is early international travel experiences or experiences gained from living outside the country of one's citizenship as a child (Cottrell & Useem, 1994). This form of international experience has been extensively discussed in the 'third country kids' (TCKs) literature (for example, Lam & Selmer, 2004; Pollock & van Reken, 2001; Eidse & Sichel, 2003) which can provide theoretical evidence that individuals, by developing extensive early international experiences, are more likely to have learning or information-processing advantages that should facilitate the learning of new behaviours and skills. TCKs are individuals who have spent a part of their childhood in countries or cultures other than their own (Pollock & van Reken, 2001):

> TCKs are raised in a neither/nor world. It is neither fully the world of their parents' culture (or cultures) nor fully the world of the other culture (or cultures) in which they were raised . . . In the process of first living in one dominant culture and then moving to another and maybe even two or three more and often back and forth between them all, TCKs develop their own life patterns different from those who are basically born and live in one place. (Ibid.: 6)

Early international travel experiences allow TCKs to develop a learning or information-processing advantage, which should facilitate the learning of new behaviours and skills. From a social learning perspective, when children travel to other countries, they learn behaviours, customs and norms of that culture through direct experience or through observations of the host nationals' behaviours (Bandura, 1997). Children with extensive travel experiences in other countries may have developed more comprehensive prior knowledge structures or sets of cognition maps about people, roles or events that govern social behaviour. The literature on the additive effect of prior knowledge (for example, Cohen & Levinthal, 1990) and cognitive learning theories (for example, Bower & Hilgard, 1981) suggest that accumulated prior knowledge increases both the ability to store new knowledge in one's memory and the ability to recall and use it.

The above discussion suggests that individuals high on openness to experience, extroversion and agreeableness, and early international travel experience, will benefit more from training and development than individuals low on these traits. Future research, however, is needed to disentangle the mechanisms that underlie these associations. A major criticism of the existing literature on international training and development effectiveness is that it is based on anecdotal evidence or broad theories and models.

There is a need to develop advanced theoretical approaches to better understand how individual differences influence the relationship between ITAs and IDAs and learning/performance outcomes. In addition future research needs to examine how non-personality individual differences, such as individual learning styles (for example, Kolb, 1984) and age (for example, Zemke, Raines & Filipczak, 2000) influence this relationship.

An issue related to cross-cultural training effectiveness should be noted. In the realm of academic research, studies that have examined the likely success of cross-cultural training have shown that cross-cultural training programmes have failed to meet performance improvement needs (Kealy & Protheroe, 1996; Mendenhall *et al.*, 2004). Kealey and Protheroe (1996), for example, reviewed empirical studies used to assess cross-cultural training effectiveness and concluded that, while cross-cultural training seems to be effective in achieving immediate learning results, its impact on expatriates' performance on the assignment is not clear. Similarly, in a recent review of cross-cultural training evaluation studies, Mendenhall *et al.* (2004: 19) concluded that 'cross-cultural training seems to be effective in enhancing knowledge and trainee satisfaction, but seems to be less effective in changing behaviors and attitudes, or in improving adjustment and performance'.

The failure of cross-cultural training to produce a significant change in cross-cultural adjustment and in performance on the global assignment can be viewed from the classical 'transfer of training problem' which is defined as the failure of the trainee to apply effectively and continually the knowledge and skills gained in training to his or her job (Broad & Newstrom, 1992). It is well known in the domestic training literature that training content often does not transfer to the actual work setting (Baldwin & Ford, 1988; Saks, 2002). For this reason, domestic research examining the ways to facilitate or improve transfer has received much attention in the past (for example, Ford & Weissbein, 1997). Meanwhile cross-cultural training scholars have largely ignored the transfer issue: to date, no research has examined the transfer problem within a cross-cultural training context. Future research needs to expand our understanding of the transfer issue within the context of cross-cultural training effectiveness.

Conclusion

This chapter provides broad discussion for both academics and human resource specialists to better understand the topic of international assignee selection and assignee training and development. The discussion of international assignee selection included the topics of individual-level antecedents of global assignee success, such as personality characteristics, language skills and prior experience of living in a different country, and the process issues for effectively selecting global assignees, such as realistic previews, self-selection and assessment. The discussion of assignee training and development covered the various interventions used to prepare international assignees to live and work in new cultural environments, with special focus on cross-cultural training programmes, still the most commonly used intervention for improving cross-national competence.

It is important to note, from a practical perspective, that many of the selection, training and development practices described in this chapter are known but not often practised in multinational firms. The most apparent reasons for multinational firms' continued oversight of these practices are that HR (in most firms) manages international assignments *after* a selection has been made (Brewster & Harris, 1999) and then with a limited budget for cross-cultural training and development activities once selected. As a consequence, the HR role in international assignment management has been relegated to administrative and tactical activities, rather than strategic ones. Using a scientist–practitioner frame of reference, it is important that the gap between theory and practice is closed through solid programme evaluation studies providing concrete financial evidence for the strategic use of the practices described in this chapter.

We believe that the key to improving success of individuals on international assignments is to understand the interaction of selection and training and development; that is, to determine who benefits the most from international training and development activities. Future research should examine more accurate methods for identifying those individuals with the requisite individual characteristics (such as personality) to succeed in other countries, the optimal level of cross-cultural training needed for international assignment success, and the long-term development of global competence that could result from the international assignments. Clearly, this is an important area that will keep researchers and practitioners alike engaged for many years to come.

References

Abe, H. & R. Wiseman. 1983. A cross-culture confirmation of the dimensions of intercultural effectiveness. *International Journal of Intercultural Relations*, 7: 5–67.
Allport, G. 1954. *The nature of prejudice*. Cambridge, MA: Perseus Books.
Amir, Y. 1969. Contact hypothesis in ethnic relations. *Psychological Bulletin*, 71: 319–42.
Baldwin, T. & J. Ford. 1988. Transfer of training: a review and directions for future research. *Personnel Psychology*, 41: 63–105.
Bandura, A. 1997. *Self-efficacy: The exercise of control*. New York: W.H. Freeman and Company.
Barrick, M. & M. Mount. 1991. The Big Five personality dimensions and job performance: a meta-analysis. *Personnel Psychology*, 44: 1–26.
Black, J. 1988. Work role transitions: a study of American expatriate managers in Japan. *Journal of International Business Studies*, 19: 277–94.
Black, J. 1990. The relationship of personal characteristics with adjustment of Japanese expatriate managers. *Management International Review*, 30: 119–34.

Black, J. & H. Gregersen. 1991. Antecedents to cross-cultural adjustment for expatriates in Pacific Rim assignments. *Human Relations*, **44**: 497–515.

Black, J. & M. Mendenhall. 1990. Cross-cultural training effectiveness: a review and a theoretical framework for future research. *Academy of Management Review*, **15**: 113–36.

Black, J., H. Gregersen & M. Mendenhall. 1992. *Global assignments*. San Francisco, CA: Jossey-Bass.

Bower, G. & E. Hilgard. 1981. *Theories of learning*. Englewood Cliffs, NJ: Prentice-Hall.

Brein, M. & K. David. 1971. Intercultural communication and the adjustment of the sojourner. *Psychological Bulletin*, **76**: 215–30.

Brewster, C. & H. Harris. 1999. *International HR*. London and New York: Routledge.

Briscoe, D. & R. Schuler. 2004. *International human resource management: policies & practices for the global enterprise*. Second edition. New York: Routledge.

Brislin, R. 1981. *Cross-cultural encounters: face-to-face interaction*. Elmsford, NY: Pergamon.

Brislin, R.W., K. Cushner, C. Cherrie & M. Yong. 1986. *Intercultural interaction: a practical guide*. Beverly Hills, CA: Sage Publications.

Broad. M. & J. Newstrom. 1992. *Transfer of training: action-packed strategies to ensure high payoff from training investments*. Reading, MA: Addison-Wesley.

Buss, D. 1991. Evolutionary personality psychology. In M.R. Rosenzweig & L.W. Porter (eds), *Annual review of psychology*, **42**: 459–92. Palo Alto, CA: Annual Reviews Inc.

Caligiuri, P. 2000a. The Big Five personality characteristics as predictors of expatriate success. *Personnel Psychology*, **53**: 67–88.

Caligiuri, P. 2000b. Selecting expatriates for personality characteristics: a moderating effect of personality on the relationship between host national contact and cross-cultural adjustment. *Management International Review*, **40**: 61–80.

Caligiuri, P. 2004. Performance measurement in a cross-national context: evaluating the success of global assignments. In W. Bennett, D. Woehr & C. Lance (eds), *Performance measurement: current perspectives and future challenges*. Hillsdale, NJ: Lawrence Erlbaum Associates.

Caligiuri, P. & D. Day. 2000. Effects of self-monitoring on technical, contextual, and assignment-specific performance: a study of cross-national work performance ratings. *Group and Organization Management*, **25**: 154–75.

Caligiuri, P. & M. Lazarova. 2001. Strategic repatriation policies to enhance global leadership development. In M. Mendenhall, T. Kuehlmann & G. Stahl (eds), *Developing global business leaders: policies, processes and innovations*. New York: Quorum Books.

Caligiuri, P. & J. Phillips. 2003. An application of self-assessment realistic job previews to expatriate assignments. *International Journal of Human Resource Management*, **14**: 1102–16.

Caligiuri, P., R. Jacobs & J. Farr. 2000. The attitudinal and behavioral openness scale: scale development and construct validation. *International Journal of Intercultural Relations*, **24**: 27–46.

Caligiuri, P., M. Hyland, A. Joshi & A. Bross. 1998. A theoretical framework for examining the relationship between family adjustment and expatriate adjustment to working in the host country. *Journal of Applied Psychology*, **83**: 598–614.

Caligiuri, P., J. Phillips, M. Lazarova, I. Tarique & P. Burgi. 2001. Expectations produced in cross-cultural training programs as a predictor of expatriate adjustment. *International Journal of Human Resource Management*, **12**: 357–72.

Church, A. 1982. Sojourner adjustment. *Psychological Bulletin*, **9**: 540–72.

Cohen, W. & D. Levinthal. 1990. Absorptive capacity: a new perspective on learning and innovations. *Administrative Science Quarterly*, **35**: 128–52.

Colquitt, J. & M. Simmering. 1998. Conscientiousness, goal orientation, and motivation to learn during the learning process: a longitudinal study. *Journal of Applied Psychology*, **85**: 678–707.

Copeland, L. & L. Griggs. 1985. *Going international*. New York: Plume.

Cottrell, A.B. & R.H. Useem. 1994. Article 5. *TCKs maintain global dimensions throughout their lives* [Electronic version]. NewsLinks – the newspaper of International Schools Services, XIII, no.4. Retrieved 17 September 2004, from http://www.tckworld.com/useem/art5.html

Csoka, L. & B. Hackett. 1998. *Transforming the HR function for global business success.* Report No. 1209-98-RR. New York: The Conference Board.

Cui, G. & N. Awa. 1992. Measuring intercultural effectiveness: an integrative approach. *International Journal of Intercultural Relations*, **16**: 311–28.

Cui, G. & S. Van den Berg. 1991. Testing the construct validity of intercultural effectiveness. *International Journal of Intercultural Relations*, **15**: 227–41.

Dalton, M. & M. Wilson. 2000. The relationship of the five-factor model of personality to job performance for a group of Middle Eastern international assignee managers. *Journal of Cross-Cultural Psychology*, **18**: 250–58.

Day D. & S. Silverman. 1989. Personality and job performance: evidence of incremental validity. *Personnel Psychology*, **42**: 25–36.

Digman, J. 1990. Personality structure: the emergence of the five factor model. *Annual Review of Psychology*, **41**: 417–40.

Dinges, N. 1983. Intercultural competence. In D. Landis & R. Brislin (eds), *Handbook of intercultural training: issues in theory and design*, Volume 1. New York: Pergamon Press.

Dowling, P. & D. Welch. 2004. *International human resource management: managing people in a multinational context.* Fourth edition. Cincinnati, OH: South-Western College Publishing.

Dunbar, E. 1992. Adjustment and satisfaction of expatriate U.S. personnel. *International Journal of Intercultural Relations*, **16**: 1–16.

Earley, P. 1987. Intercultural training for managers: a comparison of documentary and interpersonal methods. *Academy of Management Journal*, **30**: 685–98.

Eidse, F. & N. Sichel. 2003. *Unrooted childhoods. Memoirs of growing up global.* London: Nicholas Brealey Intercultural.

Evans, P., V. Pucik & J. Barsoux. 2002. *The global challenge: frameworks for international human resource management.* Boston, MA: McGraw-Hill.

Finney, M. & M. Von Glinow. 1988. Integrating academic and organizational approaches to developing the international manager. *Journal of Management Development*, **7**: 16–27.

Ford, J. & D. Weissbein. 1997. Transfer of training: an update review and analysis. *Performance Improvement Quarterly*, **10**: 22–41.

Goldberg L. 1992. The development of markers for the big-five factor structure. *Psychological Assessment*, **4**: 26–42.

Goldberg, L. 1993. The structure of phenotypic personality traits. *American Psychologist*, **48**: 26–34.

Gregersen, H., A. Morrison & J. Black. 1998. Developing leaders for the global frontier. *Sloan Management Review*, **40**: 21–32.

Gudykunst, W. 1988. Uncertainty and anxiety. In Y. Kim & W. Gudykunst (eds), *Theories in intercultural communication*: 123–56. Newbury Park, CA: Sage.

Gudykunst W. & M. Hammer. 1984. Dimensions of intercultural effectiveness: culture specific or cultural general? *International Journal of Intercultural Relations*, **8**: 1–10.

Gudykunst, W., R. Guzley & M. Hammer. 1996. Designing intercultural training. In D. Landis & R.B. Bhagat (eds), *Handbook of intercultural training*: 61–80. Second edition. Thousand Oaks, CA: Sage.

Gupta, A. & V. Govindarajan. 2002. Cultivating a global mindset. *The Academy of Management Executive*, **16**: 116–26.

Guthrie, G. 1975. A behavioral analysis of cultural learning. In R.W. Brislin, S. Bochner & W.J. Lonner (eds), *Cross-cultural perspectives on learning*. New York: Wiley.

Hammer, M.R., W.B. Gudykunst & R.L. Wiseman. 1978. Dimensions of intercultural effectiveness: an explorative study. *International Journal of Intercultural Relations*, **2**: 382–93.

Harris, P. & R. Moran. 1991. *Managing cultural differences.* Houston, TX: Gulf Publishing.

Hays, R. 1974. Expatriate selection: insuring success and avoiding failure. *Journal of International Business Studies*, **4**: 25–37.

Kealey, D. & D. Protheroe. 1996. The effectiveness of cross culture training for expatriates: an assessment of the literature on the issue. *International Journal of Intercultural Relations*, **20**: 141–65.

Kolb, D. 1984. *Experiential learning – experience as the source of learning and development.* Englewood Cliffs, NJ: Prentice-Hall.

Lam, H. & J. Selmer. 2004. Are former 'third-culture kids' the ideal business expatriates? *Career Development International*, **9**: 109–22.

Lievens, F., M. Harris, E. Van Keer & C. Bisqueret. 2003. Predicting cross-cultural training performance: the validity of personality, cognitive ability, and dimensions measured by an assessment center and a behavior description interview. *Journal of Applied Psychology*, **88**: 476–89.

McCrae, R. & P. Costa. 1987. Validation of the five-factor model of personality across instruments and observers. *Journal of Personality and Social Psychology*, **52**: 81–90.

McCrae, R. & P. Costa. 1989. More reasons to adopt the five-factor model. *American Psychologist*, **44**: 451–52.

McCrae, R. & O. John. 1992. An introduction to the five factor model and its applications. *Journal of Personality*, **60**: 175–216.

Mendenhall, M. & G. Oddou. 1985. The dimensions of expatriate acculturation. *Academy of Management Review*, **10**: 39–47.

Mendenhall, M. & G. Oddou. 1988. The overseas assignment: a practical look. *Business Horizons*, **31**: 78–84.

Mendenhall, M., T. Kuhlmann, G. Stahl & J. Osland. 2002. Employee development and expatriate assignments. In M. Gannon & K. Newman (eds), *Handbook in cross-cultural management*. London: Blackwell.

Mendenhall, M., G. Stahl, I. Ehnert, G. Oddou, J. Osland & T. Kühlmann. 2004. Evaluation studies of cross-cultural training programs: a review of the literature from 1988–2000. In D. Landis & J. Bennett (eds), *The handbook of intercultural training*. Thousand Oaks, CA: Sage

Morris, M. & C. Robie. 2001. A meta-analysis of the effects of cross-cultural training in expatriate performance and adjustment. *International Journal of Training and Development*, **5**: 112–25.

Noe, R. 2004. *Employee training and development*. Boston, MA: McGraw-Hill.

Oddou, G. 1991. Managing your expatriates: what the successful firms do. *Human Resource Planning*, **14**: 301–8.

Ones, D. & C. Viswesvaran. 1997. Personality determinants in the prediction of aspects of expatriate job success. In Z. Aycan (ed.), *Expatriate management: theory and practice*: 63–92. Greenwich, CT: JAI Press.

Ones, D. & C. Viswesvaran. 1999. Relative importance of personality dimensions for international assignee selection: a policy capturing study. *Human Performance*, **12**: 275–94.

Pollock, D. & R. van Reken. 2001. *Third culture kids*. London: Nicholas Brealey Intercultural.

Richards, D. 1996. Strangers in a strange land: expatriate paranoia and the dynamics of exclusion. *International Journal of Human Resource Management*, **7**: 553–71.

Salas, E. & J.A. Cannon-Bowers. 2001. The science of training: a decade of progress. *Annual Review of Psychology*, **52**: 471–99.

Saks, A. 2002. So what is a good transfer of training estimate? A reply to Fitzpatrick. *The Industrial–Organizational Psychologist*, **39**: 29–30.

Salgado, J. 1997. The five-factor model of personality and job performance in the European Community. *Journal of Applied Psychology*, **82**: 30–43.

Searle, W. & C. Ward. 1990. The prediction of psychological and sociocultural adjustment during cross-cultural transitions. *International Journal of Intercultural Relations*, **14**: 449–64.

Selmer, J. 2002. Practice makes perfect? International experience and expatriate adjustment. *Management International Review*, **42**: 71–87.

Stening, B. 1979. Problems of cross-cultural contact: a literature review. *International Journal of International Relations*, **3**: 269–313.

Takeuchi, R., P. Tesluk, S. Yun & D. Lepak. 2005. An integrative view of international experiences: an empirical examination. *Academy of Management Journal*, **48**: 85–101.

Tarique, I. 2002. Cross-cultural implications for instructional design, delivery, and evaluation. Panel discussion. Annual Conference of the Society of Industrial and Organizational Psychology, Toronto, Canada.

Tarique, I. & P. Caligiuri. 2002. Effectiveness of in-country cross-cultural training: role of cross-cultural absorptive capacity. Paper presented at the 62nd Annual Academy of Management Meeting, Denver, CO.

Tarique, I. & P. Caligiuri. 2003. Training and development of international staff. In A.-W. Harzing & J. Van Ruysseveldt (eds), *International human resource management*. Thousand Oaks, CA: Sage.

Tung, R. 1981. Selection and training of personnel for overseas assignments. *Columbia Journal of World Business*, **16**: 21–5.

Tung, R. 1988. *The new expatriates: managing human resources abroad*. Cambridge, MA: Ballinger.

Weissman, D. & A. Furnham. 1987. The expectations and experience of a sojourning temporary resident abroad: a preliminary study. *Human Relations*, **40**: 313–26.

Windham International & National Foreign Trade Council. 2002. *Global relocation trends 2002 survey report*.

Windham International & National Foreign Trade Council. 2003. *Global relocation trends 2003 survey report*.

Zajonc. R. 1968. Attitudinal effects of mere exposure. *Journal of Personality and Social Psychology*, 9, monograph supplement no. 2, part 2.

Zemke, R., C. Raines & B. Filipczak. 2000. *Generations at work: managing the clash of veterans, boomers, xers, and nexters in your workplace*. New York: American Management Association.

17 The evolution from repatriation of managers in MNEs to 'patriation' in global organizations
Michael Harvey and Milorad M. Novicevic

If repatriates continue to leave their organizations at (such a high rate), organizations will fail to retain the international competencies that are the very objective of many international assignments. (Leiba-O'Sullivan, 2002: 597)

Since the first academic articles on repatriation of expatriates from international assignments started appearing in the academic literature (for example, Howard, 1974; Adler, 1981; Kendall, 1981; Harvey, 1983), the competitive landscape of multinational enterprises (MNEs) has changed dramatically, thereby altering the traditional repatriation process and issues. The hallmarks of the new competitive landscape, such as abruptly increasing levels of institutional uncertainty due to deregulation, rapidly evolving technological innovations bringing about disruptive technologies, unevenly accelerating pace of competitive interactions reducing the time-frame for making decisions, and elevated levels of economic integration within regional trading blocks (EU, NAFTA, ASEAN, and the like), have engendered a heretofore unknown concept of global hypercompetition.

The requisite attempts of MNEs to shift strategic focus from economies of scale to economies of scope in the global context have only rendered their competitive advantage temporarily sustainable in this new hypercompetitive global marketplace (Griffin & Khan, 1992; Liebeskind, Oliver, Zucker & Brewer, 1996; D'Aveni, 1994, 1997, 1999; Gimeno & Woo, 1996). To gain and maintain at least a series of 'momentary' competitive advantages in these highly volatile environments, the MNEs have resorted to focusing their strategies on the development of intangible assets (which include the specific knowledge of managers utilized in cross-border assignments) and integrating them into distinct competencies (Prahalad & Hamel, 1990; Auperle, 1996; Illinitch, Lewin & D'Aveni, 1998; Makadok, 1998; Lusch, Harvey & Speier, 1998; Harvey & Lusch, 1999). Specifically the competencies of management teams and individual managers are becoming paramount in the development and dissemination of knowledge and in the enhancement of learning throughout the global network organization (Fiol, 1991; Lado & Wilson, 1994; de Vries, 1999; Hollenbeck & McCall, 2001; McCall & Hollenbeck, 2002). This integration of knowledge and emphasis on learning can in turn enable future strategic flexibility of the organization (Fiol, 1991; Hall, 1993; Miller & Shamsie, 1996). Flexibility is particularly increased when a diverse management team with global experience helps to effectuate the emergence of a unique global mindset (that is, a diverse set of experiences, perceptions and insights into how to compete effectively in the global marketplace) (Kefalas, 1998; Kedia & Mukherji, 1999; Paul, 2000).

A unique global mindset becomes specifically valuable when the structure of an MNE shifts from a multinational hierarchy to a global network organization to support the change from multi-domestic to global and transnational strategies (Baruch & Altman, 2002). Historically MNEs have been structured as home country-centred, hierarchical organizations, which foster long-term expatriation and a planned repatriation process with predictable accompanying issues. Conversely a global network organization comprising loosely affiliated complex subsidiaries is structured more as a heterarchy with a reduced influence of the home country headquarters compensated by more dynamic transfers of host country nationals, third country nationals and inpatriated managers. The dynamism of these assignments induces complexity and ambiguity in the repatriation process and issues (Harvey, Speier & Novicevic, 2001a, 2001b; Harvey & Novicevic, 2003; Caligiuri & Phillips, 2003).

Therefore successful implementation of a corporate global/transnational strategy through a global network organization requires a commensurate change in the firm's international human resource management (IHRM) (Bartlett & Ghoshal, 1992; Schuler, Dowling & De Cieri, 1993). The modifications in the traditional hierarchical IHRM system will need to address changes in key functional concerns of expatriate management as well as the repatriation process of these same managers. A competency theory frame is used in this chapter to gain insight into the modification of the repatriation process for expatriate managers and to examine the design of an appropriate process/programme to address the accompanying repatriation issues.

The goal of this chapter is fourfold: (a) to outline a competency-based view of repatriation; (b) to examine the problems associated with repatriation; (c) to discuss the impact of globalization of organizations on the fundamental precepts of repatriation; and (d) to develop an IHRM process to manage the 'patriation' (that is, the repatriation of global managers who have had numerous global assignments and after being assigned overseas for a decade or more) to the home country organization.

A competency-based view of the repatriation

A competency-based view of the repatriation of managers is grounded in the assumption that top management and corporate HR management are committed to pursuing organizational flexibility and adaptability through knowledge integration and the development of learning capabilities, which are embedded in valuable expatriate experiences. The unique combination of repatriate knowledge, relationships and experiences may be bundled into distinct competencies that allow for the flexibility of the firm resource base to generate a competitive advantage and facilitate its future global growth (Lado & Wilson, 1994; Leiba-O'Sullivan, 1999, 2002; Bernhut, 2001; Truch, 2001). Thus a competency-based perspective on repatriation addresses the dynamic nature of the global environment by acknowledging that the initial set of competencies (that is, individual and organizational) can be renewed by effectively repatriating managers from foreign assignments, as valued yet unique resources of the organization (Stroh, 1995; Stroh & Caligiuri, 1998). This augmentation of competencies achieved through integration of the expatriation and repatriation processes suggests that a global network organization needs to develop a strategic orientation to repatriation to integrate new international competencies of strategic relevance into the common knowledge base of the firm through the development of effective programmes of repatriation.

These competencies derived from the strategic repatriation management can and should be combined and recombined to provide a set of strategic choice options that can be applied in international markets different from those in which they were developed (Leiba-O'Sullivan, 2002). The strategic recombination of repatriate competencies should be assessed relative to the strategic needs of the organization for the development of a global mindset in the global organization that facilitates focused and ubiquitous actions in the global context (Kogut & Zander, 1993). In other words, a continuous sourcing of repatriation-based competencies allows the organization to develop a global mindset for competing effectively in hypercompetitive market segments (Harvey, Speier & Novicevic, 2000).

To develop dynamic capabilities through repatriation of managers, global organizations need to ensure successful reintegration of repatriated managers into the domestic organization to permit maximum utilization of their knowledge/relationships/experiences acquired during the expatriation assignment. The collective competencies of the repatriated expatriate managers thus provide the foundation for gaining a global mindset in the organization to ensure the execution of appropriate dynamic strategies by the organization. This process is cumulative as the repatriated managers provide inputs of new competencies based on their expatriation experiences that are essential to the customization of strategy executions to compete effectively against the diverse set of global competitors (Pucik & Saba, 1998; Leiba-O'Sullivan, 2002; Oddou, forthcoming).

Successful repatriation of managers is likely to create positive externalities in the domestic organization (Allen & Alvarez, 1998; Leiba-O'Sullivan,

2002). As these repatriate competencies are developed through the specific knowledge acquired on expatriate assignments, their sharing and deployment may reshape the thinking, actions and even the world view of the domestic management of the organization, making it ultimately evolve into a global mindset throughout the organization (Kefalas, 1998; Paul, 2000). Therefore successful repatriation provides the bases for a diverse set of perspectives relative to developing a corporate mindset and the transfer of knowledge to execute effective global strategies (Mahoney & Pandian, 1992; Kidger, 2002).

The importance of global assignments for expatriate managers and their successful reintegration into the domestic management team are tied to the organization's ability to transfer knowledge and cultural understanding across its global networks of relationships (Bender & Fish, 2000). Developing this multi-level competency through knowledge transfer back into the domestic organization will augment not only human capital (knowledge and experiences) but also the social capital of the organization (Wright, McMahan & Williams, 1994; Leiba-O'Sullivan, 2002).

The corporate social capital is increasingly enhanced as repatriate managers commonly possess competencies to address effectively issues in collaborative relationships with specific foreign entities and institutions (government agencies, banks, suppliers, customers, strategic alliance partners) based on their social capital created with key individuals in the host countries during their foreign assignment. This broad set of competencies augments the organization's market-based knowledge of how to compete more effectively in certain foreign markets or regions of foreign markets (Lado, Boyd & Wright, 1992; Leiba-O'Sullivan, 1999). Once successfully integrated into the domestic organization, the competencies of repatriates create a collective experience base and/or learning capability resulting in an organizational culture conducive to learning and knowledge sharing that is difficult for competitors to replicate and can therefore create a relative competitive advantage over other organizations (Taylor, Beechler & Napier, 1996; Roth & O'Donnell, 1996).

The development of social capital through transfer of the unique and valuable competencies of repatriated managers builds more diverse and pluralistic management teams in the global network (Fish & Wood, 1997). First, there may be situations outside the global organization's network of relationships which may require tacit local knowledge to explore business relationship options and exploit opportunities in a specific geographic area or culture. By utilizing successfully social capital of repatriated managers, global organizations are applying a requisite competency of such tacit knowledge that is difficult for global competitors to duplicate. Furthermore the tacit knowledge gained through repatriate networks becomes embedded into the domestic firm-specific routines as organizational capital (formal and informal structures that enable and facilitate knowledge coordination) that can increase organizational effectiveness in global competitive interactions.

In summary, by managing strategically the repatriation process to ensure a continuous inflow of repatriate unique and valuable competencies, the global network organization can configure a repertoire of strategic choices relative to a specific foreign national competitive environment, while at the same time being mindful of the need to maintain consistency across its subsidiaries. Such consistency is derived from the development of a global mindset, which in turn thrives on the creation of an adequate pool of global managers with complementary competencies (Kedia & Mukherji, 1999; Kefalas, 1998; Paul, 2000). Therefore strategic repatriation management is essential and needs to be effectively developed to help ensure that firm-specific competencies based on repatriation are renewed and maintained in the organization.

Past research on repatriation issues evolving across the expatriation–repatriation cycle: a literature review

Research studies on the repatriation of managers from foreign assignments have been episodic for the past two decades. Few of these research studies have been focused on examining the repatriation process, including the expatriation–repatriation cycle and the components/stages/elements that constitute the repatriation process. Rather most studies have focused on conceptual and empirical examination of the repatriation issues (Harvey, 1989; Black & Gregersen, 1991; Caligiuri & Phillips, 2003; Suutari & Brewster, 2003). These research efforts to date have attempted to identify why the transition back to the home country organization and sociocultural environment has been so difficult for expatriates and their families. The repatriation issues (see Table 17.1) can be divided into three categories (work issues, individual/family issues and sociocultural issues) which evolve during the three distinct stages of the expatriation–repatriation cycle (pre-expatriation, during expatriation and upon repatriation of the manager and his/her family).

The pre-expatriation challenges commonly involve the lack of preparation for the relocation of the manager/family and the lack of knowledge of what to expect once expatriated (Black & Gregersen, 1991; Black, Gregersen & Mendenhall, 1992; Gregersen & Black, 1995). The impact on the career of the expatriate appears to be the area that has not been effectively addressed in terms of planning prior to undertaking an expatriate assignment (Bennett, 1993; Handler & Lane, 1997). The lack of attention to the specific knowledge necessary to be successful in expatriate

Table 17.1   *Multifaceted issues evolving during the expatriation/repatriation cycle*

	Pre-expatriation (before)	Expatriation (during)	Repatriation (after)
Work issues	Lack of adequate training	Lack of communication/ contact	Increased tension/ conflict
	Lack of knowledge relative to what to expect during expatriation	Out of sight out of mind	Higher repatriate turnover
	Lack of career plan and role of training	Inadequate career development	Holding pattern upon return
	Assignment to career path	Loss of social capital domestically	
	Inability to identify position upon repatriation	Reduced work motivation/ performance	Lack of decision- making autonomy
Individual/ family issues	Resistance to expatriate	Educational problems with children	Potential reduction in standard of living
	Lack of training/ preparation for family members	Lack of career opportunities for trailing spouse	Reverse culture shock
	Lack of support for family	Dysfunctional behaviour of spouse/ children affecting performance	Increased marital disharmony
	Inability to address dual career issues		Job difficulties for trailing spouse
Social/cultural issues	Lack of knowledge of emerging &/or transition economies	Lack of acceptance of local culture	Difficulty of re-engaging
	Lack of insights into external constituents in country of assignment	Isolation and continuing culture shock	Lack of acceptance in home country
	Lack of language/ cultural training	Fear of hazards of the local environment (health, safety and the like)	Lack of identify in home country/ culture

assignments, coupled with the absence of career development insights, reduces both the expatriate and expatriate family's willingness to undertake a foreign assignment (Harvey, 1989, 1997a). The reluctance is compounded by the lack of attention to spouse/family training needs and preparation for repatriation upon completion of the expatriation assignment (Brislin & Van Buren, 1974; Austin, 1983; Sussman, 1986; Leiba-O'Sullivan, 2002) as well as the seeming lack of attention/concern for the expatriated dual-career couples (Harvey, 1996, 1997a, 1997b, 1998; Harvey & Buckley, 1998).

During the expatriation phase of the expatriation–repatriation cycle, as the manager and the family are 'out of sight, out of mind' for the most part, the repatriation process seems to be unattended because the adjustments issues consume most of the attention of expatriates, their families and the corporate IHRM (Black, 1990; Black, Mendenhall & Oddou, 1991; Black, Gregersen & Mendenhall, 1992). The lack of face-to-face communication with the key managers in the domestic organization and loss of domestic social capital of the expatriate manager can have a negative impact on expatriate motivation and, ultimately, performance (Harvey, 1983, 1989; Gregersen & Black, 1995). At the same time, the spouse and other family members are commonly experiencing isolation, loss of career opportunities (for the dual-career expatriate partner or spouse), and episodic dysfunctional behaviour on the part of individual family members (Gregersen & Black, 1995; Hammer, Hart & Rogan, 1998; Caligiuri & Lazarova, 2001). The culture shock and difficulties of integration into the host country culture and social environment take significant expatriate/family energy and time. This continuing attention to the present issues keeps the expatriate and family thoughts away from planning the long-term repatriation adjustment that must be initiated during the last stage of the expatriation assignment. The apprehension/fear of terrorism, health-related concerns, compatibility/change in education programmes and other issues have a tendency to compound the procrastination related to preparing for repatriation (Harvey, 1989; Tung, 1998; Peltonen, 1999).

Once the expatriate and family face the forthcoming repatriation phase tension, a latent conflict will likely arise over a number of issues that, heretofore, have been viewed as positive aspects of the expatriation experiences. The expatriate is frequently caught in a 'catch-22' stage of repatriation in that the availability of an appropriate new position will seldom be secure upon repatriating to the home country organization (Kendall, 1981; Harvey, 1983, 1989; Black, 1992; Hammer, Hart & Rogan, 1998). The holding pattern syndrome and the lack of decision-making autonomy thus become cruel 'rewards' for personal and career sacrifices made for the good of the company by the repatriated manager.

For example, the cost-of-living allowances (COLA) and other perks associated with the expatriate assignment can come as reverse culture shock to the family that became accustomed to these financial contributions that were instrumental in the adjustment to the host country (Harvey, 1989; Black & Stephens, 1989; Black & Gregersen, 1991; Black, 1992). Additionally the disharmony in the family context has a negative impact on the repatriated manager's ability to feel reintegrated into the domestic environment (Harvey, 1989; Black, Gregersen & Mendenhall, 1992). The re-engagement into the career cycle for the spouse is also a constant source of problems for the repatriate manager during the repatriation adjustment stage (Harvey, 1996, 1997a, 1997b, 1998). Furthermore the stress and tension make acceptance of the repatriated manager that much more problematic by their counterparts in the domestic organization (Hazzard, 1981; The Conference Board, 1997). This conflict reduces the transference of valuable information to the other managers: the information that was learned during the foreign assignment and is crucial in the development of global competencies and a global mindset in the organization's management team (Kefalas, 1998; Kedia & Mukherji, 1999; Paul, 2000).

· While many problems encountered in repatriation of managers and their families are well documented, the means to address these problems are less well articulated in the literature (Harvey, 1989; Black, 1992; Stroh, 1995; Black, Gregersen, Mendenhall & Stroh, 1999). The severity of the problems that are associated with the repatriation process are influenced to a degree by individual consideration, such as (a) the magnitude of the change from the home to the host culture; (b) the length of time spent in the host country; (c) the frequency of and time spent on return trips to the home country; (d) the total time away from the home country; and (e) the 'quality' of the adjustment made by the expatriate and the family members. All of these issues are accentuated when the expatriated manager is a female, compounding the stress of re-entry (Linehan & Scullion, 2002).

There are a number of organizational variables that should also be taken into consideration related to the expatriation of managers that can also influence the repatriation of managers back to the home country: (a) level and quality of communication with the expatriate once on assignment; (b) level of expatriation and repatriation training before, during and after the foreign assignment; (c) availability of a mentoring/sponsoring programme that addresses both the expatriation and repatriation phases of the assignment and is for both the expatriate manager and their spouse; (d) role clarity of the foreign assignment; and (e) organizational support/training upon repatriation of the expatriate manager as well as for the family (The Conference Board, 1997; Caligiuri & Phillips, 2003; Suutari & Brewster, 2003). While these individual and organizational variables may be helpful in predicting the level and duration of the repatriation adjustment in multi-domestic MNEs, we still know little about the way the repatriation process and issues are altered once an MNE evolves into a global network organization. The impact of this evolution on repatriation is examined in the following section of the chapter.

The evolution to global human resource management and the patriation of global managers

Most of the recent international business literature views MNEs in transition, to a different extent and through various trajectories, toward a global network form of organization (Holm, Johanson & Thilenius, 1995). The network model, viewing an MNE as an inter-organizational network of loosely coupled and interdependent subsidiaries (Bartlett & Ghoshal, 1991), posits that subsidiaries can be a source of corporate competitive advantage (Rugman & Verbeke, 1992). Originating from the field of industrial marketing (Johanson & Mattson, 1988), the network model has been adopted by the proponents of the resource-based view of the firm (Barney, 1991; Penrose, 1959; Wernerfelt, 1984) who recognize that capability development can occur at any level of the firm.

In the network perspective of an MNE, a subsidiary can be viewed as a node of a complex system of multiple linkages of internal and external relationships (Welch & Welch, 1993). The two primary network systems in which a subsidiary is embedded are identified as: between subsidiary and headquarters and among subsidiaries. The horizontal subsidiary–subsidiary network is characterized by interdependencies and interconnectedness influenced by the separate vertical headquarters–subsidiary networks (ibid.). A key component in these relational ties is the development of trust (that is, a psychological state comprising the intention to accept vulnerability based upon positive expectations of the intentions or behaviour of others) among subsidiary units (Rousseau, Sitkin, Burt & Camerer, 1998). As increased levels of trust can be maintained and built, based upon repatriate personal interactions, their informal personal relationships can contribute to the increased learning in the global network organization.

The network model provides a valuable perspective on the relevance of repatriate competencies because it reflects the reality that many subsidiaries have specialized capabilities that are understood by repatriates and on which the rest of the MNE is dependent. The repatriate manager, equipped with the unique and tacit knowledge about a specific subsidiary's dynamic capabilities, its domain of excellence and the set of its relational capabilities, is most competent to assess a subsidiary's potential to cooperate within the global network. In other words, thanks to their tacit knowledge about the stock of the subsidiary's endogenous dynamic capabilities and the availability of exogenous resources and capabilities possessed by its stake-holders, managers repatriated into the global network organization possess specific knowledge about the dynamic capabilities of the subsidiary to which they were previously assigned (Ghoshal & Bartlett, 1990; Gupta & Govindarajan, 1991; Forsgren & Pahlberg, 1992).

The utility of the repatriate managers to coordinate and cultivate infor-mal relationships among the subsidiary units depends to a degree on the match between their own capabilities and the IHRM system that supports the global network organization. The appropriate IHRM system is critical for the proactive role of repatriate managers and for their potential of achieving a global career in the MNE. An appropriate IHRM system should incorporate the repatriation process to foster perceptions of proce-dural justice in the global network (Kim & Mauborgne, 1998) that, in turn, would facilitate development of trust and cooperative relations, collective learning, and knowledge sharing among subsidiaries (Caligiuri & Phillips, 2003).

The rationale for this increasing need for a modified IHRM system for assignments is that the competencies gained on assignments by the expatri-ate managers will be too valuable to allow the organization to repatriate these managers to the home country organization where their use of newly developed competencies is more limited than when they are closer to global customers (Leiba-O'Sullivan, 2002). If competitive advantage is to be gained through the worldwide deployment of the managerial competencies, these competencies must be renewed and used continuously. By continu-ously renewing repatriate competencies, the headquarters can navigate its decision-making tasks dispersed throughout the global network to com-pensate for its diminishing influence over subsidiaries. This continuous use of repatriate potential requires a rethinking of the existing IHRM models.

Existing IHRM models (Schuler, Dowling & De Cieri, 1993; Edstrom & Galbraith, 1977; Heenan & Perlmutter, 1979; Adler & Ghadar, 1990; Milliman, Von Glinow & Nathan, 1991), although systematic and compre-hensive in their assessment of IHRM policies, processes and issues, inade-quately address strategic repatriation management in a network form of global organization. Therefore a new model addressing the increasing dynamism of expatriate assignments should capture the altered repatria-tion process and issues (Dowling & Schuler, 1990; Welch, 1994; Tayeb, 1995). The primary change that an IHRM model for a global network organization should address is the repatriate commitment to a global career throughout and post sequential assignments to specific foreign markets.

This change implies that repatriation of managers should be supple-mented by a process/programme that could be called 'patriation' (that is, the return of expatriate managers after a sequence of multiple relocations/

assignments in a global network organization) of managers. A repatriation process/programme involves organizational support to repatriated managers to help them adjust and adapt to the new work/life role in the home country organization and its sociocultural environment (Feldman, 1991; Feldman & Tompson, 1993; Baruch & Altman, 2002). The patriation process/programme goes beyond repatriation as it refers to organizational support to repatriates to help them reconstruct their new identity in the home country organization and its sociocultural environment after an absence of many years (maybe as many as 15–20 years of foreign assignments). Patriation becomes relevant when expatriate managers undergo a degree of deidentification with the domestic organization and perceive the re-entry to the home country organization to be either too disruptive to their personal/family life (entailing issues of personal identity loss in the cross-cultural re-entry) or more challenging than the original relocation abroad (entailing issues of professional identity loss in the cross-cultural re-entry) (Linehan & Scullion, 1998).

The deidentification process, manifested as an unrealistic expectation gap, can be caused by various factors, but it is most likely to occur because of the lack of a mentoring/sponsoring programme (a common case in Europe) or the lack of a formal repatriation contract (a common case in the United States) (Stroh, Gregersen & Black, 1998; Leiba-O'Sullivan, 2002). It should be noted that expatriate deidentification and identification on the 'eve' of repatriation are only the poles of a continuum, with ambivalent identification and neutral identification as intermediate stages. It is important to assess where a specific expatriate stands on this continuum to design the appropriate variation in the patriation process/programme.

As the 'patriation' process/programme is supplementary to the repatriation process/programme, it addresses specific issues occurring upon the return of expatriate managers and their family members from a sequence of global assignments. The most salient set of problems is centred on the time the expatriate is dislocated from the home country (Suutari & Brewster, 2003). The extended aggregate time in the sequential expatriation mode exacerbates the dislocation of the expatriate from the home organization, as well as from the sociocultural environment of the home country. Given that the longer aggregate time of global assignments is double or triple the time of traditional one-time expatriation in MNEs, the expatriate will have less first-hand knowledge of the culture/climate of the domestic organization. This will mean that the expatriate's knowledge of how to be successfully assimilated back into the domestic organization as well as macrocultures will be drastically diminished. The expatriate manager's frame-of-reference will be outdated and he/she will have little to virtually no social capital in the organization (Adler, 1981; Allen & Alvarez, 1998).

The magnitude of reverse culture shock will be greater, taking even longer for the 'extended' expatriate to reconstruct identity and adjust to the local business environment (Hurn, 1999). The extent of the reverse culture shock is tied not only to the length of time of the extended expatriation assignment but also to the magnitude of organizational change (new management, new ownership, new policies that could have taken place during the expatriate's absence from the organization) (Caligiuri & Phillips, 2003). This adjustment time is compounded by the extensive adjustment of the family given the potential disconnection from the domestic sociocultural environment (Harvey, 1989; Harvey & Novicevic, 2002). The potential time of decompression to the new domestic cultural/social environment accentuates the need for extensive organizational support and attention to the problems that are going to be faced by the expatriate and the family that have undergone multiple assignment experiences.

Sequential expatriation becomes much more challenging than the traditional one-time expatriation because the growth of global organizations will be tied to the emerging and transitional economies in the world marketplace (Garten, 1996, 1997a, 1997b) as opposed to the developed markets that have dominated the strategic direction of multi-domestic MNEs in the past several decades. The impact on the expatriate/family of the dramatically changing cultural distance/novelty in the sequence of expatriations will compound the adjustment back to their home country. Even successful adjustment to the initial foreign assignment to an emerging/transition country will be followed by the subsequent transfers to other potentially novel cultures, thereby making the reverse cultural adjustment back to the original home country that much more difficult. As expatriates that make these sequential transitions/adjustments become 'citizens of the world' and face the possibility of losing their home country orientation (turning formally into cosmopolitans), the 'patriation' process/programme that facilitates return back to the home country identity becomes mandatory to avoid such deidentification (Sussman, 2000). The experience of deidentification was known by British soldiers that were sent off to India or Africa for 15–20 years. Their return to Britain was a difficult and in many cases an unsuccessful adjustment transition for these career soldiers that resulted in a number of them returning to their 'adopted' home countries.

To address the issues of varying repatriate deidentification from the domestic organization, the corporate HR management needs to design a patriation programme of an appropriate scale (low-scale, medium-scale, high-scale or comprehensive patriation programme). The scale of the patriation programme will depend, not only on the degree of repatriate deidentification but also on the degree of strategic value that repatriate could present for the domestic organization (see Figure 17.1). This strategic

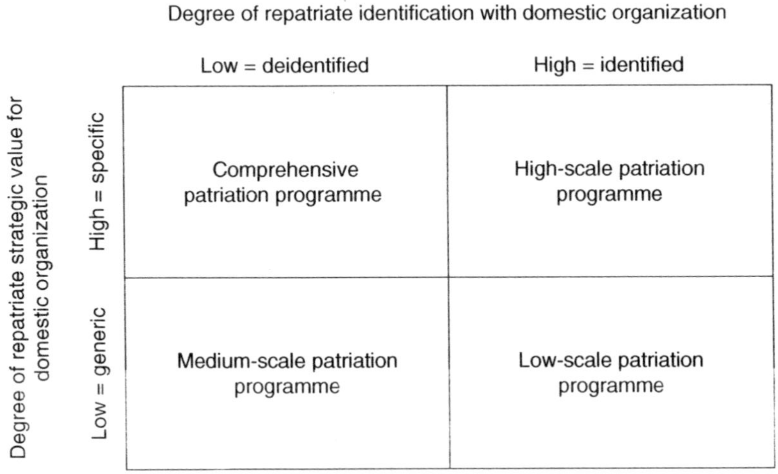

Degree of repatriate identification with domestic organization

	Low = deidentified	High = identified
High = specific	Comprehensive patriation programme	High-scale patriation programme
Low = generic	Medium-scale patriation programme	Low-scale patriation programme

(left axis label: Degree of repatriate strategic value for domestic organization)

Figure 17.1   Assessing an appropriate scale for patriation programme

orientation toward patriation necessitates a shift in IHRM focus from practices and activities to outcomes (Ulrich, 1997).

In effect, the modifications in the IHRM system components (IHRM practice such as performance appraisal, training and development, compensation and so on) will need to be shifted from the process perspective to the outcome perspective of how each of them can contribute to the IHRM system to capitalize on patriation as the process of adding value to organizational competency. Future research should contribute to a better understanding not only of the factors that mediate between the scale of patriation and the related IHRM practices (that is, IHRM system components) but also of those that contribute to the variation of the generic patriation process presented in the next section of this chapter.

The potential loss of identify with the home country culture presents a unique opportunity for the MNE to develop a strong tie with the expatriate and the organization culture of the MNE, thereby supplanting the national culture with that of the organization as the 'foundation' culture of the 'multiple' expatriate and his/her family. This 'superimposed' culture will have to be built on trust between the expatriate and the MNE. This strong organization culture can be used as a means to identify with the MNE throughout the world and, therefore, to reduce the return culture shock after an extended expatriate set of assignments. The result should be a cosmopolitan global manager with strong organizational ties to MNEs that have created a culture based upon trust in the organization throughout the world. To accomplish this goal, human resource managers must develop a process of patriating global managers returning to the home country organization. This process is described in the following section.

Development of a 'patriation' process for global managers

The evolution of an MNE from a multi-domestic to a global organization is seldom systematic. As the variations in the evolution process will affect managers' careers being expatriated sequentially to foreign assignments, new IHRM programmes and processes need to be developed to ensure that global managers are effectively supported (McCall & Hollenbeck, 2002; Suutari, 2003). This means that the process of repatriation should be supplemented by the development of a new process of 'patriation', given the length of time and cultural distances experienced by global managers. Therefore a step-by-step 'patriation' process should be instituted by organizations to facilitate the transition (see Figure 17.2). Each of these steps is briefly outlined below.

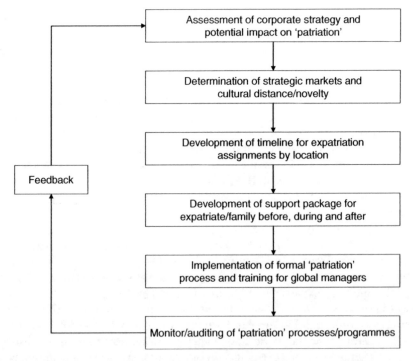

Figure 17.2   Development of a 'patriation' process for return of global managers to home country organization

1. *Assessment of corporate strategy and potential impact on patriation of global managers*   The initial step in the 'patriation' process is to determine where the organization stands in the transition from a multi-domestic to a global organization. The assessment of the transition stage will provide the international human resource management team with the time to develop properly a system that is global in perspective and able to handle the differences in expatriation of managers into the global network of organizations. The strategic shift will likely be implemented gradually over a period of years, but the international human resource management team will have to anticipate the evolution of the strategy and enact a patriation process that will coincide with the general corporate shift to a global strategy.

2. *Determination of strategic markets and cultural distance/novelty*   In the course of the MNE's transition to a global organization, one of the key considerations in developing a 'patriation' process is to ascertain what markets/countries the expatriates are most likely to be relocated to by the organization. By determining the (dis)similarities within the likely set of host countries that the expatriate will be relocated to, international human resource management can better calculate the cultural distance/novelty the expatriate will be exposed to during his/her global career. In addition some estimates can be made on the sequences of the relocation and the individual duration of specific assignments.

3. *Development of a timeline for expatriation assignments by location*   The most likely aggregate duration of sequential expatriation needs to be determined prior to the relocation of the manager/family. This timeline will provide the global manager with an anticipated roadmap of assignments or at the very least the countries to which he/she will be relocated during the overseas assignment. While it is unrealistic to provide the exact country/assignment, every effort should be made to indicate the most likely scenarios and an array of countries to which the global manager will be relocated during the expatriation tenure.

4. *Development of support package/training for expatriate/family before, during and after the series of global assignments*   Once the countries are determined for a set of expatriate managers and the various stages of the family life cycle are identified, a set of support packages can be developed by the international human resource management team. These packages will have to vary by country and by stage of the family life cycle as well as customized to the length of the assignment in each host country. The total duration of the set of expatriate assignments also will be incorporated into the appropriate support package for the expatriate. The level or degree of adjustment will vary by type of country and the length of time the expatriate has been on assignment

without returning or with a short repatriation to the home country. In addition training and development of the expatriate will be somewhat contingent on the nature and duration of the sequential expatriate assignments.

5. *Implementation of formal 'patriation' process and training for global managers*   The conversion to a strategic global human resource management (SGHRM) system will necessitate the development of an entirely new process for the 'patriation' of expatriate managers from 'deep' assignments in the global organization. This will require a rethinking of the problems and how to 'patriate' global managers effectively back to home countries after a career of global relocations. As the present repatriation philosophies and processes cannot accommodate the career expatriate, an adaptation of the repatriation process will have to be made to be effective.

6. *Monitoring/auditing of 'patriation' processes/programmes*   Given the newness of the sequential expatriation practice and the lack of adequate IHRM experience in addressing the problems/issues associated with global managers' 'patriation' back after many years of sequential expatriate assignments, an SGHRM system must be assessed on a regular, continuing basis. External benchmarking of 'patriation' programmes developed by other global organizations will become central to the success of the patriation programme developed by global organizations.

Conclusion

Repatriation of expatriate managers has been a research topic relatively neglected by academic researchers. The two decades of repatriation research have been primarily focused on conceptualization of the phenomenon and the identification of problems that are associated with returning managers/families. In multi-domestic organizations, many of the critical problems centre on addressing reverse culture shock that occurs when the manager/family have been separated from the home country for three to five years. In a global network organization, the dynamics and the aggregate length of assignment(s) will increase, thus accentuating the deidentification problems experienced by the expatriate/family upon return.

The deidentification issues will impede a catalytic role that repatriates can play in networks that foster worldwide learning, problem solving and knowledge sharing. For prevention of repatriate deidentification, the repatriation process needs to be supplemented by a process of 'patriating' returning managers. The design of a 'patriation' process/programme will necessitate a greater attention by the corporate SGHRM, as the need for organizational and social support will be increased. Moreover, as the responsibilities of the organization to monitor and prepare the expatriate/family will also be increased, the traditional form of repatriation process will have to be altered or redesigned to accommodate the problems/issues associated with deidentification of 'sequential' expatriate managers in global organizations.

References

Adler, N. 1981. Re-entry: managing cross-cultural transitions. *Group and Organization Studies*, 6(3): 341–56.

Adler, N. & F. Ghadar. 1990. Strategic human resource management: a global perspective. In R. Pieper (ed.), *Human resource management: an international comparison*: 235–60. Berlin: de Gruyter.

Allen, D. & S. Alvarez. 1998. Empowering expatriates and organizations to improve repatriation effectiveness. *Human Resource Planning*, 21(4): 29–39.

Auperle, K. 1996. Spontaneous organizational reconfiguration: a historical example based on Xenophon's anabasis. *Organization Science*, 7(4): 444–60.

Austin, C. 1983. *Cross-cultural re-entry: an annotated bibliography*. Abilene: ACU Press.

Barney, J. 1991. Firm resources and sustained competitive advantage. *Journal of Management*, 17: 99–129.

Bartlett, C.A. & S. Ghoshal. 1991. Global strategic management: impact on the new frontiers of strategy research. *Strategic Management Journal*, 12: 5–17.

Bartlett, C. & S. Ghoshal. 1992. What is a global manager? *Harvard Business Review*, September/October: 124–32.

Baruch, Y. & Y. Altman. 2002. Expatriation and repatriation in MNEs: a taxonomy. *Human Resource Management*, 41(2): 239–59.

Bender, S. & A. Fish. 2000. The transfer of knowledge and the retention of expertise: the continuing need for global assignments. *Journal of Knowledge Management*, 4(2): 125–37.

Bennett, R. 1993. Meeting the challenges of repatriation. *Journal of International Compensation and Benefits*, September–October: 2–33.

Bernhut, S. 2001. Measuring the value of intellectual capital. *Ivey Business Journal*, 65: 16–20.

Black, J.S. 1990. The relationship of personal characteristics with the adjustment of Japanese expatriate managers. *Management International Review*, 30: 119–34.

Black, J.S. 1992. Coming home: the relationship of expatriate expectations with repatriation and job performance. *Human Relations*, 45(2): 177–83.

Black, J.S. & H. Gregersen. 1991. When Yankee comes home: factors related to expatriate and spouse repatriation adjustment. *Journal of International Business Studies*, 22: 671–94.

Black, J.S. & G. Stephens. 1989. The influence of the spouse on American expatriate adjustment in overseas assignments. *Journal of Management*, 15: 529–44.

Black, J.S., H. Gregersen & M. Mendenhall. 1992. Toward a theoretical framework of repatriation adjustment. *Journal of International Business Studies*, 23(4): 773–95.

Black, J.S., M. Mendenhall & G. Oddou. 1991. Towards a comprehensive model of international adjustment: an investigation of multiple theoretical perspectives. *Academy of Management Review*, 16: 291–317.

Black, J.S., H. Gregersen, M. Mendenhall & L. Stroh. 1999. *Globalizing people through international assignments*. New York: Addison-Wesley.

Brislin, R. & H. Van Buren. 1974. Can they go home again? *International Education and Cultural Exchange*, 9(4): 19–24.

Caligiuri, P. & M. Lazarova. 2001. Retaining repatriates: the role of organizational support practice. Proceedings of the AOM, Toronto.

Caligiuri, P. & J. Phillips. 2003. An application of self-assessment realistic job previews to expatriate assignments. *International Journal of Human Resource Management*, 14(7): 1102–16.

D'Aveni, R. 1994. *Hypercompetition: manning the dynamics of strategic maneuvering*. New York: The Free Press.

D'Aveni, R. 1997. Waking up to the new era of hypercompetition. *The Washington Quarterly*, **21**(1): 183–95.

D'Aveni, R. 1999. Strategic supremacy through disruption and dominance. *Sloan Management Review*, **40**(3): 127–36.

de Vries, M.F. 1999. *The new global leaders: Richard Branson, Percy Barnevik and David Simon*. San Francisco, CA: Jossey-Bass.

Dowling, P.J. & R.S. Schuler. 1990. *International dimensions of HRM*. Boston, MA: PWS-Kent.

Edstrom, A. & J. Galbraith. 1977. Transfer of managers as a coordination and control strategy in multinational organizations. *Administrative Science Quarterly*, June: 248–63.

Feldman, D. 1991. Repatriate moves as career transitions. *Human Resource Management Review*, **1**(3): 163–78.

Feldman, D. & H.B. Tompson. 1993. Expatriation, repatriation, and domestic geographical relocation: an empirical investigation of adjustment to new job assignments. *Journal of International Business Studies*, **24**: 507–29.

Fiol, C. 1991. Managing culture as a competitive resource. *Journal of Management*, **17**: 191–211.

Fish, A. & J. Wood. 1997. Cross cultural management competence in Australian business enterprises. *Asia Pacific Journal of Human Resources*, **35**(1): 37–52.

Forsgren, M. & C. Pahlberg. 1992. Subsidiary influence and autonomy in international firms. *International Business Review*, **1**(3): 41–51.

Garten, J. 1996. The key emerging markets. *The Columbia Journal of World Business*, **31**(2): 6–31.

Garten, J. 1997a. Trouble ahead in emerging markets. *Harvard Business Review*, **75**: 38–49.

Garten, J. 1997b. *The big ten: the emerging markets and how they will change our lives*. New York: Basic Books.

Ghoshal, S. & C. Bartlett. 1990. The multinational corporation as an interorganizational network. *Academy of Management Review*, **15**(4): 603–25.

Gimeno, J. & C. Woo. 1996. Hypercompetition in a multimarket environment: the role of strategic similarity and multimarket contact on competitive de-escalation. *Organization Science*, **7**(4): 375–87.

Gregersen, H. & J.S. Black. 1995. Keeping high performers after international assignment: a key to global executive development. *Journal of International Management*, **1**(1): 3–31.

Griffin, K. & R. Khan. 1992. *Globalization and the developing world: an essay on the international dimensions of development in the post-cold war era*. Geneva: United Nations Research Institute for Social Development.

Gupta, A. & V. Govindarajan. 1991. Knowledge flows and the structure of control within multinational corporations. *Academy of Management Review*, **16**: 768–92.

Hall, R. 1993. A framework linking intangible resources and capabilities to sustainable competitive advantage. *Strategic Management Journal*, **14**: 607–18.

Hammer, M., W. Hart & R. Rogan. 1998. Can you go home again? An analysis of repatriation of corporate managers and spouses. *Management International Review*, **40**: 21–32.

Handler, C. & I. Lane. 1997. Career planning and expatriate couples. *Human Resource Management Journal*, **7**(3): 67–78.

Harvey, M. 1983. The other side of foreign assignments: dealing with the repatriation dilemma. *The Columbia Journal of World Business*, **17**(1): 53–9.

Harvey, M. 1989. Repatriation of corporate executives: an empirical study. *Journal of International Business Studies*, **20**(2): 131–44.

Harvey, M. 1996. Addressing the dual-career expatriation dilemma. *Human Resource Planning*, **19**(4): 79–86.

Harvey, M. 1997a. The impact of dual-career expatriates on international human resource management. *Journal of International Management*, **3**(4): 76–85.

Harvey, M. 1997b. Dual-career expatriates: expectations, adjustment, and satisfaction with international relocation. *Journal of International Business Studies*, **28**(3): 183–92.

Harvey, M. 1998. Dual career couples during international relocation: the trailing spouse. *International Journal of Human Resource Management*, **8**(1): 11–23.

Harvey, M. & R. Buckley. 1998. The process for developing an international program for dual-career couples. *Human Resource Management Review*, **8**(1): 89–97.

Harvey, M. & R. Lusch. 1999. Balancing the intellectual capital books: intangible liabilities. *European Management Journal*, **17**(1): 87–95.

Harvey, M. & M. Novicevic. 2002. Selecting appropriate marketing managers to effectively control global channels of distribution. *International Marketing Review*, **19**(5): 56–69.

Harvey, M. & M. Novicevic. 2003. Strategic global human resource management: its role in global networks. *Research & Practice in Human Resource Management*, **11**(1): 85–97.

Harvey, M., C. Speier & M. Novicevic. 2000. The impact of emerging markets on staffing the global organization. *Journal of International Management*, **5**(2): 32–43.

Harvey, M., C. Speier & M. Novicevic. 2001a. A theory-based framework of strategic global human resource staffing policies and practices. *International Journal of Human Resource Management*, **12**(6): 235–47.

Harvey, M., C. Speier & M. Novicevic. 2001b. Strategic human resource staffing of overseas subsidiaries. *Research & Practice in Human Resource Management*, **9**(2): 267–79.

Hazzard, M. 1981. *Study of repatriation of the American international executive.* New York: Korn/Ferry International.

Heenan, D. & H. Perlmutter. 1979. *Multinational organization devilment.* Reading, MA: Addison-Wesley.

Hollenbeck, G. & M. McCall. 2001. What makes a successful global executive? *Business Strategy Review*, **12**(4): 49–56.

Holm, U., J. Johanson & P. Thilenius. 1995. Headquarters knowledge of subsidiary network contexts in the multinational corporation. *International Studies of Management and Organization*, **25**(102): 97–120.

Howard, C. 1974. The returning overseas executive: culture shock in reverse. *Human Resource Management*, **20**(1): 22–6.

Hurn, B. 1999. Repatriation – the toughest assignment of all. *Industrial and Commercial Training*, **31**(6): 224–8.

Ilinitch, A., A.Y. Lewin & R.A. D'Aveni (eds). 1998. *Managing in times of disorder: hyper-competitive organizational responses.* Thousand Oaks, CA: Sage.

Johanson, J. & L.G. Mattson. 1988. Internalization in industrial systems – a network approach. In N. Hood & J.R. Vahlne (eds), *Strategies in global competition*: 287–314. London: Croom Helm.

Kedia, B. & A. Mukherji. 1999. Global managers: developing a mindset for global competitiveness. *Journal of World Business*, **34**(3): 230–47.

Kefalas, A. 1998. Think globally, act locally. *Thunderbird International Business Review*, **40**(6): 547–62.

Kendall, D.W. 1981. Repatriation: an ending and a beginning. *Business Horizons*, **24**: 21–5.

Kidger, P. 2002. Management structure in multinational enterprises: responding to globalization. *Employee Relations*, **24**(1): 69–85.

Kim, W.C. & R. Mauborgne. 1998. Procedural justice, strategic decision making and the knowledge economy. *Strategic Management Journal*, **19** (Special issue): 323–38.

Kogut, B. & U. Zander. 1993. Knowledge of the firm and the evolutionary theory of the multinational corporation. *Journal of International Business Studies*, **24**: 625–45.

Lado, A. & M. Wilson. 1994. Human resource systems and sustained competitive advantage: a competency-based perspective. *Academy of Management Review*, **19**(4): 699–727.

Lado, A., N. Boyd & P. Wright. 1992. A competency model of sustained competitive advantage. *Journal of Management*, **18**: 77–91.

Leiba-O'Sullivan, S. 1999. The distinction between stable and dynamic cross-cultural competencies: implications for expatriate trainability. *Journal of International Business Studies*, **30**(4): 709–26.

Leiba-O'Sullivan, S. 2002. The protean approach to managing repatriation transitions. *International Journal of Manpower*, **23**(7): 597–616.

Liebeskind, J., A. Oliver, L. Zucker & M. Brewer. 1996. Social networks, learning, and flexibility: sourcing scientific knowledge in biotechnology firms. *Organization Science*, **7**(4): 428–43.

Linehan, M. & H. Scullion. 2002. The repatriation of female international managers: an empirical study. *International Journal of Manpower*, **23**(7): 649–58.

Lusch, R., M. Harvey & C. Speier. 1998. ROI 3: building blocks for successful global companies in the 21st century. *European Management Journal*, **16**(6): 75–84.

Mahoney, J.T. & J.R. Pandian. 1992. The resource-based view within the conversation of strategic management. *Strategic Management Journal*, **13**: 363–80.

Makadok, R. 1998. Can first-mover and early mover advantages be sustained in an industry with low barriers to entry/imitation? *Strategic Management Journal*, **19**: 683–96.

McCall, M. & G. Hollenbeck. 2002. *Developing global executives: the lessons of international experience*. Boston, MA: Harvard Business School Press.

Miller, D. & J. Shamsie. 1996. The resource based view of the firm in two environments: the Hollywood film studios from 1936 to 1965. *Academy of Management Journal*, **39**: 519–43.

Milliman, J., M.A. Von Glinow & M. Nathan. 1991. Organizational life cycles and strategic international human resource management in multicultural companies: implications for congruence theory. *Academy of Management Journal*, **16**(2): 318–39.

Oddou, G. (forthcoming). International assignment experience: a framework for understanding its value. *Journal of International Business Studies*.

Paul, H. 2000. Creating a global mindset. *Thunderbird International Business Review*, **42**(2): 187–200.

Peltonen, T. 1999. Repatriation and career systems: Finnish public and private sector repatriates in their career lives. In C. Brewster & H. Harris (eds), *International HRM: contemporary issues in Europe*: 241–57. New York: Routledge Press.

Penrose, R.T. 1959. *The theory of the growth of the firm*. Oxford: Basil Blackwell.

Prahalad, C. & G. Hamel. 1990. The core competency of the corporation. *Harvard Business Review*, **68**(2): 79–91.

Pucik, V. & T. Saba. 1998. Selecting and developing the global versus expatriate manager: a review of the state-of-the-art. *Human Resource Planning*, **21**: 40–55.

Roth, K. & S. O'Donnell. 1996. Foreign subsidiary compensation strategy: an agency theory perspective. *Academy of Management Journal*, **39**(3): 678–703.

Rousseau, D.M., S.B. Sitkin, R.S. Burt & C. Camerer. 1998. Not so different after all: a cross-discipline view of trust. *Academy of Management Review*, **23**: 393–405.

Rugman, A. & A. Verbeke. 1992. A note on the transnational solution and the transaction cost theory of multinational strategic management. *Journal of International Business Studies*, **23**: 761–72.

Schuler, R., P. Dowling & H. De Cieri. 1993. An integrative framework of strategic international human resource management. *International Journal of Human Resource Management*, **4**(4): 717–64.

Stroh, L. 1995. Predicting turnover among repatriates: can organizations affect retention rates? *The International Journal of Human Resource Management*, **6**(2): 443–56.

Stroh, L.K. & P.M. Caligiuri. 1998. Increasing global competitiveness through effective people management. *Journal of World Business*, **33**: 1–16.

Stroh, L., H.B. Gregersen & J.S. Black. 1998. Closing the gap: expectations versus reality among repatriates. *Journal of World Business*, **33**: 111–24.

Sussman, N. 1986. Re-entry research and training. *International Journal of Intercultural Research*, **10**: 235–54.

Sussman, N. 2000. The dynamic nature of cultural identity throughout cultural transitions: why home is not so sweet. *Personality and Social Psychology Review*, **4**(4): 355–73.

Suutari, V. 2003. Global managers: career orientation, career tracks, life-style implications and career commitment. *Journal of Managerial Psychology*, **18**(3): 185–297.

Suutari, V. & C. Brewster. 2003. Repatriation: empirical evidence from a longitudinal study of careers and expectations among Finnish expatriates. *International Journal of Human Resource Management*, **14**(7): 1132–51.

Tayeb, M. 1995. The competitive advantage of nations: the role of HRM and sociocultural context. *International Journal of Human Resource Management*, **6**(3): 588–605.

Taylor, S., S. Beechler & N. Napier. 1996. Toward an integrative model of strategic international human resource management. *Academy of Management Review*, **21**: 959–85.

The Conference Board. 1997. *Managing expatriates' return: research report.* Report Number 1148-96-RR, New York.

Truch, E. 2001. Knowledge management: auditing and reporting intellectual capital. *Journal of General Management*, **26**: 26–40.

Tung, R. 1998. American expatriates abroad: from neophytes to cosmopolitans. *Journal of World Business*, **33**: 125–44.

Urlich, D. 1997. *Human resource champions.* Boston, MA: Harvard Business School Press.

Welch, D. 1994. HRM implications of globalization. *Journal of General Management*, **19**(4): 52–68.

Welch, D.E. & L.S. Welch. 1993. Using personnel to develop networks: an approach for subsidiary management. *International Business Review*, **2**(2): 157–68.

Wernerfelt, B. 1984. A resource-based view of the firm. *Strategic Management Journal*, **5**: 171–80.

Wright, P., G. McMahan & A. Williams. 1994. Human resources as a source of sustained competitive advantage. *International Journal of Human Resource Management*, **5**: 299–324.

PART IV

RESEARCH ON INTERNATIONAL TEAMS, ALLIANCES, MERGERS AND ACQUISITIONS

18 Decoupling and coupling in global teams: implications for human resource management
Jennifer L. Gibbs

Global teams are often formed in multinational corporations as a strategic human resource solution for bringing together people with specific knowledge, skills and expertise, regardless of their geographical location. Interaction among such diverse individuals is enabled through use of information and communication technologies (ICTs) such as e-mail, audio- and videoconferencing, knowledge management systems and archival databases. Global teams offer the promise of better and more innovative solutions and products through tapping into human resource pools worldwide, more efficient around-the-clock work across time zones, and lower-cost access to local markets and customers without the need for travel (Carmel, 1999; Gluesing & Gibson, 2004). However, in order to achieve these benefits, global teams must contend with a number of challenges due to the high level of complexity they face in working across multiple contexts: geographical, temporal, cultural and technological. This chapter addresses structural dynamics of global teams, reviewing key challenges and effective team-building strategies for managing such dynamics.

Challenges due to decoupling in global teams
Global teams are defined here as work teams that are virtual, culturally diverse, structurally dynamic, and whose members collaborate on a global task using ICTs (Gibbs, 2002; Maznevski & Chudoba, 2000). As virtual teams, they are both geographically distributed across multiple locations and dependent on computer-mediated communication (CMC) (Cohen & Gibson, 2003; Griffith, Sawyer & Neale, 2003; Lipnack & Stamps, 1997), though they may vary on the degree of each of these characteristics (Cohen & Gibson, 2003; Gibson & Gibbs, 2004). In addition global teams are often characterized by a high level of cultural diversity, as well as dynamic structural arrangements (Gibson & Gibbs, 2004), in which there is high member turnover and collaboration is temporary, informal and project-based (Townsend, DeMarie & Hendrickson, 1998).

Global team members face unique human resource management (HRM) challenges that traditional teams have not had to contend with, because of the need to coordinate tasks and processes across time, space and multiple layers of cultural complexity (Carmel, 1999). The structural characteristics defining global teams – geographic distribution, electronic dependence, cultural diversity and dynamic structure – result in more loosely coupled team interactions (Gibbs, 2002) and act as centrifugal forces that pull such teams apart through breakdown of coordination, loss of communication 'richness', cultural misunderstandings and loss of 'teamness' (Carmel, 1999). These four key elements of loose coupling (Gibbs, 2002; Weick, 1976) pose HRM-related challenges to global teams. Figure 18.1 summarizes these decoupling characteristics as well as several coupling mechanisms to help coordinate team interaction (Figure 18.1). The challenges will now be discussed in more detail, followed by a discussion of the coupling mechanisms.

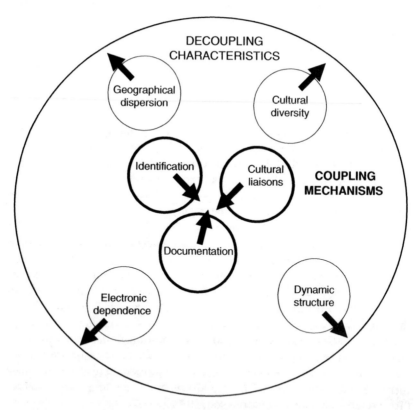

Figure 18.1   Decoupling characteristics of global teams and coupling mechanisms

Cultural diversity

Global teams face new HRM challenges due to their high degree of cultural diversity. Understanding the impacts of culture, defined broadly as a shared set of meanings or mental programming that shapes individuals' behaviour and interpretations of events (Hofstede, 1991), is even more pressing in today's global organizations, as intercultural interaction affects everyone in the organization rather than being confined to a few people (Adler, 1997). Whereas in the past only expatriates needed to develop cultural sensitivity and intercultural competence, in global firms employees do not need to go abroad or leave their own community to encounter cross-cultural contact, as 'cross-cultural dialogue has become the very foundation on which global business is conducted' (Adler, 1997: 124). Global teams are likely to be more culturally diverse than traditional collocated teams, as not only are team members working across countries and nationalities (for example, Brazilian, German and Japanese), but they are often working across organizational and functional cultures as well. For example, a global product development team may involve collaboration between multiple partner firms (such as a corporation, university and a consulting firm). Its team members are also likely to span a number of functional disciplines, such as design engineering, manufacturing or software engineering and marketing. These cultural contexts are accompanied by deep-rooted assumptions and values that provide an intuitive blueprint or set of guidelines for the way cultural members should behave, as well as helping to reduce uncertainty and normalize events (Schein, 1992). Contextual differences among team members thus lead to different norms, expectations and sets of behaviour regarding work that must be bridged in order for the team to function effectively (Maznevski, 1994).

Culturally diverse teams are likely to differ along several key dimensions, which influence their expectations about working together and are likely to create breakdowns in the communication process (Earley & Gibson, 2002). First, team members' orientation toward work may be conditioned by cultural preferences for individualism versus collectivism. Those from individualistic national cultures place more emphasis on individual goals and personal achievement, while those from collectivistic cultures give priority to group interests and maintaining group harmony (Earley, 1994; Hofstede, 1991; Triandis, 1988). Differences on this dimension may cause clashes in expectations for team interaction, level of cohesiveness, group (as opposed to individual) rewards and importance of socialization, which are all likely to be greater among those from more collectivistic cultures (Gibson & Zellmer-Bruhn, 2001; Kirkman & Shapiro, 1997). Such cultural clashes are likely to pose HRM-related challenges. For example, team members from collectivistic cultures (such as China, Singapore or Brazil) may expect more guidance, training, support and socialization from management and other team members than members from individualistic cultures (such as the USA, UK or Germany), who are more likely to prefer working autonomously and expect others to take initiative in finding their own solutions to problems. This dimension also conditions preferences for technology use, as those from collectivistic cultures are more likely to prefer collaborative technologies such as videoconferencing and face-to-face group meetings. On the other hand, those from individualistic cultures may prefer to communicate one-on-one through e-mail and voicemail, which may be considered cold and impersonal by those with a more collectivistic orientation (Gibbs, 2002).

A second key dimension on which national cultures are likely to differ is power distance, which refers to the extent to which hierarchy is valued and respected (Hofstede, 1991). Collaborators from high power distance cultures such as India, France or Japan revere hierarchy and status distinctions, whereas those from low power distance cultures such as the USA, Sweden or the Netherlands attempt to minimize hierarchy and take a more egalitarian approach. This dimension is likely to affect the level of formality expected, likelihood to share knowledge and level of participation in meetings. HRM challenges arise owing to culture clashes that occur face-to-face as well as over e-mail: for example, Americans tend to be more informal in e-mail use, addressing people by first names only, not using formal job titles and employing casual language. This may be construed as impolite or disrespectful by members of high power distance cultures, for whom formal titles indicating status and formal language are more important. Communication challenges are also likely to arise as high power distance employees of lower status may be reluctant to share important information (especially of a negative nature) with higher status managers, for fear of overstepping their bounds or causing them to lose face. While this may be frustrating for low power distance managers, team members from high power distance cultures may be equally put off by failure of low power distance members to assert authority or to recognize status differences, perceiving this as disrespectful.

HRM managers can help overcome the challenges of cultural diversity within global teams by making managers and other team members aware of cultural differences and encouraging them to adapt their communication styles accordingly. For example, managers from individualistic cultures such as the USA should make sure that employees from collectivistic cultures feel supported and have the resources they need, as they may be reluctant to ask questions or raise issues out of concern for face saving and preserving group harmony. Team managers and HRM professionals should consider such cultural differences when training employees, structuring team communication and deciding which communication media to use. Performance incentives, rewards and career opportunities should also be free of biases towards any one culture and should not exclude particular cultures (Adler & Bartholomew, 1992).

Geographical dispersion
Global teams also face unique HRM challenges because of their geographic dispersion. A key difficulty is sharing 'situated knowledge' between locations (Sole & Edmondson, 2002), as team members at different sites or locations are likely to take their own contextual knowledge for granted and be unable to articulate or share that knowledge with members from other sites (Gluesing & Gibson, 2004). This is likely to result in misunderstandings, confusion and conflicts among distant team members owing to gaps in communication resulting in different assumptions and different interpretations of messages (Armstrong & Cole, 2002), as well as the formation of divisive organizational sub-identities associated with locations (Sole & Edmondson, 2002). Additionally the fact that team members are geographically distributed across multiple time zones makes it more difficult to achieve synergy and coordinate team actions (Carmel, 1999). Geographically distributed global teams thus face challenges in sharing contextual knowledge, geographic divisiveness, and coordinating information.

The fact that team members are embedded in different geographical and organizational contexts brings about several specific HRM challenges related to team cohesion and identification. The lack of face-to-face contact among team members in different locations is likely to lead to an 'out of sight, out of mind' tendency to forget about members in other locations that hinders knowledge sharing and communication (Armstrong & Cole, 2002). Team cohesion is likely to be fragmented because of development of distinct sub-identities among locations, especially if they coincide with national differences. Allegiances to local sites rather than the team as a whole may result in competition and rivalry among different locations, rather than collaboration and synergy. Achieving identification with the global team is further problematized by tensions in team structure due to the fact that the team is embedded in different organizational contexts that may be characterized by different reporting and pay structures, policies and evaluation procedures.

Team and HRM professionals can help overcome challenges of geographical dispersion by bringing the entire team together for group meetings periodically or travelling to different locations to provide 'face time' to keep team objectives aligned, ensure that knowledge is shared and build stronger identification with the team. Although tensions due to different organizational structures and policies may not be entirely resolvable, offering incentives and rewards for team collaboration is another way of ensuring team member 'buy-in' and commitment.

Electronic dependence
Global virtual teams often rely heavily on CMC to collaborate and accomplish work, using a range of technologies, such as e-mail, phone, fax, audio- and videoconferencing, collaborative groupware and knowledge management systems (Gibson & Gibbs, 2004). This technology enables them to operate in a flexible manner and coordinate work across time zones and geographical distances (Boudreau, Loch, Robey & Straud, 1998). Technology may help structure work and organize, enhance or even create information available to the team (Griffith *et al.*, 2003). However communicating virtually rather than face-to-face creates challenges as well. Virtual team members must acquire new skills to communicate electronically, including not just becoming proficient with a variety of computer-based technologies but learning new ways to express themselves and understand others in a virtual environment with reduced social presence and cues (Townsend *et al.*, 1998). Communication via e-mail and other forms of CMC is characterized by the absence of traditional non-verbal social context cues such as facial expressions, gesture and vocal inflection or tone, making it more difficult to convey nuances and subtleties in communication (Kiesler & Sproull, 1992). Also the anonymity of CMC has been found to produce different kinds of interpersonal exchanges than face-to-face contact (Hiltz, Johnson & Turoff, 1986): on one hand, it may result in more impersonal communication owing to its reduced social cues, as less personal, tacit or informal information is exchanged; on the other, the lack of social cues may result in exaggerated hyperpersonal perceptions of others (overly positive or negative) because of overattribution of what limited cues are available (Walther, 1996; Walther & Parks, 2002).

Communicating electronically presents HRM managers with new challenges associated with building personal relationships, trust and responsiveness, because of the lack of context and reduced social cues (see the chapter by Maznevski, Canney Davison and Jonsen in the present volume for further discussion of these issues). Since global team members are physically dispersed, they lack the informal 'water cooler' talk that collocated team members take for granted, but that helps team members get to know each others' personality traits, quirks and work styles, as well as being a source of unexpected and serendipitous information exchange. Research has found that social communication and socialization processes are important for building electronic relationships (Hofner Saphiere, 1996; Knoll & Jarvenpaa, 1998). While many companies such as Boeing and

Lotus have found bringing global team members together face-to-face at the start of a project to be effective in establishing relationships and building trust (Benson-Armer & Hsieh, 1997), research has found that socialization is also possible over CMC (for example, Walther, 1992, 1995) and that it facilitates trust in virtual team development (Jarvenpaa & Leidner, 1999). Owing to the reduced cues and context present in CMC, global team members should make more pointed efforts to include personal and informal communication in e-mails and other media, to help build trust and relationships virtually. HRM professionals can play an important role in training team members in effective electronic communication.

Dynamic structure
A final decoupling characteristic that creates HRM challenges for managing global teams is their often dynamic structural arrangements. As many global teams are short-term and project-based, they tend to consist of team members working together only temporarily, with frequent change in members, roles and relationships (Kristof, Brown, Sims & Smith, 1995). Many of these teams comprise inter-firm collaboration through informal outsourcing agreements or consortia, and team members are likely to be reluctant to share knowledge across organizational boundaries because of its proprietary nature. In addition, high member turnover often leads to the loss of tacit knowledge, making it difficult to establish continuity of team processes and practices. The dynamic nature of such collaborations results in increased uncertainty, less cohesive relationships (Gluesing *et al.*, 2003), loss of or difficulty sharing knowledge, and fluid and shifting team membership that evolves according to changing task requirements and responsibilities (Kristof *et al.*, 1995; Townsend *et al.*, 1998).

Global outsourcing teams often involve short-term work arrangements with contracted employees of other nationalities (Carmel, 1999). They are also likely to be embedded within multiple employing organizations with their own distinct organizational structures and policies, making it impossible to standardize policies completely within the team. For example, software development teams at US-based companies such as Intel, Xerox and Microsoft often hire developers from lower-cost talent hubs in India, China or Brazil and bring them to work on short-term project assignments locally. Depending on the length of the assignment (which may end up lasting a year or more), this is likely to create problems for management and assessment of such temporary employees. While on assignment, their performance assessment may suffer, as their permanent managers may be unable to evaluate and assess accurately their work for someone else from thousands of miles away. At the same time, their temporary managers may be reluctant to provide performance feedback because of their low level of investment in these temporary employees as contractors and their lack of 'buy-in' to the different organizational processes and structures of their employing organizations. Even when feedback is provided, it is likely to be limited or difficult to interpret owing to different scoring procedures. As a result, decisions on salary and promotion for such employees may be adversely affected.

Managers may also be averse to provide training and other benefits needed for employees' career growth because of their low level of investment in such temporary employees, who may in turn harbour feelings of inequity and resentment toward other local permanent team members who do receive such benefits. Local team members, on the other hand, may feel their job security is threatened by outsourced employees. Conversely offering bonuses and incentives to temporary employees may prove problematic as it undermines their local pay scale (as one bonus may be the equivalent of six months' salary in their home country, for example). HRM systems should ensure that global team members receive performance appraisals and feedback so that their work is rewarded and contributes to their career development.

The next section will discuss three key coupling mechanisms that help overcome these challenges due to loose coupling in global teams.

Key coupling mechanisms for managing global team complexity

Although forming a strong, shared team culture may not be either achievable or desirable in global teams owing to their loosely coupled nature (Gibbs, 2002), certain coordination mechanisms are needed to manage cultural complexity, help bridge the loose coupling characteristics and facilitate effective team interaction. Three factors help to couple or coordinate global team interaction: assigning cultural liaisons, increasing team-level identification and documenting or formalizing team communication (Gibbs, 2002).

Cultural liaisons
Because of their dispersion across geographies and time zones, it is neither possible nor efficient for all global team members to know what every other team member knows or does, or to interact directly with every other team member. Moreover effective communication and knowledge sharing are also inhibited by cultural and language barriers. Team members are often called upon to make quick decisions without sufficient information, and formal information sources (such as reports or archival documents) are inherently limited to codified, rather than tacit, knowledge (Tushman & Scanlan, 1981). Given the cost, inefficiency and potential bias of widespread direct communication across boundaries (ibid.), informal social

mechanisms such as boundary spanners are more effective for coordinating global team interaction.

Cultural liaisons are a specific type of boundary spanner in global teams for coordinating communication across cultural boundaries. Cultural liaisons serve the role of linking or facilitating understanding and interaction among different cultural groups. They possess the skill of 'laterality', which describes the ability to work effectively with and relate to people of different cultural or functional backgrounds, work experiences, skill sets and knowledge bases (Mankin, Cohen & Bikson, 1996). Laterality has been identified as an important skill for intercultural communicators (Cohen & Gibson, 2003), who need to be able to bridge and interpret between different national or functional cultures, speak the language of those they work with, and be confident yet open to learning new things. Research has found that members of productive global teams act as cultural interpreters and mediators and suggests that this role can be taken on by more than just a few members of the team (Hofner Saphiere, 1996). Similar to weak ties in social networks, which function to connect people from diverse backgrounds (Granovetter, 1973) and provide access to a wider array of non-redundant information (Ibarra & Andrews, 1993), cultural liaisons play an important role in bridging the various cultural boundaries inherent in global teams. This strategy is particularly effective in teams consisting of two or more strong, defined subcultures, which have been found to elicit the most entrenched cultural conflicts (Earley & Mosakowski, 2000; Gibson & Vermeulen, 2003). Moderate diversity is more likely to lead to polarization along faultlines than extreme diversity, especially when that diversity is salient (Fiol & O'Connor, 2005; Lau & Murnighan, 1998).

Cultural liaisons may be assigned to the role by the team leader or human resource professional, or they may emerge informally, out of necessity or convenience. For example, a manager of a global software team distributed between the USA and Singapore may bring a few Singaporean team members to work temporarily in the USA to train them on the project and facilitate knowledge exchange in person before sending them back to continue the work in Singapore. During this time, assigning to one or more of the Singaporean team members the informal role of coordinating communication between the two sites is an effective strategy, as it helps reduce intercultural misunderstanding over e-mail, phone or videoconferencing, and helps establish a stronger relationship between the two sites by using one consistent interface which has the same cultural background and often has established personal relationships with those at the remote site. This makes mediated communication across distances much more effective than having relative strangers from different cultures interact with one another by phone, e-mail or videoconferencing. It also facilitates knowledge sharing between locations.

Cultural liaisons can also be effective in providing informal cultural orientation to team members who may be temporarily based overseas, as is common in software outsourcing teams. Although provision of formal intercultural training and orientation to assist such outsourced employees in adjusting to the foreign culture by a human resource professional is optimal, teams may not have the budget for this or have the number of members to make formal programmes cost-effective. In this case, assigning to team members with longer-term experience in the foreign culture the role of cultural mentors may be a preferable solution. Team members with greater international experience and a higher comfort level with living abroad, greater intercultural communication competence and laterality skills should be sought as cultural mentors. These cultural liaisons can help orient new arrivals: meeting them at the airport, helping them get situated and passing on cultural advice to them about their new work environment, as well as acting as intermediaries to voice their concerns to the team leader or management. These liaisons can also help bridge cultural divides within the team by organizing team-building social events, facilitating cross-cultural social interaction among team members from diverse cultures and helping mediate interpersonal conflicts among such team members.

Identification
Identification has been defined as a sense of belonging with a social category (Ashforth & Mael, 1989; Fiol & O'Connor, 2005). Through identification, individuals achieve a sense of social connectedness with others, which facilitates communication, understanding and a common purpose (Gossett, 2002). Social identification processes increase group members' identification with a strategic group (Lant & Phelps, 1999). Identification has been found to increase interpersonal trust and cooperation (Brewer, 1981; Kramer, 1993), group cohesion (Turner, 1987), internalization of organizational norms and practices, worker satisfaction (Russo, 1998) and desire to stay with the organization (Dutton, Dukerich & Harquail, 1994).

Identification has been advocated as particularly critical in virtual contexts because of the reduced physical contact among members (Wiesenfeld, Raghuram & Garud, 2001), as it facilitates coordination and control of employees, which is a key challenge owing to the lack of direct supervision or monitoring in distributed teams (Wiesenfeld, Raghuram & Garud, 1999). Organizational identification is theorized to be a new post-bureaucratic form of unobtrusive or concertive control (Tompkins & Cheney, 1985), in which individual members are influenced by organizational goals, values and information through subtle rhetorical persuasion to make decisions that reflect organizational goals (Cheney, 1983). Identification in virtual teams is argued to act as a type of social 'glue' that promotes group cohesion in the absence of face-to-face contact (Fiol & O'Connor, 2005). Wiesenfeld *et al.* (1999) examined communication behaviour as a determinant of organizational identification and found that information technologies such as e-mail and phone could help create and maintain identification or a common identity among virtual workers, helping connect them to their organizations.

Identification in global teams is further complicated by the fact that team members possess multiple identities derived from the different contexts in which the team is embedded. Identification is likely to occur at multiple levels: with one's organization, one's team, one's national culture or one's functional or professional culture (Scott, Corman & Cheney, 1998). In addition, individuals are often members of multiple teams (Townsend *et al.*, 1998), and are thus likely to struggle with multiple competing allegiances and affiliations, making it harder to induce identification with a particular team. Inducing team-level identification helps overcome divisive subidentities associated with sites or locations, as well as national or functional subcultures within the team that pose a challenge to team building (Earley & Mosakowski, 2000; Gibson & Vermeulen, 2003). It also helps build trust, which is crucial to social bonding and establishing relationships in virtual teams (see the chapter by Maznevski *et al.* in the present volume for further discussion of trust formation in global teams).

Maintaining an identified workforce requires a high level of organizational investment and effort (Gossett, 2002). Overcoming such divisive sub-cultural identities and inducing team-level identification requires continuing team-building efforts. Team and HRM managers should attempt to break up cultural cliques within the team through the use of physical space and division of work, by attempting to mix cultural groups in office arrangements and work roles to foster intercultural collaboration and linguistic desegregation. Social events and mixers are important means of team building. In addition, physical symbols such as badges and office name plates play a role in inducing identification and belonging to the team. Identification can be fostered electronically as well, through creation of a team Internet or webpage containing information about team members, such as the office layout for each location with names and photos of each team member and a brief description of their role and personal interests or hobbies. Finally, incentives should be provided for accomplishing team tasks to ensure that teamwork is valued.

Documentation
Written documentation of team processes and norms is a final important coupling mechanism in global teams. Given the high level of diversity in

team members' knowledge, skills, functional and cultural backgrounds and the high task complexity, combined with the need to collaborate virtually with dispersed others who may never meet in person, global team environments and relationships among team members are fraught with uncertainty. Regular, predictable communication has been identified as helping reduce some of this uncertainty, build and maintain trust over time (Jarvenpaa & Leidner, 1999) and provide a rhythm for team functioning that imposes structure and stability in an otherwise chaotic environment (Maznevski & Chudoba, 2000). The combination of diversity of cultural norms, establishment of new relationships in electronic environments, and spatial and temporal discontinuity makes the need for explicit and predictable communication even greater in global teams.

One way of making global team communication more predictable is through formalization and documentation of team knowledge and processes. Documentation is a coupling mechanism that helps preserve temporal as well as spatial continuity of the team, despite turnover of team members. Documentation reduces the impact of turnover by preserving knowledge. There is a greater need for explicit definition of process in virtual teams, in which communicating and establishing shared norms is not as intuitive as in face-to-face environments (Leonard, Brands, Edmondson & Fenwick, 1998). Norms and expectations for team interaction also need to be explicitly negotiated and agreed upon in culturally diverse groups in order for such groups to be effective, as these norms are culturally conditioned and not shared by all team members (Maznevski, 1994). While the process of negotiating norms for group interaction and participation is implicit and almost automatic when group members have common repertoires of norms, group members with diverse norms need to negotiate explicitly the ways in which the group will interact and operate in order to be effective (ibid.). Agreement on the way communication is coordinated and prioritized will increase predictability and help to overcome the 'out of sight, out of mind' feeling among dispersed team members (Snow, Snell, Davison & Hambrick, 1996). Establishing clear communication protocols with explicit norms for team member interaction, participation, policies and expectations for communication (how often to communicate, expected response time, which media to use, prioritization of issues, decision making and conflict resolution processes, and so on) has been found to improve global team performance (Carmel, 1999; Knoll & Jarvenpaa, 1998; Leonard *et al.*, 1998; Snow *et al.*, 1996). This can be facilitated by the use of databases and groupware (Snow *et al.*, 1996).

Written documentation also helps overcome language and cultural barriers. It is helpful in providing clear instructions, especially cross-culturally and across languages, as it allows for more time to deliberate before responding and greater understanding of messages. Documentation can thus be helpful in surfacing cross-cultural misunderstandings, especially when working remotely. It can also be used to overcome cultural differences in knowledge sharing: for example, HRM managers can develop formalized training methods consisting of standardized questions for team members who for cultural reasons are more introverted to extract knowledge they may be reluctant to volunteer. A final benefit of documentation is in formalizing team processes to motivate and bring remote workers together as a team. Documentation reduces the need for face-to-face interaction and it enables effective collaboration between geographically dispersed coworkers who have never met face-to-face. Face-to-face training is thus only necessary for transferring expertise or knowledge that was not documented.

Global team leaders require a different skill set than managers of traditional, collocated teams (see the chapter by Maznevski *et al.* in the present volume for further discussion of leadership issues). Global managers need to possess a global mindset (Gupta & Govindarajan, 2001), defined in terms of a cosmopolitan orientation or openness to diverse cultural outlooks and experiences and a sense of cognitive complexity or ability to discern the complexity of issues and reconcile apparently incongruent pieces (Boyacigiller, Beechler, Taylor & Levy, 2004). HRM professionals can play a key role in helping global team leaders develop needed process or 'group' skills in addition to technical expertise (Davison, 1994) since they play a crucial role as process facilitator that differs from the traditional role of the leader as the hierarchical authority or technical expert (Hofner Saphiere, 1996). HRM professionals should also provide team members with training on the need to develop explicit communication protocols documenting team processes and assist them in developing archival databases and knowledge management systems to preserve team knowledge. Finally HRM systems should provide incentives to encourage busy team members to invest the time and effort required to document team knowledge, as they are unlikely to do so without a perceived benefit or mandate.

Conclusion

Global teams are fragmented by decoupling characteristics of cultural diversity, geographical dispersion, electronic dependence and dynamic structural arrangements, which pose distinct international HRM challenges. To overcome such challenges, three coupling mechanisms are proposed to assist HRM professionals in coordinating global team interaction amid these decoupling characteristics: assigning boundary-spanning cultural liaisons helps to bridge cultural diversity within the team and to facilitate electronic communication among distributed team members, inducing team-level identification helps build trusting virtual relationships and overcome challenges of knowledge sharing and coordination due to geographical dispersion, and documentation of knowledge helps overcome challenges associated with turnover and temporal discontinuity due to dynamic structural arrangements. These coupling mechanisms highlight the need for both formal and informal communication in coordinating global teams.

Human resource professionals can play a key role in appointing cultural liaisons to mediate communication across cultural boundaries and providing training on effective intercultural communication to other team members. Additional training needs include effective technology use, leadership skills and global mindset in global team managers, and the need for formalization of team processes and norms through explicit communication protocols, archival databases and knowledge management systems. HRM managers should also provide incentives for sharing and documenting knowledge, as well as continuing team-building efforts and a clear reporting structure to induce and maintain team-level identification. Incentives, rewards and career opportunities should be commensurate with work performed globally (Adler & Bartholomew, 1992) and thus linked with global teamwork. Finally, ensuring that global team members' responsibilities contribute to their career development will help retain them for future projects and facilitate trust through continuity of working relationships.

Future research in this area should seek to fill gaps left by the current research on global virtual teams. First, it should make further attempts to integrate disparate literature on each of the decoupling characteristics (cultural diversity, geographical dispersion, electronic dependence and dynamic structure) and test the interactions between them. Much of the research on multicultural and virtual teams examines variables such as cultural diversity or extent of face-to-face interaction in isolation, despite the fact that many global teams are both culturally diverse and virtual in nature and thus involve complex interactions between these elements. Other research lumps these elements together under the term 'virtual' without examining their independent effects (Gibson & Gibbs, 2004) and, as a result, imprecise definitions of 'virtuality' have led to contradictory findings (Fiol & O'Connor, 2005). Several researchers have called for the need to distinguish among various features of virtual teaming (Gibson & Cohen, 2003; Griffith *et al.*, 2003), but systematic theory on the interrelationships among such features is just starting to be developed (for example, Fiol & O'Connor, 2005; Gibson & Gibbs, 2004; Martins, Gilson & Maynard, 2004).

Second, future research should examine effects and processes in different types of global teams. Theory is emerging that differentiates between pure virtual teams and 'hybrid' virtual teams involving some face-to-face contact (Fiol & O'Connor, 2005). Virtual team contexts also vary by the degree of permanence (temporary versus continuous teams), team size and the nature of work being performed (sales versus product development teams, for example). The impacts of such factors should be tested in future research to add nuance to theory on global teams and help identify strategies for overcoming specific HRM challenges related to each of these factors. More research on the way the decoupling characteristics of global teams intersect in different global team settings will assist HRM professionals in developing sophisticated solutions to the complex challenges that arise in global teams.

References

Adler, N.J. 1997. *International dimensions of organizational behavior*. Cincinnati, OH: South-Western College Publishing.

Adler, N.J. & S. Bartholomew. 1992. Managing globally competent people. *Academy of Management Executive*, **6**(3): 52–65.

Armstrong, D.J. & P. Cole. 2002. Managing distances and differences in geographically distributed work groups. In P. Hinds & S. Kiesler (eds), *Distributed work*: 167–86. Cambridge, MA: MIT Press.

Ashforth, B.E. & F.A. Mael. 1989. Social identity theory and the organization. *Academy of Management Review*, **14**(1): 20–39.

Benson-Armer, R. & T. Hsieh. 1997. Teamwork across time and space. *McKinsey Quarterly*, **4**: 18–27.

Boudreau, M.C., K.D. Loch, D. Robey & D. Straud. 1998. Going global: using information technology to advance the competitiveness of the virtual transnational organization. *Academy of Management Executive*, **12**(4): 120–28.

Boyacigiller, N., S. Beechler, S. Taylor & O. Levy. 2004. The crucial yet elusive global mindset. In H.W. Lane, M.L. Maznevski, M.E. Mendenhall & J. McNett (eds), *Handbook of global management:* 81–93. Malden, MA: Blackwell.

Brewer, M.B. 1981. Ethnocentrism and its role in interpersonal trust. In M.B. Brewer & B.E. Collins (eds), *Scientific inquiry and the social sciences:* 345–60. New York: Jossey-Bass.

Carmel, E. 1999. *Global software teams: collaborating across borders and time zones*. Upper Saddle River, NJ: Prentice-Hall.

Cheney, G. 1983. The rhetoric of identification and the study of organizational communication. *Quarterly Journal of Speech*, **69**: 143–58.

Cohen, S.G. & C.B. Gibson. 2003. In the beginning: introduction and framework. In C.B. Gibson & S.G. Cohen (eds), *Virtual teams that work: creating conditions for virtual team effectiveness:* 1–13. San Francisco, CA: Jossey-Bass.

Davison, S.C. 1994. Creating a high performance international team. *Journal of Management Development*, **13**: 81–90.

Dutton, J.E., J.M. Dukerich & C.V. Harquail. 1994. Organizational images and member identification. *Administrative Science Quarterly*, **39**: 239–63.

Earley, P.C. 1994. Self or group? Cultural effects of training on self-efficacy and performance. *Administrative Science Quarterly*, **39**: 89–117.

Earley, P.C. & C.B. Gibson. 2002. *Multinational work teams: a new perspective*. Mahwah, NJ: Lawrence Erlbaum and Associates.

Earley, P.C. & E. Mosakowski. 2000. Creating hybrid team cultures: an empirical test of transnational team functioning. *Academy of Management Journal*, **1**: 26–49.

Fiol, C.M. & E.J. O'Connor. 2005. Identification in face-to-face, hybrid, and pure virtual teams: untangling the contradictions. *Organization Science*, **16**: 19–33.

Gibbs, J.L. 2002. Loose coupling in global teams: tracing the contours of cultural complexity. Unpublished doctoral dissertation, University of Southern California.

Gibson, C.B. & S.G. Cohen. (eds). 2003. *Virtual teams that work: creating conditions for virtual team effectiveness*. San Francisco, CA: Jossey-Bass.

Gibson, C.B. & J.L. Gibbs. 2004. Unpacking the effects of loose coupling on virtual team innovation. Working paper, University of California, Irvine.

Gibson, C.B. & F. Vermeulen. 2003. A healthy divide: subgroups as a stimulus for team learning. *Administrative Science Quarterly*, **48**: 202–39.

Gibson, C.B. & M. Zellmer-Bruhn. 2001. Metaphor and meaning: an intercultural analysis of the concept of teamwork. *Administrative Science Quarterly*, **46**: 274–303.

Gluesing, J.C. & C.B. Gibson. 2004. Designing and forming global teams. In H.W. Lane, M.L. Maznevski, M.E. Mendenhall & J. McNett (eds), *Handbook of global management*. Malden, MA: Blackwell Publishing.

Gossett, L.M. 2002. Kept at arm's length: questioning the organizational desirability of member identification. *Communication Monographs*, **69**(4): 385–404.

Granovetter, M.S. 1973. The strength of weak ties. *American Journal of Sociology*, **78**: 1360–80.

Griffith, T.L., J.E. Sawyer & M.A. Neale. 2003. Virtualness and knowledge in teams: managing the love triangle of organizations, individuals, and information technology. *MIS Quarterly*, **27**(2): 265–87.

Gupta, A.K. & V. Govindarajan. 2001. Cultivating a global mindset. *The Academy of Management Executive*, **16**(1): 116–26.

Hiltz, S.R., K. Johnson & M. Turoff. 1986. Experiments in group decision making, I. Communication process and outcome in face-to-face vs. computerized conferences. *Human Communication Research*, **13**(2): 225–53.

Hofner Saphiere, D.M. 1996. Productive behaviors of global business teams. *International Journal of Intercultural Relations*, **20**(2): 227–59.

Hofstede, G. 1991. *Cultures and organizations: software of the mind*. New York: McGraw-Hill.

Ibarra, H. & S.B. Andrews. 1993. Power, social influence, and sense making: effects of network centrality and proximity on employee perceptions. *Administrative Science Quarterly*, **44**: 741–63.

Jarvenpaa, S.L. & D.E. Leidner. 1999. Communication and trust in global virtual teams. *Organization Science*, **10**: 791–815.

Kiesler, S. & L. Sproull. 1992. Group decision making and communication technology. *Organizational Behavior and Human Decision Processes*, **52**(1): 96–123.

Kirkman, B.L. & D.L. Shapiro. 1997. The impact of cultural values on employee resistance to teams: toward a model of globalized self-managing work team effectiveness. *Academy of Management Review*, **22**(3): 730–57.

Knoll, K. & S.L. Jarvenpaa. 1998. Working together in global virtual teams. In M. Igbaria & M. Tan (eds), *The virtual workplace:* 2–23. Hershey, PA: Idea Group Publishing.

Kramer, R.M. 1993. Cooperation and organizational identification. In J.K. Murnighan (ed.), *Social psychology in organizations:* 244–68. Englewood Cliffs, NJ: Prentice-Hall.

Kristof, A.L., K.G. Brown, H.P. Sims Jr & K.A. Smith. 1995. The virtual team: a case study and inductive model. In M.M. Beyerlein, D.A. Johnson & S.T. Beyerlein (eds), *Advances in interdisciplinary studies of work teams: knowledge work in teams*, vol. 2: 229–53. Greenwich, CT: JAI Press.

Lant, T.K. & C. Phelps. 1999. Strategic groups: a situated learning perspective. *Advances in Strategic Management*, **16**: 221–47.

Lau, D.C. & J.K. Murnighan. 1998. Demographic diversity and faultlines: the compositional dynamics of organizational groups. *Academy of Management Review*, **23**: 325–40.

Leonard, D.A., P.A. Brands, A. Edmondson & J. Fenwick. 1998. Virtual teams: using communications technology to manage geographically dispersed development groups. In S.P. Bradley & R.L. Nolan (eds), *Sense and respond: capturing value in the network era:* 285–98. Boston, MA: Harvard Business School Press.

Lipnack, J. & J. Stamps. 1997. *Virtual teams: reaching across space, time and organizations with technology*. New York: John Wiley and Sons.

Mankin, D., S.G. Cohen & T.K. Bikson. 1996. *Teams and technology: fulfilling the promise of the new organization*. Boston, MA: Harvard Business School Press.

Martins, L.L., L.L. Gilson & M.T. Maynard. 2004. Virtual teams: what do we know and where do we go from here? *Journal of Management*, **30**(6): 805–35.

Maznevski, M.L. 1994. Understanding our differences: performance in decision-making groups with diverse members. *Human Relations*, **47**(5): 531–52.

Maznevski, M.L. & K.M. Chudoba. 2000. Bridging space over time: global virtual team dynamics and effectiveness. *Organization Science*, **11**(5): 473–92.

Russo, T.C. 1998. Organizational and professional identification: a case of newspaper journalists. *Management Communication Quarterly*, **12**: 72–111.

Schein, E.H. 1992. *Organizational culture and leadership*. Second edition. San Francisco, CA: Jossey-Bass.

Scott, C.R., S.R. Corman & G. Cheney. 1998. Development of a structurational model of identification in the organization. *Communication Theory*, **8**(3): 298–336.

Snow, C.C., S.A. Snell, S.C. Davison & D.C. Hambrick. 1996. Use transnational teams to globalize your company. *Organizational Dynamics*, **24**(4): 50–66.

Sole, D. & A. Edmondson. 2002. Situated knowledge and learning in dispersed teams. *British Journal of Management*, **13**: 17–34.

Tompkins, P.K. & G. Cheney. 1985. Communication and unobtrusive control in contemporary organizations. In R.D. McPhee & P.K. Tompkins (eds), *Organizational communication: traditional themes and new directions*: 179–210. Beverly Hills, CA: Sage.

Townsend, A.M., S.M. DeMarie & A.R. Hendrickson. 1998. Virtual teams: technology and the workplace of the future. *Academy of Management Executive*, **12**(3): 17–29.

Triandis, H.C. 1988. Collectivism vs. individualism: a reconceptualization of a basic concept in cross-cultural social psychology. In G.K. Verma & C. Bagley (eds), *Cross-cultural studies of personality, attitudes and cognition*: 60–95. New York: St. Martin's.

Turner, J.C. 1987. *Rediscovering the social group: a self-categorization theory*. New York: Basil Blackwell.

Tushman, M.L. & T.J. Scanlan. 1981. Boundary spanning individuals: their role in information transfer and their antecedents. *Academy of Management Journal*, **24**(2): 289–305.

Walther, J.B. 1992. Interpersonal effects in computer-mediated interaction: a relational perspective. *Communication Research*, **19**: 52–90.

Walther, J.B. 1995. Relational aspects of computer-mediated communication: experimental observations over time. *Organization Science*, **6**: 186–203.

Walther, J.B. 1996. Computer-mediated communication: impersonal, interpersonal and hyperpersonal interaction. *Communication Research*, **23**: 3–44.

Walther, J.B. & M.R. Parks. 2002. Cues filtered out, cues filtered in: computer-mediated communication and relationships. In M.L. Knapp & J.A. Daly (eds), *Handbook of interpersonal communication*. Third edition: 529–63. Thousand Oaks, CA: Sage Publications.

Weick, K.E. 1976. Educational organizations as loosely coupled systems. *Administrative Science Quarterly*, **21**: 1–19.

Wiesenfeld, B.M., S. Raghuram & R. Garud. 1999. Communication patterns as determinants of organizational identification in a virtual organization. *Organization Science*, **10**(6): 777–90.

Wiesenfeld, B.M., S. Raghuram & R. Garud. 2001. Organizational identification among virtual workers: the role of need for affiliation and perceived work-based social support. *Journal of Management*, **27**: 213–29.

19 Global virtual team dynamics and effectiveness

Martha Maznevski, Sue Canney Davison and Karsten Jonsen

Virtual teams, although relatively new to the global business landscape, are already recognized as a boon to international organizations and have quickly become ubiquitous. Virtual teams are groups of people working together towards a joint outcome using communications and information technology more than the traditional face-to-face mode. Global virtual teams (GVT) have members distributed throughout the world. Recent advances in technology, especially telecommunications and the Internet, have made possible the communication of vast quantities of relatively rich information over any distance on earth. Without the time, cost and hazards of travel, groups can now share information, chat, innovate and make decisions together.

Virtual teams, therefore, can bring together the best people within any worldwide or countrywide organization or from different organizations, to work on a specific task without regard to where those members are located, and help the organization perform better. This helps respond to the increasing market expectations to transfer expertise no matter where it is located, in order to meet the demand for quick development and delivery of both products and services. In multinational organizations, these teams tend to be created especially to address international issues of strategic importance, such as global account management, strategic product development, global marketing planning and merger or acquisition integration. In the future of globalization, R&D resources will be geographically dispersed and tapped into by using virtual teams. Together the members of a virtual team have a much wider access to networks of information and expertise than if they were colocated. Moreover members of virtual teams can work on several types of tasks with different configurations of people more efficiently because location is not a constraint.

Like many organizational forms, creating effective virtual teams has also proved to be more difficult than expected. Managers cannot simply create high-performing virtual teams by assigning members and 'letting them run'. As many organizations have already discovered, without careful structuring, support and attention to processes, virtual teams do not achieve their potential and may not even get off the ground.

In this chapter we begin with some important definitions. We then identify the challenges raised by virtual teams, with particular focus on global virtual teams. We argue that resolving these challenges depends on an understanding of some important contingency factors and how they affect processes in these teams, and we follow this by identifying the success factors for managing these contingencies and obtaining high performance. We look briefly into the future and speculate on the potential of virtual teams to change the management of global organizations. We close with some recommendations for further research.

Virtual teams are groups of people who (a) work together using communications technology more often than face-to-face; (b) are distributed across space; (c) are responsible for a joint outcome and *usually* (d) work on strategic or technically advanced tasks; and (e) are multifunctional and/or multicultural. Most people focus on the first element of this definition: the use of technology. However, as we will show, each element of this definition is related to the challenges and contingencies faced by teams, and performance can only be explained by their combination.

Virtual teams face many challenges

Any kind of team faces well established challenges such as identifying clear common purpose, roles and responsibilities, creating a sense of team identity and urgency and commitment to deadlines. Specific challenges for virtual teams can range across a broad spectrum, such as access to and comfortableness with technology, technological support and online facilitation, getting team members online and away from more visible office tasks, and less frequent and less informal interaction. Here we focus on four of the most important challenges, those that have been identified as particularly important in creating effective virtual teams: *effective communication, relationship building, managing conflicts* and *leadership*. When working predominantly through communications technology, some of the key challenges of understanding each other are thrown into stark relief. By focusing on these challenges when communications technology is used, we can also deepen our understanding of how to improve our face-to-face communication: by improving virtual team effectiveness, we can improve our understanding of teams in general. Figure 19.1 shows the relationship between the processes described here, the structural dimensions, some of which are described in the next section, and performance in virtual teams.

Communication

The challenges virtual team members face with respect to communication come from two main sources. First, because technology has lower richness and social presence than the face-to-face context, team members lose much

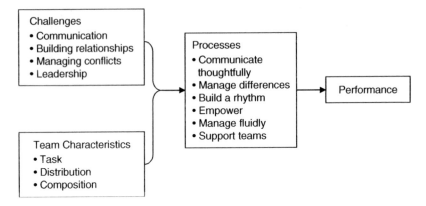

Figure 19.1   Important dimensions of global virtual team performance

of the contextual information they are accustomed to relying on. This can lead to misinterpretations, unfounded stereotypes and misunderstandings. Second, most communications over technology take place in a staggered or stepped way – asynchronously – with a lag time between one message being sent and another received. This reduces the immediacy and efficacy of feedback, yet at the same time gives people time to think through responses.

Many studies have sought to understand these challenges on communication and subsequent outcomes. Early research (for example, Hiltz, Johnson & Turoff, 1986; Siegel, Dubrovsky, Kiesler & McGuire, 1986) found that team members using only communications technology found it harder to reach consensus and paid much less attention to social norms in their communication than those working face-to-face. Verbal communication patterns, such as turn taking and deciding who speaks to whom and when, are highly dependent on social contexts which are much less rich in computer-mediated communication (Lee, 1994). Warkentin, Sayeed and Hightower (1997) found that face-to-face teams have better general communication effectiveness than virtual teams, which leads to higher levels of cohesion, satisfaction with the decision-making process and outcomes. The general conclusion of the research is that communicating effectively over technology is more difficult than in a face-to-face context. As a result, many researchers argue that the richness in face-to-face communication is indispensable, especially in ambiguous or conflictual situations (for example, Handy, 1995; Kezsbom, 2000).

Some have argued that electronic communication is best suited to routine, unambiguous tasks (Daft & Lengel, 1984; Schmidt, 1994). Pointing to the multiple failures of virtual teams reported anecdotally and discussed in research (for example, Neilson, 1997; Star & Ruhleder, 1996), many management scientists (for example, Van der Smagt, 2000) remain pessimistic about using virtual teams for non-routine activities, mainly because of the difficulty of high-level communication.

However other studies have provided more optimism and guidance. Furst *et al.* (2004) found that most virtual teams start with a sense of 'unbridled optimism' that can lead to high performance. In research conducted by Keisler, Siegel and McGuire (1984), participation was much more even, there were much broader decision shifts and there was more uninhibited verbal behaviour in computer-mediated exchanges compared with face-to-face. People online tend to express their personal opinions more freely, resulting in equalization of member participation compared with face-to-face settings: however the free expression can also lead to faster escalation of conflict and polarization of the decision process (for example, Lea & Spears, 1991). In their longitudinal field study, Maznevski and Chudoba (2000) discovered that effective teams used richer technology for more complex messages. They also discovered that complexity is not inherent in a message but is just as much a function of the extent to which the sender and the receiver share or do not share a common understanding and context. The study also found that some effective teams preferred resolving serious conflicts over the telephone and e-mail rather than face-to-face: team members argued that the loss of emotional information was helpful in preventing conflicts from escalating beyond the task to personal levels. A precondition, though, was that the relationships in the group were characterized by high levels of general *trust* and *commitment*.

A note on linguistic differences and inequalities Long-distance communication technologies currently rely heavily on the written word, and the language most often relied upon in multinational teams is English. In some ways, intercultural communication can be more effective when written than in person. E-mail can assist those who tend to prefer writing as it gives them time to digest and think through a reply. Jin, Mason and Yim (1998) suggest that most Chinese, even if they speak English, are weaker conversationally than they are working with the written word. In many cultures people prefer working through writing and, even within cultures, many people prefer the opportunity to be thoughtful and reflective before contributing. Working asynchronously avoids some of the communication patterns that create problems for those working in a second language, such as high levels of interruptions. Less fluent language readers often read more carefully than more fluent readers, and therefore may see important 'ifs' and 'maybes' that are missed by fluent readers who are skimming. On the other hand, the problem of idioms, abbreviations and different types of English remains (Canney Davison & Ward, 1999) and the business norm of fast response times for e-mail can cause difficulty for those who prefer to compose messages carefully. While much work is going into online translation software, it is still constrained and not generally in use yet.

To summarize, although communicating is more challenging through technology than it is face-to-face, it is too simplistic to conclude that communication in virtual teams is therefore less effective. Teams can learn to use a portfolio of technologies appropriately for different purposes and messages to communicate with accuracy, and even learn to use the lack of richness to their advantage (Gluesing & Gibson, 2004). Rather than continue to explore the question of the ineffectiveness of communication in virtual teams, future research should focus on the processes by which virtual teams adapt to the situation.

Building relationships: identity, trust and cooperation
High-quality relationships, characterized by trust and respect, cooperation and commitment, are important in all teams. They reduce the level of destructive conflict in the team, improve the team's ability to manage and gain value from task-related conflict, increase people's comfort in bringing diverse perspectives to the task and enhance the likelihood that people will champion and carry out the team's decisions. In some respects, high-quality relationships are even more important for virtual teams than for face-to-face ones: teams with good relationships can more easily work apart without concern for the process or outcome (Canney Davison & Ekelund, 2004).

One important source of good relationships is *identity* (see also the chapter on global teams by Gibbs). If people identify with each other and the team, they are more likely to trust, respect and cooperate with each other, and to be committed to the group. Shared identity is associated with fewer conflicts, especially in geographically distributed teams. Teams develop shared identity by getting to know each other well, and developing a shared context for their work. In a face-to-face setting it is relatively easy to get to know the other people on the team: how they approach problems, what their backgrounds are, and what they think is important and unimportant. However teams who communicate over technology generally say fewer things and have fewer contextual cues, so getting to know the other people is much more difficult. Complicating the communication constraints, people often portray themselves (deliberately, unconsciously or inadvertently) differently online than they do face-to-face (Hiltz & Turoff, 1993). Compared with face-to-face teams, members of virtual teams tend to share context and identity much less, and this less shared identity is associated with higher levels of conflict (Hinds, 1999; Mortensen & Hinds, 2001).

If shared identity is difficult to develop, trust may be even more difficult. Trust is a confident, positive expectation regarding another party's conduct (Lewicki, McAllister & Bies, 1998; Rousseau, Sitkin, Burt & Camerer, 1998). It has been called the glue of the virtual world (O'Hara-Devereaux & Johansen, 1994). Trust facilitates cooperation and enables teams to coordinate social interaction. In virtual teams, trust may be even more important than in face-to-face teams because of the absence of direct supervision (Canney Davison & Ekelund, 2004).

Much has been made of how important it is to meet face-to-face in order to build trust. However, because trust is built over multiple experiences with a person while observing both the causes and effects of the person's behaviour, it cannot even be built in a two-day team launch meeting. Experiences that contribute to trust building are much more rare in virtual teams than they are in face-to-face settings and thus the trust building is based more on performance consistency which compensates for social interaction. Rapid responses to virtual colleagues and establishing norms around communication patterns are the key to success (Kirkman *et al.*, 2002).

Helpful research focuses on the way different kinds of trust are built over technology compared with face-to-face, rather than the basic question of which type of team develops more trust. For example, researchers suggest that there are four types of trust: calculative, competence, relational and integrated (Paul & McDaniel, 2004). Calculative (such as reliability) and competence (such as expertise) trust are much more task-focused and are influenced by factors such as level of intellectual knowledge and experience, function and profession, and level of perceived competence. Relational trust is much more influenced by social, racial, gender and cultural similarities and differences. Integrative trust is multidimensional and combines all three of the other types of trust. All types of trust help build collaborative relationships, with integrated trust building the strongest collaboration. Cues for calculative and competence trust are more transparent over technology than those for relational trust, thus calculative and competence trust are easier to build online. Wilson, Straus and McEvily (1999) examined triads of students in the USA and found that, while relational trust increased after face-to-face meetings and not after electronic ones, the levels of task-based trust were the same in face-to-face and electronic groups (although the trust took longer to build in the electronic groups). A psychological willingness to be vulnerable was quickly manifested in more cooperative behaviour. Moreover the level of task-based trust was associated with important changes in group behaviour and decision making: groups with higher trust tended to structure their tasks with higher levels of interdependence.

In their study on trust in virtual teams who never met face-to-face, Jarvenpaa and her associates (Jarvenpaa, Knoll & Leidner, 1998;

Jarvenpaa & Leidner, 1999) found that trust, which was critical to the team's ability to manage decision processes, could be built quickly. Team members tended to begin their work together with a basic willingness to trust each other to get the work done with an appropriate level of quality and commitment. Early social communications, early expression of enthusiasm, coping well with uncertainties and technical problems, and individual initiative all contributed to the early creation of a basis of trust. This 'swift trust' (Meyerson, Weick & Kramer, 1996) could then be maintained and nurtured if the communication patterns became predictable and feedback and substantive information were extensive and timely. Trust was also maintained if leaders kept a positive tone, if difficulties were discussed only within the team, and if the initial focus on social interaction and team processes evolved into a strong task focus. However this type of trust was very fragile, and was broken completely after seemingly minor infractions. Jarvenpaa *et al.*'s research is consistent with a large qualitative study which found that people in virtual teams tended to take trust for granted, but talked at much more length about how trust was broken or failed (Gibson & Manuel, 2003). A further exploration of the antecedents of trust formation in virtual teams (Aubert & Kelsey, 2003) shows that there is a strong link between integrity and trust, whereas there was no significant relationship found between members' propensity to trust and the actual trust.

Trust is closely related to cooperation, especially in virtual teams. This relationship is echoed in a comprehensive list of tips from a leading online facilitator. The first item in the list is 'assume good intent', since this is crucial to set the tone of cooperation right from the start (White, 2002). Team norms are established early in a team's life (Bettenhausen & Murnighan, 1991), and cooperative norms must be consciously and explicitly developed. In an experimental setting on a short consensus-type exercise, Balthazard and Potter (2000) found that the degree to which a group developed constructive or destructive interactive styles depended in part on media type. Face-to-face groups had more constructive styles and virtual teams had a greater tendency to develop a defensive style. If the virtual teams had worked together longer, they might have developed the constructive styles on their own, but the patterns were clearly set. Face-to-face teams were more successful on performance dimensions, especially those dealing with group processes; however the main predictor of performance was interaction style (constructive versus destructive) rather than media type, demonstrating that virtual teams *can* develop constructive styles.

Virtual teams must pay much more attention to relationship building than do their face-to-face counterparts, since the medium is not very conducive to easy building of identity, trust or cooperation. However, now that research has shown there are ways to overcome this barrier and build the types of relationships needed for effective teamwork, it is important to develop a richer understanding of how those constructive processes can be built in different types of virtual teams.

Managing conflicts

Conflicts in a virtual team setting are as unavoidable as in a colocated setting. Although the word 'conflict' typically has some negative connotations, some conflicts are widely considered positive for team performance. The ability to resolve conflicts within virtual teams is crucial to their success, and conflict avoidance behaviour is related to failure.

Research has not shown whether there are more or fewer conflicts in virtual teams than in face to-face teams, but most virtual team members report that they experience more conflict because of handicapped communication and diverse composition (Baan, 2004). In addition virtual team conflicts often remain unresolved for a longer period of time because of the dispersed locations and because virtual team members often have several other tasks and functions. Mortensen and Hinds (2001), though, failed to find any positive relationship between geographic distribution and conflict. They argue that the communication of teams using technologies is more likely to stay on task. In their study, the distributed team members reported less within team communication, and less formal and clear procedures. This autonomy allowed team members to maintain greater interpersonal distance and avoid conflict.

Conflicts can be understood and managed more effectively when differentiated into categories: relationship (affective) conflicts and task (cognitive) conflicts. Relationship conflicts are rooted in personal differences and can create annoyance and hostility between team members. Task conflicts are rooted in different views on the strategic or operational elements of the team efforts.

There is little research on solving conflicts in virtual teams, and published recommendations are based more on personal experience and intuition than on empirical data. Some research does exist in this field, for example Montoya-Weiss *et al.* (2001) suggest that management behaviour based on competitive models has a significantly positive effect on virtual team performance (based on a sample of American and Japanese virtual team members). Contrary to this, other researchers found that management behaviour based on collaborative models improved participation, satisfaction and team performance (for example, Paul *et al.*, 2004: based on American and Indian virtual team members). These studies indicate that the best ways of solving conflicts in virtual teams are highly dependent on trust and culture. As we discussed in the previous section, trust is a prerequisite for effective conflict resolution. The cultural element of conflict is far more ambiguous. Owing to the diverse background of team members, the issues leading to conflicts differ between cultures, what is perceived or interpreted as conflict differs, and finally modes for resolving conflicts differ.

It is clear that developing a better understanding of conflict processes in virtual teams is vital. Research so far has only begun to suggest the complexities of conflict in this situation, and future research focusing on this area would help move the field forward significantly.

Leadership: processes, relationships and visioning
Most of what we know about leadership in virtual teams is based on qualitative research conducted with teams in the field. It is generally published in the form of recommendations to team leaders, based on benchmarking the highest performing teams. From this research, we see that the leader of a virtual team must have the same skills as any other kind of team, but the emphasis and actions differ significantly. Three aspects of team leadership are particularly important: structuring the processes, facilitating strong relationships, and maintaining and implementing the vision.

As anyone with virtual team experience knows well, processes must be explicitly and carefully managed and coordinated. Every team needs an organized workspace, defined roles, a clear task strategy and explicit interaction norms that include coming to meetings well prepared with a clear understanding of the meeting's objectives. In a face-to-face team these processes can be implicitly negotiated by team members as they observe and react to each other's facial expressions and other non-verbal behaviour. In a virtual team there is no such opportunity, and virtual teams that do not manage these processes carefully often simply fail to get off the ground. The leader must ensure that these basic processes are well structured, and that related resources – for example, shared work space on a server – are available and supported. This does not mean that the leader should run all the meetings, assign all roles and responsibilities, or monitor how well prepared everyone is before a meeting. In fact group members will feel much more committed to the team if these activities are shared and leadership for different types of tasks is spread amongst team members (Druskat & Wolff, 2001; Lipnack & Stamps, 2000).

The virtual team leader must stay engaged at each crucial step within the team's life cycle. It is the leader's job to promote timely feedback and reflection and actively to build on the team's strengths as they emerge. It can also help to create some early collaborative successes in order to boost team morale, for instance by setting 30-day goals and celebrating each achievement (Furst *et al.*, 2004). The team leader has responsibility to ensure that sponsors are kept up to date and involved in key exercises as well as engaged as important resources to access different information and contacts.

A second key role of the virtual team leader is facilitating relationships. Inside the team, it is important for team members to engage in dialogue and conversations to build social and intellectual capital. These conversations may take place in the context of formal meetings, but should also be part of the everyday life of the team in dyads and other subgroups. A virtual team leader must strike the balance between being so authoritative that s/he is copied on every e-mail between team members and clients and, at the other extreme, being so laissez-faire that the team loses direction and momentum through lack of clarity, emerging hidden agendas and subtle conflicts. The leader should not expect to take part in all internal conversations, but should facilitate, legitimate and support their occurrence. The team leader also has to be very careful in balancing online and offline relationships. For example, if the leader is in the same physical location as some team members, there is a temptation to develop closer relationships with the team members who are colocated. This is not a constructive dynamic for the team.

Good virtual team leaders spend enormous energy encouraging and facilitating relevant exchanges and keeping the team members focused on the big picture and shared goals. Creating smaller task groups is often a good way to do this. The leader of an effective virtual team also manages relationships between the team and external constituents (Druskat & Wolff, 2001). This function is often easy to ignore in virtual teams because the external constituents may also be distributed.

Finally, developing and communicating a compelling vision of the team's collective goals and potential outcome is well-established as one of the most important aspects of leadership (Bass & Stogdill, 1990; House *et al.*, 1999). When team members understand and are committed to the vision, they trust the leader and are more motivated to work towards the vision. A strong vision also allows for more autonomy and empowerment among team members: if everyone understands comprehensively the team's goals and direction, then team members trust each other to act on their own on behalf of the team. In virtual teams this latter function of visions is critical. Since the leader cannot supervise all the team members, a comprehensive vision with a related set of specific collective goals is an essential coordination mechanism.

On the other hand, the leader must often make decisions on behalf of the team. Interactional and procedural justice – the perceived fairness of the decisions – and the open consideration of perceptual biases and perspectives then become important factors influencing team members' trust in the leader. If team members feel that at least their concerns and issues were seriously and fairly considered, they will be more committed to the decisions even if they were not directly involved.

A final note on the leader's role in virtual teams is that a GVT manager must be able to use the technology the team is dependent upon, such as virtual classroom, net-meeting, e-mail and so on. This may seem fairly evident, nevertheless in the virtual world inability to use technology confidently can lead not only to inefficiency but also to lack of respect and trust from the team members. Although little research exists in this field, it has been shown (Kayworth & Leidner, 2002) that leaders of virtual teams are expected to provide a high level of continuous feedback and engage in prompt and frequent communication regarding ideas, suggestions, acknowledgments, direction and other project-related issues.

The leadership of virtual teams is one area for which practice is ahead of research. Research is now needed to dig beneath some of these best practice stories and develop a comprehensive understanding of how leadership best develops and is shared in teams, and under what conditions the role differs in different types of teams.

In this section we have focused on some of the challenges faced by virtual teams: those that have a particularly strong impact on virtual team performance and those that lead to different dynamics in virtual teams as compared to the more familiar face-to-face teams. These challenges mainly derive from two facts: team members are geographically distributed and therefore cannot coordinate their actions as closely; and team members communicate over technology, which is a less rich medium than face-to-face and requires some adaptation in communication styles. As illustrated by research, though, these challenges can be overcome by paying special attention to the factors of communication, relationships, conflicts and leadership; however research is just beginning to develop solid knowledge in these areas.

Every virtual team is different

All virtual teams face the challenges described in the previous section, but there is no simple prescription for resolving the difficulties. Every team is different on some important characteristics, and some of these differences strongly influence how a particular virtual team should develop its own best way to operate. In this section we identify two characteristics of virtual teams that influence the appropriate communication, relationship building, conflict management and leadership processes. Another important difference among virtual teams, composition, is addressed in the chapter by Gibbs in the present volume.

Task: interdependence, urgency, knowledge requirements
Different team tasks require different kinds of strategies and processes. Research on virtual teams has found that three dimensions of the task

influence virtual team processes the most: the task's inherent requirements for interdependence, urgency and knowledge (Gluesing & Gibson, 2004).

Interdependence and urgency are both associated with frequency of communication (Maznevski & Chudoba, 2000). The more a task is urgent, the more frequently team members should communicate with each other. Also, the more interdependence required, the more frequently they should communicate. Since global virtual teams are often used for tasks that require high interdependence and have a relatively high degree of urgency, most global virtual teams should communicate frequently.

The knowledge requirements of the task influence the type of relationships that must be built (Maznevski & Athanassiou, 2003) and virtual teams have greater difficulty forming collective knowledge than face-to-face teams do (Griffith *et al.*, 2003). Explicit knowledge can be codified and transferred from one person to another. We find it in books and manuals; it is 'know what'. Tacit knowledge is tied to a context and an individual's own experience and cannot be transferred directly from one person to another. The difference between explicit and tacit knowledge is the difference between reading a book about Nairobi and getting to know it by working there for a long period of time. Although tacit knowledge cannot be transferred from one person to another, it can be codeveloped. One person can help another person learn the same core of tacit knowledge by helping them to experience the same context and develop similar experiences.

Some tasks require explicit knowledge transfer: the sales and expense figures for a particular area, reports on consumer recognition surveys, and chemical or engineering formulae, for example. Explicit information can be transferred over technology relatively easily regardless of how well team members know each other. In this case, relationship building is less important to the team's performance. Other tasks require tacit knowledge codevelopment: new strategy development, merger or acquisition integration, and expansion into a new region (Athanassiou & Nigh, 2000), for example. Codeveloping tacit knowledge requires strong relationships and shared experiences, which, as we discussed above, are difficult to build in virtual teams. If the task requires tacit knowledge codevelopment, the team must build strong relationships and use a wide variety of different technologies to exchange information and different types of dialogue and interchange (Canney Davison & Ekelund, 2004; Griffith *et al.*, 2003).

Configuration: where is everyone?
Configuration refers to the physical distribution of members. For example, a team that covers many time zones must work together differently from a team located all in the same time zone or across just a few. The former team will rely more on asynchronous modes and will need to schedule

synchronous communication carefully, while the latter team can use synchronous modes much more easily.

Virtual teams also tend to be clustered in different ways. Research on networks has shown that different configurations with key managers in different positions are better for different tasks. For example, a broadly-configured network, that connects people who are connected with many others in an outward-reaching way, is better for information gathering and identifying opportunities (Burt, 1992). A more tightly configured network, with tight links among fewer people, is better for generating and maintaining mutual commitment in complex situations (Coleman, 1990).

Some virtual teams have two or more members at each of a few sites; the virtual team is, in effect, a connection of smaller face-to-face teams. Haas (2001) confirmed that communication between team members decreases significantly as a function of physical distance, so communication among clusters of closely-located but not colocated members will be greater than communication across these clusters. Members who are colocated must make efforts to connect with their peers at other locations, as the tendency will be to rely more than is appropriate on the people at one's own site. Other virtual teams have no physical clusters, but members may create informal or formal communication clusters, with subgroups who communicate more amongst each other than across subgroups (Maznevski & Athanassiou, 2003). These subgroups can help team performance if they facilitate effective information transfer and decision making within the team as a whole, but detract from performance if they become too inward-focused and block communication throughout the team.

Configuration effects are only just beginning to be studied in virtual teams and we expect this to be an important area of future research, with findings that guide many aspects of dynamics in virtual teams.

Achieving high performance
Research on virtual team performance identifies how teams overcome the four process challenges (communication, building relationships, managing conflicts, leadership), given their team characteristics. As for many other areas of virtual team research, research on performance tends to come from aggregating qualitative reports of field studies. Without the benefit of a systematic field of study, managers and team members have been 'figuring it out' on their own. In this section, we describe six practices that effective virtual teams share.

Communicating thoughtfully
Although there are many ways to use technology to communicate effectively, two general guidelines help teams communicate wisely: match

the technology with the message, and match the frequency with the type and phase of the task. The idea is to communicate in just the right ways and the right amount at the right time. Savvy leaders use natural ebbs in the task timelines to introduce reflection and tools and training for the next task phase. Using a rich medium all the time may be desirable, but prohibited by expense and logistics. Communicating frequently may be seen as important, but communicating too frequently is unproductive and results in members becoming frustrated or dropping out of the process. These two guidelines help teams match the right technology and frequency to their own situation.

The simple rule for matching technology with the message is to use richer technology for more complex messages, remembering that a message is inherently more complex to the extent that the sender and receiver have different views of the topic. A richer technology allows for more social presence and feedback, and thus conveys complex information better.

The second simple guideline for using technology effectively is to communicate more frequently to the extent that the task requires greater interdependence. If the task requires aggregating of figures and information to a single report, then enforcing norms of frequent interaction is unconstructive and the team will find that members do not comply or they become frustrated. If the task requires that pieces be done by individuals or subgroups and then handed to other parts of the team for the next step, as in many budgeting processes, frequent interaction from one subgroup to the next is required, but not among the group as a whole. However, if the task requires that all members contribute and respond continuously, continually revising the task as new information comes in (development of a merger or acquisition proposal, for example), communication should be frequent – and the task will not be achieved unless it is.

Managing differences

In the physical space it can be difficult enough to manage teams of diverse backgrounds and values, although plenty of recent research and training development has led to a better understanding of what it requires to exploit diversity in a positive sense. Managing diversity in a virtual space, however, has different and stronger implications, as the GVTs by nature are far more diverse.

Managing diversity is covered well in the chapter on global teams by Gibbs, but a few points are worth emphasizing here. The first is lack of tacit knowledge sharing in a virtual setting. When people work in the same place, they have a shared social system that includes informal exchanges. Without this system, not only can many virtual team members find it difficult to know 'how things are done around here' (here no longer exists) but this lack can also lead to social isolation, lack of identity and distinction followed by frustrations, something that can possibly be avoided if managers are paying attention to this issue. Another area to pay attention to is the ingroup versus outgroup effect of social self-categorization (Tajfel & Turner, 1985). Based on such distinctions, favouritism likely takes place even in the virtual space. However some favouritism based on social group is likely to be reduced because diverse attributes have a more equal starting point (for example, skin colour will affect dynamics less than in face-to-face teams). Categorization may instead be based on other characteristics that were previously less important, such as technological savvy. These effects of virtual teamwork on social identity and various psychological constructs are yet to be explored when it comes to experience and research.

Building a rhythm
One of the most critical questions for virtual teams is whether they need to do any of their work face-to-face and, if so, what and when. The above guidelines on technology use would suggest that teams should get together for face-to-face meetings to discuss and decide on the most complex issues. But in their longitudinal study on virtual teams, Maznevski & Chudoba (2000) found that the most effective virtual teams did not necessarily use face-to-face time for these major communication issues. Instead these teams structured their interaction over time with a rhythm created by a regular heartbeat of face-to-face meetings, interspersed with virtual interaction. One team, for example, met face-to-face for two days every three months. These meetings were arranged up to a year in advance. Maznevski & Chudoba asserted that this heartbeat was as critical to the virtual team as a heartbeat is to a human (see also Lipnack & Stamps, 2000). It pumped life-giving forces into the work of the team: trust and commitment to the relationships among members, and time to build and develop a deep level of understanding of each other's backgrounds and knowledge. These relationships and knowledge-bases then provided a foundation for interaction between meetings, no matter what the subject.

Some teams are in situations in which members will never meet all together face-to-face. In these cases the teams must find ways to create rhythms with conference calls, net meetings or other media that are as rich as possible. With current technology, and given most people's current level of comfort in building relationships and communicating over technology, it still seems to be true that a team engaging in a complex task will perform better if they are able to meet face-to-face for at least some of the heartbeats. Technology will eliminate some travel costs and time, but not all of them. Building a rhythm of heartbeats uses the expensive face-to-face time most effectively to help the team.

Empowering the team

Teams can experience empowerment in different ways, which include a perception of meaningfulness, autonomy, potential effectiveness and that the team can have an impact and make a significant organizational contribution (Kirkman & Rosen, 1997). Increased empowerment usually has a positive effect on group performance. When it comes to virtual teams, empowerment is not less important. On the contrary, among teams that rarely meet face-to-face, empowerment is critical for learning and performance. Teams that lack empowerment and rarely meet face-to-face become more passive and less performing (Kirkman *et al.*, 2004).

To implement empowerment in a virtual team, the leader must spend considerable time with the individual team members (for example, by telephone), coaching them, helping them see the larger organizational picture and how the team is aligned with the strategy of the organization, reinforcing the vision for the team and also setting the directions and boundaries for the near and long future. These dialogues help each team member to build in-depth knowledge of the task and direction, and confidence in their ability to carry it out.

Managing dynamically and fluidly

To make things even more complex, the team's task, composition, configuration and technology change continuously, requiring the team to change the way it works together. Overall, of course, there should be a strong thread of continuity on each of these structural dimensions. The main task objectives will not change, the core of the team will remain basically stable, most people will stay with the same home location and some technology infrastructure will be constant. At the same time, though, different stages of the task have different requirements even for interdependence. Core members will sometimes change following reassignments and promotions, and peripheral members should come in and out as their expertise is required. In any virtual team, members are travelling and working from airports and hotels in different time zones. And organizations, of course, change technology portfolios, upgrading software and hardware, integrating systems and sometimes shifting whole infrastructures.

In a face-to-face team, these changes are responded to with incremental shifts in team operations. In virtual teams, these changes must be noticed and attended to explicitly. A virtual team that starts off with an effective task structuring and strong relationships may find itself faltering six months later for no apparent reason. Usually this is because the team has not managed dynamically and fluidly by adjusting its task structure and relationships in accordance with new aspects of the task, composition, configuration or technology.

Supporting high performance
Finally, human resources professionals have a critical role to play here. HR managers can help teams through the initial stages with appropriate training and team building. In many organizations virtual teams start with an official face-to-face launch that combines strong relationship building with task structuring meetings and training in the different types of technology available to the team. Although expensive, these launches help virtual teams begin their work together with the greatest possible chances of success. If the task is important, the launch is worth the investment. The four success factors should help HR managers design launches that start the teams off as intended.

HR professionals can also support by playing an advocate role for virtual teams to line management. Many virtual teams work on cross-unit projects, and line managers in the members' home units resent time spent away from 'real' work on projects that seem so intangible. HR professionals can help virtual team members by working with line managers to ensure that the virtual project is given as much priority as an equally important home project would be given. HR managers can also help virtual teams obtain resources. Organizations often assume that virtual teams require no infrastructure or support, and it is common for no budget to be allocated to a virtual team's operations. Virtual teams are less expensive to the organization than expatriate assignments or extensive travel, but there are also costs involved and a virtual team will not perform well without some of these resources.

Like any team, virtual teams can reach maximum effectiveness with appropriate support from the organization. Virtual teams, though, offer potential to achieve things that colocated teams cannot achieve, so supporting them effectively can lead to even greater results.

The future
Virtual teams are currently one of the fastest-changing aspect of managing. Even as this chapter was written, findings were published to support the various arguments we proposed and the organizations we work with developed greater familiarity and confidence with virtual teams. By the time the book is published, some of our speculations may be supported or disconfirmed. We believe that the basic elements we summarize from the research here – the processes, structural conditions and key success factors – will remain a useful framework at least for the near future.

What is the future of virtual teams? Changes will come from two major directions: the technology itself and, more importantly, our familiarity with working in this mode. Technology will certainly increase in bandwidth, and parts of the world that do not have stable infrastructures will some day be connected either physically or by radio or satellite systems. The costs of connecting, of buying hardware and software, will also come down. Communicating over technology will become more and more rich, and storing and accessing information will become easier. This is all predictable, and very exciting for virtual teams. Will the need for face-to-face meetings disappear? The answer is probably 'for some teams', but that remains to be seen.

The more important idea, though, is that we are just learning to use the technology. Virtual communication seems awkward in comparison to face-to-face interaction in part because we have not used it nearly as long. Teams have been working together for thousands of years; virtual teams with possibilities of synchronous and almost synchronous communication have been with us for just over a century, and widely available and rich electronic communication has been a normal part of teamwork for only a decade.

Despite the difficulties, these are early days. People fall off a bicycle many times as they learn to ride, but they keep learning because bicycling is faster than running, which is easier. Virtual teams are the bicycles we are just learning to ride, beside the face-to-face teams that we have been running in forever. Anyone who spends time with children or teenagers can see that the next generations of virtual team members in organizations will be different. These young people have always had Internet connections, and create relationships over technology just as easily as they do with the children who live next door. Perhaps for them a 'virtual friend' can be just as important as the neighbour friend. They turn to an Internet search engine to research their projects before the word 'library' comes to mind, and find the world's most up-to-date information. They store information and create nonlinear databases naturally. Of course they must learn to use the information appropriately to build knowledge and wisdom, but it is evident that they will have different challenges with virtual teams than we experience in today's organizations.

The next wave of virtual teams research
Virtual teams research to date has focused mainly on the pragmatics of working in such teams. This made sense for the early stages, as team members struggled through the reality of needing to perform. However, in addition to providing richer explanations of processes such as conflict management and leadership, the next wave of research should focus on some of the more fundamental processes of human interaction in organizations and how they will be adapted to the virtual space. How will people identify with their organizations when they are working more with people they never see than with people they see all the time? What kind of interpersonal skills do we need to develop, given that the nature of

interpersonal interaction is inherently unpredictable? Will poor countries catch up with rich countries in technology use, and how will that change the flow of communication and ideas? Only to the extent that we explore questions like these will we be able to provide guidance to organizations to help them prepare for the future.

References

Athanassiou, N.A. & D. Nigh. 2000. Internationalization, tacit knowledge and the top management team of MNCs. *Journal of International Business Studies*, **31**(3): 471–88.

Aubert, B.A. & B.L. Kelsey. 2003. Further understanding of trust and performance in virtual teams. *Small Group Research*, **34**(5): 575–816.

Baan, A. 2004. Personal communication regarding virtual teams at Royal Dutch Shell and other companies.

Balthazard, P.A. & R.E. Potter. 2000. *Toward inclusive dialogue: participation and interaction in face-to-face and computer-mediated intellectual discourse.* Honolulu, HI: Hawaii International Conference on Systems Sciences.

Bass, B.M. & R.M. Stogdill. 1990. *Handbook of leadership: theory, research, and managerial applications.* Third edition. New York: Free Press.

Bettenhausen, K.L. & J.K. Murnighan. 1991. The development and stability of norms in groups facing interpersonal and structural challenge. *Administrative Science Quarterly*, **36**: 20–35.

Burt, R.S. 1992. *Structural holes: the social structure of competition.* Cambridge, MA: Harvard University Press.

Canney Davison, S. & B.Z. Ekelund. 2004. Effective team process for global teams. In H.W. Lane, M.L. Maznevski, M.E. Mendenhall & J. McNett (eds), *The Blackwell handbook of global management: a guide to managing complexity*: 227–49. Oxford: Blackwell Publishers.

Canney Davison, S. & K. Ward. 1999. *Leading international teams.* New York: McGraw-Hill International.

Coleman, J.S. 1990. *Foundations of social theory.* Cambridge, MA: Belknap.

Daft, R.L. & R.H. Lengel. 1984. Information richness: a new approach to managerial information processing and organization design. In L.L. Cummings & B.M. Straw (eds), *Research in organizational behaviour*: 191–234. Greenwich, CT: JAI Press.

Druskat, V.U. & S.B. Wolff. 2001. Building the emotional intelligence of groups. *Harvard Business Review*, **79**: 80–91.

Furst, S.A., M. Reeves, B. Rosen & R.R. Blackburn. 2004. Managing the life cycle of virtual teams. *Academy of Management Review*, **18**(2): 6–20.

Gibson, C.B. & J.A. Manual. 2003. Building trust: effective multicultural communication processes in virtual teams. In C.B. Gibson & S.G. Cohen (eds), *Virtual teams that work: creating conditions for virtual team effectiveness*: 59–86. San Francisco, CA: Jossey-Bass.

Gluesing, J.G. & C.B. Gibson. 2004. Designing and forming global teams. In H.W. Lane, M.L. Maznevski, M.E. Mendenhall & J. McNett (eds), *The Blackwell handbook of global management: a guide to managing complexity*: 199–226. Oxford: Blackwell Publishers.

Griffith, T.L., J.E. Sawyer & M.A. Neale. 2003. Virtualness and knowledge in teams: managing the love triangle of organizations, individuals, and information technology. *MIS Quarterly*, **27**(2): 265–87.

Haas, M.R. 2001. Acting on what others know: distributed knowledge and team performance. Working paper. Harvard Business School, Cambridge, MA.

Handy, C. 1995. *The empty raincoat: Making sense of the future.* London: Arrow Books.

Hiltz, S.R. & M. Turoff. 1993. *The network nation.* Cambridge, MA: MIT Press.

Hiltz, S.R., K. Johnson & M. Turoff. 1986. Experiments in group decision making: communication process and outcome in face to face versus computerized conference. *Human Communication Research*, **13**: 225–52.

Hinds, P.J. 1999. Perspective taking among distributed workers: the effect of distance on shared mental models of work. Paper presented at the annual meeting of the Academy of Management, Chicago.

House, R., P.J. Hanges, A. Quintanilla, P.W. Dorfman, M.W. Dickson, M. Javidan *et al.* 1999. Culture, leadership, and organizational practices. In W.H. Mobley (ed.), *Advances in global leadership*. Greenwich, CT: JAI Press.

Jarvenpaa, S.L. & D.E. Leidner. 1999. Communication and trust in global virtual teams. *Organization Science*, **10**(6): 791–815.

Jarvenpaa, S.L., K. Knoll & D.E. Leidner. 1998. Is anybody out there? Antecedents of trust in global virtual teams. *Journal of Management Information Systems*, **14**: 29–64.

Jin, Z., R. Mason & P. Yim. 1998. *Bridging US–China cross-cultural differences using internet and groupware technologies*. Paper presented at the 7th International Association for Management of Technology Annual Conference, February, Orlando, Florida.

Kayworth, T.R. & D. Leidner. 2002. Leadership effectiveness in global virtual teams. *Journal of Management Information Systems*, **18**(3): 7–40.

Keisler, S., J. Siegel & T.W. McGuire. 1984. Social psychological aspects of computer mediated communication. *American Psychologist*, **39**: 1123–34.

Kezsbom, D. 2000. Creating teamwork in virtual teams. *Cost Engineering*, **42**: 33–6.

Kirkman, B.L. & B. Rosen. 1997. A model of work team empowerment. In R.W. Woodman & W.A. Pasmore (eds), *Research in organizational change and development*, **10**: 131–67. Greenwich, CT: JAI Press.

Kirkman, B.L., B. Rosen, P.E. Tesluk & C.B. Gibson. 2004. The impact of team empowerment on virtual team performance: the moderating role of face-to-face interaction. *Academy of Management Journal*, **47**(2): 175–92.

Kirkman, B.L., B. Rosen, C.B. Gibson, P.E. Tesluk & S.O. McPherson. 2002. Five challenges to virtual team success: lessons from Sabre, Inc. *Academy of Management Executive*, **16**(3): 67–79.

Lea, M. & R. Spears. 1991. Computer mediated communication, de-individuation and group decision making. *International Journal of Man–Machine Studies*, **34**: 283–301.

Lee, A.S. 1994. Electronic mail as a medium for rich communication: an empirical investigation using hermeneutic interpretation. *MIS Quarterly*, **18**: 143–57.

Lewicki, R.J., D. McAllister & R.H. Bies. 1998. Trust and distrust: new relationships and realities. *Academy of Management Review*, **23**: 438–58.

Lipnack, J. & J. Stamps. 2000. *Virtual teams: reaching across space, time, and organizations with technology*. Second edition. New York: John Wiley & Sons.

Maznevski, M.L. & N.A. Athanassiou. 2003. Designing the knowledge management infrastructure for virtual teams: building and using social networks and social capital. In C.B. Gibson & S.G. Cohen (eds), *Virtual teams that work: creating conditions for virtual team effectiveness*: 196–213. San Francisco, CA: Jossey-Bass.

Maznevski, M.L. & K.M. Chudoba, 2000. Bridging space over time: global virtual team dynamics and effectiveness. *Organization Science*, **11**: 473–92.

Meyerson, D., K.E. Weick & R.M. Kramer. 1996. Swift trust and temporary groups. In R.M. Kramer & T.R. Tyler (eds), *Trust in organizations: frontiers of theory and research*: 166–95. Thousand Oaks, CA: Sage.

Montoya-Weiss, M.M., A.P. Massey & M. Sang. 2001. Getting it together: temporal coordination and conflict management in global virtual teams. *Academy of Management Journal*, **44**: 1251–62.

Mortensen, M. & P. Hinds. 2001. Conflict and shared identity in geographically distributed teams. Working paper. Stanford University, Palo Alto, CA.

Neilson, R.E. 1997. *Collaborative technologies and organizational learning*. Hershey, PA: Idea Group.

O'Hara-Devereaux, M. & R. Johansen. 1994. *Global work: bridging distance, culture and time*. San Francisco, CA: Jossey-Bass.

Paul, D.L. & R. McDaniel, Jr. 2004. A field study of the effect of interpersonal trust on virtual collaborative relationship performance. *MIS Quarterly*, **28**(2): 183–227.

Paul, S., P. Seetharaman, I. Samarah & P.P. Mykytyn. 2004. Impact of heterogeneity and collaborative conflict management style on the performance of synchronous global virtual teams. *Information & Management*, **41**(3): 303–21.

Rousseau, D.M., S.B. Sitkin, R.S. Burt & C. Camerer. 1998. Not so different after all: a cross-discipline view of trust. *Academy of Management Review*, **23**: 393–404.

Schmidt, K. 1994. Cooperative work and its articulation: requirements for computer support. *Le Travail Humain*, **57**: 345–66.

Siegel, J., V. Dubrovsky, S. Kiesler & T.W. McGuire. 1986. Group processes in computer mediated communication. *Organizational Behaviour and Decision Making Processes*, **37**: 157–87.

Star, S.L. & K. Ruhleder. 1996. The ecologies of infrastructures: problems in the implementation of large scale information systems. *Information Systems Research*, **7**: 111–34.

Tajfel, H. & J.C. Turner. 1985. The social identity theory of intergroup behavior. In S. Worchel & W.G. Austin (eds), *Psychology of intergroup relations*. Chicago, IL: Nelson-Hall Publishers.

Van der Smagt, T. 2000. Enhancing virtual teams: social relations vs communication technology. *Industrial Management and Data Systems*, **100**: 148–57.

Warkentin, M.E., L. Sayeed & R. Hightower. 1997. Virtual teams versus face-to-face teams: an exploratory study of web-based conference systems. *Decisions Sciences*, **14**: 29–64.

White, N. 2002. Full circle associates: http://www.fullcirc.com

Wilson, J.M., S.G. Straus & B. McEvily. 1999. All in due time: the development of trust in electronic and face to face groups. Working paper.

20 International joint venture system complexity and human resource management

Randall Schuler and Ibraiz Tarique

An increasing number of organizations are entering new global markets as they seek to develop and sustain a competitive advantage in today's highly competitive global environment (Taylor, 2004; Ernst & Halevy, 2004). To accomplish this international expansion, organizations can and do use many different market entry strategies (Narula & Duysters, 2004; Briscoe & Schuler, 2004; Beamish & Kachra, 2004; Newburry & Zeira, 1997; Child & Faulkner 1998). Prior research has shown that cross-border alliances, particularly international joint ventures (IJVs) are perhaps the most popular means of international expansion (Ernst & Halevy, 2004; Briscoe & Schuler, 2004; Schuler, Jackson & Luo, 2004).

Despite their popularity, however, IJVs are difficult to develop, organize and manage. Research has shown that a majority of IJVs fall short of their stated goals, leading to costly failures (Schuler *et al.*, 2004; Luo, 2000; Evans, Pucik & Barsoux, 2002). While external environmental forces like the legal system, political system and state of the economy, and organizational forces like partner differences and contract terms contribute to failures, a large proportion of IJV failure can be attributed to inefficient management of human resources (Arino & Reuer, 2004; Beamish & Kachra, 2004). Human resource problems stem from, among many things, the fact that IJVs involve managing the goals of two or more partner organizations, while simultaneously maintaining a competitive strength in multiple global markets (Arino & Reuer, 2004; Bouchet, Soellner & Lim, 2004). Despite their difficulties, however, IJVs have the potential to produce great benefits for companies (Bouchet *et al.*, 2004; Schuler *et al.*, 2004; Briscoe & Schuler, 2004; Evans *et al.*, 2002). Accordingly they remain a common choice among firms seeking to enter overseas markets, and an important area for scholarly study (for example, Zeira, Yeheskel & Newburry, 2004; Lajara, Lillo & Sempere, 2003; Loess & Yavas, 2003; Chen & Wilson, 2003; Chiah-Liaw, Petzall & Selvarajah, 2003; Petrovic & Kakabadse, 2003).

IJVs typically represent a long-term collaborative strategy and require active day-to-day management of a wide variety of human resource (HR) issues (Narula & Duysters, 2004; Evans *et al.*, 2002). HR issues are critical organizational concerns and problems for which human resource management expertise is required to provide effective solutions. This expertise is represented in a variety of human resource management activities. Some of the HR issues that are critical to the success of equity-based IJVs may also arise in other forms of alliances but are likely to be less central to their success (Narula & Hogedoorn, 1999; Schuler & Tarique, 2005). In IJVs, however, long-term success is impossible unless HR issues are managed effectively. While there are many lessons that can be transferred from our discussion of IJVs to managing HR issues in other forms of alliances (Schuler & Tarique, 2005), most of our discussion focuses on describing the challenges of managing human resources in IJVs. More specifically, we focus on international joint ventures by presenting a more detailed conceptualization of the IJV system and highlight its growing complexity.

Human resource management
Every IJV, from the smallest to the largest, engages in a variety of human resource management activities. These include formal policies and everyday practices for managing people and addressing HR issues. HR policies are statements that offer a general indication of how people will be managed. HR practices then take the next step and provide a more specific statement of how people will be managed. Seen another way, HR policies are the guidelines and HR practices are things that are actually implemented.

In the remainder of this chapter, we describe some HR issues that arise in several different types of IJVs and discuss their implications for a variety of human resource management activities (Schuler *et al.*, 2004). It is through an understanding of the HR issues and their specific implications that we are able to craft the most effective HRM activities for IJVs and then to identify critical research issues. In this chapter we develop a typology of IJVs as a way of illustrating the variety and complexity of IJVs and the challenge of crafting an effective set of HRM activities. Suggestions for research are made through the development of propositions based upon several theoretical perspectives.

International joint ventures
International joint ventures are legally and economically separate organizational entities created by two or more parent organizations that collectively invest financial as well as other resources to pursue certain objectives. IJVs are typically used when the required integration between the partners is high and the venture business is characterized by uncertainty and decision making urgency (Doz & Hamel, 1998; Luo, 2000; Arino & Reuer, 2004). Although an overwhelming majority of international joint ventures involve only two parent firms (one from a foreign country and the other from the local

country), some ventures may consist of multiple participants (Schuler & Tarique, 2005). Joint ventures that are launched by home country-based (foreign) and host country-based (local) firms are the dominant form of joint venture partnership (Bouchet *et al.*, 2004). Because the creation of an IJV involves establishing an independent organization, the need to establish a separate set of HR policies and practices is particularly evident.

Reasons for international joint ventures

International joint ventures have become a major form of entry into global markets (Ernst & Halevy, 2004; Evans *et al.*, 2002; Barkema *et al.*, 1997). Luo (2000), Schuler *et al.* (2004) and Harrigan (1986) suggest that there are many reasons for companies forming IJVs.

Knowledge and learning　Of the many reasons, a particularly important reason, as far as HRM is concerned, is knowledge sharing and transfer (see Sparrow elsewhere in the present volume; Foss & Pedersen, 2002; Reid, Bussier & Greenway, 2001; Child & Faulkner, 1998; Kalmbach & Roussel, 1999; Shenkar & Li, 1999). In many industries, increasing global competition and unabated technological advances have resulted in a wide range of cross-border collaborative partnerships intended to access knowledge, skills and resources that cannot be internally produced by organizations in a timely or cost-effective fashion (Narula & Duysters, 2004).

Organizational learning has long been considered a key building block and major source of competitive advantage. An IJV is not only a means by which partners trade access to each other's skills but also a mechanism for actually acquiring a partner's skills (Luo, 2000; Inkpen & Tsang, 2005). In bringing together firms with different skills, knowledge bases and organizational cultures, IJVs create unique learning opportunities for the partner firms. By definition, IJVs involve a sharing of resources. This access can be a powerful source of new knowledge that, in most cases, would not have been possible without the formal structure of an IJV. Consequently, IJVs are no longer a peripheral activity but a mainstay of competitive strategy (Bouchet *et al.*, 2004; Taylor, 2004). IJVs forge new knowledge transfer pathways, across both technologically and traditionally linked positions (Inkpen & Tsang, 2005). Kalmbach and Roussel (1999) showed that firms that formulated explicit learning objectives in their alliances generated twice the market values compared to those of non-learning-oriented alliances.

Efficiencies and economies　In addition to the growing importance of learning from IJVs another significant reason for forming alliances is to gain and retain management and organizational efficiencies and economies. These efficiencies and economies can result from combining operations, building upon the experiences of existing management and taking advantage of the latest in technologies, for example, when establishing a new facility (Luo, 2000; Newburry & Zeirra, 1997).

While there are several other reasons for establishing and operating IJVs, we propose to use efficiencies and economies as a basis for our initial extension of the relationship between IJVs and HRM to other forms of alliances because these two reasons are closely aligned with the rationale that link and differentiate varying forms and types of IJVs. But in proposing these two reasons we are obliged to incorporate two other considerations into our extension and these considerations are the need for the parent(s) to exercise control over the IJV and yet cooperate with the other partners and even the IJV itself (Luo, 2000; Geringer & Frayne, 1990; Frayne & Geringer, 2000).

Control   Without the ability to exercise control, it can be more difficult for a parent to establish conditions to maximize learning for itself and its partners, or perhaps even the IJV system, and also to gain and retain the managerial and organizational economies of scale and efficiencies, and protect shareholders' assets and 'brand image', as in the very unfortunate situation at the Union Carbide Corporation (UCC) operation in Bhopal, India that was an IJV (50 per cent UCC) in which the parent company's shareholder value and its reputation, as well as thousands of lives, were lost (Harry, 2004). As a consequence, parent companies engage in numerous strategies to maintain control (Narula & Duysters, 2004; Luo, 2000; Robson, Leonidou & Katslkeas, 2002).

Cooperation   As Narula and Duysters (2004: 199) indicate, 'globalization has affected the need of firms to collaborate, in that firms now seek opportunities to cooperate, rather than identify situations where they can achieve majority control'. Thus, while control is important, cooperation is equally critical in helping to enhance the IJV's chances of success and the learning opportunities of the parents (Inkpen & Tsang, 2005). A further element in pursuing efforts of cooperation and attempts to control is the element of trust. Indeed trust is also central to learning and management efficiencies. While an important need, the treatment of trust is left for further discussion in another chapter. It is, however, found in all stages of the four-stage model of IJVs.

The four-stage model of IJVs

The human resource issues in IJVs are clearly very extensive (Child & Faulkner, 1998; Schuler, 2001). Because these issues also reflect characteristics and qualities of the organization that are themselves closely associated with human resources, we included them together in our discussion of the four stages of IJVs. While there is an extensive set of organizational and HR issues in IJVs, they can be refined and categorized into several stages, beginning with the development of the IJV itself by the two (or more) parents and going through the advances of the IJV itself (Evans *et al.*, 2002; Schuler, 2001). The four stages of the IJV process are shown in Table 20.1, representing the entire IJV system. Shown in each stage, the organizational and human resource issues are most applicable to the IJV system. These in turn become the basis for identifying the HR implications for each stage. We propose that aspects of these stages are applicable in varying degrees to all forms of IJVs (Isabella, 2002). That is why we highlight them briefly here. Greater detail is provided elsewhere (Schuler, 2001; Schuler & Tarique, 2005). Another reason is to provide an update of the existing literature on HRM in IJVs. Future research can then tailor these HR implications to the organizational and human resource issues that are uniquely associated with varying forms of IJVs.

The four stages include the activities even before the IJV itself is formed and conclude with the relationship among the three entities, two or more partners and one IJV. While the literature generally treats one partner as being in the same country as the IJV, this need not be the case in this model. A three (or more) country IJV, however, makes the entire process more complex, and the human resource management activities more extensive and important. For another discussion of the formation and development stages of the IJV process, see Lei, Slocum and Pitts (1997) and Makhija and Ganesh (1997). For more details of each stage, see Schuler (2001) and Schuler *et al.*, (2004).

Stage 1: formation – the partnership   To manage an IJV for success, it is important to understand joint venture formation as including the several aspects shown in Table 20.1. Potential partners in an IJV need to separately determine their reasons for using an IJV as part of their business strategy. Early planning in joint ventures is especially important in order that differences in cultural and management styles between the parents and the venture are considered (Loess & Yavas, 2003; Datta & Rasheed, 1993). Without planning, the likelihood of reaping the gains from the IJV is diminished (Cyr, 1995; Pucik, 1988). Differences in partners on such qualities as culture (country and organizational can be part of an HR plan that includes an audit of these qualities) (Schuler *et al.*, 2004; Pucik, 1988).

The perspective on IJVs reflected in the discussion and propositions in this chapter and the current literature is that IJVs are intended for the longer term (Doz & Hamel, 1998; Child & Faulkner, 1998). While they may involve cooperative or competitive partners, it appears that cooperative partners

Table 20.1   Organizational/HR issues and HR implications in the four stages of the IJV system

Organizational/HR issues	HR implications

Stage 1   Formation
  Identifying reasons
  Planning for utilization
  Selecting dedicated manager
  Finding potential partners
  Selecting likely partners
  Handling issues of control,
    trust and conflict
  Negotiating the arrangement
	The more important learning is, the
	    greater the role for HRM
	Knowledge needs to be managed
	Systematic selection is essential
	Cast a wide net in partner search
	Be thorough for compatibility
	Ensure procedures and communications
	More skilled negotiators are more effective

Stage 2   Development
  Locating the IJV
  Establishing the right structure
  Getting the right senior
    managers
	Concerns of multiple sets of stakeholders
	    need to considered for long-term
	    viability and acceptance
	The structure will affect the learning and
	    knowledge management processes. These
	    are affected by the quality of IJV managers
	Recruiting, selecting and managing
	    senior staff can make or break the IJV

Stage 3   Implementation
  Establishing the vision,
    mission, values, the strategy
    and structure
  Developing HR policies and
    practices
  Dealing with unfolding issues
  Staffing and managing the
    employees
	This will provide meaning and direction to
	    the IJV and employees
	These will affect what is learned through
	    trust, control and conflict management
	Need to design policies and practices with
	    local–global considerations
	The people will make the place

Stage 4   Advancement and
    Beyond
  Learning from the partner(s)
  Transferring the new
    knowledge to the parents
  Transferring the new
    knowledge to
    other locations
	Partners need to have the capacity to learn
	    from each other
	HR systems need to be established to
	    support knowledge flow to the parent
	    and learning by the parent
	Sharing through the parent is critical

Note: © Randall S. Schuler, Rutgers University.

may help increase the chances of success and the effectiveness of the learning process itself (Narula & Duysters, 2004; Isabella, 2002; Child & Faulkner, 1998; Doz & Hamel, 1998; Cyr, 1995). Consensus has it that the very nature of joint ventures contributes to their failure: they are a difficult and complex form of enterprise (Shenkar & Zeira, 1987) and many companies initiate IJVs without fully recognizing and addressing the major issues they are likely to confront (Morris & Hergert, 1987; Arino & Reuer, 2004). Success requires adept handling of least three key issues: control, trust and conflict. Control, along with trust and learning, is one of the most important and most studied topics in the alliance literature (Luo, 2000; Schuler *et al.*, 2004; Geringer & Hebert, 1989; Yan & Gray, 1994; Inkpen & Currall, 1997). Control is defined as a purposeful and goal-oriented activity that influences the acquisition, interpretation and dissemination of information within an organizational setting (Simons, 1987; Geringer & Hebert, 1989). This definition highlights the information/knowledge qualities of IJVs. Thus, not surprisingly, Hamel (1991) and Doz & Hamel (1998) suggest that learning can be the most important lever in IJV control. Nooteboom *et al.*, (1997) suggest that trust may become a substitute for control and that, as trust increases, the need for formal control mechanisms decreases.

   Not surprisingly, the quality of IJV contract negotiations during the IJV formation can have an impact upon three consequences of importance: IJV formation satisfaction, IJV process performance and IJV overall performance (Luo, 1998; Lei, Slocum & Pitts, 1997; Arino & Reuer, 2004). Central to the quality of the contract negotiations are the bargaining processes and strategies used by each of the partners (Aldrich, 1979; Green & Walsh, 1988; Yan & Gray, 1994; Arino & Reuer, 2004). The characteristics of the contract negotiator(s) can also have an impact on the success of the IJV. These characteristics include country cultural similarities, personality and skills, and loyalty. Selecting from these characteristics and ensuring that they are supported and rewarded are important human resource management contributions (Arino & Reuer, 2004).

Stage 2: development – the IJV itself   Once the IJV process has been formed, there are several important activities that must be addressed in the development of the IJV itself, as shown in Table 20.1 (Isabella, 2002; Child & Faulkner, 1998). Where to locate is an important decision. It can be decided to locate the IJV itself in a third country or in the country of one of the partners. Locating in a third country may diminish the 'home field advantage' for either partner; however, it may increase the complexity and complications and need for more information gathering and broader expertise because several of the local stakeholders, such as trade unions, political officials, members of society and regulators, may be unknown to foreign partners (Schuler & Tarique, 2005; Narula & Hagedoorn, 1999). Locating in the country of one partner, however, may give a 'local knowledge' and control advantage. If, however, this knowledge is shared with the other partner, the advantage can move to the partnership and the IJV itself rather than one partner.

When both parents are interested in the IJV and want it to succeed, they appear to get involved in all the key decisions made early on, as reflected in the contract negotiation (Arino & Reuer, 2004). Under these conditions, the board of directors is likely to be composed equally of representatives of the parents and the IJV (internal and external to these entities). The chief operating officer, if not the managing director/general manager, may be selected from the source providing the most experience with the operation of the IJV. Of course, the more parents involved, the more complex and complicated all of this becomes.

Stage 3: implementation – the IJV itself   The implementation stage of the IJV process involves the four sets of activities shown in Table 20.1. The vision, mission, values, strategy and structure of the IJV need to support, encourage and reward learning and the sharing of knowledge (Slocum & Lei, 1993). They also need to support the other needs of the business, the needs of the parents and the needs of the other multiple stakeholders; in other words, the IJV system. With a high-quality top management team in the IJV, the vision, mission, values, strategy and structure are more likely to be crafted to fit the local needs as well as those of the parents. At this point, it is clearly not in the interest of the IJV to ignore the linkages with the parents. For the parents, willingness to trust the IJV top management team to act in their interests and at the same time the interests of the IJV is critical (Child & Faulkner, 1998; Schuler, Dowling & De Cieri, 1993; Schuler & Van Sluijs, 1992; Van Sluijs & Schuler, 1994; Inkpen & Dinur, 1998).

The entire set of the HR policies and practices needs to be created for the IJV. The factors that these policies and practices need to reflect include the following characteristics of the IJV: (a) vision, mission, values, culture, structure, strategy; (b) labour market; (c) need for global integration with parent(s) such as for knowledge transfer; and (d) differences between the country cultures of the parents and the IJV (Schuler & Tarique, 2005). As shown in Table 20.2, acceptable human resource policies and practices may vary substantially according to the cultural dimension of the countries (Hofstede, 1993; Rosenzweig & Nohria, 1994). Thus the more countries involved in the IJV system, the more variation in HR policies and practices that would be expected. And the greater the differences in country cultures, the more significant the implications for HRM policies and practices are likely to be (Robson *et al.*, 2002).

Who actually develops the HR policies and practices can range from one of the parents to the IJV exclusively. The more the development is left with the IJV, the greater the likelihood that the practices will be effective for local adaptation, but not as effective for the parents, global integration and learning transfer (Child & Faulkner, 1998). High-quality top managers, however, are likely to develop locally responsive HR policies and practices with sensitivity to the parents' considerations. Possibly some policies will be non-negotiable and have to meet parents' standards, such as ethical, safety and environmental standards, whereas other policies, such as working hours, compensation and benefits, can be much more locally adaptable. Again the more parents, the more likely that a variety of standards will exist that have to be addressed.

There are many organization and HR issues that unfold as the IJV gets set up, including the assignment of managers, managers' time-spending patterns, top management evaluation, managing loyalty issues, and career and benefits planning (Briscoe & Schuler, 2004; Zeira & Shenkar, 1990). The substance of these issues needs to be addressed explicitly by any IJV (Luo, 2000; Lorange, 1986). Each partner may place differing priorities on the joint venture; therefore a partner may assign relatively weak management resources to the venture. And the more partners there are, the more likely this may occur. To be successful, not only should the assigned managerial resources have relevant capabilities and be of adequate quality, but the overall blend of these managerial resources should reflect a balance of the interests of both parents and of the IJV. Because these assignments could be perceived as attempts to control the IJV (Pucik, 1988), it could be argued that the IJV's top management should have the final say in the staffing of any positions within the IJV itself. Sources for staffing for the IJV include parents, local country nationals, third country nationals, international itinerants (independent expatriates for hire), competitors, suppliers, customers and universities (Harry & Banai, 2005). The selection criteria certainly include knowledge of country culture and the ability to manage cultural differences (Harvey, Speier & Novicevic, 1999; Child & Faulkner, 1998).

Stage 4: advancement – the IJV and beyond   The advancement stage of the IJV process involves learning from the partners, transferring knowledge and learning to the parents, and transferring knowledge and learning to other locations. As the IJV becomes established, the partners' relationships continue to evolve (Child & Faulkner, 1998). In the view of Luo (2000) and of Doz and Hamel (1998), learning and adjustment by the partners are the key to IJV longevity and the avoidance of premature dissolution.

In general, mechanisms for knowledge and information transfer that can be used include top management support, staff rotation, staff training and

Table 20.2 Potential HR policies in countries with various cultural dimensions

HR policies	Power distance		Individualism	
	Low	High	Low	High
Staffing	Select for career progression Joint placement and career decisions	Select for specific job and level Boss places and plans employees' careers	Selection for team players Willingness to contribute to firm	Selection for individual contributions Desire to develop own career
Appraising	Joint problem solving Personal initiative in planning execution 360° feedback	Assign goals One-way communication	Not focus on task accomplishment as much as group membership and loyalty	Individual task accomplishments Set personal goals
Compensating	Employee participation and involvement in reward techniques Profit-sharing; gain-sharing	No employee participation Status distinctions accepted	Group-based contingent rewards Non-economic rewards that satisfy recognition needs	Individual-based contingent rewards Individual praise & recognition
Training & leadership	Skills for advancement	Skills for present job Direction	Skill improvement to contribute to organization Group skills Consideration	Skill improvement for self-improvement Autonomy
Work design	Provides freedom, discretion and participation	Job structure, feedback and direction by boss	Facilitates work design that includes teamwork, task significance, feedback from others	Use of task identity, autonomy, feedback from job

HR practices	Uncertainty avoidance		Masculinity	
	Low	High	Low	High
Staffing	No job descriptions General career guidelines	Clear job descriptions Clear career paths Specific rules and policies	Fit into group Fit with organization	Take personal responsibility Ability to do job
Appraising	Set of difficult and specific goals which involve high risk taking	Set easy goals with low risk taking	Use social benefit, quality of work life and equality	Job tasks & goals Work action plans Performance feedback
Compensating	Link pay to performance External equity Flexibility Broad banding	Limited use of performance-based (at risk) pay Predictability: pay consistency	Use of social benefits, quality of work life, non-zero sum, job security	Use performance pay Competitive pay, promotion and recognition
Training & leadership	General application Participative General directions	Task-specific Structure and direction	Develop social skills	Develop task skills Initiating structure
Work design	Challenge Job enrichment; personal intrinsic gain	Simple job design Limited scope of responsibility Enable group interaction	Job context important Colleagues, security and safety	Job content important Challenge, task accomplishment

Note: © Randall S. Schuler, Rutgers University.

development, site visits, rewards and recognition and repatriation management (Lei, Slocum & Pitts, 1997; Inkpen & Currall, 1997; Inkpen & Crossan,
1995; Cyr, 1995; Collins & Doorley, 1991). Again, the more parents there are,
and the more country cultures involved, the more complex this is likely to be.

Thus far, learning and knowledge transfer have occurred from one
partner to others and from the IJV itself to the parent. In both cases the
parent organizations are gaining new learning and knowledge that can be
used for their internal operations or for their next IJV process (Child &
Faulkner, 1998; Doz & Hamel, 1998). While consideration for transferring
this learning and knowledge to future IJV will enter into the complexities
of partner selection described in the first stage, transferring learning and
building social capital to other units within the organization may be more
straightforward and more under the control of the organization (Inkpen &
Tsang, 2005). Nevertheless this may become more challenging with multiple partners and multiple country cultures.

Proposed application of the four-stage model to varying forms of IJV
The organizational and human resource issues in IJVs are clearly very
extensive (Child & Faulkner, 1998; Schuler, 2001). Thus far, they have been
categorized into several stages that begin with the development of the IJV
system itself. While some variations of the two-parent IJV were mentioned,
the four stages described have been created around a generic and somewhat limited type of IJV. This appears, however, to understate the realities
of the IJV system. For example, IJVs can be differentiated on the basis of
many important characteristics, such as the number of partners (parents),
the number of countries represented in total by the IJV system and the
extent of country culture differences represented by parents in the IJV
system (Beamish & Kachra, 2004; Das & Tsang, 2000). Using these characteristics we propose that IJVs may be distinguishable on the basis of the
environmental differentiation, complexity and potential for conflict.
Furthermore this distinction can be depicted on a continuum beginning
with a simple two-party, two-country, two-country-culture IJV system and
ending with the most complex multi-party, multi-country and multi-
culture IJV system. Regardless of the particular point on the continuum,
any IJV system can still be described by adapting the four-stage generic
model. Simultaneously the organizational and HR issues can be described
and the implications and significance of HR policies and practices can also
be seen. The general relationships between the type of IJV system and the
implications for and significance of HR policies and practices are shown in
Figure 20.1.

We propose that the organizational and HR issues and the resulting
HR implications and significance can be more specifically developed by

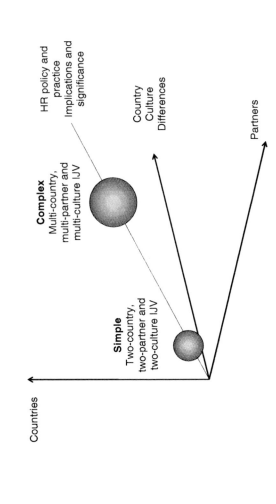

Figure 20.1   Relationships between type of IJV system complexity and the HR policy and practice implications and significance

expanding on the four-stage model of the generic IJV system. Some possibilities for this have been suggested in the description of the generic four-stage model above, but these are developed further through the explication of researchable propositions based upon several theoretical perspectives.

Theoretical perspectives for HRM–IJV relationships
We suggest that expanding upon the work of many researchers, including Beamish and Kachra (2004) and Osborn and Hagedoorn (1997) is useful in describing the relationships between HRM and IJV types. We propose to do that by using several theoretical perspectives. In the previous works, the most prevalent theoretical perspectives were: systems theory, transaction costs, agency theory, resource based, organizational learning theory, and cooperation theory (Inkpen & Tsang, 2005; Narula & Duysters, 2004; Robson *et al.*, 2002). For the purposes of this initial explication of possible relationships between HRM and IJVs we focus on transaction costs, organizational learning, and cooperation perspectives (Schuler & Tarique, 2005).

Transaction cost theory
Transaction cost theory assumes that business enterprises choose governance structures that economize transaction costs associated with establishing, monitoring, evaluating and enforcing agreed-upon exchanges. The theory has direct implications for understanding how HR activities are used to achieve a governance structure for managing the myriad implicit and explicit contracts between employers and employees in an IJV system (Schuler & Tarique, 2005; Wright & McMahan, 1992). IJV partners try to establish contractual relationships with each other to reduce their transaction costs, but they find that the preferences for explicit as opposed to implicit contracts is likely to be influenced by country culture.

Organizational learning theory
According to the organizational learning theory perspective (Kogut, 1988), prior learning facilitates the learning and application on new, related knowledge (Cohen & Levinthal, 1990). This idea can be extended to include the case in which the knowledge in question is itself a set of learning skills constituting the absorptive capacity of the IJV parents. This capacity increases as a function of the previous 'IJV formation' experience, its learning processes and the need for information the IJV system considers lacking in order to attain its strategic objectives.

Cooperation theory
Narula and Duysters (2004) suggest that globalization encourages firms to seek cooperative alliances and partnerships. This reflects an important

necessity to work, cooperate with other in orders to survive and compete in the global environment, particularly in capital and knowledge-intensive industries. Because international joint ventures offer one possible way of dealing with the 'imperative of globalization', working cooperatively becomes a significant activity for firms seeking partners for international joint ventures. Cooperation theory suggests that both partners are more likely to have successful venture relationships if they engage in cooperative rather than competitive behaviours (Loess & Yavas, 2003; Narula & Hagedoorn, 1999; Narula & Duysters, 2004; Inkpen & Tsang, 2005). Based on these three theoretical frameworks we propose the following propositions.

Propositions and research directions
As suggested earlier, the four-stage model of the IJV system may have application to many forms of IJVs because the differences among them are more of degree rather than of kind, with exceptions. Further illustrating this is Figure 20.1 which depicts the relationships between HR policy and practice significance and implications and type of IJV. These relationships are proposed because, as the IJV form moves from a simple two-country, two-partner, two-country-culture IJV to a complex multi-country, multi-partner and multi-country-cultural IJV, the amount of differentiation, complexity and conflict increases and the potential for further conflict, uncertainty and instability also increases (Bouchet, Soellner & Lim, 2004; Luo, 2000; Schuler *et al.*, 2004; Osborn & Hagedoorn, 1997). These relationships are proposed to have a one-to-one relationship as we move from the simplest IJV to the most complex IJV (Narula & Duysters, 2004; Narula & Hagedoorn, 1999). Indeed, as shown in the three dimensional Figure 20.1, there is a significant distinction between IJVs that have multiple country cultures and multiple partners and those that have only two country cultures and two partners. Many of the specific steps in the four-stage model for IJVs (Table 20.1), however, are still likely to exist, but their complexity and complications are expected to be significantly less, thus their significance and importance are substantially less (Luo, 2000).

Propositions
Based upon the description of Figure 20.1 and the three theoretical perspectives, we propose five general propositions for future research. Building upon the work of Loess and Yavas (2003), Narula and Hogedoorn (1999) and Narula and Duysters (2004), we suggest that including more partners from more countries and with more cultural distance is likely to increase the amount of differentiation, complexity and potential conflict within the IJV system.

Proposition 1: *the greater the number of partners, countries and cultures involved in an IJV, the greater the differentiation, complexity and potential for conflict with the IJV system.*

As Osborn and Hagedoorn (1997) suggest, varying forms of IJVs are linked and differentiated by their amount of uncertainty and complexity and, with these, the amount of control that can be exerted over the IJV system. In other words, as the IJV form moves from simple to complex, as depicted in Figure 20.1, we propose that complexity, complications and the potential for conflict uncertainty control and instability increase.

Proposition 2: *the challenges to learning, gaining and retaining efficiencies and exercising control increase as the form of IJV moves from simple to complex.*

As a consequence of the relationships described in Proposition 1, we further propose that increasing amounts of complexity, complications and potential for conflict, uncertainty and instability will become challenges and potential roadblocks: (a) to managing the learning processes in the alliance system; (b) to gaining and retaining efficiencies and economies of scale; and (c) to exercising control over the IJV system activities. Similarly the need for and benefit from cooperation will increase.

Proposition 3a: *the implications for and significance of HRM increase as the form of IJV moves from simple to complex.*

Proposition 3b: *the implications for and significance of HRM are much greater for complex IJVs than for simple IJVs.*

HR policies and practices have the ability of providing clarity, structure and management to organizational and human resource phenomena. Done effectively, they are able to contribute the three needs for managing the learning processes, gaining and retaining efficiencies and economies of scale, and exercising control over the IJV system activities. And as the IJV system moves from simple to complex, these three needs increase, and thus the implications for and significance of HRM will increase. While the separate HR policies and practices will all be individually and uniquely important, it is proposed that the nature of their significance will increase when done systematically across the forms of IJVs.

Proposition 4: *HR issues and implications can be developed into four stages similar to forms of IJVs from simple to complex.*

Whether an IJV system is a simple or a complex form, its activities can be categorized or staged in similar ways, each with issues and implications for HRM. For example, the formation of any IJV should be based on identifiable reasons, most of which will have implications for HRM. Partners will also have to be found and selected for the various forms of IJVs; learning and knowledge are important and selecting partners one can learn from is also important. In the development of any IJV activities, questions about where and how the venture will be located and staffed will arise. A manager for IJV management may be necessary to ensure that the IJV is managed in order to benefit the entire IJV system. In the implementation phase, additional staff may need to be added, to staff the joint venture (simple or complex) throughout the world. Many of the specific steps in the four-stage model for IJVs (Figure 20.1), however, are still likely to exist in a simple two-country, two-partner, two-country-culture IJV but their complexity and complications are expected to be significantly less, thus their significance and importance are substantially less (Luo, 2000). Throughout the various stages, HR policies and practices can help manage the differentiation, complexity and potential for conflict and thereby assist the IJV system in attaining its goals and objectives.

Conclusion

IJVs of all forms are growing in importance for organizations, and the concern for understanding and managing them as well as possible is increasing. In this chapter we have tried to highlight the role of human resource management in varying forms of IJVs. Because the existing body of work in this area has largely focused on simple two-parent–two-country–two-culture forms of IJVs, this chapter has sought to extend this focus by describing the potential relationships between HR policies and practices and several forms of IJVs, from the simple to the complex. This was done by utilizing the four-stage model used to describe the issues and implications for human resource management in international joint ventures.

Along with this model the key underlying phenomena in IJVs were identified: complexity and complications, the potential for conflict, uncertainty and instability, and the need for cooperation, all of which are proposed to increase as the form of IJV moves from the simple to the complex IJV, as illustrated in Figure 20.1. The organizational and HR issues that arise in IJVs result because these underlying phenomena become challenges and roadblocks to what are important needs in all forms of IJVs; that is, learning, efficiencies, control and cooperation. In turn, all of them have implications for human resource management, which increase in significance from simple to complex IJVs because more is at stake as the IJV becomes more complex.

Based upon the relationships shown in Figure 20.1, propositions were offered that might form a basis for further research in the area of human resource management in varying forms of IJVs. These propositions reflect the three theoretical perspectives of transaction costs, organizational learning theory and cooperation theory. Future research might reflect other theoretical perspectives as well as these three. Future research might also be based upon a generic four-stage model of human resource management in IJVs that is similar to, yet distinct from, that shown in Table 20.1.

Acknowledgements

The authors wish to thank S. Jackson, M. Moelleney, B. Kugler, G. Bachtold, W. Harry, J. Ettlie, D. Osborn, Y. Gong and I. Björkman for their suggestions and commentary in the development of this chapter.

References

Aldrich, H. 1979. *Organizations and environments.* Englewood Cliffs, NJ: Prentice Hall.
Arino, A. & Reuer, J. 2004. Designing and renegotiating strategic alliance contracts. *Academy of Management Executive,* **3**: 37–48.
Barkema, H., O. Shenkar, F. Vermeulen & J. Bell. 1997. Working abroad, working with others: how firms learn to operate international joint ventures. *Academy of Management Journal,* **40**: 426–43.
Beamish, P. & A. Kachra. 2004. Number of partners and JV performance. *Journal of World Business,* **39**: 107–20.
Bouchet, G., F. Soellner & L. Lim. 2004. Check your mindset at the border. *Worldview,* **3**: 57–67.
Briscoe, D. & R. Schuler. 2004. *International human resource management: policies & practices for the global enterprise.* Second edition. New York: Routledge.
Chen, S. & M. Wilson. 2003. Standardization and localization of human resource management in Sino-foreign joint ventures. *Asia Pacific Journal of Management,* **20**: 397–408.
Chiah-Liaw, G., S. Petzall & C. Selvarajah. 2003. The role of human resource management (HRM) in Australian–Malaysian joint ventures. *Journal of European Industrial Training,* **27**: 244–56.
Child, J. & D. Faulkner. 1998. *Strategies of cooperation.* Oxford: Oxford University Press.
Cohen, W. & D. Levinthal. 1990. Absorptive capacity: a new perspective on learning and innovations. *Administrative Science Quarterly,* **35**: 128–52.
Collins, T. & T. Doorley. 1991. *Teaming up for the 90s: a guide to international joint ventures and strategic alliances.* Homewood, IL: Business One Irwin.
Cyr, D. 1995. *The human resource challenge of international joint ventures.* Westport, CT: Quorum Books.
Das, T. & B. Teng. 2000. A resource-based theory of strategic alliances. *Journal of Management,* **26**: 31–61.
Datta, K. & A. Rasheed. 1993. Planning international joint ventures: the role of human resource management. In R. Culpan (ed.), *Multinational strategic alliances.* New York: International Business Press.
Doz, Y. & G. Hamel. 1998. *Alliance advantage: the art of creating value through partnering.* Boston, MA: Harvard Business School Press.
Ernst, D. & T. Halevy. 2004. Not by M&A alone. *The McKinsey Quarterly,* **1**: 6–10.
Evans, P., V. Pucik & J. Barsoux. 2002. *The global challenge: frameworks for international human resource management.* Boston, MA: McGraw-Hill.
Foss, N. & T. Pedersen. 2002. Transferring knowledge in MNCs: the role of sources of subsidiary knowledge and organizational context. *Journal of International Management,* **8**: 49–67.
Frayne, C.A. & J.M. Geringer. 2000. Challenges facing general managers of international joint ventures. Unpublished paper.
Geringer, J. & C. Frayne. 1990. Human resource management and international joint venture control: a parent company perspective. *Management International Review,* **30**: 37–52.

Geringer, J. & L. Hebert. 1989. Control and performance of international joint ventures. *Journal of International Business Studies*, **20**: 235–54.

Geringer, J. & L. Hebert. 1991. Measuring performance of international joint ventures. *Journal of International Business Studies*, **22**: 253–67.

Green, S. & A. Welsh. 1988. Cybernetics and dependence: reframing the control concept. *Academy of Management Review*, **13**: 287–301.

Hamel, G. 1991. Competition for competence and inter-partner learning within international strategic alliances. *Strategic Management Journal*, **12**: 83–104.

Harrigan, K. 1986. *Managing for joint venture success*. Boston, MA: Lexington.

Harry, W. 2004. Personal communication with author, 9 November.

Harry W. & M. Banai. 2005. International itinerants. In M. Morley (ed.), *International human resource management and international assignments*. Basingstoke: Palgrave Macmillan.

Harvey, M., C. Speier & M. Novicevic. 1999. The impact of emerging markets on staffing the global organization: a knowledge-based view. *Journal of International Management*, **5**: 167–86.

Hofstede, G. 1993. Cultural constraints in management theories. *Academy of Management Executive*, **71**: 81–93.

Inkpen, A. & M. Crossan. 1995. Believing is seeing: joint ventures and organizational learning. *Journal of Management Studies*, **32**: 595–618.

Inkpen, A. & S. Currall. 1997. International joint venture trust: an empirical examination in P.W. Beamish & J.P. Killing (eds), Cooperative strategies: North American perspectives. San Francisco, CA: New Lexington Press.

Inkpen A. & A. Dinur. 1998. Knowledge management processes and international joint ventures. *Organization Science*, **9**: 454–68.

Inkpen, A. & E. Tsang. 2005. Social capital, networks, and knowledge transfer. *Academy of Management Review*.

Isabella, L. 2002. Managing an alliance is nothing like business as usual. *Organizational Dynamics*, **31**: 47–59.

Kalmbach, C. & C. Roussel. 1999. Dispelling the myths of alliances. *Outlook*, Special edition (October): 5–32.

Killing, J. 1983. *Strategies for joint venture success*. New York: Praeger Publishers.

Kogut, B. 1988. Joint ventures: theoretical and empirical perspectives. *Strategic Management Journal*, **9**: 319–32.

Lajara,B., F. Lillo & V. Sempere. (2003). Human resources management: a success and failure factor in strategic alliances. *Employee Relations*, **25**: 61–80.

Lei, D., J. Slocum & R. Pitts. 1997. Building cooperative advantage: managing strategic alliances to promote organizational learning. *Journal of World Business*, **32**: 202–23.

Loess, K. & U. Yavas. 2003. Human resource collaboration issues in international joint ventures: a study of US–Japanese auto supply IJVs. *Management International Review*, **43**: 311–27.

Lorange, P. 1986. Human resource management in multinational cooperative ventures. *Human Resource Management*, **25**: 133–48.

Luo, Y. 1998. Joint venture success in China: how should we select a good partner? *Journal of World Business*, **33**: 145–66.

Luo,Y. 2000. *Guanxi and business*: Singapore: World Scientific.

Makhija, M. & U. Ganesh. 1997. The relationship between control and partner learning in learning related joint ventures. *Organizational Science*, **8**: 508–24.

Morris, D. & M. Hergert. 1987. Trends in international collaborative agreements. *Columbia Journal of World Business*, **22**: 15–21.

Narula, R. & G. Duysters. 2004. Globalization and trends in international R&D alliances. *Journal of International Management*, **10**: 199–218.

Narula, R. & J. Hagedoorn. 1999. Innovating through strategic alliances: moving towards international partnerships and contractual agreements. *Technovation*, **19**: 283–94.

Newburry, W. & Y. Zeira. 1997. Implications for parent companies. *Journal of World Business*, **32**: 87–102.

Nooteboom, J., H. Berger & N. Noorderhaven. 1997. Effects of trust and governance on relational risk. *Academy of Management Journal*, **40**: 308–38.

Osborn, R. & J. Hagedoorn. 1997. The institutionalization and evolutionary dynamics of interorganizational alliances and networks. *Academy of Management Journal*, **40**: 261–78.

Petrovic, J. & N. Kakabadse. 2003. Strategic staffing of international joint ventures (IJVs): an integrative perspective for future research. *Management Decision*, **41**: 394–401.

Porter, M. 1990. *Competitive advantage of nations*. Boston, MA: Harvard University Press.

Pucik, V. 1988. Strategic alliances, organizational learning and competitive advantage: the HRM agenda. *Human Resource Management*, **27**: 77–93.

Reid, D., D. Bussier & K. Greenway. 2001. Alliance formation issues for knowledge-based enterprises. *International Journal of Management Reviews*, **3**: 79–100.

Robson, M., L. Leonidou & C. Katslkeas. 2002. Factors influencing international joint venture performance. *Management International Review*, **42**: 385–417.

Rosensweig, P.M. & N. Nohria. 1994. Influences on human resource management practices in multinational corporations. *Journal of International Business*, 2nd quarter: 229–51.

Schuler, R. 2001. HR issues in international joint ventures. *International Journal of Human Resource Management*, **12**: 1–50.

Schuler, R. & I. Tarique. 2005. Alliance forms and HR issues, implications and significance. In O. Shenkar & J. Reuer (eds.), *Handbook of strategic alliances*. Thousand Oaks, CA: Sage.

Schuler, R., P. Dowling. & H. De Cieri. 1993. An integrative framework for strategic international human resource management. *International Journal of Human Resource Management*, **4**: 717–64.

Schuler R., S. Jackson & Y. Luo. 2004. *Managing human resources in cross-border alliances*. London: Routledge.

Schuler R.S. & E. Van Sluijs. 1992. Davidson-Marley BV: establishing and operating an international joint venture. *European Management Journal*, **10**: 28–37.

Shenkar, O. & J. Li. 1999. Knowledge search in international cooperative ventures. *Organizational Science*, **10**: 34–44.

Shenkar, O. & Y. Zeira. 1987. Human resource management in international joint ventures: direction for research. *Academy of Management Review*, **12**: 546–57.

Simons, R. 1987. Accounting control systems and business strategy: an empirical analysis, *Accounting, Organizations and Society*, **4**: 357–74.

Slocum J.W. & D. Lei. 1993. Designing global strategic alliances: integrating cultural and economic factors. In G.P. Huber & W.H. Glick (eds.), *Organizational change and redesign: ideas and insights for improving performance*. New York: Oxford University Press.

Taylor, A. 2004. Shanghai auto wants to be the world's next car company. *Fortune*, 4 October, 203–10.

Van Sluijs, E. & R. Schuler. 1994. As the IJV grows: lessons and progress at Davidson-Marley BV. *European Management Journal*, **12**: 315–21.

Wright, P. & G. McMahan. 1992. Theoretical perspectives for strategic human resource management. *Journal of Management*, **18**: 295–320.

Yan, A. & B. Gray. 1994. Bargaining power, management control and performance in United States–China joint ventures: a comparative case study. *Academy of Management Journal*, **37**: 1478–1517.

Zeira, Y. & O. Shenkar. 1990. Interactive and specific parent characteristics: implications for management and human resources in international joint ventures. *Management International Review*, **30**: 16–33.

Zeira, Y., O. Yeheskel & W. Newburry. 2004. A comparative analysis of performance assessment: international joint venture managers versus regional headquarters managers. *The International Journal of Human Resource Management*, **15**: 670–87.

21 Managing culture and human resources in mergers and acquisitions
Philip K. Goulet and David M. Schweiger

Mergers and acquisitions (M&As) have become a popular practice for firms seeking advantage in highly competitive global markets. They can quickly shape a firm's future and the dynamics of the industry in which it operates. M&As are arguably one of the most strategic of management decisions given the significant resource commitments and profound performance implications they have on the firms involved. Consequently understanding how to conduct M&As is critical to the general success of any firm undertaking this form of organizational transformation.

Research over the past two decades has significantly advanced our knowledge of M&As. Much of this work has focused on the human aspect of organizational change as a key determinant of M&A success. It is our objective to share some of this exciting work with the reader, and to further extend the discourse on this critical topic.

We have structured this chapter into four sections. The first section involves an in-depth look at the human element of M&As, and how human resource issues, particularly culture, affect M&A outcomes. The second section identifies interventions that are designed to manage some of these issues. In the third section, we propose a process model of human resource integration in cross-border M&As that synthesizes and extends the extant literature reviewed in this chapter. Finally, the fourth section offers direction for future research.

The human element of mergers and acquisitions
We are in the midst of the largest wave of M&A activity in history. It is being fuelled by globalization, technological change and deregulation. Worldwide M&A activity in merger-deal value exceeded $1.9 trillion in 2004 (*The Wall Street Journal*, 2005), and although North America and Europe account for nearly 86 per cent of M&A activity, other regions such as Asia and Latin America have also established a presence in this area (*The Wall Street Journal*, 2004).

The current wave of M&As has changed since the conglomerate wave of the 1960s. This has brought with it new issues and challenges for acquirers. The current wave of M&As represents an acquirer focus on related targets as a strategy to strengthen the acquirer's core competencies and extend its existing capabilities. Target firms can no longer be acquired and left as independent operations to accomplish these objectives. Integration of the two firms' unique capabilities is required to capture the additional value, or synergy, the acquirer hopes to achieve from these M&As. Critical to this effort is management's ability to create an environment that supports organizational interaction and change.

Although practitioners support M&As as a means to enhance firm performance, studies overwhelmingly indicate that the majority of M&As fail to achieve the performance objectives sought by the acquirer (for example, Agrawal & Jaffe, 2000). Academicians have responded to this finding by advancing knowledge of M&A phenomena and offering prescriptions for M&A success. A host of empirical studies has found that integration issues are major causal factors in explaining the less than spectacular results (for example, Chatterjee, Lubatkin, Schweiger & Weber, 1992; Datta, 1991; Larsson & Finkelstein, 1999; Pablo, 1994). These studies recognize that human integration is a key objective of the integration process, and that it is managing this process well that underlies actual value creation in M&As (for example, Haspeslagh & Jemison, 1991). In the following subsections, we review three streams of human resource research that have attempted to explain the impact of integration issues on M&A outcomes.

Autonomy removal and preserving parity
Removal of target autonomy is one stream of research dealing with human integration issues in M&As. The general findings in this area indicate that integration is smoother when employees' freedom is increased, whereas problems are created when it is reduced (Cartwright & Cooper, 1992). Centralization of activities, for example, has been found to be one of the post-M&A changes that create the most organizational problems (Bohl, 1989). Other work indicates that the removal of autonomy from target executives results in greater turnover of these executives (Lubatkin, Schweiger & Weber, 1999) and lower financial performance of the acquirer (Cannella & Hambrick, 1993). Autonomy removal is believed to signal a loss to target executives, which can cause conflict between the acquirer and target during integration. These findings, based on a sample of domestic US M&As, have been generalized to an international context by a study of cross-border French and British M&As, which also found that autonomy removal from target executives caused performance in these M&As to deteriorate (Very, Lubatkin, Calori & Veiga, 1997).

Leaving a target independent, however, is not an effective solution. As noted earlier, synergy, or acquirer–target interdependence, is a desired outcome of integration (Larsson & Finkelstein, 1999; Weber, 1996). Shying away from integration forfeits value associated with the strategic fit of the M&A.

Preserving parity between the acquirer and target is a practice designed to promote integration while avoiding negative outcomes associated with autonomy removal. It includes balancing positions assigned to acquirer and target managers in the new organization, and providing legitimate representation to both firms on the board of directors. The objective is to share power, responsibility and authority on a proportionate basis in the new organization.

However the efficacy of this practice has been challenged. A study of three Dutch and German cross-border mergers, for example, found that, although preserving parity initially eliminated conflict, it failed to lead to a true integration of the merging firms (Olie, 1994). The organizational structure that resulted from this practice did not support a reconciliation of the different styles of management between the Dutch firms (described as being congenial and informal) and German firms (described as being autocratic and formal). Furthermore, it did not break down distrust that existed between certain departments at the time of the mergers (for example, sales departments retained their pre-merger perceptions as competitors). Board members were also found to retain a greater attachment to their respective pre-merger firms than to the new organization. A true integration of the merging organizations did not occur until the parity of power, responsibility and authority between the Dutch and German firms was abandoned and board members and managers in key positions were selected on the basis of managerial capability.

The study of the successful International Computers Ltd acquisition of Nokia-Data in 1991 provides additional support for basing the new organization's structure on managerial capability rather than the practice of preserving parity (Mayo & Hadaway, 1994). In this merger between UK and Finnish firms, managerial positions were granted on the basis of capability, rather than parity, which resulted in the target overseeing a majority of the new organization's operations in Europe. The transition structure required integration teams from both companies to assess the capabilities of all employees to achieve the synergies sought from the combination. Dedicating resources to assess employee capabilities seriously and assign positions based on these assessments was found to ease the integration process.

Pre-integration mindsets

Research indicates that M&As cause dysfunctional employee mindsets that lead to numerous human resource problems during integration. Employee attitudes decline after the announcement of an M&A, and continue to deteriorate over time (Schweiger & DeNisi, 1991; Schweiger & Goulet, 2005). M&As alter the established order and pattern of activities at both firms (Haspeslagh & Jemison, 1991). These changes (anticipated or real) foster uncertainty, fear of job loss and a tendency toward self-preservation on the part of employees (Haspeslagh & Jemison, 1991; Schweiger & DeNisi, 1991). Target employees, particularly, may begin questioning the validity of their skills and knowledge in the new organization, which can lead to lowered self-esteem and feelings that they will be unable to deal with integration issues (Ivancevich, Schweiger & Power, 1987; Sinetar, 1981).

Complicating the context in which integration is to occur is the propensity of the acquirer and target to display defensive behaviour toward one another (Jemison & Sitkin, 1986). Both the acquirer and target are unfamiliar with the other's business, style and practices. This lack of knowledge can lead to frustration for both parties. Acquirer managers may want to help without knowing how, while at the same time target managers may be afraid to admit what they do not know for fear of reprisal.

The acquirer also has the propensity to display arrogant behaviour toward the target (Jemison & Sitkin, 1986). The acquirer may harbour attitudes that its firm's style, values, beliefs and practices are superior to those of the target, and thus should be imposed on it. The acquirer may also have a tendency to cast aside key cultural symbols of the target that provide continuity and meaning for target employees. The presumption is of target incompetence, rather than simply differences of opinion, style or contextual requirements (Jemison & Sitkin, 1986; Marks & Mirvis, 1985).

Acquirers need to appreciate how M&As negatively affect the pre-integration mindsets and behaviours of employees, and how its own behaviour may further distance the two firms. Understanding these human resource issues is a key first step in dealing effectively with employee resistance to change and acquirer–target conflict during integration.

Cultural orientation
Attitudes and behaviours resulting from cultural orientation differ from those resulting from pre-integration mindsets in that they are deeply rooted in the complex identity of the firms and people involved, and not in the uncertainty or arrogance induced by the M&A transaction. Culture has been generally described as the norms, values, beliefs and attitudes of a group of people. These characteristics of culture are broadly based in societies (national culture) (Hofstede, 1980) and in organizations (organizational culture) (Schein, 1985). Acquirer–target differences in cultural orientation have been associated with human resource issues during integration. Understanding and managing these differences is critical to achieving favourable integration outcomes.

National culture   National culture has long been accepted as a key variable affecting integration efforts in cross-border M&As. Indeed Norburn and Schoenberg (1994) found that 65 per cent of European cross-border acquirers that experienced serious problems with integration said that the difficulties were due to national culture differences.

Research on national culture distance between the acquirer and target has provided an array of interesting results. In Western European and US cross-border M&As, for example, targets with a national culture high on uncertainty avoidance (Hofstede, 1980) were found to perform more profitably when subjected to lower levels of integration (Morosini & Singh, 1994). Conversely targets with a national culture low on uncertainty avoidance were found to perform more profitably when subjected to higher levels of integration. These results suggest that in cross-border M&As acquirers will have greater difficulty achieving synergies from integration when targets are from countries that rate high on uncertainty avoidance. They also suggest that acquirers will unnecessarily forfeit synergies from integration when higher levels of autonomy are granted to targets from countries that rate low on uncertainty avoidance.

In highly individualistic societies (Hofstede 1980) lower levels of integration were also associated with higher productivity (Morosini & Singh, 1994). Therefore several dimensions of a target's national culture may need to be considered by the acquirer when determining the nature of integration. However, it is unclear how an acquirer should integrate a target that possesses national culture traits that are not complementary (that is, possessing cultural traits of both low uncertainty avoidance and high individualism).

To address the complexity of national culture research, a composite index of cultural distance (Kogut & Singh, 1988) based on Hofstede's (1980) dimensions has been developed and subsequently used by various studies within an M&A context (for example, Brouthers & Brouthers, 2000; Morosini, Shane & Singh, 1998). However this measure has recently been criticized for oversimplifying the conceptual and methodological properties of cultural distance, which has led to inconsistent and flawed results (Harzing, 2003; Shenkar, 2001). Research has yet to develop and widely embrace an efficient and effective means of measuring and interpreting the effects of national culture on M&A phenomena.

National culture has also been found to affect the integration practices of acquirers. A study of US, British and French acquirers of Western European targets, for example, found that French acquirers exercise higher formal control over targets than both British and US acquirers (Calori, Lubatkin & Very, 1994). This is consistent with the national culture dimension of uncertainty avoidance, on which France scores higher than both the US and UK (Hofstede, 1980).

Other findings associated with national culture indicate that French, more so than British, acquirers rely on centralized headquarters–subsidiary controls over targets, so that power and influence resides at the hierarchical top (Lubatkin, Calori, Very & Veiga, 1998). These integration practices have been attributed to the French not only expressing a greater need for uncertainty avoidance but also having a greater acceptance of power distance (Hofstede, 1980).

Conversely US acquirers have been found to rely more on informal communication and cooperation than the French, and to rely more on formal control by procedures than the British (Calori *et al.*, 1994). US managers have also been found to provide a higher level of personal effort to support merger success. They become more involved with target employees than the British. This 'hands-off' attitude of acquirer managers was found to be typically British. More important, the use of these informal integration mechanisms was found to yield higher post-M&A attitudinal and economic measures of performance (*ibid.*).

These findings indicate that acquirers may be culturally predisposed in the way they approach integration, and that targets may be culturally predisposed in the way they respond to integration. They also indicate that some differences in national culture may elicit perceptions of attraction rather than resistance. Therefore similarity of national culture traits in cross-border M&As may not necessarily be a harbinger of more successful integration results. Indeed a study of Italian cross-border M&As found that national culture distance was associated with performance based on sales growth over a two-year period following the M&A (Morosini *et al.*, 1998).

There are some indications, however, that the effects of national culture distance may be giving way to the use of 'best practices' in cross-border M&As. Convergence in some human resource practices was found in a study of US, Japanese, German, French and UK acquirers of UK targets (Faulkner, Pitkethly & Child, 2002). Practices such as performance-related pay, formal planning systems, tighter cost control and overall financial management, and greater investment in training were common across nationalities.

Considerable differences, though, still remain. US acquirers were found to have a shorter-term employment and termination philosophy than the other countries surveyed, and to practise the least open communications, preferring a 'need to know' formal approach to the more open approach found to be practised by Japanese, German and French acquirers. Differences were also found in the way training was performed, with the US and UK favouring courses and the Japanese, German and French favouring on-the-job training. Although more closely related to US acquirers, UK acquirers were less short-term in employment philosophy and showed less of a tendency towards a 'need to know' communication style. Furthermore the Japanese were found to be less likely than the Americans to employ a formal and transparent personnel appraisal system, whereas the French were found to be the most formal in planning career development. Conversely the Germans were found to be the most ad hoc in career development, and the least likely to employ job rotation practices.

In sum, although some homogenization of human resource practices has occurred in cross-border M&As, there remains a significant nation-specific bias in the way acquirers apply human resource practices to integration.

Organizational culture   Organizational culture has been further defined as the special way an organization and its members think about what they do and why they do it (Bower, 2001) and what they consider to be appropriate business practices (Schein, 1985). Differences between acquirer–target organizational cultures are associated with anxiety, negative evaluations of counterparts and ethnocentrism between acquirer and target employees (for example, Sales & Mirvis, 1984), which can lead to employee perceptions that place M&A partners into 'us' and 'them' categories. Often members of one culture attempt to dominate members of the other, particularly in related M&As where the acquirer has experience in the target's industry (Berry, 1980). Target employees are made to feel like second-class citizens in the new organization (Ulrich, Cody, LaFasto & Rucci, 1989). This can lead to conflict and dysfunctional employee outcomes, including lack of trust in management, lack of commitment to the new organization, lack of cooperation between the acquirer and target firms, and increased turnover among target executives (for example, Lubatkin *et al.*, 1999; Nahavandi & Malekzadeh, 1988; Schweiger & DeNisi, 1991).

Acquirers have responded to the problems that differences in organizational culture can create by favouring similar M&A partners. A study of Dutch managers, for example, found that they prefer acquiring a firm with a similar organizational culture, and that cultural similarity is positively related to degree of integration (van Oudenhoven & de Boer, 1995). Managers were found to show a greater willingness to merge with a similar partner, estimate the chance of success to be higher and expect less resistance to the merger within their own company.

These findings suggest that acquirers should strive for a less intensive form of integration when there is a large cultural gap between merging firms. Implementing integration in this fashion, however, limits synergies that can be realized from M&As. Also acquirers risk developing a false sense of security when focusing on targets that have similar characteristics. Similarities found in related M&As, for example, imply that M&A relatedness should lead to greater performance. However a meta-analysis of M&A

studies between 1921 and 2002 found no post-M&A performance effect due to relatedness (King, Dalton, Daily & Covin, 2004). The benefits of relatedness do not always exceed the greater costs of implementing a higher level of integration and the impediments in this process that can cause the loss of anticipated synergies (Jemison & Sitkin, 1986; Larsson & Finkelstein, 1999).

Similarity based on the cultural relatedness of acquirer–target business practices has even been found to have negative consequences for M&A outcomes. Similarities can lead to redundancies and conflict between the acquirer and target (Krishnan, Miller & Judge, 1997). Combining complementary rather than similar operations is likely to be seen as much less threatening to employees (Walter, 1985). Indeed complementary M&A partners with moderately discrepant capabilities have been found to evoke relatively little resistance when compared to similar partners (van Oudenhoven & de Boer, 1995).

Research indicates that successful M&As are driven more by how well integration is managed than by the pairing of acquirers and targets based on the similar cultural characteristics of business practices. Similarity of organizational cultures seems to be less important than the complementarity of organizational cultures. Each firm needs to be valued for its unique contribution to the new organization, and this requires the acquirer to understand and deal effectively with complex human resource issues during integration.

Interventions to smooth integration
The above section provided a literature review of significant human resource issues that affect integration outcomes. This section provides a review of the literature that offers insights into the efficacy of interventions designed to mitigate negative preintegration mindsets and negative outcomes associated with autonomy removal and culture clash during integration.

Acquirer communication
Communication is the most basic intervention available to acquirers. Employee anxiety, uncertainty, lack of trust and other negative feelings following the announcement of an M&A often result from a lack of reliable information about the future (Marks & Mirvis, 1985; Napier, 1989) and it is often this uncertainty, rather than the changes themselves, that is so stressful.

To deal with dysfunctional employee mindsets, immediate, honest and consistent disclosure of information to employees is advocated (for example, Ford & Ford, 1995). Formal communication has been associated with positive reactions toward the acquirer, stabilization of volatile situations and minimization of management resignations (Bastien, 1987). Communicating the organization's intentions increases employee perceptions that the company is trustworthy, honest and caring (Schweiger & DeNisi, 1991), and communication that organizes helps employees understand their work and roles in the new company (Sinetar, 1981). Realistic merger previews that communicate specific information about the way the M&A would affect employees have been found to reduce employee uncertainty (Schweiger & DeNisi, 1991). Merger workshops that engage employees in understanding the logic or rationale of the M&A have also been found to reduce negative employee feelings (Leroy & Ramanantsoa, 1997).

M&A integration has been described as a process of identity building, and communication is fundamental to this process (Kleppestø, 1998; Vaara, Tienari & Säntti, 2003). Kleppestø (1998), for example, argues that, in situations of crisis, turmoil and change associated with integration, the need for a (re)negotiation of meaning, identity and relations increases, while the applicability of previous understandings decreases and comes under debate. Communication is critical in the formation of identities and in the development of a world view and relationships in the new organization.

Kleppestø warns acquirers that they must understand the complexity of communication to be successful at integration. It is not possible not to communicate. The absence of speech and physical presence is not equivalent to non-communication; it is merely another set of signals. Moreover communication involves the simultaneous passing of messages at two levels: the report level and the command level. The report level conveys the information proper, whereas the command level negotiates the relationship between the actors involved. Communications can also be highly contextual, and therefore difficult to translate, which can lead to varying interpretations and problems during integration. Effective communication is knowing what is being communicated at both the report and command levels, as well as how this information is being interpreted.

Additional impediments to effective communication occur in cross-border M&As when the firms involved do not have a common mother tongue. Especially below the top management level, the foreign language skills of employees involved in integration are typically limited. As a result, employees frequently find it difficult to express themselves verbally or to understand the nuances in what employees from the other firm are saying. Also written documents drafted in a foreign language tend to become more abstract and limited in scope when compared to those written in one's mother tongue (Vaara, 2003). Unfortunately language skills and communicative competencies are often neglected areas in cross-border M&As (Gertsen & Söderberg, 1998).

Communication also has its limitations. While communication was found to stabilize negative employee reactions subsequent to an M&A

announcement, it was not found to return employee attitudes to pre-announcement levels (Schweiger & DeNisi, 1991). Communication is necessary but not sufficient in eliminating employee uncertainty and suspicion surrounding the motives of management during M&As, and in improving the ultimate outcomes of integration (for example, Buono, Weiss & Bowditch, 1989; Putnam & Pacanowsky, 1983). Other interventions are needed to complement acquirer communication.

Employee involvement and cross-firm interaction
Research clearly indicates that involvement of both acquirer and target employees in the integration process aids integration effectiveness. Employee involvement reduces the psychological trauma individuals experience during post-M&A transitions (Marks, 1994), leads to more successful integration of functional areas (Gerpott, 1995), facilitates partnerships and collaborative working environments (Hakanson, 1995) and is a key predictor of synergy realization in domestic and cross-border M&As (Larsson & Finkelstein, 1999). Fostering open information exchange and developing face-to-face personal relationships between acquirer and target employees is a part of this process, as is providing employees with a sense of control and ability to manage organizational change successfully.

As an intervention to enhance employee involvement and interaction, an acquirer can identify employees that advance the integration process, and then retain and support them. These 'integration entrepreneurs' (Empson, 2000) explore opportunities for cooperation between the merging firms. Their efforts help to forestall the demonization of the merging partner firm by establishing personal relationships with their merger-partner colleagues. Their actions also encourage their more resistant colleagues to participate in the integration process.

Another intervention that aids employee involvement and interaction is the use of in-house integration teams consisting of managers from both firms that work together on proposals regarding organization, process and people in the new organization. Other interventions include training in national intercultural understanding between cross-border firms, utilizing an integration structure involving an integration manager position in headquarters that assists and supports (not directs) the efforts of full-time local integration managers, and granting managerial positions based on capability, rather than parity (Mayo & Hadaway, 1994; Schweiger, 2002). The headquarters' integration manager, especially, should be capable of communicating to many levels of authority and bridging gaps in culture and employee perceptions, because this individual will be responsible for educating employees about their counterpart's organization and forging social connections between the two organizations (Ashkenas & Francis, 2000).

Each intervention described above distributes responsibility and authority to a wider swath of employees across both firms, thereby enhancing acquirer–target interaction and favourable integration outcomes.

Cultural learning
The basis of most conflict in M&As has been attributed to lack of knowledge and understanding of each partner's concerns and organizational culture (Arnold, 1983; Buono & Bowditch, 1989). Cultural conflict poses threats to effective integration and occurs when employees of merging firms have to work together without a shared understanding of their partner's culture (David & Singh, 1993).

To minimize cultural conflict, an understanding of culturally defined behavioural norms and procedural routines of the acquirer and target is necessary (Pablo, Sitkin & Jemison, 1996; Schweiger & Goulet, 2005). Learning as a part of the integration process must occur to bridge cultural differences that can lead to conflict and poor integration outcomes. This entails more than the simple communication of information and feelings to identify differences. Compatibility between M&A partners is achieved through interorganizational learning that results in the construction of an adequately 'shared set' of understandings (David & Singh, 1993).

Learning in this manner supports the acculturation process, or the convergence of the acquirer and target cultures into a new, unified culture. To achieve acculturation, M&A partners must develop a mutuality of interest, but, more important, they must develop a common language and a shared understanding of the business reality (Sales & Mirvis, 1984).

To develop an accurate picture of the business reality, a deep form of learning is necessary, one that entails introspective learning in which both M&A partners learn not only about their partner but also about themselves by understanding what each firm truly values and how each firm explicitly and implicitly functions. Stepping outside of one's own organizational culture is necessary before one can discover the limitations of one's own present culture and the possibilities inherent in other cultures (Schein, 1993). This deep form of cultural learning ensures that key elements of the acquirer and target will be valued and preserved in the new organization.

Identifying cultural differences and learning from them are the building blocks behind shared understandings, a common focus for the new organization and a shared identity. What is good from the acquirer and target cultures should win acceptance in the new organization's culture on its own account, rather than be forced (Mayo & Hadaway, 1994). Employees from both firms will be more accepting of change as a result of integration, because the proposed change will be framed more as an addition to or an extension of existing cultural elements of their pre-M&A firms. This new synthesis that retains the old with the new establishes a form of partial stability to allow change to occur (Schein, 1985) and acculturation to begin.

Convergence on a shared culture offers the greatest opportunity for synergy realization (David & Singh, 1993), because it involves the highest form of integration. Interventions that promote cultural learning are critical to the effective management of the integration process, and to the realization of better solutions for the new organization. Collaborative problem solving and inter-group mirroring workshops between the merging management teams have been found to facilitate integration by reducing misperceptions and inter-group conflict (Blake & Mouton, 1984; Blumberg & Weiner, 1971). Merger workshops that engage employees to participate jointly in determining best practices for the new organization have also been found to result in enhanced teamwork, cooperation and commitment to cultural change and integration (Leroy & Ramanantsoa, 1997).

However these interventions should be complemented and preceded by deep cultural learning interventions that help employees truly understand culture. These interventions have been found to help employees learn about each other and their organizations, break down stereotypes and minimize conflicts (Schweiger & Goulet, 2005). They include an inter-group cultural mirroring exercise and weekly follow-up meetings. The inter-group cultural mirroring exercise is designed to help employees from both firms constructively explore cultural similarities and differences among themselves, and to discuss how they could be managed. Through mirroring and discussion, tangible cultural similarities and dissimilarities can be identified and inaccurate stereotypes can be clarified and eliminated. Those aspects of culture from each firm that would best serve the new organization and those actions necessary to converge the two cultures are jointly determined. These deep cultural learning interventions have been found to be an effective means to resolve cultural differences between merging firms and to overcome several dysfunctional outcomes associated with cultural misalignments.

Another intervention to achieve deep learning during the cultural identity-building process involves the use of metaphors. In a study of a Finnish–Swedish merger, for example, Vaara *et al.* (2003) found that a special metaphor exercise aided the culturally diverse organizations to understand images of 'us' and 'them' and to construct images of a common future. Metaphors are important linguistic vehicles that allow for effective communication of meaning that is difficult or impossible to express otherwise. They are a figurative comparison: for example, an organization as a home or a spider's web. The images are produced in a process of interpretations that involves not only employees' first-hand experiences, but also the reconstruction of historical stereotypes, myths and legends from different social domains. As a result, they reveal cognitive, emotional and political aspects of the cultural identity-building process that characterize the merger context. More traditional approaches to identity building tend to focus on the cognitive aspects of these processes, whereas the metaphor perspective also allows one to see the emotional and political elements (Vaara *et al.*, 2003).

As a part of the metaphor exercise, participants from the merging companies were asked to write down metaphors that best described their view of the acquirer, the target and the merged organization in the future. A summary of the individually produced metaphors was given to the participants in the exercise along with other materials, including readings on Finnish–Swedish cultural differences, which were used to reflect on cultural issues inherent in the merger. The metaphors offered insights into the cultural identity development challenges and suggested new ways of building mutual value base, trust and commitment.

A process model of human resource integration

Human resource management policies are frequently neglected as a functional strategy to help companies integrate M&As. More salient have been policies associated with business strategy, structure, market selection and product development (Faulkner *et al.*, 2002). In this section, we propose a process model that focuses on human resource integration in cross-border M&As, based on a synthesis of the above literature reviews (see Figure 21.1). The model is designed to advance discourse on the nature and sequence of integration interventions in promoting favourable M&A outcomes.

The literature clearly indicates that learning is critical to bridging acquirer–target differences that can impede the integration process. However it is less clear how this learning process should unfold. Below we make the argument that learning in cross-border M&As occurs as a five-stage process: performing culture and human resource due diligence, communicating the logic of the M&A, bridging national culture distance, reconciling organizational culture differences and determining best practices to be implemented.

Stage 1: performing culture and human resource due diligence
Even though it is often emphasized in the literature that cultural aspects should be taken into account early in the decision process, the same literature has little to say about how to carry out such a cultural analysis quickly and effectively (Gertsen, Söderberg & Torp, 1998). As soon as it is known that there is an interest in acquiring a company, a closed course of negotiation is usually begun; most of the flow of information between the two partners ends, apart from what the negotiators discuss among themselves and the publicly available information (*ibid.*). In addition often only a few

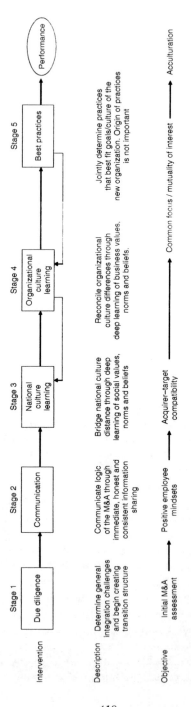

Figure 21.1 Human resource integration in cross-border mergers and acquisitions

specialist employees are involved in the negotiations, making it difficult to conduct a broader, pre-M&A study of culture in the companies involved (Forstmann, 1994). Therefore, although the effects of cultural differences can be present as early as the negotiation stage of an M&A (Chu, 1996), they will be perceived more clearly and will be more accurately assessed during the period of post-M&A management.

Even so, there are a few actions that the acquirer can take prior to the deal announcement to get the integration process off on a good footing. Literature on national differences is readily available to practitioners. A general national culture analysis can be performed by acquirers to determine, for example, how each firm may be culturally predisposed in their approach to problem solving. Understanding the implications of these types of cultural differences will help determine the effectiveness of alternative integration strategies (Forstmann, 1994).

Although organizational culture is unique to each firm and less transparent than national culture, organizational culture differences can also be generally assessed through a variety of secondary and primary sources (Schweiger, 2002). Secondary sources include information gleaned from the Internet, publications, speeches by target management, and interviews with acquirer employees and other trusted business brokers who are knowledgable about the target firm. Primary sources include observation of target management behaviours during M&A meetings and negotiations, examination of target documents (for example, organizational charts, human resource management policies, meeting minutes) and interviews with and surveys of target managers and employees. However, at this stage, access to primary sources and depth of cultural assessment may be very limited, requiring the acquirer to settle for a more generalized view of the target's culture (*ibid.*) in assessing cultural differences and determining the effectiveness of alternative integration strategies.

Additionally acquirer middle managers should be involved at this early stage of the M&A process to generate buy-in of integration problems and process (Haspeslagh & Jemison, 1991). It also helps acquirer top managers to assess further the nature of integration and potential synergies, and to further refine the strategic vision for the M&A. An integration manager, preferably an acquirer executive, who has a deep understanding of the acquirer and is well-connected to key resource holders, should also be selected at this stage. This individual should have strong communication and networking skills, which will be used to forge social connections between the merging firms and to establish integration teams of acquirer and target employees once the deal is announced. The integration teams will be responsible for integration at the functional level within the new organization (Ashkenas & Francis, 2000).

Stage 2: communicating the logic of the M&A
Immediately following the deal announcement, the acquirer should communicate the logic of the M&A to employees of both firms to mitigate negative pre-integration mindsets. Employees need to understand the
rationale, or vision, behind this strategic transaction, given that it will affect
their work environment, and possibly how they perform their jobs.
Acquirer communication that is honest and consistent will help to allay
some of the initial uncertainty and anxiety that M&As create, and begin to
elicit employee trust and confidence in acquirer management that is needed
to influence favourably employee mindsets. Merger previews and workshops should be used as interventions to ensure complete and accurate
communication, and to encourage employees to explore opportunities in
the M&A. Identifying, retaining and supporting integration entrepreneurs
should begin in this stage, as should training for both firms in national
intercultural understanding.

Stages 3 & 4: bridging national culture distance and reconciling
organizational culture differences
No two firms have the same organizational culture, because each firm's
culture is uniquely shaped by its members' shared history and experiences
(Schein, 1985). Cultural differences and the need to reconcile those
differences will therefore exist in all M&As. Cross-border M&As create an
additional dimension of complexity in that national culture distance
between the acquirer and target will also need to be managed.

Research indicates that national and organizational culture should not
be treated in isolation, which further complicates the integration process.
The results of a study of European and US cross-border M&As involving
Italian firms, for example, suggested that performance was an outcome of
access to diverse routines and practices (organizational culture characteristics) that are embedded in national culture (Morosini *et al.*, 1998).
Moreover, in domestic M&As, differences in organizational culture have
been found to affect adversely attitudinal and behavioural variables that are
believed to cause conflict and poor post-M&A performance, whereas, in
cross-border M&As, differences in organizational culture have been found
to have a positive effect on variables believed to aid synergy realization
(Weber, Shenkar & Raveh, 1996).

Other studies have also indicated that some cultural problems associated
with M&As are amplified in domestic, rather than cross-border, settings
(Very, Lubatkin & Calori, 1996; Very *et al.*, 1997). Cross-border M&As
have even been found to reduce marginally employee resistance (Larsson &
Finkelstein, 1999). Two explanations have been advanced for these findings.
First, combination potential may be more complementary and, thus, less

threatening in cross-border M&As than in domestic M&As with overlapping operations. Second, cultural differences that can negatively affect integration in domestic M&As may be more carefully attended to in cross-border M&As (Larsson & Finkelstein, 1999).

These findings suggest that, early on during integration, differences in national culture are perceived to be more acceptable to M&A partners than differences in organizational culture: whereas in the former these differences may be perceived as complementary or perhaps tolerable, in the latter they may be perceived as a form of risk that needs to be controlled. Differences in national culture are also more evident to the acquirer at the time of the deal. Therefore they may be factored into the M&A decision and given greater attention early on during integration.

We argue that implementing interventions to bridge national culture distance should precede the implementation of interventions to reconcile differences in organizational culture. The above findings suggest that M&A partners are more accepting of and more attentive to national culture distance, and therefore are predisposed to working toward developing shared understandings involving these cultural differences. An initial focus on national culture distance will be a good starting point for engaging employee involvement in the new organization, promoting employee understanding of the new organization's business reality, encouraging employee cooperation between firms and developing employee trust in the new organization's management. More important, given that some organizational values are rooted in values of national culture, it is necessary to gain an understanding of differences in national culture before differences in organizational culture can be understood and reconciled.

Understanding why values of national culture are important to each M&A partner will help the two merging firms perceive national culture differences to be more complementary in nature, and therefore more capable of providing a foundation upon which the new organization's culture can be constructed. National culture learning interventions involving cultural learning mirroring exercises at all levels of anticipated human integration should be implemented early after the M&A to communicate to employees in both firms that bridging national culture distance is a serious matter and fully supported by top management.

Organizational culture learning interventions should be implemented once shared understandings of national culture differences are achieved. Cultural learning mirroring exercises as well as metaphor exercises to support the cultural identity-building process should be implemented at all levels and across each department of anticipated human integration. The depth at which these interventions are implemented supports subsequent learning required at the departmental level to determine best practices in the new organization. Shared understandings of differences between organizational cultures, and how national culture affects these differences, will help the acquirer and target develop a common focus for, and mutual interest in, the new organization. Both firms will be working effectively toward a shared identity and acculturation. Difficulties reconciling organizational culture issues may indicate the need for additional work identifying and reconciling issues of national culture.

It is not the objective of cultural learning interventions to dilute national culture values, but to merge effectively values of organizational culture that drive employee perceptions of acceptable business practices. National culture is less malleable than organizational culture, because it is based on social values individuals learn from birth, and these values continue to play a key role in establishing context for employees of both firms after the M&A. As a result, acculturation in cross-border M&As represents organizational culture integration supported by national culture compatibility.

Stage 5: determining best practices

Although managers have been found to focus on task-related criteria when making integration decisions (Pablo, 1994), studies indicate that reconciling cultural issues prior to technical issues smoothes the integration process. Studies of US domestic and European cross-border M&As have found that, when the acquirer and target management teams first reconcile interpersonal issues (for example, values, philosophy, perceptions of one another), they are better able to manage technical issues (Birkinshaw, 1999; Marks & Mirvis, 1985) and that, when they focus only on the task issues associated with integration early in the integration process, ethnocentric attitudes and defensiveness develop (Buono & Bowditch, 1989). These negative outcomes contribute to the failure of integration teams. Teams that address interpersonal issues early on perform well.

Once cultural learning has occurred, and a common focus and mutual interest in the new organization have been achieved, the process of reconciling technical issues associated with the tasks of identifying and implementing best practices will be more manageable. Whereas the prior two stages of integration involve deep learning to develop shared understandings of cultural differences, this stage of integration involves shared understandings in action. Departmental meetings involving employees from both firms should be used to identify best practices at the work-unit level. The practices adopted should complement those aspects of culture that have been chosen to achieve the new organization's goals; however no constraints should be placed on the origin of those practices. Furthermore positions granted to employees to manage the implementation and operation of these practices should be based on capability, not parity. This should minimize the negative effects of autonomy removal during integration by making changes that may affect personal freedoms appear as just. Difficulties determining best practices may indicate the need for additional work identifying and reconciling cultural issues at the organizational and national levels.

Future research
The literature has only begun to address the multitude of cultural and human resource issues that can plague M&As. This section offers suggestions for future research that can advance knowledge in this important area of integration. We proposed that national culture distance should be reconciled prior to organizational culture differences. Empirical work is needed to confirm the efficacy of this cultural learning sequence. Work is also needed to determine whether there are multiple stages to national and organizational culture understanding and, if so, how they may affect the cultural learning process and M&A outcomes. Moreover very little is known about organizational culture in terms of its relation to national culture (Very, Lubatkin & Calori, 1996). Theoretical and empirical work is needed to develop an understanding of this complex relationship and inter-action effects on the integration process.

There are also a number of specific weaknesses in M&A research that tend to challenge some of our existing, and to some extent fundamental, knowl-edge of M&A phenomena. We have already mentioned that the validity of the composite cultural distance index derived from Hofstede's (1980) cul-tural dimensions has been questioned (Harzing, 2003; Shenkar, 2001), thus casting doubt on results of studies that have used this measure. However the concept of national culture and its methodological implementation in research have also come under debate. Harzing (2003), for example, argues that researchers should both let go of a mechanistic view of cultural distance and consider institutional factors in cross-border research. An argument can be advanced that it is management's perception (based on international experience, for example) of the level of cultural distance between specific countries that influences integration decisions and outcomes. Therefore studies that incorporate a primary measure of cultural distance may be more informative in identifying the effects of national culture on the integration process. M&A studies also need to consider institutional factors, such as government restrictions, legal frameworks, the market for corporate control and ownership structures, which may provide alternative explanations for the influence of national culture on integration decisions.

Indeed the general concept of culture has even been called into question. The classic anthropological literature views culture as an empirical category, a system of assumptions, values and norms which can be objectively described, and something that members of a group, an organization or a nation have or bear collectively (Gertsen *et al.*, 1998). The management literature tends to reduce the concept of culture to its behavioural elements, which implies that culture is a fairly stable property or attribute of an organization and hence amenable to quantitative measurement (Cartwright, 1998). However some argue that culture is learned through socialization, and that it is too complex to be simply regarded as just another management variable (for example, Cartwright & Cooper, 1992).

Many anthropologists now argue that culture is based on shared or partly shared patterns of interpretation, which are produced, reproduced and continually changed by the people identifying with them (Gertsen *et al.*, 1998). Culture is seen as being made up of relations and 'the constantly ongoing attempt of the collective to define itself and its situation' (Kleppestö, 1993: 23), which implies that a culture comes into existence in relation to and in contrast with another culture and that it is an interpretive process rather than a relatively constant structure of values and norms. In effect, culture is a social construction that may be ambiguous, unclear and changeable, and may contain contradictions.

From this perspective, M&A research should interpret 'culture conflict' as a confrontation between two groups' attempts to create, mediate and defend their respective social identities and self-images rather than as a threat to the norms and values of a particular organizational culture. As a result, initial similarity or dissimilarity between merging-company cultures does not play the role that present research asserts (*ibid.*: 194). This was evident in a study of a Finnish–Swedish cross-border acquisition, which found that nationalistic interpretations and national confrontation appeared to escalate when it gradually became clear to both groups that the people on the other side had contradictory views concerning the integration efforts and the scope and content of specific changes (Vaara, 2003).

Clearly the national and organizational culture constructs require additional development based on strong theory and empirical verification to achieve agreement in this critical area of M&A integration research. Several questions must be (re)addressed as a part of this effort. First, is culture a stable state and can it be objectively described and analysed in quantitative, empirical research, or is culture an ambiguous and evolving phenomenon that may only be captured through longitudinal, qualitative (case) studies? Second, what truly causes conflict between merging companies? Is it a threat to the norms and values of a cultural system, or is it competition between two groups to establish and maintain their social identities and self-images, or perhaps their political interests? Third, can both be active participants in what the literature has referred to generally as culture conflict? Fourth, how do subcultures or social identities linked to departments, professions and other communities of interest within the organization affect the integration process? Research in these areas could have a profound effect on advancing theory of the integration process and have far-reaching implications for practice.

There are several other issues that have also plagued M&A research that warrant mention here. Little is still known about the way performance is achieved in M&As. First, there is little agreement on what measures should determine M&A performance. Secondary financial and market-returns data, and primary behavioural and financial perceptions data, are used, with secondary data measures predominating in the literature due to convenience rather than empirical rigour. Second, there is little overlap in the variables used by researchers to explain performance. This lack of replication of known effects is slowing knowledge accumulation in the M&A area (King *et al.*, 2004). In this sense, future research needs to be more focused, and less 'broad brush' in its approach to M&A (Cartwright, 1998). Third, further studies are needed to determine the specific mechanisms of national and organizational culture, including human resource management practices, that lead to post-M&A performance across varying levels of integration sought. Fourth, a better understanding is needed of the conditions under which M&As, as opposed to internal innovation, for example, make sense as a path to superior performance (King *et al.*, 2004). Fifth, research needs to focus on different types of M&As (relative size and strategic objective) to determine the true dynamics and challenges of the integration process. Focusing research in these areas and on performance outcomes will help to identify best practices and interventions for effective integration.

Since specific functions, rather than entire organizations, are often integrated (Schweiger, 2002), it would be useful to incorporate functional area cultures into a process model of cultural learning. With few exceptions (for example, Gerpott, 1995; Schweiger & Goulet, 2005), however, M&A studies have focused on the top management level rather than the functional or operational level of the organization, thus leaving this area of M&A research relatively weak. Additional work focusing on functional-level integration issues and how these issues are affected by national culture distance and organizational culture differences would add depth to our understanding of the cultural learning process in cross-border M&As.

Sample imbalances and underspecified models also plague M&A research. There is a need for more research outside a North American and European context. Many samples are also biased in terms of the home and host countries included. Additionally, research variables of demonstrated importance are regularly excluded from M&A studies. Therefore underspecification of research models may represent the norm in M&A studies (King *et al.*, 2004).

These are just some of the many research opportunities that remain to be addressed in our quest for knowledge of the M&A integration process (see also Schweiger & Goulet, 2000, for a critical review of the extant research in M&As). Even though much work has been performed over the past three decades to increase our understanding of M&A phenomena, clearly much more work is needed. Our knowledge of the integration process, including antecedent, process and outcome variables, remains relatively weak. More collaborative efforts on the part of teams of researchers across countries may be needed to hone theory and apply empirical rigour that future studies will require.

Conclusion

Given the failure rate of M&As, it is clear that much needs to be learned about the successful merging of two organizations. Identifying the strategic fit behind an M&A is a rather simple task in comparison to grasping the complexity of human resource issues that accompany integration. Unlocking synergies in M&As requires introspective learning on the part of both the acquirer and the target as a prelude to bridging national culture distance and reconciling organizational culture differences. Involvement of employees from both firms will be necessary to achieve the depth of cultural learning necessary to navigate the many obstacles that plague the integration process. Building shared understandings in this fashion will influence favourably employee aspirations for change and enhance the effectiveness and efficiency with which this change can occur.

Not all acquirers are created equal. Each acquirer may be predisposed to behaviours that are counterproductive to realizing synergies in M&As. Acquirers that understand integration as a learning process and perceive targets as possessing complementary rather than redundant values and capabilities will fare better at securing the organizational fit needed to realize post-M&A performance. They will understand that successful integration is a function of how well the human element of M&As is managed.

References

Agrawal, A. & J.F. Jaffe. 2000. The post-merger performance puzzle. In C. Cooper & A. Gregory (eds), *Advances in mergers and acquisitions*: 7–42, Volume 1. New York: JAI Press.
Arnold, J.D. 1983. Saving corporate marriages: five cases. *Mergers and Acquisitions*, **23**: 55–8.
Ashkenas, R.N. & S.C. Francis. 2000. Integration managers: special leaders for special times. *Harvard Business Review*, Nov.–Dec.: 108–16.
Bastien, D.T. 1987. Common patterns of behavior and communication in corporate mergers and acquisitions. *Human Resource Management*, **26**(1): 17–33.
Berry, J.W. 1980. Social and cultural change. In H.C. Triandis & R.W. Brislin (eds), *Handbook of cross-cultural psychology*: 211–79, Volume 5. Boston, MA: Allyn & Bacon.
Birkinshaw, J. 1999. Acquiring intellect: managing the integration of knowledge-intensive acquisitions. *Business Horizons*, May–June: 33–40.

Blake, R.R. & J.S. Mouton. 1984. *Solving costly organizational conflicts: achieving intergroup trust, cooperation and teamwork*. San Francisco, CA: Jossey-Bass.

Blumberg, A. & W. Weiner. 1971. One from two: facilitating an organizational merger. *Journal of Applied Behavioral Science*, 7: 87–102.

Bohl, D.L. 1989. *Tying the corporate knot*. New York: American Management Association.

Bower, J.L. 2001. Not all M&As are alike – and that matters. *Harvard Business Review*, 79(3): 93–101.

Brouthers, K.D. & L.E. Brouthers. 2000. Acquisitions or greenfield start-up? Institutional, cultural and transaction cost influences. *Strategic Management Journal*, 21: 89–97.

Buono, A.F. & J.L. Bowditch. 1989. *The human side of mergers and acquisitions: managing collision between people, cultures and organizations*. San Francisco, CA: Jossey-Bass.

Buono, A.F., J.W. Weiss & J. L.Bowditch. 1989. Paradoxes in acquisition and merger consulting: thoughts and recommendations. *Consulting*, 8(9): 145–59.

Calori, R., M. Lubatkin. & P. Very. 1994. Control mechanisms in cross-border acquisitions: an international comparison. *Organization Studies*, 15: 361–79.

Cannella, A.A. Jr & D.C. Hambrick. 1993. Effects of executive departures on the performance of acquired firms. *Strategic Management Journal*, 14: 137–52.

Cartwright, S. 1998. International mergers and acquisitions: the issues and challenges. In M.C. Gertsen, A.-M. Söderberg & J.E. Torp (eds), *Cultural dimensions of international mergers and acquisitions*: 5–15. Berlin: Walter de Gruyter.

Cartwright, S. & C. L. Cooper. 1992. *Mergers and acquisitions: the human factor*. Oxford: Butterworth Heinemann.

Chatterjee, S., M.H. Lubatkin, D.M. Schweiger & Y. Weber, 1992. Cultural differences and shareholder value in related mergers: linking equity and human capital. *Strategic Management Journal*, 13: 319–34.

Chu, W. 1996. The human side of examining a foreign target, *Mergers & Acquisitions*, Jan.–Feb.: 35–9.

Datta, D.K. 1991. Organizational fit and acquisition performance: effects of post-acquisition integration. *Strategic Management Journal*, 12: 281–97.

David, K. & H. Singh. 1993. Acquisition regimes: managing cultural risk and relative deprivation in corporate acquisitions. In D.E. Hussey (ed.), *International review of strategic management*: 227–76, Volume 4. New York: John Wiley & Sons.

Empson, L. 2000. Mergers between professional services firms: exploring an undirected process of integration. In C. Cooper & A. Gregory (eds), *Advances in mergers and acquisitions*: 205–37, Volume 1. New York: JAI Press.

Faulkner, D., R. Pitkethly & J. Child. 2002. International mergers and acquisitions in the UK 1985–94: a comparison of national HRM practices. *The International Journal of Human Resource Management*, 13(1): 106–22.

Ford, J.D. & L.W. Ford, 1995. The role of conversations in producing intentional change in organizations. *Academy of Management Review*, 20(3): 541–70.

Forstmann, S. 1994. *Kulturelle Unterschiede bei grenzüberschreitenden Akquisitionen*. Konstanz: Universitätsverlag Konstanz.

Gerpott, T.J. 1995. Successful integration of R&D functions after acquisitions: an exploratory empirical study. *R&D Management*, 25(2): 161–78.

Gertsen, M.C. & A.-M. Söderberg. 1998. Foreign acquisitions in Denmark: culture and communicative dimensions. In M.C. Gertsen, A.-M. Söderberg & J.E. Torp (eds), *Cultural dimensions of international mergers and acquisitions*: 167–96. Berlin: Walter de Gruyter.

Gertsen, M.C., A.-M. Söderberg & J.E. Torp. 1998. Different approaches to the understanding of culture in mergers and acquisitions. In M.C. Gertsen, A.-M. Söderberg & J.E. Torp (eds), *Cultural dimensions of international mergers and acquisitions*: 17–38. Berlin: Walter de Gruyter.

Hakanson, L. 1995. Learning through acquisition: management and integration of foreign R&D laboratories. *International Studies of Management and Organization*, 25: 121–57.

Harzing, A.-W. 2003. The role of culture in entry mode studies: from neglect to myopia. *Advances in International Management*, 15: 75–127.

Haspeslagh, P.C. & D.B. Jemison. 1991. *Managing acquisitions: creating value through corporate renewal.* New York: The Free Press.

Hofstede, G. 1980. *Culture's consequences: international differences in work-related values.* Beverly Hills: Sage Publications.

Ivancevich, J.M., D.M. Schweiger & F.R. Power. 1987. Strategies for managing human resources during mergers and acquisitions. *Human Resource Planning*, **10**(1): 19–35.

Jemison, D.B. & S.B. Sitkin. 1986. Acquisitions: the process can be a problem. *Harvard Business Review*, **64**(2): 107–16.

King, D.R., D.R. Dalton, C.M. Daily & J.G. Covin. 2004. Meta-analyses of post-acquisition performance: indications of unidentified moderators. *Strategic Management Journal*, **25**: 187–200.

Kleppestø, S. 1993. *Kultur och identitet vid företagsuppköp och fusioner.* Stockholm: Nerenius och Santèrus.

Kleppestø, S. 1998. A quest for social identity – the pragmatics of communication in mergers and acquisitions. In M.C. Gertsen, A.-M. Söderberg & J.E. Torp (eds), *Cultural dimensions of international mergers and acquisitions*: 147–66. Berlin: Walter de Gruyter.

Kogut, B. & H. Singh. 1988. The effect of national culture on the choice of entry mode. *Journal of International Business Studies*, **19**: 411–32.

Krishnan, H.A., A. Miller & W.Q. Judge. 1997. Diversification and top management team complementarity: is performance improved by merging similar or dissimilar teams? *Strategic Management Journal*, **18**: 361–74.

Larsson, R. & S. Finkelstein. 1999. Integrating strategic, organizational, and human resource perspectives on mergers and acquisitions: a case survey of synergy realization. *Organization Science*, **10**(1): 1–26.

Leroy, F. & B. Ramanantsoa. 1997. The cognitive and behavioral dimensions of organizational learning in a merger: an empirical study. *Journal of Management Studies*, **34**: 871–94.

Lubatkin, M., D.M. Schweiger & Y. Weber. 1999. Top management turnover in related M&As: an additional test of the theory of relative standing. *Journal of Management*, **25**(1): 55–67.

Lubatkin, M., R. Calori, P. Very & J.F. Veiga. 1998. Managing mergers across borders: a two-nation exploration of a nationally bound administrative heritage. *Organization Science*, **9**: 670–84.

Marks, M.L. 1994. Regrouping after downsizing. In A.K. Korman (ed.), *Human dilemmas in work organizations: strategies for resolution*: 125–48. New York: The Guilford Press.

Marks, M.L. & P.H. Mirvis. 1985. Merger syndrome: stress and uncertainty. *Mergers and Acquisitions*, **20**: 50–55.

Mayo, A. & T. Hadaway. 1994. Cultural adaptation – the ICL–Nokia–Data merger 1991–2. *Journal of Management Development*, **13**(2): 59–71.

Morosini, P. & H. Singh. 1994. Post-cross-border acquisitions: implementing 'national culture-compatible' strategies to improve performance. *European Management Journal*, **12**: 390–400.

Morosini, P., S. Shane & H. Singh. 1998. National cultural distance and cross-border acquisition performance. *Journal of International Business Studies*, **29**: 137–58.

Nahavandi, A. & A.R. Malekzadeh. 1988. Acculturation in mergers and acquisitions. *Academy of Management Review*, **13**: 79–90.

Napier, N.K. 1989. Mergers and acquisitions, human resource issues and outcomes: a review and suggested typology. *Journal of Management Studies*, **26**: 271–89.

Norburn, D. & R. Schoenberg. 1994. European cross-border acquisitions: how was it for you? *Long Range Planning*, **27**(4): 25–34.

Olie, R. 1994. Shades of culture and institutions in international mergers. *Organization Studies*, **15**: 381–405.

Pablo, A.L. 1994. Determinants of acquisition integration level: a decision-making perspective. *Academy of Management Journal*, **37**: 803–36.

Pablo, A.L., S.B. Sitkin & D.B. Jemison. 1996. Acquisition decision-making processes: the central role of risk. *Journal of Management*, **22**: 723–46.

Putnam, L. & M. Pacanowsky. 1983. *Communication and organizations: An interpretive approach.* Beverly Hills, CA: Sage.

Sales, A.L. & P.H. Mirvis. 1984. When cultures collide: issues in acquisition. In J.R. Kimberly & R.E. Quinn (eds), *Managing organizational transitions:* 107–33. Homewood, IL: Irwin.

Schein, E.H. 1985. *Organizational culture and leadership: a dynamic view.* San Francisco, CA: Jossey-Bass.

Schein, E.H. 1993. How can organizations learn faster? The challenge of entering the green room. *Sloan Management Review*, Winter: 85–92.

Schweiger, D.M. 2002. *M&A integration: a framework for executives and managers.* New York: McGraw-Hill.

Schweiger, D.M. & A.S. DeNisi. 1991. Communication with employees following a merger: a longitudinal field experiment. *Academy of Management Journal*, **34**: 110–35.

Schweiger, D.M & P.K. Goulet. 2000. Integrating mergers and acquisitions: an international research review. In C. Cooper & A.Gregory (eds), *Advances in mergers and acquisitions:* 61–91. Greenwich, CT: JAI Press.

Schweiger, D.M & P.K. Goulet. 2005. Facilitating aquisition integration through deep-level cultural learning interventions: a longitudinal field experiment. *Organization Studies*, **26**(10): 1479–502.

Shenkar, O. 2001. Cultural distance revisited: towards a more rigorous conceptualization and measurement of cultural differences. *Journal of International Business Studies*, **32**(3): 519–36.

Sinetar, M. 1981. Mergers, morale and productivity. *Personnel Journal*, **60**: 863–7.

The Wall Street Journal, Mergers Snapshot/Regional Volume, 3/24/2004, Sec. C., p.5.

The Wall Street Journal, Simmering M&A sector reaches a boil, 1/3/2005, Sec. R., p.10.

Ulrich, D., T. Cody, F. LaFasto & T. Rucci. 1989. Human resources at Baxter Healthcare Corporation merger: a strategic partner role. *Human Resource Planning*, **12**(2): 87–103.

Vaara, E. 2003. Post-acquisition integration as sensemaking: glimpses of ambiguity, confusion, hypocrisy and politicization. *Journal of Management Studies*, **40**(4): 859–94.

Vaara, E., J. Tienari & R. Säntti. 2003. The international match: metaphors as vehicles of social identity-building in cross-border mergers. *Human Relations*, **56**(4): 419–51.

van Oudenhoven, J.P. & T. de Boer. 1995. Complementarity and similarity of partners in international mergers. *Basic and Applied Social Psychology*, **17**(3): 343–56.

Very, P., M. Lubatkin & R. Calori. 1996. A cross-national assessment of acculturative stress in recent European mergers. *International Studies of Management & Organizations*, **26**(1): 59–86.

Very, P., M. Lubatkin, R. Calori & J. Veiga. 1997. Relative standing and the performance of recently acquired European firms. *Strategic Management Journal*, **18**: 593–614.

Walter, G.A. 1985. Culture collisions in mergers and acquisitions. In P. Frost, G. Moore, M. Reis Louis, C. Lundberg & J. Martin (eds), *Organizational culture:* 301–14. Beverly Hills, CA: Sage.

Weber, Y. 1996. Corporate cultural fit and performance in mergers and acquisitions. *Human Relations*, **49**(9): 1181–1202.

Weber, Y., O. Shenkar & A. Raveh. 1996. National and corporate cultural fit in mergers/acquisitions: an exploratory study. *Management Science*, **42**: 1215–27.

PART V

THEORETICAL PERSPECTIVES ON INTERNATIONAL HUMAN RESOURCE MANAGEMENT

22 A resource-based view of international human resources: toward a framework of integrative and creative capabilities

Shad S. Morris, Scott A. Snell and Patrick M. Wright

Few will argue against the importance of international human resource management (IHRM) in today's multinational corporation (MNC). A wide range of issues, which varies from global sourcing and off-shoring to regional trade agreements and labour standards to strategic alliances and innovation, all point to the vital nature of IHRM in today's global economy. In fact some observers have suggested that how firms manage their workforces is among the strongest predictors of successful as opposed to unsuccessful MNCs (cf. Bartlett & Ghoshal, 1989; Doz & Prahalad, 1986; Hedlund, 1986).

Researchers have adopted a number of different theoretical approaches for studying IHRM. Not surprisingly, the resource-based view (RBV) of the firm has emerged as perhaps the predominant perspective (Wright, Dunford & Snell, 2001). RBV is particularly attractive to IHRM researchers in that it focuses directly on the potential value of a firm's internal asset stocks for conceiving and executing various strategies. This perspective departs from traditional Input/Output (I/O) economic models of competitive advantage that focus on the structure of markets as the primary determinant of firm performance (Barney, 1991; Wernerfelt, 1984). Also in contrast with I/O economic models, the RBV is based on the assumption that resources are (a) distributed heterogeneously across firms, and (b) remain imperfectly mobile over time. Because these asset stocks are unequal, there is the potential for comparative advantage. And when the resources are immobile, that advantage may be difficult to appropriate or imitate, thereby conferring a sustainable advantage.

In the context of MNCs, the premises of resource heterogeneity and immobility have particular relevance. While the RBV typically focuses on resource heterogeneity across firms, MNCs are unique in that they possess heterogeneity *within* their asset stocks as well. Because they operate in multiple environments, MNCs are likely to possess variations in both their people and the practices that reflect local requirements, laws and cultures.

This variation is a potential source of advantage at a local level, and can provide a global advantage to the MNC as a whole if the knowledge, skills and capabilities can be leveraged appropriately.

However, while heterogeneous resources are potentially immobile across firms, they may also be immobile within firms (MNCs). Given that scholars have consistently noted the difficulties of integrating people and practices within MNCs (for example, Szulanski, 1996; McWilliams, Van Fleet & Wright, 2001) the challenge of integration remains one of the more perplexing organizational and strategic issues. It is therefore somewhat surprising that IHRM researchers have not addressed this issue more directly.

The purpose of this chapter is to summarize the literature on RBV and IHRM by addressing the ways in which resource heterogeneity and immobility provide potential advantages to MNCs. However, we also hope to extend the RBV in this context by addressing some of the primary challenges and necessary capabilities to create resources and integrate them across business units within the MNC. In this sense, we draw upon the knowledge-based view of the firm (KBV) and organizational learning perspectives to look at the way practices are created and integrated on a global scale (Grant, 1996; Teece, Pisano & Shuen, 1997). To organize this discussion, we break the chapter down into three sections. First, we review how the RBV has been applied to IHRM issues to date and discuss the underlying assumptions of this research. Second, we extend the RBV logic to deal more appropriately with issues of practice integration and creation within a globally dynamic environment by turning our focus to aspects of learning capabilities. Finally, we discuss the implications for future research and where this extended view of RBV might improve research on a firm's human resources.

IHRM, people, practices and competitive advantage

Discussions of IHRM within the RBV framework focus on both the workforce (that is, the people) and the HR function (that is, the structures, policies and practices) (for example, Evans, Pucik & Barsoux, 2002; Fey & Björkman, 2001; MacDuffie, 1995; Schuler, Dowling & De Cieri, 1993). To have a sustainable competitive advantage a firm must first possess people with different and better skills and knowledge than its competitors or it must possess HR practices that allow for differentiation from competitors. Second, these practices or skills and abilities should not be easy for competitors to duplicate or imitate (Wright, Dunford & Snell, 2001).

Managing global workforces

Building on the assumptions of heterogeneity and immobility, scholars systematically stress the strategic contributions of people's knowledge and skills to the performance of firms and sustained competitive advantage

(Boxall, 1996). In fact Barney (1991) developed a model to show how specific assets can be strategically identified to lead to sustainable competitive advantage. Building on this model, McWilliams, Van Fleet and Wright (2001) argue that human resources, defined as the entire pool of employees, present a unique source of advantage in comparison to domestic labour pools in terms of value, rarity, inimitability and nonsubstitutability (VRIN).

Given the VRIN framework, McWilliams *et al.* (2001) argued that firms can benefit from a global workforce in two ways: capitalizing on the global labour pools, and exploiting the cultural synergies of a diverse workforce. First, global (heterogeneous) labour pools potentially provide superior human capital. This is because firms can draw from different labour pools to match the different needs of the firm (Bartlett & Ghoshal, 1989). For example, some labour pools may have workers who, on average, have higher cognitive ability or have had greater access to education and training. An MNC could potentially draw from the highest quality labour pools for those functions that require high cognitive ability and education and training (McWilliams *et al.*, 2001).

Second, the use of heterogeneous labour pools potentially increases the quality of global business decision making. When an MNC draws from its multiple labour pools it has the potential to build a diverse and flexible cadre of managers that are better able to bring different perspectives to a decision than a management group based solely on the parent country (Ricks, 1993). That diversity also enables management to be flexible in applying their skills throughout the different parts of the firm. Wright and Snell (1998) discussed these advantages in terms of resource flexibility and coordination flexibility.

While McWilliams *et al.* (2001) highlighted the benefits of human resource heterogeneity and immobility; they also pointed out the difficulty in transferring and integrating these resources within the MNC. Drawing on Szulanski's (1996) concept of stickiness, they noted that the exchanges are made more difficult by 'the lack of absorptive capacity of the recipient, causal ambiguity, and an arduous relationship between the source and the recipient' (Szulanski, 1996: 36). Yet little research exists discussing how internal stickiness can be overcome in order to maximize the benefits of a global workforce while overcoming the challenges of integration and coordination.

Managing global HR functions

Placing people as the source of sustainable competitive advantage moves us to the dilemma of how best to manage their knowledge, skills and abilities. Within the RBV literature, issues of resource heterogeneity and immobility underlie the inevitable tension between local responsiveness and global integration in MNCs (cf. Bae & Lawler, 2000; Brewster, 1999; Fey & Björkman, 2001; Sparrow, Schuler & Jackson, 1994). Local responsiveness and the value derived from customization imply variation (heterogeneity) within the MNC. Global efficiency, on the other hand, requires integration across business units. However, given the assumption of resource immobility, this integration is not always easy to achieve.

Schuler *et al.* (1993) captured the essence of these tradeoffs by highlighting the relationships between *internal operations* and *inter-unit linkages*. From the standpoint of internal operations, each overseas affiliate must operate as effectively as possible relative to the competitive strategy of the MNC. This means that these affiliates can offer advantages to the MNC by recognizing and developing HR practices that are appropriate for their local markets, employment laws, cultural traditions and the like.

While internal operations at the local level are important, the MNC must also establish inter-unit linkages to gain efficiencies of scale and scope across several different countries. This suggests that, while overseas affiliates can generate advantages locally, there are also substantial advantages that can be gained globally through integrated HR practices. Each is important, but each carries with it a different set of organizational requirements. These requirements point directly to issues relevant for HRM.

Extending these ideas, Taylor, Beechler and Napier (1996) describe how MNCs might develop a more *integrative* approach to HRM. The objective of this strategy is to share best practices from all parts of the firm (not just corporate) to create a worldwide system. While there are allowances for local differentiation, the focus is on substantial global integration. Differentiation provides both the potential for local response and customization and the variety of ideas and practices needed for innovation at the global level.

However integration through coordination, communication and learning is not always easily achieved in this context. Ironically the very characteristics that provide resource-based advantage at the local level actually complicate integration at the global level. The ability of firms to gain efficiencies of scope and scale at the global level is made more difficult by resource heterogeneity, and this challenge is exacerbated by resource immobility.

The challenge then for the transnational firm is to identify how firms can preserve variety (and local customization) while simultaneously establishing a foundation for integration and efficiency. As mentioned by McWilliams *et al.* (2001), very few scholars have addressed the 'stickiness' issue involved in balancing the global and local tension. Taylor *et al.* (1996) allude to such integration difficulties when they note:

The reason firms move toward an exportive rather than an integrative SIHRM orientation . . . is that the mechanisms to identify and transfer the best HRM practices in their overseas affiliates are not in place. Such mechanisms as having regional or global meetings of affiliate HR directors, transferring HRM materials (e.g., performance appraisal forms to affiliates) or posting of the HR director of the affiliates to the HQs of the firm were not developed. (ibid.: 972)

These same capability issues are raised by McWilliams *et al.* (2001) when they discuss the major causes of internal stickiness being lack of absorptive capacity, causal ambiguity and arduous relationships between the source and recipient. In both examples, barriers to global practice integration are raised and discussed, but not resolved. This issue is addressed more fully below.

IHRM and capabilities
Given the importance (and difficulty) of integrating human resources at a global level, while preserving the uniqueness and heterogeneity at the local level, it seems reasonable to discuss these issues in the context of *competitive capabilities*. Using the knowledge-based view (KBV) of firms, that emphasizes the need to acquire and integrate knowledge, we suggest two such capabilities (see Table 22.1). First, knowledge integration capability refers to a firm's ability to transfer and coordinate human resources across affiliates in a way that utilizes economies of scale and scope while allowing and promoting responsiveness to the local environment. Second, knowledge creation capability refers to a firm's ability to create new and potentially innovative practices at the local level.

Knowledge integration capability
Ironically, while learning capability is one of the key dimensions of the Bartlett and Ghoshal (1989) framework of transnational organizations, most IHRM researchers have made only passing mention of the way firms share and integrate best practice within the MNC. Snell, Youndt and Wright (1996) argued that, particularly in dynamic environments, organizational learning may be the only way to ensure that resources sustain their value and uniqueness over time. In essence, the capability to integrate HR practices better than competitors may be a key source of sustainable competitive advantage (cf., Kogut & Zander, 1992). In the subsections below, we frame the key factors underlying knowledge integration capability in terms of organizational capital, social capital and human capital.

Organizational capital Youndt, Subramaniam and Snell (2004) define organizational capital as the institutionalized knowledge and codified

Table 22.1 IHRM: people, practices and capabilities

Focus	Theories	Strategic question	Sources
People	*RBV*: Focus on individual resources of knowledge, skills and abilities	*Workforce*: What are the knowledge, skills and abilities that are heterogeneous and immobile?	McWilliams, Van Fleet & Wright, 2001
Practices	*RBV and competencies*: Focus on combined resources of HR practices	*HR practices and systems*: What are the HR practices and systems that are heterogeneous and immobile?	Taylor, Beechler & Napier, 1996
Capabilities	*KBV and organizational capabilities*: Focus on learning processes and capabilities	*Learning capabilities*: How can HR practices and systems be created and integrated to preserve heterogeneity and immobility?	Chadwick & Cappelli, 1999

experiences residing within an organization. Artifacts of organizational capital include an organization's reliance on manuals and databases to preserve knowledge, along with the establishment of structures, processes and routines that encourage repeated use of this knowledge (Hansen, Nitin & Tierney, 1999). As an integration mechanism, organizational capital allows the firm to preserve knowledge as incoming employees replace those leaving. An example of such an artifact might be a 'lessons learned' database to ensure that lessons learned by one group can be made accessible for all groups.

Using MNC research, in order to improve the integration of knowledge within an MNC relative to the speed of its diffusion or imitation by competitors, firms invest in ways to make knowledge explicit by encoding its use and replicating it in rules and documentation (Kogut & Zander, 1993). Other forms of organizational capital are likely to represent detailed, company-wide routines on the way new HR practices should be integrated by all affiliates. These routines may detail how practices should be shared to reduce the variance and time it takes to implement each new approach and, thereby, improve the overall efficiency of knowledge integration

(March, 1991). Similarly, organizations typically implement information systems to provide affiliates with a common platform for HR processes and practices (Snell, Stueber & Lepak, 2002). These systems, processes and routines ensure that (a) practices are implemented routinely through established data collection procedures, and (b) practices are rapidly disseminated throughout the entire MNC with minimal costs (Daft & Weick, 1984). In terms of integration capability, then, organizational capital provides a basis for sharing and institutionalizing knowledge across affiliates. However it may work against efforts to preserve heterogeneity at the subunit level.

Social capital   Social capital, defined as the knowledge embedded within social networks, also plays a potentially valuable role in the integration capability of MNCs (Nahapiet & Ghoshal, 1998). For example, Szulanski (1995) found that one of the biggest obstacles to transfer of knowledge in MNCs is the poor relationship between sources and recipients of information. Along this line, Ghoshal and Bartlett (1988) empirically showed that knowledge sharing and integration could not occur without the existence of strong social connections.

The importance of social capital for integration capability is found in research by Kostova and Roth (2002), who concluded that successful practice adoption is largely dependent upon relationships based on trust and shared identity. Trust provides the motive to interact with others, while shared identity provides an overlapping understanding of what it is important to share. Both of these elements of social capital would seem vital for integration capability. And, importantly, neither of them would de facto require the loss of local autonomy.

Human capital   While organizational and social capital are both potentially important resources underlying a firm's integration capability, Teece (1977) argued that one of the principal obstacles to transfer and integration is lack of prior experience and knowledge (that is, human capital). Research by Szulanski (1996) and Tsai (2002), for example, has shown that knowledge sharing and integration is facilitated when respective parties have the absorptive capacity or prior experience to understand related ideas (Szulanski, 1996; Tsai, 2002). In the context of MNCs, Haas (2004) showed that groups with great international experience are more likely to integrate knowledge from other parts of the organization than those that have not. Similarly, Gregersen and Black (1992) found that, not only is international experience important for integration, but when it is coupled with experience in corporate headquarters affiliates are more likely to maintain allegiance to the overall goals of the firm.

These international and corporate skills and knowledge are often gained through transfers and rotational assignments that enable the HR function to develop a more complex and global orientation. This provides them with the ability to manage the integration process more systematically (Kedia & Bhagat, 1988). Such forms of human capital can also correct any tendency of HR subunits to assume that the situation in the host country is unique, thus avoiding the 'not-invented-here' syndrome.

The upshot of this discussion is that a firm's integration capability likely depends on a combination of human, social and organizational capital. Social and organizational capitals are alternative – and potentially complementary – resources for knowledge and practice sharing. Human capital, in turn, is important for absorbing or acquiring that knowledge. As firms develop the capability to integrate existing practices they can achieve economies of scale and scope through HRM. And when these integrative mechanisms preserve resource heterogeneity at a local level, it may lead to a more rapid response to a global environment and greater potential for competitive advantage.

Knowledge creation capability

In the context of organizational learning and the KBV, it is important to distinguish knowledge integration capability from knowledge creation capability. Just because a firm is able to integrate practices across affiliates, this does not mean that it will be able to create new practices as well (see Table 22.2). Creation capabilities allow the MNC to develop new practices that lead to resource heterogeneity in the first place. While few HRM researchers have mentioned the importance of integration mechanisms, fewer still have discussed the importance of creation mechanisms that renew a firm's stock of HR practices. This is despite the fact that, as firms continually integrate practices, it is imperative that new practices are created and developed that allow for innovation and continuous improvement in a changing environment. Therefore, in global environments characterized by rapid change and increasing competition, static concepts of heterogeneity may no longer be sufficient to explain (and sustain) a competitive advantage.

A continuing source of debate in strategy is whether any static view of resources can really explain a competitive advantage that is sustainable over time (Lippman & Rumelt, 1982). For example, Grant (1996) argues that idiosyncratic advantages naturally erode over time. This debate is especially relevant in the global environment where what might create a competitive advantage at one point or in one location, may not at another point or location. Hence it is vital that MNCs develop the capability to create and renew HR practices in order to maintain a competitive advantage.

Table 22.2 Capabilities: creative and integrative

Focus	Market assumption	Value proposition	Sources
Integrative capabilities	*Stable market:* Resources must be combined and integrated to maintain an advantage	Combining resources in ways that others cannot copy creates benefits arising from scarcity	Taylor, Beechler & Napier, 1996; McWilliams, Van Fleet & Wright, 2001
Creative capabilities	*Dynamic market:* Resources must be reconfigured and created to maintain an advantage	Developing new resources that competitors do not yet have creates benefits arising from innovation	Chadwick & Cappelli, 1999; Snell, Youndt and Wright, 1996

Ghoshal & Bartlett (1988) stated that MNCs 'create' new products, practices or systems locally, using specific mechanisms to respond to local circumstances. Creating local HR practices lies at the heart of an MNC's capability to be responsive to the unique and changing opportunities of different environments. Below we discuss how human capital, social capital and organizational capital might influence the knowledge creation capability of new HR practices. (See Figure 22. 1 for an overview of mechanisms that influence knowledge integration and creation capabilities.)

Human capital   The knowledge and experience, that is, human capital, of the people within the HR function is a key factor in new HR practice creation, whether of new practice ideas or of improvements in the practices (Lepak & Snell, 1999). For example, HR functions possessing large amounts of local knowledge and experience should be able to create practices effectively on their own in response to the various, changing environments. This localized experience helps them to understand the needs of local clients and suppliers, which allows them to develop practices that are unique to each region or country and, hence, heterogeneous across the firm.

International experiences are also important for creating new HR practices. For example, because international experience is often highly valued in MNCs (for example, Mendenhall & Stahl, 2000), people with international skills and knowledge are more likely to be seen by others as being confident and willing to share divergent opinions and advocate for their own position (Stasser, Stewart & Wittenbaum, 1995). Moreover Gregersen and Black (1992) showed that people with strong experience in many international settings and limited experience in corporate headquarters are more likely to

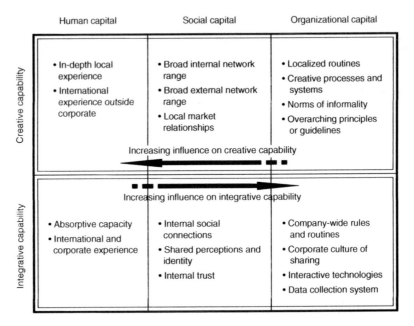

Figure 22.1   Capabilities: Human, social and organizational capital

make changes based on local demands rather than on pressures from central parts of the firm. This is most likely due to the people's array of international experiences that have detached them from an allegiance with the company as a whole.

Social capital   Specific aspects of social capital have been argued to play a role in knowledge creation. For example, while Hansen (2002) argued that social networks provide an important conduit for the sharing of knowledge, he also argued that such networks play a role in knowledge creation because they inform network members about the existence, location and significance of new knowledge. Burt (1982) found that networks comprising a broader range of contacts will have a more heterogeneous base of information and knowledge to draw from. While such wide networks may not always facilitate a deep flow of knowledge, they offer different reference points for HR members to make comparisons and explore new ideas.

   A firm's ability to find new opportunities is likely to be a function of multiple local contacts. HR affiliates often have critical links with local vendors and, perhaps, competing HR groups that allow them to pursue local opportunities (Bartlett & Ghoshal, 1989; Hedlund, 1986). Birkinshaw (1997) refers to these as relationships within the 'local market'. Within the local market an affiliate is likely to be embedded in different types of relationships (Ghoshal & Bartlett, 1990; Ghoshal & Nohria, 1989). McEvily and Zaheer (1999) argue that, because each part of the MNC maintains different local patterns of network linkages, they are exposed to new knowledge, ideas and opportunities.

Organizational capital   In many cases, organizational capital may actually hinder knowledge creation capability. The formalized processes, systems, structures and so on have a tendency to reinforce existing routines and work against variation and change that engender creativity. However, in some instances, organizational capital may facilitate flexibility in the course of actions that allow a firm to attend to environmental cues. This is especially true when employees are encouraged to take action that supersedes company-wide, standardized routines in favour of localized response that allows knowledge assimilation from the local environment (Daft & Weick, 1984). Grant (1996) argued that such creative routines and processes offer an efficient framework for people to create new, situation-specific practices by utilizing local perspectives in developing practices for the firm.

Though potentially problematic for the integrative capability, localized routines and creative processes help affiliates relate better to local vendors, clients and competitors by providing a set of expectations and processes that encourage HR groups to turn to the surrounding environment. For example, an HR affiliate may have developed a simple manual or informal norm of what to do when developing a new practice. Such a routine is likely to leave many gaps in exact steps to follow, but provide an overview or value to help the HR group be innovative. This simple routine allows the local HR group to assimilate knowledge more quickly from its employees and develop practices to meet their needs.

In summary, these aspects of human capital, social capital and organizational capital help us identify how the knowledge integration and creation capabilities might occur within an MNC. Some of these forms of capital are more useful, depending upon the capability it is supporting, and, ironically, some of these mechanisms that influence integration might actually hinder knowledge creation and vice versa. For example, firms heavy in local knowledge and experiences and weak in international experiences might have a negative effect on a firm's ability to integrate practices across the various parts of the firm. Such strong human capital is likely to promote the 'not-invented-here' syndrome through the affiliate's strong belief and experience base dealing exclusively with the local environment. Similarly, rigid forms of organizational capital, in terms of standardized routines and shared electronic databases, might deter the various parts of HR to develop and create practices on their own. This could largely stem from the fact that so much structure and support for integration is in place that HR groups fail to find time to bring about new practices or adapt existing practices to the local environment.

Implications for research and theory

The unique complexities and challenges faced by today's global firms present different implications for the RBV and its application to strategic IHRM. For example, because a large amount of the international management literature focuses on variances in cultural, geographical and institutional pressures, the implications for applying the RBV become more complex. As MNCs struggle to create and integrate their practices across borders, they are faced with unique challenges that push either for global efficiency or for local responsiveness. These challenges open the discussion for ways to actually manage both the creation and the integration of knowledge on a global scale.

This means that the questions typically asked by strategic IHRM scholars (for example, about HR practices and performance) should be augmented with questions on how HR practices are created and integrated in ways that lead toward resource heterogeneity and immobility. To create a sustainable competitive advantage, firms must not only be able to respond to their local environments or standardize their practices across the firm. They must be able to balance a tension of practice heterogeneity through local practice creation and immobility of those practices through their integration across the firm.

One theoretical implication of this discussion calls for a greater understanding of the rents found through the creation and integration of HR practices. As Chadwick and Dabu (2004) explain, a marriage of rent concepts with theories of the firm (that is, RBV) is essential in describing the firm's competitive advantages and particularly in understanding how actors within firms can take conscious steps toward a sustainable competitive advantage. The current strategic IHRM literature alludes strongly to the importance of integration and being able to organize heterogeneous resources in a way that is difficult for competitors to imitate. The assumption here is that heterogeneity and immobility of resources create greater performance or rents arising from scarcity: Ricardian rents (cf. Carpenter, Sanders & Gregersen, 2001). In essence, Ricardian rents can be rooted in the cross-border integration of various HR practices. The integration of such practices ensures not only that some of them will be unique to the firm, but that they will be difficult for others to imitate, making them scarce in the market.

The advantages that come from constant creation of HR practices operates under a different principle than traditional resources leading to Ricardian rents. Rather than rents arising from scarcity, the creation capability perspective emphasizes rents arising from market discontinuities: Schumpeterian rents (cf., Carpenter *et al.*, 2001). Schumpeterian rents derive from a firm's ability to exploit or leverage resources to address changing environments (Teece *et al.*, 1997; Amit & Schoemaker, 1993). Based on Schumpeterian rents, a focus on the continuous creation of resources can enable a firm to achieve competitive advantage on a sustainable basis by developing new practices that lead to practising heterogeneity across a complex and ambiguous global network. Hence, as mentioned by Lado and Wilson (1994), and Teece *et al.* (1997), turning to these dynamic capabilities as an extended approach to the RBV offers a closer understanding of the actual *sources* of competitive advantage in a changing global environment.

While we discuss the main mechanisms driving knowledge creation and integration (Grant, 1996), aspects of integration tend to focus on a broad array of learning processes, including knowledge sharing, transfer, codification, adoption and/or institutionalization. Further research should look at the way different aspects of the integration process might be influenced by specific human, social and organizational capital mechanisms. For example, Hansen and Haas (2001) showed that many firms have little difficulty in sharing knowledge across various units of the firm, but that the actual application or institutionalization of this knowledge is a completely different matter. While other scholars such as Kogut and Zander (1992) and Schulz (2001) have theoretically separated integration to include transfer and integration (or combination), very little practical research has been done on what factors might influence the transfer and what factors might influence the integration of knowledge. Clearly there must be differences since research such as Hansen and Haas (2001) notice the disparity between knowledge that is shared and knowledge that is actually applied.

Also, while the ideas presented in this chapter are rooted in theory, empirical research is needed to determine the impact of human, social and organizational capital on knowledge creation and integration capabilities. While theory suggests that aspects of all three of these factors will influence both capabilities, it is most probable that aspects of human capital will more strongly influence the creative capability. This is largely due to the fact that people and their knowledge and skills are what allows the different HR affiliates the ability to develop local practices on their own, without interference or supervision from regional or corporate headquarters. Similarly social and organizational capital should have their strongest influences on the integrative capability. This is due, in part, to the conduits and repositories created from aspects of social capital and organizational capital, respectively. In fact, as we mentioned earlier, some aspects of organizational capital might have a negative effect on the firm's ability to create new practices (knowledge), while some aspects of human capital may have a negative effect on the firm's ability to integrate those practices across affiliates.

Conclusion

The purpose of this chapter has been to summarize the literature on RBV and IHRM in multinational firms by addressing the ways in which resource heterogeneity and immobility provide potential advantages to MNCs. However we have also attempted to extend the RBV in this context by addressing some of the primary challenges to be met and capabilities needed to integrate resources across business units within the MNC.

The solution frequently used by firms has been to standardize HR practices and policies at a global level, but this solves the integration problem while destroying the advantages of local variety. The challenge as we see it is identifying how firms can preserve variety (and local customization) while simultaneously establishing a foundation for integration and efficiency.

The ability of HR managers to balance this tension lies in the development of capabilities to create and integrate practices across the global HR function. We extended traditional views of RBV to include aspects of practice integration and creation. Such capabilities allow firms constantly to renew their HR practices in a way that allows them to respond to multiple external pressures while being coordinated and integrated to ensure that these practices drive the firm's sustainable competitive advantage.

References

Amit, R. & P.J.H. Schoemaker. 1993. Strategic assets and organizational rent. *Strategic Management Journal*, **14**: 33–46.

Bae, J. & J.J. Lawler. 2000. Organizational and HRM strategies in Korea: impact on firm performance in an emerging economy. *Academy of Management Journal*, **43**: 502–17.

Barney, J.B. 1991. Firm resources and sustained competitive advantage. *Journal of Management*, **17**: 99–120.

Bartlett C. A. & S. Ghoshal. 1989. *Managing across borders: the transnational solution*. Boston, MA: Hutchinson Business Books.

Birkinshaw, J. 1997. Entrepreneurship in multinational corporations: the characteristics of subsidiary initiatives. *Strategic Management Journal*, **18**: 207–29.

Boxall, P. 1996. The strategic HRM debate and the resource-based view of the firm. *Human Resource Management Journal*, **6**: 59–75.

Brewster, C. 1999. Different paradigms in strategic HRM: questions raised by comparative research. In P. Wright, L. Dyer, J. Boudreau and G.Milkovich (eds). *Research in personnel and HRM*. Greenwich, CT: JAI Press, pp. 213–38.

Burt, R.S. 1982. *Toward a structural theory of action*. New York: Academic Press.

Carpenter, M., W. G. Sanders & H.B. Gregersen. 2001. Bundling human capital with organizational context: the impact of international assignment experience on multinational firm performance and CEO pay. *Academy of Management Journal*, **44**: 493–511.

Chadwick, C. & P. Cappelli. 1999. Alternatives to generic strategy typologies in strategic human resource management. In L.D. Dyer, P.M. Wright, J.W. Boudreau & G.T. Milkovich (eds), *Strategic human resource management in the twenty-first century*. Stamford, CT: JAI Press.

Chadwick, C. & A. Dabu. 2004. Rent theories, human assets, human resource management, and competitive advantage. working paper.

Daft, R.L. & K.E. Weick. 1984. Toward a model of organizations as interpretation systems. *Academy of Management Review*, **9**: 284–95.

Doz, Y. & C.K. Prahalad. 1986. Controlled variety: a challenge for human resource management in the MNC. *Human Resource Management*, **25**: 55–72.

Evans, P., V. Pucik & J.-L. Barsoux. 2002. *The global challenge: frameworks for international human resource management*. New York: McGraw-Hill Irwin.

Fey, C.F. & I. Björkman. 2001. The effect of human resource management practices on MNC subsidiary performance in Russia. *Journal of International Business Studies*, **32**: 59–75.

Ghoshal, S. & C.A. Bartlett. 1988. Creation, adoption, and diffusion of innovation by subsidiaries of multinational corporations. *Journal of International Business Studies*, **19**: 365–88.

Ghoshal, S. & C.A. Bartlett. 1990. The multinational corporation as an interorganizational network. *Academy of Management Review*, **15**: 603–25.

Ghoshal, S. & N. Nohria 1989. International differentiation within multinational corporations. *Strategic Management Journal*, **10**: 323–37.

Grant, R.M. 1996. Toward a knowledge-based theory of the firm. *Strategic Management Journal*, **17**(S2): 109–22.

Gregersen, H.B. & J.S. Black. 1992. Antecedents to commitment to a parent company and a foreign operation. *Academy of Management Journal*, **35**: 65–91.

Hansen, M.T. 2002. Knowledge networks: explaining effective knowledge sharing in multiunit companies. *Organization Science*, **13**: 290–302.

Hansen, M.T. & M.R. Haas. 2001. Competing for attention in knowledge markets: electronic document dissemination in a management consulting company. *Administrative Science Quarterly*, **46**: 1–28.

Hansen, M.T., N. Nitin & T. Tierney. 1999. What's your strategy for managing knowledge? *Harvard Business Review*, **77**: 106–17

Hedlund, G. 1986. The hypermodern MNC: a heterarchy? *Human Resource Management*, **25**: 9–35.

Kedia, B.L. & R.S. Bhagat. 1988. Cultural constraints on transfer of technology across nations: implications for research in international and comparative management. *Academy of Management Review*, **13**: 559–72.

Kogut, B. & U. Zander. 1992. Knowledge of the firm, combination capabilities, and the replication of technology. *Organization Science*, **7**: 502–18.

Kogut, B. & U. Zander. 1993. Knowledge of the firm and the evolutionary theory of the multinational corporation. *Journal of International Business Studies*, **24**: 625–45.

Kostova, T. & K. Roth. 2002. Adoption of an organizational practice by subsidiaries of multinational corporations: institutional and relational effects. *Academy of Management Journal*, **45**: 215–33.

Lado, A.A. & M.C. Wilson. 1994. Human resource systems and sustained competitive advantage: a competency-based perspective. *Academy of Management Review*, **19**: 699–727.

Lepak, D.P. & S.A. Snell. 1999. The human resource architecture: toward a theory of human capital allocation and development. *Academy of Management Review*, **24**: 31–48.

Lippman, S. & R. Rumelt. 1982. Uncertain imitability: an analysis of interfirm differences in efficiency under competition. *Bell Journal of Economics*, **13**: 418–38.

MacDuffie, J.P. 1995. Human resource bundles and manufacturing performance: organizational logic and flexible production systems in the world auto industry. *Industrial and Labor Relations Review*, **48**: 197–221.

March, J.G. 1991. Exploration and exploitation in organizational learning. *Organization Science*, **2**: 71–87.

McEvily, B. & A. Zaheer. 1999. Bridging ties: a source of firm heterogeneity in competitive capabilities. *Strategic Management Journal*, **20**: 1133–45.

McWilliams, A., D.D. Van Fleet. & P.M. Wright. 2001. Strategic management of human resources for global competitive advantage. *Journal of Business Strategies*, **18**: 1–23.

Mendenhall, M.E. & G. K. Stahl. 2000. Expatriate training and development: where do we go from here? *Human Resource Management*, **39**: 251–66.

Nahapiet, J. & S. Ghoshal. 1998. Social capital, intellectual capital, and the organizational advantage. *Academy of Management Review*, **23**: 242–66.

Ricks, D. 1993. *Blunders in international business*. Cambridge: Blackwell Business.

Schuler, R.S., P.J. Dowling & H. De Cieri. 1993. An integrative framework of strategic international human resource management. *Journal of Management*, **19**: 419–60.

Schulz, M. 2001. The uncertain relevance of newness: organizational learning and knowledge flows. *Academy of Management Journal*, **44**: 661–81.

Snell, S.A., D. Stueber & D.P. Lepak. 2002. Virtual HR departments: getting out of the middle. In R.L. Heneman & D.B. Greenberger (eds), *Human resource management in virtual organizations*. Greenwich, CT: Information Age Publishing.

Snell, S.A., M.A. Youndt & P.M. Wright. 1996. Establishing a framework for research in strategic human resource management: merging resource theory and organizational learning. *Research in Personnel and Human Resource Management*, **14**: 61–90.

Sparrow, P., R.S. Schuler & S.E. Jackson, 1994. Convergence or divergence: human resource practices and policies for competitive advantage worldwide. *International Journal of Human Resource Management*, **5**: 267–99.

Stasser, G., D.D. Stewart & G.M. Wittenbaum. 1995. Export roles and information exchange during discussion: the importance of knowing who knows what. *Journal of Experimental Social Psychology*, **31**: 244–65.

Szulanski, G. 1995. Unpacking stickiness: an empirical investigation of the barriers to transfer best practices inside the firm. *Academy of Management Journal*, best paper proceedings: 437–42.

Szulanski, G. 1996. Exploring internal stickiness: impediments to the transfer of best practice within the firm. *Strategic Management Journal*, **17**: 27–44.

Taylor, S., S. Beechler & N. Napier. 1996. Toward an integrative model of strategic international human resource management. *Academy of Management Review*, **21**: 959–85.

Teece, D. 1977. Time–cost tradeoffs: elasticity estimates and determinants for international technology transfer projects. *Management Science*, **23**: 830–37.

Teece, D.J., G. Pisano & A. Shuen. 1997. Dynamic capabilities and strategic management. *Strategic Management Journal*, **18**: 509–34.

Tsai, W. 2002. Social structure of cooperation within a multiunit organization: coordination, competition, and intraorganizational knowledge sharing. *Organization Science*, **13**: 179–92.

Wernerfelt, B. 1984. A resource-based view of the firm. *Strategic Management Journal*, **5**: 171–80.

Wright, P.M. & S.A. Snell. 1998. Toward a unifying framework for exploring fit and flexibility in strategic human resource management. *Academy of Management Review*, **22**(4): 756–72.

Wright, P.M., B.B. Dunford & S. A. Snell. 2001. Human resources and the resource based view of the firm. *Journal of Management*, **27**: 701–21.

Youndt, M.A., M. Subramaniam & S.A. Snell. 2004. Intellectual capital profiles: an examination of investments and returns. *Journal of Management Studies*, **41**: 335–61.

23 International human resource management and economic theories of the firm
Marion Festing

International human resource management (IHRM) is a discipline characterized by a variety of perspectives. Three main research areas will be described in the first section of the chapter: human resource management (HRM) in multinational enterprises (MNEs), cross-cultural HRM and comparative international HRM (Dowling & Welch, 2004).

The three perspectives are characterized by different paradigms: the universalist and the contextual paradigm. The universalist paradigm suggests that rules derived from theoretical approaches can be applied independently of contextual considerations in order to improve HRM. In contrast, the contextual paradigm suggests that there are different views on HRM and implies that it is more important to explain differences than to focus on firm performance (Brewster, 1999).

Economic theory largely reflects the basic assumptions of the universalist paradigm. It is characterized by cost/benefit arguments and may include a variety of theoretical perspectives. Consistent with other chapters in this volume, the focus of this chapter is on new institutional economics, that is, transaction cost theory, agency theory and property rights. Proponents implicitly assume that the reasoning of the new institutional economic perspectives is valid in all contexts and that local uniqueness (for example, a particular legal or cultural environment) either can be included in the respective frameworks or is inconsequential. Economic approaches may include contextual factors but, nevertheless, the universalist perspective dominates. The basic reasoning of the new institutional economic approaches is outlined in the second section of the chapter.

Insights from the three perspectives on IHRM and from economic theories provide the basis for the third section. Applications of economic theory to IHRM are outlined, and the limitations and potential of these perspectives for IHRM are discussed. Since economic explanations do not represent a core focus within IHRM research, only a limited number of papers can be found dealing with economic explanations of IHRM issues. The main theoretical focus of existing papers appears to be on transaction cost theory and agency theory. The chapter concludes with a summary of the economic arguments in IHRM studies and discussion on potential future research directions for IHRM.

Perspectives on international HRM

Human resource management in the multinational firm focuses to a large extent on the management of expatriates, their recruitment and selection, training and development, and compensation. This emphasis is complemented by strategic approaches to HRM in MNEs (for example, the relationship between HRM activities in headquarters and subsidiaries) (Dowling & Welch, 2004). A common feature of these approaches is that they look at issues that may not exist in a domestic context, but have emerged from a firm's operations in different cultural or national contexts, and/or with people from different countries (Morgan, 1986).

The cross-cultural perspective of IHRM analyses the effect of culture on HRM practices. The concept of culture is often operationalized by using the cultural dimensions identified by Hofstede (1980), sometimes also by other prominent intercultural researchers such as Hall and Hall (1990) or Trompenaars and Hampden-Turner (1997). Important fields of research include intercultural aspects in recruitment and selection (Kühlmann, 2004), in training (Black & Mendenhall, 1989) and compensation issues (Schuler & Rogovsky, 1998).

The comparative approach to IHRM describes and compares HRM practices in different countries. It adds to our understanding of local HRM practices and more and more often interprets the results using country-specific explanations such as neoinstitutionalist approaches. Examples of this approach include Gooderham and Nordhaug (1997) or Wächter *et al.* (2003).

An economic theory of the firm

The basis for the development of the neoclassical perspective of microeconomic analysis has been the behavioural assumption of 'bounded rationality' (Simon, 1957). In a world characterized by perfect information the rules developed in the context of the neoclassical economic analysis of institutions would be unnecessary (Hegmann, 2004). However, limited information combined with limited information processing capacity have led to the emergence of new institutional economics (Williamson, 1985). These theoretical approaches explain and analyse institutions, which in turn make exchanges more efficient. The main objective of new institutional economics is to explain the structure, behavioural consequences, efficiency and changes in economic institutions. Key questions include the following:

- What are the most cost-effective and efficient institutions when considering a certain kind of coordination problem?

● What effect do coordination problems, cost and efficiency considerations have on institutional change (Ebers & Gotsch, 1995)?

The basic ideas of economic analysis of institutions have been summarized in Figure 23.1. In HRM, the working contract is in the centre of consideration (Jones & Wright, 1992). This contract is the legal basis of any exchanges between employers and employees, and its primacy suggests costs and efficiency of employment relations are dependent on such contracts. The different approaches within new institutional economics (such as transaction cost theory, agency theory or property rights theory) place other concepts at the centre of consideration (for a more detailed overview, see Furubotn & Richter, 2000).

Transaction costs include costs occurring within the processes of specifying, negotiating and enforcing contracts. According to Williamson (1985) it is possible to analyse any contractual problem of economic organization with transaction cost theory. The approach seeks to identify the environmental factors that, together with a set of related human factors, explain how companies can organize transactions to reduce the costs associated with these transactions. The most important human factors are bounded rationality and opportunism: 'Bounded rationality suggests that due to limited information and constraints on information processing, decision

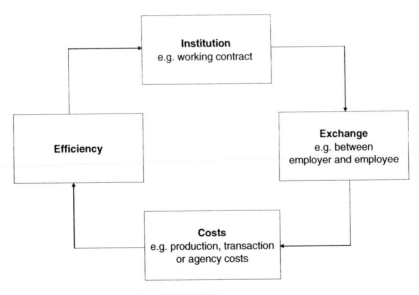

Source: Based on Ebers & Gotsch (1995: 186).

Figure 23.1 Basic concept of the economic analysis of institutions

makers are not always capable of making decisions that maximize utility. Individuals are not always forthcoming with information, and absent effective monitoring mechanisms, may opportunistically take advantage of parties to exchange' (Grossman & Schoenfeldt, 2001: 60–61). The most important environmental factors are asset specificity and uncertainty. High asset specificity reflects the fact that some transactions are character-ized by a high focus on company needs which can only be fulfilled through unique, company-specific assets. Uncertainty may include either outcome or behavioural uncertainty (Williamson, 1985). Transaction cost theory acknowledges that all exchanges involve costs and suggests that various organizational solutions vary in their transaction costs, some being more expensive than others.

The application of transaction cost theory to HRM issues starts with the assumption that employees exchange performance for remuneration (Jones & Wright, 1992). These exchange relationships differ according to firm and industry-specific environmental factors: the nature of work which results from these environmental factors can be more or less company-specific and more or less observable. The efficiency of the exchange between employer and employee will differ when using different governance struc-tures. Often different types of internal labour markets are discussed (Williamson, 1984). Respective HRM strategies are an important part of governance structures in labour market transactions: 'The role of HRM practices is to allow for the measurement of unique contributions and to provide adequate rewards for individual employee performance' (Wright & McMahan, 1992: 309). For a multinational enterprise aiming at an efficient work organization this means that IHRM policies and practices should match the requirements of the work (for a more detailed description of the theory, see Williamson, 1984; Grossman & Schoenfeldt, 2001).

Agency theory places the relationship between principals and agents in the centre of the contractual analysis (Pratt & Zeckhauser, 1985). The main agency problems may occur (a) because goals of principals and agents may not be congruent and (b) because of the problem of appropriately moni-toring or verifying the behaviour of the agent. If both principals and agents are utility maximizers, agents may pursue goals that do not necessarily cor-respond to the goals of the principals. The literature essentially suggests three mechanisms for solving the 'agency problem'. Monitoring systems represent one alternative to align the principal's and agent's goals. They are associated with relatively low agency costs when behaviour is directly observable. However, in situations characterized by information asymmetry (that is, when agents have more specialized knowledge than principals) monitoring costs may increase. A second mechanism is the design of an incentive system which encourages the agent to share the principal's goal.

A third approach for reducing goal differences relates to intensive socialization processes, aimed at creating a clan organization (for more detailed description, see Eisenhardt, 1989; Roth & O'Donnel, 1996; Bender, 2004).

Property rights theory has only rarely been applied to IHRM and will not be discussed in detail in this chapter. For an outline of the theory, see Alchian (1961); for an exemplary application to different types of codetermination, readers are referred to Furubotn (1988).

Economic theory and international HRM

While economic explanations of international HRM are limited, this is not true for HRM activities on a national level. An impressive body of knowledge has been created representing an important field in HRM research (Lazear, 1999). Although the economic perspectives that follow do not reflect the emphasis on new institutional economics found elsewhere in this chapter, these examples provide an important overview. Recruiting situations are interpreted as situations characterized by information asymmetries where signalling plays an important role. When training issues are discussed the economic school mainly looks at investments in human capital. Career issues are discussed in the context of tournament theory. Understanding the conditions where incentives are the most intense and have the comparably highest effects is the focus of much compensation research. Studies on teamwork address the potential for free riding. Outsourcing of HR activities is seen as a make-or-buy decision (for an overview, see Backes-Gellner, Lazear & Wolf, 2001). A discussion of IHRM research based on transaction cost and agency theory will now follow.

Economic theory and HRM in MNEs

Using transaction cost theory, Festing (1997) has developed a model explaining strategic IHRM in multinational firms in the context of corporate strategy. This model follows arguments outlined by Wright and McMahan, when they assert: 'It seems intuitive that a firm's strategy can have an effect on the nature of work. To the extent that the nature of work changes . . . the types of HRM systems necessary to monitor inputs, behaviors and outputs also change' (Wright & McMahan, 1992: 310). Consequently Festing suggests that the extent to which work is either specific or non-specific, and the degree to which outcomes can be either easy or difficult to measure, are dependent on the corporate strategy. High human capital specificity leads to mutual dependence of both the employee and the company (Williamson, 1985).

Whereas general qualifications increase the employability of the individual by other employers, this usually is not the case for firm-specific human capital. Firms which lose their firm-specific human capital cannot replace those employees with candidates from the external labour market; rather these firms are forced to carry out reinvestment in order to develop the unique equipment, process, informal team and/or communication capabilities required by strategy (Williamson, Wachter & Harris, 1975). The higher the degree of a transaction's specificity, the greater the loss in value arising when the necessary human and tangible assets are not employed pursuing company goals. Hence a firm's specifically qualified employee will, other things being equal, be interested in permanent employment. The same is true of the company (Williamson, 1984). Festing (1997) has identified several strategic situations related to human asset specificity in the context of MNEs, and outlined their implications and requirements for different IHRM strategies as reflected in organizational issues of labour market transactions. Other work in the area of IHRM based on transaction cost theory includes international staffing (Erdener & Torbiörn, 1999) or expatriate management in international joint ventures (Kabst, 2004).

In addition to transaction cost approaches, agency theory has been applied to conceptualize IHRM practices in MNEs. The main focus here is on compensation issues. Roth and O'Donnel (1996) show in their study on compensation strategies in foreign subsidiaries of MNCs that agency problems (particularly information asymmetries due to the cultural distance between the country of origin and the host country and the extent of commitment of the subsidiary's management to the parent company) influence the choice of pay practices (Roth & O'Donnel, 1996). Björkman and Furu (2000) add to this line of theorizing by including the subsidiary role as well as the institutional environment in their study of top management compensation strategies in MNEs. They have found empirical evidence that the strategic role of a subsidiary contributes to pay practices. For example, they showed that managers of sales subsidiaries had a higher percentage of variable pay. This was attributed to the fact that, for these subsidiaries, the task was highly programmable and that outcomes were easy to measure. However the effect of the cultural distance between the country of origin of the MNE and the host country could not be confirmed. Instead the influence of the institutional environment seemed to be quite important within the sample.

An example of the agency perspective on international assignments is found in the work of Yan, Zhu and Hall (2002). In the present chapter, issues of possible opportunism, on the side either of the agent or of the principal, and the alignment of organizational and individual goals concerning international assignments are presented in the context of international careers. Agency theoretical arguments are here combined with the idea of the psychological contract.

Table 23.1   *Candidate pool preferences based on agency theory predictions regarding parent–subsidiary relationship*

	Goal congruency	
	Low	High
Asymmetry of knowledge (low)	Third-country nationals	Local nationals
Asymmetry of knowledge (high)	Expatriates	Inpatriates

Source: Harvey, Speier & Novicevic (2001: 903).

Harvey, Speier and Novicevic (2001) combine agency theory with expectancy when explaining staffing policies in MNEs. They identify asymmetries in the knowledge about effort–outcome relationships and goal congruence about effort–outcome standards as the two sources of agency problems. Information asymmetry results from differing information levels between the headquarters and the subsidiary, due either to increased autonomy or to a significant cultural distance, e.g. regarding performance goals. Goal congruence relates to the extent to which the subsidiary's top management is committed to the top management goals of the MNE (Harvey, Speier & Novicevic, 2001). Using these two dimensions the authors predict preferences for candidate pools and associated selection choices (Table 23.1).

This section has outlined the benefits of analysing HRM problems in MNEs based on an economic perspective. Transaction cost and agency theory represent comprehensive explanatory concepts providing a differentiated argumentation background for a variety of IHRM decisions. These economic frameworks provide insights and give importance to variables that might have been neglected in another context. Yet it must be admitted that the quantification of transactions and agency costs, and attendant measures of administrative efficiency, still remain problematic.

Economic theory and intercultural HRM
The effect of cultural differences on HRM has yet to become the centre of economic analysis (Wolff & Pooria, 2004; Casson, 1993). How cultural differences affect management practices is not yet understood in terms of economic theories.

There is no general definition of the term 'culture'. Hofstede (1980: 25) defines it as the 'collective programming of the mind . . . '. However, when using economic theory, culture is discussed from a utility perspective and it is suggested to define the term 'in a way that is compatible with the view that individuals optimize, and that their behaviour sustains an economic equilibrium . . . In economic terms, culture may be defined as collective subjectivity' (Casson, 1993: 419–20). Subjectivity of values means that individual preferences are not directly measurable, but rather are expressed through observable behaviour. 'The second use of subjectivity is in the context of probabilities. In the absence of information about relative frequencies, an individual may attach a purely personal probability to an event. This probability cannot be directly measured, but when an individual maximizes expected utility, changes in his behaviour may be attributed to the modification of his attributed probability' (ibid.: 420).

Economic theories focus on cultural norms and regulations, including legal norms, common right, codes of conduct, culture-specific attitudes, signals and cultural and social capital. The main focus is on the way the different aspects influence social relationships and economic performance of a society (Hegmann, 2004; Casson, 1993). An example of this approach can be found in the study by Knack and Keefer (1997). The analysis of the cultural phenomenon in the context of economic theories requires the development of a thorough understanding of culture including the corresponding system of rules, as far as this is possible with limited information-processing capacities. These rules can then be explained by microeconomic perspectives.

A popular approach is to interpret culture as an informal aspect of institutional regulations (for example, North, 1990). Following this idea, Wolff and Pooria (2004) differentiate three levels of regulations. It is proposed that the formal as well as the informal institutional context have influences on the governance structures. These governance structures are established to coordinate individual action within firms, such as the working contract. Furthermore the institutional context is supposed to influence the individual preferences of actors in the contract, including their respective utility functions. Wolff and Pooria (2004) summarize the influence of the implicit context on behaviour as cultural socialization (Figure 23.2).

Wolff and Pooria suggest that intercultural problems in international management arise from differing socialization of the various actors. At the centre of economic reasoning is the problem of efficient resource allocation. If the relevant actors are socialized by cultures in different ways, the meaning of appropriate (that is, efficient) resource allocation may differ between individuals. Hence assumptions about acceptable and effective coordination and motivation measures may differ as well. An employee's lack of understanding of the coordination and motivation measures established by a manager from a different culture may result in an inefficient resource allocation. Allocation errors result from the so-called 'cultural gap' between differently socialized actors in a common contract. This cultural gap is interpreted as an information asymmetry, potentially leading to

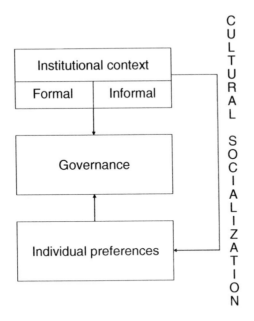

Source: Based on Wolff & Pooria (2004: 452).

Figure 23.2 Levels of regulation

problems with (a) misunderstanding, potentially involving inefficient resource allocation, and (b) the increasing risk of opportunistic behaviour which may result from a difference in culture-specific information.

Grossman and Schoenfeldt (2001) suggest that cultural differences may involve ethical breaches, which increase the perception of opportunism. Opportunism results in an increase in organizational transaction costs, and is associated with lower performance. The suggestion is that differing degrees of 'ethical distance', 'defined as differences in the way the cultures assess the ethical ramifications of a decision' (ibid.: 63) should be managed by different IHRM strategies.

In summary, economic theory offers a classification of intercultural problems but it does not specify the content of culture. The focus is not on value systems but rather on property rights. Jones argues that the design of property rights 'constitutes the culture and that the norms and values that govern organizational action emerge from the way in which property rights are distributed, enforced, and guaranteed' (Jones, 1983: 455). In explanations based on transaction costs theory the variable 'transaction atmosphere' would also include cultural, religious and social norms and values. Different types of 'transaction atmospheres' may influence the level of transactions costs associated with certain coordination and motivation measures (Picot, Dietl & Franck, 2002). Thus a cultural gap would lead to an increase in transaction costs.

As culture is not an objective concept, but socially constructed reality acquired by individuals through socialization processes, there are limits to the economic analysis of culture. Thus even decontextualization becomes difficult (Hegmann, 2004). Furthermore culture not only consists of explicit knowledge but also comprises implicit knowledge, which by definition is difficult to analyse (Polanyi, 1967). Consequently it is difficult for members of a culture always to consider the implicit aspects of their culture in economic action. Here a risk of misinterpretation is emerging (Hegmann, 2004). There seems to be consensus about the fact that 'a comprehensive economic theory of culture has not been worked out, but existing analysis makes it possible to identify with some accuracy the key characteristics of a culture that determines the economic performance of a group' (Casson, 1993: 423).

Economic theory and comparative IHRM
Explanations of country-specific differences in IHRM are dominated by neoinstitutionalism perspectives such as Whitley (1992, 1999) or Powell and DiMaggio (1991) or the country-of-origin effect (Ferner, 1997). These approaches follow a context-oriented paradigm which interprets differences in HR practices in the context of the institutional environment perceived as typical of a certain country or region.

Economic theories often focus on the firm as the unit of analysis, and do not assume a deterministic relationship between firm environment and HR activities. Instead they suggest that firms decide about their HRM practices with respect to major strategic decisions for reasons of efficiency. An empirical study about qualification and competitive strategies in Germany and Great Britain by Backes-Gellner (1996) shows that no systematic country-specific variations can be found in the qualification level of the technical staff in both countries. Controlling for production/service strategies as well as marketing strategies in different industries, the author finds these two strategies the most important determinants of the level of qualification for firms. This finding challenges the cultural as well as the neoinstitutionalism perspectives. However Backes-Gellner shows that there are differences in the ways qualifications are acquired. The dual system in Germany is contrasted with the more training-oriented approaches in the UK and France. In summary, her conclusion is that 'institutions do matter' when the goal is to explain how qualification requirements are developed in different countries. However, when it comes to the explanation for firm-specific behaviour with respect to the qualification strategy and the resulting level of qualification in a firm, the competitive strategy and especially the production and marketing decisions are more important predictors. In this context 'institutions don't matter' (ibid.: 303).

The work by Backes-Gellner points out the weaknesses of the dominating cultural and institutional explanations in international comparative HRM as central assumptions and complements these approaches with a firm-level explanation applying new institutional economics. In summary, she states that firm-specific aspects (related to strategic choices) matter much more in explaining firm behaviour than the larger institutional environment. This result is consistent with the arguments posited by Lawler *et al.* (1995) that economic analysis mainly focuses on market-related factors when explaining HRM practices. However, in their comparative study on HRM in India and Thailand, Lawler *et al.* (1995) have found evidence that long-term differences in this area are mainly related to non-market factors. This may be seen as an indicator that it is difficult to capture all relevant variables in IHRM with an economic approach. In other papers we have seen that institutionalist perspectives have the potential to increase our understanding of IHRM decision processes (see, for example, the arguments outlined in Roth & O'Donnel, 1996; Björkman & Furu, 2000). This potential is yet to be fully realized.

Conclusion

Economic theory adds to our understanding in all three research areas of IHRM. It explicitly links the perspectives of the two main actors, employee and organization, by taking a contractual perspective, assuming an exchange relationship and giving hints for efficient governance structures. The main focus is on cost and efficiency aspects, which are often neglected when the international dimension of HRM is discussed. Furthermore, based on this theoretical perspective, investments in firm-specific human capital and their amortizations have proved to be of major importance when taking IHRM decisions and designing appropriate strategies.

In economic explanations cross-border issues such as the cultural or institutional context of IHRM are thought to be included in the regulatory environment influencing the contracts between employer and employee. It is argued that there is no need for a complementary theoretical perspective (Backes-Gellner, 1996). The economic perspective on IHRM may have limits. As pointed out in the context of cross-cultural IHRM, it is only possible to integrate cultural assumptions in the economic framework as long as these assumptions are explicit, or at least as long as their influence on behaviour can be identified. Furthermore, when discussing international comparative HRM, it has become very clear that economic explanations depend on the research focus.

In summary, IHRM explanations may very well be rooted in economic theory, especially when the firm level is concerned. However the state of the art in economic IHRM research indicates that it may not be useful to pursue a purely universalist paradigm. With respect to global compensation, Bloom, Milkovich and Mitra (2003) have outlined that successful firms have considered company-specific as well as external variables. The research considered within this chapter indicates that economic theory cannot claim – no theory can claim – to provide a complete explanation of IHRM phenomena (Bender, 2004). In contrast, the integration of multiple theoretical perspectives has proved to explain pay practices better (Tremblay, Coté & Balkin, 2003). Which IHRM issues can be explained by economic theories and which theories can best complement arguments of economic theory? Further research needs to be focused on this central question. In the research considered within this chapter, the choice of the combined theories reflected the weaknesses of economic theory. The request for further elaboration of the behavioural assumptions and political processes or an explicit consideration of the institutional and cultural environment, especially when international HRM issues are to be explained, highlights this weakness. As this chapter has shown, we already find research where economic arguments are combined with motivation theories, resource dependence perspectives or cultural and institutional concepts (see, for example, Bender, 2004; Tremblay, Coté & Balkin, 2003; Grossman & Schoenfeldt, 2001; Roth & O'Donnel, 1996; Björkman & Furu, 2000).

To balance the potential for combining economic theory with other theories, we must reiterate that, as economic explanations of IHRM do not represent a major research field, there are many research issues that may gain new insights when analysed solely from an economic perspective. For example, the centralization/decentralization problem of IHRM activities could be analysed from an agency perspective. Furthermore cultural aspects within the principal–agent relationship would be an interesting topic. This list could be extended. In addition, the section about economic theory and IHRM referred to approaches which are not part of new institutional economics. These approaches (such as signalling perspectives or tournament theory) may also be applied in an IHRM context. Consequently the economic analysis of IHRM provides a wide and promising field for future research and may further expand our knowledge in the future.

References

Alchian, A.A. 1961. *Some economics of property rights.* Santa Monica, CA: Rand Corporation.

Backes-Gellner, U. 1996. *Betriebliche Bildungs- und Wettbewerbsstrategien im Deutsch-Britischen Vergleich.* Munich/Mering: Rainer Hampp Verlag.

Backes-Gellner, U., E.P. Lazear & B. Wolff. 2001. *Personalökonomik: Fortgeschrittene Anwendungen für das Management.* Stuttgart: Schäffer-Poeschel.

Bender, R. 2004. Why do companies use performance-related pay for their executive directors? *Corporate Governance*, **12**(4): 521–33.

Björkman, I. & P. Furu. 2000. Determinants of variable pay for top managers of foreign subsidiaries in Finland. *International Journal of Human Resource Management*, **11**(4): 698–713.

Black, J.S. & M. Mendenhall. 1989. A practical but theory-based framework for selecting cross-cultural training methods. *Human Resource Management*, **28**(4): 511–39.

Bloom, G., G.T. Milkovich & A. Mitra. 2003. International compensation: learning from how managers respond to variations in local host contexts. *International Journal of Human Resource Management*, **4**(8): 1350–67.

Brewster, C. 1999. Strategic human resource management: the value of different paradigms. *Management International Review*, Special issue, **39**(3): 45–64.

Casson, M. 1993. Cultural determinants of economic performance. *Journal of Comparative Economics*, **17**: 418–42.

Dowling, P.J. & D.E. Welch. 2004. *International human resource management. Managing people in a multinational context.* Fourth edition. Sydney: Thomson Learning.

Ebers, M. & W. Gotsch. 1995. Institutionenökonomische Theorien der Organisation. In A. Kieser (ed.), *Organisationstheorien*: 185–236. Second edition. Stuttgart: Kohlhammer.

Eisenhardt, K.M. 1989. Agency theory: an assessment and review. *Academy of Management Review*, **14**: 57–74.

Erdener, C. & I. Torbiörn. 1999. A transaction cost perspective on international staffing patterns: implications for firm performance. *Management International Review*, Special issue, **39**(3): 89–106.

Ferner, A. 1997. Country of origin effects and HRM in multinational companies. *Human Resource Management Journal*, **7**(1): 19–37.

Festing, M. 1997. International human resources management strategies in multinational corporations: theoretical assumptions and empirical evidence from German firms. *Management International Review*, Special issue, **1**: 43–63.

Furubotn, E.G. 1988. Codetermination and the modern theory of the firm: a property-rights perspective. *Journal of Business*, **61**(2): 165–81.

Furubotn, E. & R. Richter. 2000. *Institutions and economic theory: the contribution of the new institutional economics.* Ann Arbor, MI: University of Michigan Press.

Gooderham, P.N. & O. Nordhaug. 1997. Flexibility in Norwegian and UK firms: competitive pressure and institutional embeddedness. *Employee Relations*, **19**(6): 568–80.

Grossman, W. & L.F. Schoenfeldt. 2001. Resolving ethical dilemmas through international human resource management, a transaction cost economics perspective. *Human Resource Management Review*, **11**: 55–72.

Hall, E.T. & M. Hall, 1990. *Understanding cultural differences.* Yarmouth: Intercultural Press.

Harvey, M., C. Speier & M.M. Novicevic. 2001. A theory-based framework for strategic global human resource staffing policies and practices. *International Journal of Human Resource Management*, **12**(6): 898–915.

Hegmann, H. 2004. Implizites Wissen und die Grenzen mirkoökonomischer Analyse. In G. Blümle, N. Goldschmidt, R. Klump, B. Schauenberg & H. von Senger (eds), *Perspektiven einer kulturellen Ökonomik*: 11–29. Münster: LIT Verlag.

Hofstede, G. 1980. *Culture's consequences: international differences in work related values.* Beverly Hills, CA: Sage.

Jones, G.R. 1983. Transaction costs, property rights, and organizational culture: an exchange perspective. *Administrative Science Quarterly*, **28**: 454–67.

Jones, G.R. & P.M. Wright. 1992. An economic approach to conceptualizing the utility of human resource management practices. *Research in Personnel and Human Resource Management Practices*, **10**: 271–91.

Kabst, R. 2004. Human resource management for international joint ventures: expatriation and selective control. *International Journal of Human Resource Management*, **15**(1): 1–16.

Knack, S. & P. Keefer. 1997. Does social capital have an economic payoff? A cross-country investigation. *The Quarterly Journal of Economics*: 1251–87.

Kühlmann, T.M. 2004. *Auslandseinsatz von Mitarbeitern*. Göttingen: Hogrefe.

Lawler, J.J., H.C. Jain, V. Ratnam & V. Atmiyanandana. 1995. Human resource managing in developing economies: a comparison of India and Thailand. *International Journal of Human Resource Management*, 6(2): 319–46.

Lazear, E.P. 1999. Personnel economics: past lessons and future directions. Presidential address to the society of labor economists. *Journal of Labor Economics*, 17(2): 199–236.

Morgan, P.V. 1986. International human resource management – fact or fiction. *Personnel Administrator*, 31(9): 43–7.

North, D.C. 1990. *Institutions, institutional change and economic performance*. Cambridge: Cambridge University Press.

Picot, A., H. Dietl & E. Franck. 2002. *Organisation. Eine ökonomische Perspektive*. Second edition. Stuttgart: Schäffer-Poeschel.

Polanyi, M. 1967. *The tacit dimension*. New York: Doubleday.

Powell, W.W. & P.J. DiMaggio. (eds). 1991. *The new institutionalism in organizational analysis*. Chicago, IL/London: University of Chicago Press.

Pratt, J.W. & R.J. Zeckhauser. 1985. Principals and agents. An overview. In J.W. Pratt & R.J. Zeckhauser (eds), *Principles of agents: the structure of business*: 1–35. Boston, MA: Harvard Business School Press.

Roth, K. & S. O'Donnel. 1996. Foreign subsidiary compensation strategy: an agency theory perspective. *Academy of Management Journal*, 39: 678–703.

Schuler, R.S. & N. Rogovsky. 1998. Understanding compensation practice variations across firms: the impact of national culture. *Journal of International Business Studies*, 29(1): 159–77.

Simon, H.A. 1957. *Models of man*. London: Wiley.

Tremblay, M., J. Coté & D.B. Balkin. 2003. Explaining sales pay strategy using agency, transaction cost and resource dependence theory. *Journal of Management Studies*, 40(7): 1651–82.

Trompenaars, F. & C. Hampden-Turner. 1997. *Riding the waves of culture. Understanding cultural diversity in business*. Second edition. London: Nicholas Brealey Publishing.

Wächter, H., M. Müller-Camen, A. Tempel & R. Peters. 2003. *Personalpolitik US-amerikanischer Unternehmen in Deutschland*. Munich/Mering: Hampp Verlag.

Whitley, R.D. 1992. *European business systems: firms and markets in their national contexts*. London: Sage.

Whitley, R. 1999. *Divergent capitalisms: the social structuring and change of business systems*. Oxford: Oxford University Press.

Williamson, O.E. 1984. Efficient labor organization. In F.H. Stephen (ed.), *Firms, organisation and labour*: 87–118. London: Macmillan.

Williamson, O.E. 1985. *The economic institutions of capitalism*. New York/London: Free Press.

Williamson, O.E., M.L. Wachter & J.E. Harris. 1975. Understanding the employment relation: the analysis of idiosyncratic exchange. *Bell Journal of Economics*, 6: 250–78.

Wolff, B. & M. Pooria. 2004. 'Kultur' im Internationalen Management aus Sicht der Neuen Institutionenökonomik. In G. Blümle, N. Goldschmidt, R. Klump, B. Schauenberg & H. von Senger (eds), *Perspektiven einer kulturellen Ökonomik*: 451–71. Münster: LIT Verlag.

Wright, P.M. & G.C. McMahan. 1992. Theoretical perspectives for strategic human resource management. *Journal of Management*, 18(2): 295–320.

Yan, A., G. Zhu & D.T. Hall. 2002. International assignments for career building: a model of agency relationships and psychological contracts. *Academy of Management Review*, 17(3): 373–91.

24 International human resource management research and institutional theory
Ingmar Björkman

Until the early 1990s, international HRM researchers made few references to institutional theory. However, in their influential paper on organizational theory and strategic HRM, Wright and McMahan (1992) discuss institutional theory and argue: 'the idea of institutionalization may help in understanding the determinants of HRM practices' (p 313). Since this was written, institutional theory has been used in international HRM research mostly to examine the HRM practices found in foreign-owned subsidiaries of multinational corporations (MNCs) (for example, Rosenzweig & Nohria, 1994; Hannon, Huang & Jaw, 1995; Björkman & Lu, 2001; Fenton-O'Creevy, Gooderham & Nordhaug, 2004). Institutional arguments have also been used in comparative studies of HRM practices across countries (for example, Gooderham, Nordhaug & Ringdal, 1999). Nonetheless, this chapter argues that institutional theory is still underexploited in IHRM research, and that the application of this theory could significantly augment our understanding of a range of important research questions. Below, I provide an overview of key aspects of institutional theory and review work carried out within an institutional theory framework. The main objective is to propose ways in which this theory can be used in future research on MNCs, while questions related to comparative international HRM research are examined elsewhere in this *Handbook* (Brewster, 2005; for recent reviews, see also Budhwar & Sparrow, 2002; Schuler, Budhwar & Florkowski, 2002).

Institutional theory
Although theorists differ in their views of institutional theory (DiMaggio & Powell, 1991; Scott, 1987, 2001; Tolbert & Zucker, 1996), most scholars today share 'an interest in understanding the bases of stability of social forms and the meanings associated with them' (Scott, 2003: 119) and point to the influence that socially constructed beliefs, rules and norms exert over organizations. A common point of departure for most 'new institutionalists' (DiMaggio & Powell, 1991) is thus that organizations (and suborganizations) are under pressure to adapt and be consistent with their institutional environment. They are assumed to search for legitimacy and recognition,

which they do by adopting structures and practices defined as and/or taken for granted as appropriate in their environment (Meyer & Rowan, 1977). Institutional theory shares this emphasis on the exchange relationship with the environment with resource dependency theory (Pfeffer & Salancik, 1978) and efforts have been made to integrate the two (Oliver, 1991). A central assumption in institutional theory is that organizations sharing the same environment – who thus are members of the same organizational field (DiMaggio & Powell, 1983; Westney, 1993) – are characterized by shared systems of meanings and tend to become 'isomorphic' with each other.

DiMaggio and Powell (1983) suggest that there are three major ways in which isomorphism is produced: coercive isomorphism, where a powerful constituency (for example, the government) imposes certain patterns on the organization; mimetic isomorphism, where organizations in situations of uncertainty adopt the pattern exhibited by organizations in their environment that are viewed as successful; and normative isomorphism, where professional organizations such as universities, consultancy firms and professional interest organizations act as disseminators of appropriate organizational patterns which are then adopted by organizations under the influence of the professional organizations. More recently, Scott (1995, 2001) has suggested that there exist three 'pillars' of institutional processes: regulatory (corresponding to DiMaggio and Powell's coercive mechanisms), cultural–cognitive (cf. mimetic) and normative processes.

'Institutionalization' is the process through which activities are repeated and given common meaning (Scott, 2001), but institutionalization is also a property variable (Zucker, 1977). Tolbert and Zucker (1996) propose that institutionalization processes can be divided into three stages: preinstitutionalization, semi-institutionalization and full institutionalization (see Greenwood, Suddaby & Hinings, 2002 for a related model of the stages of institutional change). At the preinstitutionalization phase the adoption of organizational practices and structures is likely to be driven by instrumental considerations (and possibly coercive and mimetic factors) and adoption can be predicted by organizational characteristics that make the change economically and technically viable. At the full institutionalization phase, when there is general social consensus about the value of the focal activity or structure, the impetus for adoption is predominately normative and the adopters more heterogeneous (Tolbert & Zucker, 1996). Further a distinction can be made between 'ceremonial adoption' (Meyer & Rowan, 1977), where organizational actors do not believe in the value of the practice/structure that therefore may be only loosely coupled with everyday activities and behaviour, and 'internalized adoption' (Kostova & Roth, 2002) where the practice/structure is seen as valuable and organizational actors are committed to it.

Most organization scholars working within an institutional perspective have focused on the relationship between organizations and their environments, conducting comparative and historical studies of how the institutional environment shapes organizational forms and practices. Institutional theorists have generally shared scepticism toward rational choice and efficiency-based perspectives, and instead stressed that organizational practices are to be understood against the background of socially constructed views of appropriate organizational forms. They have historically played down the importance of organizational agency, and in particular in the early work focused more on institutional stability and similarity across organizations and their subunits than on institutional changes.

However, as exemplified in the special issue on institutional theory published in *Academy of Management Journal* (2002), recently more emphasis has been placed on institutional changes, including processes of birth, change and deinstitutionalization. More attention has also been paid to the roles played by interests and agency and to institutional analyses of organizational phenomena at different levels of analysis, including organizations and their subunits, social fields and industries, and national as well as international levels (Scott, 2001; Dacin, Goodstein & Scott, 2002). The interaction of top-down processes (from societal institutions) and bottom-up processes (focusing on actors and how they invent and negotiate institutions) in institutional creation and diffusion is also increasingly examined in the literature (for recent reviews, see Tolbert & Zucker, 1996; Scott, 2001; Dacin *et al.*, 2002).

Institutional theory and MNC HRM practices

Institutional theory has been used to shed light on a wide variety of organizational phenomena (Scott, 2001). Over the last decade, a number of scholars have responded to calls (cf. Rosenzweig & Singh, 1991; Westney, 1993; Kostova & Zaheer, 1999) also to use institutional theory to address issues in the international management field. Several studies have been conducted on the HRM practices found in foreign subsidiaries. Foreign-owned subsidiaries can be seen as being influenced both by institutional factors in the local environment and by international isomorphic processes, including pressures from the MNC parent company (Westney, 1993). In the local context, the labour laws and regulations restrict the range of possible HRM practices, local managers have taken-for-granted views about good management practices that influence the policies and practices that they suggest for the subsidiary, strong local professional norms may exist, and processes of institutionalization might also take place among MNCs in the focal country. Hence cultural–cognitive and normative institutional processes enfolding in the local context may play important roles in explaining the HRM practices found in situations of uncertainty (DiMaggio & Powell, 1983; Levitt & March, 1988). At the same time, there may be coercive pressures from the MNC parent organization and taken-for-granted practices may be diffused through organizational actors to foreign subsidiaries (Westney, 1993).

Researchers have typically examined subsidiary HRM practices in terms of their degree of global 'integration' or MNC 'standardization' versus local 'responsiveness' or 'local adaptation' (Prahalad & Doz, 1987; see also Rosenzweig, 2005), although it has also been argued that an MNC some-times may blend global standardization with local responsiveness (Hannon *et al.*, 1995; Taylor, Beechler & Napier, 1996). In empirical studies, sub-sidiary managers have usually been asked to estimate the extent to which the HRM practices resemble those of local firms and the MNC parent organization, respectively. Studies of foreign-owned subsidiaries in the United States (Rosenzweig & Nohria, 1994) and Taiwan (Hannon *et al.*, 1995) showed that the HRM practices of MNCs overall were more localized than globally standardized, indicating stronger local than international institutional pressures. On the other hand, a study of Chinese–Western joint ventures revealed that the HRM practices were more similar to those of the MNC parent company than to those of local firms (Björkman & Lu, 2001), perhaps in part because the study focused on professionals and managers rather than rank-and-file employees. These studies have examined the relationship between possible explanatory factors consistent with the institutional perspective and subsidiary HRM practices. The results indicate that, among other things, the subsidiary establishment form (greenfield investment rather than acquisition) and the number of expatriates in the subsidiary – both indicating cultural–cognitive and/or normative institutional factors – are positively associated with a high degree of MNC standardization (Rosenzweig & Nohria, 1994; Björkman & Lu, 2001).

The relationship between MNC home country and subsidiary HRM practices has been examined in a number of studies, and there exists much evidence that MNCs from different countries differ systematically in their overseas operations (for example, Yuen & Hui, 1993; Rosenzweig & Nohria, 1994; Guest & Hoque, 1996; Bae, Chen & Lawler, 1998; Muller, 1998; Björkman & Lu, 2001; Faulkner, Pitkethly & Child, 2002). Several of these studies were conducted within an institutional framework, and authors have presented several explanations for the home country effects.[1] Firstly, expatriate managers tend to have taken-for-granted views of the kind of practices that are efficient. As a consequence, they may attempt to introduce patterns from their home organization when functioning in overseas settings (Bartlett & Ghoshal, 1989). The taken-for-granted views may, in turn, have their roots in, for example, the MNC's home country culture (Westney, 1993) or national business system (Ferner & Quintanilla, 1998). It is therefore possible that the tendency to attempt to introduce MNC practices varies according to the home country of the MNC. Secondly, MNC units may mimic the organizational patterns exhibited by foreign companies in their local environment. Many foreign managers interact socially and professionally with other expatriates, and such interaction can provide the vehicle for a diffusion of 'rationalized myths' (Meyer & Rowan, 1977) concerning appropriate practices. For instance, in China, expatriate networks are at least to some extent to be structured according to nationality (Björkman & Lu, 2001).

In spite of the contributions made by the studies reviewed above, they can be criticized on several different grounds and much work remains to be done. First, much extant work on HRM practices in MNC subsidiaries abroad has used a single measure of the degree of MNC standardization and/or localization of HRM practices. However different HRM practices differ in their level of MNC standardization and localization (Rosenzweig & Nohria, 1994). Therefore there is arguably a need to describe and analyse each practice separately rather than (as has often been done in international HRM research so far) only using an aggregate measure of the subsidiary's HRM system.

Second, HRM practices have typically been operationalized in a relatively simplistic manner using perceptual data, often collected from one respondent per unit only. Indicators of actual practices in the foreign subsidiary as well as in the parent organization would give better measures of the degree of resemblance of HRM practices.

Third, to date scholars have failed to disentangle the relative influence of MNC internal and external regulative, normative and cultural–cognitive processes. In which situations do these processes work together and in which situations may, for example, efforts by MNC headquarters to pressure foreign subsidiaries to adopt HRM policies in fact backfire (cf. Martin & Beaumont, 1998)? The methodology used in Kostova and Roth's (2002) research on the adoption of organizational practices by MNC subsidiaries could be used as a model of the way to measure the strength of different institutional processes.

Fourth, more work should also be carried out on the tension between MNC internal institutional pressures and the HRM practices that would be most efficient within a rational choice perspective. There exist a number of potential drawbacks to standardizing HRM practices across foreign subsidiaries (and, conversely, of extreme local responsiveness). First, global standardization by definition precludes the possibility of being responsive to the local institutional environment. As pointed out by Oliver (1997), firms that are better than their competitors in handling institutional pressures may attain a competitive advantage. Second, labour market considerations may favour different HRM solutions in different countries. Third, a blind standardization of practices across MNC units may lead to a lack of fit between the characteristics of the focal subsidiary's operations and its HRM system. Hence it may be more difficult to achieve a high degree of strategic HRM fit in the subsidiary. Fourth, there may be a backlash against 'headquarters imperialism' if subsidiaries are forced to fully adopt standardized MNC practices rather than contribute to the development of the unit's own policies and practices (Martin & Beaumont, 1998). Finally, if there are strong pressures to standardize HRM throughout the MNC this may stifle local experimentation and development of the HRM system, thereby reducing the capacity of the MNC as a whole to develop new innovative HRM practices.

Fifth, researchers need to be careful in terms of the level of analysis. A distinction can be made between HRM system architecture (level one), HRM policies (level two) and HRM practices (level three) (Becker & Gerhart, 1996). Using employee compensation as an example of a specific HRM function, at the HRM architecture level of analysis the focus can be on the extent to which employee performance is valued in the firm; at the policy level data may be collected on the extent to which incentive pay is used throughout the firm; and typical questions at the practices level of analysis could be whether 360 degree performance appraisals are used to determine bonuses on the part of the total financial incentive achievable by an employee that is based on the performance of the team that she/he is part of (ibid.). Research on the transfer of HRM within the MNC has predominately been conducted at levels two and three (although with some researchers using the term 'practices' also at level two). All three levels of analysis are relevant, but the results are likely to differ both in terms of the degree of HRM standardization and concerning the determinants of subsidiary HRM practices and policies. To date there is a dearth of research on the relationship between the different levels of analysis.

Finally, most research on subsidiary HRM policies and practices has centred on how much the foreign affiliate's HRM system resembles that of the home country organization of the MNC. However, as pointed out by Taylor *et al.* (1996), the 'exportation' of HRM from the parent organization to the foreign unit is not the only possible MNC internal transfer of HRM policies and practices; MNCs may also have an 'integrative' approach to IHRM by attempting to identify 'the best' practices and policies within the MNC as a whole, and then transfer these to the other MNC units. In this conceptualization of IHRM, transfer of HRM policies and practices can occur between foreign affiliates as well as between headquarters and foreign subsidiaries (ibid.).

Other areas to be pursued in future research

Few efforts have been made in IHRM research to examine processes of institutionalization and diffusion of practices and structures. Such processes could be studied at different levels of analysis and for a range of issues in HRM. For instance, scholars could study macro- and meso-level processes of institutionalization and diffusion of 'high performance' work/HRM practices (Becker & Gerhart, 1996), the HR scorecard (Becker, Huselid & Ulrich, 2001), outsourcing of HRM tasks (Greer, Youngblood & Gray, 1999) and the structure and roles of the HR department in the MNC (Stiles, 2005). Institutional theorists remind us that organizations imitate each other in situations of uncertainty. Organizations are particularly likely to mimic others perceived as successful, but imitation is also likely to be influenced by the mental and social closeness of the firms to each other. For instance, companies belonging to the same industry, being from the same home country, using the same consultants and employing HR executives with the same education and professional background could be particularly likely to imitate each other.

It would also be of interest to carry out explanatory analyses of the extent to which organizations and organizational units such as foreign subsidiaries of MNCs engage in ceremonial adoption (Meyer & Rowan, 1977) or internalized adoption (Kostova & Roth, 2002). Such work would require scholars to look beyond the general adoption of general HRM policies and instead investigate the internalization of policies by the people who implement the policies in their daily work. Longitudinal work would be particularly interesting as it would enable analyses of the way patterns of adaptation change as the practice/structure becomes increasingly institutionalized.

To date, IHRM scholars have paid little attention to agency in their analyses. More emphasis on the role played by organizational actors will add to the explanatory power of institutional arguments in IHRM research. For instance, studies of HRM in MNC subsidiaries would be advised to investigate the role of organizational actors who are in a position to influence organizational structures and practices. The extent to which MNC subsidiaries adopt certain organizational practices/structures is likely not only to be a result of the extent to which organizational actors have internalized a belief in these practices but also to be a function of the influence that these actors have on firm decision making (cf. Dacin *et al.*, 2002). One could, for instance, hypothesize that the more highly regarded the subsidiary's HR department is and the more deeply the department is involved in strategic planning, the more this is likely to influence the affiliate's HRM practices.

Another path could be to integrate an institutional perspective with work already under way on symbolic and reputational considerations in HRM (see, for example, Ferris *et al.*, 1999). Galang and Ferris (1997) show how HR departments in US firms may actively engage in symbolic activities with the aim of acquiring additional influence in the organization. Recently the roles played by the HR function in MNCs have also received increased research attention (for example, Ferner & Varul, 2000; Scullion & Starkey, 2000; Kelly, 2001; Novicevic & Harvey, 2001), but few efforts have been made to approach the phenomenon from a well developed theoretical perspective. Institutional theory might offer important insights into ways the HR department in different contexts can increase its influence in the organization. For instance, HR managers may try to ascertain whether top management perceives the HRM practices implemented in the firm as both progressive and appropriate, thus enhancing the reputation of the department. These perceptions are not only likely to be affected by institutionalization processes at meso and macro levels, but may also be actively influenced by the HR department through 'management of meaning' (Pfeffer, 1981) in the organization.

Stinchcombe (1965) was probably the first scholar to draw our attention to the impact of the founding conditions on the firm's subsequent operations. According to Stinchcombe, organizations are significantly moulded by the specific context prevailing at the time of their birth. He proposed further that organizations are subsequently likely to retain many of the features acquired when they were established. The term 'organizational imprinting' refers to this tendency on the part of organizations (Scott, 1987). Several factors may contribute to organizational imprinting. Gray and Yan (1997) refer to the initial resource mix that an organization acquires at its founding, and to the institutional forces that prevail at that moment. As argued by Scott (1987), initial structures and processes may become institutionalized as 'the way things are done', thus being an important reason for the persistence of organizational features over time. Students of IHRM could for instance investigate whether imprinting effects can be found in analyses of foreign subsidiary HRM practices.

There is a long-standing debate about the impact of MNCs on the host country (Moran, 1993). Most of this discussion has been on the direct economic implications of MNCs and there has been much less work on the impact of foreign firms' operations on non-economic aspects of the local society. Although numerous studies have shown that considerable differences in HRM remain across countries owing to cultural and institutional factors, there are also indications of some convergence across countries (Brewster *et al.*, 2004). MNCs may through their activities significantly contribute to the diffusion of foreign HRM practices (Westney, 1993), but there is a paucity of research on the effects that foreign-owned firms have on the host country's people management practices, in particular in developing countries (Schuler *et al.*, 2002). For instance, several scholars (for example, Warner 1996; Benson & Zhu, 1999; Goodall & Warner, 1998) have described and analysed some of the changes taking place in HRM practices and policies in domestic Chinese firms during recent years, but little empirical research has specifically aimed at investigating the process of diffusion of Western-style HRM practices and policies among local Chinese organizations (Benson & Zhu, 1999; though see Zhu & Warner, 2000). Björkman (2003) has developed a series of testable propositions that can be used as a foundation for future empirical research in the Chinese context and a similar set of propositions could also be tested in other locations.

Finally, there is a need to combine institutional theory with other theoretical perspectives. During the last decade, several efforts have been made to go beyond individual theoretical perspectives to build integrative models of the determinants of HRM in MNCs (for example, Schuler, Dowling & De Cieri, 1993; Taylor, Beechler & Napier, 1996). These models have built on a variety of theoretical perspectives. For instance, the model proposed by Taylor *et al.* (1996) draws on resource-based theory of the firm (Barney, 1991) and resource dependency theory (Pfeffer & Salancik, 1978). Both the Schuler *et al.* (1993) and the Taylor *et al.* (1996) models specify a number of mediating and moderating factors that may influence the HRM policies and practices in MNCs, and their work has been instrumental in furthering empirical work on international HRM. The development of a similar conceptual model based squarely on institutional theory would offer a suitable challenge for theorists interested in augmenting our understanding of the determinants of HRM in MNCs.

Conclusions

The main message of this chapter is that, although institutional theory has already been instrumental in helping us to understand better the forces influencing HRM in MNCs, the theory has great potential to make additional contributions within the field of IHRM. Although the discussion in this chapter has been limited to HRM within the context of MNCs, an examination of institutional mechanisms can inform comparative studies of HRM as well as research on HRM in domestic settings (see also Paauwe & Boselie, 2003). My prediction is that students of IHRM will increasingly use institutional theory as their theoretical framework in the years ahead.

Acknowledgments
The author would like to thank Mats Ehrnrooth and Günter Stahl for helpful comments on earlier drafts and the Wallenberg Foundation for financial support.

Note

1. Scholars (for example, Ferner & Quintanilla, 1998) have also examined MNC home country effects within a business system approach (Whitley, 1999). For a comparison of neoinstitutional and business system approaches to studying HRM in MNCs, see Tempel and Walgenbach (2004).

References

Bae, J., S.-J. Chen & J.L. Lawler. 1998. Variations in human resource management in Asian countries: MNC home-country and host-country effects. *International Journal of Human Resource Management*, **9**: 653–70.
Barney, J.B. 1991. Firm resources and sustained competitive advantage. *Journal of Management*, **17**: 99–120.
Bartlett, C.A. & S. Ghoshal. 1989. *Managing across borders: the transnational solution.* Boston, MA: Harvard Business School Press.
Becker, B. & B. Gerhart. 1996. The impact of human resource management on organizational performance: progress and prospects. *Academy of Management Journal*, **39**: 779–801.
Becker, B., M.A. Huselid & D. Ulrich. 2001. *The HR scorecard: linking people, strategy and performance.* Boston, MA: Harvard Business School Press.
Benson, J. & Y. Zhu. 1999. Markets, firms and workers in Chinese state-owned enterprises. *Human Resource Management Journal*, **9**(4): 58–74.
Björkman, I. 2003. The diffusion of Western-style human resource management practices among Chinese firms: the role of Western multinational corporations. *Asia–Pacific Business Review*, **9**(2): 43–60.
Björkman, I. & Y. Lu. 2001. Institutionalization and bargaining power explanations of human resource management practices in international joint ventures – the case of Chinese–Western joint ventures. *Organization Studies*, **22**: 491–512.
Brewster, C. 2005. Comparing HRM policies and practices across geographical borders. In G. Stahl & I. Björkman (eds), *Handbook of research in international human resource management.* Cheltenham, UK and Northampton, MA, USA: Edward Elgar.
Brewster, C., W. Mayrhofer & M. Morley. (eds). 2004. *Human resource management in Europe: evidence of convergence?* Oxford: Elsevier.
Budhwar, P.S. & P.R. Sparrow. 2002. An integrative framework for understanding cross-national human resource management practices. *Human Resource Management Review*, **12**: 377–403.
Dacin, M.T., J. Goodstein & W.R. Scott. 2002. Institutional theory and institutional change: introduction to the special research forum. *Academy of Management Journal*, **45**: 45–56.
DiMaggio, P.J. & W.W. Powell. 1983. The iron cage revisited: institutional isomorphism and collective rationality in organizational fields. *American Sociological Review*, **48**: 147–60.
DiMaggio, P.J. & W.W. Powell. 1991. Introduction. In P.J. DiMaggio & W.W. Powell (eds), *The new institutionalism in organizational analysis*: 1–38. Chicago, IL: University of Chicago Press.
Faulkner, D., R. Pitkethly & J. Child. 2002. International mergers and acquisitions in the UK, 1985–94: a comparison of national HRM practices. *International Journal of Human Resource Management*, **13**: 106–22.
Fenton-O'Creevy, M., P. Gooderham & O. Nordhaug. 2004. HRM in US subsidiaries in Europe: centralization or autonomy? Paper presented at the AoM Meeting, New Orleans, 6–11 August.
Ferner, A. & J. Quintanilla. 1998. Multinationals, national business systems and HRM: the enduring influence of national identity or a process of 'Anglo-Saxonization'. *International Journal of Human Resource Management*, **9**: 710–31.
Ferner, A. & M.Z. Varul. 2000. Internationalisation and the personnel function in German multinationals. *Human Resource Management Journal*, **10**(3): 79–96.
Ferris, G.R., W.A. Hochwarter, M.R. Buckley, G. Harrel-Cook & D.D. Frink. 1999. Human resource management: some new directions. *Journal of Management*, **25**: 385–415.

Galang, M.C. & G.R. Ferris. 1997. Human resource department power and influence through symbolic action. *Human Relations*, **50**: 1403–26.

Goodall, K. & M. Warner. 1998. HRM dilemmas in China: the case of foreign-invested enterprises in Shanghai. *Asia–Pacific Business Review*, **4**(4): 1–21.

Gooderham, P.N., O. Nordhaug & K. Ringdal. 1999. Institutional and rational determinants of organizational practices: human resource management in European firms. *Administrative Science Quarterly*, **44**: 507–31.

Gray, B. & A. Yan. 1997. Formation and evolution of international joint ventures: examples from U.S./Chinese partnerships. In P.Beamish & P.Killing (eds), *Global perspectives on cooperative strategies: Asian perspectives:* 57–88. San Francisco, CA: The New Lexington Press.

Greenwood, R., R. Suddaby & C.R. Hinings. 2002. Theorizing change: the role of professional associations in the transformation of institutionalized fields. *Academy of Management Journal*, **45**: 59–80.

Greer, C.R., S.A. Youngblood & D.A. Gray. 1999. Human resource management outsourcing: the make or buy decision. *Academy of Management Executive*, **12**(3): 85–96.

Guest, D. & K. Hoque. 1996. The influence of national ownership in human resource management practices in UK greenfield sites. *Human Resource Management Journal*, **6**(4): 50–74.

Hannon, J.M., I.-C. Huang & B.-S. Jaw. 1995. International human resource strategy and its determinants: the case of subsidiaries in Taiwan. *Journal of International Business Studies*, **26**: 531–54.

Kelly, J. 2001. The role of the personnel/HR function in multinational corporations. *Employee Relations*, **23**: 536–57.

Kostova, T. & K. Roth. 2002. Adoption of organizational practice by subsidiaries of multinational corporations: institutional and relational effects. *Academy of Management Journal*, **45**: 215–33.

Kostova, T. & S. Zaheer. 1999. Organizational legitimacy under conditions of complexity: the case of the multinational enterprise. *Academy of Management Review*, **24**: 64–81.

Levitt, B. & J.G. March. 1988. Organizational learning. *Annual Review of Sociology*, **14**: 319–40.

Martin, G. & P. Beaumont. 1998. Diffusing 'best practice' in multinational firms: prospects, practice and contestation. *International Journal of Human Resource Management*, **9**: 671–95.

Meyer, J. & B. Rowan. 1977. Institutionalized organizations: formal structures as myth and ceremony. *American Journal of Sociology*, **83**: 340–63.

Moran, T.H. 1993. Introduction: governments and transnational corporations. In T.H.Moran (ed.), *Governments and transnational corporations*. London: Routledge.

Muller, M. 1998. Human resource and industrial relations practices of UK and US multinationals in Germany. *International Journal of Human Resource Management*, **9**: 732–49.

Novicevic, M.M. & M. Harvey. 2001. The changing role of the corporate HR function in global organizations of the twenty-first century. *International Journal of Human Resource Management*, **12**: 1251–68.

Oliver, C. 1991. Strategic responses to institutional processes. *Academy of Management Review*, **16**: 145–79.

Oliver, C. 1997. Sustainable competitive advantage: combining institutional and resource-based views. *Strategic Management Journal*, **18**: 697–713.

Paauwe, J. & P. Boselie. 2003. Challenging 'strategic HRM' and the relevance of the institutional setting. *Human Resource Management Journal*, **13**(3): 56–70.

Pfeffer, J. 1981. Management as symbolic action: the creation and maintenance of organizational paradigms. In L.L. Cummings & B.M. Staw (eds), *Research in organizational behavior*, vol. 3: 1–52. Greenwich, CT: JAI Press.

Pfeffer, J. & G.R. Salancik. 1978. *The external control of organizations: a resource dependence perspective*. New York: Harper & Row.

Prahalad, C.K. & Y. Doz. 1987. *The multinational mission: balancing global demands and global vision*. New York: Free Press.

Rosenzweig, P.M. 2005. The dual logics behind international human resource management: pressures for global integration and local responsiveness. In G. Stahl & I. Björkman (eds), *Handbook of research in international human resource management*. Cheltenham, UK and Northampton, MA, USA: Edward Elgar.

Rosenzweig, P.M. & N. Nohria. 1994. Influences on human resource management practices in multinational corporations. *Journal of International Business Studies*, **25**: 229–51.

Rosenzweig, P.M. & J.V. Singh. 1991. Organizational environments and the multinational enterprise. *Academy of Management Review*, **16**: 340–61.

Schuler, R.S., P. Budhwar & G.W. Florkowski. 2002. International human resource management: review and critique. *International Journal of Management Reviews*, **4**: 41–70.

Schuler, R.S., P.J. Dowling & H. De Cieri. 1993. An integrative framework of strategic international human resource management. *Journal of Management*, **19**: 419–59.

Scott, W.R. 1987. The adolescence of institutional theory. *Administrative Science Quarterly*, **32**: 493–511.

Scott, W.R. 1995. *Institutions and organizations*. Thousand Oaks, CA: Sage.

Scott, W.R. 2001. *Institutions and organizations*. Second edition. Thousand Oaks, CA: Sage.

Scott, W.R. 2003. *Organizations: rational, natural, and open systems*. Fifth edition. London: Prentice-Hall.

Scullion, H. & K. Starkey. 2000. In search of the changing role of the corporate human resource function in the international firm. *International Journal of Human Resource Management*, **11**: 1061–81.

Stiles, P. 2005. The human resource department: roles, co-ordination, and influence. In G. Stahl & I. Björkman (eds), *Handbook of research in international human resource management*. Cheltenham, UK and Northampton, MA, USA: Edward Elgar.

Stinchcombe, A. 1965. Social structure and organizations. In J.G. March (ed.), *Handbook of organizations*. Chicago, IL: Rand McNally.

Taylor, S., S. Beechler & N. Napier. 1996. Toward an integrative model of strategic international human resource management. *Academy of Management Review*, **21**: 959–85.

Tempel, A. & P. Walgenbach. 2004. Comparing institutionalist approaches to the study of human resource management in multinational corporations. Paper presented at the AoM Meeting, New Orleans, 6–11 August.

Tolbert, P.S. & L.G. Zucker. 1996. The institutionalization of institutional theory. In S.R. Clegg, C. Hardy & W.A. Nord (eds), *Handbook of organization studies*. London: Sage.

Warner, M. 1996. Human resources in the People's Republic of China: the 'three systems' reforms. *Human Resource Management Journal*, **6**(2): 32–43.

Westney, D.E. 1993. Institutionalization theory and the multinational corporation. In S. Ghoshal & D.E. Westney (eds), *Organization theory and the multinational corporation*. New York: St Martin's Press.

Whitley, R. 1999. *Divergent capitalisms: the social structuring and change of business systems*. Oxford: Oxford University Press.

Wright, P.M. & G.C. McMahan. 1992. Theoretical perspectives for strategic human resource management. *Journal of Management*, **18**: 295–320.

Yuen, E. & T.K. Hui. 1993. Headquarters, host-culture and organisation influences on HRM policies and practices. *Management International Review*, **33**: 361–83.

Zhu, Y. & M. Warner. 2000. An emerging model of employment relations in China: a divergent path from the Japanese? *International Business Review*, **9**: 345–61.

Zucker, L.G. 1977. The role of institutionalization in cultural persistence. *American Sociological Review*, **42**: 726–43.

25 International human resource management and social network/social capital theory

Mark L. Lengnick-Hall and
Cynthia A. Lengnick-Hall

Work gets done through relationships embedded in larger networks. The intricate network of relationships both within and outside an organization forms the circulation system that carries information and ideas to those who need it, when they need it (Lengnick-Hall & Lengnick-Hall, 2002). Connections among people both within and across organizations have received increasing attention in the recent past thanks to some groundbreaking research in sociology and management (for example, Burt, 1992; Coleman, 1988; Granovetter, 1974; Krackhardt 1990). As Brass (1995) noted, a social capital/social network perspective is not offered as a substitute or competing view to the traditional HR focus on individual attributes. Rather combining this perspective with the traditional one may broaden our understanding of the complexities of behaviour in organizations and offer new avenues for research in IHRM.

The purpose of this chapter is to guide IHRM scholars interested in incorporating social network/social capital theory in their future research. We begin by defining key concepts. Next, we describe the relationship between social capital and competitive advantage in international firms. Finally, we propose an agenda for IHRM research focused on the role of IHRM in using social capital and social networks to achieve strategic capabilities in multinational corporations. Figure 25.1 illustrates the essential relationships.

Relationships: the foundation for social capital

A relationship represents a lasting association between two or more individuals, groups or organizations (Lengnick-Hall & Lengnick-Hall, 2003). Relationships have four distinctive characteristics. One, they occur over time and are built on a history of interaction. Past events shape expectations and provide a context for evaluating the present. Expectations about the future also are shaped by the level of commitment and closeness between the partners in the relationship. Two, relationships often involve mutual influence. One party in a relationship may influence the other on

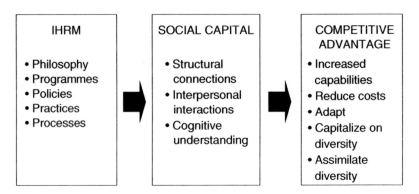

*Figure 25.1   Relationships among IHRM, social capital and competitive
advantage*

some issues, while the roles are reversed on other issues. Three, relationships
can range from one-dimensional to multifaceted. For example, a worker
may have only a task-oriented relationship with one coworker, but may
have several relationships with a different coworker (for example, colleague,
friend and neighbour). Four, relationships are usually embedded in wider
social networks. Having a relationship with one person provides potential
access to others whom you do not even know.

Relationships are receiving increasing attention in the IHRM literature.
Researchers have examined the relationships between supervisors and
employees (for example, Graen & Uhl-Bien, 1995), the relationships among
employees on teams (for example, Chen & Klimoski, 2003) and the relationship between an individual and an organization (for example, Rousseau,
1995). However, until recently, this research did not address how relationships embedded in networks affect knowledge sharing, job and organizational performance and sustained competitive advantage.

Social capital
The concept of social capital has the potential to explain how human
resources may be leveraged to create competitive advantage. Portes (1998)
provides a clear distinction among different forms of capital: 'Whereas economic capital is in people's bank accounts and human capital is inside their
heads, social capital inheres in the structure of their relationships. To
possess social capital, a person must be related to others, and it is those
others, not himself, who are the actual source of his or her advantage.'
Nahapiet and Ghoshal (1998) define social capital as the sum of the actual
and potential resources embedded within, available through, and derived
from the network of relationships possessed by an individual or a social

unit. Adler and Kwon (2002) define social capital as the goodwill available to individuals or groups; its source lies in the structure and content of the actor's relations; its effects flow from the information, influence and solidarity it makes available to the actor.

We integrate these ideas and define social capital in the international context as *the intangible resource of structural connections, interpersonal interactions and cognitive understanding that enables a firm to (a) capitalize on diversity and (b) reconcile differences.* These two capabilities provide a foundation for an international organization to develop dynamic capabilities, to manage the inherent tension between pressures toward cost reduction on a global scale and pressures toward local adaptation, and to navigate the challenges that arise from diverse national values, economic systems and workplace conditions that are inherent in a multinational setting.

Social capital can either facilitate or constrain organizational effectiveness. It may facilitate organizational effectiveness by (a) providing a form of social control – people will do things for others without close monitoring, (b) providing a source of support – people have others to turn to in times of need, and (c) providing access to information and other assets (advice, political opportunities, and so on). On the other hand, social capital may constrain organizational effectiveness (Portes, 1998). One, strong ties that benefit group members also can be used to exclude outsiders. For an international firm, ingroup versus outgroup behaviours can be devastating. Two, it is difficult to find the correct balance between investing in creating social capital and using it to achieve organizational objectives. Too much emphasis on building relationships can place excessive demands on group members, making it difficult for them to accomplish other important objectives. A recent study demonstrated that there is a threshold beyond which more relationships and stronger relationships both exhibited diminishing returns in terms of knowledge creation (McFadyen & Cannella, 2004). Three, participating in a community can create demands for conformity. International firms must remain open to diverse ideas that contradict prevailing expectations. Relationships can form a buffer that prevents novel ideas from being heard. And, four, there can be pressures exerted causing downward levelling norms. In an attempt to find common ground across diverse cultures and peoples, there may be a tendency toward lowering expectations rather than raising them to a supranational standard.

Kostova and Roth (2003) differentiate social capital as both a private and a public good. As a private good, social capital is only available to the individual who has developed a network of relationships. This network is only accessible by others in the organization at the discretion of the individual and any organizational benefits are secondary or by-products of individual benefits. On the other hand, as a public good, social capital is available not only to those who created it, but also to others in the organization or community. Being a member of an organization or community entitles each individual to enjoy the benefits of relationships created by all other organization or community members.

Individual-level social capital may explain why some people have better access to employment than others, why some have more mobility through occupational ladders than do others, and why some entrepreneurs succeed where others fail (Portes, 1998). Granovetter (1974) proposed that multiple 'weak ties' (relationships that are more superficial: that is, acquaintances) could expand an individual's information base. Acquaintances are likely to have access to social networks different from those of friends, thus extending the potential range of information available to an individual. Weak ties may serve as bridges to other social networks enabling employees to solve problems and leverage their own job performance (Hansen, 1999; Inkpen & Tsang, 2005).

Burt (1992) identified 'structural holes' as positions between two social networks, each with dense connections within, but weak ties between them. An individual in a 'structural hole' can control information and benefits (that is, decide what information to provide either party or negotiate from a position of privileged information). Burt *et al.* (2000) found similar benefits to individuals in structural holes in both American and French manager samples. More recently, Burt (2004) proposed that individuals in 'structural holes' can act like brokers between groups and are more likely to express their ideas, less likely to have their ideas dismissed and more likely to have their ideas evaluated as valuable. In an international context, organizations that are dependent upon individuals in structural holes may find themselves operating from a weakened competitive position. Research is needed to determine whether this hypothesis is supported.

Dutton and Heaphy (2003) argue that 'high-quality connections' are important in many organizational situations. High-quality connections have *higher emotional carrying capacity* (that is, the expression of more emotion and of both positive and negative emotions), *tensility* (the capacity to withstand strain and to function in a variety of circumstances) and a high degree of *connectivity* (an atmosphere of buoyancy, creating expansive emotional spaces that open possibilities for action and creativity). Gittell (2003) showed that high-quality connections facilitate coordination of highly interdependent work units. The creation of high-quality connections poses challenging problems for international organizations since relationships are weakened by less frequent interactions and lack of physical proximity. Research is needed to assess whether the use of expatriates and job rotation schemes may help overcome some of these barriers.

Social capital in international organizations

Kostova and Roth (2003) propose a contingency perspective specifying the level of social capital needed in different types of interdependencies between headquarters and foreign subunits found in multinational corporations. They distinguish between simple and complex interdependence. Simple interdependence requires fewer and more easily specified points of interaction as well as readily codifiable exchanges. In contrast, complex interdependence requires many points of interaction and the exchanges are not easily codifiable. As the degree and complexity of interdependence between headquarters and a foreign subunit increase, higher levels of social capital will be required. They predict that the level of social capital required will be highest for transnationals, followed by international MNCs, then global MNCs, and that MNCs would require the lowest levels of social capital.

Relationships at different levels in the organization have the potential for affecting organizational performance in different ways. For example, social capital at top management levels facilitates successful partnerships, alliances, mergers and acquisitions. A history of repeated exchanges leads to strong ties which, in turn, promote trust, reciprocity and a longer-term perspective, making strategic alliances more effective. Moreover, as Inkpen and Tsang (2005) propose, social ties among individuals are the foundation for inter-member ties across firms within an industrial district. More research is needed to explain how top management social capital facilitates and constrains strategic choice and execution.

Social capital at organizational levels below top management can affect organizational performance through its impact on efficiency and innovation. Social ties augment more formal links, facilitate effective decentralization and offer a hedge against undesirable employee turnover (Dess & Shaw, 2001). Relationships also create commonalities that lead to shared vision, collective goals, preservation of organizational memory and a more stable platform for knowledge work (Inkpen & Tsang, 2005). While these propositions are logical, empirical research is needed to determine whether they are supported.

Although increased social capital at all organizational levels may be necessary for international organizations to succeed, there may be limits on how much can be created. For example, international organizations that operate in fewer countries may be able to create sufficient social capital for effective operations, while those operating in many countries may find it difficult to create sufficient social capital. We propose that an organization's stock of social capital creates upper limits on how expansive an organization can be in its international efforts.

Social capital and competitive advantage

The intersection of social capital/social network theory and competitive advantage offers a rich opportunity for IHRM research. Social capital contributes to competitive advantage in a number of ways that are particularly crucial for international operations.

First, to compete in a global economy, firms require dynamic capabilities (Eisenhardt & Martin, 2000). This means they must move beyond the frictionless dissemination of information and develop an ability to transfer, share and use knowledge throughout the enterprise. Social capital provides the links among people and competencies that contribute to an organization's combinative capacity. As Kogut and Zander (1992) explain, the essence of combinative capability is the capacity to synthesize and apply knowledge currently within the firm as well as a talent for integrating and using newly acquired knowledge. We propose that (a) links formed by the structural dimension of social capital reinforce workflow interdependencies and can draw knowledge to relevant sites; (b) the relationship dimension provides a basis for developing trust and interpersonal bonds that underlie rich flows of tacit knowledge, the process through which one network member is affected by the experience of another (Argote & Ingram, 2000); and (c) the cognitive dimension creates a basis for interpreting and translating ideas and know-how across cultures and diverse settings.

One potentially productive avenue for research is understanding how specific IHRM policies and practices shape the structural, relationship and cognitive elements of social capital and consequently influence a firm's ability to learn and exploit what it knows despite cultural differences and geographic distance. For example, Hofstede (1985) demonstrates substantial differences across cultures in their desire to accommodate complexity and ambiguity. Can IHRM make a more powerful contribution to a firm's ability to develop dynamic capabilities by developing programmes to augment the cognitive complexity of all employees regardless of their prevailing national culture or rather by designing work structures that translate cognitively complex ideas into more structured organizational routines?

Social capital is a source of incentives and motivation for employees to engage in extra-role, voluntary behaviours such as knowledge sharing and other types of organizational citizenship behaviours that also lead to dynamic capabilities. Kelloway and Barling (2000) argue that, since knowledge work is discretionary behaviour in organizations, firms will thrive to the extent they are able to increase employees' ability, motivation and opportunities to undertake these voluntary or optional activities. Bolino, Turney and Bloodgood (2002) present a comprehensive model showing how organizational citizenship behaviours can contribute to all three dimensions of social capital (as identified by Nahapiet & Ghoshal, 1998). They argue that organizational citizenship behaviours (a) bring people together in ways that increase the number and usefulness of ties they have with others in the firm, (b) they 'infuse the connections among employees with an affective component', thereby augmenting the relational dimension of social capital, and (c) make it easier for individuals to understand each other and develop a common language. The reciprocal relationship between social capital and organizational citizenship behaviours can be a powerful source of competitive advantage and an important point for IHRM intervention in international organizations. However, currently, there is no research that demonstrates this relationship. Consequently one area for future research is to test the proposition that there is a reciprocal relationship between social capital and organizational citizenship behaviour and that this leads to improved organizational performance and competitive advantage.

Second, international operations typically face two competing forces: pressure to reduce costs through globalization and pressure to be locally responsive and adaptive. Social capital can enable effective responses to both of these forces. Social capital contributes to efficiency by smoothing coordination problems and reducing transaction costs between individuals, across units and among organizations (Lazenga & Pattison, 2001; Putnam, 1993). When people are willing to cooperate and collaborate and determine how to make things work through mutual adjustment, organizations and markets run more efficiently. However research needs to establish whether there are limits to the impact of social capital on organizational efficiency in an international organization. Can you have too much social capital, such that inefficiencies are created by too much attention being paid to the maintenance of relationships at the expense of accomplishing organizational objectives?

Social capital also helps firms enhance their responsiveness to local conditions. Social capital contributes to adaptation by capitalizing on the cognitive diversity offered by an international workforce. Social capital enables role versatility in individuals and units, allowing them to be both senders and recipients of knowledge and reducing barriers to effective knowledge flow such as 'not-invented-here' syndrome and information hoarding. Without the familiarity and trust that comes from strong relationships, individuals are often reluctant to ask for information, believing it exposes their ignorance. Without the understanding that comes from social ties, people may have difficulty putting themselves in the shoes of the recipient of information with sufficient insight to make an effective translation of ideas from one context to another. Social capital is a key mechanism for

eroding barriers to communication based on hierarchy, functional orientation, geographic distance or cultural distinctions. The specific mechanisms
by means of which IHRM can help a firm transform social capital into specific cost reduction activities or effective responses to local conditions need
further exploration.

Moreover social capital is a key factor shaping intracorporate networks,
strategic alliances and industrial districts (Inkpen & Tsang, 2005). Social
capital transforms other factors such as proximity, exchange history, norms
and patterns of accommodation, into routines for knowledge exchange and
collaboration. Research has demonstrated that organizations and units
with deep social capital can create channels for resource exchanges more
quickly and easily than those without such social ties (Tsai, 2000). Social
capital helps reconcile differences in local cultures and diverse goals.
Furthermore, as market transactions are infused with social ties, such
exchanges encourage the trust and reciprocity that lead to effective alliances
and joint ventures.

Third, firms that operate in multiple locations inevitably increase the
level of diversity and complexity they face. This situation can be dealt with
by efforts to reduce complexity and assimilate diversity (a melting pot
approach) or it can be managed by efforts to increase the firm's ability to
absorb complexity and adopt a multicultural attitude that accentuates and
capitalizes on diversity. Social capital is an important element in each of
these approaches. A fruitful area for IHRM research is to determine the
contingencies that are favourable to an assimilation rather than absorption
approach to managing diversity.

Social capital offers a basis for developing commonalities across diverse
groups by providing incentives for fostering a global mindset (Sparrow
et al., 2004). Common goals, recognition of key reciprocal relationships
and understanding the enterprise-wide consequences of local actions
provide a basis for capitalizing on interdependencies. Social capital creates
interpersonal interactions that promote knowledge and understanding of
diverse cultures and markets and it provides a mechanism for reconciling
diverse perspectives and experiences (Gupta & Govindarajan, 2004). When
individuals see each other as part of the same team, regardless of cultural,
national or experiential differences, there is an incentive for bridging
differences to capitalize on the variety of ideas and options available.
Relationships are the foundation for developing this orientation. However
it is unlikely that the creation of social capital alone will lead to the creation
of a global mindset. IHRM researchers may discover what role social
capital plays in the creation of a global mindset.

Social capital also helps a firm capitalize on diversity and complexity
through its contribution to absorptive capacity among individuals and

units. Absorptive capacity reflects the realization that what an individual or organization already knows influences what it is able to learn readily (Cohen & Levinthal, 1990). The accumulation of prior knowledge enhances the ability of individuals and organizations to acquire and use new knowledge. Since diversity in prior knowledge facilitates novel associations, international organizations have a tremendous potential for high levels of absorptive capacity. Moreover diversity coupled with structural, relationship and cognitive commonalities helps individuals and organizations deal with uncertainty by enabling people to recognize the value of new ideas and to understand how new information is related to current expertise and routines. The breadth and depth of an international organization's social capital may determine its absorptive capacity. For example, we propose that narrow and deep social capital (that is, less diverse total knowledge stock) may be useful for some organizational environments, while broad and shallow social capital (that is, more diverse knowledge stock) may be more useful in other environments.

The frequency, openness and strength of the interactions among an organization's people determine to a great extent the firm's ability to integrate diverse talents to develop new competitive capabilities, combine diverse ideas to arrive at new insights and take advantage of investments in technology. Social capital, like many other intangible resources, is both difficult to imitate and non-substitutable. Therefore the way in which a firm manages its human resources and the manner in which people interact to form an organizational community have a significant influence on competitive outcomes.

HR's role in creating and sustaining social capital

Integrating these various ways in which social capital contributes to strategic advantage yields an interesting research agenda for IHRM scholars. Traditionally HR has focused its efforts on the attraction, selection, development and utilization of individuals to accomplish tasks within the structure of jobs. More recently this focus has expanded to include the creation and use of groups or teams to accomplish organizational goals. Relationships, and the creation of social capital, have not received as much attention.

An important first step in a research agenda is to identify and evaluate IHRM policies, programmes, practices, and processes to bridge individual, functional and national boundaries effectively and create effective structural connections, interpersonal interactions and cognitive associations.

A range of traditional and non-traditional HR practices has been proposed to facilitate relationship building and the formation of social capital (Cross & Parker, 2004; Lengnick-Hall & Lengnick-Hall, 2003). However many of the traditional HR activities need to be revised from the perspective of social capital and international concerns. For example, HR can use organization design to foster relationship building and social capital formation. Gittell (2003), advocates (a) using boundary spanners to build relationships among participants in a given work process, (b) altering the role of supervisor to relationship builder, and (c) the use of routines, in the form of process maps, that can increase the level of shared knowledge among employees by illustrating where each task fits in the overall work process, and how each employee's work relates to the work of others. Others have suggested using expatriates to transfer knowledge and to extend the reach of social networks. While there are many ideas regarding ways IHRM can contribute to creating social capital in multinational firms, research is needed to determine the conditions under which specific practices are effective.

Second, reorienting IHRM's role toward relationship building and the formation of social capital enables HR to contribute directly to the creation of competitive advantage (Lengnick-Hall & Lengnick-Hall, 2003). Relationships, which integrate human capital and other intangible aspects of a firm leverage the human talent that falls within traditional HR responsibilities to create more powerful competencies. What one person knows (or can do) is multiplied when others can tap into that knowledge or capability in their own jobs. Relationships, and the resulting organizational capabilities they create, can be an important source of sustained competitive advantage because they are heterogeneous, reflect individual differences and are relatively immobile since they are embedded in a firm's culture and climate. However this new perspective creates challenges for IHRM researchers. For example, how do you measure relationships and the social capital they generate? Currently available social network analysis tools are limited in the number of individuals that can be studied. And, while they can describe social networks, they do not measure social capital.

A third set of research issues surround the role of social capital in managing costs versus the role of social capital in fostering responsiveness to local conditions and issues. It would be useful to know more precisely how specific activities that create social capital might also encourage or restrict the ways in which it is applied. Do some IHRM practices, such as facilitating communities of practice, have a positive effect on responsiveness but little influence on cost containment? Do other practices, such as cross-cultural career paths, encourage global best practices that facilitate cost control, but inhibit diversity and responsiveness at the local level? Research into which practices have a robust impact and which are more specialized is important for designing effective IHRM strategies to fit specific competitive strategies.

Fourth, research is needed to articulate and assess IHRM's role in the tension between diversity assimilation and diversity exploitation. One route is to better understand the mechanisms by which IHRM practices can enable an organization to use social capital to increase the firm's ability to absorb and capitalize on the complexity of the rich and diverse repertoire of behaviours, values, actions and ideas that become available from operating in an international arena. An important research question is under what conditions a firm should emphasize its ability to absorb and capitalize on differences and under what conditions it should emphasize its ability to reduce and overcome differences. For example, Hofstede (1985) demonstrated that power distance, the degree to which inequality in power is accepted, varies considerably across nations. What are the tradeoffs in developing IHRM practices that enable managers to use social capital as a mechanism for adapting their behavior to accommodate a local preference for direction and hierarchical distinction as opposed to developing IHRM practices to use social capital as a mechanism for developing a common corporate value regarding power distance that overcomes local variations?

A fifth useful task is to identify the specific IHRM practices that transform the potential for social capital inherent in a firm's social networks into a realized organizational capability that leverages knowledge, connections and other tangible and intangible resources. This is the essence of transforming social capital from a private good to a public good. For example, enterprise resource planning systems create a network of structural, relationship and cognitive links across the organization. However this potential is only transformed into realized social capital if actions are taken to build upon the impersonal connections to create integrative bonds and emotional ties. Little is known about the specific actions IHRM can take to ensure that social networks become social capital.

Sixth, we need a clearer understanding of what types of social capital are desirable for different organizational situations. Research reviewed earlier suggests a trend toward developing a contingency perspective on social capital. Strong ties (or high-quality connections) are necessary in workgroup situations of high interdependency, as well as within multinational corporations that require high interdependency among units. Weak ties, on the other hand, may be useful for capitalizing on an organization's knowledge base by facilitating the flow and transfer of knowledge among individuals and units. These relationships need further clarification and empirical testing.

Conclusion
So what is the current state of knowledge about social capital and its importance to IHRM? At present, social capital and social network theory

and research offer interesting potential for adding to the explanation of the 'black box' of strategic human resource management. A focus on social capital and social networks may add to our understanding of how people make a difference and why the intangible assets of a firm are so crucial to success, particularly in global, knowledge-intensive enterprises and industries.

The underlying theme of strategic human resource management is that people matter; that the way a firm manages and capitalizes on its human talent can make the difference between success and failure. Human resource professionals have accomplished a great deal with regard to developing and nurturing a firm's human capital, but, just as resources are more powerful once they are combined to form strategic capabilities, human capital is more powerful once it is leveraged through relationships to form communities and networks of engaged individuals applying their talents collaboratively.

International operations guarantee diversity; however diversity alone is no guarantee of organizational success. Diversity applied toward a common objective is the key to synergy. Diversity directed toward different purposes is a source of flexibility. Social capital provides a bridge to connect the various capabilities, perspectives, purposes and settings that drive a global enterprise. Effective international human resource management must be as concerned with creating and directing a firm's social capital as it is with creating and guiding its human capital. This is a largely unexplored area of research providing many opportunities for discovery.

References

Adler, P.S. & S-W. Kwon. 2002. Social capital: prospects for a new concept. *Academy of Management Review*, **27**(1): 17–41.

Argote, L. & P. Ingram. 2000. Knowledge transfer: a basis for competitive advantage in firms. *Organizational Behavior and Human Decision Processes*, **82**(1): 150–69.

Bolino, M.C., W.H. Turney & J.M. Bloodgood. 2002. Citizenship behavior and the creation of social capital in organizations. *Academy of Management Review*, **27**(4): 505–22.

Brass, D.J. 1995. A social network perspective on human resources management. *Research in personnel and human resource management*, **13**: 39–79.

Burt, R. 1992. *Structural holes.* Cambridge, MA: Harvard University Press.

Burt, R.S. 2004. Structural holes and good ideas. *American Journal of Sociology*, **110**: 349–99.

Burt, R.S., R.M. Hogarth & C. Michaud. 2000. The social capital of French and American managers. *Organization Science*, **11**: 123–47.

Chen, G. & R.J. Klimoski. 2003. The impact of expectations on newcomer performance in teams as mediated by work characteristics, social exchanges, and empowerment. *Academy of Management Journal*, **46**(5): 591–607.

Cohen, W.M. & D.A. Levinthal. 1990. Absorptive capacity: a new perspective on learning and innovation. *Administrative Science Quarterly*, **35**: 128–52.

Coleman, J. 1988. Social capital in the creation of human capital. *American Journal of Sociology*, **94**: S95–S120.

Cross, R. & A. Parker. 2004. *The hidden power of social networks: understanding how work really gets done in organizations.* Boston, MA: Harvard Business School Press.

Dess, G.G. & J.D. Shaw. 2001. Voluntary turnover, social capital, and organizational performance. *Academy of Management Review*, **26**(3): 446–57.

Dutton, J.E. & E.D. Heaphy. 2003. The power of high quality connections. In K.S. Cameron, J.E. Dutton & R.E. Quinn (eds), *Positive organizational scholarship*. San Francisco, CA: Berrett-Koehler Publishers.

Eisenhardt, K.M. & J.A. Martin. 2000. Dynamic capabilities: what are they? *Strategic Management Journal*, **44**(6): 1229–50.

Gittell, J.H. 2003. A theory of relational coordination. In K.S. Cameron, J.E. Dutton & R.E. Quinn (eds), *Positive organizational scholarship*. San Francisco, CA: Berrett-Koehler Publishers.

Graen, G.B. & M. Uhl-Bien. 1995. Relationship-based approach to leadership: development of leader–member exchange (LMX) theory of leadership over 25 years: applying a multi-level domain approach. *Leadership Quarterly*, **6**(2): 219–47.

Granovetter, M. 1974. *Getting a job: a study in contacts and careers*. Chicago, IL: University of Chicago Press.

Gupta, A.K. & V. Govindarajan. 2004. *Global strategy and organization*. New York: John Wiley & Sons.

Hansen, M.T. 1999. The search-transfer problem: the role of weak ties in sharing knowledge across organization subunits. *Administrative Science Quarterly*, **44**(1): 82–111.

Hofstede, G. 1985. The interaction between national and organizational value systems. *Journal of Management Studies*, **22**: 347–57.

Inkpen, A.C. & E.W.K. Tsang. (2005). Social capital, networks, and knowledge transfer. *Academy of Management Review*, **30**: 146–65.

Kelloway, E.K. & J. Barling. 2000. What have we learned about developing transformational leaders? *Leadership and Organizational Development Journal*, **21**(3): 157–61.

Kogut, B. & U. Zander. 1992. Knowledge of the firm, combinative capabilities, and the replication of technology. *Organization Science*, **3**(3): 383–97.

Kostova, T. & K. Roth. 2003. Social capital in multinational corporations and a micro–macro model of its formation. *Academy of Management Review*, **28**(2): 297–317.

Krackhardt, D. 1990. Assessing the political landscape: structure, cognition, and power in organizations. *Administrative Science Quarterly*, **35**(2): 342–69.

Lazenga, E. & P.E. Pattison. 2001. Social capital as social mechanisms and collective assets: the example of status auctions among colleagues. In N. Lin, K.C. Cook & R.S. Burt (eds), *Social capital theory and research*. New York: de Gruyter.

Lengnick-Hall, M.L. & C.A. Lengnick-Hall. 2002. *Human resource management in the knowledge economy: new challenges, new roles, new capabilities*. San Francisco, CA: Berrett-Koehler Publishers.

Lengnick-Hall, M.L. & C.A. Lengnick-Hall. 2003. HR's role in building relationship networks. *Academy of Management Executive*, **17**(4): 53–63.

McFadyen, M.A. & A.A. Cannella Jr. 2004. Social capital and knowledge creation: diminishing returns of the number and strength of exchange relationships. *Academy of Management Journal*, **47**(5): 735–46.

Nahapiet, J. & S. Ghoshal. 1998. Social capital, intellectual capital, and organizational advantage. *Academy of Management Review*, **23**: 242–66.

Portes, A. 1998. Social capital: its origins and applications in modern sociology. *Annual Reviews of Sociology*, **24**: 1–24.

Putnam, R. 1993. The prosperous community: social capital and public life. *American Prospect*, **4**(13): 35–42.

Rousseau, D. 1995. *Psychological contracts in organizations: understanding written and unwritten agreements*. Newbury Park, CA: Sage.

Sparrow, P., C. Brewster & H. Harris. 2004. *Globalizing human resource management*. London: Routledge.

Tsai, W. 2000. Social capital, strategic relatedness and the formation of intraorganizational linkages. *Strategic Management Journal*, **21**: 925–39.

26 International human resource management, fairness and trust: an organizational support theory framework

Ellen Whitener

P&G [Proctor and Gamble] has implemented a global candidate management system [selection system] which uses a common set of assessment factors and common assessment tools, such as a scorable application with an embedded biodata instrument, a problem solving test, an English proficiency test, and a structured interview . . . Variations across regions can occur due to local practices, local labor pools, or lack of trust in validated assessment tools. Generalizing across cultures, P&G tends to find that applicants generally prefer biodata instruments to cognitive tests . . . [and] P&G finds that local candidates . . . have trust issues based on their lack of experience with new selection tools or practices. (Wiechmann, Ryan & Hemingway, 2003: 79)

International Human Resource Management (IHRM) is 'the set of distinct activities, functions, and processes that are directed at attracting, developing, and maintaining . . . [a multinational corporation's (MNC)] . . . human resources. It is thus the aggregate of the various HRM systems used to manage people in the MNC, both at home and overseas' (Taylor, Beechler & Napier, 1996: 960). As P&G has experienced, IHRM embodies fundamental tensions between global and local practices and corporate and local cultures (Schuler, Dowling & De Cieri, 1993), tensions that result in 'trust issues' that can derail the effectiveness of the IHRM system.

Executives work hard to create a corporate human resource system that selects, develops and manages applicants, candidates and employees efficiently and effectively throughout the organization and builds trust in the organization (Whitener, 1997). To direct and support their efforts, HR researchers have taken a pragmatic approach, trying to identify the best practices and the best features of those practices by estimating relative effectiveness. The HR literature therefore is full of studies that estimate and compare the validities of selection practices, improvements in training outcomes of different training methods and learning practices, performance outcomes of different compensation schemes, and reactions and biases associated with different performance feedback/management processes. Researchers then recommend specific practices based on their relative effectiveness on the appropriate measure. Strategic HR researchers also take a pragmatic approach but at a higher level, demonstrating the impact of systems of HR practices on organizational and financial measures and identifying the appropriate HR architecture to meet strategic goals. Their research also provides corporate executives with information on how to design and implement an efficient and effective HR system. Finally international HR researchers conduct comparative research, searching for the 'best international HRM practices' given specific cultural contexts: asking how HR practices fare given cultural differences (Geringer, Frayne & Milliman, 2002).

Human resource management, however, is more than a mechanical system designed to optimize the efficiency and effectiveness of the human input into the enterprise. It is also a meaning-making system that sends messages to employees, messages that optimally achieve three levels of consistency (Baron & Kreps, 1999): (a) single-employee consistency which emphasizes that the different parts of the overall HR system should be consistent with each other; (b) among-employee consistency which emphasizes that the treatment of different workers should be consistent; and (c) temporal consistency which emphasizes consistency over time.

Achieving consistency across all three levels is difficult enough for the domestic organization, but the added layer of local cultural interpretation faced by MNCs makes achieving consistency in these ways across all aspects of global operations a Herculean task.

This chapter explores whether one way to address this task is to focus less on the specific HR activities and more on the content of a message that can stay consistent across cultures, employees and time even if the HR system on its face looks inconsistent: that the organization values employees and is supportive of and committed to them. Organizational support theory (OST) recognizes this aspect of human resources, proposing that employees interpret organizational policies, practices and treatment (including human resource practices) as indicators of the organization's support of and commitment to them (Eisenberger, Fasolo & Davis-LaMastro, 1990; Eisenberger, Huntington, Hutchison & Sowa, 1986). Relying on the tendency of employees to personify the organization, assigning it human-like characteristics, OST applies the notions of social exchange and reciprocity to the relationship between employees and the organization (Eisenberger *et al.*, 1990; Eisenberger *et al.*, 1986) and predicts that employees reciprocate, matching their attitudes toward the organization with their perceptions of their treatment (Rhoades & Eisenberger, 2002). In particular employees' perceptions of organizational support (Whitener, 2001) and fairness and equity of outcomes and procedures (Dirks & Ferrin, 2002; Konovsky & Pugh, 1994) affect their trust in the organization.

Trust involves positive expectations about a target and a willingness to make oneself vulnerable to that target (Rousseau, Sitkin, Burt & Camerer, 1998). It evolves over time from interpretive assessments of the trustworthiness of the target (Mayer, Davis & Schoorman, 1995). When the target is an individual, people interpret the individual's behaviour to determine whether he or she is trustworthy (Whitener, Brodt, Korsgaard & Werner, 1998).

Cultural differences affect their interpretive frameworks: their propensity to trust and their expectations of trustworthy behaviour (for example, Doney, Cannon & Mullen, 1998; Johnson & Cullen, 2001; Whitener *et al.*, 1998). Individuals from different cultures have different propensities to trust (for example, Downes, Hemmasi, Graf, Kelley & Huff, 2002; Huff & Kelley, 2003; Inglehart, 1997; Inglehart, Basanez & Moreno, 1998). More specifically, propensity to trust is higher in countries with high power distance, high uncertainty avoidance and low individualism (Johnson & Cullen, 2001; Hofstede, 1980). Individuals from different cultures also have different expectations of what constitutes trustworthy behaviour. Although some elements of leader trustworthiness, such as integrity, competence and benevolence, may be universal (Den Hartog, House, Hanges, Ruiz-Quintanilla, Dorfman *et al.*, 1999; House, Hanges, Ruiz-Quintanilla, Dorfman, Javidan & Dickson *et al.*, 1999), others, such as delegation of control, may be culture-specific (Whitener, Maznevski, Hua, Saebo & Ekelund, 1999).

When the target is an organization, people interpret the organization's actions and practices, including its human resource policies and procedures, to decide whether it is sufficiently trustworthy to warrant their trust (Blunsdon & Reed, 2003; Gould-Williams, 2003; Eisenberger *et al.*, 1990; Rhoades & Eisenberger, 2002; Whitener, 2001). Therefore the MNC faces a complicated meaning-making system because employees from different cultures present multiple, and diverse, interpretive frameworks, rooted in their cultural norms and values, that affect their interpretations of their experiences (their perceptions of organizational support and fairness) and have an impact on their trust (Doney *et al.*, 1998). This diversity creates a tension for the MNC between its desire for consistency in its human resource practices across its international operations and its need to adapt its human resource practices for local interpretations of those practices.

This tension will be difficult to resolve if IHRM research continues to focus on comparisons of the effectiveness of HR practices across different cultures without looking into the features of the meaning systems that affect employees' interpretations of those practices. OST's foundation in interpretation, social exchange and reciprocity, and the research on fairness and trust, provide direction beyond that associated with describing cultural differences for identifying the features of meaning systems and for designing IHRM practices to respond effectively.

Organizational support theory

Organizational support theory (Eisenberger *et al.*, 1986; Rhoades & Eisenberger, 2002) takes a 'relational' perspective that relies on social exchange theory (Blau, 1964; Homans, 1961) and the norm of reciprocity (Gouldner, 1960) and describes HR practices as messages interpreted by employees of the organization's support of and commitment to its employees. Social exchange theory originally focused on the way that two individuals build their relationship by trading 'favours' and reducing tension: a person receiving a favour from another feels tension from the relationship being out of balance, which obliges him or her to reciprocate by returning the favour. Organizational support theory applies the notions of exchange and reciprocity to the relationship between employees and the personified organization predicting that the extent to which employees perceive that they have received beneficial and favourable treatment from the organization (their perceptions of organizational support) affects their attitudes toward the organization. For example, if they feel that the employer is committed to them, then they reciprocate with their commitment to the employer.

Empirical work has supported the theory: supportive human resource practices, procedural justice, trust in the employer and perceptions of organizational support interact in increasing employee commitment (Allen, Shore & Griffeth, 2003; Rhoades, Eisenberger & Armeli, 2001; Whitener, 2001) which mediates the impact of these variables on intentions and actual behaviour, such as turnover (for example, Allen *et al.*, 2003; Rhoades *et al.*, 2001). The evidence then suggests that organizational support theory ties together the interactions among human resource practices, organizational fairness and trust into a framework (Albrecht & Travaglione, 2003; Allen *et al.*, 2003; Ambrose & Schminke, 2003; Erdogan, 2002; Rhoades *et al.*, 2001; Wayne, Shore, Bommer & Tetrick, 2002; Whitener, 2001): employees' trust in the organization and its leadership is rooted in the fairness and support they perceive in the organization's human resource policies and practices.

This framework provides the backbone for exploring the features of meaning making in interpreting human resource management practices in the international, multi-national context. It includes four links, between (a) international human resource practices and perceptions of organizational support, (b) international human resource practices and perceptions of organizational fairness, (c) perceptions of organizational support and trust, and (d) perceptions of organizational fairness and trust. Consideration of each of these links provides direction for future research on understanding how to design human resource practices across cultures, balancing the tension between global and local interpretations and practices and conveying a consistent message of organizational commitment and support.

International human resource practices and perceptions of organizational support

Eisenberger *et al.* (1986) devised the construct, perceptions of organizational support (POS), to measure employees' perception that the organization values and cares about them. The construct validity of POS and its relationships with predicted antecedents and consequences are well-established (Rhoades & Eisenberger, 2002). Coefficient alpha reliabilities with US samples (the country of construct origin) often hit the 0.90s (for example, Wayne *et al.*, 2002). Meta-analyses have yielded significant correlations with human resource practices (Rhoades & Eisenberger, 2002) as well as organizational fairness and trust (Dirks & Ferrin, 2002; Rhoades & Eisenberger, 2002).

A little work has explored POS in cross-cultural contexts: with American expatriates (Kraimer & Wayne, 2004), Turkish school teachers (Erdogan, Kraimer & Liden, 2004) and Belgian workers (Eisenberger, Stinglhamber, Vandenberghe, Sucharaski & Rhoades, 2002; Stinglhamber & Vandenberghe, 2003). However this work has been, like much before it, primarily descriptive and comparative and does not provide direction in understanding the meaning-making process by which individuals from different cultures interpret the supportiveness of the organization's human resource practices.

Features of OST provide direction for exploring some of the fundamental ways that cultural differences affect the interpretation of human resource practices. For example, OST assumes that employees personify and reify the organization, seeing it as a person or actor and a concrete, holistic entity. When employees personify the organization, they generalize from organizational practices and treatment they receive from individuals who represent the organization to the organization itself. However individuals from different cultures may vary in the extent to which they personify or anthropomorphize organizations. Consider that individuals from familistic societies have strong bonds among members of ingroups but weak bonds between members of different groups (that is, 'low trust' societies: Fukayama, 1995). People in these cultures do not build strong relationships with individuals attached only by their organizational affiliation. Because they do not identify closely with the individuals, they seem unlikely to build an attachment to the organization or personify it. And if they are not personifying the organizations, they also seem unlikely to be interpreting their experiences as unified messages of personal support. In contrast individuals from societies that freely and regularly develop bonds across a variety of associations and communities (that is, 'high trust' societies: ibid.) would be more likely to have strong relationships and identification with individuals, generalize from those individuals to the organization as actor, and interpret the organization's actions as a coherent message of the organization's support (or lack thereof). These individuals, from personifying cultures, would then evoke their local cultural values to interpret the message they see, whereas individuals from non-personifying cultures would not even see a message from the organization that they need to interpret. The local–global tension would therefore be much more relevant to employees in personifying cultures than non-personifying cultures, such that we may present the following proposition.

Proposition 1: organizations would need to adapt HR practices to local customs in cultures that have a tendency to personify and attach to organizations but could focus on global HR practices in cultures that rarely personify and attach to organizations.

In addition, OST predicts that employees interpret HR practices. Value congruence affects interpretation, suggesting that the fit between employees' and the organization's values will affect their interpretation of the supportiveness of HR practices. Jackson (2002) described a 'locus of human value' as the value that cultures place on human beings within their work organizations. He proposed two opposing loci of human value: *instrumentalism*, which considers employees valuable for their ability to achieve the objectives of the organization, and *humanism*, which considers employees valuable for who they are. In their extremes they lead to different human resource practices. Organizations with a strong instrumental locus of human value (such as in Hong Kong: Jackson, 2002) are likely to craft job descriptions carefully, pay by results and use objective or results-oriented performance appraisals. In contrast, organizations with a strong humanistic locus of human value (such as in Japan: Ibid.) are likely to provide extensive job rotation, seniority-based pay and holistically developmental performance appraisals.

Jackson suggests that employees are likely to interpret their treatment as unsupportive if human resource practices do not fit their locus of human value: 'Inappropriate HR policies and practices . . . may lead to alienation, poor motivation, and labor strife where staff see themselves as stepping out of their own culture into an alien one when they go to work in the morning' (ibid., 471). However appropriateness may not be strictly based on match/mismatch. Individuals from instrumentalist cultures that value employees for their contribution to organizational objectives may be willing to interpret HR practices favourably, regardless of whether they are 'instrumental' or 'humanistic' practices, as long as the practices are consistent with organizational objectives. Individuals from humanist cultures that value employees for who they are as people may only interpret HR practices favourably if they are humanistic practices. Therefore the tension between local and global practices would be more relevant in humanistic than in instrumental cultures:

Proposition 2: organizations would need to adapt HR practices to local customs in humanistic cultures but could focus on global HR practices in cultures that have an instrumental locus of human value, being sure to clarify how the practices meet organizational objectives.

International human resource practices and fairness or justice

OST predicts that concerns about fairness or justice in the workplace are fundamental in interpreting the extent to which the organization (as represented by its treatment, including HR practices) is supportive of its employees (Folger & Cropanzano, 1998; Rhoades & Eisenberger, 2002). People are concerned about distributive justice, whether their outcomes are fair (Adams, 1965) and procedural justice, whether the process by which outcomes are distributed is fair (Thibaut & Walker, 1975). To determine the fairness of their outcomes, people engage in a social exchange and comparison process, comparing the ratio of what they give (their inputs) and what they receive (their outcomes) in an exchange relationship to a 'comparison other's' input–outcome ratio. They apply decision rules to judge the fairness of input–outcome ratios (for example, equity, equality or need) and of the process by which outcomes are achieved (for example, consistency, bias suppression, accuracy, correctability, representativeness and ethicality (Adams, 1965; Levanthal, 1976). They then use their fairness judgments to guide their interpretation of the organization's support and commitment (Rhoades & Eisenberger, 2002). Indeed two different meta-analyses (Cohen-Charash & Spector, 2001; Rhoades & Eisenberger, 2002) found significant and large relationships between fairness perceptions and perceived organizational support (average weighted correlations of 0.54 and 0.62, respectively).

Although concern about fairness of treatment in the workplace may be universal and its impact on employees' attitudes significant, the importance, definition, prevailing norms and rules and social/political context of justice vary by culture (Greenberg, 2001; Steiner, 2001). Researchers have explored these variations by comparing differences in fairness dimensions and perceptions between members from different countries or among people of different cultural orientations (Kluckhohn & Strodtbeck, 1961) or cultural values (Hofstede, 1980; Schwartz, 1994). But cultural differences may more subtly underlie differences in specific aspects of perceived fairness. For example, although earlier work suggested that people in most cultures valued participation in decisions ('voice': Greenberg, 2001), a set of recent studies indicates that the importance of voice in determining perceptions of fairness varies, depending on cultural norms associated with power distance. Individuals who were not comfortable with large power distances (Hofstede, 1980) were more sensitive to the extent to which participation in decisions was allowed (Brockner, Ackerman, Greenberg, Gelfand, Francesco, Chen, Leung, Bierbrauer, Gomez, Kirkman & Shapiro, 2001).

This research suggests that cultural differences (for example, collectivism, individualism and power distance: Hofstede, 1980) affect the application of rules and weighting of fairness dimensions:

Proposition 3: cultural values and orientation influence the fairness rules used across local operations, which in turn affect fairness perceptions of HR practices. For example, individuals from cultures with small power distances may be more likely to base their fairness perceptions of procedural justice on representativeness and voice than individuals from cultures with large power distances. They may also be more likely to base their fairness perceptions of distributive justice on equality than individuals from cultures with large power distances.

In addition, cultural differences may also affect perceptions of fairness through their impact on preferred styles of information processing. For example, Steiner and Gilliland (1996) found that American subjects trusted scientific process and empirical data significantly more than French subjects, who relied more heavily on argumentation and reasoning in judging the fairness of selection instruments. Similarly cultural differences may affect judgment biases, cognitive shortcuts used to manage information processing, which have long been assumed to be biologically based and universal. In four separate studies, American subjects (representing a high individualism culture) were significantly more likely to display a self-serving bias than Japanese subjects (representing a high collectivism culture: Gelfand, Higgins, Nishii, Raver, Dominguez, Murakami, Yamaguchi & Toyama, 2002).

Therefore recent work implies that culture affects complex processes, such as employees' information processing and judgment rules, which may have an impact on the extent to which employees interpret IHR practices as fair, and ultimately supportive.

Proposition 4: cultural values and orientation influence information process-
ing preferences and judgment biases used across local operations, which in
turn affect fairness perceptions of HR practices. For example, individuals
from individualistic cultures may be more likely to use a self-serving bias and
focus on distributive justice than individuals from cultures with large power
distances.

Perceptions of organizational support and trust

Numerous research studies have explored the relationship between POS
and trust. Indeed the original articulation of OST predicted that trust
would play a key role in influencing employees' responses to their perceptions of their treatment. A recent meta-analysis (Dirks & Ferrin, 2002)
found a weighted average correlation of 0.69 between POS and trust in
organizational leadership.

In the cross-cultural, international context, the relationship between
perceived organizational support and trust may be affected by the relationship between culture and exchange ideology (and its related components
such as the norm of reciprocity). Although biologists have hailed social
exchange and reciprocity, the backbones of OST, as central to every area of
life across all cultures, sociologists have explored their nuances and found
some differences (Buchan, Croson & Dawes, 2002; Redding, 1990). For
example, although a norm of reciprocity may govern social interactions
across cultures, the timing, level and extent of reciprocation may vary by
cultures. Indeed, in an experiment manipulating conditions of ingroup and
outgroup and direct and indirect exchange using an investment task,
Buchan *et al.* found that participants from China and Korea were more
likely to reciprocate than participants from Japan and the USA.

The small number of cultures makes it difficult to speculate, but it seems
plausible that perhaps the same mechanism associated with Fukayama's
high and low trust societies may be associated with this result. Individuals
in low trust societies may reciprocate easily within their groups but not
outside their groups; individuals in high trust societies may reciprocate
easily, even with strangers. We therefore might see a similar difference in the
tendency to reciprocate the organization's treatment.

Proposition 5: individuals from high trust cultures may be more likely to rec-
iprocate positive treatment from the organization than those from low trust
cultures. In particular, the relationship between perceptions of organizational
support and trust in the organization will be stronger in high trust cultures
than in low trust cultures. Organizations would need to adapt HR practices to
local customs in high trust cultures but could focus on global HR practices in
low trust cultures.

Perceptions of organizational fairness and trust

Finally, other factors being equal, experiences associated with fairness are likely to influence trust (Brockner, Siegel, Daly, Tyler & Martin, 1997; Konovsky & Pugh, 1994). Indeed, three recent meta-analyses found significant and moderate (0.43–0.61) weighted mean correlations between procedural and distributive justice and trust (Cohen-Charash & Spector, 2001; Colquitt, Conlon, Wesson, Porter & Ng, 2001; Dirks & Ferrin, 2002).

Several studies have explicitly explored the universality of this relationship (Aryee, Budhwar & Chen, 2002; Lind, Tyler & Huo, 1997; Pillai, Williams & Tan, 2001). In surveys and experiments involving German, American, Hong Kong Chinese, Japanese and Indian subjects, these researchers found that trust and procedural justice were significantly related to each other. They also found that the factor structures of the measures and the strength of the relationships were sufficiently similar to conclude 'the universal importance of trust as it relates to organizational justice' (Pillai *et al.*, 2001: 325). Indeed Lind *et al.* sounded rather surprised at the result: 'Given the sometimes substantial cross-cultural differences that social psychologists have reported . . . and given hypotheses in the literature about how the very meaning of justice might change radically across cultures . . . we had little reason to think a priori that the processes that drive procedural justice judgments were so robust across cultures. But in all four cultures [that we tested], procedural fairness appeared to be defined largely in terms of the relational variables', including trust (Lind *et al.*, 1997: 777).

OST-related constructs, however, go beyond cultural comparisons like this. In particular, the theory predicts that differences in perceptions of fairness may be rooted in culturally related social identity. Several studies of fairness of HR practices (for example, selection outcomes and procedures and negotiation outcomes and procedures) suggested that perceptions of fairness were affected by whether social exchange was important to self-identification. Individuals with cultural norms where social exchange significantly affects identity were more sensitive to justice process and outcomes (Brockner, Chen, Mannix, Leung & Skarlicki, 2000) than individuals with cultural norms where social exchange has a weak relationship with identity.

Proposition 6: individuals from cultures where identity is strongly rooted in social exchange will be more responsive to fairness perceptions than those from cultures where identity is not strongly rooted in social exchange. In particular, the relationship between perceptions of organizational fairness and trust in the organization will be stronger in cultures with high exchange-based social identity than in cultures with low exchange-based social identity.

Organizations would need to adapt HR practices to local customs in cultures with high exchange-based social identity but could focus on global HR practices in cultures with low exchange-based social identity.

Conclusion

Organizational support theory, connecting international human resource practices, and trust through the interpretation of the fairness and support of those practices, suggests some different avenues for future research than a 'mere' comparison of cultural differences. Organizational support theory relies on several important mechanisms: interpretation, social exchange and reciprocity. Each of these mechanisms can capture some of the nuances associated with assessing the effectiveness of human resource practices in international and cross-cultural contexts. First, cultural values (for example, locus of human values, power distance, individualism, collectivism and societal trust/propensity to trust) affect the interpretation of human resource practices. If human resource practices fit their cultural values, then employees will be more likely to interpret those practices as fair and supportive. Second, interpretation is subject to information and judgment processes. Recent research has just cracked open the door to exploring how cultures vary in their information and judgment processes. Third, the whole notion of organizational support theory relies on social exchange and reciprocity. Yet social exchange may not be important to individuals in some cultures and reciprocity rules may vary widely across cultures. Researchers who broaden our awareness of the role of the social exchange ideology across cultures will facilitate our understanding of how to craft and modify human resource practices that effectively bridge the global and local divide by sending a unified and strong message of organizational support and commitment.

References

Adams, J.S. 1965. Inequity of social exchange. In L. Berkowitz (ed.), *Advances in experimental social psychology*, vol. 2: 267–99. New York: Academic Press.

Albrecht, S. & A. Travaglione. 2003. Trust in public-sector senior management. *International Journal of Human Resource Management*, **14**: 76–92.

Allen, D.G., L.M. Shore & R.W. Griffeth. 2003. The role of perceived organizational support and supportive human resource practices in the turnover process. *Journal of Management*, **29**: 99–118.

Ambrose, M.L. & M. Schminke. 2003. Organizational structure as a moderator of the relationship between procedural justice, interactional justice, perceived organizational support, and supervisory trust. *Journal of Applied Psychology*, **88**: 295–305.

Aryee, S., P.S. Budhwar & Z.X. Chen. 2002. Trust as a mediator of the relationship between organizational justice and work outcomes: test of a social exchange model. *Journal of Organizational Behavior*, **23**: 267–85.

Baron, J.N. & D.M. Kreps. 1999. Consistent human resource practices. *California Management Review*, **41**(3): 29–53.

Blau, P.M. 1964. *Exchange and power in social life*. New York: Wiley.

Blunsdon, B. & K. Reed. 2003. The effects of technical and social conditions on workplace trust. *International Journal of Human Resource Management*, **14**: 12–27.

Brockner, J., Y. Chen, E.A. Mannix, K. Leung & D. Skarlicki. 2000. Culture and procedural justice: when the effects of what you do depend on how you do it. *Administrative Science Quarterly*, **45**: 138–59.

Brockner, J., P.A. Siegel, J. Daly, T.R. Tyler & C. Martin. 1997. When trust matters: the moderating effect of outcome favorability. *Administrative Science Quarterly*, **42**: 558–83.

Brockner, J., G. Ackerman, J. Greenberg, M.J. Gelfand, A.M. Francesco, Z.X. Chen, K. Leung, G. Bierbrauer, C. Gomez, B.L. Kirkman & D. Shapiro 2001. Culture and procedural justice: the influence of power distance on reactions to voice. *Journal of Experimental Social Psychology*, **37**: 300–315.

Buchan, N.R., R.T.A. Croson & R.M. Dawes. 2002. Swift neighbors and persistent strangers: a cross-cultural investigation of trust and reciprocity in social exchange. *American Journal of Sociology*, **108**: 168–206.

Cohen-Charash, Y. & P.E. Spector. 2001. The role of justice in organizations: a meta-analysis. *Organizational Behavior and Human Decision Processes*, **86**: 278–321.

Colquitt, J.A., D.E. Conlon, M.J. Wesson, C.O.L.H. Porter & K.Y. Ng. 2001. Justice at the millennium: a meta-analytic review of 25 years of organizational justice research. *Journal of Applied Psychology*, **86**: 425–45.

Den Hartog, D.N., R.J. House, P.J. Hanges, S.A. Ruiz-Quintanilla, P.W. Dorfman, *et al.* 1999. Culture-specific and cross-culturally generalizable implicit leadership theories: are attributes of charismatic/transformational leadership universally endorsed? *Leadership Quarterly*, **10**: 219–56.

Dirks, K.T. & D.L. Ferrin. 2002. Trust in leadership: meta-analytic findings and implications for research and practice. *Journal of Applied Psychology*, **87**: 611–28.

Doney, P.M., J.P. Cannon & M.R. Mullen. 1998. Understanding the influence of national culture on the development of trust. *Academy of Management Review*, **23**: 601–20.

Downes, M., M. Hemmasi, L.A. Graf, L. Kelley & L. Huff. 2002. *International Journal of Management*, **19**: 614–21.

Eisenberger, R., P. Fasolo & V. Davis-LaMastro. 1990. Perceived organizational support and employee diligence, commitment, and innovation. *Journal of Applied Psychology*, **75**: 51–9.

Eisenberger, R., R. Huntington, S. Hutchison & D. Sowa. 1986. Perceived organizational support. *Journal of Applied Psychology*, **71**: 500–507.

Eisenberger, R., F. Stinglhamber, C. Vandenberghe, I.L. Sucharaski & L. Rhoades. 2002. Perceived supervisor support: contributions to perceived organizational support and employee retention. *Journal of Applied Psychology*, **87**: 565–73.

Erdogan, B. 2002. Antecedents and consequences of justice perceptions in performance appraisals. *Human Resource Management Review*, **12**: 555–78.

Erdogan, B., M.L. Kraimer & R.C. Liden. 2004. Work value congruence and intrinsic career success: the compensatory roles of leader–member exchange and perceived organizational support. *Personnel Psychology*, **57**: 305–32.

Folger, R. & R. Cropanzano. 1998. *Organizational justice and human resource management*. Thousand Oaks, CA: Sage.

Fukuyama, F. 1995. *Trust: the social virtues and the creation of prosperity*. New York: Free Press.

Gelfand, M.J., M. Higgins, L.H. Nishii, J.L. Raver, A. Dominguez, F. Murakami, S. Yamaguchi & M. Toyama. 2002. Culture and egocentric perceptions of fairness in conflict and negotiation. *Journal of Applied Psychology*, **87**: 833–45.

Geringer, J.M., C.A. Frayne & J.F. Milliman. 2002. In search of 'best practices' in international human resource management: research design and methodology. *Human Resource Management*, **41**: 5–30.

Gould-Williams, J. 2003. The importance of HR practices and workplace trust in achieving superior performance: a study of public-sector organizations. *International Journal of Human Resource Management*, **14**: 28-54.

Gouldner, A.W. 1960. The norm of reciprocity: a preliminary statement. *American Sociological Review*, **25**: 161–78.

Greenberg, J. 2001. The seven loose can(n)ons of organizational justice. In J. Greenberg & R. Cropanzano (eds), *Advances in organizational justice*. Stanford, CA: Stanford University Press.

Hofstede, G. 1980. *Culture's consequences: international differences in work-related values.* Beverly Hills, CA: Sage.

Homans, G.C. 1961. *Social behavior: its elementary forms.* New York: Harcourt, Brace & World.

House, R., P.J. Hanges, A. Ruiz-Quintanilla, P.W. Dorfman, M. Javidan, M.W. Dickson, *et al.* 1999. Cultural influences on leadership and organizations: project GLOBE. In W.H. Mobley, M.J. Gessner & V. Arnold (eds), *Advances in global leadership*, Greenwich, CT: JAI Press.

Huff, L. & L. Kelley. 2003. Levels of organizational trust in individualist versus collectivist societies: a seven-nation study. *Organization Science*, **14**: 81–90.

Inglehart, R. 1997. *Modernization and postmodernization: cultural, economic, and political change in 43 societies*. Princeton, NJ: Princeton University Press.

Inglehart, R., M. Basanez & A. Moreno. 1998. *Human values and beliefs. A cross-cultural sourcebook*. Ann Arbor, MI: The University of Michigan Press.

Jackson, T. 2002. The management of people across cultures: valuing people differently. *Human Resource Management*, **41**: 455–75.

Johnson, J.L. & J.B. Cullen. 2001. Trust in cross-cultural relationships. In M.J. Gannon & K.L. Newman (eds), *The Blackwell handbook of cross-cultural management*. Oxford: Blackwell.

Kluckhohn, F.R. & F.L. Strodtbeck. 1961. *Variations in value orientations*. Evanston, IL: Row, Peterson.

Konovsky, M. & S.D. Pugh. 1994. Citizenship behavior and social exchange. *Academy of Management Journal*, **37**: 656–69.

Kraimer, M.L. & S.J. Wayne. 2004. An examination of perceived organizational support as a multidimensional construct in the context of an expatriate assignment. *Journal of Management*, **30**: 209–37.

Levanthal, G.S. 1976. The distribution of rewards and resources in groups and organizations. In L. Berkowitz & W. Walster (eds), *Advances in experimental social psychology*, vol. 9: 91–131. New York: Academic Press.

Lind, E.A., T.R. Tyler & Y.J. Huo. 1997. Procedural context and culture: variation in the antecedents of procedural justice judgments. *Journal of Personality and Social Psychology*, **73**: 767–80.

Mayer, R.C., J.H. Davis & F.D. Schoorman. 1995. An integrative model of organizational trust. *Academy of Management Review*, **20**: 709–34.

Pillai, R., E.S. Williams & J.J. Tan. 2001. Are the scales tipped in favor of procedural or distributive justice? An investigation of the U.S., India, Germany, and Hong Kong (China). *The International Journal of Conflict Management*, **12**: 312–32.

Redding, S.G. 1990. *The spirit of Chinese capitalism*. New York: W. de Gruyter.

Rhoades, L. & R. Eisenberger. 2002. Perceived organizational support: a review of the literature. *Journal of Applied Psychology*, **87**: 698–714.

Rhoades, L., R. Eisenberger & S. Armeli. 2001. Affective commitment to the organization: the contribution of perceived organizational support. *Journal of Applied Psychology*, **86**: 825–36.

Rousseau, D.M., S.B. Sitkin, R.S. Burt & C. Camerer. 1998. Not so different after all: a cross-discipline view of trust. *Academy of Management Review*, **23**: 393–404.

Schuler, R., P. Dowling & H. De Cieri. 1993. An integrative framework of strategic international human resource management. *Journal of Management*, **19**: 419–59.

Schwartz, S.H. 1994. Beyond individualism/collectivism: new cultural dimensions of values. In U. Kim, H.C. Triandis & G. Yoon (eds), *Individualism and collectivism*. London: Sage.

Steiner, D.D. 2001. Cultural influences on perceptions of distributive and procedural justice. In S. Gilliland, D. Steiner & D. Skarlicki (eds), *Theoretical and cultural perspectives on organizational justice*. Greenwich, CT: Information Age Publishing.

Steiner, D.D. & S.W. Gilliland. 1996. Fairness reactions to personnel selection techniques in France and the United States. *Journal of Applied Psychology*, **81**: 134–41.

Stinglhamber, F. & C. Vandenberghe. 2003. Organizations and supervisors as sources of support and targets of commitment: a longitudinal study. *Journal of Organizational Behavior*, **24**: 251–70.

Taylor, S., S. Beechler & N. Napier. 1996. Toward an integrative model of strategic international human resource management. *Academy of Management Review*, **21**: 959–85.

Thibaut, J.W. & L. Walker. 1975. *Procedural justice: a psychological analysis*. Hillsdale, NJ: Erlbaum.

Wayne, S. J., L.M. Shore, W.H. Bommer & L.E. Tetrick. 2002. The role of fair treatment and rewards in perceptions of organizational support and leader–member exchange. *Journal of Applied Psychology*, **87**: 590–98.

Whitener, E.M. 1997. The impact of human resource activities on employee trust. *Human Resource Management Review*, **7**: 389–404.

Whitener, E.M. 2001. Do 'high commitment' human resource practices affect employee commitment? A cross-level analysis using hierarchical linear modeling. *Journal of Management*, **27**: 515–35.

Whitener, E.M., S.E. Brodt, M.A. Korsgaard & J.M. Werner. 1998. Managers as initiators of trust: an exchange relationship framework for understanding managerial trustworthy behavior. *Academy of Management Review*, **23**: 513–30.

Whitener, E.M., M.L. Maznevski, W. Hua, S. Saebo & B. Ekelund. 1999. Testing the cultural boundaries of a model of trust: subordinate–manager relationships in China, Norway and the United States. Paper presented at the 59th Annual Meeting of the Academy of Management, Chicago, IL, August.

Wiechmann, D., A.M. Ryan & M. Hemingway. 2003. Designing and implementing global staffing systems: Part I: leaders in global staffing. *Human Resource Management*, **42**: 71–83.

27 Gender and international human resource management

Jeff Hearn, Beverly D. Metcalfe and Rebecca Piekkari

Niall Fitzgerald, co-chairman [*sic.*] of Unilever . . . brought together for a week-long leadership exercise . . . the multinational's top 100 managers . . . In an interview in the Financial Times (17/06/03), he recalls his dismayed reaction when he discovered not one woman was to be found in the group:
'My God, how can we have put so much work into gender diversity and I see no reflection of it in the top leadership?' (Cited in EFQM, 2003)

International Human Resource Management (IHRM) is not usually examined from a gender perspective. In contrast, this chapter addresses the relation of gender to IHRM, primarily in the context of multinational corporations (MNCs). Although IHRM as a field encompasses cross-cultural management and comparative research on HR systems and industrial relations in different countries, much of the field, both practically and academically, focuses on human resource activities and implications in multinationals (see, for example, Dowling & Welch, 2004). As Schuler, Budhwar and Florkowski (2004: 356) write, 'The purpose of IHRM is to enable the firm, the multinational enterprise, to be successful globally.' This does not mean that gender and IHRM would be unimportant for small- and medium-sized companies, yet these issues have received even less scholarly attention in small and medium enterprises (SMEs) and in companies in early stages of internationalization.

This chapter examines the following issues. First, what is gender? Second, what is meant by gendered organizations and gendered management? Third, what has gender to do with IHRM? Next, the relations of gender, diversity and IHRM are discussed, followed by placing IHRM into the context of globalization. Finally, some possible future directions for gendering IHRM are presented, before brief concluding remarks.

What is 'gender'?

Gender and gendered power relations are major defining features of most organizations and managements, including IHRM. Organizations, managements and IHRM are not just structured by gender but pervaded and constituted by and through gender; at the same time, organizational and managerial realities construct and sometimes subvert dominant gender relations. When gender is referred to, it is usual to think of 'men and women' and 'relations between them'; these are certainly part of gender, but only a part. Gender is just as relevant in relations between women and between men, for example, in gendered hierarchies within genders. Gender has also taken on other more complex meanings. These wider understandings of gender are both contested and central to analysing organizations.

Sex and sex differences are often naturalized as fixed in biology. The distinction between sex and gender was recognized in the 1960s in feminist and other critical accounts of women's and men's positions in society. It highlighted how what was often thought of as natural and biological was also social, cultural, historical and political. 'Sex' as biological sex differences was distinguished from 'gender' as sociocultural constructions of sex differences (Oakley, 1972).[1] This has led on to much research on sex/gender differences and indeed their relative absence (Jacklin & Maccoby, 1975; Durkin, 1978), psychological scales measuring 'masculinity–femininity', sex/gender roles and gender socialization. There are, however, many problems with these approaches (Eichler, 1980; Carrigan *et al.*, 1985), including their cultural specificity and relative lack of attention to power, change and social structures. Paradoxically the sex/gender approach can easily take us back to biology.

Even with such difficulties, the sex/gender model has prompted path-breaking work on gender relations, some attending to attitudes, self-concepts and identity, some focusing on social categories and structural relations. In this, gender has often been understood as a way of recognizing sociocultural relations, as relatively autonomous from biology. Such approaches articulate structural concepts of gender relations, as in sex/gender classes, patriarchy, gender systems and gender orders. However, about the same time as sex role approaches were being criticized, there were also, in the late 1970s and early 1980s, critiques of the concept of patriarchy and of relatively fixed 'categorical' approaches to gender (Rowbotham, 1979; Connell, 1985).

The outcome of these simultaneous, if somewhat separate, critiques of, first, social psychological concepts of sex role and, second, overly structuralist or societal concepts of gender as determined within patriarchy, has been a movement to more differentiated, more pluralized approaches to gender. In these, power issues remain central, as encapsulated in the notion of gendered power relations. This reformulation of gender fits closely with revisions of patriarchy/ies as historical, multiple structures (Walby, 1986, 1990; Hearn, 1987, 1992) and with moves to post-structuralism and some versions of postmodernism. In recent years there has been increasing attention to gendered practices, processes and discourses; multiple/ composite masculinities and femininities; interrelations of gendered unities and differences; life stories and subjectivities; and the social construction of sexualities. Construction of difference, such as by age, class, ethnicity and occupation assists in reproducing gendered asymmetrical power between men and women, between men and between women, as such differences often carry gendered meanings and reinforce gender inequalities.

Many complications remain in conceptualizing gender, particularly within positivist paradigms. A pervasive constraint is the persistence of dualisms and dichotomies, such as female/male, woman/man, feminine/ masculine, femininity/masculinity and girls/boys. While these are clearly important differentiations, they only speak to part of the possibilities of what gender is or might be in different situations and societies (Edwards, 1989). Perhaps the greatest challenges to a simple, dualist view of gender come from sexuality studies and queer theory. Gender and sexuality are intimately connected with each other: 'without a concept of gender there could be, quite simply, no concept of homo- or hetero-sexuality' (Sedgwick, 1991: 31).

The very distinction between sex and gender also brings difficulties. The distinction may closely parallel nature–culture and body–mind dichotomies, even reinforcing them and repositioning male/masculinity as the norm, and may imply that biology is pre-social or free of the social, though biology is constituted in the social (Bondi, 1998). The sex–gender distinction can be seen as a sociocultural construction: gender is not the cultural arrangement of *given* sex difference; rather sex/gender difference is a cultural arrangement, dominantly constructed by way of the heterosexual matrix (Butler, 1990). Gender is not one 'thing'; it is contested, complex, differentiated. Moreover, while our focus is on gender, this should not be isolated from other social divisions and oppressions, such as class or age, in relation to which gender is formed.

Gendered organizations, gendered managements

Debates about the meaning of gender have continued at the very time that the field of gender, organizations and management has expanded greatly and become more established. In identifying organizations, management and IHRM as gendered, a number of assumptions and emphases are made. First and obviously, there is some kind of focus on gender. Social relations between and amongst genders, interpersonal and structural, material and discursive, are understood as significant. Gendering occurs in both distributions of gendered people and gendered practices, and applies even when organizations and managements totally comprise men or indeed women.

While organizations and management can be gendered in many ways, typical patterns include the following:

- *The valuing of organizations and management themselves over work in the private domains.* This is frequently gendered in valuing men's work over women's.
- *Gendered divisions of labour*, both formal and informal. Women and men may, through inclusion and exclusion, specialize in particular types of labour, creating vertical and horizontal divisions within organizations and management.
- *Gendered divisions of authority*, both formal and informal. Women and men may be valued differently in terms of both formal authority, by virtue of their post and position, and informal authority, from their status and standing in the organization (Kanter, 1977/1993).
- *Gendered processes between the centre and margins.* These may be literally or metaphorically spatial in the distribution of power and activity between the centre and margins of organizations and management. 'Front-line' activities are often staffed by women, 'central' activities more often performed by men. The 'main aim' of organizations tends to be dominantly defined by men (Cockburn, 1991).
- *The gendered relations of organizational participants to domestic and related responsibilities.* Women typically continue to carry the double burden of childcare and unpaid domestic work, and even a triple burden of care for the dependants, including parents, older people and people with disabilities (Harlow *et al.*, 1995).
- *Gendered processes in sexuality*, including the dominance of various forms of sexuality over others. Most organizations and managements reproduce dominant heterosexual norms, ideology and practices. Indeed (hetero)sexual arrangements in private domains generally provide the base infrastructure for organizations and managements, principally through women's associated unpaid reproductive labour.
- *Gendered processes in violence*, including harassment, bullying and physical violence (Hearn & Parkin, 1987, 1995, 2001).
- *Gendered processes in interactions between individuals, and individuals' internal mental work.*
- *Gendered symbols, images and forms of consciousness*, for example, in media, advertising and corporate logos (Acker, 1992).

In specific organizations and managements these elements interact, often reinforcing, sometimes contradicting, each other. Many organizations and managements are characterized by definite gendered patterns, defined by and reproducing social relations of age, class, disability, ethnicity and so on. Gendered processes and their interrelations are not monolithic, but often paradoxical and open to multiple interpretations. Although men's dominance is profound, it is not unresisted (Cockburn, 1991; Thomas *et al.*, 2004); it has to be continually re-established and can be challenged, subverted and destabilized. There is also recognition of the gendering of men in management (Collinson & Hearn, 1994); gendered practices and 'doing gender' (Rantalaiho & Heiskanen, 1997); and the ambiguous, contradictory and paradoxical nature of gendered selves in organizations (Kondo, 1990).

Gender, HRM and IHRM
Locating HRM

Management, HRM and IHRM are gendered in many ways. Most obviously, there is the continuing dominance of men in management, especially at the very top and highest pay levels. Yet despite, or perhaps because of, this, in many organizations, management has been and continues to be represented as gender-neutral, whether as part of supposedly non-gendered bureaucracy or as taken-for-granted managerial imperative.

Management often involves homosocial practices, with men's preference for men and men's company, and the use of masculine models, stereotypes and symbols in management, often from sport, the military and evolution, such as the 'law of the jungle'. Male homosociality that combines emotional detachment, competitiveness and viewing women as sexual objects, and perpetuates hegemonic masculinity, also suppresses subordinate masculinities and reproduces a pecking order among men. Management and especially what is often understood as effective business management have often been assumed to be consistent with characteristics traditionally valued in men (Alimo-Metcalfe, 1993). There have been significant historical transformations of management, from male near-monopoly, to dominant traditional managerial masculinities, and to more modern forms of gendering (Kerfoot & Knights, 1993; Roper, 1994; Collinson & Hearn, 1996).

There is evidence of some increase in women's representation in middle management, small business ownership, and management in total (Davidson & Burke, 2000; Vinnicombe, 2000). There are signs of some change in SMEs. While in 1996, 50 per cent of SMEs in the European Business Survey (1996) countries had only men in management, the 2002 figure was 44 per cent; and the proportion of SMEs with one or two women in management had also increased (*European Business Survey*, 2002). However, according to Eurostat (2002), only in Italy, the Netherlands and Austria was the proportion of men employed as 'Directors and chief executives' less than three times that for women. In Sweden it was 15 times higher. There are clear national policy pressures, especially in Norway, to address and change this situation, particularly in relation to the membership of boards of directors.

At CEO and highest executive levels the very low numbers of women appear to be changing very little (Institute of Management, 1995; Veikkola *et al.*, 1997; Institute of Management/Remuneration Economics, 1998). In 2003, only one woman was CEO and one woman chaired the board of a FTSE 100 company (Singh & Vinnicombe, 2003). Men managers are more likely than women managers to be better paid, to be in more secure employment, to be on higher grades, to be less stressed, to be older at each responsibility level and to have not experienced prejudice and sexual discrimination (Davidson & Cooper, 1984; Institute of Management, 1995; Institute of Management/Remuneration Economics, 1998).

Within management strong gender specializations persist, often underwritten by gender divisions in education and training: for example, men's domination of most engineering and technology. Though men have been very prominent in the institutional development of personnel management (Trudinger, 2004), in many countries HRM is an area of management in which women are relatively more represented (Legge, 1987). HRM is subject, and contributes, to workplace gender power relations within and across hierarchies. Those parts of HRM practice that involve corporate management–labour relations can be rethought in terms of gender relations, often meaning cooperations and conflicts between groups dominated by men. Many studies on gender in HRM have focused on recruitment, appointments, promotion, team building, communication, power, authority, equal opportunities policies (EOPs) and sexual harassment (Adler & Izraeli, 1988b, 1994; Powell, 1993; Davidson & Burke, 1994, 2000; F. Wilson, 1995, 2003; E. Wilson, 2000; Ely *et al.*, 2003; Powell & Graves, 2003). These are also very relevant for IHRM.

The question of remuneration and other personnel rights and benefits, fair or unfair, is another central aspect of IHRM. A key gender issue for HR policy and outcomes is the gender pay gap. In the OECD, women are still paid 16 per cent less per hour than men, on 'raw' unadjusted figures.[2] There are some signs of slow narrowing of the gender gap in some Western European countries, but the most recent figures suggest a widening in Austria, Portugal and Sweden. IHRM may also include the development of gender-sensitive policies and practices, gender equality plans, EOPs, family-friendly policies, gender training, and harassment, bullying and violence policies. For both management and employees, IHRM contributes to processes of gendered identity formation.

Mainstream texts on IHRM

Though studies of gender, organizations and management have predominantly focused on the nationally based, single organization in the last ten years or so, there have been some moves towards more consideration of international, transnational and multinational organizations. Even so, most mainstream approaches to IHRM have remained silent on the question of gender.[3] Gender analysis is absent, at least in an explicit way, from most mainstream IHRM texts and, when it is introduced, it is often in a very limited way, for example in terms of women as expatriates. To illustrate the way in which gender is treated in mainstream textbooks and contributions on IHRM, we have selected a few recent, but well-established, publications in the field: a textbook by Dowling and Welch (2004) and an edited volume by Harzing and Van Ruysseveldt (2004), both entitled *International Human Resource Management*, and an edited volume by Punnett and Shenkar (2004) entitled *Handbook for International Management Research*, in which there is a chapter dedicated to IHRM.

First, it should be emphasized, indeed it cannot be emphasized too much, that the dominant tradition is certainly one of supposed 'gender-neutrality' or 'gender-absence' (Hanmer & Hearn, 1999) in description, analysis and explanation. Interestingly, apparent or supposed or assumed gender-neutrality is itself often a form of gendering, in the sense of obvious gender divisions not being talked about.

When, rather unusually, questions associated with gender are explicitly addressed, they are interpreted as, first, related to women, and second, related to expatriates rather than the mass of gender issues that continue within and between corporations. Gender is made 'other' in two senses: as woman and as expatriate. Thus gender is mainly discussed in two different, albeit related, contexts: women themselves as candidates for expatriate assignments; and women as spouses, partners or family members of male expatriates. These are now examined in more detail, prior to some remarks on silences and assumptions.

Women as candidates for expatriate assignments

Despite increasing demand for expatriates, the number of women in such positions remains low. This might be surprising given the characteristics identified for effective international managers, such as interpersonal, intuitive and cooperative styles of management which are often associated with women (Harris, 2004; also in this volume). Research has identified a number of factors that explain the underrepresentation of women in international assignments. Fischlmayr (2002) divides the barriers faced by potential female expatriates into self-established and external ones. The former barriers refer to the unwillingness of women to relocate, the challenges associated with dual career couples and women's self-reinforcing behaviour that tends to follow traditional, gender-based rules. The external barriers in turn encompass factors such as HR or line managers' reluctance to select female candidates and the nature of the target location as culturally too demanding, effectively precluding female expatriates. It is assumed that, while on assignment in such a location, female expatriates will experience problems. Scullion and Paauwe (2004) state that the assumption that women will experience such problems is worrying because, in the light of recent research, female expatriates are generally successful in their global assignments.

Women as spouses, partners or family members of male expatriates
Transnational organizations and managements function partly by the globalization of staff movements in relocations, expatriations and repatriations of managers and workers (Welch, 2003). Given the barriers that women are perceived to face when striving for international career opportunities, the typical expatriate today tends to be male. Not surprisingly, the importance attached to the support of the spouse and the family in various phases of the expatriate assignment still rests on the assumption that the spouse is female and will not work abroad in a career-related position (Punnett *et al.*, 1992). For example, in expatriate selection, discussions with spouse and family are emphasized (Schuler *et al.*, 2004). It is also acknowledged that international mobility is becoming increasingly a problem in many companies and countries particularly owing to factors associated with spouse and family. More specifically, the growing unwillingness to disrupt the education of children, and the problems associated with dual-income and dual-career couples are seen as major barriers to transferring staff across borders. Moreover many families are less willing to disrupt their personal and social lives (Scullion & Paauwe, 2004). Overall, the family is recognized as a very significant factor in expatriate performance and success (Schuler *et al.*, 2004).

The absent presence of men
Gender is generally related, first, to women, and, second, to expatriates rather than other gender issues between subunits within and between MNCs in business-to-business transactions. When reviewing many aspects of IHRM in these texts, such as international compensation and performance management, gender was not discussed. The many and various gender issues within and between corporations (gendered management, hierarchies, authority, informal relations, processes and so on) rather than those concerning some expatriates are generally left unanalysed. Gender is externalized, in a relatively individualized expatriate cultural space elsewhere.

It appears that in these texts the assumption was often made that top managers are or almost all are of a similar gender: male. Men, masculinities and their social construction and social power were generally left unspoken; they are, in that sense, invisible, an 'absent presence' (Hearn, 1998), despite (and perhaps because of) their dominance, especially at the highest levels, and within expatriate policy, practice and discourse. The 'transnational capitalist class' (Sklair, 2001) is in practice very much a male transnational capitalist class. Questions of difference and diversity among men, such as by age, class, ethnicity, locality, nationality and religion, are usually left in silence, as are matters of the complex interconnections between power, unities and differences amongst and between men. Differences within and amongst management, men and masculinities may be intertwined with other social differences. These are important issues in both the practice of IHRM and its academic study.

Peltonen (this volume) points out that in IHRM 'key employees' – experts and professionals, often in administrative or developmental tasks in the corporate hierarchy – are more likely to be men than women. Yet this is rarely interrogated. Key employees tend to be ethnically closer to the 'ideal' appreciated in corporate cultures based on middle-class values of white North American or European professionals. Harris (2004: 358) makes an important observation: 'The most significant feature of the research into expatriate failure rates and reasons for failure is that it is based on a *male* population.' In their study of a European oil company operating in China and Colombia, Goodall and Roberts (2003) identified the strength of expatriate networks, often meaning male expatriate networks. The close bonds between them delivered trust and cooperation across geographical locations as well as swift and efficient responses. They also led to selective recruitment in hiring other similar expatriates. Schuler *et al.* (2004) call for combating management ethnocentrism in expatriate selection and opening up the recruitment process. Davison and Punnett (1995) argue that international managers and researchers need to avoid an 'ostrich-like' attitude of 'gender and race blindness' when dealing with international assignments.

Moving beyond these various silences, neglects and very partial approaches to IHRM involves analysing gender and diversity more fully. This leads us to a further level of complexity that is rather rapidly developing in IHRM. Changing current expatriate selection and recruitment processes is a slow process.

Gender, diversity and IHRM

A key part of contemporary IHRM is diversity management, highlighting diverse social divisions, such as ethnicity, gender, language (Piekkari, this volume), nationality and 'race', but also sometimes age, class, disability or religion. However prominent discussion of diversity management is gener-ally absent from mainstream textbooks on IHRM. While 'domestic' writ-ings on leadership and HRM are replete with references to advantages stemming from diversity management, IHRM textbooks largely equate diversity with an appropriate mix of nationalities and organizational per-spectives. A major challenge in composing an international staff is to find a suitable balance between the number of parent country nationals, third country nationals and host country nationals (Harzing & Van Ruysseveldt, 2004; Dowling & Welch, 2004; Schuler *et al.*, 2004). Originating from various parts of the MNC, these groups of employees may also represent different organizational interests. Thus 'diversity' can be a way of obscur-ing gender (Hearn & Collinson. 2005).

Diversity management can be understood as the result of both global corporate initiatives, on the one hand, and social movement pressures, on the other. It can also be seen as part of gendered management, and con-tradictions therein. As with debates on multiculturalism, there are many ways of promoting and conceptualizing diversity management that are less or more challenging to existing power structures, including gender power (Goldberg, 1994; McLaren, 1994; Prasad & Mills, 1997; Prasad *et al.*, 1997). Diversity management can, at one level, be conceptualized as a men's/managerial project. It can be used to play down gender power, and as a means of diversion from gender, women and men, by focusing on 'diversity' that can mean everything, anything or nothing. Just as Okin (1997) asked, 'Is multiculturalism bad for women?', so we might add, 'Is multiculturalism – or diversity – good for men?', that is, in obscuring and promoting men's power and dominant interests.

Diversity management and programmes might also be a contradictory gender project, both incorporating gender and other social divisions into mainstream agendas and having potential to deconstruct and threaten dominant gender powers. Diversity debates can often be strangely gender-less or free of the taint of gender. We have found this is in interviewing HR and other managers in global companies on gender and diversity corporate policies (Hearn & Piekkari, 2004, 2005). Analyses of diversity discourses in international corporate settings have tended to show generally a relatively non-challenging and 'content-less' character, without social divisions, rather than championing social movement expectations and aspirations.[4]

On the other hand, variations in the theory and practice of diversity man-agement (Thomas & Ely 1996; Kirton & Greene, 2000) resonate with different frameworks for gender intervention, including 'fixing the women', 'celebrate differences', 'create equal opportunities' and 'revise work culture' (Ely & Foldy, 2003; Fletcher & Ely, 2003; Kolb *et al.*, 2003). These present more or less fundamental engagements with gender arrangements. The main perspectives on gender adopted in research on diversity implicitly reflect either women's differences from men as international managers ('celebrate differences') or barriers to women's recruitment and international career advancement in corporations ('create equal opportunities').[5]

An aspect of diversity and IHRM that is certainly gendered, yet still often hidden, is sexuality and the predominance of heterosexual organizational culture. Many studies have reported on the marginalization and subordination of lesbians and gay men in business and workplaces more generally. On the other hand, the UK Gay and Lesbian Census (ID Research, 2001) found that, while 15 per cent of lesbians and gay men in the workplace who responded believe their sexuality has hindered their job prospects, a surprisingly large number – 43 per cent – had managerial roles.[6] Bringing issues of sexuality and sexual diversity into IHRM is a complex task, not least because of cultural and religious variation in sexual mores and attitudes internationally.

In diversity frameworks, both practical and analytical, there are crucial questions: Who constructs 'diversity'? Who defines it? Who decides? And which forms of diversity are legitimate (Cockburn, 1991)? These can be seen as part of the interrogation of dominant gendered organizational cultures within the long agenda of equal opportunities.[7] We can ask which men and women, and which masculinities and femininities are favoured or not in diversity programmes, in their management, implementation, consumption and effects. Diversity management and programmes provide space for the development of further paradoxes around gender and power, including relations of gender and other powers, such as enactment of white men's racism against other men. Such contradictions can be reproduced in detailed structures and practices of diversity management and programmes, such as the discriminatory practice of instructing training programme participants who belong to a subordinated category, such as 'black people', to speak on behalf of that category, but not doing likewise with members of dominant social categories, such as 'white people'.

Gender, IHRM and globalization

In gendering IHRM it is important to consider the form, development and location of specific corporate systems within a broader, often global, context. Though studies of gender, organizations and management have predominantly focused on the nationally based, single organization, there have been growing moves towards more consideration of international, transnational and multinational organizations. The state of IHRM in a particular corporation is but one of a range of social processes, internal and external to the organization, which have an impact on women's prospects and those of men in relatively subordinated social categories.

IHRM operates at the intersections of international/global, national, regional and local traditions and strategic international management, and is thus subject to contradictory gendered pressures.

Key global issues are the gendering of organizations and management within globalization, MNC expansion, global diffusion of ICTs, environmentalism, postcolonialism and 'Third World' development. Such global issues both change the business environment of MNCs and reconstruct internal structures and processes of MNCs. Concentrations of capital are increasing (Korten, 1998), with gendered forms and effects (Banerjee & Linstead, 2001; Hearn & Parkin, 2001). There are few signs that the world is becoming more equal, in gender or other terms. At the same time, MNCs are themselves vulnerable to huge risks, ranging from terrorism to financial scandals and computer hacking and viruses. These are part of the global context of IHRM.

Gendered production networks are evolving as a result of globalization processes and major changes in international political economy. While IHRM commentators have reviewed global management policies in terms of training, development, recruitment and selection, there is little critique of gendered implications of new and indeed transitional or composite forms of political economies (Hearn, 2004). Within the broader academic community, for example political scientists, development economists and sociologists, there is a growing concern about management policies of MNCs and the gender, organizational and societal inequalities they perpetuate. Researchers and policy actors have focused on women's increasing capabilities in education, entrepreneurship, technology, management and so on, and discussed the risks and rights of women in a globalizing economy (Walby, 2002).

While the corporate rhetoric promotes adherence to a global management system and global philosophy this is not neither necessarily universally applied nor supported by local legal frameworks. Standing (1999) suggests that new forms of employment in developing regions such as Eastern Europe, Asia and Latin America are less regulated whereas, in the EU for example, there has been growing regulation on equal treatment and diversity. Labour market variations and changes operate in a wide variety of ways, and some contrasting examples follow.

One example is the way MNCs have used changes in trade and financial agreements to move their production and services around the globe. Much production, such as electronics, toys, shoes and sports goods, and business services, such as call centres and ticket reservation, have become part of the 'global assembly line'. Much of this relies on low-paid low-skilled female labour (Pyle & Ward, 2003), from data entry in Trinidad and Tobago (Freeman, 2000) to telesales work in Asia (Kelkar, 2002). There are also hidden production relationships which MNCs manage in less developed countries through subcontracting networks employing low-paid female workers (Pyle & Ward, 2003).

Another aspect of change concerns how governments in developing and transitional economies generally have tended to ignore gender and employment issues permitting MNCs to reproduce gendered divisions of labour (ibid.). For example, restructuring by the Russian Federation administration since the Gorbachov era has restricted women in chemical manufacturing, affiliated industries and some technical occupations on health and fertility grounds. Putin continued this and there have been concerted efforts to reduce the number of women in the Duma and state secretariat, and replace them with male intelligentsia and military officials. In place of the former strict quotas for female representation in economic and political systems, the new gender regime involves recruitment and promotion processes that openly restrict women's participation. Rather than challenge these and similar practices, foreign investors in these regions often support them (Kay, 2002; Metcalfe & Rees, 2002).

A third scenario centres on the intersection of local cultural and religious patterns with global restructuring. Singapore has encouraged major foreign investment and seen increasing numbers of (Chinese) women entering the labour market at the professional and managerial level, yet culturally issues of gender and 'race' rarely figure in HR systems. Confucian ideology combines equality and ethical values in society, along with given societal, including gender, hierarchies; thus programmes and interventions that tackle race or gender are not deemed relevant or necessary (see Lee & Pow, 1999; Lyons, 2000; Metcalfe & Linstead, 2001). This HR practice is adhered to by local Singaporean organizations and also MNCs. Even with their international profile, PriceWaterhouseCoopers in Singapore, for example, do not have an HR/diversity policy (see Metcalfe & Linstead, 2001) and there is limited evidence to suggest that the practice is similar in Hong Kong as well (Chiu & Ng, 1999). Indeed one of the lessons of taking a broad global context into account is the need to be aware of the great variations in HR practice and policy in different localities, even within MNCs and their subsidiary and associated companies.

Some future research directions
Having said all this, there is gradually growing interest in the intersection of gender analysis and IHRM, and a number of future directions for research and practice.

The gendering of IHRM
Given the multifaceted nature of HRM embedded within global organization and societal contexts, it is difficult to determine the extent to which

IHRM models are themselves gendered (Dickens, 1998). An organization's approach to IHRM is but one of a range of social processes, both internal and external to the organization, which have an impact on women's prospects. They are likely to affect, in a different way, the prospects of men from relatively subordinated social categories, such as ethnic minority men. The conceptual ambiguity and fluidity of HRM also make it difficult to apply universally to diverse global settings. As Woodall states: 'Far from being merely androgynous, HRM is gender blind. Its underlying features are insensitive to the gender aspects of employment . . . At the centre is the unitarist managerialism that cannot admit the diversity or plurality of workforce interests' (Woodall, 1996: 349). IHRM policies and practices can also be reread in terms of their implicit or explicit assumptions about the gender of management, models of gendered management in use and the relations of gender policy and diversity policy. In this context, the implications and impact of women's relatively strong participation in HRM and IHRM need to be further researched.

Gendered impacts of IHRM
There is still a major lack of studies on the gendered impacts of gender and EOP policies, home–work reconciliation initiatives and other policies. More generally, while there has been debate about the well-respected 'soft' and 'hard' models of HRM (Legge, 1995), as representing developmental humanism and utilitarian instrumentalism approaches, respectively, to managing employees, there is very little consideration of the way HRM can shape gendered employment experiences, practices and opportunities, at national or international level. This remains a research priority. There are, however, notable exceptions. For example, Truss (1999) has researched HRM practices in Lloyds Bank and raised doubts about the ability of so-called 'soft' HRM to deliver sustained advantages to women in the area of training and development for example, since HRM practices focused almost exclusively on a generic view of employees. The way in which gender and diversity agendas are culturally deployed or sidetracked in IHRM policy development is evidence of the way in which MNCs reinforce varying forms of social inequalities.

Corporate structures, IHRM and gender policy
Another promising arena for research is the implications of different forms of corporate internal structures for IHRM, gender policy and diversity management. Different kinds of corporate internal structures have an impact on gender policy and IHRM more generally, through more or less centralized control systems. IHRM operates at the intersections of international, national, regional and local HRM traditions and strategic

international management, and consequently is subject to contradictory gendered pressures. Internal corporate structures create differences in gender relations in management and policy implementation. Relations between different units within MNCs have further impacts, depending on whether they are highly integrated globally, local networks or strongly centralized. Corporations with strong headquarters may contrast with polycentric corporations, where head office issues looser guidelines to local subsidiaries on, say, corporate EOPs. Centralized global corporations may develop some sort of EOP, even if these have insignificant impacts in some local areas and at high levels. Decentralized corporations may be more likely to respond to local conditions, with more autonomous, variable structures within local or functional units (Hearn & Parkin, 2001; Hearn & Piekkari, 2004).

Gendering global–local relations
Closely linked to the previous area is the relevance of gender in relations between global and local practices and processes. Recruitment and appointment processes can sometimes be seen as contradictory processes of gendered organizational and individual resistance, with local units sometimes resisting expatriate recruitment or standardization in methods, whatever corporate policies may say. The earlier discussion of the way globalization and international business have supported gender segregation in labour markets and subsequent inequalities raises research questions on how MNCs interpret and implement gender policies in diverse regions and localities. Such research can be assisted by attention to transnational cultural change and various forms of deterritorialization and hybridity (Ong, 1999; Hearn, 2004). Space and culture, and gendered social space and culture, are not strictly experienced or understood in terms of the geographical space of the nationally located place that the people concerned occupy. There is much scope to build on these insights in developing more accurate analyses of gender issues in IHRM practices, and transnational corporate cultures more generally.

Mergers and acquisitions
Another area of increasing interest is the gender dimensions of international mergers and acquisitions. Such (re)organizing takes place across both national/cultural and institutional/organizational boundaries (Morgan et al., 2001). There are a growing number of detailed and in some ways theoretically sophisticated research texts on the cultural, linguistic and ethnic complexities of M&As (Säntti, 2001; Read, 2004), yet even such texts often seem not to notice that the cultures are intensely gendered (Harlow & Hearn, 1995). It is commonplace to talk of 'strategic fit' in such international

M&As, and increasingly some notion of 'cultural fit' is also recognized (Nahavandi & Malekzadeh, 1988; Cartwright & Cooper, 1993; Elsass & Veiga, 1994; Vaara, 2000). However a key aspect of culture is gender relations, so it would seem appropriate also to consider what we might call 'gender fit' in such processes. The meeting of very different gender structures, cultures and practices in M&As is likely to be significant in subsequent corporate development, and this is attracting growing attention (Søderberg & Vaara, 2003; Tienari *et al.*, 2003). Moreover there is immense scope for far greater attention to IHRM in relation to the gendering of international business-to-business activity, alliances, partnerships, supply chains, financial dependencies and other intercorporate relations – formal or informal and often involving men at the high levels.

Gender and diversity
The intersection of gender and diversity is an important area for both further research and policy development in IHRM. Research on diversity and intersectionality needs to be linked with a focus on structured asymmetrical power relations between men and women. A challenge is to maintain this double focus on difference without neglecting gender and other structural powers (Foldy & Creed, 1999; Holvino, 2001).

Concluding comments
IHRM is located within more general globalizing changes in work, organizations and management. The very notion of organization and management is becoming more complex with transnationalization, globalization and new information and communication technologies. Organizational workplaces increasingly involve transnational organizations, interorganizational relations, networks, network organizations, net organizations and virtual organizations. Such historical globalizing conditions create many more possible positions and forms of gender power, predominantly, though not exclusively, for men.

We should also acknowledge the very real attempts to produce more gender-equal IHRM policy and practice being developed by some corporations, for example through various business networks and government–business alliances committed to gender equality, and through engagement with the links between gender equality, diversity and sustainability (Triple Value Strategy Consulting, 2003).

Perhaps the key question that remains is how it is that IHRM and research on IHRM usually manage *not* to attend explicitly to gender issues and the very obvious gender structuring of international business. Is this mere carelessness or something more significant? This is indeed itself a form of gendering of knowledge, in both practice and theory.

Acknowledgments

We are grateful to research cooperation with David Collinson, to Ingmar Björkman and Denice Welch for comments on an earlier draft, and to Eero Vaara for bibliographic advice.

Notes

1. It should be noted that the meanings and connotations of words, such as 'sex' and 'gender', differ in different languages. For example, in Finnish there is a single word for both 'sex' and 'gender': 'sukupuoli'; and the same word for 'he' and 'she': 'hän'.
2. This is the figure unadjusted for the effects of the remuneration rates by observed characteristics of jobs and the whole national wage structure. If these factors are taken into account, the gender wage gap as measured is altered, for example, to a lower figure by 2–4 per cent for the UK, and by a higher figure of up to 6 per cent in the Netherlands (*OECD Employment Outlook*, 2002: 94–106).
3. Even critical texts on HRM (for example, Watson, 2004) may fail to discuss gender issues.
4. Zanoni and Janssens (2003) show how diversity discourses can be understood as products of management practices (in devaluing diversity through seeing difference as lack of valued attributes; or constructing difference as providing additional value) or as producers of management practices (in reaffirming them as those practices as they exist now, or challenging inter-group practices).
5. These parallel Adler and Izraeli's (1988a:4) twin characterization of assumptions made about women in management as based on 'complementarity' (to men) and 'equity' (with men) respectively.
6. These figures are not representative.
7. Distinctions have been made between the long and short agendas of equal opportunities (Jewson & Mason, 1986; Cockburn, 1990).

References

Acker, J. 1992. Gendering organizational theory. In A.J. Mills & P. Tancred (eds), *Gendering organizational analysis*: 248–60. Newbury Park, CA: Sage.

Adler, N. & D. Izraeli. 1988a. Women in management worldwide. In N. Adler & D. Izraeli (eds), *Women in management worldwide*: 3–16. New York: M.E. Sharpe.

Adler, N. & D. Izraeli. (eds). 1988b. *Women in management worldwide*. New York: M.E. Sharpe.

Adler, N. & D. Izraeli. (eds). 1994. *Competitive frontiers: women managers in a global economy*. Cambridge, MA: Blackwell.

Alimo-Metcalfe, B. 1993. Women in management: organizational socialization and assessment practices that prevent career advancement. *International Journal of Selection and Assessment*, **1**: 68–82.

Banerjee, S.B. & S. Linstead. 2001. Globalization, multiculturalism and other fictions: colonialism for the new millennium? *Organization*, **8**: 683–722.

Bondi, L. 1998. Sexing the city. In R. Fincher & J.M. Jacobs (eds), *Cities of difference*: 177–200. New York: Guilford Press.

Butler, J. 1990. *Gender trouble: feminism and the subversion of identity*. New York/London: Routledge.

Carrigan, T., R.W. Connell & J. Lee. 1985. Towards a new sociology of masculinity. *Theory and Society*, **14**: 551–604.

Cartwright, S. & C.L. Cooper. 1993. The role of culture compatibility in successful organizational merger. *Academy of Management Executive*, **7**: 57–70.

Chiu, W.C.K. & C.W. Ng. 1999. Women friendly HRM: a study among women and men of organizations in Hong Kong. *Journal of Occupational and Organizational Psychology*, **72**: 485–502.

Cockburn, C.K. 1990. 'Equal opportunities' intervene. In J. Hearn & D. Morgan (eds), *Men, masculinities and social theory*: 72–89. London and Boston, MA: Unwin Hyman.

Cockburn, C.K. 1991. *In the way of women: men's resistance to sex equality in organizations.* Basingstoke: Macmillan.

Collinson, D.L. & J. Hearn. 1994. Naming men as men: implications for work, organizations and management. *Gender, Work and Organization*, **1**: 2–22.

Collinson, D.L. & J. Hearn. (eds). 1996. *Men as managers, managers as men: critical perspectives on men, masculinities and managements.* London: Sage.

Connell, R.W. 1985. Theorising gender. *Sociology*, **19**: 260–72.

Davidson, M.J. & R.J. Burke. (eds). 1994. *Women in management: current research issues.* London: Paul Chapman.

Davidson, M.J. & R.J. Burke. (eds). 2000. *Women in management: current research issues II.* London: Sage.

Davidson, M.J. & C.L. Cooper. 1984. Occupational stress in female managers: a comparative approach. *Journal of Management Studies*, **21**: 185–205.

Davison, E.D. & B.J. Punnett. 1995. International assignments: is there a role for gender and race in decisions? *International Journal of Human Resource Management*, **6**: 411–41.

Dickens, L. 1998. What HRM means for gender equality. *Human Resource Management Journal*, **8**: 23–40.

Dowling, P.J. & D.E. Welch. 2004. *International human resource management: managing people in a multinational context.* Fourth edition. London: Thomson.

Durkin, J.J. 1978. The potential of women. In B.A. Stead (ed.), *Women in management*: 42–6. Englewood Cliffs, NJ: Prentice-Hall.

Edwards, A. 1989. The sex-gender distinction: has it outlived its usefulness? *Australian Feminist Studies*, **10**: 1–12.

EFQM (European Foundation for Quality Management). 2003. *Womenisation at work – the next frontier.* Available at http://www.aboveclouds.org/pdf/women_eng.pdf

Eichler, M. 1980. *The double standard: a feminist critique of feminist social science.* London: Croom Helm.

Elsass, P.M. & J.F. Veiga. 1994. Acculturation in acquired organizations: a force-field perspective. *Human Relations*, **47**: 431–53.

Ely, R.J. & E.G. Foldy. 2003. Diversity: overview. In R. Ely, E. Foldy & M. Scully (eds), *Reader in gender, work and organization*: 321–6. Oxford/New York: Blackwell.

Ely, R.J., M. Scully & E. Foldy. (eds) 2003. *Reader in gender, work and organization.* Oxford/New York: Blackwell.

European Business Survey. 1996. *Proportion of SMEs with no women in management.*

European Business Survey. 2002–10 years of a single European market. 2002. Hong Kong: Grant Thornton. Available at http://www.gthk.com.hk/eng/resources/misc2/section2/page1.asp

Eurostat. 2002. *The life of women and men in Europe. A statistical portrait. Data 1980–2000.* Luxembourg: Eurostat/European Commission.

Fischlmayr, I.C. 2002. Female self-perception as barrier to international careers? *International Journal of Human Resource Management*, **13**: 773–83; reprinted in Dowling & Welch, 2004.

Fletcher, J.K. & R.J. Ely. 2003. Introducing gender: overview. In R. Ely, E. Foldy & M. Scully (eds), *Reader in gender, work and organization*: 3–9. Oxford/New York: Blackwell.

Foldy, E.G. & W.E.D. Creed. 1999. Action learning, fragmentation, and the interaction of single-, double-, and triple-loop change: a case of gay and lesbian workplace advocacy. *Journal of Applied Behavioral Science*, **35**: 207–27.

Freeman, C. 2000. *High tech and high heels in the global economy: women, work and pink collar identities in the Caribbean.* Durham, NC: Duke University Press.

Goldberg, D.T. (ed.). 1994. *Multiculturalism: A critical reader.* Malden, MA: Blackwell.

Goodall, K. & J. Roberts. 2003. Only connect: teamwork in the multinational. *Journal of World Business*, **38**: 150–64.

Hanmer, J. & J. Hearn. 1999. Gender and welfare research. In F. Williams, J. Popay & A. Oakley (eds), *Welfare research: a critical review*: 106–30. London: UCL Press.

Harlow, E. & J. Hearn. 1995. Cultural constructions: contrasting theories of organisational culture and gender construction. *Gender, Work and Organization*, **2**: 180–91.

Harlow, E., J. Hearn & W. Parkin. 1995. Gendered noise: organizations and the silence and din of domination. In C. Itzin & J. Newman (eds), *Gender, culture and organizational change*: 89–105. London: Routledge.

Harris, H. 2004. Women's role in international management. In A.-W. Harzing & J. Van Ruysseveldt (eds), *International human resource management*: 357–86. Second edition. London: Sage.

Harzing, A.-W. & J. Van Ruysseveldt. (eds). 2004. *International human resource management*. Second edition. London: Sage.

Hearn, J. 1987. *The gender of oppression: men, masculinity and the critique of Marxism*. Brighton: Wheatsheaf/New York: St Martin's.

Hearn, J. 1992. *Men in the public eye: the construction and deconstruction of public men and public patriarchies*. London/New York: Routledge.

Hearn, J. 1998. Theorizing men and men's theorizing: men's discursive practices in theorizing men. *Theory and Society*, **27**: 781–816.

Hearn, J. 2004. Tracking 'the transnational': studying transnational organizations and managements, and the management of cohesion. *Culture and Organization*, **10**(4): 273–90.

Hearn, J. & D.L. Collinson. 2005. Men, masculinities and workplace diversity/diversion: power, intersections and contradictions. In A. Konrad, P. Prasad & J. Pringle (eds), *Handbook of workplace diversity*: 299–322. London: Sage.

Hearn, J. & W. Parkin. 1987. *'Sex' at 'work': the power and paradox of organization sexuality*. Brighton: Wheatsheaf/New York: St Martin's.

Hearn, J. & W. Parkin. 1995. *'Sex' at 'work': the power and paradox of organization sexuality*. Revised and updated. Hemel Hempstead: Prentice Hall/Harvester Wheatsheaf.

Hearn, J. & W. Parkin. 2001. *Gender, sexuality and violence in organizations: the unspoken forces of organization violations*. London: Sage.

Hearn, J. & R. Piekkari. 2004. Gender divisions, gender policies and gender practices in top management: interviewing chief HR managers of large Finnish corporations. European Academy of Management Conference, University of St Andrews. May.

Hearn, J. & R. Piekkari. 2005. Gendered leaderships and leaderships on gender policy: national context, corporate structures, and chief human resources managers in transnational corporations. *Leadership*, **1**(4): 429–54.

Holvino, E. 2001. *Working paper no. 14*. Center for Gender in Organizations, Simmons School of Management, Boston.

ID Research 2001. *Gay and lesbian census*. London: ID Research.

Institute of Management 1995. *National management salary survey*. Kingston-on-Thames: Institute of Management.

Institute of Management/Remuneration Economics 1998. *UK national management survey*. London: Institute of Management.

Jacklin, C.N. & E.E. Maccoby. 1975. Sex differences and their implications for management. In E. Gordon & M.H. Strober (eds), *Bringing women into management*: 23–38. New York: McGraw-Hill.

Jewson, N. & D. Mason. 1986. The theory and practice of equal opportunities policies: liberal and radical approaches. *The Sociological Review*, **34**: 307–34.

Kanter, R.M. 1977/1993. *Men and women of the corporation*. New York: Basic Books.

Kay, R. 2002. A liberation from emancipation? Changing discourses on women's employment in Soviet and post-Soviet Russia, *Journal of Communist Studies and Transition Politics*, **18**(1): 51–72.

Kelkar, G. 2002. Women and the digital divide. *Gender, Technology and Development*, **6**: 1–21.

Kerfoot, D. & D. Knights. 1993. Management masculinity and manipulation: from paternalism to corporate strategy in financial services in Britain. *Journal of Management Studies*, **30**: 659–79.

Kirton, G. & A.M. Greene. 2000. *The dynamics of managing diversity*. Oxford: Butterworth Heinemann.

Kolb, D., J.K. Fletcher, D.E. Meyerson, D. Merrill-Sands & R.J. Ely. 2003. Making change:

a framework for promoting gender equity in organizations. In R. Ely, M. Scully & E. Foldy (eds), *Reader in gender, work and organization*: 10–15. Oxford/New York: Blackwell.

Kondo, D. 1990. *Crafting selves: power, gender, and discourses of identity in a Japanese workplace*. Chicago, IL: University of Chicago Press.

Korten, D. 1998. *Taming the giants*. Available at wysiwyg://191/http://www.geocities.com/RainForest/3621/KORTEN.HTM

Lee, J.S.K. & J.C.I. Pow. 1999. Human resource policies for women – a study in Singapore. *The Journal of Management Development*, **18**: 326–41.

Legge, K. 1987. Women in personnel management: uphill climb or downhill slide? In A. Spencer & D. Podmore (eds), *In a man's world*. London: Tavistock.

Legge, K. 1995. *Human resource management: rhetorics and realities*. Basingstoke: Macmillan.

Lyons, L. 2000. The limits of feminist political intervention in Singapore. *Journal of Contemporary Asia*, **30**: 67–83.

McLaren, P. 1994. White terror and oppositional agency: towards a critical multiculturalism. In D.T. Goldberg (ed.), *Multiculturalism: A critical reader*: 45–74. Malden, MA: Blackwell.

Metcalfe, B. & A. Linstead. 2001. Bondmaids becoming feminists? Women coming out in Singapore. Paper presented to Critical Management Studies Conference, University of Manchester, July.

Metcalfe, B. & C. Rees. 2003. Gendering human resource development: the case of the Russian Federation. Paper presented at European Academy of HRD, Toulouse University.

Morgan, G., P. Hull Kristensen & R. Whitley. (eds). 2001. *The multinational firm: organizing across institutional and national divides*. Oxford: Oxford University Press.

Nahavandi, A. & A.R. Malekzadeh. 1988. Acculturation in mergers and acquisitions. *Academy of Management Review*, **13**: 79–90.

Oakley, A. 1972. *Sex, gender and society*. London: Temple Smith. Revised edition 1985. Aldershot: Gower.

OECD Employment Outlook. 2002. OECD. Available at http://www.oecd.org/dataoecd/36/7/17652667.pdf

Okin, S.M. 1997. Is multiculturalism good for women? *Boston Review*, **22**: 25–8.

Ong, A. 1999. *Flexible citizenship: the cultural logics of transnationalism*. Durham, NC: Duke University Press.

Powell, G.N. 1993. *Women and men in management*. Third edition. Thousand Oaks, CA: Sage.

Powell, G.N. & L.M. Graves. 2003. *Women and men in management*. Third edition. Thousand Oaks, CA: Sage.

Prasad, P. & A.J. Mills. 1997. From showcase to shadow: understanding the dilemmas of managing workplace diversity. In P. Prasad, A.J. Mills, M. Elmes & A. Prasad (eds), *Managing the organizational melting pot: dilemmas of workplace diversity*: 3–18. Thousand Oaks, CA: Sage.

Prasad, P., A.J. Mills, M. Elmes & A. Prasad. (eds). 1997. *Managing the organizational melting pot: dilemmas of workplace diversity*. Thousand Oaks, CA: Sage.

Punnett, B.J. & O. Shenkar. (eds). 2004. *Handbook for international management research*. Second edition. Ann Arbor, MI: University of Michigan Press.

Punnett, B.J., O. Crocker & M.A. Stevens. 1992. The challenge for women expatriates and spouses: some empirical evidence. *International Journal of Human Resource Management*, **3**: 585–92.

Pyle, J.L. & K.B. Ward. 2003. Recasting our understanding of gender and work during global restructuring. *International Sociology*, **18**: 461–89.

Rantalaiho, L. & T. Heiskanen. (eds). 1997. *Gendered practices in working life*. London: Macmillan.

Read, S. 2004. Managing the merger integration process: a social constructionist perspective. PhD thesis, Victoria University of Wellington.

Roper, M.R. 1994. *Masculinity and the British organization man since 1945*. Oxford: Oxford University Press.

Rowbotham, S. 1979. The trouble with 'patriarchy'. *New Statesman*, **98**: 970.

Säntti, R. 2001. How cultures interact in an international merger. PhD thesis. Acta Universitatis Tamperensis 819, Tampere.

Schuler, R.S., P.S. Budhwar & G.W. Florkowski. 2004. International human resource management. In B.J. Punnett & O. Shenkar (eds), *Handbook for international management research*: 356–414. Second edition. Ann Arbor, MI: University of Michigan Press.

Scullion, H. & J. Paauwe. 2004. International human resource management: recent developments in theory and empirical research. In A.-W. Harzing & J. Van Ruysseveldt (eds), *International human resource management*: 65–88. Second edition. Thousand Oaks, CA: Sage.

Sedgwick, E.K. 1991. *The epistemology of the closet*. Berkeley, CA: University of California Press.

Singh, V. & S. Vinnicombe. 2003. *The 2003 female FTSE report: women directors moving forward*. Cranfield: Cranfield School of Management.

Sklair, L. 2001. *The transnational capitalist class*. Oxford: Blackwell.

Søderberg, A.-M. & E. Vaara. (eds). 2003. *Merging across borders: people, cultures and politics*. Copenhagen: Copenhagen Business School Press.

Standing, G. 1999. *Global labour flexibility: seeking distributive justice*. Basingstoke: Macmillan.

Thomas, D.A. & R.J. Ely. 1996. Making differences matter: a new paradigm for managing diversity. *Harvard Business Review*, September/October: 79–90.

Thomas, R., A. Mills & J. Helm Mills. (eds). 2004. *Identity politics at work: resisting gender, gendering resistance*. London: Routledge.

Tienari, J., C. Holgersson, A.-M. Söderberg & E. Vaara. 2003. An uneasy coupling – reflections on women and management in merging organization. In A.-M. Söderberg & E. Vaara (eds), *Merging across borders: people, cultures and politics*: 229–51. Copenhagen: Copenhagen Business School Press.

Triple Value Strategy Consulting. 2003. Sustainable development and gender issues. A report for the Netherlands Ministry of Social Affairs and Employment. Available at http://www.triple-value.com/SZW%20final%20report%20update%2020030916.pdf

Trudinger, D. 2004. The comfort of men: a critical history of managerial and professional men in post-war modernisation, Australia 1945–1965. PhD thesis, Department of History, University of Sydney.

Truss, C. 1999. HRM: gendered terrain? *International Journal of HRM*, **10**: 180–98.

Vaara, E. 2000. Constructions of cultural differences in postmerger change processes: a sense-making perspective on Finnish-Swedish cases. *M@n@gement*, **3**: 81–110.

Veikkola, E.-S., E. Hänninen-Salmelin & S. Sinkkonen. 1997. Is the forecast for wind or calm? In E.-S. Veikkola (ed.), *Women and men at the top: a study of women and men at the top*: 82–7. Gender Statistics 1997:1. Helsinki: Statistics Finland.

Vinnicombe, S. 2000. The position of women in Europe. In M.J. Davidson & R.J. Burke (eds), *Women in management: current research issues II*: 9–25. London: Sage.

Walby, S. 1986. *Patriarchy at work*. Cambridge: Polity.

Walby, S. 1990. *Theorising patriarchy*. Cambridge: Polity.

Walby, S. 2002. Gender and the new economy: regulation and deregulation. ESRC Seminar, Work Life and Time in the New Economy, LSE, October.

Watson, T.J. 2004. HRM and critical social science analysis. *Journal of Management Studies*, **41**: 447–67.

Welch, D.E. 2003. Globalisation of staff movements: beyond cultural adjustment. *Management International Review*, **43**: 149–69.

Wilson, E. (ed). 2000. *Organizational behaviour reassessed: the impact of gender*. London: Sage.

Wilson, F. 1995. *Organizational behaviour and gender*. London: McGraw-Hill.

Wilson, F. 2003. *Organizational behaviour and gender*. Aldershot: Ashgate.

Woodall, J. 1996. HRM and women: the vision of the gender blind. In B. Towers (ed.), *The handbook of HRM*. Oxford: Blackwell.

Zanoni, P. & M. Janssens. 2003. Deconstructing difference: the rhetoric of human resource managers' diversity discourses. *Organization Studies*, **25**: 55–74.

28 Critical theoretical perspectives on international human resource management
Tuomo Peltonen

International human resource management (IHRM) is a branch of management studies that investigates the design and effects of organizational human resource practices in cross-cultural contexts. The field has evolved from its fragmented beginnings when, for example, Laurent (1986) was able to define international human resource management as being a discipline in its infancy. International personnel questions have since then become a new professional sub-specialism for the human resource people and the discovery of the international people management problems has helped the occupation to regain some authority in the political struggle over management expertise.

However, despite the recent advances, international human resource management is rarely approached from a critical theoretical perspective, unlike many other sub-specialisms of management studies. There is a growing interest in critical approaches to management and organizations. Critical theories aim in general to uncover and change societal structures, ideologies and power relations that constitute and shape the organizational phenomena and workplace relations (for example, Alvesson & Willmot, 1996; Alvesson & Deetz, 2000) and their understanding of 'management' emphasizes control and governing dimensions of administrative activities (Willmot, 1997; Grey, 1999). 'Human resource management', in turn, is seen in critical theories as a way of ensuring employees' commitment to the economic goals of the business enterprises instead of being treated as a mere functional response to individual, organizational and environmental needs (Townley, 1994; Legge, 1995). Additionally international management has also recently seen critical deconstructions of its uses of the concept of 'culture' in organizational discourses (for example, Prasad, 1997; Westwood, 2001).

The purpose of this chapter is to introduce critical theories to the field of international HRM. The chapter is structured as follows. The first section presents an introduction to critical theoretical perspectives, their adaptations in management studies and some of the more specific themes and questions relevant to a critical engagement with the role of HRM and international HRM in the structuring of organizations. The second section first reviews briefly the current state of critical approaches in the current discourses on IHRM research. The section develops tentative directions for critical theoretical research in the context of two important debates within IHRM, namely research into HRM in MNC subsidiaries and the study of expatriate assignments. A short section concludes.

The case for critical study of international human resource management
The field of management and organization studies was long dominated by functionalist paradigms (Burrell & Morgan, 1979). The last 15 years have seen a steady increase in critical contributions to management theorizing and organizational analysis (Alvesson & Willmot, 1996; Grey & Fournier, 2000), together with the birth of several scholarly communities specializing in non-orthodox theories and studies, including for example the International Critical Management Studies Conference and the Critical Management Studies division within the American Academy of Management. Critical management research draws from a number of theoretical inspirations. We will briefly introduce three of them here.

The so-called 'labour process theory' is a research programme that emerged after the publication of Harry Braverman's influential *Labor and Monopoly Capital* (1974). Labour process theory explores the deskilling hypothesis according to which rational management techniques, including also HRM practices, are used to mechanize and simplify work and thus to make control of work more efficient. Critical theory, in turn, is a social theory movement rooted in the Frankfurt School of social philosophy. Critical theory aims to uncover the suppressed conflict in modern society by analysing how the established understandings of social life are contaminated by ideological discourses and technocratic consciousness, a theme which has been developed particularly in the writings of Jürgen Habermas (1984). Poststructuralism, on the other hand, stems from French philosophy and is influenced by the ideas of semiotics and structuralism but also by other continental theories such as the philosophical works of Nietzsche (Schrift, 1999). Poststructuralism is in a very generalized sense interested in engaging with hierarchies and dualisms, that is, with strategies of power, inscribed in our institutionalized notions of truth and subjectivity, and the approach has become known to English audiences mainly through the writings of Michel Foucault (1977, 1978) and Jacques Derrida (1981).

Despite their profound differences, one can argue that the various critical theories share the broadly common aim of looking at the tensions and contradictions between the dominant and dominated groups and the ways in which rationality, science and discourse are used to affirm the power of the ruling group in society. Recently more emphasis has been laid on the construction of differences along the lines of gender, race, ethnicity, sexuality and nationalism, as well as on the power relations and subjectivities emerging from the discursive constructions of sameness and otherness. This orientation has gone hand in hand with the increasing interest in post-structuralist approaches to the critical study of society and culture, and also in the development of gender and feminist studies as a viable stream of social research (for example, Calhoun, 1995; see also the chapter by Hearn, Metcalfe & Piekkari in the present volume). Following the shift toward postmodern ideas in social sciences, the field of management and organization studies has also witnessed an increasing interest in the issues related to knowledge, discourse, power and identity (for example, du Gay, 1996; Chia, 1996; Jacques, 1996). Calás and Smirchich (1999) have argued that the introduction of postmodern and poststructuralist approaches has already influenced the way in which sociological management research is conducted, most of all in the form of situated reflexivity towards the commonsense categories and knowledge claims prevalent in the authorial articulations on the nature of organizations and organizational management. Poststructuralist critique of regimes and discourses of truth has also affected earlier, broadly neo-Marxist, streams of critical theorizing by making them more aware of the complexities of social power and the heterogeneity of the human subject (for example, Clegg 1989; Knights & Willmot, 1989).

It is also important to note that critical theories have been used not only to deconstruct the established understandings of management and organizations in general, but also to reframe critically the various sub-specialisms of management (Alvesson & Willmot, 1996). An interesting observation in the context of this chapter is that the field of human resource management, a thematic area closest to the emerging discipline of IHRM, has been approached recently from critical theoretical perspectives. For example, Legge (1995) has argued that, although the rhetoric of personnel management has seemingly shifted from the earlier emphasis on pluralism and industrial relations conflict to the prevalence of unitarist paradigms, the old contradictions and tensions associated with the management of paid work in the late modern societies still influence the realities of human resource management in organizations. On the other hand, Townley (1994) has provided another influential critique in which she has used the work of Foucault to look at the ways in which HRM practices assist in making employees manageable through a number of different techniques that situate employees as objectified 'cases' or 'problems' in the organizational grids of intelligibility. Both Legge (1995) and Townley (1994) demonstrate, from their own slightly different critical theoretical perspectives, how seemingly neutral organizational arrangements and techniques associated with the state-of-the-art HRM may be understood as part of the workings of power and ideology.

Similarly techniques and expertise of IHRM can be scrutinized in a critical examination that reveals the hidden intentions and interests behind the seemingly neutral façade of HRM, international management and IHRM. The field of IHRM studies and constitutes organizational practices that are similar to those found in domestic HRM, including the techniques of personnel selection, training, rewarding and career development as well as the issues related to strategic HRM. However, in contrast to domestic HRM, in IHRM, many personnel techniques are legitimized with reference to cultural differences and cross-cultural adjustment instead of a more general concern with organizational effectiveness or employee well-being (for example, Adler, 2002). A critical take on IHRM would pay attention to the ways in which culture tends to be represented as an uncontaminated fact on which IHRM systems can be built, although a closer reading might reveal how 'culture' is often made to serve particular interests. Culture can, for example, be used to describe the social context of the less developed, non-Western countries, whereas the Western world may be assumed to be 'civilized'. Alternatively, 'culture' can be used politically as a motive with which management can introduce HR practices that serve a control function. Human resource function or organizational leadership can, for example, install international performance-monitoring systems in order to be able to better watch over the doings of an individual manager or expert while he or she is abroad.

The central role of cultural difference in the discourse of IHRM could be seen as broadening the scope of critical dialogues beyond the power-oriented analysis of HR practices. In the context of multiple national cultures and cultural identities, a potential further use of critical theories would be to give voice to the marginalized groups and ignored constituencies, and thus to challenge what is currently taken for granted in academic theorizing on and practical orientations to organizational management (for example, Calás & Smirchich, 1991; Nkomo, 1992). This type of critical inquiry could scrutinize the groups typically made visible in the IHRM research to reflect critically what are the significant groups and voices missing in contemporary representations of the 'human resources' of the internationally operating companies. One could, for example, observe that the employee categories present in the IHRM discourse include top executives, human resource managers and the valued experts and professionals, often in administrative or developmental tasks in the corporate hierarchy. 'Key employees' are more often men than women and they also tend to be ethnically closer to the ideal persons cherished in the corporate cultures based on the middle-class values of white North American and North European professionals. The discourse of international human resource management rarely pays attention to the ways in which the supposedly neutral categories sustain and reproduce existing societal asymmetries based on race, ethnicity, class, nationality or gender, despite their relevance to understanding international diversity (Prasad, Mills, Elmes & Prasad, 1997).

Another specific feature of *international* HRM that could be reframed from a critical theoretical perspective is the failure problematics within international mobility and job assignments. It is not common in IHRM research to try to understand international personnel failures as manifestations of deeper social, cultural and political forces in societies and organizations. In most cases, failures among expatriates and repatriates are individualized as personal adjustment problems that can be solved with 'better' selection, training and mentoring of the internationally mobile staff. The contribution of critical theories in this context would be to direct attention to more fundamental structures and processes behind failures and human resource problems, including an analysis of social structures, corporate ideologies and workplace power relations and the way in which they produce 'dysfunctional' outcomes such as career catastrophes, discrimination based on gender or ethnicity, or oppression of the non-Western countries by the centres of global capitalism (cf. Alvesson & Willmot, 1996). While such critical explanations of the HR failures may not be translatable into rational management techniques and HRM models (in fact, they often challenge the taken-for-granted), they do offer advice to practitioners by arousing critical reflection on deeper tensions and contradictions that produce unwanted outcomes related to the management of human resources. Although it seems that there is considerable potential for critical theoretical studies on the various aspects of IHRM, it might be useful first to review briefly the extent to which critical discourses inform current research debates on international dimensions of human resource management.

Toward a critical research programme within IHRM: current debates and future avenues

A quick look at some of the most recent books reveals that there is very little written explicitly on issues of power, domination and ideology in international human resource management. For example, Evans, Pucik and Barsoux (2002) note in the final pages of their book that 'inequality between the rich and poor, both within nations and between nations . . . has worsened during the last quarter century, and notably during the 1990s', but they also pinpoint that 'After all, the HR function cannot do anything about such complex issues.' The interpretations put forward here by Evans *et al.* may seem self-evident to the students of an MBA class. However many students critical of organization start with the assumption that management techniques and models are ideologically biased and that they are indeed part of the public moulding of social relations in the name of managerial rationality (Deetz, 1992; Alvesson & Willmot, 1996). As noted earlier, HRM cannot be regarded as neutral or instrumental in its relation to the objects of managing. Instead it is deeply implicated in the steering of organizational members' thoughts and behaviours – a point demonstrated, for example, by Townley (1994) in her rereading of the role of HR techniques in the management of organizations. Following the credo of such critical thinking, it can be argued that, although the macro-level inequalities of the world portrayed in the textbooks as demonstrations of global ethical issues may be too grand for the organizational behaviour concerns of the IHRM scholars, there are plenty of opportunities to engage critically with the organizational distortions and injustices that are evident at the workplace level of international business enterprises.

If we then explore the emerging debates from other scholarly sources, especially journals, the range of available critical interrogations of IHRM seems to be even narrower than in the context of textbooks. I searched for critically pitched articles from the *International Journal of Human Resource Management* (IJHRM), the current house journal for the IHRM discipline, by entering the keywords 'power', 'ideology' and 'critique' to the electronic database search covering all volumes of IJHRM (date: 10.8.04). My assumption was that the existence of some of these three keywords in the titles of the papers might indicate that the contents of the full paper would contain some sort of engagement with the critical debates on IHRM phenomena. However the search did not produce any hits from the archives of the past issues of IJHRM. It is of course possible that I could have missed the articles that engage with the non-orthodox perspectives despite their conventionalist titles, but, on the other hand, it is more probable that the result from the journal database search reveals a wider paucity of critical studies of international human resource management phenomena in the journals devoted to the advancing of the discipline.

HRM practices in MNC subsidiaries

At the same time, however, some of the recent research contributions within the field do engage with critically loaded concepts such as organizational power. One such IHRM debate where power has appeared recently concerns the structuring of HRM practices in the MNCs (Rosenzweig & Nohria, 1994; Hannon *et al.*, 1995; Ferner & Quintanilla, 1998). The standard research contributions in this stream of IHRM research are based on relatively straightforward empiricist analyses of the structural forms of

MNCs in relation to the organization of HRM. Often, the adopted approach to the structuring of HRM in MNCs is interrogated by surveying to what extent a particular HR practice (for example, performance appraisal) is adjusted to the cultural and institutional demands of the host country context. As Ferner and Quantanilla (1998) have proposed, HRM practices that are transferred from the headquarters to the subsidiaries can remain rooted in the corporate or home country norms and values or can be adapted to the local context, depending on the organizational–contextual contingencies.

Empirical studies tend to suggest that, in general, MNCs prefer centralization to differentiation (Bonache, 2000), although results vary across contexts. Anyway, given that there is at least tentative bias towards standardization in MNC behaviour, there is a need to explain why corporations resort to global uniformity when the literature on transnational HR management suggests that contextual variety of the different organizational units needs to be taken into account in the implementation of management policies at the local level (for example, Sparrow & Hiltrop, 1997). Organizational power comes into the picture here as a way of theoretically and empirically accounting for the resources that the MNC headquarters and their managers use to impose their preferred HR norms and standards on the local unit. One of the most articulate contributions to a power explanation comes from Björkman and Lu (2001), who, in their study of the Chinese–Western joint ventures, introduce a framework from organization theory that employs ideas from institutional theory (Scott, 2001) and a resource dependency approach to organizational power (Pfeffer & Salancik, 1978). They argue that standardization of HRM follows to a large extent from the process during which the Western parties acquire power resources with which to impose their parochial preferences on the Chinese organizations and actors, along with the adaptation of institutionalized managerial beliefs, which put global unity on a pedestal.

Critical accounts of MNC power in host country subsidiaries would differ from the existing notions in that social power would be seen as being deeper and more constitutive than in the views approaching power as an empirically observable resource (cf. Frost & Egri, 1991). Instead of analysing power as external to the emergence of a particular HR design, the focus in critical theories, especially in approaches influenced by Foucault's (1982) conception of 'positive power', tends to be more on how power is constructed in the course of organizing the relations and identities of main actors (Clegg, 1989; Hardy & Clegg, 1996). Thus, rather than understanding 'power' as a mechanism or structure that explains whether a locally tailored or globally integrated human resources strategy gets implemented in a given institutional context, the emergence of the more fundamental, prior asymmetry between the actors is seen as something that needs to be described and accounted for. This implies a view where 'power' of the multinational corporations and their central management apparatus is seen as not being possible before other actors have joined the evolving collectivity and accepted the proposed roles and responsibilities as the basis of their participation in the 'transfer' of management techniques (Latour, 1986).

For example, post-colonial theory (Said, 1978; Prasad, 2003) starts with the assumption that power relations between colonizers and colonized cannot be fully understood by focusing on resources and structural forces leading to coercion of the behaviour of the dominated. Instead power emerges in this approach as an effect of constructing and moulding the identity of both of the participants in a relation, implying that the colonized are also playing a part in crafting, internalizing and living the conditions that make power and asymmetry possible in an evolving organizational connection.

Equipped with a positive or relational view on social power, critical analysis of global homogenization could start by asking more specific questions about the construction of core/periphery relations and the structuring of power in decision making on IHRM. The research questions could include the following, who defines the reality of organization? How are the identities of headquarters and various subsidiaries negotiated and how do subsidiary managers take on the role of local executives representing something smaller and more peripheral than the units in the symbolic and political core of the contemporary world economy? How are different national, cultural and ethnic groups of employees defined and talked about and are there visible differences between the identities of the Western/developed and the non-Western/developing managers and experts? How is the need for Western/rational/standardized HR practices in the remote subsidiaries legitimated and naturalized? Whose rationality prevails and how are consents to corporate imperialism manufactured in the non-Western subsidiaries? What kind of resistance emerges in the subsidiaries and how is it tempered into revolt behaviour?

These are just some questions that might advance the study of power and HRM in MNCs from a critical theoretical perspective. Whereas the dynamics of the relations between the centre and the periphery of transnational corporations lead relatively easily to considering power analytics and critical investigations of international business management as research frameworks, the study of expatriates, repatriates and cultural adjustment has usually been seen as a province of psychologistic and individualistic research debates. However processes related to expatriate life could also provide some interesting insights into the workings of power, discourse and identity in the international settings.

Expatriate research

Expatriates and their adjustment, performance and repatriation constituted a central topic for IHRM research in its formative years (for example,
Mendenhall, Dunbar & Oddou, 1987) and the debate still goes on in the
field. Studies in this area typically look at the individual-level processes and
problems related to international job mobility of corporate professionals,
often within big multinational companies (Thomas, 1998). However the
focus of the debate has shifted slightly from the psychological issues
around cross-cultural and practical problems to an emphasis on expatriates
as part of the human capital of the firm. The extraordinary quality of international assignments is beginning to vanish in connection with this change
of perspective as contemporary expatriate studies tend to look at the
globally mobile employees as 'strategic resources' and future global
managers, rather than as 'complex humans' encountering adjustment problems and career discontinuities (for example, Inkson, Arthur, Pringle &
Barry, 1997).

The transition towards a more strategic or HRM perspective on international assignments means, to some extent, that the research discourse on
expatriates has moved away from the theoretical traditions of cross-
cultural and social psychology that informed the early stages of expatriate
research. While the conventional organizational and work psychology that
conceptualizes individuals as atomistic units might have little to offer to
critical social theories of management and business, the recent currents in
psychology of organizations, as well as in psychology proper, put more
emphasis on social and contextual underpinnings of human behaviour
(Nord & Fox, 1996). At a relatively general level, the recent development in
expatriate research could then be criticized on the basis that its leaning on
the theories of strategic human resource management makes it more
difficult to think about and theorize expatriates as individuals-in-context,
especially to understand how internationally mobile employees' work and
career processes are affected and affect the wider circuits of power and
control in international business.

One example of the way critical ideas about identities could inform the
empirical investigation of expatriates comes from my own work. In a theoretical synthesis of my work on expatriates, repatriates and their career
processes (Peltonen, 1998), I try to conceptualize the negotiation of the organizational and personal identities as a struggle over the stability and change
of power positions in a Finnish subsidiary of a multinational corporation
used as the case company. With the help of extensive qualitative material, I
look at the discursive attempts of expatriates and repatriates to challenge,
resist and change the established hierarchies among professional engineers
and managers in an engineering corporation. My study relates beliefs,

meanings and identity work of the expatriate employees to the current construction of power relations. The empirical focus is on the self-categorizations and accounts that expatriates and other employees gave about their standing in the social web of organization as well as on their views about their professional and managerial motivations and orientations. However the interpretation given to qualitative data seeks to reveal patterns in the identities constructed and to find links between observed subject positions and organization and industry-level social structures and power relations.

In a relatively different context, albeit in a fashion similar to my analyses, David Boje presents an interesting interpretation of a story of expatriate failure as one of five scholars invited to give a response to the issues raised by a short case description of a troublesome expatriate assignment (Keough, 1998; Sypher, Shwom, Boje, Rosile & Miller, 1998). While the other academics provide advice based on the seeming shortcomings in communication, planning of the assignment and intercultural training, Boje focuses instead on the construction of the expatriate's story of international relocation, especially from the viewpoint of latent tensions and contradictions inscribed in the narrative. Boje thus takes a broadly discursive methodological path to uncover deeper structures and hierarchies that are implicit in the female expatriate's story but that do not come across in the normalized interpretations available in the form of conventional IHRM models and theories of expatriation/repatriation. In this vein, Boje finds a number of silenced voices and marginalized truths such as the tendency of a corporation to use home country expatriates to control the foreign subsidiaries, the lack of ideas about the use of repatriating expatriates and the overall colonial attitude of the North American headquarters towards the foreign subsidiaries. Boje's interpretation of a normalized 'case description' of an expatriate story opens up other possible stories to be told about the reality of IHRM and multinational corporations, which, in turn, help us to see deeper structures and power relations of the global workplace. Furthermore these alternative perspectives and representations of expatriate lives could be used to explain some of the puzzling outcomes in a way that is more enlightening and engaging than the interpretations of the conventional human resource models and theories of international working.

The influences flowing from social structures to expatriate life notwithstanding, the practical circumstances surrounding expatriates and other internationally mobile 'key persons' have a constitutive role in the changing material arrangements of globalization. At the same time as international networking and global careers are becoming 'business as usual' for the professional and managerial employees of the corporate sector, the rest of workforce, especially in low-income jobs, is still very much tied to its local community. Most of the expatriate employees studied within IHRM are white-collar experts and corporate executives for whom moving from one location to another is not a particular problem since they are considered 'okay' in the eyes of the global political and safety institutions. Unlike the experience of masses of immigrant workers who are forced to seek better opportunities in the industrial countries, the authorities of the host countries normally welcome the corporate and business expatriates. As sociologist Zygmunt Bauman (1998, 2000) has noted in this context, the business traveller or expatriate and the immigrant worker could be seen as the two sides of the same coin of globalization, in that, without the existence of the global army of low-paid 'susceptible persons', there would not be the phenomenon of corporate expatriation and international business travelling. However, I am not aware of any published paper in the IHRM field that would have contrasted corporate expatriates with immigrant workers, although the issue is topical in the more general dialogues on transnational organizations and globalization (Sassen, 1998; Banerjee & Linstead, 2001; Hearn, 2004). Overall, lifestyles and social arrangements surrounding expatriates and other internationally mobile professionals could be a fruitful topic for future critical analyses on globalization of work and employment management (cf. Peltonen, 2005).

Conclusions

This chapter has provided some preliminary openings to the study of IHRM from the perspective of critical theories. In conclusion, it is perhaps useful to note that the overall scholarly spirit which I hope passes from the engagement with critical theories to the IHRM research is openness and creativity. The chapter has suggested two specific lines of critical inquiry within IHRM (construction of power relations in connection with the organization of HRM in MNC subsidiaries, and the changing role of expatriates in the transnational organizations and labour markets) but, by doing so, it has in no way intended to ignore other potentially interesting lines of critical analyses and interrogations of IHRM. Instead various critical theoretical approaches illuminate different aspects of the workings of power and ideology within international human resource management, and, rather than establishing an exclusive programme, it is more fruitful for the advancement of theoretical dialogues in the field to let critique enter into international HRM research in its many forms and styles.

Acknowledgments

I would like to thank the comments of Ingmar Björkman, Jeff Hearn and Rebecca Piekkari. Wihuri Foundation and the Finnish Foundation for Economic Education have supported my research work.

References

Adler, N. 2002. *International dimensions of organizational behaviour*. Cincinatti, OH: South Western.
Alvesson, M. & S. Deetz. 2000. *Doing critical management research*. London: Sage.
Alvesson, M. & H. Willmot. 1996. *Making sense of management. A critical introduction*. London: Sage.
Banerjee, S.B. & S.A. Linstead. 2001. Globalization, multiculturalism and other fictions: colonialism for the new millennium? *Organization*, **8**(4): 683–722.
Bauman, Z. 1998. *Globalization*. Cambridge: Polity Press.
Bauman, Z. 2000. *Liquid modernity*. Cambridge: Polity Press.
Björkman, I. & Y. Lu. 2001. Institutionalization and bargaining power explanations of HRM practices in international joint ventures. *Organization Studies*, **22**(3): 491–512.
Bonache, J. 2000. The transfer of an idea–suggestion system: against radical relativism in international HRM. *International Studies of Management and Organization*, **29**(4): 24–44.
Braverman, H. 1974. *Labor and monopoly capital*. New York: Monthly Review.
Burrell, G. & G. Morgan. 1979. *Sociological paradigms and organisational analysis*. London: Heinemann.
Calás, M. & L. Smirchich. 1991. Voicing seduction to silence leadership. *Organization Studies*, **12**(4): 567–604.
Calás, M. & L. Smirchich. 1999. Past postmodernism? Reflections and tentative directions. *Academy of Management Review*, **24**(4): 649–72.
Calhoun, C. 1995. *Critical social theory*. London: Blackwell.
Chia, R. 1996. *Organizational analysis as deconstructive practice*. Berlin: de Gruyter.
Clegg, S. 1989. Radical revisions: power, discipline and organizations. *Organization Studies*, **10**(1): 97–115.
Deetz, S. 1992. Disciplinary power in the modern corporation. In M. Alvesson & H. Willmot (eds), *Critical management studies*. London: Sage.
Derrida, J. 1981. *Positions*. Chicago, IL: University of Chicago Press.
du Gay, P. 1996. *Consumption and identity at work*. London: Sage.
Evans, P., V. Pucik & J-L. Barsoux. 2002. *The global challenge. Frameworks for international human resource management*. New York: McGraw-Hill/Irwin.
Ferner, A. & J. Quintanilla. 1998. Multinationals, national business systems and HRM: the enduring influence of national identity or a process of Anglo-Saxonization? *International Journal of Human Resource Management*, **34**(3): 343–61.
Foucault, M. 1977. *Discipline and punish*. NewYork: Pantheon.
Foucault, M. 1978. *The history of sexuality. Vol 1. an introduction*. Harmondsworth: Penguin.
Foucault. M. 1982. The subject and power. In H. Dreyfus & P. Rabinow (eds), *Michel Foucault: Beyond structuralism and hermeneutics*. Chicago, IL: University of Chicago Press.
Frost, P.J. & C.P. Egri. 1991. The political process of innovation. *Research in Organizational Behavior*, **13**: 229–95.
Grey, C. 1999. 'We are all managers now/we always were': on the development and demise of management. *Journal of Management Studies*, **36**(5): 561–86.
Grey, C. & V. Fournier. 2000. At the critical moment: conditions and prospects for critical management studies. *Human Relations*, **53**(1): 7–32.
Habermas, J. 1984. *The theory of communicative action*. vol. 1. London: Heinemann.
Hannon, J., I.-C. Huang & B.-S. Jaw. 1995. International human resource strategy and its determinants: the case of subsidiaries in Taiwan. *Journal of International Business Studies*, **26**(3): 531–54
Hardy, C. & S. Clegg. 1996. Some dare call it power. In S.R. Clegg, C.Hardy & W.R. Nord (eds), *Handbook of organization studies*. London: Sage.
Hearn, J. 2004. Tracking 'the transnational': studying transnational organizations and managements, and the management of cohesion. *Culture and Organization*, **10**(4): 273–90.
Inkson, K., M. Arthur, J. Pringle & S. Barry. 1997. Expatriate assignment versus overseas experience. *Journal of World Business*, **32**: 351–68.
Jacques, R. 1996. *Manufacturing the employee*. London: Sage.

Keough, C.M. 1998. The case of the aggrieved expatriate. *Management Communication Quarterly*, **11**(3): 453–9.

Knights, D. & H. Willmot. 1989. Power and subjectivity at work. From degradation to subjugation in social relations. *Sociology*, **23**(4): 535–58.

Latour, B. 1986. The powers of association. In J. Law (ed.), *Power, action and belief: a new sociology of knowledge?* 264–80. London/Boston/Henley: Routledge and Kegan Paul.

Laurent, A. 1986. The cross-cultural puzzle of international human resource management. *Human Resource Management*, **25**(1): 91–102.

Legge, K. 1995. *Human resource management: rhetorics and realities*. London: Macmillan.

Mendenhall, M., E. Dunbar & G. Oddou. 1987. Expatriate selection, training and career-pathing: a review and critique. *Human Resource Management*, **26**(3): 331–45.

Nkomo, S. 1992. The Emperor has no clothes: rewriting 'race' in organizations. *Academy of Management Review*, **17**(3): 487–514.

Nord, W. & S. Fox. 1996. The individual in organization studies. In S.R. Clegg, C. Hardy & W.R. Nord (eds), *Handbook of organization studies*. London: Sage.

Peltonen, T. 1998. *Expatriate experience and career*. Doctoral dissertation. Acta Oeconomia Helsingiensis, series A-139. Helsinki: Helsinki School of Economics Press.

Peltonen, T. 2005. The speedy business traveler and the others of time/space compression: making of the flying professional in global business and academia. In P. Case, S. Lilley & T. Owens (eds), *The speed of organization*. Copenhagen: Liber Press.

Pfeffer J. & G.R. Salancik 1978. *The external control of organizations: a resource dependency perspective*. New York: Harper and Row.

Prasad, A. 1997. The colonizing consciousness and representations of the other: a postcolonial critique of the discourse of oil. In P. Prasad, A. Mills, M. Elmes & A. Prasad (eds), *Managing the organizational melting pot: dilemmas of workplace diversity*. London/Thousand Oaks/New Delhi: Sage.

Prasad, A. (ed.). 2003. *Postcolonial theory and organizational analysis*. London: Sage.

Prasad, P., A. Mills, M. Elmes & A. Prasad. (eds) 1997. *Managing the organizational melting pot: dilemmas of workplace diversity*. London/Thousand Oaks/New Delhi: Sage.

Rosenzweig, P. & N. Nohria. 1994. Influences on human resource management practices in multinational corporations. *Journal of International Business Studies*, **25**(2): 229–51.

Said, E. 1978. *Orientalism*. New York: Pantheon Books.

Sassen, S. 1998. *Globalization and its consequences. Essays on the new mobility of people and money*. New York: The Free Press.

Schrift, A.D. 1999. *Nietzsche's French legacy. A genealogy of poststructuralism*. London: Routledge.

Scott, W.R. 2001. *Institutions and organizations*. London: Sage.

Sparrow, P. & J.-M. Hiltrop. 1997. Redefining the field of European human resource management: a battle between national mindsets and forces of business transition. *Human Resource Management*, **36**(2): 201–20.

Sypher, B., B. Shwom, D. Boje, G.A. Rosile & V. Miller. 1998. The case of the aggrieved expatriate: case analyses. *Management Communication Quarterly*, **11**(3): 460–85.

Thomas, D. 1998. The expatriate experience: a critical review and synthesis. *Advances in International Comparative Management*, vol.12: 237–73. Cincinnati, OH: JAI Press.

Townley, B. 1994. *Reframing human resource management*. London: Sage.

Westwood, R. 2001. Appropriating the other in the discourses of comparative management. In R. Westwood & S. Linstead (eds), *The language of organization*. London: Sage.

Willmot, H. 1997. Rethinking management and managerial work: capitalism, control and subjectivity. *Human Relations*, **50**: 1329–59.

29 Language effects in multinational corporations: a review from an international human resource management perspective
Rebecca Piekkari

Many multinational corporations (MNCs) today adopt a common corporate language to facilitate the process of internal communication between headquarters and foreign subsidiaries as well as directly between foreign units. From a top management perspective, such 'language standardization' (Marschan-Piekkari *et al.*, 1999a: 379) has many advantages: for example, it may support formal reporting between units in various foreign locations, improve access to company documents and create a stronger sense of belonging to a global corporate 'family'. Indeed the issue is not only one of efficiency but one of corporate control (SanAntonio, 1987: 199). A common corporate language is thus seen to operate as an integrative mechanism among the geographically scattered, multilingual workforce. In this context, English is frequently chosen as the 'lingua franca' owing to the importance of Anglophone markets, the economic power of the USA and the Internet. 'Lingua franca' is defined as an idiom that non-native speakers use with other non-native speakers, rendering it a foreign language for all parties concerned (Vandermeeren, 1999: 276), or among native and non-native speakers. For example, pan-Nordic corporations increasingly choose English as their corporate language (Louhiala-Salminen *et al.*, 2005).

A standardized English-language approach adopted by many multinational corporations, including General Electric, Nokia and Electrolux, however, does not resolve language diversity associated with daily operations. The level of proficiency in the common corporate language is likely to vary and lower-level employees are likely to speak only their local language. As Vandermeeren (1999) argues, international business interaction is rarely a monolingual event. In reality, communication across linguistic boundaries is frequently carried out in a mixture of languages. Accordingly, Barner-Rasmussen and Björkman (2003) conceptualize the multinational corporation as a multilingual organization.

Thus there seem to be two counter forces operating for and against the language strategy chosen by top management of multinational corporations:

those that lead to the standardized use of one language, and others that suggest the use of multiple languages in an adaptive way. Nevertheless, as Vandermeeren (1999: 276) points out, 'standardization' and 'adaptation' are not 'all or nothing' phenomena because most companies mix their strategies of language choice.

Until recently, language as a separate variable has gained very limited attention in the field of international business in general, and in IHRM in particular. This is because language, if considered at all, is often subsumed into the broader concept of culture. It seems that the term 'culture' is frequently used as a general explanation for the various problems experienced by internationalizing companies. This is in sharp contrast to the early research by Johanson and Wiedersheim-Paul (1975: 307–8) who coined the term 'psychic distance' in order to explain why internationalizing companies first enter similar foreign markets in terms of language, culture, political and educational systems and levels of industrial development and so on. By analytically separating language from other factors, the respective causes of disturbances in information flows between markets may be made easier to identify. In line with this, the present chapter considers language a more specific and precise variable than culture more generally.

The purpose of this chapter is, then, to review the implications of language policy and language use for international human resource management (IHRM) at different levels of analysis: for example, individual managers and employees, cross-cultural teams, foreign subsidiaries and the firm as a whole. Inevitably, given that language skills reside in individuals, the focus is on managing people (Marschan-Piekkari *et al.*, 1999a). Since much of the relevant literature seeks to analyse aspects of IHRM in multinational corporations (see, for example, Dowling & Welch, 2004), I shall focus on this particular organizational context. This chapter argues that recent research on language in international business and IHRM has adopted multiple perspectives, problematizing language effects beyond its role as a mere medium of communication. I shall proceed by first defining language and reviewing the various perspectives adopted on language in the field. Thereafter I shall examine language effects at multiple levels of analysis in order to demonstrate explicitly how language effects extend beyond the individual, and provide an agenda for future research.

Language and languages in multinational corporations

If we take a closer look at language diversity in multinational corporations, it is not only the multiplicity of idioms which is evident, but also the various forms of language found in the workplace. Welch, Welch and Piekkari (2005) divide them into three forms or layers, the first being everyday written and spoken language, such as English or German, which is the main focus of the present chapter. For example, in their study of Japanese-owned subsidiaries in Scotland Wright, Kumagai and Bonney (2001) identify a specific form of everyday spoken language, 'broken English' or 'pidgin English', used in the communication between local staff and Japanese expatriate management. Second, many firms use so-called 'company speak' which is replete with acronyms and special terms typical of the organization in question (Welch *et al.*, 2005). For example, General Electric uses abbreviations such as N-1 and N-2 to indicate the person's status in the organizational hierarchy. The third layer of language is technical, professional or industry jargon used by, for example, IT engineers. These layers of language are intertwined. For example, in-depth knowledge of the professional language or 'company speak' may actually compensate for the person's limited skills in the foreign language itself.

Drawing on translation studies, Janssens, Lambert and Steyaert (2004) describe the evolution of perspectives on language in international management. They summarize this historical evolution from three perspectives: the instrumental (or mechanical), the cultural and the political.

According to the instrumental perspective, the presence of multiple languages complicates internal communication processes within the multinational corporation. As mentioned previously, multinational corporations respond to this challenge by selecting one common language that every employee is assumed to be able to speak. This 'lingua franca' is considered to be a neutral tool to communicate more 'easily'. In this approach, language is typically regarded as a means of transferring information and presented as a pragmatic problem related to top management's concerns about organizational effectiveness. It is assumed that imposing one language, that is standardizing language choice, will resolve the difficulties experienced in international communication (Janssens *et al.*, 2004). Much of the work in international business and IHRM has adopted such an instrumental perspective on language. For example, Fixman's (1990) study of foreign language needs in US-based multinationals suggests that foreign language skills per se were rarely considered in staff selection and career advancement. Instead they were viewed as a mechanical skill to be acquired if necessary and secondary to the candidates' technical skills.

The cultural perspective, as Janssens *et al.* (2004) describe, adopts a different view on the multiplicity of languages. Multinational corporations are understood as culturally embedded and linguistically diverse. These authors argue that such an approach avoids imposing one common language. Instead different languages will be encouraged in various local contexts allowing adaptation of the language strategy. Language is seen as a key to the understanding of different foreign cultures and an essential aspect of the cultural context (Brannen, 2004). Therefore proficiency in the local language is often related to expatriates' cross-cultural ability and performance (Dowling & Welch, 2004). For example, in his study of Western expatriates assigned to China, Selmer (2004) found that expatriates' proficiency in Chinese was positively related to their sociocultural adjustment. He argues that learning a Chinese language reduced expatriates' feelings of being outsiders and improved their relationships with host country nationals. At the same time, learning the local language was also a vehicle to enhance communication between groups of employees and to reduce social exclusion. This suggests a certain degree of overlap between the instrumental and the cultural perspectives.

The political perspective introduces the explicit relationship between language and power. It argues that the selection of a given 'lingua franca' is a political process, not a neutral act, as suggested by the instrumental view. Recent research on international mergers and acquisitions clearly demonstrates the political play associated with language issues (Bruntse, 2003; Gertsen *et al.*, 1998; Piekkari *et al.*, 2005). The choice of a common corporate language raises questions and emotions about national dominance and may even undermine integration efforts. This is particularly true in the case of mergers that are announced as a 'marriage of equals' (Vaara & Tienari, 2003). The case study of a Nordic financial institution shows that the chosen corporate language, Swedish, sent an implicit symbolic message regarding the division of power between the merging parties (Björkman, Tienari & Vaara, 2003; Piekkari *et al.*, 2005). It restricted equal opportunities between employees and caused unfavourable disintegration.

Scandinavian Airlines (SAS), which is a pan-Scandinavian organization originating from Sweden, Denmark and Norway, did not formally appoint a common language partly in an attempt to maintain the power balance between the three nations (Bruntse, 2003). Janssens *et al.* (2004) write that the equality of languages can never be taken for granted in international companies: there is always a degree of manipulation, persuasion, resistance and negotiation. Even in organizations such as the European Union, in which the equality of languages is stated in writing (Wagner *et al.*, 2002), there is a constant competition between languages of large and small countries. As will be discussed later, the political perspective on language is not only associated with the process of choosing a common corporate language but also with its use.

The three perspectives – instrumental, cultural and political – introduced by Janssens *et al.* (2004) demonstrate different approaches to language in the MNC context. As discussed above, they are not mutually exclusive but sometimes overlapping. We now discuss more specifically language effects from an international human resource management perspective.

IHRM implications of language
Prior research on language and its implications for IHRM is here divided
into four broad groups based on the level of analysis: (1) the individual,
(2) cross-cultural teams, (3) headquarters–subsidiary and inter-subsidiary
relationships, and (4) the MNC as a totality. Moreover our aim is to classify previous research in the field according to the authors' perspective on
language.

Individual managers, employees and relationships between them
As companies introduce network structures and encourage direct horizontal communication between subsidiary units, there is an increasing need to
use foreign languages in the daily work. This applies not only to the top ech-
elons of the organization but also further down the hierarchy (Charles &
Marschan-Piekkari, 2002). Such a 'democratization' process of international communication has a number of consequences. For example, once
a common corporate language is in place, it becomes a requirement for
being admitted to corporate training and management development programmes, potential international assignments and promotion (Marschan-
Piekkari *et al.*, 1999a). In this way, multiple incentives are created for
learning the corporate language, which demonstrates an instrumental perspective on language. However providing corporate training in one standardized language such as English may exclude groups of subsidiary staff
who still lack the necessary language skills. This may also affect their
opportunities to create and expand networks of personal relationships
within the MNC.

Language ability is one of the selection criteria used in expatriate postings as it is regarded as an important aspect of expatriate performance.
Dowling and Welch (2004) refer to the expatriate's skills in the local language of the host country as well as in the common corporate language of
the MNC. In this context, Marschan-Piekkari *et al.* (1999a) found parent
country nationals who sometimes became what they termed 'language
nodes'. These persons were comfortable operating across several language
interfaces, such as the host country language, the common corporate language and the parent country language. They communicated, often informally, with colleagues in other subsidiary and headquarters units and their
language-based linkages tended to extend beyond the host and home units.
For example, a third country national based in a subsidiary in Singapore of
a Finnish MNC called his Finnish colleague 'our pet Finn', indicating the
conduit role that this expatriate had in the local office (Marschan, 1996:
139–40). Goodall and Roberts (2003a) add another dimension to the discussion by emphasizing expatriates' proficiency in the 'company speak'.
This contributed to the strength of expatriate networks and made them

virtually impermeable to outsiders such as host country nationals. The importance of language skills in foreign assignments may result in selective recruitment if particular nationalities or groups of employees are preferred over others. A recent survey shows that, even in a national context such as the UK, English class and regional accents may be a disadvantage, as they raise concerns about a person's competence and success in business (Aziz Management Communications Index, 2003). Such findings reveal political considerations associated with language use in recruitment practices.

Language skills may also influence the employee's chances of advancing his or her career within the MNC (SanAntonio, 1987). For example, in a study of a Finnish–Swedish merger it was found that Swedish as the common corporate language operated as a 'glass ceiling' effectively excluding non-Swedish-speaking individuals from climbing up the corporate ladder (Piekkari *et al.*, 2005). Research on Japanese-owned subsidiaries in different parts of the world provides supporting findings (Lincoln *et al.*, 1995; Negandhi *et al.*, 1985; Wright *et al.*, 2001; Yoshihara, 2001). Japanese companies are very ethnocentric in their staffing policies. Senior positions in most Japanese foreign subsidiaries are filled by Japanese expatriates, making the Japanese language a significant source of power. In Japanese-owned companies, such a 'glass ceiling' restricts the upward mobility of local staff and makes them pursue different career paths. In this context, foreign language skills can be seen as a feature distinguishing between corporate elites and non-elites (Odendahl & Shaw, 2002; Welch *et al.*, 2002). On the other hand, an individual who is competent in a key language of the organization may gain a strategically important position beyond his or her formal, hierarchical status (Marschan *et al.*, 1997; SanAntonio, 1987).

Related to career advancement and promotion, it may be particularly challenging for managers to carry out performance appraisal of employees with whom they do not have a shared language. Such situations are not uncommon in MNCs which operate under a global matrix structure. But even in organizations with unitary command structures operating primarily within one geographical region, such as the Nordic countries, serious language-related challenges may emerge. Piekkari *et al.* (2005) describe a situation in which a Swedish manager responsible for a Finnish-speaking unit found himself conducting appraisal interviews through an interpreter. After the introduction of Swedish as the corporate language of the merged organization, many Finns had to operate professionally without adequate levels of proficiency in the common corporate language (see also Björkman, Tienari & Vaara, 2003). At the time, investments in language training had not yet materialized. Consequently these otherwise capable and useful employees appeared unintelligent in their encounters with the Swedes. They often remained silent although professionalism would have required active participation. In a way, their professional competence was hidden behind the language barrier and they seemed to be underperforming (Piekkari *et al.*, 2005).

In line with the political approach, language may also complicate the power dynamics of performance appraisal interviews in situations in which the subordinates have the linguistic edge. For example, an interview study of Japanese-owned subsidiaries in Germany shows how Japanese managers were reluctant to conduct direct appraisals of their German subordinates. The language of the workplace among Japanese subsidiaries in Germany was English and the Germans tended to enjoy a relaxed facility with English that few of their Japanese managers shared (Lincoln *et al.*, 1995). Indeed previous research shows that relationships between expatriates and local employees are likely to be negatively affected in the case where the subordinate group (local employees) possess a significant linguistic advantage (Lincoln *et al.*, 1995; Wright *et al.*, 2001).

The above discussion demonstrates an instrumental approach on language in expatriate selection, the use of expatriates as 'language nodes' and conduits in cross-border communication. In addition, the acknowledgment of language effects on career advancement and social inclusion/exclusion reveals political considerations.

Cross-cultural teams

On the next level of analysis, the recognition of belonging to a particular group and the categorization of others into ingroups and outgroups is a social process in which language plays a major role prior (Gudykunst *et al.*, 1989). Research on cross-cultural teams has examined cultural, national and functional diversity as a factor affecting team dynamics and performance (for example, DiStefano & Maznevski, 2000; Salk & Brannen, 2000; Schweiger *et al.*, 2003). On the one hand, it is often argued that diversity is a potential source of new ideas. On the other hand, extreme diversity among team members may slow down communication, operate as a barrier to interactions and negatively affect team performance.

However language diversity per se has received little specific attention in research on cross-cultural teams. Henderson Kassis (2005) argues that the importance of the language factor is often overlooked. In many studies the actual process of interpersonal interaction taking place through language is generally left unexamined. Cross-cultural teams, however, are composed of individuals who speak a variety of mother tongues and belong to different language communities. Drawing on sociolinguistics and discourse analysis, Henderson Kassis explains that language diversity is produced as team members not only speak several languages but also hear in a variety of different ways; that is, they use different interpretive mechanisms.

In particular, language use has been found to be associated with the socialization of team members and trust building (Lagerström & Andersson, 2003). Language and cultural diversity may also intersect with gender, as teams from a certain country or region such as the Middle East may largely be composed of males (see the chapter by Hearn, Metcalfe & Piekkari in this volume).

In MNCs, the use of English as the working language of the team is very common since many large corporations have adopted English as the official corporate language. Yet the two interview studies conducted by Schweiger *et al.* (2003) and Lagerström and Andersson (2003) demonstrate that language was a major source of problems for cross-cultural teams. Rather unexpectedly, the level of proficiency in English among the team members varied significantly. While one of the interviewees in Schweiger *et al.*'s study (2003: 134) admitted that 'we did not tap the full depth of the number of members' capabilities' owing to the problems associated with English, Lagerström and Andersson (2003: 91) report that one global team member had to be dismissed for the same reason.

Indeed cross-cultural teams are simultaneously both multilingual and monolingual since English is frequently used as a 'lingua franca' among native and non-native speakers (Henderson Kassis, 2005). However, when English is used as a working language of the team, participants are often under the false impression that they are sharing the same context as if they had a common mental space (Henderson Kassis, 2005). The widespread use of English in MNCs may create a sense of artificial confidence and familiarity; consequently team members may fail to perceive that they are culturally distant (Welch *et al.*, 2001). In this stream of research, language is primarily considered a barrier to effective communication between team members rather than a doorway into understanding the very cultural differences that may lie behind the communication challenges. Such an approach suggests an instrumental perspective on language.

Headquarters–subsidiary and inter-subsidiary relationships
Research on language and international business has also examined the implications of language for foreign subsidiaries, particularly from the viewpoint of control, communication and coordination challenges. This reflects the recent shift in MNC management research to study the foreign subsidiary as the central unit of analysis (see Birkinshaw & Hood, 1998; Holm & Pedersen, 2000, for reviews of research on subsidiaries).

Much of the earlier work regards language as a barrier to the effective functioning of the MNC (Feely & Harzing, 2003). Barner-Rasmussen (2003) examined the relationship between a Finnish-based headquarters and its foreign subsidiaries and found evidence for the mental and physical distance created by the lack of a shared language. The interview with the CEO demonstrated not only that he does not visit the subsidiary in France because he does not speak French, but also a certain degree of ignorance towards the French unit (Barner-Rasmussen, 2003: 71). Similarly, in their study of Danish subsidiaries in France, Andersen and Rasmussen (2004) identified a number of problems faced by headquarters in communicating and controlling its French units because of the language barrier. Yoshihara's (2001) study of Japanese multinationals shows that one way of solving language-related communication and control challenges in headquarters–subsidiary relationships is to use parent country nationals. He argues that the Japanese model of globalization primarily relies on managing foreign operations by sending Japanese expatriates and by using the Japanese language. This removes the language barrier between the headquarters and the foreign subsidiary but introduces it lower down in the organization. But even in the case of using parent country nationals, these very same expatriates may lose their ability to communicate in the right 'company speak' after working in the periphery of the MNC. This may further magnify the perceived distance between headquarters and foreign subsidiaries (Goodall & Roberts 2003b).

Research on knowledge sharing and transfer in MNCs has largely been silent about the role of individuals and language in this process. However recent work in the area does incorporate language as a factor. For example, Buckley, Carter, Clegg and Tan (2005) examined how corporate social knowledge, along with language, promotes the transfer of knowledge between the Western headquarters and the Chinese subsidiary units. Corporate social knowledge is defined as knowledge held by individuals, or groups of individuals, that enable them to interpret, understand and predict the behaviour of others in the corporate context. Their evidence from four cases suggests that a common language alone is unable to secure effective knowledge transfer between the parties. Corporate social knowledge, which is often expressed in 'company speak', is essential for the articulation and assimilation of foreign knowledge. Knowledge transfer between headquarters and subsidiaries in China was achieved through the presence of expatriates, the circulation of staff internationally and the use of multinational teams (Buckley *et al.*, 2005). In this study, language was very much seen as a medium of knowledge transfer, as suggested by the instrumental view.

Similarly, in relationships between subsidiaries, Barner-Rasmussen and Björkman (2005) found that the intensity of communication among foreign-owned subsidiaries in Finland and China was related to the subsidiary managers' fluency in the shared language, and the extent to which they participate in corporate training. Overall the accumulation of social capital in MNC subsidiaries has been found to be positively influenced by language skills (Barner-Rasmussen, 2003).

On the other hand, the cultural and political perspectives are perhaps more evident in a multiple case study conducted by Mäkelä, Kalla and Piekkari (2004). The authors discovered how informal subsidiary clusters such as the Germanic, the Latin and the Scandinavian explain much of the knowledge sharing within MNCs. Within these clusters, linguistically and culturally similar subsidiaries were inclined to exchange best practices and collaborate on a number of issues. At the same time, units outside these clusters remained isolated and distant from major information exchanges owing to the language and cultural barriers. Their findings depict the MNC as a clustered organization in which language skills of subsidiary staff are considered as part of the unit's competence base (Mäkelä *et al.*, 2004; Marschan-Piekkari *et al.*, 1999b). In this context, expatriates who possess multiple memberships in several clusters may be used to effectively transcend cluster boundaries (Mäkelä *et al.*, 2004).

The multinational corporation as a totality
At the corporate level of analysis, it has been shown that language may influence the internationalization pattern of the company and produce particular paths of foreign market expansion. Building on Johanson and Wiedersheim-Paul's (1975) work, Welch *et al.* (2001) argue that there is a strong tendency for companies to stay within the same language cluster in their initial foreign expansion as a way of minimizing the risks involved. These authors compare hypothetical company patterns between Finnish, Japanese, Spanish and Canadian companies. They suggest that companies headquartered in English-speaking countries may undertake extensive internationalization and yet remain within the English-speaking world. Compared to the Finnish and Japanese companies, the Canadian company is likely to cross the language frontier at a far later stage in its internationalization process and postpone its decisions regarding the selection, recruitment and training of language-competent staff (Welch *et al.*, 2001; see also Johanson & Wiedersheim-Paul, 1975).

Research on language effects in MNCs reveals broad and subtle influences on control and coordination of foreign subsidiaries. For example, Marschan-Piekkari *et al.* (1999b) found that subsidiary units formed what the authors termed a 'shadow structure' based on language clusters that lay behind the formal organizational structure. Owing to the lack of fluency in the common corporate language, English, subsidiaries in these language clusters worked together on a range of activities such as joint management development and technical training by communicating in various subsidiary languages. Such regionalization within the MNC raises questions about the strength of corporate culture and the overall corporate cohesion. Research at this level of analysis touches upon the cultural perspective on language.

Language effects also extend beyond the boundaries of the MNC. Looking from outside at the MNC, the choice of the common corporate language may shape its corporate identity (Barner-Rasmussen, 2003) and its attractiveness as a potential employer from the viewpoint of future recruits.

For analytical purposes, the above review of language effects in multinational corporations was carried out at different levels of analysis. Obviously there is considerable interplay between these levels, which may be an attractive avenue for future research efforts.

Conclusion

The study of language and languages in MNCs has only just begun and offers considerable potential for making a contribution to the field. Given that language is a 'soft' issue associated with managing people, various attempts to measure and quantify its effects seem particularly promising. In the following we organize some suggestions for future research under the four levels of analysis discussed in the chapter.

At the first level of analysis, future research could examine how employees' language fluency influences performance appraisal ratings or outcomes of recruitment decisions. Previous research drawing on qualitative methods suggests that asymmetry in language skills has an effect on these practices. Moreover the relationship between 'language as a glass ceiling' and career development deserves further research. Given the emphasis placed on language in selecting suitable expatriates for foreign postings, researchers should move beyond the study of adjustment and focus on the effect of language on expatriate performance.

At the next level of analysis, language diversity among members of cross-cultural teams is still in its infancy. For example, a study of the control of language use in teams (that is who talks most, whose opinions are considered, and so on) can be supported by existing research in communication studies. Moreover interplay between language diversity and other forms of diversity such as gender, functional and educational background is unclear. It can be argued that the common professional culture binding, for example, engineers from different countries is transnational, facilitating communication between team members. On the other hand, based on her comparative study of three cross-cultural teams with engineers from several European countries, Chevrier (2003) warns against overestimating the power of professional cultures in teams. It would also be very interesting to explore the effect of language diversity on team performance. Traditionally research on cross-cultural teams has adopted an instrumental perspective on language, offering significant potential for examining language issues from political or cultural perspectives.

Much of the research in this area examines the effect of language on internal headquarters–subsidiary and inter-subsidiary relationships. The subsidiary operations under study have largely been wholly-owned units, or in rare cases joint ventures (Buckley *et al.*, 2005). Anecdotal evidence suggests that, for example, British MNCs have outsourced call centre activities to India primarily on the basis of language considerations, that is English. This may offer a novel platform for investigating language issues from an IHRM perspective.

At the level of the multinational corporation as a whole, one may ask how the home country of the MNC is likely to shape and characterize its language use. It is worth noting that a considerable bulk of studies in this field has been conducted on multinationals headquartered in the Nordic countries which tend to apply a fairly flexible and adaptive language policy. This is in sharp contrast to the explicit English-only language policy adopted by an American company in Japan (SanAntonio, 1987). Given this, a comparative study of the effects of language on human resource practices in MNCs originating from English and non-English-speaking countries would be an interesting research avenue to follow. The importance of context needs to be acknowledged in this type of research.

In addition to inviting more empirical studies on the subject, the potential for theoretical and methodological contributions should not be neglected. The study of language in MNCs could successfully be grounded in organization theory such as agency theory, organizational learning and institutional theory (see Ghoshal & Westney, 1993, on the integration between international management and organization theory). For example, in line with the institutional theory (Björkman in the present volume), which emphasizes fit between the organization and its environment, Brannen (2004) introduces the concept of 'semantic fit'. She explains that 'semantic fit depends on how the firm assets are understood in each new cultural context' (Brannen, 2004: 597). Whether the firm wishes to transfer personnel policies or teamwork concepts, language is the vehicle of communication and semantic fit is often the determinant of success. From a methodological perspective, West and Graham (2004) propose a measure of linguistic distance as a valuable tool for assessing cultural distance in future research on international management issues. Finally, it is worth noticing that language is likely to permeate all facets of conducting any international research project (see also Marschan-Piekkari & Welch, 2004).

Acknowledgments
The author would like to thank Ingmar Björkman, Jeff Hearn and Jaap Paauwe for very helpful comments on an earlier draft of this chapter.

References

Andersen, H. & E.S. Rasmussen. 2004. The role of language skills in corporate communication. *Corporate Communication: An International Journal*, **9**(3): 231–42.

Aziz Management Communications Index 2003. New survey finds English regional accents a disadvantage in business. Press release: http://www.azizcorp.com/info/releases/azizrel49. htm. 22 October 2003.

Barner-Rasmussen, W. 2003. Knowledge sharing in multinational corporations: a social capital perspective. PhD thesis no.113. Swedish School of Economics and Business Administration, Helsinki.

Barner-Rasmussen, W. & I. Björkman, 2003. The impact of language and interaction ties on interunit social capital in the MNC. In W. Barner-Rasmussen, Knowledge sharing in multinational corporations: a social capital perspective. PhD thesis no. 113, Swedish School of Economics and Business Administration, Helsinki.

Barner-Rasmussen, W. & I. Björkman. 2005. Surmounting interunit barriers: factors associated with interunit communication intensity in the multinational corporation. *International Studies Management and Organization*, Special issue, **35**(1) .

Birkinshaw, J. & N. Hood. 1998. *Multinational corporate evolution and subsidiary development*. London: Macmillan.

Björkman, I., J. Tienari & E. Vaara. 2003. Trapped in the past or making use of experience? In A-M. Søderberg & E. Vaara (eds), *Merging across borders: people, culture and politics*: 203–28. Copenhagen: Copenhagen Business School Press.

Brannen, M.Y. 2004. When Mickey loses face: recontextualization, semantic fit and the semiotics of foreignness. *Academy of Management Review*, **29**: 593–616.

Bruntse, J. 2003. It's Scandinavian: dansk–svensk kommunikation i SAS. MSc thesis, November, Institut for Nordisk Filologi, University of Copenhagen.

Buckley, P., M.J. Carter, J. Clegg & H. Tan. 2005. Language and social knowledge in foreign knowledge transfer to China. *International Studies of Management and Organization*, Special issue, **35**(1).

Charles, M. & R. Marschan-Piekkari. 2002. Language training for enhanced horizontal communication: a challenge for MNCs. *Business Communication Quarterly*, **65**(2): 9–29.

Chevrier, S. 2003. Cross-cultural management in multinational project groups. *Journal of World Business*, **38**(2): 141–9.

DiStefano, J.J. & M.L. Maznevski. 2000. Creating value with diverse teams in global management. *Organizational Dynamics*, **29**(1): 45–61.

Dowling, P.J. & D.E. Welch. 2004. *International human resource management: managing people in a multinational environment*. Fourth edition. London: Thomson Learning.

Feely, A.J. & A-W. Harzing. 2003. Language management in multinational companies. *Cross-Cultural Management: an International journal*, **10**(2): 37–52.

Fixman, C. 1990. The foreign language needs of U.S.-based corporations. *Annals*, 511, September: 25–46.

Gertsen, M.C., A.-M. Søderberg & J.E. Torp. 1998. Different approaches to understanding culture in mergers and acquisition. In M.C. Gertsen, A.-M. Søderberg & J.E. Torp (eds). *Cultural dimensions of international mergers and acquisitions*: 17–38. Berlin: de Gruyter.

Ghoshal, S. & D.E. Westney. 1993. *Organization theory and the multinational corporation*. Basingstoke: Macmillan.

Goodall, K. & J. Roberts. 2003a. Only connect: teamwork in the multinational. *Journal of World Business*, **38**(2): 150–64.

Goodall, K. & J. Roberts. 2003b. Repairing managerial knowledge-ability over distance. *Organization Studies*, **24**(7): 1153–75.

Gudykunst, W.B., S. Ting-Toomey, B.J. Hall & K.L. Schmidt. 1989. Language and intergroup communication. In M.K. Asante & W.B. Gudykunst (eds), *Handbook of international and intercultural communication*: 145–61. Newbury Park, CA: Sage.

Henderson Kassis, J. 2005. Language diversity in international management teams. *International Studies of Management and Organization*, Special issue, **35**(1).

Holm, U. & T. Pedersen. 2000. *The emergence and impact of MNC centres of excellence: a subsidiary perspective*. London: Macmillan.

Janssens, M.J., J. Lambert & C. Steyaert. 2004. Developing language strategies for international companies: the contribution of translation studies. *Journal of World Business*, **39**: 414–30.

Johanson, J. & F. Wiedersheim-Paul. 1975. The internationalization of the firm: four Swedish cases. *Journal of Management Studies*, October: 305–22.

Lagerström, K. & M. Andersson. 2003. Creating and sharing knowledge within a transnational team: the development of a global business system. *Journal of World Business*, **38**(2): 84–95.

Lincoln, J.R., H.R. Kerbo & E. Wittenhagen. 1995. Japanese companies in Germany: a case study in cross-cultural management. *Industrial Relations*, **34**(3): 417–40.

Louhiala-Salminen, L., M. Charles & A. Kankaanranta. 2005. English as a lingua franca in Nordic corporate mergers: two case companies. *English for Specific Purposes*, Special issue. **24**(4): 401–22.

Mäkelä, K., H. Kalla & R. Piekkari. 2004. The clustered multinational: who shares knowledge with whom? Paper presented at the Annual Conference of the European Academy of Management, Governance in Managerial Life, University of St Andrews, May.

Marschan, R. 1996. New structural forms and inter-unit communication in multinationals: the case of Kone Elevators. PhD thesis A-110, Helsinki School of Economics.

Marschan, R., D.E. Welch & L.S. Welch. 1997. Language: the forgotten factor in multinational management. *European Management Journal*, **15**(5): 591–8.

Marschan-Piekkari, R. & C. Welch. 2004. *Handbook of qualitative research methods for international business*. Cheltenham, UK and Northampton, MA, USA: Edward Elgar.

Marschan-Piekkari, R., D.E. Welch & L.S. Welch. 1999a. Adopting a common corporate language: IHRM implications. *International Journal of Human Resource Management*, **10**(3): 377–90.

Marschan-Piekkari, R., D.E. Welch & L.S. Welch. 1999b. In the shadow: the impact of language on structure, power and communication in the multinational. *International Business Review*, **8**(4): 421–40.

Negandhi, A.R., G.S. Eshghi & E.C. Yuen. 1985. The management practices of Japanese subsidiaries overseas. *California Management Review*, **27**(4): 93–105.

Odendahl, T. & A.M. Shaw. 2002. Interviewing elites. In J.F. Gubrium & J.A. Holstein (eds), *Handbook of interview research: context and method*: 299–316. Thousand Oaks, CA: Sage.

Piekkari, R., E. Vaara, J. Tienari & R. Säntti. 2005. Integration or disintegration? Human resource implications of the common corporate language decision in a cross-border merger. *International Journal of Human Resource Management*, **16**: 333–47.

Salk, J.E. & M.Y. Brannen. 2000. National culture, networks and individual influence in a multinational management team. *Academy of Management Journal*, **43**(2): 191–202.

SanAntonio, P.M. 1987. Social mobility and language use in an American company in Japan. *Journal of Language and Social Psychology*, **6**(3–4): 191–200.

Schweiger, D.M., T. Atamer & R. Calori. 2003. Transnational project teams and networks: making the multinational organization more effective. *Journal of World Business*, **38**(2): 127–40.

Selmer, J. 2004. Do you speak Chinese? Language proficiency and adjustment of business expatriates in China. Paper presented at the Annual Conference of the Academy of International Business, Stockholm School of Economics, July.

Vaara, E. & J. Tienari. 2003. The 'balance of power' principle: nationality, politics and the distribution of organizational positions. In A-M. Søderberg & E. Vaara (eds), *Merging across borders: people, culture and politics*: 87–110. Copenhagen: Copenhagen Business School Press.

Vandermeeren, S. 1999. English as lingua franca in written corporate communication: findings from a European survey. In F. Bargiela-Chiappini & C. Nickerson (eds), *Writing business: genres, media and discourses*: 273–91. Harlow: Pearson.

Wagner, E., S. Bech & J.M. Martinéz. 2002. *Translating for the European Union institutions*. Manchester, UK and Northampton, MA: St Jerome Publishing.

Welch, C., R. Marschan-Piekkari, H. Penttinen & M. Tahvanainen. 2002. Corporate elites as informants in qualitative international research. *International Business Review*, **11**(5): 611–28.

Welch, D.E., L.S. Welch & R. Marschan-Piekkari. 2001. The persistent impact of language on global operations. *Prometheus*, **19**(3): 193–209.

Welch, D.E., L.S. Welch & R. Piekkari. 2005. Speaking in tongues: language and international management. *International Studies of Management and Organization*, Special issue, **35**(1), Spring.

West, J. & J.L. Graham. 2004. A linguistic-based measure of cultural distance and its relationship to managerial values. *Management International Review*, **44**(3): 239–60.

Wright, C., F. Kumagai & N. Bonney. 2001. Language and power in Japanese transplants in Scotland. *Sociological Review*, 236–53.

Yoshihara, H. 2001. Global operations managed by Japanese and in Japanese. In J.H. Taggart, M. Berry & M. McDermott (eds), *Multinationals in a new era*: 153–65. Chippenham: Palgrave.

Index

Abe, H. 254, 255, 303, 304, 305
absorptive capacity 483
Acherman, G. 495
Acker, J. 505
Adams, G.A. 168, 268
Adams, J.S. 166, 494
adjustment *see* expatriate adjustment
    and performance
Adler, N.J. 149, 153, 204, 207, 208, 239,
    265, 266, 270, 273, 323, 333, 349,
    507, 526
Adler, P.S. 486
agency theory 171–2, 452, 455, 469
    and compensation 454
Agrawal, A. 406
Ahlstrand, B. 49, 73
Aikin, K.J. 233
Albrecht, S. 491
Alchian, A.A. 453
Aldrich, H. 391
Alimo-Metcalfe, B. 274, 506
Allen, D. 325, 333
Allen, D.G. 491
Allen, T.D. 268
alliances 5, 385, 386
Allport, G.W. 231, 315
Altemeyer, B. 235
Altman, Y. 324, 333
Alvarez, S. 325, 333
Alvesson, M. 523, 524, 525, 527, 528
Ambrose, M.L. 491
American Express 284
Amir, Y. 315
Amit, R. 445
Anastasi, A. 207
Andersen, H. 544
Anderson, P. 76
Anderson, V. 141
Andersson, M. 543
Andreason, A.W. 247
Andrews, S.B. 355
Ang, S. 254
Applebaum, E. 72
Aram, J.D. 258

Argote, L. 480
Arino, A. 385, 386, 391, 392
Arkin, A. 150
Armeli, S. 491
Armstrong, D.J. 351
Arnold, J.D. 415
Arnold, V. 204
Aron, A. 237, 238
Arthur, J.B. 4, 94, 98
Arthur, M.B. 254, 265, 531
Aryee, S. 158, 159, 254, 497
Ashby, W.R. 199
Ashforth, B.E. 356
Ashkenas, R. 68, 414, 419
assessment 180
assignments
    non-standard 283, 300
    short-term 165
Athanassiou, N.A. 121, 126, 375, 376
attitudes
    monitoring 70, 71
    versus norms 195–6
Aubert, B.A. 370
Auperle, K. 323
Austin, C. 329
Awa, N. 306
Aycan, Z. 249, 252
Aziz Management Communications
    Index 541

Baack, S.A. 143, 144, 146, 253, 256,
    258, 259
Baan, A. 371
Baba, M.L. 115, 125, 126
Bacharach, S.P. 237
Backes-Gellner, U. 453, 458, 459
Baden-Fuller, C. 113
Bae, J. 436, 466
Bagozzi, R.P. 121, 200
Bailey, E. 189
balanced scorecard techniques 91
Baldwin, T. 317
Balkin, D.B. 93, 460
Balthazard, P.A. 370

Bamber, G.J. 79, 80
Bamberger, P.A. 237
Banai, M. 393
Bandura, A. 316
Banerjee, S.B. 513, 533
Barham, K. 200
Barkema, H.G. 25, 387
Barling, J. 268, 480
Barner-Rasmussen, W. 536, 543, 544, 545, 546
Barnett, T. 228
Barney, J.B. 4, 49, 51, 93, 172, 331, 433, 434, 471
Baron, J.N. 489
Barrett, M. 120
Barrick, M. 304, 315
Barry, S. 254, 531
Barsky, A. 237, 238, 239
Barsoux, J.-L. 3, 5, 44, 309, 385, 434, 527
Bartholomew, S. 351, 360
Bartlett, C.A. 3, 30, 36, 37, 38, 40, 42, 51, 53, 116, 121, 123, 199, 200, 324, 331, 332, 433, 435, 437, 439, 441, 443, 466
Bartunek, R.M. 202
Baruch, Y. 324, 333
Basanex, M. 490
Bass, B.M. 373
Bastien, D.T. 412
Bateson, G. 215
Batt, R. 99
Baum, J.A.C. 107
Bauman, Z. 533
Beamish, P.W. 200, 385, 396, 398
Beatty, R.W. 25, 49
Beaumont, P. 50, 467, 468
Becker, B.E. 28, 49, 70, 91, 468, 469
Becker, T.H. 158
Beckman, T.J. 113
Beechler, S. 4, 16, 53, 199, 200, 326, 359, 436, 466, 471, 488
Beehr, T.A. 256, 259
Beer, M. 3, 49, 106
Belgium 75
Bell, J.H.J. 25
Bender, R. 453, 460
Bender, S. 326
Bendix, R. 72
Bennett, N. 49

Bennett, R. 327
Bennis, W.G. 218
Bensedrine, J. 77
Benson, J. 15, 471
Benson-Armer, R. 353
Berman, M. 215
Bernardin, H.J. 179, 183
Bernhut, S. 325
Bernstein, I.H. 207
Bernthal, P.R. 177
Berry, I. 272
Berry, J.W. 411
Berscheid, E. 226
Berthon, P. 120
'best fit' model 102–7
best practice 91, 92, 93, 96, 107, 410
    mergers and acquisitions 422–3
Bettenhausen, K.L. 370
Bettis, R. 21
Bhagat, R.S. 440
Bhardwaj, A. 235
Bhaskar-Shrinivas, P. 249, 250, 254, 257
Bhatt, B. 254
Bhawuk, D.P.S. 223, 239
Bierbrauer, G. 495
Bierman, L. 228
Bies, R.H. 369
Bikson, T.K. 355
Bird, A. 7, 207
Birkinshaw, J.M. 53, 116, 117, 118, 200, 422, 443, 543
Bishko, M.J. 158
Bisqueret, C. 309–10
Björkman, A. 25, 27
Björkman, I. 21, 91, 95, 141, 190, 434, 436, 454, 459, 460, 463, 466, 467, 471, 529, 536, 539, 541, 544
Black, J.S. 2, 29, 30, 147, 153, 158, 159, 166, 169, 199, 207, 208, 249, 250, 251, 252, 253, 254, 255, 256, 258, 265, 272, 303, 304, 305, 306, 307, 309, 312, 327, 329, 330, 333, 439, 441, 450
Blackburn, V.B. 227
Blake, R.R. 416
Blake, S. 224
Blaschke, S. 76, 80
Blau, P.M. 228, 491
Block, C.J. 187

Bloodgood, J.M. 480
Bloom, G. 460
Bloom, M. 172
Blumberg, A. 416
Blunsdon, B. 490
boards
    HR representation on 52, 81, 82
    and mergers and acquisitions
        407
Bobo, L. 231, 232, 233
Bochner, S. 272
Bohl, D.L. 406
Boje, D. 532
Bolino, M.C. 480
Bommer, W.H. 491
Bonache, J. 121, 142, 146, 147, 159,
    163, 165, 166, 168, 170, 529
Bondi, L. 504
Bonney, N. 538
Boocock, G. 141
Borgatti, S.P. 126
Borman, W.C. 176
Boselie, P. 91, 93, 94, 96, 97, 99, 101
Bossink, C.J.H. 267
Boswell, W.R. 260
Bouchet, G. 385, 387, 399
Boudreau, J.W. 28
Boudreau, M.C. 352
'boundaryless career' concept 265
'bounded rationality' 450, 451
Bouquet, C. 200, 212
Bowditch, J.L. 414, 415, 422
Bowen, D.E. 52, 54, 64, 100
Bower, G. 316
Bower, J.L. 411
Boxall, P.F. 4, 22, 49, 68, 70, 94, 435
Boyacigiller, N. 147, 148, 170, 199, 200,
    359
Boyd, N. 326
Boyer, R. 76, 77, 78
Brake, T. 204
Brands, P.A. 358
Brannen, N.Y. 539, 542, 547
Brass, D.J. 475
Braun, W. 114
Braverman, H. 524
Brein, M. 306
Brewer, M.B. 323
Brewster, C. 4, 5, 15, 21, 24, 30, 51, 52,
    68, 69, 71, 73, 74, 76, 79, 116, 117,
121, 127, 134, 142, 143, 147, 148,
    167, 251, 295, 296, 298, 308, 318,
    327, 330, 333, 436, 449, 470
Brief, A.P. 187, 232, 234, 236, 237, 238,
    239
Briggs, J. Peat 216
Brigham, J.C. 231
Brimm, M. 204
Briscoe, D.R. 5, 149, 152, 178, 191,
    309, 385, 393
Brislin, R.W. 253, 254, 255, 258, 272,
    306, 313, 329
Broad, M. 317
Brockner, J. 495, 497
Brodt, S.E. 490
Bross, A. 307
Brouthers, K.D. 409
Brouthers, L.E. 409
Brown, J.S. 127
Brown, K.G. 353
Brown, M. 26
Brunstein, I. 74, 79
Bruntse, J. 539
Buchan, N.R. 496
Buckley, M.R. 151, 183
Buckley, P.J. 20, 544, 547
Buckley, R. 329
Budhwar, P.S. 4, 73, 74, 84, 122, 497,
    502
Buono, A.F. 414, 415, 422
Burgi, P. 312
Burke, R.J. 268, 506, 507
Burnell, P. 76
Burns, S. 158
Burrell, G. 524
Burt, R.S. 331, 369, 376, 442, 475, 478,
    490
business development 54
business leaders, goals 78
business performance, and HRM 49
Buss, D. 303, 304
Bussier, D. 387
Butler, J. 504
Buttram, R.T. 239
Buyens, D. 75
Byrne, D. 226
Byrnes, E.C. 247

Calás, M. 525, 526
Caldwell, R. 52, 62

Calhoun, C. 525
Caligiuri, P.M. 2, 16, 25, 50, 153, 158,
    169, 211, 212, 251, 253, 255, 256,
    258, 259, 265, 268, 269, 303, 304,
    306, 307, 308, 312, 314, 315, 324,
    325, 327, 329, 330, 332, 334
Callaham, J.D. 239
Calof, J.L. 200
Calori, R. 200, 406, 409, 410, 420,
    423
Camerer, C. 331, 369, 490
Campbell, A. 53, 149
Campbell, D.T. 231
Campbell, J.P. 176
Candace, J. 126
Cannella, A.A. Jr 27, 406, 477
Canney Davison, S. 367, 368, 369,
    375
Cannon, J.P. 490
Canon-Bowers, J.A. 123, 315
capabilities
    creative and integrative 441
    development 53
    and IHRM 437–44
Cappelli, P. 99
Cappleman, S. 120
Capra, F. 214, 215, 216
career planning initiatives 165
Carlson, D.S. 268
Carmel, E. 347, 348, 351, 353, 358
Carpenter, M. 444, 445
Carrigan, T. 503
Carter, M.J. 544
Cartwright, S. 406, 424, 425, 517
Cascio, W.F. 169, 177, 179, 189, 269
Casson, M. 455, 456, 458
Cateora, P.R. 273
Cavusgil, S.T. 74
Cendant Mobility 24
centralization 406, 529
    and decentralization 52
centres of excellence
    knowledge management 115–19
    and MNEs 116–17
Cerdin, J.-L. 121
ceremonial adoption 469
Cervino, J. 142
Chadwick, C. 444
Chadwick, K. 227, 228
Chang, W.C. 252

change
    over time 76
    path dependence 78
Charan, R. 204
Charles, M. 540
Chattanooga model of global
    leadership development 216–19
Chatterjee, S. 406
Chen, C.C. 160, 163, 166, 169
Chen, G. 476
Chen, S. 385
Chen, S.-J. 466
Chen, Y. 497
Chen, Z.X. 495, 497
Cheney, G. 356, 357
Cheng, J.L.C. 2, 24, 248
Cherrie, C. 313
Chevrier, S. 546
Chia, R. 525
Chiah-Liaw, G. 385
Chiesa, V. 120
Child, J.D. 18, 19, 20, 21, 77, 385, 387,
    388, 389, 391, 392, 393, 396, 410,
    466
China 43–4, 46, 56, 58, 60, 141, 163,
    168, 271, 514
Chiu, W.C.K. 514
Christiansen, N.D. 256
Chu, P. 269
Chu, W. 419
Chudoba, K.M. 347, 358, 367, 375,
    378
Church, A.T. 248, 249, 252, 303, 305
Chusmir, L.H. 271
Clark, P. 71
Clarke, C. 256, 258, 259
Clases, C. 154
Clegg, J. 544
Clegg, S. 525, 529
Coase, R.H. 167
Cockburn, C.K. 505, 506, 512
Cody, T. 411
Coff, R.W. 21
cognitive consensus 124
Cohan, S.G. 360
Cohen, R.R. 232, 234, 236
Cohen, S. 123, 125
Cohen, S.G. 347, 355
Cohen, W. 316, 398, 483
Cohen, Y. 18, 19

Cohen-Charash, Y. 494, 497
Colbert, B. 21
Cole, P. 351
Coleman, J.S. 376, 475
Colgate-Palmolive 42
collective bargaining 79, 80
collective cognition 124
collectivism 185–8, 349–50, 495
Collins, H. 114
Collins, T. 396
Collinson, D.L. 506, 511
Colquitt, J.A. 315, 497
Comaroff, J. and Comaroff, J. 80
communication 125
    and mergers and acquisitions
        412–14
    in virtual teams 365–7
communities of practice 127, 134
comparative human resource
        management (HRM)
    compared to international human
        resource management 68, 84
    research 15, 74
        explaining national differences
            74–6
comparative international human
        resource management (IHRM)
        450
    and economic theory 458–9
comparative research 4
compartmentalization 296–7
compensation 460, 468
    and agency theory 454
    of expatriates 158–75
    satisfaction with 166–7
competitive advantage 92–3, 107, 118,
        122, 172, 323, 331, 332, 434–7,
        440, 444
    and social capital 480–483
competitive pressures 108
conditions of employment 75
Conference Board 330
configurational models 93–4
Conger, J. 210
Conlon, D.E. 497
Connell, R.W. 503
Connor, J. 51, 54
consumer demand 17
consumer electronics 37–8
contact or association hypothesis 315

contextual paradigm 69, 71, 72–3, 449,
        458
contextually based human resource
        theory (CBHRT) model 102–8
    environmental fit 105
    horizontal fit 105
    organizational fit 105
    strategic fit 103
contingency models 92, 93, 95, 108
convergence 75, 76
    directional 81, 82
    evidence of 77–83
    literature 77–8
    majority 81
    meaning of 80
    and non-convergence in the HR
        literature 78–80
    regional 77–8
Cooke, N.J. 124
Cooper, C.L. 26, 406, 424, 507, 517
Cooper, G. 73
Cooper, H. 24
cooperation theory 398–9
Copeland, L. 313
Corman, S.R. 357
corporate governance 25, 27
corporate structure, IHRM and gender
        policy 515–16
corporate wrongdoing 25
cost-of-living-allowance (COLA) 330
Costa, P. 303
costs of employing expatriates 167–8
Coté, J. 460
Cottrell, A.B. 316
Covin, J.G. 412
Cox, C. 73
Cox, T.H. 224, 226
Crandall, C.S. 233
Crandall, L.P. 158, 169
Cranfield Network on European
        Human Resource Management
        (Cranet-E) 43, 52, 81
Creed, W.E.D. 517
critical theoretical perspective, HRM
        525
critical theory 524
Cropanzano, R. 494
Crosby, F.J. 223
Croson, R.T.A. 496
Cross, R. 483

cross-cultural development 302–22
cross-cultural differences
  global performance management
    systems 185
  in performance feedback 187–93
cross-cultural management issues 15
cross-cultural perspective, IHRM 450
cross-cultural teams 542–3
  and language 542–3, 546
cross-cultural training 302–22
cross-national coaching or mentoring
    310
cross-national transfer 16
cross-racial friendships 237–8
Crossan, M. 396
Csoka, L. 309
Cui, G. 305, 306
Cullen, J.B. 490
Culpan, O. 270
cultural differences 3, 95, 197, 419,
    420–422, 455, 490, 495, 526
cultural distance 148
cultural distance index 409, 423
cultural diversity, in global teams 347,
    348–51
cultural environment 43
cultural intelligence 254
cultural issues 51
cultural learning 415–17, 422
cultural orientation, and mergers and
    acquisitions 408
culture 526
  definitions of 455–6
  and institutions 76
  national, and mergers and
    acquisitions 409–11
Currall, S. 391, 396
Cushner, K. 253, 254, 255, 258, 313
customers 70
Cyr, D. 389, 391, 396
Czinkota, M.R. 17, 29

Dabu, A. 444
Dacin, M.T. 107, 466, 469
Daft, R.L. 366, 439, 443
Daily, C.M. 27, 159, 412
Dalton, D.R. 27, 412
Dalton, M. 204, 255, 307
Darbishire, O. 24, 80
d'Arcimoles, C.H. 102

Das, A. 74
Das, T. 396
Datta, D.K. 389, 406
D'Aunno, T. 80
D'Aveni, R. 323
Davenport, T.H. 120
David, K. 306, 415, 416
Davidsen, O.M. 248
Davidson, M.J. 506, 507
Davis, B.L. 184
Davis, D.D. 190, 193
Davis, J.H. 490
Davis-LaMastro, V. 489
Davison, E.D. 510
Davison, S.C. 358, 359
Dawes, R.M. 496
Day, D.V. 184, 255, 304
de Boer, T. 411, 412
De Cieri, H. 4, 15, 18, 22, 23, 24, 27,
    28, 324, 332, 392, 434, 471, 488
De Marie, S. 24
de Vries, M.F. 323
Deal, J. 204
Dean, J.W. Jr 40
Debrah, Y.A. 74
Debroux, P. 55, 62
decentralization 5, 43, 52, 149
decision making 99, 495
Decker, S. 120
Deephouse, D.L. 107
Deetz, S. 523, 528
DeFidelto, C. 52
DeFrank, R.S. 286, 288, 289, 292,
    298
Deitch, E.A. 187
Delery, J.E. 21, 92, 93, 94
DeMarie, S.M. 347
Den Hartog, D.N. 490
Denisi, A. 159, 160, 169
DeNisi, A.S. 408, 411, 413, 414
Derrida, J. 524
Desousa, K.C. 113, 127
Dess, G.G. 479
Devanna, M.A. 3, 69
Dewe, P. 150
Di Santo, V. 211, 212
DiBella, A.J. 113
Dickens, L. 515
Dickson, M.W. 490
Dietl, H. 458

Dietz, G. 93, 94, 99
Dietz, J. 223, 232, 234, 235, 236, 239
Digh, P. 198
Digman, J. 303
DiMaggio, P.J. 18, 38, 77, 78, 96, 458, 463, 464, 466
Dinges, N. 303, 304, 305
Dinur, A. 392
Dirks, K.T. 489, 492, 496, 497
discrimination 231–2, 233
  eliminating 238
DiStefano, J.J. 542
diversity 51, 486
  business case for 223
  and gender 517
  racial 228
diversity management 223–43
  Cox's model 224–5
  curvilinear hypothesis 228–30
  eliminating discrimination 237–8
  empirical research 226, 230
  IHRM and gender 510–512
  justification factors 234, 239–40
  linear hypothesis 226–8
  macro models 224–31
  macro or organizational level approach 223–4
  micro approach 224, 231–40
    research 234–6
  stereotypes, prejudice and discrimination 231–2
  suppression factors 232–3, 239
  Thomas and Ely's model 225–6
diversity training 310
Djelic, M.-L. 77
Doh, J.P. 29
Dominguez, A. 495
Doney, P.M. 490
Dooley, K. 214
Doorley, T. 396
Dore, R. 72, 73
Dorfman, P.W. 204, 490
Doty, D.H. 92, 93, 94
double ABCX model 270
Dovidio, J.F. 233, 234, 235, 236, 237, 238
Dowling, P.J. 4, 5, 6, 15, 18, 23, 24, 25, 26, 27, 43, 43–4, 46, 68, 79, 141, 147, 154, 160, 162, 164–5, 188, 192, 298, 309, 324, 332, 392, 434,

449, 450, 471, 488, 502, 508, 511, 537, 539, 540
Downes, M. 490
Doz, Y. 3, 4, 5, 24, 36, 37, 39, 141, 199, 200, 386, 389, 391, 393, 396, 433, 466
Druskat, V.U. 372, 373
du Gay, P. 525
dual-career couples 154, 158, 268–9, 283, 329, 509
Dubrovsky, V. 366
Due, J. 79
Duguid, P. 127
Dukerich, J.M. 356
Dumville, B.C. 115, 124
Dunbar, E. 306, 531
Dunford, B.B. 22, 433, 434
Durham, C.C. 179
Durkin, J.J. 503
Durup, M.J. 268
Dutton, J.E. 356, 478
Duxbury, L. 268
Duysters, G. 385, 387, 388, 391, 398, 399
Dwyer, S. 227, 228
Dyer, L. 26, 49, 73

e-commerce 119
e-enablement, and HRM 51–2, 54, 60
Eagle, B.W. 268
Earley, P.C. 254, 255, 256, 309, 349, 355, 357
Ebers, M. 451
economic theory
  and comparative IHRM 458–9
  and HRM in MNEs 453–5
  and IHRM 453–9
  and intercultural HRM 455–8
  theories of the firm, and IHRM 449–62
economic transformation 24
Edmondson, A. 114, 351, 358
Edström, A. 42, 143, 163, 170, 332
Edström, P.E. 1, 3
Edwards, A. 504
Edwards, J.R. 268
Edwards, P. 53
Edwards, T. 107
EFQM (European Foundation for Quality Management) 502

Egan, T.D. 236
Egri, C.P. 529
Eichler, M. 503
Eidse, F. 316
Eisenberger, R. 489, 490, 491, 492, 494
Eisenhardt, K.M. 51, 171, 453, 480
Ekelund, B.Z. 368, 369, 375, 490
Elder, J. 74
Elkjaer, B. 134
Elmes, M. 527
Elsass, P.M. 517
Ely, R.J. 225, 226, 227, 230, 239, 507, 511
Emerson, V. 197
emic approach 75
emotional stability 304
employee benefits, and local practices 41
employee development 94
employment practices, transfer 94
Empson, L. 414
England, G.W. 74
Engle, A.D. 16
equity theory 169, 170
Erdener, C. 454
Erdogan, B. 491, 492
Ernst, C.T. 204, 207
Ernst, D. 385, 387
Eshleman, A. 233
Esses, V.M. 235, 239
ethnocentric (home country-oriented) approach 2
    to staffing 146
etic approach 75
Europe 73, 79
    change in selected HRM practices 82
    compensation of expatriates in MNEs 164
    international staffing 142
    parent country nations (PCNs) 147
    selected HRM practices 81
European model of HRM 79
European Union 77–8, 79
Eurostat 506
Evans, P. 3, 4, 39, 44, 144, 145, 149, 151, 152, 309, 387, 389, 434, 527
Evans, P.A. 51, 53, 62
Evaristo, R. 113, 120
Everett, M. 126

Ewing, J.R. 25
expatriate adjustment and performance 1, 2, 158, 247–64
    adjustment 258–9
        definitions of 249
        historical basis for study 247–9
        measurement of 249–53
        psychological and sociocultural aspects 251–2
    adjustment–performance relationship 255–7
    causal chain issues 259–60
    cross-sectional studies 257–8
    intention to remain 253–4
    interaction with hosts 254
    job attitudes 254
    performance 141, 255
        measurement 253–5, 259
    performance appraisal 190–193
    performance management systems 176
    self-report data 258
expatriate compensation 158–75
    in European MNEs 164
    global approach 161–2
    home-country approach 162
    host-country approach 161
    and justice 168–9
    satisfaction with compensation packages 166–7
expatriate failure 142, 532
expatriate management 2, 26, 42
expatriate research 531–3
expatriates
    advice networks 121–3
    costs of employing 167–8
    dual-career couples 154, 158, 268–9, 283, 329, 509
    incentives 171
    management of 2
    motives for using 143–6
    pay package design 159
    premiums and allowances 170–171
    use of 24
expatriation, sequential 334
expatriation-repatriation cycle 327–31
Eylon, G. 215

face-to-face communication 353, 359, 361, 366, 369, 378

Fagan, C. 287
fairness 182, 193, 490–491, 491, 492,
495
and IHR practices 494–5
and trust, perceptions of 497
family considerations 267–70, 278,
308
repatriation 327, 329–30, 334, 337–8,
339
separation 287–9
family system approach, double ABCX
model 270
Farr, J. 304
Farr, J.L. 187
Fasolo, P. 490
Faulkner, D. 385, 387, 388, 389, 391,
392, 393, 396, 410, 417, 466
FDI 46
Feely, A.J. 543
Feldman, D.C. 254, 255, 259, 333
Fell, R. 50
Fenton-O'Creevy, M. 463
Fenwick, J. 358
Fenwick, M.S. 22, 24, 28, 29
Fernandez, J. 58, 59, 60
Fernandez, Z. 142, 146, 163, 165, 170
Ferner, A. 3, 16, 22, 49, 54, 55, 56, 62,
63, 79, 143, 458, 467, 470, 528,
529
Ferrin, D.L. 489, 492, 496, 497
Ferris 21
Ferris, G.R. 55, 63, 64, 103, 168, 470
Ferris, S.P. 228
Festing, M. 20, 204, 453, 454
Festinger, L. 166
Fey, C.F. 21, 91, 95, 434, 436
Filipczak, B. 317
finance function 39
Finkelstein, S. 170, 406, 412, 414, 420,
421
Finland 166
Finney, M. 304
Fiol, C.M. 323, 324, 355, 356, 357, 360,
361
firm performance
and HRM 92–7, 100
'best fit' model 102–7
linkage between 97–9
performance measurement 105–8
professional performance 106

societal performance 106
strategy 100–101
time-lag issue 101–2
and IHRM 91–112
Fischlmayr, I.C. 508
Fish, A. 326
Fiske, S.T. 233
Fixman, C. 538
Fletcher, J.K. 511
Florent-Treacy, E. 207, 208, 212
Florkowski, G.W. 29, 502
Foldy, E.G. 511, 517
Folger, R. 494
Fombrun, C.J. 3, 69, 70
Ford, J.D. 317, 412
Ford, L.W. 412
foreign subsidiaries, staffing 146–50
Forsgren, M. 332
Forster, N. 154, 283
Forstmann, S. 419
Foss, N. 387
Foti, R.J. 184
Foucault, J. 524, 529
founding conditions 470
Fournier, V. 524
Fox, S. 531
frame of reference (FOR) training
183–4
France 52
Francesco, A.M. 495
Francis, S.C. 414, 419
Franck, E. 458
Franko, L.C. 255
Franko, L.G. 2, 148
Frayne, C.A. 388, 489
Freeman, C. 513
Freeman, K. 158, 159, 161, 163
Frone, N.R. 268
'front–back' organization 44
Frontczak, N.T. 271
Frost, A. 116
Frost, P.J. 529
Fukuda, K. 269
Fukuyama, F. 492
Fulkerson, J. 213
Furnham, A. 307
Furst, S.A. 120, 367, 372
Furu, P. 454, 459, 460
Furubotn, E.G. 451, 453
Futoran, G.C. 274

Gaertner, S.L. 233, 234, 235, 236, 237, 238
Galang, M.C. 55, 63, 64, 470
Galbraith, J.R. 1, 3, 42, 44, 143, 163, 170, 332
Ganesh, U. 389
Gardner, T.M. 27, 91, 97, 101
Gargiulo, M. 24
Garonzik, R. 158
Garten, J. 141, 334
Garud, R. 356
Gelfand, M.J. 495
gender
    composition of management, and local practices 41
    and diversity 517
    gendered organizations and managements 504–6
    and HRM 506–7
    and IHRM 502–22
    mainstream texts 508
    IHRM and diversity 510–512
    IHRM and globalization 512–14
    meanings of 502–4
    and mergers and acquisitions 516–17
    pay gap 507
    policy, IHRM and corporate structure 515–16
    see also women
Gentile, M.C. 239
geocentric (world-oriented) approach 2
    to staffing 146
Geppart, M. 79
Gerhart, B. 70, 97, 101, 230, 468, 469
Geringer, J.M. 388, 391, 489
Germany 79, 82, 458
Gerpott, T.J. 414, 425
Gertsen, M.C. 413, 417, 424, 539
Gessner, M. 204
Ghadar, F. 149, 332
Ghemawat, P. 57, 58, 61
Ghoshal, S. 3, 30, 37, 38, 40, 42, 51, 53, 116, 121, 123, 199, 200, 324, 331, 332, 433, 435, 437, 439, 441, 443, 466, 476, 481, 547
Ghosn, Carlos 197
Giacalone, R. 215

Gibbs, J.L. 347, 348, 350, 352, 354, 360
Gibson, C.B. 124, 347, 349, 351, 352, 355, 357, 360, 368, 370, 375
Giddens, A. 76
Gilley, K.M. 251
Gilliland, S.W. 182, 495
Gimeno, J. 323
Gittell, J.H. 478, 484
Glase, M.B. 176
Glick, P. 233
global coordination (integration) 16
global expertise networks 127, 134
global human resource management 331–6
global human resource strategies 79
global integration 68
    and local responsiveness 5, 30, 36–48
    and pressures by industry 37
    see also integration-responsiveness framework
global knowledge economy 24
global knowledge management
    and HRM 113–40
    systems 119–21
    theorized outcomes as integration mechanisms 128–33
global leadership 197–222
    challenges 218
    competencies
        in empirical research 209
        and international assignments 212–13
    definition of 204
    development 212–14
        Chattanooga model 216–19
    empirical research 205–6
    global mindset, literature review 199–204
    literature review 204–11
    'non-linear' perspective on development 214–19
    programmes 53
    selection for 212
    selection and succession 213–14
global mindset 324, 325, 326, 359
    definition of 202–3
    development 211–12
    empirical research 201–2
    literature review 199–204

global networks/network organizations 51, 324, 325, 331, 332–3
global performance management systems 176–96
  appraisal for expatriates 190–193
  assessment 180
  collectivism 185–7
  cross-cultural differences 185
    in performance feedback 187–93
  current status 177–8
  defining performance 179–80
  encouraging performance 181–2
  evaluation goals 178–9
  facilitating performance 180–181
  goal setting 179–80
  for host-country nationals 188, 190
  implementation 178
  individualism 185–7
  performance appraisal in USA, Saudi Arabia and Korea 189
  purposes 178–9
  rewards 181–2
  training for 182–7
  training of raters 182–4
global risks 24
global shared services 26
global staffing 141–57
  approaches to 142
  expatriate selection 142
  literature on 141–2
  motives for using expatriate employees 143
  staffing foreign subsidiaries 146–50
  top management staffing and inpatriation 151–2
global task forces 53
global workforces, management 434–5
globalization 15, 18, 24, 197, 198, 533
  gender and IHRM 512–14
global–local relations, gendering 516
GLOBE project 204
Gluesing, J.C. 115, 125, 347, 351, 353, 368, 375
GMAC Global Relocation Services 24, 265
goals 185, 186–7, 188
  of business leaders 78
  setting 179–80
Goddon, J.R. 202

Goldberg, D.T. 511
Goldberg, L. 303
Goldsmith, M. 207, 208
Gomez, C. 95
Gómez-Mejia, L.R. 93, 158, 166, 167, 171
Gong, Y. 146, 148
Goodall, K. 471, 510, 540, 544
Gooderham, P.N. 72, 74, 94, 450, 463
Goodstein, J. 465
Goold, M.C. 53, 149
Gossett, L.M. 356, 357
Gotsch, W. 451
Gould, J.M. 113
Gould-Williams, J. 490
Gouldner, A.W. 491
Goulet, P.K. 408, 415, 416, 425, 426
government policies 17
Govindarajan, V. 153, 170, 199, 211, 309, 332, 359, 482
Graen, G.B. 476
Graf, J. 223
Graf, L.A. 490
Graham, J.L. 547
Granovetter, M.S. 355, 475, 478
Grant, R.M. 113, 434, 440, 443, 445
Gratton, L. 63, 100
Graves, L.M. 507
Gray, B. 391, 470
Green, S. 391
Greenaway, K. 113, 115
Greenberg, J. 494, 495
Greene, A.M. 511
Greenhaus, J.H. 268
Greenway, K. 387
Greenwood, R. 96, 464
Greer, C.R. 469
Gregersen, H.B. 119, 158, 199, 207, 212, 249, 251, 252, 254, 255, 272, 306, 307, 309, 312, 327, 329, 330, 333, 439, 441, 444, 445
Grensing-Pophal, L. 180
Grey, C. 523, 524
Grey, D.A. 469
grievance procedures 70
Griffeth, R.W. 491
Griffin, K. 323
Griffith, T.L. 347, 352, 360, 375
Griggs, L. 313

Grossman, W. 357, 452, 460
Gudykunst, W.B. 252, 254, 304, 305, 313, 314, 542
Guest, D.E. 3, 63, 70, 73, 91, 97, 99, 100, 101, 102, 106, 466
Guillén, M. 18
Gulati, R. 24
Gunnigle, P. 43
Gupta, A.K. 153, 170, 199, 211, 309, 332, 359, 482
Gupta, V. 204
Gutek, B.A. 268
Guthrie, G. 306
Gutteridge, T. 254
Guzley, R. 313, 314
Guzzo, R.A. 169

Haas, M.R. 119, 376, 439, 445
Habermas, J. 524
Hackett, B. 309
Hadaway, T. 407, 414, 415
Hagan, C.M. 179
Hagedoorn, J. 386, 392, 398, 399, 400
Hakanson, L. 414
Halevy, T. 385, 387
Hall, D.T. 212, 454
Hall, E.T. 450
Hall, M. 450
Hall, P.A. 72
Hall, R. 324
Hall, W.S. 233
Hambrick, D.C. 170, 358, 406
Hamel, G. 68, 323, 386, 389, 391, 393, 396
Hamil, J. 160, 166
Hammer, M.R. 254, 256, 258, 259, 304, 305, 313, 314, 329
Hampden-Turner, C. 450
Hancock, P.A. 260
Handler, C. 327
Handy, C. 366
Hanges, P.J. 490
Hanges, P.W. 204
Hanmer, J. 508
Hannerz, U. 77, 202
Hannon, J.M. 42, 463, 466, 528
Hansen, M.C. 119
Hansen, M.T. 438, 442, 445, 478
Harari, E. 2
Harding, S. 215

Hardy, C. 529
Harlow, E. 505, 516
Harpaz, I. 74
Harquail, C.V. 356
Harrigan, K. 387
Harris, H. 5, 24, 52, 68, 79, 116, 117, 127, 134, 270, 273, 274, 275, 276, 295, 308, 318, 508, 510
Harris, J.E. 454
Harris, M. 309–10
Harris, P. 313
Harrison, D.A. 158, 249, 250, 251, 255, 257, 313
Harry, W. 388
Hart, W. 329
Hartog, D.N. 103
Harvard school 3
Harvey, B. 239
Harvey, M. 2, 21, 25, 26, 56, 63, 125, 134, 141, 148, 151, 152, 158, 159, 160, 268, 269, 295, 323, 324, 325, 327, 329, 330, 334, 393, 455, 470
Harzing, A.-W. 2, 3, 5, 26, 79, 142, 143, 145, 146, 147, 148, 253, 258, 266, 409, 423, 508, 511, 543
Haspelagh, P.C. 406, 408, 419
Hass, R.G. 233
Hauenstein, N.M. 184
Hayles, N.K. 214
Hays, R.D. 248, 312
Hazzard, M. 330
headquarters' international orientation 25
headquarters–subsidiary/intersubsidiary relationships 543–5
health issues 290
Heaphy, E.D. 478
Hearn, J. 503, 505, 506, 508, 510, 511, 513, 516, 533
Hebert, L. 391
Hechanova, R. 256, 259, 272
Hedlund, G. 3, 25, 45, 294, 433, 443
Heenan, D.A. 2, 146, 332
Hegewisch, A. 21
Hegmann, H. 450, 456, 458
Heilman, M. 274
Heineken 42
Heiskanen, T. 506

Hemingway, C.A. 27
Hemingway, M. 488
Hemmasi, M. 490
Henderson Kassis, J. 542, 543
Hendrickson, A.R. 347
Hendry, C. 15, 72
Hergert, M. 391
heroic leadership 210
Hewlett Packard 117
Higgins, M. 495
high performance work systems
    (HPWS) 72, 94
Hightower, R. 366
Hilgard, E. 316
Hill, C.J. 266
Hiller, J.S. 228
Hiltrop, J.M. 26, 101, 529
Hiltz, S.R. 352, 366, 368
Hinds, P. 368, 371
Hinds, P.J. 368
Hinings, C.R. 96, 464
Hippler, T. 249, 250, 251
Hite, J.M. 255
Hitt, M.A. 21, 24, 123
Hochschild, A.R. 287
Hocking, B.J. 26
Hodgetts, R. 158
Hodgkinson, G. 115, 123, 124
Hodson, G. 235, 236
Hofner Saphiere, D.M. 352, 355, 359
Hofstede, G. 3, 75, 78, 142, 186, 188,
    349, 350, 392, 408, 409, 410, 423,
    450, 455, 480, 485, 490, 495
Hollenbeck, G.P. 204, 208, 210, 213,
    323, 336
Hollingsworth, J.R. 76, 77, 78
Holm, U. 331, 543
Holm, U.I.F. 116
Holman, D. 253
Holtbrügge, D. 22
Holvino, E. 517
Holzmüller, H.H. 75
Homans, G.C. 491
home-country expatriates 42
homosexuality 512
Hong Kong 76
Hood, N. 53, 543
Hoque, K. 466
host-country
    autonomy in 42

impact of MNEs 470–471
host-country nationals (HCNs) 145,
    146
    attitudes to women 270–272
    performance management systems
        176, 188, 190
House, R.J. 75, 204, 373, 490
Hout, T. 37
Howard, C. 323
Howard, G.C. 248
Hsieh, T. 353
Hua, W. 490
Huang, I.-C. 42, 463
Huff, L. 490
Huffcut, A.I. 183
Hui, T.K. 466
human capital 439–40, 441–2, 454
human resource department 49–67
    as administrative expert 52
    ambiguities in role 49–50
    business development 54
    capability development 53
    case studies 56–61
    as change agent 52
    cooptation 55
    devolution and coordination 53–5,
        59, 62
    effectiveness of 99
    as employee champion 52
    function 49
    and international business travellers
        295–9
    'parenting' style/role 43, 59, 60
    power and influence 55–6, 63, 64
    pressures for change 63–4
    roles in MNEs 50–53, 54, 62
    status 52
    as strategic partner 52, 54
    strategic role 51
    transactional work 54
    value creation 49, 52
    and virtual teams 380
human resource management (HRM)
    114
    balanced scorecard techniques 91
    best practices 91, 92, 93
    and business performance 49
    characteristics of good practice 70
    compared to other functions
        39–40

comparison of policies and practices
　across geographical borders
　68–90
and complexity 43
contextual paradigm 69, 71, 72–3
critical theoretical perspective 525
and cultural environment 43
e-enablement 51–2, 54, 60
and firm performance 92–7
and gender 506–7
and global knowledge management
　113–40
integration–responsiveness
　framework 38–9
and international joint ventures 386
and justice 168–70
local influences 72
and local practices 39–40
meaning of 99
national differences 71–83
and organizational performance 27
and organizational strategy 25
regional convergence 79
reliance on home country 43
strategic role 3–4
universalist model 69–71
see also strategic human resource
　management
human resource management (HRM)
　practices 26–7, 100, 102
development and transfer 107–8
host-country pressures 42
and integration–responsiveness
　framework 40–44
interpretation 493
in MNE subsidiaries 528–30
in MNEs, and institutional theory
　465–8
human resources (HR)
managing global functions 435–7
and social capital 483–5
tripartite approach 58
human resources (HR) policies, in
　various cultural dimensions
　394–5
humanism 493
Hunt, J. 49
Hunter, B.A. 233
Huntington, R. 489
Huo, Y.J. 497

Hurn, B. 334
Huselid, M.A. 4, 28, 40, 49, 70, 91, 93,
　95, 98, 101, 469
Hutchings, K. 28
Hutchison, S. 489
Hyland, M. 307
Hyman, R. 73
Hymer, R.M. 158

Ibarra, H. 355
IBM 3, 117
Ichniowski, C. 95
ICT (information and communication
　technologies) 347
identities 531–2
Iles, P. 227
Ilinitch, A. 323
ILO 79
Imaizumi, A. 256
immersion cultural experiences 310
incentive alignment 171
incentive-based payment systems 94
India 46, 141
individualism 185–7, 350, 394, 409
industrial relations theory 79–80
informal networks 120–121
information processing 495–6
information sharing 124
information sharing systems 70, 82, 99
information systems 114
Inglehart, R. 490
Ingram, P. 480
Inkpen, A. 387, 388, 391, 392, 396,
　398, 399, 478, 479, 482
Inkson, K. 254, 265, 531
Inohara, H. 76
inpatriation 141, 151–2
Institute of Management 507
institutional pressures 107
institutional regulations 456, 457
institutional theory 91, 463–5
　and IHRM research 463–74
　and MNE HRM practices 465–8
institutionalism perspective 18–19
institutionalization 464, 469
institutions, and culture 76
instrumentalism 493, 494
integration–responsiveness framework
　36–8, 50
　assessment 44–7

change in ownership patterns 46
China and India 46
convergence among local
environments 46
and European MNCs 43
extension 40–44
and HRM 38–9
and HRM practices 40–44
link to performance 45–6
intercultural HRM, and economic
theory 455–8
internalized adoption 469
international assignments 24, 143–4,
247–64, 311
and global leadership competencies
212–13
individual-level antecedents for
success 303–6
motives for 2–3
non-traditional forms 154
selection for 302–22
training and development for
309–14
and women 265–82, 508–9
international business 15, 25, 36
experience in 25
international business travel 284–6
international business travellers
family separation 287–9
health issues 290
and IHRM 283–301
organizational support 294–5, 300
positive factors 292–4
role of HR department 295–9
safety concerns 291
study of 285–6
training for 295
travel stress 289–90
International Computers Ltd 407
International Human Resource
Management Conferences 1
international human resource
management (IHRM) 15, 324,
332
and capabilities 437–44
comparative approach 450
compared to comparative human
resource management 68, 84
corporate structure and gender
policy 515–16

critical research programme 527–33
critical theoretical perspectives
523–35
cross-cultural perspective 450
and economic theories of the firm
449–62
and economic theory 453–9
failure within 527
and firm performance 91–112
and gender 502–22
gender
and diversity 510–512
and globalization 512–14
and gender, mainstream texts 508
gendered impacts of 515
gendering of 514–15
for global network organizations
332–3
globally distributed teams 123
and international business travellers
283–301
and language 536–50
language implications 540–546
and MNEs 453–5
organizational support theory
framework 488–501
and patriation 335
perspectives on 450
and property rights theory 453
resource-based view 433–48
and social capital theory 475–87
and social network theory 475–87
see also strategic international
human resources management
international human resource
management (IHRM) practices,
and fairness or justice 494–5
international human resource
management (IHRM) research
1–5
and institutional theory 463–74
international joint ventures 385–404,
454
control 388
cooperation 388
cooperation theory 398–9
efficiencies and economies 387–8
four-stage model 388–96
applications 396–8
future research 399–401

and HRM 386
HRM–IJV relationship 398–9
knowledge and learning 387
organizational learning theory 398
reasons for 387
transaction costs theory 398
international management cadres 51
international mobility 153–4, 159
international non-governmental
    organizations (INGOs) 29
international organizations, social
    capital in 479
international staffing 2
international training and development
    activities 309–11
interorganizational networks and
    alliances 24
'intraorganizational information
    market' 119
Ireland, R. 123
Isabella, L. 389, 391
isomorphism 80, 96, 464
ITT 117
Ivancevich, J.M. 2, 286, 408
Izraeli, D.N. 273, 507

J-Electric
    case study 56–7
    internship programme 60
    three-part HR function 58
Jacklin, C.N. 503
Jackson, S.E. 19, 28, 63, 73, 93, 385,
    436
Jackson, T. 493
Jacobs, R. 304
Jacques, R. 525
Jaffe, J.F. 406
James, E.H. 232, 236
Jansen, P.G.W. 267
Janssens, M.J. 193, 538, 539
Japan 4, 40, 42, 54–5, 56, 62, 73, 76, 79,
    167, 271, 544
    'kaizen' 190
    parent country nations (PCNs) 147
Jarillo, J.C. 42
Jarvenpaa, S.L. 352, 353, 358, 369, 370
Javidan, M. 204, 490
Jaw, B.-S. 42, 463
Jaworski, R.A. 256
Jeannet, J. 200

Jemison, D.B. 406, 408, 412, 415, 419
Jensen, C.S. 79
Jewson, N. 274
Jin, Z. 367
job design 70, 94
job performance 1176
job satisfaction 166–7, 299
Johansen, R. 39, 369
Johanson, J. 331, 537, 545
John, O. 303
Johnson, C. 296
Johnson, G. 200
Johnson, J. 239
Johnson, J.L. 490
Johnson, K. 352, 366
joint ventures, international 385–404
Jones, G.R. 167, 451, 452, 457
Joshi, A. 307
Joshi, C. 235
Judge, W.Q. 21, 412
justice
    and expatriate compensation 168–9
    and HRM 168–70
    Rawls' theory of 170

Kabst, R. 20, 454
Kachra, A. 385, 396, 398
Kaiser, J. 239
Kakabadse, N. 385
Kakuyama, T. 179
Kalla, H. 545
Kalleberg, A. 72, 98
Kalmbach, C. 387
Kamoche, K.N. 16, 21, 23, 73, 74
Kane, J. 158, 159, 161, 163
Kane, J.S. 179
Kanfer, R. 100
Kanter, R.M. 505
Kanungo, R.N. 121
Katslkeas, C. 388
Katz, H.C. 24, 80
Katz, I. 233
Kawakami, K. 235, 236
Kay, R. 514
Kayworth, T.R. 374
Kealey, D.J. 253, 256, 311, 317
Keats, B. 24
Kedia, B.L. 200, 324, 327, 330, 440
Keefer, P. 456
Keenoy, T. 73

Kefalas, A.G. 200, 324, 326, 327, 330
Keisler, S. 367
Kelkar, G. 513
Kelley, L. 490
Kelloway, E.K. 268, 480
Kelly, G.A. 276
Kelly, J. 470
Kelsey, B.L. 370
Kendall, D.W. 323, 329
Kennedy, A. 251, 252
Keough, C.M. 532
Kerfoot, D. 506
Kerr, C. 79
Kets de Vries, M. 204, 207, 208, 212
Kezsbom, D. 366
Khan, R. 323
Kidger, P.J. 25, 326
Kieser, A. 77
Kiesler, S. 352, 366
Kim, W.C. 24, 332
Kinder, D.R. 233
King, D.R. 412, 425
King, Z. 63
Kirkman, B.L. 349, 369, 379, 495
Kirton, G. 511
Kittel, B. 76, 80
Kleppestø, S. 413, 424
Klimoski, R.J. 123, 476
Kluckholn, F.R. 495
Knack, F. 456
Knight, G. 179
Knight, G.A. 17
Knights, D. 506, 525
Knoll, K. 352, 358, 369
Knoll, M. 228
knowledge 483
  acquisition and creation 113
  and belief 122–3
  capturing and storage 113
  cultural dependence 114–15
  diffusion and transfer 113
  meaning of 114–15
  tacit knowledge 120, 326–7, 331, 375
knowledge creation capability 440–441
knowledge integration capability 437
knowledge and learning, international
    joint ventures 387
knowledge management 51, 113–40
  centres of excellence 115–19
  informal networks 120–121
  initiatives 119
  integration mechanisms 115
  nature of 114–15
  within international and globally
      distributed teams 123–6
knowledge management systems 120
  global 119–21
knowledge sharing, and language 544
knowledge-based view of the firm 434,
    437
Kobayashi, N. 39
Kobrin, S.J. 121, 147, 200
Koch, M.J. 73, 98
Kochan, T. 49, 70, 73, 228
Kocharekar, R. 119
Kogut, B. 325, 398, 409, 437, 438, 445,
    480
Kolb, D. 317, 511
Kondo, D. 506
Konopaske, R. 286
Konovsky, M. 489, 497
Konrad, A.M. 227
Kopp, R. 142, 162, 167
Korea, performance appraisal 189
Korsgaard, M.A. 490
Korten, D. 513
Kossek, E.E. 213
Kostova, T. 121, 439, 464, 465, 467,
    469, 477, 479
Kotter, J. 208
Krackhardt, D. 475
Kraimer, M.L. 256, 492
Kramer, R.M. 356, 370
Kreps, D.N. 489
Krishnan H.A. 412
Kristof, A.L. 353
Kryson, M. 232
Kühlmann, T.M. 204, 311, 450
Kuhn, T. 69
Kumagai, F. 538
Kwon, S.-W. 477

labour markets, deregulation and
    decontrol 79
'labour process theory' 524
Lado, A.A. 323, 325, 326, 445
LaFasto, F. 411
Lagerström, K. 543
Lajara, B. 385
Lam, H. 316

Lambert, J. 538
Lammers, C.J. 105
Lane, H.W. 7, 197, 198, 199, 200
Lane, I. 327
Langdon, J.C. 182
language
  and cross-cultural teams 542–3
  diversity in MNEs 537–9
  and individual managers and
      employees 540–542
  instrumental, cultural and political
      perspectives 539
  and knowledge sharing 544
  language effects in MNEs 536–50
  and power 539
  and promotion 541
  standardization 536, 537
  training 310
Lansbury, R.D. 80
Lant, T.K. 356
Laroche, P. 91
Larsson, R. 406, 412, 414, 420, 421
Latham, G.P. 179
Latour, B. 530
Lau, D.C. 355
Laurent, A. 1, 3, 15, 39, 523
Lawler, E.E. 51, 178, 184
Lawler, J.J. 436, 459
Lawler, J.L. 466
Lawrence, P. 36
Lazarova, M. 2, 153, 268, 312, 329
Lazear, E.P. 453
Lazenga, E. 481
Lea, M. 367
leader–member exchange (LMX)
    model 272–3
leadership
  in virtual teams 372–4
  see also global leadership
learning 323–4, 325
  cultural 415–17
  styles 317
Lee, A.S. 366
Lee, J.S.K. 514
Lefkowitz, J. 230, 238
Legge, K. 49, 50, 55, 70, 96, 507, 515,
    523, 525
Lei, D. 21, 389, 391, 392, 396
Leiba-O'Sullivan, S. 323, 325, 326, 329,
    332, 333

Leidner, D.E. 353, 358, 369, 370,
    374
Leiter, M.P. 268
Lengel, R.H. 366
Lengnick-Hall, C.A. 121, 127, 475,
    483, 484
Lengnick-Hall, M.L. 121, 127, 475,
    483, 484
Lenway, S.A. 121, 200
Leonard, D.A. 358
Leonidou, L. 388
Lepak, D.P. 40, 306, 439, 441
LePine, M.A. 260
Leroy, F. 413, 416
Leslie, J. 204
Leung, K. 495, 497
Levanthal, G.S. 494
Levinthal, D.A. 316, 398, 483
Levitt, B. 466
Levitt, T. 69
Levy, O. 200, 202, 359
Lewicki, R.J. 369
Lewin, A.Y. 323
Li, J. 21, 387
Lichtenstein, B. 214, 215, 216
Liden, R.C. 492
Liebeskind, J.P. 127, 323
Liesch, P.W. 17
Lievens, F. 309–10
Lillo, F. 385
Lim, L. 385, 399
Lin, N. 126
Lincoln, J.R. 72, 541, 542
Lind, E.A. 497
line management 49, 296
Linehan, M. 5, 153, 266, 269, 270, 273,
    278, 330, 333
Linnehan, F. 227, 239
Linstead, S.A. 513, 514, 533
Lipnack, J. 347, 372, 378
Lippman, S. 440
Lippman, W. 231
Lobel, S.A. 226
local practices, and HRM 39
local responsiveness (differentiation)
    68, 466
  and global integration 16, 36–49
  see also integration–responsiveness
      framework
local staff, development 44

local-level participation procedures 70
Loch, K.D. 352
Locke, E.A. 179–80
Locke, R. 79
Loess, K. 385, 389, 399
London, M. 187
Lorange, P. 149, 393
Lord, M.D. 294
Lorsch, J. 36
Louhiala-Salminen, L. 536
Lowe, K.B. 167, 266, 267
Lu, Y. 190, 463, 466, 467, 529
Lubatkin, M.H. 406, 409, 410, 411,
    420, 423
Luk, D.M. 250
Lundstedt, S. 247
Luo, Y. 385, 386, 387, 388, 391, 393,
    399, 401
Lusch, R. 323
Luthans, F. 158, 181
Lyons, L. 514
Lysgaard, S. 248, 258

McAllister, D. 369
McCall, M.W. Jr 204, 208, 210, 213,
    323, 336
McCline, R.L. 239
McCloy, R.A. 176
Maccoby, E.E. 503
McConahay, J.B. 233, 234
McCrae, R. 303
McCubbin, H.L. 270
McCurry, L. 94
McDaniel R. Jr 369
MacDuffie, J.P. 4, 94, 434
McEvily, B.W. 121, 369, 443
McEvoy, G.M. 250, 252, 256
MacEwan, K.E. 268
McFadyn, M.A. 477
McGrath, R.G. 73, 98
McGuire, T.W. 366, 367
McIvor, R. 94
McKeen, J.D. 113, 115
Maclagan, P.W. 27
McLaren, P. 511
McLaughlin-Volpe, T. 237, 238
McLeod, P.L. 226
McMahan, G.C. 5, 16, 20, 21, 49, 51,
    69, 70, 230, 326, 398, 453, 463
McMillan, A. 227

McNabb, R. 99
McNett, J. 197
McWilliams, A. 16, 25, 434, 435, 436,
    437
Madsen, J.S. 79
Mael, F.A. 356
Mahoney, J.T. 326
Makadok, R. 323
Makela, A.K. 121
Mäkelä, K. 545
Makhija, M. 389
Malekzadeh, A.R. 411, 517
management development 51
management practices, transfer across
    borders 3
managers
    embeddedness 78
    locally hired 42
    repatriation of 153
managing diversity 377–8
Mankin, D. 125, 355
Mannix, E.A. 497
Manual, J.A. 370
manufacturing function 39
Manzini, R. 120
March, J.G. 439, 466
Marginson, P. 53
marketing function 39
Marks, M.L. 408, 412, 414, 422
Marschan, R. 540, 541
Marschan-Piekkari, R. 536, 537, 540,
    545, 547
Martin, C. 497
Martin, G. 50, 467, 468
Martin, J.A. 480
Martin, R. 79
Martinez, J.I. 42
Mason, D. 274
Mason, R. 367
Matsui, T. 179
Matten, D. 79
Mattson, L.G. 331
Mauborgne, R. 24, 332
Maurer, F. 120
Maurice, M. 78
Mayer, R.C. 490
Mayne, L. 21
Mayo, A. 407, 414, 415
Mayrhofer, W. 4, 74, 79, 81, 147, 153,
    167

Maznevski, M.L. 7, 125, 197, 199, 200, 347, 349, 358, 359, 367, 375, 376, 378, 490, 542
Mead, C. 204
Meertens, R.W. 233
Meiskins, P. 69, 77
Meiss, J.D. 215
Mendenhall, M.E. 2, 7, 190, 191, 193, 197, 204, 209, 212, 213, 214, 215, 216, 249, 252, 253, 255, 303, 304, 307, 309, 311, 314, 317, 327, 329, 330, 441, 450, 531
Mento, A.J. 180
mergers and acquisitions 5, 150, 405–29
  acquirer communication 412–14
  autonomy removal 406–7
  best practices 422–3
  cultural learning 415–17
  cultural orientation 408
  employee involvement 414–15
  gender dimension 516–17
  human element 405–12
  model of HR integration 417–23
  national culture 409–11
  organizational culture 411–12
  performance measures 425
  pre-integration mindsets 407–8
Merton, R. 202
Metcalfe, B. 514
Meyer, J.W. 18, 77, 78, 464, 467, 469
Meyerson, D. 370
Michailova, S. 294
Michigan school 3
Milkovich, G.T. 168, 172, 460
Miller, A. 412
Miller, D. 324
Miller, E. 160
Miller, E.L. 2, 248
Miller, V. 532
Milliman, J.F. 15, 149, 332, 489
Mills, A.J. 511, 527
mindset, defined 199
Mintzberg, H. 207
Minuchin, S. 269, 270
Mirvis, P.H. 408, 411, 412, 415, 422
Mischel, W. 248, 253, 258
Mitra, A. 460
Mitroff, I. 248
Mitsuhashi, H. 21

MNE subsidiaries, in HRM practices 528–30
MNEs 1, 30, 36–7
  adaption to local differences 43
  and centres of excellence 116–17
  competitive landscape 323
  concerns and goals 27–8
  effects of nationality 54
  Europe, compensation of expatriates 164
  and the HR function 50–61
  HRM practices and institutional theory 465–8
  and IHRM 453–5
  impact on host country 470–471
  in language effects 536–50
  local needs 37
  as networks 331
  and parent country nationals 148–9
  pay system design 159
  senior management 141
  senior staff in subsidiaries 146–50
  staffing decisions 1–2
  standardization 467
  strategic IHRM in 15–35
  sustainability 27
  transfer of knowledge within 120
Mobley, W. 58, 59, 60, 204
Mohammed, S. 115, 123, 124
Mohrman, A. 123
Mohrman, S. 123, 125
Mohrman, S.A. 51
Moingeon, B. 114
Montoya-Weiss, M.M. 371
Moody, J.W. 98
Moore, K. 117, 118
Moran, R. 313
Moran, R.T. 204
Moran, T.H. 470
Morely, M. 74
Moreno, A. 490
Morgan, G. 516, 524
Morgan, P.V. 450
Morisihma, M. 73
Morley, M. 4, 79
Morosini, P. 409, 410
Morris, C. 260
Morris, D. 391
Morris, M. 311

Morrison, A. 199, 200, 207, 309
Mortensen, M. 368, 371
Mosakowski, E. 355, 357
motivation 266–7
Motowidlo, S.J. 176
Mount, M.K. 184, 304, 315
Mouton, J.S. 416
Moynihan, L.M. 27
Mueller, F. 69, 71
Mukherji, A. 200, 324, 327, 330
Mullen, M.R. 490
Müller, M. 72, 78, 466
multinational corporations *see* MNEs
    (multinational enterprises)
Murakami, F. 495
Murnighan, J.K. 355, 370
Murtha, T.P. 121, 200
Murthi, B.P.S. 228, 229, 230

Nahapiet, J. 439, 476, 481
Nahavandi, A. 411, 517
Napier, N.K. 4, 16, 271, 326, 412, 436,
    466, 471, 488
Narula, R. 385, 386, 387, 388, 391,
    392, 398, 399
Nathan, M. 15, 332
nation states, role 77
national differences 79
    cultural explanation 74–5
    HRM 71–83
        explaining 74–6
    institutional explanation 74–5
National Foreign Trade Council 24
nationality, effects of 54
Neale, M.A. 347, 352
Negandhi, A.R. 541
Neilson, R.E. 366
neoinstitutional theory 96, 458
    'North-American phenomenological
        neoinstitutionalism' 77
Netherlands 99, 407
networks 127
    informal 120–121
    interorganizational 24
    MNEs as 331, 332
Neumark, D. 99
Nevis, E.C. 113
new institutional economics 450–451
Newbury, W. 385, 388
Newell, S. 120

Newman, J.E. 254, 259
Newman, J.M. 168
Newstrom, J. 317
Ng, C.W. 514
Ng, K.Y. 497
Ngui, M. 74
Nicholson, N. 256, 259
Nigh, D. 121, 126, 375
Nisbett, R.E. 258
Nishii, L.H. 100, 495
Nitin, N. 438
Nkomo, S. 526
Noe, R. 313
Noelle, G.F. 3
Nohria, N. 3, 16, 41, 54, 72, 119, 392,
    443, 463, 465, 466, 467, 528
non-linearity 215–19
Nonaka, I. 115
Noonan, L.E. 183
Nooteboom, J. 391
Norburn, D. 409
Nord, W. 531
Nordhaug, O. 94, 450, 463
norms, versus attitudes 195–6
North, D.C. 456
Novicevic, M.M. 21, 25, 26, 56, 63,
    125, 134, 295, 324, 325, 334, 393,
    455, 470
Nueno, P. 57, 58, 61
Nummela, N. 200
Nundi, D.I. 2
Nunnaly, J.C. 207

Oakley, A. 503
Oberg, K. 248, 249
Obloj, K. 24
O'Connor, E.J. 355, 356, 357, 360, 361
Oddou, G. 2, 190, 191, 193, 213, 252,
    253, 255, 303, 304, 312, 325, 329,
    531
Odendahl, T. 541
O'Donnell, S.W. 149, 163, 171, 326,
    453, 454, 459, 460
Oguri, M. 252
O'Hara-Devereaux, M. 39, 369
Ohmae, K. 116, 199, 200
Okazaki-Ward, L. 73
Okin, S.M. 511
Olie, R. 407
Oliver, A. 323

Oliver, C. 78, 96, 107, 464, 467
Olson, D.H. 270
Olson-Buchanan, J.B. 260
Ondrack, D. 142
Ones, D. 191, 303, 304, 307
Ong, A. 516
Onglatco, M.L.T. 179
open systems approach 97, 105
openness or intellect 304–5
Oppler, S.H. 176
O'Reilly, C.A. 223, 236
O'Reilly, M. 158, 161
Organization Resources Counselors,
    Inc (ORC) 162
organizational behaviour, and strategic
    management 114
organizational capital 437–9, 442, 443–4
organizational culture 25–6, 411–12
organizational heritage 103
organizational imprinting 470
organizational learning 115, 398
organizational performance 16, 28
organizational processes, and women
    272–8
organizational strategy, and HRM 25
organizational support theory 491–9
    and IHRM 488–501
Orr, J.E. 127
Osborn, R. 398, 399, 400
Osland, J.S. 7, 145, 204, 207, 209, 212,
    213, 311
Osterman, P. 93
Ostroff, C. 100
Ostroff, C. Bowen 64
Oswald, F.L. 176
Ouchi, W.G. 76
outsourcing 53, 453, 469
Ozeki, C. 213

Paauwe, J. 27, 91, 93, 95, 96, 97, 98, 99,
    101, 102, 103, 106, 150, 509
Pablo, A.L. 406, 415, 422
Pacanowsky, M. 414
Pahlberg, C. 332
paid time off, and local practices 41
Paillai, R. 497
Pandian, J.R. 326
parent country nations (PCNs) 146,
    147, 148
    Europe and Japan 147

Park, H.J. 21, 92, 95
Parker, A. 483
Parker, B. 250, 252, 256
Parker Follet, M. 216
Parker, P. 265
Parkin, W. 505, 513, 516
Parks, M.R. 352
Parsons, T. 75
part-time workers 81
Pate, J. 154
'patriation' 331–6
    development of process 336–8
Patterson, J.M. 270
Pattison, P.E. 481
Patton, M.Q. 285
Paul, D.L. 369
Paul, H. 199, 200, 324, 326, 327,
    330
Paul, S. 371
Pausenberger, E. 3
pay system design 159
Peace Corps 247–8
Peat, D. 216
Peccei, R. 91, 99, 100, 106
Pedersen, T. 116, 117, 387, 543
Pelled, L.M. 51
Peltonen, T. 329, 510, 531
Pennings, J.M. 25
Penrose, E.T. 18, 22
Penrose, R.T. 331
perceptions of organizational
    support (POS) 492
    and trust 496
performance
    definition of 176
    task and contextual 176
    see also expatriate adjustment
        and performance
performance appraisals 70
performance incentives 171
performance management systems
    176–96
    expatriates 176
    host-country nationals 176
    and rewards 178
performance measurement 105–7
performance related pay 102
Perlmutter, H.V. 1, 2, 146, 200, 332
Perrewe, P.L. 268
Perry, E.L. 275

Peters, T.J. 76
Petersen, L.-E. 223, 231, 232, 234, 235, 237, 238, 239
Peterson, M.F. 125
Peterson, R.B. 152
Petrovic, J. 295, 385
Pettigrew, A.M. 24
Pettigrew, T.F. 233
Petzall, S. 385
Pfeffer, A.M. 18, 19
Pfeffer, J. 49, 91, 92, 93, 95, 464, 470, 529
Phelps, C. 356
Phelps, M.I. 158, 169
Philips
  case study 57–8
  'Dutch mafia' 42
  management development process 60–61
  One Philips programme 61
  succession planning 61
  three-part HR function 58–9, 60
Philips, C. 198
Phillips, J. 306, 307, 308, 312, 324, 327, 330, 332, 334
Phillips, M. 256
Picot, A. 458
Piekkari, R. 510, 511, 516, 529, 537, 539, 541, 542, 545
Pieper, R. 70, 73, 74, 79
Piore, M. 80
Pisano, G. 434
Pitkethly, R. 410, 466
Pitt, L. 120
Pitts, R. 389, 391, 396
Pla, J. 168
Podsiadlowski, A. 223
Polanyi, M. 458
political risk 267
Pollock, D. 316
polycentric (host-country-oriented) approach 2
  to staffing 146
Poole, M. 70, 74, 78
Pooria, M. 455, 456
Porter, C.O.L.H. 497
Porter, M. 37
Portes, A. 476, 477, 478
post-colonial theory 530
poststructuralism 524, 525

Pot, F. 106
Potter, R.E. 370
Pow, J.C.I. 514
Powell, G.N. 507
Powell, W.W. 18, 38, 77, 78, 96, 458, 463, 464, 466
power distance 394, 410, 485, 490
Power, F.R. 408
Powers, R.L. 16
Prahalad, C.K. 3, 5, 16, 36, 37, 68, 141, 199, 200, 323, 433, 466
Prasad, A. 523, 527, 530
Prasad, P. 511, 527
Pratt, J.W. 452
Pratto, F. 231
prejudice 233–4
  against women 273
  eliminating 237–8
  research on 234–6
Prescott, C.E. 116, 117, 118
Preston, J. 115
PricewaterhouseCoopers 265, 283, 514
Pringle, J. 254, 531
Proctor and Gamble 488
professional performance 106
promotion and compensation schemes 70
property rights 453, 457
Protheroe, D. 311, 317
Prusak, L. 120
psychic distance 537
psychology 251–2, 531
public ownership 76
Pucik, V. 3, 4, 5, 44, 49, 51, 144, 309, 325, 385, 389, 393, 434, 527
Pudelko, M. 79
Pugh, S.D. 234, 239, 489, 497
Pulakos, E.D. 182
Punnett, B.J. 269, 508, 509, 510
Purcell, J. 22, 49, 70, 73, 94, 101
Putnam, L. 414
Putnam, R. 481
Puumalainen, K. 200
Pyle, J.L. 513

Quintanilla, J. 3, 16, 22, 54, 55, 62, 79, 467, 528, 529

racial diversity 228
Raghuram, S. 356

Raines, C. 317
Ramanantsoa, B. 413, 416
Ramia, G. 29
Ranft, A.L. 294
Rantalaiho, L. 506
Rasheed, A. 389
Rasmussen, E.S. 544
Ratner, H. 115, 125
Raveh, A. 420
Raver, J.L. 495
Rawls' theory of justice 170
Read, S. 516
Ready, D. 207, 208, 210
Reagans, R. 121
recruitment 51, 52–3, 70, 71, 94, 453
Redding, S.G. 496
Reed, K. 490
Reed, M. 20
Rees, C. 514
Reger, K.R. 276
regiocentric approach 2
   to staffing 146
regional convergence 77–8
   HRM 79
Reid, D. 387
Reizenstein, R.M. 239
relatedness, versus rationality 186
relationships 475–9, 484
rent concepts 444–5
repatriate competencies 326
repatriation of managers 153, 323–43
   competency-based view 324–7
   deidentification process 333, 334–5,
      338
   literature review of research 327–31
   patriation process 331–8
   reverse culture shock 334
Repertory Grid analyses 276
reputation 103
research
   comparative 4
   development of 1–5
resource allocation decisions 28
resource dependence perspective 19
resource-based view, and IHRM
   433–48
resource-based view of the firm 4,
   21–2, 49, 51, 93, 103, 331
rewards 181–2, 186–7
Reynolds, C. 2, 152, 158, 160, 163

Rhinesmith, S.H. 199, 200, 204
Rhoades, L. 489, 490, 491, 492, 494
Ricardian rents 444–5
Richard, O.C. 227, 228, 229, 230
Richards, D. 304
Richardson, R. 97, 98, 101
Richter, R. 451
Ricks, D. 435
Riesenberger, J.R. 204
Ringdahl, K. 463
risk management 17
Ritchie, J.B. 213
Riusala, K. 121
Robert, C. 28
Roberts, J. 510, 540, 544
Roberts, K. 213
Robertson, L. 187
Robey, D. 352
Robie, C. 251, 311
Robock, S.H. 2
Robson, M. 388, 392, 398
Rogan, R. 329
Rogers, J. 252
Rogers, R.W. 177
Rogovsky, N. 450
Romani, L. 76
Ronen, S. 75
Roper, M.R. 56
Ropp, S.A. 237, 238
Rose, M.J. 77
Rosen, B. 379
Rosen, R. 198, 208
Rosenzweig, P.M. 3, 5, 16, 38, 39, 41,
   54, 72, 392, 463, 465, 466, 467,
   528
Rosile, G.A. 532
Roth, K. 121, 171, 326, 439, 453, 454,
   459, 460, 464, 467, 469, 477, 479
Rothbard, N.P. 268
Rousseau, D.M. 265, 331, 369, 476,
   490
Roussel, C. 387
Rowan, B. 78, 464, 467, 469
Rowan, R. 18
Rowbotham, S. 503
Rowley, C. 15
Ruben, B.D. 212, 253, 256
Rubin, I.M. 258
Rubin, J. 274
Rucci, T. 411

Rudden, E. 37
Rueur, J. 385, 386, 391, 392
Ruggles, R. 113
Rugman, A. 331
Ruhleder, K. 366
Ruiz-Quintanilla, S.A. 490
Rumelt, R. 440
Russia 95
Ruysseveldt, J. van 5
Ryan, A.M. 251, 488

Saarenketo, S. 200
Saba, T. 325
Sabal, C. 80
Sackmann, S.A. 114
Saebo, S. 490
Sager, C.E. 176
Said, E. 530
Saks, A. 317
Salancik, G.R. 19, 464, 529
salary
    inequity 169, 169–70
    satisfaction with 166
Salas, E. 123, 315
Sales, A.L. 411, 415
Salgado, J. 315
Salk, J.E. 542
Sambharya, R. 200
SanAntonio, P.M. 536, 541, 547
Sanchez, J.I. 26
Sanders, D. 74
Sanders, W.G. 444, 445
Sano, Y. 73
Santos, J. 24
Säntti, R. 413, 516
Sarnin, P. 200
Sassen, S. 533
Saudi Arabia, performance appraisal
    189
Sawyer, J.E. 347, 352
Sayeed, L. 366
Scanlan, T.J. 354
Scarborough, H. 114, 115, 120
Schein, E.H. 349, 408, 411, 415, 416
Schein, V.E. 276
Schleicher, D.J. 184
Schmidt, K. 366
Schminke, M. 491
Schneider, C. 49
Schoemaker, P.J.H. 445

Schoenberg, R. 409
Schoenfeldt, L.F. 452, 457, 460
Schoorman, F.D. 490
Schrift, A.D. 524
Schuler, R.S. 4, 5, 15, 16, 17, 19, 23, 27,
    28, 29, 49, 51, 63, 73, 79, 80, 93,
    141, 146, 147, 149, 150, 152, 160,
    162, 164–5, 178, 191, 309, 324,
    332, 385, 386, 387, 388, 389, 391,
    392, 393, 396, 398, 399, 434, 436,
    450, 471, 488, 502, 509, 510, 511
Schulz, M. 445
Schuman, H. 232
Schumpeterian rents 445
Schwartz, D.G. 120
Schwartz, M. 233
Schwartz, S.H. 75, 495
Schweiger, D.M. 406, 408, 413, 414,
    415, 416, 419, 425, 426, 542, 543
Scott, C.R. 357
Scott, W.R. 18, 77, 463, 464, 465, 470,
    529
Scullion, H. 5, 43, 50, 51, 53, 141, 142,
    143, 147, 148, 149, 151, 153, 154,
    159, 295, 330, 333, 470, 509
Searle, W. 249, 251, 252, 303, 306, 307
Sears, D.O. 233
security 24, 273
Sedgwick, E.K. 504
Seike, A. 73
Sekaran, U. 74
selection 70, 88, 164–5, 180, 181
    of expatriates 142
    for global leadership 212
    for international assignments
        302–22
        candidate assessment 308–9
        intersection with training 314–17
        personality characteristics 303–5,
            315–16
        prior international experience
            305–6, 316–17
        realistic previews 306–7
        self-selection 307–8
    language criteria 305, 540–541
    typology of international manager
        selection schemes 275–8
    and women 273–8
self, definition of 185
Selmer, J. 253, 306, 316, 539

Selvarajah, C. 385
Sempere, V. 385
Senko, J. 158, 162
sequential expatriation 334, 339
Sewell, W.H. 248
Shaffer, M.A. 158, 159, 249, 250, 251,
    252, 253, 256, 259
Shalev, M. 68
Shamsie, J. 324
Shane, S. 409
Shapiro, D.L. 120, 349, 495
shared cognition 126
shareholder-driven model 72
shareholders 70
Shaw, A.M. 541
Shaw, J.D. 479
Shaw, K. 95
Shay, J.P. 143, 253, 256, 258, 259
Shenkar, O. 387, 391, 393, 409, 420,
    423, 508
Sherif, M. 231
Sherman, S. 181
Shirkey, E.C. 260
Shoib, G. 120
Shore, L.M. 491
Shrader, C.B. 227
SHRM Global Forum 24
Shuen, A. 434
Shuetz 247
Shurygailo, S. 177
Shwom, B. 532
Sichel, N. 316
Sidanius, J. 231
Siegel, J. 366, 367
Siegel, P.A. 497
Silverman, S. 304
Simmering, M. 315
Simmonds, K. 2
Simms, H.P. Jr 353
Simon, H.A. 450
Simons, R. 391
Sinangil 191
Sinetar, M. 408, 413
Singer, M. 198
Singh, H. 409, 415, 416
Singh, J. 38, 465
Singh, V. 507
Sisson, K. 49
Sitkin, S.B. 331, 369, 408, 412, 415,
    490

Skarlicki, D. 497
Sklair, L. 510
Skovbro, C. 283
Slater, I. 52
Slocum, J.W. 389, 391, 392, 396
Smale, A. 121
SMEs 502, 506
    internationalization 141
Smirchich, L. 525, 526
Smith, A.B. 177
Smith, C. 69, 77
Smith, C.R. 265, 271, 273
Smith, K.A. 353
Smith, M.B. 247, 248, 253, 255, 258
Smith, P. 76
Snell, S.A. 22, 40, 69, 230, 358, 433,
    434, 435, 437, 439, 441
Snow, C.C. 358
social capital 326, 439, 442–3
    and competitive advantage
        480–483
    concept 476–8
    and HR 483–5
    in international organizations 479
    relationships 475–9, 484
social capital theory 121, 126
    and IHRM 475–87
social comparison theory 166
social exchange theory 491
social network theory 121
    and IHRM 475–87
socialization 456–7
societal expectations 96
societal performance 106
Söderberg, A.-M. 413, 417, 517
Soellner, F. 385, 399
Sole, D. 351
Sorge, A. 74
Soskice, D. 72
Sowa, D. 489
Spain 52
Sparrow, P.R. 4, 5, 53, 63, 68, 79, 84,
    116, 117, 121, 122, 123, 124, 127,
    134, 143, 147, 253, 436, 482,
    529
Spears, R. 367
Spector, P.E. 26, 494, 497
Speier, C. 323, 324, 325, 393, 455
Spradley, J. 256
Spreitzer, G.M. 120

Sproull, L. 352
Srinivas, K.M. 200
staffing 454
    foreign subsidiaries 146–50
    global 141–57
Stahl, G.K. 160, 204, 213, 251, 265,
    311, 441
stakeholder approach 99, 106
Stamoulis, D.T. 184
Stamps, J. 347, 372, 378
Staples, D.S. 113, 115, 120
Star, S.L. 366
Starkey, K. 26, 43, 50, 53, 149, 151,
    295, 470
Stasser, G. 441
'state of the art' compensation policies
    170, 172
Stedman, Y. 16
Steeh, C. 232
Steiner, D.D. 494, 495
Stening, B. 303
Stephens, G.K. 249, 250, 251, 330
Stewart, D.D. 441
Steyaert, C. 538
Stiglitz, J. 79
Stiles, P. 469
Still, L.V. 265, 271, 273
Stinchcombe, A. 470
Stinglhamber, F. 492
Stockdale, M.S. 223
Stodtbeck, F.L. 495
Stogdill, R.M. 373
Stone, R.J. 254, 271
Stoner, J.A.F. 258
Storey, J. 4, 50, 62, 73, 149
Stouffer, S.A. 247
strategic choice perspective 20–21
strategic flexibility 324
strategic global staffing 53
strategic human resource management
    (HRM) 69
    definition of 70
    HR function strategy and practices
        26–7
    in MNEs
        development of research on 22
        future directions for 28–30
        implications for research 29–30
        integration–differentiation balance
            23

strategic international human
    resources management
    definitions 16
    external factors 24–5
    framework 23, 29
    institutionalism perspective 18–19
    internal/organizational factors
        25–6
    in MNEs 4, 15–35
        concerns and goals 27–8
        theoretical perspectives 18–22
    resource dependence perspective
        19
    resource-based perspective 21–2
    strategic choice perspective 20–21
    theoretical model 16–17
    transaction cost perspective 20
strategic management, and
    organization behaviour 114
strategy 100–101
Straud, D. 352
Straus, S.G. 369
Stroh, L.K. 25, 50, 272, 273, 325, 330,
    333
Stueber, D. 439
Subramaniam, M. 437
subsidiaries
    headquarters–subsidiary/
        intersubsidiary relationships
        543–5
    staffing foreign subsidiaries
        146–50
    strategic role 170–172
Sucharaski, I.L. 492
Suddaby, R. 464
Suder, G.G.S. 24
Sulsky, L.M. 183, 184
Sundaram, A.K. 29, 30
supplies 17
support functions 39
Sussman, N. 329, 334
sustainability, MNEs 27
Suutari, V. 159, 160, 165, 166, 197, 199,
    204, 212, 251, 255, 327, 330, 333,
    336
Swan, J. 115, 120
Sweden 52
Swim, J.K. 233
symbolic activities 469, 470
synergy 53, 54

Sypher, B. 532
Szulanski, G. 434, 435, 439

tacit knowledge 120, 326–7, 331, 375
Tahvanainen, M. 255
Tajfel, H. 226, 231, 378
Takeuchi, H. 115, 204
Takeuchi, R. 254, 306
talent management 51
Tan, H. 544
Tan, J.J. 497
Tarique, I. 2, 312, 386, 387, 389, 392, 398
taxation 165
Tayeb, M. 332
Taylor, A. 385, 387
Taylor, S. 4, 16, 17, 19, 25, 53, 153, 199, 200, 212, 213, 271, 326, 359, 436, 466, 468, 471, 488
Teagarden, M.B. 30
team cognition 123
teams
    cross-border global 311
    cross-cultural 542–3
    global
        challenges due to decoupling 347–54
        coupling mechanisms 348, 354–9
        cultural diversity in 347, 349–51
        cultural liaisons 354–6, 360
        decoupling and coupling in 347–64
        documentation 357–9
        dynamic structure 353–4
        electronic dependence 352–3
        face-to-face meetings 353, 359, 361
        geographical dispersion 351–2
        identification 356–7
        power distance 350
    global outsourcing teams 353
    global team processes 134
    global virtual 364–84
    globally distributed teams (GDTs) 125–6
    see also virtual teams
teamwork 79, 94, 453
Teece, D.J. 434, 439, 445
Teegan, H. 29
Ten Have, K. 95

Teo, S.T.T. 99
terrorism 17, 29, 153, 159
Tesluk, P.E. 254, 306
Tetrick, L.E. 491
Thal, N.L. 273
Tharp, C.G. 25
Thibaut, J.W. 494
Thilenius, P. 331
third-country nationals (TCNs) 146
Thomas, A. 2, 75
Thomas, D. 531
Thomas, D.A. 227, 230, 239, 511
Thomas, D.C. 147, 150, 247, 249, 250, 253, 254, 255, 259, 260
Thomas, R. 506
Thomas, R.J. 218
Thomas, R.R. 225, 226
Thurley, K. 73
Tichy, N.M. 3, 69, 204
Tienari, J. 413, 517, 539, 541
Tierney, T. 119, 438
Tillery, K.R. 266
Toh, S.M. 159, 160, 169
Tolbert, P.S. 463, 464, 465
Tomlinson, J. 77
Tompkins, P.K. 356
Tompson, H.B. 333
top management 146
    staffing and inpatriation 151–2
Torbiorn, I. 1, 141, 146, 147, 160, 250, 454
Tornikoski, C. 159, 160, 163, 165, 166
Torp, J.E. 417
Torrington, D. 49
Townley, B. 55, 523, 525, 528
Townsend, A.K. 167
Townsend, A.M. 352, 353, 357
Toyama, M. 495
Toynbee, P. 77
trade unions 73, 75
training 51, 70, 82, 99, 453
    cross-cultural 302–22, 310, 311–14
    and development for international assignees 309–14
    frame of reference (FOR) training 183–4
    for global performance management systems 182–7
    for international business travellers 295

intersection with selection for
    international assignees 314–17
and local practices 41
of raters for global performance
    management systems 182–4
transaction cost theory 20, 77, 167–8,
    398, 449, 451, 452, 453–4, 457–8
transactional work 54
transactive memory 124
transfer
    of employment practices 94
    of people across units 2–3
'transnational solution' 37
Travaglione, A. 491
Traxler, F. 76, 80
Tregaskis, O. 19, 21, 43, 74
Tremblay, M. 460
Triandis, H.C. 185, 223, 233, 347
Triple Value Strategy Consulting 517
Trompenaars, F. 450
Truch, E. 325
Trudinger, D. 507
Truss, C. 49
Truss, K. 100
trust 439, 488, 490, 491, 492–3, 543
    and fairness, perceptions of 497
    leader trustworthiness 490
    and perceptions of organizational
        support (POS) 496
Tsai, W. 3, 382, 439
Tsang, B. 396
Tsang, E. 387, 388, 396, 398, 399, 478,
    479, 482
Tsui, A. 53, 55, 62, 64, 236
Tubbs, M.E. 179
Tung, R.L. 1, 2, 25, 142, 147, 160, 248,
    253, 254, 258, 259, 265, 283, 304,
    307, 329
Turkey 271
Turner, F. 215
Turner, J.C. 231, 356, 378
Turney, W.H. 480
Turoff, M. 352, 366, 368
Tushman, M.L. 354
Tyler, T.R. 497
Tyson, S. 50

Uhl-Bien, M. 476
UK, mergers and acquisitions 410
UK Gay and Lesbian Census 512

Ulrich, D. 28, 49, 51, 52, 54, 62, 69,
    335, 411, 469
uncertainty 17, 466
UNCTAD 141, 151
Union Carbide Corporation, Bhopal
    388
universalistic models 69–71, 93, 449
Urbina, S. 207
USA 77, 79, 142
    Department of Labor 70
    models of HRM 73, 78–9
    Peace Corps 247–8
    performance appraisal 189
Useem, R.H. 316

Vaara, E. 413, 416, 417, 424, 517, 539,
    541
Vachani, S. 29
value congruence 493
value, rarity, inimitability and
    nonsubstitutability (VRIN) 435
Van Buren, H. 329
Van den Berg, S. 305
van der Merwe, R. 120
Van der Smagt, T. 367
Van der Velde, M.E.G. 267
Van Fleet, D.D. 16, 434
Van Keer, E. 309–10
van Oudenhoven, J.P. 411, 412
van Reken, R. 316
Van Ruysseveldt, J. 508, 511
Van Sluijs, E. 392
Vandenberghe, C. 492
Vandermeeren, S. 527, 536
Varma, A. 272
Varul, M.Z. 470
Vashdi, D.F. 237
Vaslow, J.B. 234, 239
Veiga, J.F. 406, 410, 517
Veikkola, E.-S. 507
Verbeke, A. 331
Verburg, R.M. 103
Vermeulen, F. 355, 357
Very, P. 406, 409, 410, 420, 423
Vickerstaff, S. 79
Villanova, P. 179
Vinnicombe, S. 506, 507
virtual assignments 24
virtual teams 125, 154, 177, 347, 353–3,
    360–361

achieving high performance 376–80
communication 365–7, 376–7
configuration 375–6
conflict management 371–2
dynamic and fluid management 379
empowerment 379
face-to-face communication 366,
    369, 378
and the HR department 380
identity 368
leadership in 372–4
linguistic differences 367–8
managing diversity 377–8
relationships 368–71, 373
task requirements 374–5
trust 369–70
Visweswaran, C. 303, 304, 307
Von Glinow, M.A. 15, 120, 204, 304,
    332

Wächter, H. 79, 450, 454
Wagner, E. 539
Wagner, K.H. 115, 125
Walby, S. 503, 513
Walker, L. 494
Walsh, J.S. 266
Walsham, G. 120
Walster, E.H. 226
Walter, G.A. 412
Walther, J.B. 352, 353
Wang, X.Y. 121
Ward, C. 249, 251, 252, 303, 306, 307
Ward, K.B. 367, 513
Warkentin, M.E. 366
Warner, M. 15, 471
Wasti, S.A. 28
Waterman, R.H. 76
Watson, T. 50, 63
Wayne, S.J. 256, 492
Weatherby, R.P. 202
Webb, J. 274
Weber, Y. 406
Wederspahn, G.M. 169
Weick, K.E. 202, 348, 370, 439, 443
Weiner, W. 416
Weinstein, M. 24
Weiss, J.W. 414
Weissbein, D. 317
Weissman, D. 307
Welbourne, T. 167

Welch, C. 541, 547
Welch, D.E. 5, 6, 15, 24, 25, 26, 27, 79,
    141, 147, 149, 154, 163, 188, 192,
    283, 285, 295, 298, 300, 309, 331,
    332, 449, 450, 502, 508, 509, 511,
    537, 538, 539, 540, 543, 545
Welch, L.S. 154, 285, 295, 300, 331,
    547
Welge, M.K. 3, 22
Welsh, A. 391
Wentland, D. 158, 165
Werner, J.M. 490
Werner, S. 158
Wernerfelt, B. 331, 433
Wesson, M.J. 497
West, J. 547
Westney, D.E. 464, 465, 466, 467, 470,
    547
Westwood, R. 523
Wheatley, M. 214
White, N. 370
Whitener, E.M. 488, 489, 490, 491
Whitfield, K. 99
Whitley, R.D. 55, 62, 71, 72, 93, 458
Wicker, A.W. 254
Wiechmann, D. 488
Wiedersheim-Paul, F. 537, 545
Wiese, D. 269
Wiesenfeld, B.M. 356, 357
Williams, A. 326
Williams, E.S. 497
Williams, K. 79
Williams, K.Y. 223
Williamson, O.E. 18, 20, 167, 450, 451,
    452, 453
Williamson, P. 24
Willmot, H. 523, 524, 525, 527, 528
Wills, S. 200
Wilson, E. 507
Wilson, F. 507
Wilson, J.M. 369
Wilson, M. 255, 307, 323, 325, 385, 445
Wilson, T.D. 258
Windham International and National
    Foreign Trade Council 269, 309
Wirdenius, H. 73
Wiseman, R.L. 254, 255, 303, 304, 305
Wittenbaum, G.M. 441
Woehr, D.J. 183
Wolf, J. 25

Wolff, B. 453, 455, 456
Wolff, S.B. 372, 373
Wolfram Cox, J. 22
women 223, 239, 506–7, 513–14
  at higher executive levels 507
  cross-cultural adjustment 265, 266
  desire to terminate assignments
    265–6
  family considerations 267–70, 278
  host national's attitudes to 270–272
  individual motivation 266–7
  on international assignments
    265–82, 508–9
  in international management 153
  managers' attitudes towards 273
  and organizational processes 272–8
  performance 265, 266
  and selection 273–8
  as spouses/partners/family members
    of male expatriates 509
  supervisor-subordinate relationship
    272–3
  see also gender
Woo, C. 323
Wood, J. 326
Wood, R.E. 180
Wood, S. 97, 103
Woodall, J. 515
work systems 79
work–family conflict 268–9
Workplace Employee Relations Survey
  (WERS) 49
Worldwide Survey of International
  Assignment Policies and Practices
  162
Worm, V. 283, 285, 294, 300
Woywode, M. 79
Wright, C. 541, 542
Wright, G. 270
Wright, P.M. 5, 16, 20, 21, 22, 25, 27,
  49, 69, 70, 91, 93, 97, 99, 100, 101,
167, 172, 228, 230, 326, 398, 433,
  434, 435, 437, 451, 452, 453, 463
Wright, S.C. 237, 238
Wyer, R.S. 274

Xin, K.R. 51
Xiucheng, F. 25, 27, 95, 141

Yamaguchi, S. 495
Yan, A. 165, 212, 391, 454, 470
Yavas, U. 385, 389, 399
Yeheskel, O. 385
Yeung, A. 207, 208
Yim, P. 367
Yip, G.S. 68
Yong, M. 313
Yoshihara, H. 541, 544
Yoshimura, N. 76
Youndt, M.A. 40, 437
Young, S. 147
Youngblood, S.A. 469
Yuen, E. 466
Yun, S. 254, 306

Zack, M. 114
Zaheer, A. 443
Zaheer, S. 465
Zajonc, R. 315
Zander, U. 325, 437, 438, 445,
  480
Zanko, M. 74
Zeckhauser, R.J. 452
Zeira, Y. 2, 385, 388, 391, 393
Zellmer-Bruhn, M. 349
Zemke, R. 317
Zhang, M. 16
Zhu, C.J. 24, 43–4, 46
Zhu, G. 212, 454
Zhu, Y. 471
Zimmermann, A. 253
Zucker, L.G. 323, 463, 464, 465